Letters to Friends,
Family, and Editors

FRANZ KAFKA

Letters to Friends, Family, and Editors

Translated by RICHARD *and* CLARA WINSTON

SCHOCKEN BOOKS · NEW YORK

First published by SCHOCKEN BOOKS 1977

Copyright © 1958, 1977 by Schocken Books Inc.

The original German edition, BRIEFE 1902–1924,
was edited by Max Brod.

Library of Congress Cataloging in Publication Data

Kafka, Franz, 1883-1924.
  Letters to friends, family, and editors.

  Translation of Briefe, 1902-1924.
  Includes bibliographical references.
  1. Kafka, Franz, 1883-1924—Correspondence.
  2. Authors, Austrian—20th century—Correspondence.
  I. Title.

PT2621.A26Z5313   1977   833'.9'12   [B]   77-3136

Manufactured in the United States of America

Publisher's Note

This volume is based on the collection of Kafka's *Briefe,* edited by Max Brod and published in 1958. At that time, *Briefe an Milena* had already appeared (1952), edited by Willy Haas; an English version was published in 1962. Later, in 1967, appeared *Briefe an Felice und andere Korrespondenz aus der Verlobungszeit,* edited by Erich Heller and Jürgen Born. The English version, *Letters to Felice,* edited by Heller and Born and translated by James Stern and Elisabeth Duckworth, was issued in 1973. The volume includes the letters to Grete Bloch. "Letter to His Father" appeared in 1954 in the volume *Dearest Father,* edited by Max Brod; a bilingual edition of this "Letter" was published in 1966.

Of the letters in the present volume, the majority are addressed to Max Brod, Kafka's lifelong friend, companion, and helper. The friendship with Oskar Pollak, Kafka's schoolmate, was short-lived. Of a permanent nature was the friendship with the philosopher Felix Weltsch, the blind writer Oskar Baum, and, from 1921 on, Robert Klopstock, a medical student, later a physician, whom he met at the sanatorium in Matliary.

Among the addressees were important women, among them Hedwig W. (1907–9) and Minze Eisner (1919–23). Kafka corresponded vigorously with Kurt Wolff, one of the directors of Rowohlt Verlag and later owner of the publishing house that bore his name.

Fortunately some new material could be secured and included in the English edition: e.g., the full text of the letter to the sister of Julie Wohryzek (November 24, 1919); it replaces the fragment tentatively addressed in *Briefe* "To the parents of J.W. (?)." Further additions are seven letters to Martin Buber, of which four (dated May 25, 1914, and June 28, July 20, and August 3, 1917) are published here for the first time, with the kind assistance of the Jewish National and University Library in Jerusalem, who own the originals; a letter concerning the printing history of *The Metamorphosis* (probably addressed to Robert Musil); a letter to Felix Weltsch; a letter to his parents written in the last days of his life and preserved by Max Brod in his Kafka biography; fifteen short letters or postcards sent to Brod from 1905 to 1909, also from the biography; a letter to René Schickele; and one to Otto Stoessl.

Briefe included four letters to Kafka's favored sister Ottla which are retained in the present volume (with corrected dates). Additional letters to Ottla are now available in *Briefe an Ottla und die Familie,* edited by Hartmut Binder and Klaus Wagenbach, Frankfurt a.M., 1974.

As in the original German edition, this version concludes with a selection from the slips of paper on which Kafka, advised in the last few weeks of his life to speak as little as possible, noted his observations and wishes.

The editorial work was a joint effort by Beverly Colman, Nahum N. Glatzer, Christopher J. Kuppig, and Wolfgang Sauerlander. The translators wish to thank Mr. Sauerlander for his invaluable help in clarifying obscurities, deciphering private references, and interpreting the eccentricities of Kafka's language and character; he has also made extensive additions to Max Brod's original notes and has succeeded in dating many letters that were dated incorrectly in the German edition.

All Kafka material is copyrighted by Schocken Books Inc., New York.

Contents

Letters to Friends,
Family, and Editors

1900

To Selma Kohn[1]

[Entry in an album]

How many words in this book.

They are meant for remembrance. As though words could carry memories.

For words are clumsy mountaineers and clumsy miners. Not for them to bring down treasures from the mountains' peaks, or up from the mountains' bowels.

But there is a living mindfulness that has passed gently, like a stroking hand, over everything memorable. And when the flame shoots up out of these ashes, hot and glowing, strong and mighty, and you stare into it as though spellbound by its magic, then—

But no one can write himself into this kind of pure mindfulness with unskillful hand and crude pen; one can write only in such white, undemanding pages as these. I did so on September 4, 1900.

Franz Kafka

1902

To Oskar Pollak[1]

[Prague, February 4, 1902]

While we were walking together Saturday, I realized what it is we need. But I have not written you about it until today because such things have to lie awhile and stretch. When we talk together, the words are hard; we tread over them as if they were rough pavement. The most delicate things acquire awkward feet and we can't help it. We're almost in each other's way; I bump into you and you— I don't dare and you—. When we come to things that are not exactly cobblestones or the *Kunstwart*,[2] we suddenly see that we are in masquerade, acting with angular gestures (especially me, I admit), and then we suddenly become sad and bored. Does anyone make you as bored as I do? You often become quite sick. Then I feel sympathy and cannot do anything and say anything, and jerky, silly words come up, the sort of remarks you'd get from anyone, only better said; then I fall silent and you fall silent and you become bored, and I become bored and it's all like a stupid hangover and there's no use lifting a hand. But neither wants to say this to the other, out of shame or fear or— You see, we're afraid of each other, or I am—.

Of course I understand it. It's boring, to stand for years in front of an ugly wall and it just won't crumble away. Of course, but the wall is afraid for itself, for the garden (if there is one), and you get out of sorts, yawn, have headaches, don't know where to turn.

You must surely have noticed, whenever we see each other again after a longish time we're disappointed, irritated, until we get used to the irritation. Then we have to put up a front of words, so that our yawns won't be noticed.

. . . .

The fear creeps over me that you won't understand this whole letter—what's its aim? Without flourishes and veils and warts: When we talk together we're hampered by things we want to say and cannot say just like that, so we bring them out in such a way that we misunderstand. even ignore, even laugh at each other. (I say: The honey is sweet, but I talk so low or so stupidly or inadequately, and you say: Nice weather today. The conversation has already taken a wrong turn.) Since we are always trying and always without success, we become tired, dissatisfied, stiff-jawed. If we tried to do it in writing, we would be more at ease than when we talk—we could then discuss the cobblestones and the *Kunstwart*, without shame, for the better part would be in safety. That is the point this letter is trying to make. Is that prompted by jealousy?

I had no way of knowing that you would read the last page also; that's why I have scribbled this odd bit, although it doesn't belong to the letter.

We have been talking together for three years; so in many things we no longer distinguish between mine and thine. Often I would not be able to say what comes from me and what from you, and perhaps it's the same for you too.

Now I am extremely glad that you are keeping company with that girl. For your sake; she means nothing to me. But you often talk with her, not only for the sake of talking. You walk around with her somewhere here or there, or in Roztok, and I sit at my desk at home. You talk with her, and in the middle of a sentence somebody jumps up and makes a bow. That is me with my untrimmed words and angular faces. That lasts only a moment, and then you go on talking. I sit at my desk at home and yawn. I've been through it already. Wouldn't that separate us? Is that so strange? Are we enemies? I am very fond of you.

To Oskar Pollak

[Liboch;[3] postmarked on arrival: August 12, 1902]
If someone flies through the world on seven-league boots from the Bohemian to the Thuringian forests, it's quite a feat to catch him or even so much as touch the tip of his coat. No cause for offense. So it's now too late for Ilmenau.[4] But in Weimar—can there be some hidden intention here?—a letter will be waiting for you, stuffed full of strange things which will have become stronger and finer from having waited so long in the aforesaid town. Let us hope so.

Yours, Franz

To Oskar Pollak

[Prague; postmarked on arrival: August 24, 1902]
I sat at my fine desk. You don't know it. How could you? You see, it's a respectably minded desk which is meant to educate. Where the writer's knees usually are, it has two horrible wooden spikes. And now pay attention. If you sit down quietly, cautiously at it, and write something respectable, all's well. But if you become excited, look out—if your body quivers ever so little, you inescapably feel the spikes in your knees, and how that hurts. I could show you the black-and-blue marks. And what that means to say is simply: "Don't write anything exciting and don't let your body quiver while you write."

So I was sitting at my fine desk and writing my second letter to you. You know, a letter is like a bellwether; it at once draws twenty baaing letters after it.

Whoosh, the door flew open. Who came in without knocking? Some ruffian? Ah, a beloved guest. Your postcard. It is odd about this first card that I have received here. I've read it countless times, until I know your whole ABC; and only after I'd read more out of it than was actually in it was it time to stop and tear up my letter. Rish-rosh, it went, and was dead.

But I read one thing in your card that stood out and was not at all nice to read: You are traveling around with that wicked accursed bug of criticism biting you, which is something one should never do.

But what you write about the Goethe National Museum[5] seems to me totally twisted and wrong. You went there filled with conceits and schoolboy ideas, and began right off by griping about the name. Now I think the name "museum" is good, but "national" seems to me even better, not at all tasteless or sacrilegious or anything of the sort, as you write, but the subtlest, most marvelously subtle irony. For what you write about the study, your holy of

holies, is again nothing more than a conceit and a schoolboy idea with just a
dash of German lit.—may it roast in hell.[6]

Damn it all, there was nothing to it, keeping his study in order and then
setting it up as a "museum" for the "nation." Any carpenter and
wallpaperer—supposing he were the right sort who knew enough to
appreciate Goethe's bootjack—could do it, and that's all there was to praise.

But do you know what really is the holiest thing we could have of
Goethe's as a memento—the footprints of his solitary walks through the
country—they would be it. And here comes a joke, a marvelous one, that
makes God in His heaven weep bitterly and sends hell into hellish convulsions
of laughter. It's this: We can never have another person's holy of holies, only
our own—that's a joke, a marvelous one. Once before I gave you a chance to
nibble at tiny bits and pieces of it—in the Chotek gardens.[7] You neither wept
nor laughed. That's how it is—you're neither God in heaven nor the wicked
devil.

Only the wicked criticaster (talking down Thuringia) inhabits you, and
he is a subordinate devil whom, however, you should shake off. And so, for
the good of your soul, I shall tell you the strange tale of how once upon a
time [...], may God bless him, was overcome by Franz Kafka.

He was always running after me wherever I went, wherever I was. If I lay
on the vineyard wall, looking out over the countryside and maybe seeing or
hearing something lovely far off beyond the mountains, you can be sure that
suddenly someone rose up behind the wall, with considerable noise, solemnly
bleated, and gravely stated his view that the beautiful landscape decidedly
stood in need of a treatise. Elaborately, he explicated his plan for a
comprehensive monograph or a charming sketch and drove home his point.
My only argument against it was myself, and that was little enough.
. . . .

[...] You cannot imagine how all this torments me now. Everything I've
written you is nothing but gallows whimsy and country air, and what I'm
writing you now is glaring daylight that hurts the eyes. My uncle from
Madrid (railroad manager)[8] was here; I came to Prague because of him.
Shortly before his arrival I had the weird, unfortunately very weird notion of
begging him, no, not begging, asking, whether he mightn't know some way
to help me out of this mess, whether he couldn't guide me to someplace
where at last I could start afresh and do something. All right, I began
cautiously. No need to tell you the whole story in detail. He began to talk
unctuously, although ordinarily he's a truly kind person; he comforted me,
nicey-nicey. Let it pass. I dropped into silence at once, without really wanting
to, and in the two days that I have been in Prague on his account I didn't say
another word about it, although I have been with him all the time. He leaves

this evening. I am going to Liboch for another week, then to Triesch[9] for a week, then back to Prague, and then to Munich, to attend the university, yes, the university. Why are you making faces? Yes, I mean to go to the university. Why am I writing all this to you. Perhaps I knew it was a hopeless thing; what do people have their own feet for. Why have I written to you about it? So that you will know how I feel about the life outside that goes stumbling over the cobblestones like the poor mail coach that limps from Liboch to Dauba.[10] You simply have to have pity on and patience with

your Franz

Since I haven't written to anybody else I wouldn't like it if you were to talk to anybody about my endless letters. You won't. If you want to answer, which would be very nice, you can write to the old address for another week, c/o Windischbauer, Liboch. Later Zeltnergasse 3, Prague.[11]

To Oskar Pollak

[Liboch; autumn 1902]
It's a strange time I've been spending here, as you must have noticed, and I needed a strange time like this, a time in which I lie for hours on a vineyard wall and stare into the rain clouds which don't want to leave here, or into the wide fields, which grow even wider when you have a rainbow in your eyes, or where I sit in the garden and tell the children (especially a blonde little six-year-old, whom all the women call adorable) fairy tales or build sand castles or play hide-and-seek or whittle tables that—as God is my witness—never turn out well. A strange time, isn't it?

Or where I go through the fields which now lie brown and mournful with abandoned plows but which all the same glisten silvery when in spite of everything the late-afternoon sun comes out and casts my long shadow (yes, my long shadow, maybe by means of it I'll still reach the kingdom of heaven) on the furrows. Have you noticed how late-summer shadows dance on dark, turned-up earth, how they dance physically? Have you noticed how the earth rises toward the grazing cow, how trustfully it rises? Have you noticed how rich, heavy soil crumbles under too delicate fingers, how solemnly it crumbles?

To Oskar Pollak

[Prague; postmark: December 20, 1902]
Prague doesn't let go. Either of us. This old crone has claws. One has to yield, or else. We would have to set fire to it on two sides, at the Vyšehrad and at

the Hradčany; then it would be possible for us to get away. Perhaps you'll give it some consideration up to Carnival time.

You've read a great deal, but you don't know the tale of Shamefaced Lanky and Impure in Heart.[12] Because it's new and is hard to tell.

Shamefaced Lanky had crept off to hide his face in an old village, among low houses and narrow lanes. The lanes were so small that whenever two people walked together they had to rub against each other friendly-neighborly-like, and the rooms were so low that when Shamefaced Lanky stood up from his stool his big angular head went right through the ceiling, and without his particularly wanting to he had to look down on the thatched roofs.

Impure in Heart lived in a big city that got drunk night after night and was frantic night after night. For you see that is the joy of cities. And Impure in Heart was just like the city. For you see this is the joy of the impure.

One day before Christmas Lanky sat stooped at the window. There was no room for his legs inside so he'd stuck them out of the window for comfort; there they dangled pleasantly. With his clumsy, skinny, spidery fingers he was knitting woolen socks for the peasants. He had almost spitted his gray eyes on the knitting needles, for it was already dark.

Someone knocked daintily at the plank door. That was Impure in Heart. Lanky gaped. The guest smiled. And at once Lanky began feeling ashamed. He was ashamed of his height and his woolen socks and his room.—But in spite of that he did not blush, but remained as lemon-yellow as he has been. And with difficulty and shame he set his bony legs into motion and shamefully extended his hand to the guest. It reached across the whole room. Then he stammered some friendly mutterings into his woolen socks.

Impure in Heart sat down on a flour sack and smiled. Lanky also smiled, and his eyes crawled bashfully along his guest's glistening waistcoat buttons. Impure in Heart turned his eyelids toward the ceiling, and the words emerged from his mouth. Those words were fine gentlemen with patent-leather shoes and English cravats and glistening buttons; and if you furtively asked them, "Do you know what blood of blood is?" one would answer with a leer, "Yes, I have English cravats." And as soon as those little gentlemen were out of the mouth, they stood up on tiptoe and were tall; they then skipped over to Lanky, climbed up on him, tweaking and biting, and worked their way into his ears.

Lanky began acting restive; his nose sniffed the air of the room. God, how stuffy, stale, and unaired the air was!

The stranger did not stop. He told stories about himself, about waistcoat buttons, about the city, about his feelings—a merry mix. And as he talked he incidentally kept stabbing his pointed cane into Lanky's belly. Lanky trembled and grinned. Then Impure in Heart stopped; he was content and smiled. Lanky grinned and politely led his guest to the plank door. There they shook hands.

Lanky was alone again. He wept. He wiped his big tears away with his socks. His heart ached and he could not tell anyone. But sick questions crawled up his legs to his soul.

Why did he come to me? Because I am lanky? No, because I . . . ?

Am I weeping out of pity for me or for him?

Do I like him after all or do I hate him?

Has my god or my devil sent him?

The question marks throttled Shamefaced Lanky.

Once again he set to work on the socks. He almost pierced his eyes with the knitting needles. For it was even darker.

So think it over until Carnival.

Yours, Franz

1903

To Oskar Pollak

September 6 [1903?]

It might have been more sensible for me to have waited with this letter until I saw you and knew what the two months have made of you, for these summer months move me—I think—a good way along. And then too this summer I haven't received so much as a postcard from you, and in the last half year I haven't spoken a word with you that was worth the trouble. So it may well be that I am sending the letter to a stranger who will be annoyed by the importunity, or to a dead man who cannot read it, or to a clever person who will laugh at it. But I must write the letter; for that reason I'm not waiting until it becomes clear that I ought not write it.

For I want something from you, and I don't want it out of friendship or intimacy, as might be imagined; no, purely out of selfishness, plain selfishness.

Perhaps you noticed that I entered on this summer with high hopes; perhaps you were even dimly aware of what I wanted out of this summer. I'll say it: to bring out at one stroke what I believe I have in me (I don't always believe it). You could be aware of it only dimly, and I ought to have kissed your hands for having gone along with me, for it would have been most uncomfortable to be walking beside someone whose mouth was nastily pursed. But it was not nastily pursed.

Well the summer has forced *my* lips to part somewhat—I've become healthier (today I'm not feeling so well), become stronger, been with people a good deal, can talk with women—I have to say all this here—but the summer has brought me none of the miracles.

Now, however, there's something that's tearing my lips wide apart, or is it a gentler feeling, no, tearing is right—and someone who is standing behind the tree says softly to me: "You won't do anything without others." But I am now writing solemnly and with choice sentence structure: "Solitariness is repulsive; honestly lay your eggs out in the open and the sun will hatch them; better to bite into life than bite your tongue; honor the mole and its ilk but don't make it into one of your saints." Then someone who is no longer behind the tree says to me: "Is that the truth after all and one of summer's miracles?"

(Listen, just listen to a clever opening to a cunning letter. Why is it clever? A poor man who had not previously begged writes a begging letter with an elaborate opening in which he piteously describes the toilsome road that led to the insight that not to beg is a vice.)

Tell me, do you understand the feeling one must have when one's task is to pull a yellow mail coach full of sleeping people through an interminable night? One is sad, one has a few tears in the corners of one's eyes, hobbles slowly from one white milestone to the next, has a crooked back and has to keep looking down the highway, although there is nothing on it but night. Damn it all, how one would like to wake up those wretches in the coach, if only one had a post horn.

Now, now you can listen to me, if you're not tired.

I'll put together a bundle for you; it will contain everything I have written up to now, original or derivative. Nothing will be missing except the childhood things (as you see, this misery's been on my back from early on), then the stuff I no longer have, then the stuff I regard as worthless in this context, then the plans, since they are whole countries to him who has them and sand to everyone else, and finally the things I cannot show even to you, for we shudder to stand naked and be fingered by others, even if we have begged on our knees for that very thing. Anyhow, this whole past year I have written almost nothing. Whatever remains, and I don't know how much it is, I'll give to you if you write or say yes to me in answer to this request of mine.

You see that is something special, and although I am very clumsy about expressing such things (very ignorant), perhaps you already know. What I want to hear from you is not whether one might happily wait a bit or whether to go ahead and burn it all up with a light heart. In fact I don't even want to know what your attitude toward me is, for I'd have to force that out of you too; what I want is something easier and harder, I want you to read the pages, even if indifferently and reluctantly. For there are also indifferent and reluctant passages among them. Because—this is why I want it—what is dearest and hardest of mine is merely cool, in spite of the sun, and I know that another pair of eyes will make everything warmer and livelier when they look at it. I say only warmer and livelier, for that is divinely certain, since it is written: "Glorious is autonomous feeling, but responsive feeling brings strength to others."

Well, why all the fuss, eh—I am taking a piece (for I can do more than this and I shall—yes), a piece of my heart, packing it neatly in a few sheets of inscribed paper, and sending it on to you.

To Oskar Pollak

[Prague, November 9, 1903]

Dear Oskar,

Perhaps I am glad you have left,[1] as glad as people would have to be if someone climbed to the moon to look at them from there, for this sense of being observed from such height and distance would give people some small assurance that their movements and words and wishes are not altogether comical and foolish, as long as astronomers in their observatories hear no laughter from the moon.
. . . .
[. . .] We are as forlorn as children lost in the woods. When you stand in front of me and look at me, what do you know of the griefs that are in me and what do I know of yours. And if I were to cast myself down before you and weep and tell you, what more would you know about me than you know about hell when someone tells you it is hot and dreadful. For that reason alone we human beings ought to stand before one another as reverently, as reflectively, as lovingly, as we would before the entrance to hell.
. . . .
[. . .] If, like you, one dies for a while, one has the benefit of suddenly seeing clearly in either a pleasant or ugly light all the relationships that inevitably look so hazy when one is inside them. But the survivor also has that strange experience.

I have really spoken with you alone, among all the young people, and when I did talk to others it was only incidental or for your sake or through you or in reference to you. For me, you were, along with much else, also something like a window through which I could see the streets. I could not do that by myself, for tall though I am I do not yet reach to the windowsill.

Now that's going to change, of course. I now talk to others also, more awkwardly but more independently, and I see to my considerable surprise what your standing here was. Hence in this city which is foreign to you there are some quite intelligent people to whom you were someone to be revered. That's the truth. And I am vain enough to be pleased by that.

I don't know why that was so, whether because you were reticent, or seemed so, or receptive, or suggested potentialities, or really radiated power. At any rate, some think you left them, although after all you only left the girl.

Your letter is half sad and half glad. You really didn't go to the boy, but to the fields and the forest. But you are seeing these fields and forests, whereas we barely see their spring and their summer, and know no more about their autumn and their winter than about God in ourselves.

Today is Sunday, when the clerks always come down Wenzelsplatz across the Graben,[2] and clamor for Sunday quiet. I think their red carnations and their stupid and Jewish faces and their clamor is something highly significant; it is almost as if a child wanted to get to heaven and bawled and barked because no one was bothering to hand him the footstool. But the child doesn't want to get to heaven at all. The others, however, who walk on the Graben smiling because they do not know how to use even their Sunday—I'd slap their faces if I had the courage and didn't smile myself. But you in your castle may laugh, for there heaven is close to the earth, as you write.

I am reading Fechner, Eckhart.[3] Some books seem like a key to unfamiliar rooms in one's own castle.

The things I wanted to read to you and that I will send to you are fragments from a book, *The Child and the City*, which I myself have only in fragments. If I am to send them to you, I must copy them, and that takes time. So I'll be sending you only a few pages with every letter (if I don't see the thing making visible progress, I'll soon lose interest). Then you may read them in context; the first fragment is coming in the next letter.

By the way, no writing's been done for some time. It's this way with me: God doesn't want me to write, but I—I must. So there's an everlasting up and down; after all, God is the stronger, and there's more anguish in it than you can imagine. So many powers within me are tied to a stake, which might possibly grow into a green tree. Released, they could be useful to me and the country. But nobody ever shook a millstone from around his neck by complaining, especially when he was fond of it.

Here are some verses. Read them when you are in the proper mood.

This present day is cool and hard.
The clouds congeal.
The winds are ropes tugging.
People congeal.
Footsteps sound metallic
On brazen pavements,
And our eyes behold
Wide white lakes.

Standing in the Christmassy square
Of an ancient little town,
The crèche's colored windows stare
Out upon the snowy ground.
Walking in the moonlight goes
A man in silence in the snow,
And the wind his shadow blows
Tall along the crèche's wall.

People who dark bridges cross,
    passing saints
    with feeble candles.
Clouds that parade across gray skies,
    passing churches
    with darkening towers.
One who leans on the squared stone railing,
    looking into the evening waters,
    hands resting upon ancient stone.

Yours, Franz

To Oskar Pollak

[1903]

Dear Oskar,

    [...] Cool morning postscript to a painful evening madness. I see nothing unnatural in your not having helped the woman; perhaps uncorrupted people wouldn't have done so either. But it is unnatural that you brood on it and what is more enjoy this brooding and this inner conflict, enjoy your self-laceration. You skewer yourself on every brief emotion for a long time, so that in the end you live for only an hour, since you have to mull for a hundred years about that hour. Granted, perhaps I don't live at all in that case. Once I had the impudence to write somewhere that I was living swiftly, offering this for proof: "I look into a girl's eyes, and it was a long love story with thunder and kisses and lightning;" whereupon I was vain enough to write: "I am living swiftly." Like a child with picture books behind a curtained window. Sometimes the child catches a glimpse of the street through a crack, and at once turns back to its precious picture books.—In making comparisons I am merciful toward myself.

To Oskar Pollak
                                    [Prague; postmark: December 21, 1903]
No, I want to have written to you before you come yourself. Letter-writing is like being looped together by a rope; when we stop, the rope is broken, even if it was no more than a thread, so I want to tie the ends together quickly and provisionally.

You see, this was the image that seized hold of me last night. People keep themselves at a tolerable height above an infernal abyss toward which they gravitate only by putting out all their strength and lovingly helping one another. They are tied together by ropes, and it's bad enough when the ropes around an individual loosen and he drops somewhat lower than the others into empty space; ghastly when the ropes break and he falls. That's why we should cling to the others. I suspect that girls keep us from falling because they are so light, and therefore we must love the girls and they should love us.

Enough, enough—with good reason I am afraid of starting a letter to you, because it always stretches out and never comes to a good end. That's why I stopped writing to you from Munich,[4] although I had so much to write. Besides, I can't write at all when I am in foreign parts. All words are wildly dispersed and I can no longer corral them into sentences, and then everything new is pressing in on me so hard that I cannot fend it off and cannot ignore it.

Well, now you are coming in person. I don't want to waste the whole Sunday afternoon sitting at the desk—I've been sitting here since two o'clock and now it's five—when I'll so soon be able to talk with you. I'm so glad. You will bring cold air that will do all our stuffed heads good. I'm so happy. See you soon.

                                                          Yours, Franz

1904

To Max Brod[1]

[1903 or 1904]

Dear Max,

Since I skipped class yesterday I must write to explain why I did not go along with the bunch of you on the night of the fancy-dress ball, though I may have promised to.

Forgive me, I wanted to give myself the pleasure of bringing you and Přibram[2] together for an evening, because I thought some neat counterpoint would result if you, in the stress of the moment, made sardonic remarks—as you do in company—and he with his rational overview, which he has about almost everything except art, took an opposite stand.

But when I conceived of that, I had forgotten your crowd, the clique you were with. To a stranger's first glance it does not show you off to advantage. For partly it is dependent on you, partly independent. Insofar as it is dependent it surrounds you like responsive mountain country with a ready-made echo. That upsets the listener. While his eyes would like to deal quietly with an object in front, his back is being pummeled. He inevitably loses the capacity to enjoy either, especially if he is not too limber.

But insofar as your companions are independent, they do you even more harm, because they distort you. They put you in a false position. To the listener you are refuted by yourself; opportunity is lost if your friends behave in the usual way. A mob of friends is useful only in revolutions, when all act together and simply; but if what you have is only a small uprising by flickering light at a table, such friends will spoil it. You may want to show your scenery "Morning Landscape," and set it up for the backdrop; but your friends think your "Wolf's Gorge" fits the occasion better and they set that up for the wings. Granted, you're the one who has painted both, as any viewer can recognize, but what disturbing shadows fall on the meadow in "Morning Landscape" and what horrible birds fly over the field. That's how it is, I think. Rarely, but sometimes, it will happen (I admit I don't fully understand this yet) that you say: "Look at Flaubert. All he has is perceptions of facts, you know, no sentimental vaporings." How nasty I could make you seem if I turned such a remark against you at the opportune moment. You say, "What a wonderful thing *Werther* is." I say, "But to tell the truth there's a lot of sentimental vaporing in it." That is a silly, disagreeable remark, but I am your friend; I am saying it not to hurt you, but only to let the listener know your full views on such matters.

Often it can be a sign of friendship not to think through a friend's statements. But in the meantime the listener has grown sad, tired.

I have written this because I would feel worse if you didn't forgive me for not having spent the evening with you than if you didn't forgive me for this letter.—Warm regards.

Yours, Franz K.

Don't put it aside yet, I've read through it once more and see that it isn't very clear. I wanted to write: What for you is supreme happiness, namely, in a spell of exhaustion to let yourself go slack and yet, through the aid of one likeminded to be steered without any effort on your part to where you want to be, just this, at a social occasion, puts you in what I feel is a bad light. I was thinking this in connection with P. Enough for now.

To Oskar Pollak

[January 10, 1904]
Evening, half past ten

I am putting Marcus Aurelius aside, putting him reluctantly aside. I think I could not live without him now, for reading two or three maxims in Marcus Aurelius makes me more composed and more disciplined, although the book as a whole only shows a man who with prudent speech and a hard hammer and sweeping view would like to make himself into a controlled, steely, upright person. But we can't help but become skeptical when we hear a person continually urging himself: "Be calm, be indifferent, cast passion to the wind, be steadfast, be a good emperor." It's fine if we can use words to cover ourselves up from ourselves, but even better if we can adorn and drape ourselves with words until we have become the kind of person that in our hearts we wish to be.

In your last letter you reproach yourself unjustly. When someone extends a cool hand to me, it makes me feel good, but when he takes my arm I find it embarrassing and incomprehensible. Do you think that is because it has seldom happened? No, no, that isn't true. Do you know what is special about some people? They are nothing, but they cannot show it, cannot even show it to their own eyes, that is what is special about them. All these people are brothers of the man who went about the city, knew nothing, could not bring out a sensible word, could not dance, could not laugh, but constantly carried about, clutched tightly in both hands, a locked box. If some sympathetic person asked, "What are you carrying in the box so carefully?" the man drooped his head and said uncertainly: "I know nothing, that's true, and I can't bring out a sensible word, I can't dance either and I can't laugh, but I must not tell you what is in this locked box, no, no, I won't tell." After an answer like that all the sympathetic people naturally drifted away, but a certain curiosity, a certain suspense, lingered in a good many of them so they went on asking themselves, "What is in the locked box?" And for the sake of the box they came back to see the man every so often, but he would not say. Well, curiosity, that kind of curiosity, doesn't last, and suspense dissipates; by and by everybody cannot help smiling when an insignificant-looking locked box is everlastingly guarded with inexplicable anxiousness. Then again, we've given the poor man a halfway decent disposition, maybe he'll come round to smiling himself, though somewhat crookedly.—Now instead of the curiosity there is indifferent, distant pity, worse than indifference and distance. The sympathizers, fewer in number than in the past, now ask: "Whatever are you carrying around in the box so cautiously? Maybe a treasure, eh, or a prophecy? Anyhow, open it up; we need both; oh well, leave it closed, we believe you anyhow." Whereupon suddenly someone screams piercingly; the man looks around startled; it was himself. After his death, the box was found to contain two milk teeth.

Franz

To Oskar Pollak

[January 27, 1904]

Dear Oskar,

You've written me a dear letter that should have been answered soon or not at all, and now two weeks have passed without my having written you; that would be unforgivable, but I had reasons. First of all, I wanted to write you only after careful reflection, because the answer to your letter seemed to me more important than any other previous letter to you (unfortunately I didn't get to it); and secondly I read Hebbel's diaries[3] (some 1800 pages) all at once, whereas previously I had always just bitten out small pieces that struck me as insipid. All the same, I started to read consecutively. At first it was just a game, but eventually I came to feel like a caveman who rolls a block in front of the entrance to his cave, initially as a joke and out of boredom, but then, when the block makes the cave dark and shuts off the air, feels dully alarmed and with remarkable energy tries to push the rock away. But by then it has become ten times heavier and the man has to wrestle with it with all his might before light and air return. I simply could not take a pen in hand during these days. Because when you're surveying a life like that, which towers higher and higher without a gap, so high you can scarcely reach

it with your field glasses, your conscience cannot settle down. But it's good
when your conscience receives big wounds, because that makes it more
sensitive to every twinge. I think we ought to read only the kind of books
that wound and stab us. If the book we're reading doesn't wake us up with a
blow on the head, what are we reading it for? So that it will make us happy,
as you write? Good Lord, we would be happy precisely if we had no books,
and the kind of books that make us happy are the kind we could write
ourselves if we had to. But we need the books that affect us like a disaster,
that grieve us deeply, like the death of someone we loved more than
ourselves, like being banished into forests far from everyone, like a suicide. A
book must be the axe for the frozen sea inside us. That is my belief.

But you are happy; your letter actually glitters; I think in the past you
were unhappy only because of poor company. It was quite natural; we cannot
sun ourselves in the shade. Surely you don't think that I am responsible for
your happiness. At most this way: A wise man whose wisdom had remained
hidden from himself met a fool and talked with him for a while about
seemingly remote matters. When the conversation was over and the fool
wanted to go home—he lived in a dovecote—the wise man threw his arms
around him, kissed him, and cried out: Thanks, thanks, thanks. Why? The
fool's folly had been so great that it showed the wise man his wisdom.

I feel as if I have wronged you and must ask your forgiveness. But I know
of no wrong.

Yours, Franz

To Max Brod

[Prague,] August 28 [1904]
It is so easy to be cheerful at the beginning of summer. One has a lively heart,
a reasonably brisk gait, and can face the future with a certain hope. One
expects something out of the Arabian Nights, while disclaiming any such
hope with a comic bow and bumbling speech—an exciting game that makes
one feel cosy and all aquiver. One sits in one's tossed bedding and looks at the
clock. It reads late morning. But we paint the evening with subdued colors
and distant views that stretch on and on. And we rub our hands red with
delight because our shadow grows long and so handsomely crepuscular. We
adorn ourselves, secretly hoping that the adornment will become our nature.
And when people ask us about the life we intend to live, we form the habit,
in spring, of answering with an expansive wave of the hand, which goes limp
after a while, as if to say that it was ridiculously unnecessary to conjure up
sure things.

If we were to be totally disappointed, that would be sad, of course, but then again it would be the fulfillment of our daily prayer that the consistency of our life may be preserved as far as external appearances go.

But we˙are not disappointed; this season which has only an end but no beginning puts us into a state so alien and natural that it could be the death of us.

We are literally carried by a vagrant breeze wherever it pleases, and there is a certain whimsicality to the way we clap our hands to our brows in the breeze, or try to reassure ourselves by spoken words, thin fingertips pressed to our knees. Whereas we are usually polite enough not to want to know anything about any insight into ourselves, we now weaken to some extent and go seeking it, although in the same manner as when we pretend to be trying hard to catch up with little children who are toddling slowly in front of us. We burrow through ourselves like a mole and emerge blackened and velvet-haired from our sandy underground vaults, our poor little red feet stretched out for tender pity.

On a walk my dog came upon a mole that was trying to cross the road. The dog repeatedly jumped at it and then let it go again, for he is still young and timid. At first I was amused, and enjoyed watching the mole's agitation; it kept desperately and vainly looking for a hole in the hard ground. But suddenly when the dog again struck it a blow with its paw, it cried out. *Ks, ks*, it cried. And then I felt—no, I didn't feel anything. I merely thought I did, because that day my head started to droop so badly that in the evening I noticed with astonishment that my chin had grown into my chest. But next day I was holding my head nice and high again. Next day a girl put on a white dress and fell in love with me. She was very unhappy over it and I did not manage to comfort her; you know how hard it is to do that. On another day when I opened my eyes after a short afternoon nap, still not quite certain I was alive, I heard my mother[4] calling down from the balcony in a natural tone: "What are you up to?" A woman answered from the garden: "I'm having my teatime in the garden." I was amazed at the stalwart technique for living some people have. Another day I exulted painfully in the drama of overcast weather. Then a week or two or even more whisked away. Then I fell in love with a woman. Then once there was dancing in the tavern and I didn't go. Then I was down in the dumps and very stupid, so that I stumbled on the country roads, which are very steep around here. Then once I read this passage in Byron's diaries (I am only paraphrasing because the book is already packed up): "For a week I have not left my house. For three days I have been boxing four hours daily with a boxing master in the library, with the windows open, to calm my mind."[5] And then, and then the summer was over and I find it is getting cool, getting to be time to answer the summer letters, that my pen has skidded a little and that I might as well lay it down.

Yours, Franz K.

To Max Brod

[On a visiting card. Probably 1904]

Please wait awhile. I'll surely be here by half past ten. You know, I forgot that today is a holiday, and Přibram won't let go of me. But I'll surely come.

Yours, Franz K.

To Max Brod

[1904?]

My dear Max,

I'm sorry, it must really have been very much à la cabaret yesterday, because when I came there at half past nine after the Italian class everything was already closed up.

My mother has a vague impression in her waltz-addled memory that you said you would be coming over to see me today. If you mean to, let me rather come over to your place today, for we have a convalescing aunt in the apartment and in the evening we would be stumbling too often over sleepers. So let me know, and all the more nicely because I am sending you the Lucian.

Yours, Franz

To Max Brod

[1904]

I wondered that you did not write a word to me about "Tonio Kröger."6 But I told myself: "He knows how happy a letter from him makes me, and one has to say something about 'Tonio Kröger.' So he must have written, but there are accidents, cloudbursts, earthquakes; the letter must have gone astray." But immediately afterward this idea annoyed me, because I was not in a mood for writing, and cursing at having to answer a possibly unwritten letter I began to write. When I received your letter, I considered in my perplexity whether to go to you or to send you flowers. But I did neither, partly from negligence, partly because I was afraid of doing something stupid, since I have slipped out of phase a bit and am as gloomy as rainy weather.

But then your letter did me good. For when somebody tells me a sort of truth, I find an arrogance there. He is edifying me, humiliating me, expects me to muster difficult arguments, without himself running any risk, since he considers his own truth unassailable. But solemn, sincere, and touching though it is when someone states a prejudice, it is even more touching when it is justified, especially when it is in turn justified by other prejudices.

Perhaps you have also written about the resemblance to your story *Excursions into Dark Red.*[7] Before my recent rereading of "Tonio Kröger," I too thought there was such a broad resemblance. For the novelty of "Tonio Kröger" consists not in the discovery of that antithesis (thank God I no longer have to believe in that antithesis; it robs one of courage) but in the peculiar profit to the artist (to quote the poet in *Excursions)* of infatuation with this antithesis.

If I now assume that you have written about these matters, I do not understand why your letter is on the whole so excited and breathless. (Perhaps I am merely remembering that this is how you were on Sunday morning.) I beg you, calm down a bit.

Yes, yes, it's just as well that this letter will go astray also.

Yours, Franz K.

After two days wasted on studying.

1905

To Max Brod
[Prague; postmark: May 4, 1905]
Since things turned out well without my presence, you must not be annoyed with me. Especially since I could not help thinking, because of the nasty weather, that the meeting would be in the café. Anyhow, since you spent the time reading Stefan George,[1] you were appeased. And now at eleven o'clock the weather is so lovely but nobody is consoling me.

Yours, F.K.

To Max Brod
[Picture postcard. Zuckmantel;[2] postmarked on arrival: August 24, 1905]
Dear B.,
Certainly, I would have written you if I had stayed in Prague. But as it is I

am frivolous; this is my fourth week in a sanatorium in Silesia, where I mingle a great deal with people and womenfolk, and have become rather lively.

Franz K.

To Max Brod

[Prague; postmark: October 21, 1905]

Now I am almost pleased to be studying at last,[3] for which reason I won't be coming to the café this week. I would gladly spend the evening there, for I never go on studying after seven o'clock, but that kind of relaxation impairs my studying all the next day. And I dare not waste any time. So it is better that I read my Kügelgen[4] in the evening—a good occupation for a narrow spirit, and one that makes for sound sleep, when it comes.

Fondly, Franz

1906

To Max Brod

[Prague; postmark: February 19, 1906]

Dear Max,

What with one thing and another I almost failed to write you that I cannot go to the exhibition tomorrow, and in fact not at all. I've let myself be seduced into accepting a foolishly early date,[1] while my knowledge is not even infinitesimal. A rash act, and therefore very nice, if only I did not keep thinking about the medical certificate I want soon in order to be able to quit. How about the *Amethyst?*[2] I have my money ready.—Do look around the exhibition for something pretty that can be bought for a small sum. Perhaps useful as a wedding present.

Yours, Franz

To Max Brod

[Prague; postmark: March 16, 1906]

Dear Max,

I really should have written you during my examination,[3] for there's no doubt you saved me three months of my life for some other purpose than learning finance. Only your notes saved me, for thanks to them I shone to M. as his own reflection, even one with an interesting Austrian hue; and in spite of the fact that he was still wrapped up in the masses of stuff he has lectured on this semester, and I had only your small slips of paper in my memory, we arrived at the loveliest rapport. But the others were fun too, although I did not know very much.

Many regards, yours, F.K.

Přibram did very well.

To Max Brod

[Probably May 1906]

Dear Max,

Since I have not been to your place for so long (carrying crates and dusting, for we are moving the business;[4] little girl; very little studying; your book,[5] prostitutes, Macaulay's *Lord Clive*;[6] even so it adds up to a whole)— since I have not been to your place for so long I am coming today so as not to disappoint you and because I think it's your birthday,[7] in the absurdly lovely metamorphosis of *The Happy Ones*.[8] You will receive me well.

Yours, Franz K.

To Max Brod

[Prague; postmark: May 29, 1906]

Dear Max,

Since I do have to study now after all (don't pity me; that's wasting time on what is a waste of time) and since it is an effort for me to take off my rags during the day and put on street clothes, I have to live like a nocturnal animal. But still I would like to see you again some evening, perhaps tomorrow, Wednesday, or whenever else you like. Incidentally I am writing chiefly because I want to know how you are feeling, because Monday you went to the doctor's.

Franz

To Max Brod

[Prague; postmark: June 7, 1906]

From now on, my friend, I won't be able to go anywhere for a while. The dean[9] has been so rash as to advance my date slightly, and since I was ashamed to be more cautious than he, I made no objection. Yesterday a literary critic said to me very firmly: Max Brod is an authentic poet. Warm greetings.

Franz

To Max Brod
                                [Zuckmantel; postmark: August 13, 1906]
Dear Max, I have vanished for a long time; now I am reappearing, although
still breathing heavily. First a brief report in regard to where you will stay.
Hotel Edelstein, two minutes from the sanatorium, close to the woods, has a
room for 5 fl. a week, room with excellent board for 45 fl. a month for one
person. From the eighteenth on it may be even cheaper. In the sanatorium
annex rooms may be had for 7 to 8 fl. a week.

                                                           Yours, Franz

To Max Brod
                                  [Prague; postmark: October 31, 1906]
Dear Max,
    Please forgive me for last night—I'll come to see you at five o'clock. My
excuse will be a bit comical, so that you'll surely believe it.

                                                           Yours, Franz

To Max Brod
            [Pneumatic tube postcard.[10] Prague; postmark: December 11, 1906]
Dear Max,
    My interesting cousin from Paraguay, whom I have told you about and
who during this stay in Europe spent a few days in Prague just when you
were about to take your final examination, turned up in Prague again on his
way back. He wanted to leave this evening, but since I wanted to show him
to you I managed to persuade him, with a great effort, not to leave until
tomorrow morning. I am very glad and will fetch you this evening to meet
him.

                                                           Yours, Franz

To Max Brod
                                             December 16 [1906?]
My dear Max,
    When are we going to the Indian dancing girl, since the other young
woman has escaped us, her aunt for the present being stronger than her talent.

                                                                 Franz

1907

To Max Brod

[Prague,] February 12, 1907

Dear Max,

I am glad to be writing to you before going to sleep; it is only four o'clock.

I read *Die Gegenwart* yesterday, although nervously, for people were around and what was printed in *Die Gegenwart* is meant to be whispered into the ear.[1]

Well, it is Carnival, pure Carnival, but of the most amiable sort.—Good, so this winter I have taken a dance step after all.

I am especially glad that not everyone will see why my name is mentioned where it is. For he would have to read the first paragraph with that in mind and take note of the passage that deals with the felicity of sentences. He would then find: a list of names that ends with Meyrink[2] (obviously a curled-up hedgehog) is impossible at the beginning of a sentence if the following sentences are to be able to breathe. Hence a name with an open vowel at the end—here inserted—was needed to save those words. My own merit in that context is minimal.

A pity, though—I know you did not mean it that way—that it will now become an indecent act for me to publish something later, for that would blast the delicacy of this first public appearance. And I would never achieve an effect equal to the one assigned me in your sentence.

However, that is only a minor consideration today; I am more concerned with establishing the radius of my present fame, since I am a good child and a lover of geography. I don't think I can count very much on Germany. For how many people read a review down to the last paragraph with unslackening eagerness. That is not fame. But it is another matter with Germans abroad, in the Baltic Provinces, for example, or still better in America, or most of all in the German colonies; for the forlorn German reads his magazine through and through. Thus the center of my fame must be Dar es Salaam, Ujiji, Windhoek. But just to reassure these people who are so quick to take an interest (farmers, soldiers: how nice), you should have written parenthetically: "This name will have to be forgotten."

I kiss you; take your exam soon.

Yours, Franz

To Max Brod

[Prague; postmark: May 1907; day illegible]

My dear Max,

I really am hopeless, but nothing is going to change me. Yesterday afternoon I wrote you a tube postcard reading: "Here in the tobacco shop on the Graben I ask you to forgive me for not coming to see you tonight. I have a headache, my teeth are rotting away, my razor is dull; it adds up to an unpleasant sight. Yours, F."

This evening I lie down on the sofa thinking I have apologized and that a measure of order has been restored to the world, but as I am considering this I remember that I wrote Wladislaw Gasse instead of Schalengasse.[3]

Please be angry about it and don't speak to me anymore. My future is not rosy and I will surely—this much I can foresee—die like a dog. I too would be glad to avoid myself, but since that isn't possible I can at least rejoice in not having any self-pity, and so have at last become an egotist. We ought to celebrate this great moment, you and I, I mean; as a future enemy you certainly are entitled to celebrate it.

It is late. I want you to know that tonight I wished you a good night.

Yours, Franz

To Max Brod

[Probably May 1907]

Dear Max, Be calmer about your Goethe research! We can be sure that Goethe would never have written: "Goethe would never have done that"; but might he not have admitted to his birthday at the last moment, at the gate? Now really! On the contrary, you would have been able to write to Goethe that I never would have done it. I wouldn't have done it either (a birthday is a matter more bothersome than indifferent) if it had not just happened that it was significantly linked with the mention of the twenty-three-year-old girl (what an immense age that used to seem to us!) who provided me with a miracle of a Sunday the very next day. That was some Sunday.

Tell me, why do you constantly bother me with those two chapters?[4] Rejoice with me that you write incomprehensible things, and let the other stuff alone.

Yours, Franz

To Max Brod

[Triesch, mid–August 1907]

My dear Max,

When I came home last night from the outing (jolly, jolly), your letter was here and threw me into a quandary, in spite of my tiredness. I know all about indecision; it's the one thing I do know about, but whenever something is reaching out for me, I keel right over, so worn out am I from the pros and cons of a thousand earlier trivia. I myself would not be able to resist the decisiveness of the world. So it would not be right for me even to try to change your mind.

Your temperament and mine are altogether different, so it is of no significance that when I came to the passage, "I decided not to accept," I felt such terror—as if I were reading an account of a battle—that I could not read further. But the damnable infinitude of advantages and disadvantages in all things soon made me feel calmer about this, as it does about everything.

I told myself: You need a great deal of activity. I am sure about your requirements in this respect, even though I cannot comprehend them. For a whole year to have nothing but forest to walk to would not satisfy you; and after all, isn't it all but certain that during your year of court clerking in the city you will obtain a place in literature that will obviate the need for anything else?

Of course I would have run like a madman to Komotau.[5] I need no occupation, the more so since I am not capable of it. And although a forest might not satisfy me either, I nevertheless—that is clear—have accomplished nothing at all during my year of court clerking.

Then again, a profession becomes harmless as soon as one is able to cope with it. I would make a constant fool of myself during working hours—even though there are only six of them. If, as you write, you think that I could handle a job of this kind, you have some pretty wild ideas.

But then, take the shop and the consolation in the evening. Ah yes, if consolation made one happy, and if a bit of luck were not also necessary for happiness.

No, if my prospects don't improve by October I shall take the advanced course at the commercial school and learn Spanish in addition to my French and English. If you want to join me in this, it would be nice. I would make up for the edge you have over me at studying by my impatience; my uncle would have to find us a position in Spain, or else we would go to South America or the Azores, to Madeira.

For the present I can stay here until August 25. I am riding around on the motorbike a good deal, swimming a lot, lying nude in the grass by the pond for hours, hanging about the park until midnight with a bothersomely infatuated girl, have already tedded hay in the meadow, have set up a merry-go-round, helped trees after a storm, taken cows and goats to pasture and driven them home in the evening, played a lot of billiards, taken long walks, drunk a lot of beer, and I have even been in the temple too. But I have spent most of the time—I have been here six days—with two girls, very bright girls, students, extremely Social Democratic, who have to keep their teeth clenched lest they come out with a conviction, a principle, on the least provocation. One is named A.; the other, H.W., is short, her cheeks are constantly and boundlessly red; she is very nearsighted, and not only for the sake of the pretty gesture with which she places her pince-nez on her nose—whose tip is really beautifully composed of tiny planes; last night I dreamed of her plump little legs. Such are the roundabout ways by which I recognize a girl's beauty and fall in love. Tomorrow I shall read to them from *Experiments*;[6] it is the only reading matter I have with me, aside from Stendhal[7] and *Die Opale*.[8]

Ah yes, if I also had some issues of the *Amethyst* I would copy the poems for you, but the magazines are in the bookcase at home and I keep the key with me to prevent discovery of a savings bank book that nobody at home knows about and that for me determines my rank in the family. So if you cannot wait until August 25, I'll send you the key.

And now I must express my gratitude, my poor boy, for the trouble you went to persuading your publisher of the excellence of my drawing.[9]

It is hot and this afternoon I am to dance in the woods.

Please give your family my regards.

Yours, Franz

[THERE FOLLOWED COPIES OF SEVERAL POEMS[10] BY MAX BROD]

To Max Brod

[Postcard. Prague; postmark: August 28, 1907]

My dear Max, That was not good, for it is wrong of you not to write how you are doing in Komotau, but to ask me how I am, how I spent the summer— The view of the Erzgebirge may be beautiful and all that, even across the green baize of the office table, and I would have been pleased to visit you if the fare were not so high. It's possible that you have found a person whose handwriting is like mine used to be, but now my writing has changed[11] and only as I write to you do I recall the way I used to form my letters. Aren't you coming Sunday? I'd be pleased.

Yours, Franz K.

To Hedwig W.[12]

[Prague,] August 29 [1907]

My dear, I am tired and perhaps a little sick.

Now I have opened the shop and am trying, by writing to you in the office, to make this office a little pleasanter.[13] And everything around me is subject to you. The table presses against the paper as if in love with it; the pen lies in the hollow between thumb and index finger like a willing child; and the clock strikes like a bird.

But I feel I am writing to you from a war or something of the sort, from events that cannot easily be imagined because the factors that make them up are so unusual and their tempo so jangled. Involved in the most painful tasks I transfer——

evening, eleven o'clock

Now the long day has passed, and unworthy of it though it is, it has this beginning and this end. But at bottom nothing has changed since I was interrupted, and although the stars are now in the open window to my left, the intended sentence can be completed:

—I transfer my headaches from one firm resolution to another equally firm but of an opposite sense. And all these resolutions come to life, give birth to upsurges of hope and visions of a contented life; this confusion of consequences is even worse than the confusion of resolutions. Like rifle bullets I fly from one to the other, and the accumulated excitement that soldiers, spectators, rifle bullets, and generals distribute among one another in this struggle of mine is quite enough to make me tremble.

But you want me not to miss you at all, to tire my feelings and soothe them by taking them for a long walk, while you continually agitate yourself and in summer put on your fur coat only because in the winter it may turn cold.

Anyhow, I have no social life, no distraction; I spend my evenings on the small balcony above the river; I do not even read the *Arbeiterzeitung*[14] and I am not a good person. Years ago I wrote this poem:

> In the evening sun
> We sit with bowed backs
> On the benches in the park.
> Our arms dangle,
> Our eyes blink sadly.

And people in their clothes
Walk swaying on the gravel
Under this great sky
Which spreads from hills in the distance
On and on to distant hills.

And so I do not even have that concern with people that you require.

You see, I am a ridiculous person; if you are a little fond of me, it's out of pity; my part is fear. How little use meetings in letters are; they're like splashings near the shore by two who are separated by an ocean. The pen has glided over the many slopes of all the letters and now it has come to an end; it is cool and I must go to my empty bed.

Yours, Franz

To Hedwig W.

[Prague, early September 1907]

In spite of everything, my dear, your letter has come late. You thoroughly thought over what you wrote. I had no way of forcing it to come earlier, not by sitting up in bed at night, not by sleeping in my clothes on the sofa and coming home more often than was proper during the day. Until this evening when I stopped all that and felt a desire to write to you, but first I was fussing with some papers in a pigeonhole and found your letter there. It had come earlier, but someone while dusting had taken the precaution of putting the letter into the pigeonhole.

I said that writing a letter is like splashing in the water by the shore, but I did not say the splashing could be heard.

And now sit down and read quietly and let me, instead of my script, look into your eyes.

Imagine that A receives letter after letter from X, and in each one X tries to refute the existence of A. He builds his case with ever-mounting force, using complicated arguments, dark in color, to such a point that A feels almost walled in, and even feels particularly aggrieved, to the point of tears, by the gaps in the arguments. At first all of X's intentions are masked; he merely says he thinks A is quite unhappy, that he has this impression, but knows nothing about the details of the matter; what is more, he comforts A. However, he goes on, if that were so it would not be surprising, because A is a dissatisfied person, as Y and Z well know—says X. After all, it might be admitted that he has cause for his dissatisfaction; just look at him, look at his situation, and there seems no reason to contradict—says X. In fact, if you observe his situation closely you would be forced to say that A is not dissatisfied enough, for if he were to examine his predicament as thoroughly as X is doing, he could not go on living. At this point X is no longer offering consolations. And A sees, sees with open eyes, that X is the best person in the world, and yet he writes me letters of this tenor, so what for God's sake can he want but to kill me? How good he is even at the last moment, since he tries not to betray himself, in order to spare me grief, but he forgets that a light once lit sheds its illumination indiscriminately.

What is the sentence from *Niels Lyhne* supposed to mean, and the sand without the castle of happiness.[15] Of course the sentence is right, but would not one who speaks of flowing sand be right? But the person who sees the sand running is not in the castle; and where is the sand flowing to?

What am I to do now? How am I going to keep myself in one piece? I am in Triesch also, am walking across the square with you; someone falls in love with me, I receive this letter, read it, hardly understand it. Now I must bid goodbye, I hold your hand, run away, and disappear in the direction of the bridge. Oh please, it's enough.

I bought nothing in Prague for you because from October 1 on I shall probably be in Vienna.[16] Forgive me.

Yours, Franz K.

To Hedwig W.

[Prague, early September 1907]

My dear girl, once again it is late evening before I have a chance to write, and it is cool because we are after all in fall, but I am thoroughly warmed by your good letter. Yes, white dresses and sympathy become you best of all, whereas furs conceal the timid girl and ask to be admired for themselves and cause suffering. And what I really want is you, and even your letter is only an ornamental wallpaper, white and pleasant, behind which you are sitting in the grass somewhere or taking a walk, and one has to push through it to capture and hold you.

But just now, when everything is going to become better and the kiss I received on my lips is the best start for all the good things in the future, you are coming to Prague; just when I would like to visit you and stay with you, you impolitely say goodbye and take off. I would have left my parents here, a few friends and other things that I will miss; now you will be in this damned city and it seems to me it will be impossible for me to slink through all the many streets to the railroad station. And yet Vienna is more necessary for me than Prague for you. I'll be studying at the Export Academy for a year; I'll be up to my neck in unusually strenuous work, but I won't mind that. You'll have to let me put off reading the newspapers a bit longer, for I'll need time to take walks and write you letters; otherwise I mean to allow myself no pleasures.

But I'll go on so very gladly taking part in yours, only you must give me a greater chance to do so than you did in describing the last party. For there are so many things highly important to me that you do not write about at all. At what time did you arrive, when did you leave, how were you dressed, along what wall did you sit, did you laugh and dance a great deal, into whose eyes did you look for a quarter of a minute, were you tired at the end and did you sleep well? And how could you write and then—that is the worst of all— suppress a letter that belongs to me. That alone was what weighed on your spirits, when in this beautiful New Year weather you walked to the temple with your mother and grandmother, over the pavement and up the two steps and the stone slabs. You didn't consider that it takes more courage not to hope than to hope, and that when such courage is possible for a certain kind of temperament, a mere change in the wind can give courage the most favorable direction.

I send you my kisses with all the good things I think I have in me.

Yours, Franz

To Hedwig W.

[Prague, September 8, 1907]

Dearest,

They have taken away my ink and are already asleep. Permit the pencil to write to you, so that everything I possess has some share in you. If only you were here in this empty room in which only two flies against the window are making noise, I could be close to you and lay my neck against yours.

But as it is I am unhappy to the point of confusion. A few minor ailments, a little fever, a little frustrated expectation put me to bed for two days, so I wrote a dainty fever-letter to you, but then on this fine Sunday I tore it up, leaning over the windowsill. For, my poor dear, you have enough agitation. You wept for many hours in the night, didn't you, while I ran around the streets by starlight to prepare everything for you (by day I had to study); in the end it doesn't matter whether people live a street away from each other or a province. How different everything around us was. There I was self-assuredly standing at the railroad station Thursday morning, and then again Thursday afternoon (the train does not come at half past two, but at three, and was fifteen minutes late) and you were trembling in Triesch and then you wrote that letter that I received on Friday, whereupon I could think of nothing better to do than to go to bed. It isn't bad, for without sitting up I can see the Belvedere[17] and green slopes from my pillow.

In the end all that has happened is that we have danced a quadrille between Prague and Vienna, one of those figures in which couples bow so much they do not come together, no matter how much they want to. But sooner or later the round dances must come too.

I do not feel at all well. I do not know what will happen. If I get up early and see a fine day in the offing, it's bearable, but later—

I close my eyes and kiss you.

Yours, Franz

To Hedwig W.

[Prague,] September 15 [1907]

You know, love, people live oddly in Triesch, and therefore it's not surprising that today I put a red dot on my globe at the approximate location of Triesch. It was rainy today, so I took down the globe and decorated it like that.

In Triesch someone is flushed from crying without having shed tears; someone goes to a party and doesn't want to be seen there; someone has put on a silk sash I have never seen; someone writes a letter and does not mail it. Where was this letter written? Probably with pencil, but on the lap or against the wall, on the leaf of the table? And was the light in the hall sufficient for writing a letter? But I am not curious; I would be curious, to give an example, if I insisted on knowing whom Fräulein Agathe danced with. That would be improper and you would be right not to answer me.

But it so happens that you stand in some close relationship with everybody in Triesch—though it may be by a roundabout route through other persons. Even with the bellboy in the hotel or some watchman in whose field you are stealing turnips. You give them orders or let them make you cry. But I have to read that as though I were an exile—as yet I know no other kind of exile—one hungers for news about big changes back home but can scarcely read because one is so miserable about being cut off from any possibility of action there, and so delighted to be finding out something at last. Here I may say that I have no sympathy for patients whom you take care of.

The decision concerning myself, the final one, is coming tomorrow, but this letter is impatient; as soon as I write "love" on it, it comes to life and doesn't want to wait any longer. You misunderstand me nicely if you think that striving for ideal usefulness is consonant with my nature; in fact I am not in the least interested in practical usefulness.

I know you must get away from Vienna, but just the way I must from Prague; the two of us might well spend this year in Paris, for example. But the following is the correct way to put it: We are beginning to move in the right direction, and if we continue that way, will we not necessarily have to come to each other?

Please write me in precise terms about your future in Prague; perhaps I'll be able to make some arrangements after all. I'll gladly do so.

                                                                Yours, Franz

To Hedwig W.

                                          [Prague,] September 19 [1907]

Dear,

How you misunderstand me, and I don't know whether it takes a certain measure of dislike for someone to want to misunderstand him. You won't believe me, but I wasn't being at all ironic; all the things I wanted to know and that you have reported on in your letters were and are important to me. And the very sentences you call ironic were aiming at nothing but imitating the tempo with which I was permitted to caress your hands on several lovely days. Whether in those sentences I spoke about watchmen or Paris was almost beside the point.

Again interrupted in the morning and now, after midnight and very tired, continued:

Yes, the decision has come, but only today. Other people make decisions rarely and then take pleasure in their decisions during the long times between. But I an forever deciding, as often as a boxer, only I'm not boxing, that's true. Incidentally, that's only the way things look, and I hope that my affairs will soon assume the look appropriate to their nature.

I am staying in Prague and within a few weeks will in all probability obtain a position with an insurance company.[18] These next weeks I shall have to study insurance incessantly, but it is highly interesting. I'll wait till you come to tell you the rest, but of course I have to be careful not to make Providence nervous, now that it is occupied with me. So you may not tell anyone about it, not even my uncle.

When are you coming? What you write about room and board is not very clear. My readiness to help you is not any the less because the paper has a margin—you know this and yet you don't say so—but as I've told you, unfortunately I know very few people and wherever I asked it was no use, for there are teachers from earlier years around. At any rate, I'll see that this ad appears in the *Tagblatt* and the *Bohemia*[19] on Sunday:

"A young woman specializing in French, English, philosophy, and education, formerly at Vienna University, now at Prague University, available to give lessons to children, at which she believes, on the basis of past successful experience, she can achieve excellent results, or for employment as reader or companion."

I'll collect the answers from the papers myself. I would give the address Triesch, general delivery, but perhaps you will already be in Prague by next week.

Of course I'll continue looking, for one can't count too much on ads of this sort; chance in Prague must wish you as much luck as I do.

Yours, Franz

To Max Brod

[Prague,] September 22, 1907

My dear Max,

This is how it is. Other people make decisions once in a considerable while, and in between take pleasure in their decisions. But I make decisions from moment to moment, like a boxer, without doing any boxing. Yes, I am staying in Prague.

In the near future I shall probably obtain a position here (nothing the least unusual), and it's only not to make Providence nervous while it operates that I have written nothing definite about it and do not do so now.

I'm looking forward to seeing you.

Yours, Franz

To Hedwig W.

[Prague,] September 24 [1907]

Remarkably, your letter came in the evening, love, so I write in haste now for you to receive this in time.

The idea that Uncle should write to Mama is very good, and I alone am at fault for not having myself thought of it.

What's this now, you want to run away from me again, or are at any rate threatening that? Is it enough for me to stay in Prague to discourage you about your plans? Please, come; just before your letter arrived I thought how lovely it would be for us to meet on Sunday mornings and read that French book I am in the midst of reading (I have so little time at present), which is written in a chilling yet tattered French, the way I love it, so come, please.

Your notion that you should pay for everything I am doing for you for my pleasure was gladdening. But the cost of the ads, copies of which I enclose (so that you can see how clumsy and poor they look), is too trivial. However, I shall have you sent the bill for the champagne I drank to your health last night—didn't you notice?

The trifles that bother and tire you now are only bad the first time; by the second time they are expected and therefore already interesting. It takes only half a turn to have courage. Come.

Yours, Franz

To Hedwig W.

[Prague,] September 24 [1907]

At any rate a mild success, as you see, love.

I opened the letters because I thought I could help you with inquiries. Well, one of them, as you can see, looks reassuringly Jewish and I'll try to find out what kind of people they are; at any rate, I'll write to them.

The other sounds a little like something from a novel. You are to write—I'm translating it for you—to the indicated code number what your terms would be for carrying on German conversation with a young lady of twenty-one three times a week, possibly on walks. You might answer it after all, for the sake of the joke.

But both would have to be answered quickly; I don't think there will be any more replies coming. At any rate, we'll run it again in the next few days.

My best to you; have Mama write, don't forget, and come.

Yours, Franz

To Max Brod

[Prague; postmark: October 4, 1907]

Dear Max, You know I have a job,[20] so a new year has begun and my afflictions, assuming that up to now they walked on foot, are now walking appropriately on their hands. I would very much like to meet you tomorrow at half past two at the Mary statue on the Ring;[21] punctually, please; make it possible.

Yours, Franz K.

To Max Brod

[Postcard. Prague; postmark: October 8, 1907]

Dear Max, Written in the street to answer you quickly.—Why have you so bad a memory for your leisure time, so good a one for lent books. I'm coming Friday, remember.—I knew nothing about the operation, I merely ask (which is why I'm writing just on a card) why God is punishing Germany, Blei, and us so hard. Especially me, who after all until 6:15 P.M.——

Yours, Franz

To Hedwig W.

[Prague, early October 1907]

Now I have to write to you in gray strokes again because those who have already locked themselves into sleep have the ink, whereas the pencil, which has fallen in love with you, came to hand right off. Dear one, dear one, how nice that summer weather should have appeared in the middle of autumn, and how grateful we must be, for the shift of seasons would be hard to endure if one could not keep in inward equilibrium with them. Dear one, dear one, my way home from the office is worth telling about, all the more so because it is the only thing about me that is worth telling. I come tearing out of the big portal at 6:15, regret the wasted quarter-hour, turn to the right and go down Wenzelsplatz, then meet an acquaintance who walks along with me and tells me a few interesting things, come home, open the door of my room, your letter is there, I enter into your letter like someone who is tired of paths through fields and now walks into the woods. I lose myself, but that doesn't worry me. If only every day would end this way.

October 8

Dear child, another evening after several evenings that passed so quickly. May this ink-blot boldly usher in the excitement of letter-writing.

My life is completely chaotic now. At any rate I have a job with a tiny salary of 80 crowns and an infinite eight to nine hours of work; but I devour the hours outside the office like a wild beast. Since I was not previously accustomed to limiting my private life to six hours, and since I am also studying Italian and want to spend the evenings of these lovely days out of doors, I emerge from the crowdedness of my leisure hours scarcely rested.

Am in the office now. I am in the Assicurazioni Generali and have some hopes of someday sitting in chairs in faraway countries, looking out of the office windows at fields of sugar cane or Mohammedan cemeteries; and the whole world of insurance itself interests me greatly, but my present work is dreary. And yet it is sometimes very nice, sitting there, to lay down the pen and imagine, for example, that I am placing your hands one atop the other and enclosing them in one of my hands, knowing that I would not let go even if my hand were unscrewed from my wrist.

Adieu.

Yours, Franz

To Max Brod

[Prague; postmark: October 16, 1907]

Dear Max, Written in the street, as we shall always be writing each other from now on, because the jostlings of passersby enliven the handwriting.

Looking at the photograph of Paula K. Yesterday I saw her several times in the flesh. She stood still for a while and walked for a while, all in white, down Hybernergasse with a young man who wore creased trousers. Only to have some firm impressions to cling to: her teeth are crooked; she has a dimple, but only in the right cheek; her complexion is moderately weatherbeaten, covered with ashes, not powder. Evidently her skin rests by day.—I'll be coming Thursday. Do me the favor of working hard.

                                                                        Franz

To Max Brod

                              [Prague; postmark: October 21, 1907]
A quick note in the office; we've really earned our lunch. Forgive me if I don't come today; I had something I had to do Sunday and didn't get it done because Sunday is short. Mornings for sleep, afternoons for washing hair, dusk for strolling like an idler. I always use Sunday as a prelude to pleasures; that is pretty silly. Write me when you will be free, except Thursday and Friday are no good for me.

                                            All the best, yours, Franz

To Max Brod

                              [Prague; postmark: October 21, 1907]
My dear Max, We are having a contest in unreliability and unpunctuality. Of course I haven't the slightest intention of being the winner, for I am just naïvely unpunctual from Italian diligence, you from sheer hedonism. But since you are trying to balance that out by coming to see me (Wednesday, yes?), I don't mind. Maybe you are doing it only because it is easier to call off a visit than an invitation.

                                                            Yours, Franz

To Max Brod

                        [Postcard. Prague; postmark: October 26, 1907]
Dear Max, The earliest I can come will be half past ten or eleven o'clock, because they want to take a look at my body there.[22] Since it is now almost certain that I will continue in my unhappy state, unhappy while laughing at my own expense, they are looking at my body merely for the fun of it.

                                                            Yours, Franz

To Hedwig W.

[Prague, probably November 1907]

Dear girl, Forgive me for not having answered you right off, but I still have not developed the technique for making good use of my few hours; midnight comes apace, as now. Don't think the beautiful weather has driven you out of my mind; it only drives out the pen, love. But I'll answer all your questions.

I can't say whether I am going to be transferred soon and far away; hardly before a year is out. Best of all would be to be transferred right out of the firm. That isn't altogether impossible.

I don't complain about the work so much as about the sluggishness of swampy time. The office hours, you see, cannot be divided up; even in the last half hour I feel the pressure of the eight hours just as much as in the first. Often it is like a train ride lasting night and day, until in the end you're totally crushed; you no longer think about the straining of the engine, or about the hilly or flat countryside, but ascribe all that's happening to your watch alone, which you continually hold in your palm.

I am learning Italian, for I shall probably be sent to Trieste first.

During my first few days I must have presented a most pathetic sight to anyone alert to such matters. Whatever it's actually been, I felt declassed; people who have not lazed away at least part of their time up to their twenty-fifth year are greatly to be pitied, for it's my belief that it's not the money you have earned that you take with you into your grave, but your idle time.

I am at the office at eight o'clock, leave at half past six.

Cheerful people without inner complications? All people in this sort of work are like that. The springboard for their cheerfulness is the last moment in the office; unfortunately, it's just such people I don't associate with.

Erotes will soon be published under the title of *The Path of a Lover*,[23] but without my title page, which has proved not reproduceable.

What you write about the young writer is interesting, but you exaggerate the points of similarity. I merely try casually and in a hit-and-miss way to dress well; but many people in many countries have already become adept at that; they take care of their nails, and some even use fingernail polish. If he speaks French beautifully, that is in itself one significant difference between us; and that he is able to see you is a damnable difference.

I have read the poem, and since you give me leave to judge it I can say that there is much pride in it, but unfortunately pride that walks very much alone. On the whole it seems to me a childlike and therefore endearing expression of admiration for admirable contemporaries. Voilà. But all too sensitive to the balance of a scales you are holding in your dear hands, I am sending along a poor trifle,[24] perhaps a year old, which he can judge under the same terms (you won't mention any names, or offer any other clue, will you?). It will give me great pleasure if he thoroughly ridicules me. Then send the page back to me, as I am doing with his.

Now I have answered everything and more; it's time for me to assert my rights. What you write about yourself is as unclear as it must be to you also. Am I to blame for their tormenting you, or are you tormenting yourself and the others merely not giving you help? "A man I find very likable," "both should have made concessions." All that I can visualize of that huge and blurred city of Vienna is you alone, and I cannot help you at all now, so it seems. May I not close this letter while the clock is dismally striking one?

Yours, Franz

To Hedwig W.

[Prague, November 1907]
12 o'clock

Tired, but obedient and grateful: thank you. So all is well. The transitions from fall to winter are often this way. And now that it's winter we sit in one room—it's really that way—except that the walls by which we are each sitting are a trifle far apart; but that's merely incidental and doesn't have to be so.

What stories! How many people you know, and all the walks and the plans. I have no stories, see no people; for my daily walk I scurry down four streets whose corners I have already rounded off, and across a square. I'm too tired for plans. Perhaps I'll gradually turn to wood from my frozen fingertips on up—I wear no gloves. Then you'll have a nice letter-writer in Prague and my hand will be a pretty knickknack for you. And for that reason, because I'm living so brutish a life, I must ask you twice over to forgive me for inflicting myself on you.

22nd

For heaven's sake, why didn't I mail the letter? You will be angry, or merely uneasy. Forgive me. And be a bit charitable toward my laziness, or whatever you want to call it. But it isn't laziness alone, it's also fear, generalized fear of writing, of this horrible pursuit; yet all my unhappiness now is due to my being deprived of it. But above all: only shaky things have to be stabilized by some arrangement every so often. I should like to think that our relations are not in that category.

And in spite of everything I would have written you long since, instead of carrying the half-finished letter around with me folded small, but I have suddenly got mixed up with a whole crowd. Army officers, Berliners,

Frenchmen, painters, cabaret singers, and they have taken away my few evening hours in the merriest fashion. And not only the evening hours; last night, for example, I didn't have a kreuzer for a tip to give a band leader so I lent him a book instead. And so it goes. It makes one forget that time is passing and that one is losing the days, so it can be commended on those grounds. Greetings, my love, and thanks.

Yours, Franz

To Max Brod

[Prague; postmark: December 21, 1907]

Dearest Max, I am feeling so rotten that I think I can manage only if I don't talk to anyone for a week, or as long as proves necessary. If you don't try to answer this card in any way I'll know you care for me.

Yours, Franz

To Max Brod

[Prague, end of 1907]

Dear Max,

In the joy of having met all of you I made a few careless remarks, and when I left you I suddenly started to worry about the following. You will take care that it doesn't happen, won't you?

It's settled, then, that your father will intercede with Herr Weissgerber for Herr Bäuml;[25] he can also give my name, although I don't particularly like the idea, but please, in no case is he to say that I am dissatisfied, will be leaving my job, will be taking a job with the post office, and other things of the sort. I would be terribly sorry about that, because Herr Weissgerber went to considerable trouble to place me in the Assicurazioni, and, as was only to be expected, after my initial despair I was most excited and thanked him wildly. He more or less vouched for me at the company, and the very first words the senior officials spoke in the presence of Herr Weissgerber expressed their assumption that if I were hired, which at the time was by no means certain, I would remain with the company forever. Naturally I more than nodded assent.

Of course, if I do get a job in the post office, which is still highly dubious, explanations will have to be made; but for the present, please, I would rather not hurt my past providence with so much as my fingertip.

Yours, Franz

To Felix Weltsch[26]

[Visiting card. Probably 1907]

After all, our nervous system does take in the entire city. And I have always felt a painful twinge at the spot where your room is, because you studied so desperately there. Now it's over. Thank God!

Yours, Franz K.

1908

To Max Brod

[Prague; postmark: January 11, 1908]

I beg you, my dear, dear Max, even if you had other plans for the evening, wait for me so that I don't have to fetch anyone from the theater, not ride in a rubber-tired hack, not sit upstairs in some coffeehouse balcony, not go into any bar, not have to look at that striped dress. If only you had time for me every evening!

To Hedwig W.

[Prague, probably early 1908]

Dear, For once in the office to typewriter music, in haste and with graceful mistakes. I should have thanked you long ago for your letter and now it is again so very late. But I think you have already forgiven me forever in such matters, for when things are going well with me I write quickly enough—it's quite some time back and at the time I didn't need to—otherwise, slowly. And although you dealt with me kindly in your letter, you forbore to compliment me on the verve with which I bury my head in any old road gravel and refuse to pull it out again. Hitherto I've lived quite decently, though at intervals, for in ordinary times it is not difficult to build oneself a sedan chair and feel that it is being carried down the road by good spirits. But then if (so I wanted to continue, but it was already 8:15 and I went home)— but then if one wooden brace breaks, especially in poorish weather, one is standing on the highway, can no longer accomplish anything, and is still far from the phantom city one wanted to reach. Permit me to pull such stories over me as a sick man draws sheets and blankets over himself.

That was written some time ago. Then today your letter came, love.

Herewith the third script; one of the three ought to soothe the overstrung child. Now we are gathering under this three-script flag, blue gray black, and together recite the following, taking care to coordinate every word: "Life is disgusting." Very well, it's disgusting, but it's no longer so dreadful if we say it in pairs, for the feeling that blows one of us to smithereens collides with the other person, is prevented by him from expanding, and one surely says: "How prettily she says 'disgusting life' and stamps her foot as she says it." The world's a sad place, but still it's a bit flushed with sadness, and is animated sadness so very far from happiness?

You know, I've had an abominable week, a terrible lot to do at the office. Perhaps that will always be so; I suppose one must earn one's grave. And there have been other troubles too; I'll tell you about them some time. In short I've been chased around like a wild animal, and since I'm not one at all, how tired I must be. Last week I really belonged in this street I live on,[1] which I call "Suicide Lane," for the street traces a broad path down to the river; there a bridge[2] is being built, and the Belvedere on the other bank, with its hills and gardens, will be tunneled under, so that by following the street across the bridge it will be possible to walk under the Belvedere. For the present, however, only the framework of the bridge has been erected; the street stops at the river. But all this is only a joke, for it will always be finer to go across the bridge to the Belvedere than to go through the river into heaven.

I understand your situation; it's ridiculous how much you have to study, and you have every right to become nervous without anyone's saying so much as a single word of reproach to you on that account. But look, at any rate you are making visible progress. You have a goal that cannot run away from you like a girl and that, even if you try to fend it off, will make you happy. Whereas I shall remain one of those humming tops forever, for a while distressing the eardrums of a few people who may come too close to me, that's all.

It delighted me that there is an obvious mistake in your letter, which you'll have to admit at once, for this week we are having only one holiday. The other must be some piece of Lower Austrian good luck. In these matters you must not argue with me, for I know all the holidays by heart up to the beginning of May. In all other matters you may argue with me or even worse you may refuse to argue with me, but let me insert the marginal plea here, don't do so.

Yours, Franz

To Max Brod

[Letterhead: Assicurazioni Generali*]
[Prague; postmark: March 29, 1908]

My dear Max,

What an inconvenient initial letter your name has. The way I hold the pen, I cannot write it decently, although I would like to.

But since I have too much to do and it is sunny here in this deserted office, I have had an almost excellent idea which can be carried out very cheaply. Instead of our planned nightlife from Monday to Tuesday we could arrange a nice morning life, meeting at five o'clock or half past five at the Mary statue— then we won't have to let the women down—and go to the Trocadero or to Kuchelbad or to the Eldorado.³ Then, depending on how we feel, we could have coffee in the garden by the Moldau or else leaning against Joszi's shoulder. Both possibilities have their points. For at the Trocadero we wouldn't cut a bad figure. There are millionaires and even richer people whose pockets are empty by six o'clock in the morning, and it would be just as if we had been picked clean by all the other bars and were now coming to this last one for that teeny cup of coffee and are able to pay for a second cup only because we were millionaires or still are—who can tell in the morning?

As you see, all one needs for this is an empty wallet, and I can lend you that if you like. But if you're not brave enough, stingy enough, energetic enough for such an undertaking, don't bother to write me, just meet me Monday at nine. But if you are ready for it, send me a postcard by pneumatic post stating your conditions.

* [IN THE BLANK SPACE OF THE PRINTED "___ DEPARTMENT":] Sad Sunday-morning work . . .

To Max Brod

[Prague, probably May 1908]

Here, dear Max, are two books and a pebble. I've always tried hard to find something for your birthday that is of such neutral nature that it cannot be changed, be lost, be spoiled, and be forgotten. And after having pondered the problem for months I once again could think of nothing but sending you a book. But books are a vexation; if on the one hand they are neutral, on the other hand they are all the more interesting; and then only my convictions attracted me to the neutral ones, but with me convictions are by no means the decisive factor, and at the end I found myself, still changing my mind, holding in my hand a book that simply burned with sheer interestingness. Once I deliberately forgot your birthday. That was of course better than sending a book, but it wasn't good. Therefore, I am sending you the pebble now, and will send one to you as long as we live. Keep it in your pocket; it will protect you. If you leave it in a drawer, it won't be inactive either; but if you throw it away, that will be best of all. For you know, Max, my love for you is greater than myself and I dwell in it rather than it dwells in me. And if it has only a feeble support in my insecure nature, by means of the pebble it comes to occupy an abode in rock, even if only in a crack in the sidewalk on Schalengasse.[4] For a long time this love has saved me more often than you know, and right now, when I am more puzzled about myself than ever and when fully conscious feel half asleep, but so extremely light, barely existing—I go around as though my guts were black, you know—at such a time as now it feels good to throw a pebble like this into the world and thus divide certainty from uncertainty. What are books compared with that! Once a book begins to bore you, it goes on doing so, or your child tears it up, or, like Walser's book,[5] it's already falling apart when you receive it. But the pebble cannot bore you; a pebble also cannot disintegrate, or if it does, only in times far in the future. You also cannot forget it because you are not supposed to remember it. Finally, you can never lose it for good, since you'll find it again on any old gravel path because it is just any old pebble. And I could not harm it by even greater praise. For praise is harmful only when the praise crushes, injures, or embarrasses the object of praise. But a pebble? In short, I have found the finest of birthday presents for you, and convey it to you with a kiss which is meant to express awkwardly my thanks that you exist.

Yours, Franz

To Max Brod

[Letterhead: Assicurazioni Generali]
Prague, June 9, 1908

Dear Max,

Thank you. I am sure you forgive unhappy me for not having thanked you sooner. Sunday morning and early afternoon I uselessly, terribly uselessly, applied for a job, although solely by my posture; sat with my grandfather[6] for the rest of the afternoon, though often painfully conscious of the leisure hours, and then in the twilight, and then in the dusk on the sofa beside dear H.'s bed while she pummeled her boyish body under the red blanket, in the evening at the exhibition with the other girl, at night in bars, home at half past five. Only then did I see your book,[7] for which I thank you again. I've read only a little, the part I already knew. What a noise, what controlled noise.

Yours, Franz

To Max Brod

[Postcard. Prague; postmark: August 22, 1908]
I sincerely thank you, my dear Max, but must tell you that the murkiness of the facts is clearer than your explanations. The one convincing thing I can make out of it is that we must go together often and long to see the cinema, the factory, and the geishas before we understand the business not only for our own benefit but also for the world's. I can't Monday, but every day from Tuesday on. I'll expect you Tuesday at four o'clock.[8]

Yours, Franz

To Max Brod

[Picture postcard. Tetschen on the Elbe;[9] postmark: September 2, 1908]
My dear Max,

Now at five o'clock drinking down with milk the boredom of six hours' work—that also makes some marginal sense. But otherwise. Otherwise there are a few additional matters: very good food morning, noon, and night and living in the hotel room. I like hotel rooms; I'm at home at once in hotel rooms, more than at home, really.

Yours, Franz

I'll be coming back Thursday afternoon.

To Max Brod

[Picture postcard. Černošic;[10] postmark: September 9, 1908]
At that time I lay in bed until twelve, nor was it any better in the afternoon. The day before and the subsequent night were to blame. That I am in Černošic is not remarkable. I hope you all are better off than I am.

F.K.

To Max Brod
        [Picture postcard. Spitzberg,[11] Bohemian Forest, September 1908]
My dear Max,
    I am sitting under the veranda roof; it's about to rain. I prop my feet on a table brace to protect them from the cold brick floor and abandon only my hands to the cold by writing. And I write that I am very happy and that it would be a great joy to me if you were here, for in the woods are things one could meditate on for years, lying in the moss. Adieu, I'll be coming soon.
                                                        Yours, Franz

To Max Brod
                                            [Prague, September 1908]
My dear Max, It is half past twelve at night, an unusual time for letter-writing, even when the night is as hot as today's. Not even moths come to the light.
    After the happy week in the Bohemian Forest—the butterflies there fly as high as the swallows here—I have been in Prague for four days, and so defenseless. Nobody can stand me and I can stand no one, but the latter is only the consequence. Your book[12] alone, which I am at last reading straight through, does me good. It is a long time since I have been so plunged in inexplicable unhappiness. As long as I am reading I cling to the book, although it was never meant to help the unhappy; but otherwise I am so urgently driven to find someone who will merely touch me in a friendly manner that yesterday I went to the hotel with a prostitute. She is too old to still be melancholy, but feels sorry, though it doesn't surprise her, that people are not as kind to prostitutes as they are to a mistress. I didn't comfort her since she didn't comfort me either.

To Max Brod
                        [Postcard. Prague; postmark: October 25, 1908]
Yes, my dear Max, how glad I will be to come Tuesday, and very early. I have only one question now and wish you could answer it right away. If, for example, eight persons sit within the periphery of a conversation, when and how is one supposed to take the floor in order not to be considered taciturn.

For heaven's sake, one surely cannot plunge in at random, even if one is as impartial as an Indian. If only I had asked you sooner!

Yours, Franz

N.B. My Papa[13] has not bought me a dress-circle seat to *La Sorcière!*[14]

To Oskar Baum[15]

[Prague,] November 6, 1908

Dear Herr Baum,

You give me pleasure simultaneously by the publication of your book[16] (I have not read it yet, am eager to do so) and by yesterday's invitation. Thank you very much; of course I will come. Don't think it ingratitude on my part if I bring a book along and want to read aloud rather a lot.

I hope it isn't inconvenient for you if we come Wednesday instead of Monday, as Max has already written you.

I kiss your charming wife's hand.

Yours, F. Kafka

To Max Brod

[Prague; postmark: November 12, 1908]

My dear Max, I guess I won't be able to come. This morning, just as I was looking forward to the afternoon and evening, I was told to come to the office in the afternoon; at noon, when I was still looking forward to the evening, I was told that I'll have to be in the shop during the afternoon and evening. There is a great deal to do because a clerk is sick and Father isn't feeling well. It would be murder if I didn't stay in the shop until eight, and probably if I left at night.

So make excuses for me nicely, please.

To Max Brod

[Postcard. Prague; postmark: November 21, 1908]

My dear Max, According to the newspapers everything seems to be going splendidly for you, and of course I congratulate you and myself and all of us. Although, as I've already said, I don't know where happiness resides on this earth, I cannot help rejoicing that you will have a chance at a similar insight.

Yours, Franz

To Max Brod

[Picture postcard (reproduction of Hiroshige's[17] *Fujiyama*).
Prague; postmark: November 21, 1908]

My dearest Max,

Here on a smeared picture postcard, but the most beautiful I have, I send you a kiss—before the eyes of the whole populace, that is. Since I believe you more than I do myself, I thought yesterday I was really at fault, only I thought it doesn't matter all that much since we're going to live for a long time. But if what you write is so, and I have already become convinced of that again, then things are better than I thought and you'll shortly be coming up in the elevator. Anyhow, I'm feeling very good today, as though I were just beginning to live, so your card fits right in, for what a fine acquaintanceship it is that begins in such a way.

Yours, Franz

That date you mention doesn't worry me because you'll surely get the job before that, and if not your *Maidservant*[18] will be published, though it will be published in any case, so what more do you want? One can ask for more at night, but in the morning?

To Max Brod

[Letter-card. Prague; postmark: December 10, 1908]

My dear Max, If I had come to you today—it doesn't matter, I'll just come tomorrow—I would have asked you, as I am now doing, for there would be no point to my springing such a surprise, to arrange things somehow, in some decent manner, so that I won't have to go tomorrow evening. For as I realized before washing up this morning, I have been in despair for two years, and only the greater or lesser extent of this despair determines the nature of my mood at any given time. And I am at the café, have read a few nice things, am feeling well, and am therefore not writing as determinedly as I wished to at home. But that in no way belies the fact that, for the past two years, each time I get up in the morning I cannot think of anything with power enough to provide consolation for me, who am strong in consolation.

Franz

I won't go anywhere, absolutely not.

To Max Brod

[Prague,] December 15, 1908

My dear Max,

Before tomorrow comes I must thank you for Diderot.[19] I really needed such a pleasure which always remains ahead of one when one heads toward it, but which at the same time closes more and more around one, the farther one moves.

Recently I wrote the following sentence about Kassner[20] and some other matters:

There are things we have never seen, heard, or even felt, whose existence moreover cannot be proved—although no one has as yet tried to prove them—which we nevertheless run in pursuit of, even though the direction of their course has never been seen, and which we catch up with before we have reached them, and into which we someday fall with clothes, family mementos, and social relationships as into a pit that was only a shadow on the road.

But this is meant only as a pretext to send you greetings and to wish you the best of luck with your work.

Yours, Franz

To Elsa Taussig[21]

[Prague, December 28, 1908]

Dear Fräulein,

Do not be alarmed; I merely want to remind you as I promised, in good time but as late as possible so that it won't slip your mind, that you intended to go to the Orient[22] with your sister this evening.

It is superfluous for me to write more, and actually diminishes the importance of the preceding lines, but I have always found it easier to do the superfluous than the almost necessary. You see, I have always neglected the almost necessary, I confess. I can confess that because it is natural.

For we are so glad to have accomplished the absolutely necessary (which of course we must always do pronto, for how otherwise could we keep ourselves alive for going to the cinematograph—don't forget this evening—for gymnastics and showers, for living alone, for good apples, for sleeping when we have already had all the sleep we need, for being drunk, for a few past things, for a hot bath in winter when darkness has fallen, and for who knows what else)— we are then so glad, I think, that just because we are so glad we go ahead and do the superfluous but omit the almost necessary.

I mention this only because after the evening in your flat I knew that it was almost necessary for me to write you. Yet I procrastinated, for after the last cinematograph show—you must keep these two strands apart—that letter was still almost necessary, but this incidental necessity was already somewhat in the past, although in another and less significant direction than the direction in which the superfluous is located.

When, however, you recently told me to write to you in order to give you a specimen of my handwriting, you provided me at once with all the prerequisites for the necessary, and thus for the superfluous.

And yet that almost necessary letter would not have been a bad thing. You must consider that the necessary always happens, the superfluous just usually, the almost necessary rarely, at least in my case; with the result that, stripped of all context, it can easily become slightly pitiful, meaning entertaining.

So it's a pity about that letter because it's a pity to be deprived of your laughter at that letter. In saying which—surely you'll believe me—I don't mean anything against your laughter in general, nor am I against the laughter to which you will be stirred today by *The Gallant Guardsman*, let alone *The Thirsty Policeman*.

Yours, Franz K.

To Max Brod

[Prague,] December 31, 1908

My dear Max, No, thanks, not that, better not.

(By the way, I did not receive your card until four o'clock, when I was on the point of going to you; I went to sleep, have now got up at a quarter past six and am still, so to speak, a bit sleepy.)

I know you have guests; who says that they want to have me or could even tolerate me? What is more, every time I woke up for the past four days I have consoled myself by looking forward to today's sleep. And above all, we would get to the tea but not to *Saint Anthony*[23] and there would be no chance for *The Happy Ones*.[24]

But at the present time there's nothing that would mean more to me than *The Happy Ones*, and therefore I wish you a Happy New Year with particular earnestness and ask you not to stay up late working.

Adieu, my dear Max; give your family New Year's wishes from me and write to tell me when I can listen again.

Yours, Franz

To Max Brod

[Prague, 1908]

My dear Max,

Wouldn't you like me to fetch you tomorrow, Wednesday, evening; you will want to bid goodbye to Přibram, so that would fit in well. I've already come out of my Saturday night unconsciousness. You don't know that state; part of the reason, of course, is that I haven't been in society for so long. But it's not only that; something could be done about that. The same thing happened to me that time in the London[25] with Joszi and Maltschi. I was on my feet again Sunday. I went to see *The Vice Admiral*,[26] and I maintain that if plays must be written, the way to learn about them is from operettas. And even if things bog down on stage, down below the conductor has something afoot, beyond the bay all kinds of cannon are crossfiring away, the tenor's arms and legs are weapons and flags, and in the four corners the chorus girls, including some pretty ones in sailor costume, are laughing.

By the way, if you will come tomorrow and drop me a note to that effect, I'll show you my new overcoat, if it's ready and if we have moonlight.

Yours, Franz

1909

To Hedwig W.

[Prague,] January 7, 1909

My dear Fräulein,

Here are the letters; I am also including today's card and no longer have a single line of yours[1] in my possession.

May I therefore tell you that you would give me pleasure by letting me talk with you. You are free to regard that as a lie, but if so it would take a certain friendliness on your part to think me capable of so big a lie. What is more, your taking it as a lie would necessarily induce you to talk with me; not that I mean to say that my possible pleasure at the favor might prompt you to refuse.

In any case, no such considerations can force you to see me. (It would be a pleasure for me, don't forget that.) You might of course be afraid of being disgusted or bored; perhaps you are leaving tomorrow; it's also possible that you haven't even read this letter.

You are invited to our house for lunch tomorrow. I am no obstacle to your accepting the invitation; I never come home before a quarter past two. If

I hear that you mean to come, I'll stay away until half past three. That's happened before, so nobody will wonder.

F. Kafka

To Max Brod

[Postcard. Prague; postmark: January 13, 1909]
My dear Max, Yesterday I went to see B., so it was your fault and the beautiful night's that I was up late and am so tired I'm stupid with sleepiness. God knows why, I no longer have any stamina. I'm going to sleep now and will *come around six;* in the evening I want to go to Příbram to study. It's not only that I need the subject, that it interests me a little, that I really must help P. who is so pressed now, but also I prefer not to lose sight of him on account of the job.[2] It wouldn't amount to much, but it would be something and of late you've become nervous, so it seems to me, although for my part I cannot comprehend why you should.

Yours, Franz

To Max Brod

[Postcard. Prague; postmark: January 21, 1909]
My dear Max, You will recall that I told you about the *Bohemia,* rather too confidently, it now seems to me. Well, a rebuff would be very depressing, not so much on account of the rebuff as on account of the cause. Hence I want to do everything possible to put myself on a secure footing, and I cannot help it that this "I want to do everything possible" means only "please help me." So I'll come to your place between four and five, I think, tomorrow—Friday—afternoon. The whole business will take at most a quarter of an hour. I know that's a great deal of time for you now, but do forgive me since I do not forgive myself for it.

Yours, Franz

To Max Brod

[Prague; postmark: March 12, 1909]
But your memory, dear Max! I remember perfectly! Outside your house Sunday night I shook myself and said: Tuesday I'll be going to this place and that place. You said: Come Wednesday. I: I'll be tired, besides I want to see Př[ibram]. You: Then come Thursday. Good. Thursday I came. Anyhow, the state I'm in now, even deserved reproaches would be too harsh for me.

Yours, Franz

To Max Brod
                    [Postcard. Prague; postmark: March 13, 1909]
My dear Max, I cannot come this evening. Don't you realize that? This
evening we, a small company of three betrayed cronies, are going to the
varieté to amuse ourselves. What's this about doubting? When I came to you
Thursday I wanted first to ignore my own pain and congratulate you on the
post office.[3] There are bound to be doubts in this matter, but you have to
have made up your mind long beforehand. The post office, a government job
without ambition, is the only thing that suits you. In a week you'll have
disabused yourself of the idea of lots of money and a high position, and then
all will be well. Please, no more doubts. Incidentally, I'll pay my debts and
then you'll have money again.
    I'll come Monday at six.

                                                          Yours, Franz

To Max Brod
                            [Prague; postmark: March 23, 1909]
My dearest Max, You see how it is, all the people I like are going to be angry
with me except one, and she doesn't like me anyhow. The story of my life
yesterday is simple. I was there until ten o'clock and in the bar until one
o'clock. I was awake enough to hear the clock strike half past seven, when
your music probably started. Father and Mother are not quite well,
Grandfather[4] is sick, the dining room is being painted, and the family lives in
my room as in a gypsy caravan. This afternoon I must go to the office. I
haven't the courage to apologize to Baum. Don't abandon me.

                                                          Yours, Franz

To Hedwig W.
                                         [Prague, mid-April 1909]
Dear Fräulein,
    You were in a bad state when you wrote that letter, but surely not
permanently so. You are alone, you write, and perhaps there is some intent
behind your being so—such intentions naturally have neither beginning nor
end. And lonesomeness looks bleak when viewed from outside, when
someone sits confronting himself as we often do, but inside the walls, so to
speak, it has its comforts. However, it certainly shouldn't be filled with
having to study; that's dreadful, especially when one is still upset about other
things. I know that. In such states we imagine—I remember that so well—that
we are forever stumbling through unfinished suicides; we're continually done

in and have to start from scratch from moment to moment. That kind of studying becomes the very center of this dismal world. But for me it has always been hardest in winter. When in winter I had to light the lamp right after dinner, I would draw the curtains, sit down resolutely at the desk, black through and through with unhappiness, only to stand up after all, having to cry out, and while standing raise my arms as if about to take flight. Good Lord. And just to make sure that one got away with nothing, some good-hearted acquaintance would drop in, from the skating rink, say, chat a little, and when he left the door would jiggle ten times before shutting. In spring and summer it is quite different; windows and doors are open and the same sun and air are in the room in which you're studying and in the garden where others are playing tennis; you no longer thrash about in hell within the four walls of your room, but occupy yourself like a living person between two walls. That is an enormous difference; you should be able to break through whatever hellishness remains. And you will surely manage to, if I could, who can only manage to do anything while literally plunging to my doom.

If there is anything you want to know about me: that story about Fräulein Kral is a fairy tale—whether it's a pretty one I don't know; my mother is due for an operation next week; my father is more and more on the downgrade; my grandfather collapsed unconscious today; and I'm not so well myself.

Yours, Franz K.

To Max Brod

[Prague, mid-April 1909]

My dear Max,

Yes, I couldn't come last night. Our family is practically a battlefield; my father is worse, and my grandfather collapsed unconscious in the shop.

As dusk came on today, around six, I read "Stones, Not People"[5] at the window. It leads one out of the human realm in an engaging way; it is not sin and not discontinuity, but a public exit, though a rather narrow one, with each separate step accompanied by its own justification. While firmly embracing the poem one imagines that without any effort of one's own, realer than real because of the joy of the embrace, one can emerge from unhappiness.

Yesterday we talked about a story by Hamsun.[6] I spoke of how the man took his seat in a cab in front of the hotel. That was not the essential thing. Rather, the man is sitting with a girl he loves, at a table somewhere in a restaurant. But at another table in this restaurant sits a young man whom the girl herself is in love with. By some trick the man brings the young man over to his table. The young man sits down beside the girl; the man stands up, although only after a while; probably he holds the arm of the chair as he does so, and says with as close as possible an approximation to the truth: "Sir, ma'am—I am very sorry—you, Elisabeth, utterly bewitched me again today, but I realize that I cannot have you—it's a mystery to me——" This last phrase, you know, is a point at which the story, before the reader's eyes, destroys itself or at least obscures itself, no, diminishes, moves away, so that the reader, in order not to lose it, must walk into the obvious trap.——

If you're not feeling well, let me know at once.

Yours, Franz

To Max Brod

[Postcard. Prague; postmark: April 21, 1909]

My dear Max, Going downhill. The operation went well, as far as anyone can tell so far. Thank you very much, but you know quite well that I am always tentative. I accompanied W. from the Altneu Synagogue[7] to the bridge; if the toll collector[8] had addressed me, I would have started all over again. My craving to do so is not especially strong; small resistance would suffice, but I cannot summon that up. Add to this the pleasure of being able to talk about oneself in boundless generalities.

Adieu, yours, Franz

Yes, Thursday, but I'll have to go to see Mother afterward.

To Max Brod

[Postcard. Prague; postmark: May 8, 1909]

My dear Max, Since things have been going well for you in all respects recently, you will easily forgive me for not having kept two promises, although to be sure both are utterly trivial. I am too tired. I am so tired that I prefer agreeing to everything and anything right away so as not to have to give any thought to the matter. That's what happened Sunday; my head isn't going to improve quickly, if it improves at all. Yesterday after supper I wanted to lie down on the sofa and take a fifteen-minute nap but slept with the light out—though around ten my father made several futile efforts to rouse me—until half past one, when I transferred to bed. If waiting for me last night bothered you, I'm very sorry.

Yours, Franz

To Max Brod[9]

[Letter-card. Prague; postmark: June 2, 1909]
My dear Max, I've just received your card this evening. That's really incomprehensible. How are we to explain that? Is Herr Kalandra anxious to keep the probationary workers busy, or are the highest circles, once set in motion, now bent on advancing your career? The affair comes as a surprise, of course, but it need not alarm you. You'll have to ease up on your nightlife for a while; mornings you'll laze around in a somewhat more disciplined way than hitherto, while you'll have most afternoons for writing, which after all is the main thing for you and for us. On the whole, only the summer months are affected; they are almost upon us and we never get any work done during the summer anyhow, I think. In recompense you have the afternoons and twilit evenings undisturbed; one certainly could have more but hasn't. the right to demand more; and apparently you'll be legally entitled to vacations from now on. So the whole effect of the decree is that one young lady will be somewhat cross for a while. Good heavens!

Yours, Franz

To Max Brod

[Prague, early July 1909]
My dear Max, Quickly, because I'm so sleepy. I am sleepy! I don't know what I did a moment ago and what I will do a moment from now and I haven't the faintest idea what I am doing at present. For fifteen minutes I unravel the problems of a district and then, with sudden presence of mind, put away a file I have for a long time been rummaging about for, which I need and haven't yet used. And on the chair lies such a heap of unfinished business that I cannot open my eyes wide enough to take in the heap at one glance.

But your Dobřichowitz.[10] That is something absolutely brand new. What great things you bring off out of this feeling! Only the first paragraph may possibly, at least for these days, be somewhat unreal. "Everything is sweet-smelling," etc.—here you're plunging into a depth in the story that hasn't yet been established. "The silence of a great region—" etc. The friends in the story did not say that, I think; if they are torn to pieces they didn't say that. "The villas of this night."

But after that everything is good and real; it is as if we were witnessing the creation of night. I liked best: "He looked for a pebble, but did not find one. We hurried," etc.

The novel[11] I gave you is my curse, I see; what should I do. If some pages are missing, which I was well aware of, it's quite all right, and even more telling than if I had torn the whole manuscript up. Do be reasonable. What this young woman says means nothing, you know. As long as your arm's around her waist, back, or neck, in this heat she will either like everything all at once or not at all. What has that to do with the novel's very center which I know so well and which I still feel, in most unhappy hours, somewhere within myself. And now no more about it; we're agreed on that.

I see that I'd like to go on writing forever only in order not to have to work. I really shouldn't.

Franz

To Oskar Baum
[Prague,] July 8, 1909

Dear Herr Baum, No, no, it's not at all true that I have little to do, and if you assume so, it's probably because when a person is idling he cannot very well imagine work and because on a hot day in the country work and idleness tend to coincide. But it doesn't matter that I have a great deal to do, for even if I didn't I would not have anything to say but this: that I would be glad to be in the country because there it is like being in heaven, as I have verified on occasional Sundays and as you and your wife are fully conscious of right now.

All to the good that the epilogue[12] won't get finished. Let this epilogue stretch out in the sun in every sense, and you bid the reader goodbye with a splendidly tanned face. I say that somewhat out of self-interest, for I was not really convinced by your conclusion "but don't write a novel about it," etc. Of course it is fine, very fine, when toward the end of such a story a few characters come together and begin laughing heartily, but not that way; that isn't the right kind of laughter for a story that has worked its way up so serenely only to be thrust back at this point into an unhealthy obscurity. What in the world do you have against the reader, that good soul, or at least that for-the-present still good soul?

What most pleased me in your card was the allusion to your "remorse," for this remorse is nothing but a hunger for different work, which is something that at bottom you yourself understand. But first rest up thoroughly for a while; you deserve it. I'm not asking for a long letter either, because anything is better than writing letters. Lying in a meadow and eating grass is better. On the other hand, it really is awfully nice to receive letters, especially in town.

Continue happy, you and your wife.

Yours, Franz Kafka

To Max Brod

[Prague; postmark: July 15, 1909]

Dearest Max, Not because the subject itself has to be dealt with right away and cannot be postponed, but because it is after all an answer to your question, and yesterday's walk was too short for the answer to the answer. (Not "yesterday's," for it is already two-fifteen A.M.) You said she loves me. Why so? Was that a joke, or the sobriety of sleepiness? She loves me and it does not occur to her to ask whom I was with in Stechowitz,[13] what I do, why I cannot go on an outing on a weekday, etc. Perhaps there was not enough time in the bar, but on the outing there was time and to spare, yet any answer satisfied her. Apparently anything can be refuted, but it's impossible even to attempt a refutation of the following: In D. I was afraid of running into Frau Weltsch,[14] whereupon she immediately became afraid also, became afraid for me of my running into Frau Weltsch. From this we can derive a simple geometrical diagram. Her attitude toward me is of the greatest friendliness, as incapable of development as anything could be, and equally remote from the most intense and the slightest love, since it is of a totally different nature. Naturally I must not put myself into the diagram if it is to remain clear.

Now I have earned my sleep.

Yours, Franz

To Max Brod

[Postcard. Prague; postmark: July 19, 1909]

Dear Max, Just to set matters straight right off: I have that pressure in my stomach, as if the stomach were a person and wanted to cry. Is this the right way to put it? But the cause is not so noble; think what it would be like if it were noble? In general this sublime pressure in the stomach is something whose absence I don't have to lament; if only all other pangs were on the same level.

Franz

To Max Brod

[Letterhead: Workers' Accident Insurance Institute]
[Prague, summer 1909]
In the office, too, but at 4:30

My dearest Max, Just as I was thinking over your letter, which reached me at noon, and was so astonished that this time contrary to all the rules I had not helped you win her, and just as I was considering how I would go about comforting you were I your mother and knew what had happened (for the noonday meal strawberries with sugared sour cream, afternoon sending you into the woods between Mnichovic and Stranschitz[15] for a nap, in the evening a liter of Pschorr) your card arrived with good news and one item the very best, that Miss Songstress is letting the novel alone for two weeks, for even the best novel could not for long survive the same girl's constantly exerting pressure on it, and doing so simultaneously from inside and from outside. It's also good that the other young lady will breathe a sigh of relief, for she suffers because of the other one without knowing it, without deserving it, and through no fault of her own.

I gathered from your letter that I was supposed to go to Baum on Thursday and bowed to the necessity. From your card I am glad to see the chance of being let off, for I shall no more be able to on Thursday than I would have been on Monday. His novel delights me so, you know, and if I have worked my way out of my stuff there is nothing I would rather do on Thursday than go; but I hope he and his wife will not be angry if I don't turn up. For I've got so much to do! In my four districts—apart from all my other jobs—people fall off the scaffolds as if they were drunk, or fall into the machines, all the beams topple, all embankments give way, all ladders slide, whatever people carry up falls down, whatever they hand down they stumble over. And I have a headache from all these girls in porcelain factories who incessantly throw themselves down the stairs with mounds of dishware.

By Monday I may have the worst of it behind me. I'm almost forgetting: If you can, come tomorrow, Wednesday, to meet me at the shop around eight, to advise me about Nowak.[16]

If you're agreed, let's turn the feast into a trophy and award it after the completion of your novel. And now to the files.

Yours, Franz

To Max Brod

[Prague, August 1909]

Dear Max, All that last night was nothing. If anybody made such a fuss with me for a whole evening, as I did yesterday, I would think twice whether I would take him along to Riva.[17] But don't give it a thought. Of course it wasn't she, nor was it another girl, but the good fortune of being allowed to name it!

Yours, Franz

To Max Brod

[Prague, end of August 1909]

My dear Max, I cannot come this evening; until noon today I thought my family were due at three in the afternoon, and in that case I would have come, although it would have been difficult. But now they are not due until seven; if I left right afterward, the fuss would be incredible. So I'll come tomorrow evening; if you're home and have time, well and good; if not, I have no right to mind.—Yes, the trip. So we won't be leaving until Tuesday, since you'll certainly be content with that and I can then bid goodbye to the one person who is not arriving until Monday.

Yours, Franz

To Max Brod

[Postcard. Prague; postmark: October 11, 1909]

My dear Max, I did not read your "Visit"[18] until I was on my way to the office Saturday, and reading it as I did in curiosity and haste a good many things seemed to me to have been cooked too hot, some passages actually burnt. But when I read it again last night and then again, it was a joy to see how the essential matter remained serene and right amid the hurly-burly of all those many points. Especially the story about the banquet, the inquiry about Bouilhet[19] and what follows, the farewell. For a somewhat in-completely informed reader, however, it may be that this passion is brought somewhat too suddenly and too close to his face, so that he might possibly see nothing at all. What does it matter?

Adieu, Franz

I'll come Wednesday. We might consider whether we oughtn't to attend the Kestranek trial.[20]

To Max Brod

[Postcard. Prague; postmark: October 13, 1909]

My dear Max, Don't be angry with me; I can't help it. Dr. F.[21] is on the point of becoming reproachful to me because I have been letting his, our business go unattended to, although there isn't very much I can be reproached about as yet, at most for taking Sunday off, since on Monday I was at the office for another reason. I started today, but unless I warm to it I can't manage it, and if I should warm to it I won't be able to fit *Saint Anthony* in and won't be able to come to see you tomorrow. Yes, Saturday, after so many afternoons like today I could allow myself a good afternoon, but then you might have no time. For the rest, fresh diversions are threatening. Rauchberg[22] is giving a seminar on insurance.—Baum has read to me a small, very fine section of the novel.[23]

To Oskar Baum

[Prague, end of 1909]

Dear Herr Baum, I am writing this at twelve o'clock in the Kontinental,[24] the first quiet place I've found this Saturday. What a fine book[25] that is; much as I expected it to be, it nevertheless surprises. And in its strong, grave format it seems to correspond to the intention with which it was written. For that you ought to forgive the publisher for everything; the book turned out well against his nature and perhaps against his will. Now let the world open its arms to receive these dear children. I should think it can't help doing so.

   Till we meet again.

To Max Brod

[Picture postcard (Pilsen). Postmark: December 21, 1909]

My dear Max, It's good that the tour[26] is almost over and tomorrow evening we return to Prague. I thought it would be different. I've felt bad the whole while, and classifying from morning milk to evening rinsing one's mouth is not a cure. Good that you have your novel in the desk and are working.

                                                        Yours, Franz

To Director Eisner[27]

[Prague, probably 1909]

Dear Herr Eisner, Thank you for the package, my professional education is rather scanty anyhow. You say Walser knows me? I don't know him. I have read *Jakob von Gunten*[28]—a good book. I haven't read the other books, for which you are partly to blame since in spite of my advice you did not want to buy *The Tanner Youngsters*.[29] Simon is, I think, a character in that book. Doesn't he run around everywhere, up to his ears in happiness, and in the end nothing comes to him except that he provides amusement to the reader? That is a very poor career, but only a poor career gives the world the light that an imperfect but pretty good writer wants to generate—at all costs, unfortunately. Viewed superficially, of course, such people are running around everywhere; I could list a few of them for you, myself among them, but they are distinguished by nothing but that lighting effect in fairly good novels.

One might say that they are people who were somewhat slower at emerging from the last generation than others; you cannot demand that all people should follow the regular leaps of time with equally regular leaps of their own. But the laggard in a march never catches up with the rest of the marching column. The step left behind soon acquires such an appearance that you would be willing to wager it is not a human step, but you would lose the wager. Consider that the view from a racing horse on the track—if you can keep your eyes on it—the view from a horse leaping the hurdle, say, certainly shows you the utmost presence, the veritable essence of racing. The unity of the stands, the unity of the living spectators, the unity of the surrounding region at that certain time of year, etc., even the last waltz of the orchestra and the way people like to play it nowadays. But if my horse turns back and won't take the jump and shuns the hurdle or runs off and disports inside the arena, or even throws me, naturally the total view will seemingly have gained a great deal. There are gaps among the spectators; some fly, others fall, hands wave back and forth as though responding to every possible wind, a rain of fleeting interrelationships falls upon me, and it is quite possible that some spectators feel it and concur with me while I lie on the grass like a worm. Would that prove anything?[30] [FRAGMENTARY]

To Max Brod

[Postcard showing the Mt. Jeschken toboggan run. Maffersdorf,[31] 1909]
Dear Max, Again I have a few terrific days behind me! But I don't want to write about that; even while they were going on it would have taken effort to write about them properly.—Today at half past six I rode to Gablonz, from Gablonz to Johannesberg, then to Grenzendorf, now I am going on to Maffersdorf, then to Reichenberg, then to Röchlitz, and toward evening to Ruppersdorf and back.

To Max Brod

[Prague, probably 1909]
My dear Max, What if you were to come right over to the Arco,[32] not for long, God forbid, just to please me. You know, Př. is there. Please, dear lady, please Herr Brod, be so kind as to let Max go.

Franz K.

To Max Brod

[Prague, possibly 1909]
My dear Max, You are lucky you're not home; you are spared several

kindnesses you might have wanted to do for me. I am lucky because I can ask you all the more easily and boldly to forgive me and make my excuses to the world for not being able to come to Baum's tomorrow until around nine. There are some relatives visiting us. By the way, I shall be dropping by your place for a moment on Monday at five; if I happen to disturb you in the midst of your work, pretend you're not home.

Yours, Franz

1910

To Max Brod

[Prague; postmark: January 5, 1910]

My dear Max (In the office where people will disturb me ten times over these ten lines—no matter), what I meant when I said that was this: A person who assents to your novel[1]—as it is rising up anew in its greatness it will dazzle many people, and must therefore depress them—a person who assents to your novel—"assent" meaning here to grasp it with all the love he can muster—a person who assents to your novel must all the while he is reading it increasingly long for a solution of the kind you have presented in the half chapter you read aloud. But he is bound to see this solution as lying in the novel's most dangerous direction—not dangerous for the novel, only dangerous for his blissful connection with it—and that this solution now, as he feels convinced, has taken place just on that outermost frontier where the novel still receives what it must demand, but the reader also receives what he has not yet managed to make himself forgo. And only the intimations of the possible solutions—to which you who so penetrate the innermost nature of the novel would have been entitled—still seem to alarm him even when they are still far off. It will not be a bad comparison if the novel is later compared to a Gothic cathedral, not a bad comparison assuming, of course, that for every passage in the dialectical chapters one can show that there is a passage in one of the other chapters which supports the first, and that it requires precisely the load that the other exerts. My dearest Max, how fortunate you are and how fortunate you will be at the end, and we through you.

Yours, Franz

I wanted to add something about Milada, but I am afraid.

To Max Brod
> [Postcard. Prague; postmark: January 29, 1910]

Dear Max, Lest I forget—if your sister[2] is going to be in Prague Monday, you must write me today; if she is coming later, there is time, of course, for you to tell me on Monday. Tomorrow I am treating myself to having my stomach pumped; I have a feeling that disgusting things will come out.

> Yours, Franz

To Max Brod
> [Postcard. Prague; postmark: February 18, 1910]

Dear Max, You've forgotten me completely. You don't write me—

> Franz

To Max Brod
> [Postcard. Prague; postmark: March 10, 1910]

I won't be coming to the Lucerna,[3] Max. Now, at four o'clock, I'm in the office writing and tomorrow afternoon I'll be writing[4] and this evening and tomorrow evening and so on. I can't ride either. All that's left to me is doing Müller exercises,[5] and barely that. Adieu.

> Yours, Franz

To Max Brod
> [Prague; postmark: March 12, 1910]

My dear Max, Don't rush into the expense of a tube postcard to let me know that you cannot be at the Franz Joseph Station at 6:05 A.M. because you must be, since the train on which we are going to Wran leaves at 6:05. At 7:15 we take our first step in the direction of Davle, where we'll eat a goulash at Lederer's, at 12 o'clock lunch in Stechowitz, from 2–3:30 we'll tramp through the forest to the rapids where we'll paddle around. At 7 o'clock we take the steamer back to Prague.[6] Don't think it over but be at the station at 5:45.

By the way you might write a tube postcard after all, saying that you want to go to Dobřichowitz or somewhere else.

[A DRAWING OF A PEN] This is a pen point from Soennecken;[7] it's not part of the story.

To Max Brod
                          [Postcard. Prague; postmark: March 18, 1910]
Dear Max, I cannot quite make out from your card whether you have
received mine. Nor could I pull myself together sufficiently to write to Baum
all this while. Didn't I write recently that all I could still do was Müller
exercises. Well, I can't even do them anymore. Recently I had rheumatic
pains in my shoulders, then they slid down to the small of my back, then into
my legs, but instead of going on into the ground as you might expect, they
went up into the arms. It's perfectly in accord with all this that the raise in
salary I expected today hasn't come, won't come next month either, but only
after I'm so tired of waiting for it that I don't give a damn. What pleases me
most about the novella,[8] dear Max, is that I have it out of the house.
Tomorrow I'll come over to see you around seven o'clock (it's six o'clock
now and I'm still in the office), also because of *Bohemia*.[9] You'll show me
poems; it will be a lovely evening.
    So long.
                                                          Yours, Franz

To Max Brod
                               [Postcard. Prague, probably March 1910]
Dear Max, I should have known it—the Realists[10] don't stop until they're
finished, and Dr. Herben[11] wasn't finished until a quarter after ten. Then I
went to Stockhausgasse, checked the lights in Baum's windows, and went
home. Should I have come up anyhow at that hour? I need the sleep so badly.
Perhaps you don't know that previously for one and a half days I had fasted,
aside from a little tea. About Smolová,[12] *Čas*[13] says: *Její útlý, čistý procitlivělý*
*hlásek arci příjemně se poslouchal.** And that after they have already heaped
praise on the predictable filth of the rest of the evening.

* Her pure, clear, emotional little voice did indeed sound pleasant.

To Max Brod
                                                 [Prague, April 1910]
Dear Max, This is writing pretty fast, wouldn't you say—though it is getting
on toward one. Please send this to Matras; a review in *Deutsche Arbeit*[14]
would particularly delight Marschner, of course. But it will also be
particularly difficult to get it in, I'm afraid. At any rate, he would like you to
write to Matras asking him to reply yes or no as quickly as possible. Of course
he may change whatever he likes, even write the whole thing over if it gives

him pleasure, but it is his duty (so you must tell him) to print something about the book. Thanks very much.

Yours, Franz

To Max Brod

[Spring 1910][15]

My dear Max, I know nothing about the Tarnowska trial; on the other hand I understand Wiegler's comments very well, but Handl's opinion is even more important than Wiegler's, since he already takes the public into consideration.

You comfort me more than you know with word that you have written two poems for me. I need comfort. Just at the right time stomach pains and the like have started, and of such an intensity as is commensurate with a body strengthened by Müller exercises. All the interminable afternoon I lay on the sofa with tea inside me instead of dinner and after a quarter of an hour's nap had nothing to do but feel peevish because the dusk was slow in coming. Toward half past four a streak of brightness formed and simply would not go away. When dusk finally fell, it was still not the right thing. Cut it out, Max, stop complaining about girls. Either the pain they inflict on you is a good pain or if it is not, then you will muster your defenses, throw off the pain, and be the stronger for it. But what about me? Everything I possess is directed against me; what is directed against me is no longer a possession of mine. If, for example—this is purely an example—if my stomach hurts, it is no longer really my stomach but something that is basically indistinguishable from a stranger who has taken it into his head to club me. But that is so with everything. I am nothing but a mass of spikes going through me; if I try to defend myself and use force, the spikes only press in the deeper. Sometimes I am tempted to say: God knows how I can possibly feel any more pain, since in my sheer urgency to inflict it upon myself I never get around to perceiving it. But often I must say: I know I am really feeling no pain, I am truly the most pain-free person anyone could imagine. So I was not in pain as I lay on the sofa, I was not irritated at the brightness which ended in due time, and the same with the darkness. But, dear Max, you must believe me even if you don't want to, that everything was so ordered on this afternoon that I, if I had been I, would have had to experience all those pains in that exact order. From today on, I shall believe firmly and continually, accepting no counterargument: a bullet would be best. I shall simply shoot myself away from the place I am not. All right, that would be cowardly; granted, what is cowardly remains cowardly, even in a case in which there is no alternative to cowardice. This is a situation which has to be done away with at all costs, but nothing but cowardice can do away with it; courage leads only to cramps. And we will stay with our cramps, don't be worried.

To Max Brod

[Letter-card. Prague; postmark: April 30, 1910]

Good luck with the writing, dearest Max, for all our sakes! Hasn't it occurred to you that the force with which you've thrown yourself at your story[16] might make the second girl incomprehensible just as it made the first sick? That fever you were still in on Wednesday! In the meantime she will have been well preserved for you in the medical student's atmosphere. Just cool off and she will come running again. May the awareness of that give you the courage to really cool off until you cannot stand it otherwise. But what do I know—perhaps in the meantime the silly girl has run right into the middle of the story. If only I could hold her back by clutching at her skirts.

Yours, Franz

To Max Brod

[Postcard. Prague; postmark: May 11, 1910]

My dear Max, Your card didn't reach me until this noon. All right, then I won't visit until Saturday. Good Lord, those drawings![17]

Yours, Franz

To Max Brod

[Picture postcard. Saaz; postmark: August 22, 1910][18]

In spite of everything it isn't bad, you know, to lie against a pile of sheaves for a while and bury your face in them!

Franz

To Max Brod

[Prague, September 1910]

Dear Max, I first of all wanted to see how you were—your bed actually has a nervous expression—and secondly wanted to ask you to go to the French woman[19] tomorrow again by yourself because my lecture[20] is becoming more urgent (the announcement is in the newspaper between the "scoundrels and knaves" of the election notice and an appeal by the Salvation Army). In short—what's going to come of it? Just writing this note, I lose the thread. I bring more anxiety to this than is needed to make it a success.

To Max Brod

[Prague, late September/early October 1910] [21]
Dear Max, I don't want either to upset you or make you wait, so since I cannot come at five I will make a stab at coming tomorrow at five, with no obligation on your part. For today I have an appointment with the doctor at a quarter past five—ah yes, you don't know all my ailments (dislocated big toe).

F

To Max Brod

[Letterhead: Workers' Accident Insurance Institute]
[Prague, early October 1910]
Dear Max,
When I received your letter, I was lying stretched out on the sofa with my bad leg. It doesn't look very pretty. The foot in particular is enormously swollen—but it is not very painful. It is well bandaged and will improve. But whether my leg will be ready for travel as early as Saturday, I don't know. If the wish for a trip can be strong enough to make me well, I'll be well by Saturday, I assure you, for I [FRAGMENTARY]

To Max and Otto Brod

[Three picture postcards [22] addressed to Otto Brod in Paris. Prague; postmark: October 20, 1910]
Dear Max, I arrived safely [23] and I am very pale only because everybody regards me as an improbable apparition. A brief fainting spell deprived me of the pleasure of shouting at the doctor. I had to lie down on his sofa, and during that time—it was very odd—I felt so much like a girl that I tried with my fingers to tug down my skirt. For the rest, the doctor declared himself horrified by the appearance of my backside; the five new abscesses are no longer so important since a skin eruption has appeared which is worse than all the abscesses, will take a long time to heal, and is and will be the real cause of the pain. My idea, which of course I did not reveal to the doctor, is that the international pavements of Prague, Nuremberg, and above all Paris have caused this eruption. And so I am now sitting at home in the afternoon as in a tomb (I cannot walk around because of my tight bandage; I cannot sit still because of the pain, which the healing makes even worse), and only in the

mornings do I overcome this hereafter for the sake of the office, to which I must go. I'll be getting to see your parents tomorrow.

During the first night in Prague I dreamt, all through the night, I think (my sleep hung around this dream like a scaffolding around a new building in Paris)—I dreamt that I had been quartered for the night in a large building that consisted of nothing but Paris cabs, automobiles, omnibuses, etc., which had nothing to do but drive close by each other, over each other, under each other, and nobody talked or thought about anything but fares, junctions, connections, tips, directions, cambios, counterfeit money, etc. Because of this dream I could not sleep, but since I was muddled about the essential questions, I was able to endure the dreaming only with the greatest effort. I inwardly complained because they had put me up in such a house, when after my travels I so badly needed a rest; but at the same time there was a partisan within me who acknowledged, along with the ominous bows of French doctors (they keep their smocks buttoned) the necessity for this night. Please count over your money to make sure I haven't cheated both of you; by my admittedly not wholly certain reckoning I spent so little that it looks as if I used all my time in Paris for washing my sores.

Ugh. That hurts again. It was high time I returned. For you as well as for myself.

Yours, Franz K.

To Max Brod

[Picture postcard. Berlin; postmark: December 4, 1910]

Dearest Max,

The difference is this: in Paris one is cheated, here one cheats; it is sort of comical. On Saturday I went almost directly from the train to the Kammerspiele; I've acquired a taste for buying tickets in advance. Today I am going to see *Anatol*.[24] But nothing is as good as food in the vegetarian restaurant here. The place itself is a little dreary; people eating fried eggs and cabbage (the most expensive dish); the architecture is nothing; but what contentment one feels here. I keep sounding my inner state; at the moment, to be sure, I still feel very bad, but how will I feel tomorrow? This place is so thoroughly vegetarian that even tips are forbidden. Instead of rolls, there is only Simons' bread.[25] Right now the waiter is bringing me semolina pudding with raspberry syrup. But I am also having lettuce with cream, which will go well with gooseberry wine, and I'll finish off with a cup of strawberry-leaf tea.

Adieu.

To Max Brod

> [Picture postcard (self-portrait of Goethe in his Frankfurt study).
> Berlin; postmark: December 9, 1910]

A well-appointed study, dear Max, isn't it? Basically furnished only with five pieces of furniture and their shadows. At any rate, an unhealthy blaze of light falls on the desk. The bottle is comfortably placed on the side table where it can be conveniently reached from the desk by leaning over. The feet rest on the table stretcher, not on the floor. If painting is on the program, the easel replaces the desk.

> Yours, Franz

To Oskar Baum

> [Picture postcard (Rubens: *The Son of the Artist, with
> Bird)*. Berlin; postmark: December 9, 1910]

Cordial greetings, and for the house this rival to little Leo.[26] I know there is no need for him to worry; rather it should increase his self-assurance.

> Yours, Franz K.

To Max Brod

> [Picture postcard. Berlin; postmark: December 9, 1910]

Max, I have seen a performance of *Hamlet,* or rather heard Bassermann.[27] For whole quarter-hours I actually had another person's face; every so often I had to look away from the stage into an empty box, in order to compose myself.

> Yours, Franz

To Max Brod

> [Prague, December 15, 1910]

My dear Max, In order not to have to talk again about this week I shall first repeat what you already know, so that it will all be in your head at one time.—Everything this week has fallen out better for me than my situation has ever allowed before, and than, to all appearances, it will ever allow again. I had been in Berlin, and after my return fitted so loosely into my usual surroundings that had it been in my nature I could easily have gone on a rampage.—I had eight perfectly free days.[28] Not until last night did I begin to dread the office, although then the dread hit me so hard that I felt like hiding under the table. But I myself don't take that seriously, for it's not an autonomous dread. I almost never quarrel with my parents, who are now in good health and good spirits. My father is annoyed with me only when he sees me sitting too late at my desk, because he thinks I am overworking.—My health was better than it has been for months, at least at the beginning of the week. All the greens went so deeply and peacefully into my stomach that it seemed sheer good luck had been feeding me up for the sake of this past week. Things at home have been singularly peaceful. The wedding[29] is over, and the new relatives are being digested. The young lady downstairs whose piano-playing is occasionally audible is supposed to be away for several weeks, and all these benefits have been given me just now, as the end of fall is nearing—in other words, in a period in which I have always felt at my most vigorous.

December 17

This funeral oration I started day before yesterday will not come to an end. To make matters worse, in terms of it there is the additional misery that I am evidently incapable of sustaining a mournful, totally demonstrable emotion for a few days at a stretch. No, I'm just not capable of that. Now that I've been keeping watch over myself for a week, I am in such a rush of feeling that I am flying. I am simply drunk with myself, which is hardly to be wondered at under the circumstances, given even the weakest wine. Yet little has changed for the past two days, and what has is for the worse. My father has not been quite well. He is at home. When the breakfast clatter ceases on the left, the lunch clatter begins on the right. Doors are now being opened everywhere as if walls were being smashed. But above all, the center of all the misery remains. I cannot write; I have not done a line I respect; on the other hand, I have excised everything I wrote after Paris—it wasn't much! My whole body warns me against every word; every word, before it lets me write it down, first looks around in all directions. The sentences literally crumble before me; I see their insides and then have to stop quickly.

The fragment of the novella[30] enclosed is something I copied out day before yesterday, and now I am letting it be. It is already old and certainly not flawless, but it very well carries out the ultimate intention of the story.

I won't be coming this evening. Until Monday morning I want to remain alone up to the very last moment. Keeping hard at my own heels still is a joy that warms me—and a healthy joy at that, for it stirs in me that general excitement which produces the only possible equilibrium. If it went on like this, I could look anybody in the eye, which before the Berlin trip, and even in Paris, I could not do with, for example, you. You noticed that. I am so fond of you and could not look you in the eye.—Here I come with my stories and perhaps you have your own worries. Might I have a card from you about your affair Monday, at the office? Also, I have not yet congratulated your sister. I'll take care of that on Monday.

Yours, Franz

1911

To Max Brod

[Postcard. Prague; postmark: January 27, 1911]
Dear Max, I am going to Friedland Monday.[1] It has turned out that I must go to the dentist tomorrow. So I can hardly make it to your place before six. I am reading Kleist; he fills me as if I were an old pig's bladder. To keep things under control, and because I have made up my mind to do it, I'm now going to the Lucerna.

Franz

To Max Brod

[Picture postcard (Friedland Castle). Postmark: February 1, 1911]
The castle[2] is smothered in ivy; it climbs halfway up the loggias. The drawbridge resembles the kind of bric-a-brac with chains and wires that you want not to pay attention to, just because it is bric-a-brac, even though you've been conscientious about your sightseeing of everything else. You need not necessarily believe in that red roof at the bottom of the picture.

Franz

To Max Brod

[Picture postcard (Friedland). Postmark: February 2, 1911]
Are you too, like me, best able to imagine an unfamiliar region when you have heard about a quiet occupation of the kind possible anywhere else in the world, which someone has practiced somewhere in that region? I explain this to myself on the grounds that the region is not left behind, but that also not a single characteristic element is forcibly detached from it, and therefore the whole remains intact. I went to the Imperial Panorama and saw Brescia, Mantua, and Cremona, the smooth pavements of the cathedrals lying almost at the tip of one's tongue.

Franz K.

To Oskar Baum

Friedland, February 25, 1911
Today I was in Neustadt an der Tafelfichte,[3] a village where if you walk on

the main street with your trousers strapped at the cuffs, you become totally bogged down in snow, whereas if they are unstrapped the snow comes up inside as far as your knees. One could be happy here.

Best regards.

To Max Brod

[Picture postcard. Grottau;[4] postmark: February 25, 1911]
A few novelties, dear Max: People have already heard blackbirds singing in the park—the court coaches have such powerful springs that the footmen have to hold on to the chassis at the rear when their lordships alight—as I was arriving here today I saw a duck standing in the water at the river's edge—I rode with a woman who very closely resembled the slave dealer from *The White Slave*,[5] etc.

To Sophie Brod

[Picture postcard ("Interior of the Vegetarian Restaurant
Thalysia in Reichenberg"). Postmark: February 26, 1911]
For the library of your new home, dear Fräulein Sophie, let me recommend the novel *The Day of Requital* by A. K. Green,[6] which a man opposite me in the train today was reading. Isn't that a portentous title?

The "Day" is a flagpole; the "The" can be the pegs at the bottom; the "of" is the fastening for the rope at the top; the "Requital" is the flag itself, perhaps not quite black but very dark, whose ripplings for *e* to *i* to *a* are provoked by a wind of middling force. (The *l* particularly weakens it.) So you see, tired as I am, even during the journey I am keeping an eye out for things that might be useful to you, and would of course be very proud if when I next visit you were already in possession of the day of requital.

Franz K.

To Max Brod

[Picture postcard. Prague; postmark: March 2, 1911]
Dear Max, When you come tomorrow would you be so kind as to bring the *Hyperion* along with you. I would like to lend it to Eisner. His issues of the *Rundschau*[7] have again accumulated in my hands and it will do my conscience good, when I at last return them, if I can include something which might interest him.

Franz

To Max Brod
[Picture postcard. Prague; postmark: March 5, 1911]
Thank you, my dear Max, I know what the stuff[8] is worth. It's the same as always, of course. Its faults stick deeper into my flesh than its good points. But here is something more important that concerns the world: our chronology has gone awry. Although the tube mail received my postcard by ten o'clock, the card didn't arrive in time to forestall [the manuscript's] being lent out. As a postal official you have a share in the blame.

Yours, Franz K.

To Max Brod
[Picture postcard. Zittau; postmark: April 23, 1911]
Here on Mount Oybin[9] sit more than two hundred sulky guests. I am still writing my postcards as, relatively speaking, a southerner. But only cards. The article[10] is still undone.

Franz

To Max Brod
[Prague,] May 27, 1911
My dear Max, Today is your birthday, but I am not even sending you the usual book, for it would be only a sham. At bottom, I am no longer even capable of giving you a book. I am writing only because I feel so strong a need to be in your presence for a moment today, if only with this card; and I have begun with this plaint only so that you will recognize me right off.

Yours, Franz

To Max Brod
[Sanatorium Erlenbach, Switzerland,[11] September 17, 1911]
My dear Max, When you insisted that I was to write the story here, you only showed your ignorance of the arrangements in a sanatorium, whereas when I promised to write it I must somehow have forgotten sanatorium life, which after all I know quite well. For the day here is filled with "activities," as the bathing, being massaged, gymnastics, etc., are called, and with the preparatory rest before these activities and the recuperative rest after them. The meals, at any rate, do not take up much time, since they consist of applesauce, mashed potatoes, vegetable juices, fruit juice, etc. If you like, they can be taken quite unnoticeably, but also can slide down enjoyably and only slightly delayed by

whole-grain bread, omelettes, puddings, and above all nuts. In recompense, the evenings, especially now that it's turned rainy, are spent sociably. Sometimes we are entertained by gramophone programs, for which ladies and gentlemen sit separately as they do in the Zurich minster, and when the songs are loud, as for example for a Socialist march, the gramophone horn is directed more toward the gentlemen, but for tender selections, or those that require close attention, the gentlemen move over to the ladies' side, either returning after the selection is finished or, in certain cases, remaining there forever, sometimes by (if you want to check this sentence grammatically you will have to turn the page) a Berlin trumpeter's playing, to my great delight, or by some mountain dweller unsteady on his feet reading a dialect piece not by Rosegger but by Achleitner,[12] or finally by an amiable person who gives his all in reciting a humorous novel in verse of his own composition, in the course of which by old habit my eyes fill with tears. Now you may think I don't have to be present at these entertainments, but that is not true. For in the first place one has somehow to show one's thanks for the relative effectiveness of the cure (consider that I took the medicine on the last evening in Paris and by today, three days later, its effects are gone), and secondly, there are so few guests here that one can't, at least intentionally, disappear. And finally, the lighting is pretty bad. I can't imagine where I would be able to be alone and write. Even for this letter some eyesight is being sacrificed.

Of course if I were to feel the compulsion to write within myself, as I do for lengthy periods only once in a long while, as I did for a moment in Stresa where I felt wholly like a fist with the nails pressing into the flesh—I cannot put it differently—then of course none of these obstacles would exist. I simply would not put up with the "activities," could take my leave right after meals, as a very peculiar eccentric after whom people turn their heads, go up to my room, put the chair on the table, and write by the light of the feeble bulb high up in the ceiling.

When I consider that, in your opinion—I won't say following your example—one should even be able to write on promptings from outside, I can see that you are quite right in your injunction to me, whether or not you know sanatoria, and in spite of my elaborate excuses everything really comes back to me—or to put it better, it reduces itself to a small difference of opinion or a large difference in ability. Incidentally, it is only Sunday evening, so I shall have approximately one and a half days, though the clock here in the reading room, in which I have at last been left alone, has a remarkably rapid stroke.

In one respect my stay here is useful aside from my health. The guests consist chiefly of elderly Swiss women of the middle class, which is to say, people among whom ethnological idiosyncrasies are displayed most delicately and tenuously. But if we do manage to observe such traits in them, we should therefore hold tight to what we have seen. My ignorance of their dialect also helps in my observation, I think, for they are less individualized. I see more this way than we would see from a train window, although it is not really different. To put it briefly and tentatively, in forming an opinion of Switzerland I would prefer to follow Meyer rather than Keller[13] or Walser.

For your article on war, while I was in Paris I copied the title of a book, along with the publisher's blurb: Colonel Arthur Boucher, *La France victorieuse dans la guerre du demain*. The author, a former chief of operations, states that if France is attacked, "she will know how to defend herself with an absolute certainty of victory." I wrote this down in front of a bookstore on the Boulevard St. Denis in my capacity as German literary spy. May it be useful to you. If your stamp collector is not dearer to you than mine is to me, save the envelope for me.

Yours, Franz

To Oskar Baum

Erlenbach, September 19, 1911

Dear Herr Baum,

Our travels, as Max has surely told you, were so variegated that no time was left for remembering people back home. But now that my vacation is nearing its end, one of my illnesses is beginning to dissolve while the others look on in astonishment, and everybody takes the view that I should be returning to the office, now—that is, yesterday—on a rainy cold evening, at the open window, under the thin blanket, I began to feel warm.

To Max Brod

[Postcard. Prague; postmark: October 12, 1911]

Dear Max, We certainly hit it right. *Sulamith*[14] by Goldfaden is being played. Joyfully, I squander a card to tell you what you have already read. I only hope you have also written me.

Franz

To Max Brod

[Prague, probably 1911]

My dear Max, Once again I cannot come tomorrow; who knows whether I can come in the evening. If I don't come to your house at six, I'll go directly to the lecture. If I am not at the lecture, I'll pick you up at the

Rudolphinum.[15] A pity you are not home; even though my teacher of Czech is waiting for me I would have liked to have read a few poems. *"Die Kinder, ein ewiger Ball"* keeps running through my head. Work, dear Max, work!

Yours, F

1912

To Max Brod

[Postcard. Prague; postmark: February 19, 1912]

My dear Max, Your uncle's money—I'd already been secretly mourning it, but back home found it in my breast pocket. Your first remark, that he had sent it through the Postal Savings System, made such an impression upon me that the envelope in my hand no longer signified. Please thank your parents once more; I only went through the motions, but they were the ones who actually arranged the evening.[1] Which evening can I come over? It's a long time since I've had a really good visit with you.

Franz

To Max Brod

[Postcard. Prague, probably early 1912]

Dear Max, As soon as I got home yesterday I remembered that there are a few small but ugly typing and dictating errors in "Unhappiness"[2] which I have removed from my copy but which remain in yours. Since they worry me, send it right back to me. You will receive the piece again, improved.

Yours, Franz

To Max Brod

[Prague, end of March 1912]

Dear Max, I have considered the matter[3] back and forth. A lawsuit on your part seems to me highly disadvantageous, don't go to court! There remains the possibility of putting up with it. That's what I would do. But not you. Better than suing would be to be sued. You could then, since you feel the requisite detestation of him, publicly call him a liar. After his *Bohemia* statement, you would be justified in doing so, if he does not yield. But in my opinion it would be best for you to send to the newspapers, in the form of an advertisement, a statement of this sort: "I have learned that someone is showing around an anonymous letter in which he is accused of scandalous behavior during a concert arranged by me, and is saying that I wrote this letter or prompted it. I have neither the time nor the desire to take this affair into court. The matter also seems to me too trivial to be settled in another manner. I therefore content myself with stating publicly that that letter was neither written by me nor at my prompting nor with my knowledge." At any rate, I cannot regard the matter as so dreadful. Only your face yesterday alarmed me.

Franz

To Max Brod

[Letter-card. Prague; postmark: May 7, 1912]

Dear Max, Your book[4] has given me such pleasure, even late last night when I leafed through it at home. That blessed railroad journey you told me about has plainly left its impress. You were afraid it is too quiet, but there's life in it. I am tempted to say, by night and day. The way everything successively moves toward Arnold and comes back from him again; everything is alive without added melodramatics. It is certainly a summation and at the same time a link to *Death to the Dead*[5] on a higher level. I embrace you.

Yours, Franz

To Kafka's family

[Picture postcard of the room in which Goethe died. Weimar;[6] postmark: June 30, 1912]

Dear Parents and Sisters,[7] We have arrived safely in Weimar, are staying in a quiet, pretty hotel with a view of a garden (all for 2 marks), and are living and sightseeing happily. I only wish I had some news from all of you.

Yours, Franz

To Max Brod

[Picture postcard of Gleim's house in Halberstadt.[8] Halberstadt; postmark: July 7, 1912]

How well off these German poets were! Sixteen windows on the street! Even if the house swarmed with children, which my sense of literary history tells me was probably the case.

To Max Brod

[Picture postcard. Halberstadt; postmark: July 7, 1912]

Dear Max, This first morning greeting to your office. Don't take it too hard.

I'm not exactly blissful, in spite of this incredibly old city. I am sitting on a balcony above the fish market and twining my legs to wring the fatigue out of them.

Regards to all, yours, Franz

To Max Brod

[Letterhead: Sanatorium Rudolf Just, Jungborn in the Harz Mountains, P.O. Stapelburg][9]
July 9 [1912]

My dear Max, Here is my diary.[10] As you will see, I faked a little because it was not intended for me alone. I can't help that; at any rate, such faking is not in the least deliberate. Rather, it came from my inmost nature and I really ought to look down there with respect. I like it here quite well; the independence is so pleasant and an inkling of America is pumped into these poor bodies. When I walk on the country roads and set my sandals beside the heavy plowboots of a passing old peasant, I don't feel particularly proud of myself. But when I walk alone in the woods or lie in the meadows, all is well. Only for the time being none of this stimulates the desire to write. If that is on its way, at any rate it hasn't yet arrived in the mountains. Perhaps it's waiting for me in Weimar. I have just written three picture postcards to it.

Be well and regards to all.

Yours, Franz

To Max Brod

Jungborn, July 10, 1912

My dearest Max, I an answering at once because your letter is burning in my hands from sheer joy. Your poem[11] will remain the adornment of my hut, and when I wake up at night, which often happens, for I am not yet used to the noises in grass, tree, air, I will read it by candlelight. Perhaps I will eventually be able to recite it by heart. And it will help to elevate me if only in my own estimation, as I sit unrecognized over my nuts. The poem is pure (only the "rich grapes" brings a slightly dubious note of superfluity into the two lines; there you ought still to tinker a bit), but in addition you meant it for me, didn't you, are perhaps making a gift of it to me, not having it published at all, for, you know, even the most dreamlike of companionships is for me the most important thing in the world.

How good, clever, and competent Rowohlt[12] is! Emigrate, Max, emigrate from Juncker,[13] taking everything or as much as possible with you. He has held you back—not within yourself, I don't think that, there you're on the right course—but certainly in public terms. The typography of the Kleist *Anecdotes*[14] fits in perfectly; printed in this dry type, the tumult of "intensity of feeling"[15] will be heard all the better.

You say nothing about the *Yearbook*[16] and "On the Cheap."[17] Is Rowohlt taking *Concept*[18] for nothing? Of course I am pleased that he is thinking about my book,[19] but write him from here? I would not know what I ought to write.

If the office torments you a little, that doesn't matter. That's what it exists for; one can't expect anything different, but one can expect that in the near future Rowohlt or someone else will come along and wrest you out of your office. But he ought to leave you in Prague and you ought to want to stay there! Here it is nice enough, but I am hapless and sad. That doesn't have to be final; I know that. At any rate, I'm a long way from being up to writing as yet. The novel[20] is so huge, as if sketched across the whole sky (also as colorless and vague as today's), and I get in a tangle with the very first sentence I want to write. I have already discovered that I must not let the dreariness of what I have already written deter me, and yesterday profited a good deal from this knowledge.

On the other hand, my house is giving me a great deal of pleasure. The floor is perpetually covered with grass which I bring in. Yesterday before falling asleep I thought I heard women's voices. If one is unfamiliar with the slap of bare feet in the grass, when one lies in bed a person passing by sounds like a stampeding buffalo. I cannot learn how to scythe.

Be well and regards to all.

Yours, Franz

To Max Brod

[Jungborn,] July 13, 1912

My dear Max, Who is insisting that you write to me? I give myself the pleasure of writing to you and so drawing tighter the connection between you and me (in saying this I am also thinking of Weltsch and Baum; I cannot bring myself to write separately to them, for there would be so much I would have to repeat before finding the special focus for each) and certainly would not want to take your time. When I return to Prague, you will simply read me the passages from your short diary, with explanations, and I will be fully content. Only send me a little card now and then so I don't find myself singing my letters so all alone in the open fields.

So you thought Fräulein Kirchner[21] stupid. But now she has written me two cards which at least come from some lower heavenly sphere of the German language. I copy this one word for word:

My dear Herr Doktor Kafka,

   May I express my thanks to you for your kind cards and friendly remembrances. I had a lovely time at the ball and it was half past four in the morning before I returned home with my parents. The Sunday in Tiefurt[22] was also very nice. You ask whether I enjoy receiving cards from you, to which I can only reply that it will be a great pleasure for me and my parents to hear from you. I am fond of sitting in the garden by the pavilion and remembering you. How are you? Well, I hope.

   Cordial good wishes and friendly regards from me and my parents.

                                              Sincerely,
                                              Margarethe Kirchner

   I have reproduced it perfectly, including the signature. Well? Above all consider that these lines are literature from beginning to end. For if I am not, in her eyes, unpleasant, I am at any rate of no more importance to her than a pot. But then why does she write as I would wish it? Do you suppose it is true that one can attach girls to oneself by writing? In your card you don't mention the *Yearbook*. Please send me a bit of news about Weltsch. Pat him for me. And my regards to Fräulein Taussig and all the Baums.

                                              Yours, Franz

No less than seven diary pages.

To Max Brod

                                        [Jungborn,] July 17, 1912

My dear Max, You're not exactly cheerful, as I think I gather from your letter. But what is wrong? You're working on "Noah's Ark"[23] and getting on with it, in my expectations making it so lovely that I want to ask you to send me a carbon of it. In addition you're firmly entrenched with Rowohlt. Surely Lissauer's[24] nasty comments don't make you turn a hair. Are you by any chance envious of me?

   My chief affliction consists in my eating too much. I am stuffing myself like a sausage, rolling in the grass and swelling up in the sun. I have the silly idea of wanting to make myself fat, and from there on curing myself in general. As if the latter, or even the former, were possible at all! The good effect of the sanatorium shows up in the fact that, with all that, I am not really spoiling my stomach; it merely becomes insensitive. There is definitely a connection that my scribbling goes more slowly than in Prague. On the other hand, or rather in addition, yesterday and today some insights into the inferiority of my writing dawned on me and, I am afraid, will not again vanish. But it does not matter, I cannot stop writing; it is therefore a pleasure that can be tested to the core without harm.

So you have the *Yearbook* in hand! I would not call it "Arkadia"; up to now only taverns have been called that. But it is easily possible that the name, once established, will be compelling.

Why are you sitting alone at the Louvre[25] on Sunday night? Why are you not in Schelesen[26] with Baum? That would suit you better.

So I will write Weltsch. But won't you put in a good word with him for me? I suppose his sickness is like what his sister had recently?

Be well, dear Max, and don't be sad. It certainly is true that the life I am now leading is largely designed to circumvent sadness, but still I would a thousand times prefer to plunge straight into it, as I do almost every evening in the writing room where I sit for an hour and a half, usually alone and without writing. It is one of the ideas at Jungborn, which seems to me more important than the really basic principles, that no talking is allowed in the writing room. However, there is also the rule, or the superstition, that the windows must be closed at nine. You are allowed to remain there until nearly ten. But at nine o'clock a maid comes—sometimes it seems to me that I wait from eight o'clock on for this femininity—and closes the windows. One maid has short arms and I have to help her. It is particularly still here when the doctor gives a talk in the lecture hall (three times a week). Faced with the choice of two pleasures, I choose the silence, even though I would like very much to go to the lectures. Recently he declared that breathing from the diaphragm contributes to the growth and stimulation of the sexual organs, for which reason female opera singers, for whom diaphragm breathing is requisite, are so immoral. But it is also possible that of all people they are forced to employ straightforward chest-breathing. Take it as you like.

Regards to all, yours, Franz

Three enclosures.

To Max Brod

[Jungborn,] July 22, 1912

My dear Max, Are we once more to play the game of the unhappy children? One points to the other and repeats his old refrain. Your momentary opinion about yourself is a philosophical whim; mine about myself is no ordinary bad opinion. Rather, my only goodness is to be found in this opinion. After properly establishing its boundaries in the course of my life, it is the one thing I must never, never doubt. It introduces order into me. Since I immediately go to pieces in the face of the unmanageable, it gives me a certain calm. After all, you and I are close enough to be able to see into the basis for each other's opinion. I have succeeded with some details, I grant you, and I have rejoiced in them even more than you would think proper—how else could I go on holding the pen in my hand? I have never been the sort of person who carried something out at all costs. But that is just it. What I have written was written in a lukewarm bath. I have not experienced the eternal hell of real writers, aside from a few exceptions which I can leave out of the reckoning in spite of their possibly boundless intensity because they are great rarities and because they display only feeble energies.

I am also writing here, though very little, bewailing myself and also enjoying myself. This is the way pious women pray to God, but in the biblical stories God is found differently. You must understand, Max, if only as a favor to me, that I am still a very long way from being able to show you what I am writing now. It is being worked in small pieces, more strung together than interwoven, and will go on straight ahead for a long while before it gets around to turning in the still highly desired circle, and then at that moment toward which I am working things will by no means become easier. Rather, it is possible that after so much groping I will then completely lose my head. For that reason, only after the first version[27] is finished will it be something we can talk about.

Didn't you have the "Ark" copied on the typewriter? Can't you send me a carbon after all? And doesn't the successful completion deserve a word?

Is Weltsch still in bed? How that has knocked him down! And I still have not written to him and still am not writing to him! Please do tell Fräulein T.[28] and Weltsch, and if possible the Baums, that I love them all and that love has nothing to do with letter-writing. Tell them in such a way that it will be better and received in more friendly fashion than three actual letters. If you want to, you can do it.

In our joint story,[29] aside from details I enjoyed only the sitting beside you on Sundays (discounting the fits of despair, of course), and this pleasure would immediately tempt me to go on with the project, but you have more important things to do, even if it were only the Ulysses.[30]

I lack all organizational talent and so cannot even find a title for the Yearbook. Don't forget that titles which seem either neutral or bad take on a good appearance as the result of probably unpredictable influences from the real world.

Don't say anything against sociability! I came here partly for people and am satisfied that at least in that respect I have not been disappointed. How do I live in Prague, after all? This craving for people, which I have and which is transformed into anxiety once it is fulfilled, finds an outlet only during vacations. Certainly I have changed a little. Incidentally, you did not read my account of the schedule carefully. I write little up to eight o'clock, but after eight, nothing, in spite of my then feeling most liberated. I would write more about that if I had not squandered today in a particularly stupid manner, on ball games and card games and sitting around and lying in the garden. And I do not go on any outings. There is the gravest danger that I will not even see the Brocken[31] at all. If you only knew how the short time passes! If only it passed as distinctly as water, but it passes like oil.

I am leaving here Saturday afternoon (but would like very much to have a card from you by then), will stay in Dresden Sunday and arrive in Prague in the evening. I am not going by way of Weimar only because of perfectly obvious weakness. I have received a short letter from her, with regards from her mother in her own hand and three enclosed photographs. In all three she can be seen in different poses, ever so much more clearly than in the earlier photographs, and how beautiful she is. And I am going to Dresden as though it had to be, and will have to look at the Zoological Garden, in which I belong.

Franz

Nine diary pages.

Max, do you know the song "Now fare thee well . . ."?[32] We sang it early this morning, and I have copied it. I am putting the copy away very carefully. What purity and what simplicity; every stanza consists of an exclamation and a nod of the head.

I am adding a forgotten page from the trip.

To Max Brod

[Prague, August 7, 1912][33]

My dearest Max,

After tormenting myself for a long time, I am stopping. I am unable and in the near future will scarcely be able to complete the remaining pieces.[34] Since I can't do it now, but undoubtedly will be able to do it someday, in a good spell, would you really advise me—and how could it possibly be justified?—to have something bad published with my eyes open, something which would then disgust me, like the "Conversations" in *Hyperion*?[35] What has so far been written on the typewriter is probably not sufficient for a book, of course; but after all, is going unpublished—and are even worse outcomes—not far less bad than this damnable forcing oneself? In these short pieces there are a few passages for which I would like to have ten thousand advisers; but if I hold them back, I need no one but you and me and am content. Tell me I am right! This artificial working and pondering has bothered me all along and makes me needlessly miserable. We can allow bad things to remain finally bad only on our deathbed. Do tell me that I am right, or at least that you aren't angry with me about it. Then I shall be able to begin something else with a clear conscience and also be reassured about you.

Yours, Franz

To Max Brod

[Dictated to Kafka's sister Ottla]
[Prague, probably from the second half of 1912]

Dearest Max, I really no longer know whether I shall be coming over tomorrow, Sunday morning, at best with a lie, because I am afraid of you. I cannot endure the kind of face you made the night before your departure. I now regularly sleep until a quarter past eight, and I also properly gave instructions that today I was to be waked at seven, and they did wake me at seven, as I was dimly able to recall when I finally woke at a quarter past eight. But this waking disturbed me no more than my nowadays terribly distinct dreams. (Yesterday, for example, I had a furious conversation with Paul Ernst.[36] We were going at it hammer and tongs. He was much like Felix's father. From tomorrow on, he will write two stories daily.) I have not received a letter for two days. You have not answered two cards and a letter of mine, and although both facts are not very difficult to explain, I mention this because I have no better excuse for my own unpunctuality.

To Max Brod

[Prague, August 14, 1912]

Good morning! Dear Max, while arranging the little pieces yesterday, I was under the young woman's[37] influence, and it may well be that some silliness resulted, perhaps only a secretly comic sequence. Please look it over once more and let my thanks for that be included in the enormous thanks I owe you.

Yours, Franz

There are also a number of petty errors in it, as I now see when, alas, I am for the first time reading over one of the copies. And the punctuation! But perhaps there is still time for correcting these matters. Only this: Cut "That's a good one" in the children's story, and put a question mark after the "Afraid" four words back.[38]

To Ernst Rowohlt

Prague, August 14, 1912

Dear Herr Rowohlt,

I am herewith transmitting to you the short prose pieces you wished to see. They might well make a small book. While I was assembling them for this purpose I sometimes had the choice between appeasing my sense of responsibility and my eagerness to have a book of my own among your fine books. Certainly my decisions have not been perfectly pure. But now, of course, I would be happy if you liked the things only to the extent of your publishing them. Ultimately, even with the greatest experience and the greatest keenness, the flaws in these pieces do not reveal themselves at first glance. And the personal mark of each writer consists in his having his own special way of concealing his flaws.

Yours sincerely, Dr. Franz Kafka

Manuscript follows separately by parcel post.

To Rowohlt Verlag

[Letterhead: Workers' Accident Insurance Institute]
Prague, September 7, 1912

Dear Sir,

Many thanks for your friendly letter of the 4th.[39] Since I can easily imagine the commercial prospects of publishing such a small first book, I gladly agree to any conditions you wish to propose. Conditions that limit your risk as far as possible will also be those I prefer.

I have too much respect for the books you have published to interfere with any proposals in regard to this book. I would only ask for the largest possible typeface[40] consistent with your plans for the book. If it were possible to give the book a dark cardboard binding with tinted paper somewhat like the Kleist *Anecdotes*, I would like that very much—always assuming, however, that this would not disturb your plans.

Looking forward to further word from you, I am,

Sincerely yours, Dr. Franz Kafka

To Elsa Taussig

Prague, September 18, 1912

Dear Fräulein Elsa, Many thanks! That's the way it is in the south.

Just reading this diary,[41] my blood begins to boil, although after its fashion, rather feebly.

Do write me a word about where and when I can see you, and I shall come with pleasure. But I would not want to take you by surprise; there are no pleasant surprises. By the way, how would it be if one of these days we would go together to visit the old uncle; since Max has gone away from us all, we do belong together.

Cordially yours, Franz K.

To Felix Weltsch and Max Brod

[Letterhead: Workers' Accident Insurance Institute]
Prague, September 20, 1912

Dear Lucky Ones,

I am giving myself the pleasure—a very nervous one, to be sure—of writing to you in the middle of office hours. I would not do so if I were still able to write letters without a typewriter, but this pleasure is irresistible. If mood isn't quite sufficient, as is usual, the fingertips are always there. I must assume that that greatly interests you, because I am writing this in such great haste.

Thank you, Max, for the diary. Your fiancée was so kind as to send it to me at once. It arrived at the same time as your first card. I also thanked her promptly and I must confess promptly asked her for a rendezvous, for which, I hope as you would wish it, I have proposed your uncle's apartment, so that we three inconsolables can get together.

You must not stop the diary. And it would be better still if all of you would keep diaries and send them. Since we are already writhing with envy, we want to know why. Just from those few pages, I have begun to understand the south a little, and I have been powerfully affected by those Italians in the compartment. Whom you, with your incessant good living, probably no longer even remember.

Last night, Max, I visited your parents. Your father, however, was at a club, and at the moment I felt too weak to insist that your brother produce your letters. As for news [HERE THE TYPESCRIPT ENDS]

At this suspenseful passage I was interrupted. A delegation of the Provincial Association of Lumbermill Proprietors is coming—nothing less, for the sake of the impression it will make on you too—and will stay forever.

So farewell.

Yours, Franz

Regards to Herr Süssland.

My sister Valli celebrated her engagement[42] Saturday; give her the pleasure of congratulating her on a picture postcard, without saying how you knew.

To Rowohlt Verlag

[Letterhead: Workers' Accident Insurance Institute]
Prague, September 25, 1912

Dear Sirs,

Enclosed I take pleasure in returning to you, with thanks, the signed contract form. I kept it for a few days because I wanted simultaneously to send you a correction for the piece entitled "The Sudden Walk"; near the present end of the first paragraph there is one passage that repels me.[43] Unfortunately I do not have this correction quite right yet, but will certainly send it in the next few days.

One more request: since no publication date is mentioned in the contract—it does not matter in the least to me that this should be done—but since I naturally would very much like to know when you mean to bring out the book, may I ask you to be so kind as to write me about this when occasion offers.

With cordial regards, yours sincerely, Dr. Franz Kafka

To Max Brod

[Prague, autumn 1912]

Dearest Max, Where in the world are you? I was going to catch some sleep on the sofa while waiting for you, but sleep did not come, nor did you. By now it's time for me to go home; but I do want to see you tomorrow morning, at any rate. I'll be at the office until twelve, and although I don't like to tell you to visit or call for me there, that way I would see you sooner, and perhaps you can arrange your errands to make it possible. But in any case I'll come to your place after twelve. If you could manage to be home—I would take you out for a walk in our sun.—Fräulein B.[44] sends you regards, and I am glad to lend her my mouth for the purpose.

Franz

To Max Brod

[Prague, autumn 1912]

Dear Max, Here I am sending you the second chapter,[45] without me.

It was the only good spell that I have had with it since Saturday. I cannot come because my father is not well and wants me to stay with him. Maybe I can come in the evening.

Yours, Franz

To Rowohlt Verlag

[Letterhead: Workers' Accident Insurance Institute]
Prague, October 6, 1912

Dear Sirs,

Enclosed I am sending you the correction for the piece "The Sudden Walk." Will you be so kind as to enter it into the manuscript in place of the earlier passage.

At the same time may I repeat my request of some time ago that you inform me concerning the publication date you have in mind for *Meditation*. I would be much obliged if I might hear from you soon about this.

Cordially yours, Dr. F. Kafka

To Max Brod

[Prague, October 7, 1912]

My dearest Max,

After writing well Sunday night—I could have written all through the night and the day and the night and the day, and finally have flown away, and could certainly have written well today also—one page, really just an exhalation of yesterday's ten, is actually finished—I had to stop for the following reason: my brother-in-law,[46] the manufacturer, this morning left for a business trip which is going to take from ten to fourteen days. (In my happy distraction I had scarcely noticed that this was impending.) During this period, the factory is actually left to the foreman alone, and no investor, especially so nervous a one as my father, would have any doubts that fraud must now be running rampant in the factory. For that matter, I think the same, though not so much because I am worried about the money as because I am uninformed and uneasy in conscience. But actually, even a neutral person, insofar as I can imagine one such, might see a certain justification for my father's anxiety, although I should not forget that in the final analysis I do not at all see why a foreman from Germany would not be able to run everything with his usual efficiency even in the absence of my brother-in-law, to whom he is inordinately superior in all technical and organizational matters, for after all we are human beings and not thieves.

Now in addition to the foreman, my brother-in-law's younger brother[47] is also here. Granted, he is a fool in all matters except business, and even in business matters to a considerable extent. But still he is competent, hardworking, attentive, a livewire, I might say. But of course he has to be in his office a great deal, and in addition manage the agency, for which purpose he has to run around the city half the day and therefore has little time left for the factory.

Recently, when I told you that nothing coming from outside could disturb my writing now (that, of course, was not so much boasting as an attempt to comfort myself), I was thinking only of how my mother whimpers to me almost every evening that I really should look in on the factory now and then to reassure Father, and of how my father has also said it to me much more strongly by looks and in other roundabout ways. In large part such pleas and reproofs were not without a certain rationale, for supervising Brother-in-law would certainly do him and the factory a great deal of good; except that I— and herein lay the irreducible irrationality of such talk—cannot perform any such supervision, even in my clearest states of mind.

For the next two weeks, however, that is not what is really involved. For this period, no more really is needed than any pair of eyes going about the factory, and even mine will do. There cannot be the slightest objection to this demand's being directed to me in particular, for in everybody's opinion I bear the chief blame for the establishment of the factory—though I must have assumed this blame in a dream—and in addition there is no one else around who could look into the factory, for my parents, who in any case would be out of the question, are in the midst of the busiest season at the store (the store also seems to be going better in its new location), and this afternoon, for example, my mother was not even home for dinner.

This evening, therefore, when my mother once again began with the old lament and, aside from blaming me for my father's bitterness and sickness, also brought up this new argument about Brother-in-law's departure and the orphaned state of the factory, and my youngest sister, who ordinarily sides with me, correctly sensing the change of feeling that I have recently had on this subject, and simultaneously displaying monstrous obtuseness, deserted me in my confrontation with Mother, and while bitterness—I don't know whether it was only gall—passed through my whole body—I realized with perfect clarity that now only two possibilities remain open to me, either to jump out of the window once everyone has gone to sleep, or in the next two weeks to go daily to the factory and to my brother-in-law's office. The first would provide me with the opportunity of shedding all responsibility, both for the disturbance of my writing and for the orphaned factory. The second would absolutely interrupt my writing—I cannot simply wipe from my eyes the sleep of fourteen nights—and would leave me, if I had enough strength of will and of hope, the prospect of possibly beginning again, in two weeks, where I left off today.

So I did not jump, and the temptations to make this a farewell letter (my ideas for it take another direction) are not very strong. I stood for a long time at the window and pressed against the pane, and there were many moments when it would have suited me to alarm the toll collector on the bridge by my fall. But all the while I really felt too firm to let the decision to smash myself to pieces on the pavement penetrate to the proper decisive depth. It also seemed to me that my staying alive interrupts my writing less than death—even if I can speak only, only of interruption—and that between the beginning of the novel and its continuation in two weeks somehow, in the factory especially and especially in relationship to my satisfied parents, I shall move and have my being within the innermost spaces of my novel.

Dearest Max, I am putting this whole thing before you not for your opinion, for of course you could have no opinion of it, but since I was firmly determined to jump without leaving a farewell letter—before the end one has a right to be just tired—I wanted, since I am about to step back into my room as its occupant, to write you instead a long letter of reunion, and here it is. And now just a kiss and goodnight, so that tomorrow I am a factory boss, as they demand.

                                                              Yours, Franz

Tuesday, 12:30 A.M., October [8,] 1912
And yet, now in the morning, I must not conceal this, I hate them all, one after the other, and think that in these fourteen days I shall scarcely be able to summon up the good-mornings and good-evenings. But hatred—and this again is directed against myself—really belongs more outside the window than peacefully sleeping in bed. I am far less sure than I was during the night.[48]

To Rowohlt Verlag

                      [Letterhead: Workers' Accident Insurance Institute]
                                              Prague, October 18, 1912
Dear Sir,

The sample page which you so kindly sent me is altogether beautiful. Let me speedily and by registered mail express my approval of the typeface and thank you from the bottom of my heart for your solicitude toward my little book.

The page numbering on the sample is, I hope, only provisional, for "Children on a Country Road" should be the first piece. It is my fault for not sending along a table of contents, and the worst of it is that I cannot make up for this omission, since aside from the opening piece and the closing piece,

"Unhappiness," I no longer remember the sequence of the pieces in the manuscript.

I hope the revised version of "The Sudden Walk" has reached you.

Cordially yours, Dr. F. Kafka

To Max Brod

[Prague, autumn 1912]

Dear Max, Yesterday I completely forgot one principal item—our telephone. You cannot imagine how urgently we need it, or at least how urgently we needed it two weeks ago, when I stopped going to the factory. I still go to the office fairly often. You know, I'd like to reduce as far as possible the excuses for failure, a possibility I don't yet see in actuality but that I catch glimpses of in the faces of my brothers-in-law.

Yours, Franz

To Max Brod

[Postcard. Prague; postmark: November 7, 1912]

Dearest Max, Why is that person interfering with us, when after so long a time we have a chance to see each other alone and have a good talk. To be sure, he would have interested me, if only because he was once mentioned in my correspondence. But he wasn't worth my dragging myself out of bed when I am tired almost to death. That is why it was already nine before I came to the Arco, where I learned that you had already left, at which I turned around and went back home. You aren't working? It grieves me that in the course of time so many obstacles have collected around you. One of these days you must clear a great space around yourself with one vigorous swing of your arms. Your poems look very good in the *Herder-Blätter*.[49] Well then, I will come Friday.

Yours, Franz

To Max Brod

[Prague,] November 13, 1912

Dearest Max (I am dictating this as I lie in bed, out of laziness and because the letter concocted in bed should find its way on to paper at the same spot). I just want to tell you that I will not be reading at Baum's Friday. At present the whole novel is in an uncertain state. Yesterday I had to force myself to finish the sixth chapter,[50] and so it turned out crude and bad. I had to exclude two characters who should have entered into the chapter. So all the while I was writing, they were pursuing me, and since in the novel they were supposed to raise their arms and clench their fists, they threatened me with the same gestures. All this time, they were more alive than what I was writing. So today I am not writing anything, not because I don't want to but because I am too hollow-eyed. Besides, there's been not a word from Berlin. But what fool could have expected otherwise? There you did your best; you offered whatever one could offer in the way of goodness, understanding, and sense. But had an angel made that telephone call instead of you, he still could not have undone the effect of my venomous letter. Well, on Sunday the messenger boy of a Berlin flower-shop will deliver a note without salutation or signature.[51]

To add to my usual agony, I glanced through the third chapter and saw that I would need a strength I altogether lack to drag that cart out of the mud. And even such strength would not suffice to overcome my unwillingness to read the chapter aloud in its present state. Of course I cannot skip over it either. And so you have no choice but to repay me for breaking my promise by two acts of kindness. First, not to be angry with me, and secondly, to read aloud yourself.

So long. (I must now go for a walk with my secretary Ottla. She came here straight from work this evening and like a pasha I have been dictating to her from my bed, and moreover have constrained her to silence, for she keeps on saying that she too wants to add a word.) The best thing about such letters as this is that their beginnings cease to be true by the time they reach their end. I feel a great deal better than I did when I began.

Yours, Franz

To Willy Haas

[Prague,] November 25, 1912

Dear Herr Haas,

Of course I accept the invitation of the Herder Society. It will give me great pleasure to read for you. I will read the story in *Arkadia;*[52] it takes not quite half an hour. What sort of audience will there be? Who else will be reading? How long is the whole program? Would a business suit be sufficient? (The last is a superfluous question, since that is all I have to wear.) But please do reply to my other questions.

With cordial greetings, Dr. F. Kafka

To Max Brod

[End of 1912]

Dearest Max, I don't know whether you have received my letter of yesterday, but in any case I want to tell you that the account of the chief matter is by today already false and everything has turned out unimaginably well.

Franz

To Oskar Baum

[Picture postcard. Prague, probably 1912]

Dear Herr Baum,

Max must attend a goodbye party for a colleague on Monday and I must try to reconcile my father to a matter which I am going to tell you about. So the following Monday we will both be coming.

Be well!

F. Kafka

1913

To Otto Stoessl [1]

[Prague,] January 27, 1913

Dear Dr. Stoessl,

Rowohlt Verlag has sent you my book *Meditation*.[2] Please regard it as a small token of the affection I feel for your writings. You probably scarcely recall ever having spent any time with a person by my name, and yet you did. It was in Prague, in the tavern called "At the Sign of the Two Blackbirds," and my friend Max Brod was kind enough to introduce me to you.[3] Seeing and hearing you was a great encouragement to me at that time, and a remark you made then, "The novelist knows everything," still rings in my mind to this day.

Cordially yours, Dr. F. Kafka

To Elsa and Max Brod [4]

[Picture postcard, addressed to Monte Carlo. Prague; postmark: February 4, 1913]

My dears, I have no need for a nightwatchman, being one myself in respect to sleepiness, walks in the dark, and being chilled to the bone. Are you properly warming yourselves in the sun? Please look out for a place for summer or autumn where I could live in vegetarian style, stay healthy, where I could be alone without feeling forlorn, where even a blockhead can learn Italian and so forth, in short a lovely and improbable sort of place. Be well. You are in our thoughts.

Franz

To Elsa and Max Brod

[Picture postcard, addressed to Saint-Raphaël.
Prague; postmark: February 14, 1913]

Only a few days ago the realization came to me that you will be away for eighteen days. So long! It is going on forever. Are the two of you at least keeping a journal? If you have not yet done so, you must begin today. Sit down somewhere along the shore and together draw up an account of your trip so far, even if it takes you from morning to night. I warn you there will be war between us unless you do this. And come back soon.

Franz

To Gertrud Thieberger [5]

[Postcard. Prague; postmark: February 20, 1913]

Dear Fräulein Thieberger,

I am sorry that I will not be able to go to *Carmen* after all, for today I have to be on duty in the afternoon. I forgot to mention this on the telephone, as I forget most everything when I am on the phone. Once again, many thanks for your kindness. Incidentally, is it economical to obliterate the memory of a good performance by a probably inferior one? With warm greetings to you and your sister.

F. Kafka

To Kurt Wolff Verlag [6]

[Prague,] March 8, 1913

Dear Herr Wolff,

I am sending the proofs for *Arkadia* by return mail. I am grateful to you for having sent me the page proofs since there was a ghastly printer's error on page 61—"bride" instead of "breast."

With thanks, yours sincerely, Dr. F. Kafka

To Kurt Wolff

[Postcard. Charlottenburg; postmark: March 25, 1913][7]

BEST GREETINGS FROM A PLENARY SESSION OF AUTHORS OF YOUR HOUSE.

OTTO PICK   ALBERT EHRENSTEIN   CARL EHRENSTEIN[8]

Dear Herr Wolff,

Pay no attention to what Werfel[9] tells you. He does not know a word of the story.[10] As soon as I have had a clean copy made, I will of course be glad to send it to you.

Sincerely, F. Kafka

[CORDIAL GREETINGS FROM PAUL ZECH; (A DRAWING BY ELSE LASKER-SCHÜLER,[11] SIGNED:) ABIGAIL BASILEUS III]

To Max Brod

[Prague,] April 3, 1913

Dearest Max,

If it didn't seem so stupid without adequate explanation—and how could I possibly explain it in words?—I would simply say that for me, such as I am, the best thing is to keep out of sight. That would be the most exact answer. In the past, if there was no other way, I could at least hold tight to the office. Nowadays, however, I know that if I followed my inner biddings—and my inhibitions are pretty faint—I would throw myself down at my boss's feet and beseech him not to fire me. I would beg him on grounds of pure humanity— for I myself can see no other grounds, though others apparently see the matter quite differently, for which I have to be thankful. My mind is daily prey to fantasies, for example that I lie stretched out on the floor, sliced up like a roast, and with my hand am slowly pushing a slice of the meat toward a dog in the corner. Yesterday I sent my great confession to Berlin.[12] She is a real martyr and it is clear that I am undermining the entire basis on which she previously used to live, happy and in tune with the whole world.

I would have liked to come today, Max, but must take care of an important errand. I am going to Nusle[13] to look up a market gardener there and ask to be taken on for part-time work. So I will come tomorrow, Max.

Franz

To Kurt Wolff

[Prague,] April 4, 1913

Dear Herr Wolff,

Your very kind letter has just reached me late this evening. Under the circumstances I cannot get the manuscripts[14] to you by Sunday even with the best will in the world, and even though I would find it more bearable to send off a still-unfinished piece of work rather than to let it seem that I was being in the least disobliging. To be sure, I cannot see in what way or what sense these manuscripts could be a favor to you, but for that reason I ought to send them all the more readily. I will indeed send you the first chapter of the novel, since most of it has already been copied; by Monday or Tuesday the manuscript should be in Leipzig. Whether it can be published by itself I do not know. To be sure, this first chapter does not expose the total failure of the next five hundred pages, but on the other hand it probably lacks sufficient coherence. It is a fragment and will stay that way; this prospect gives the chapter what coherence it has. My other story, *The Metamorphosis*, is not yet transcribed, since lately everything has combined to keep me away from writing and from my pleasure in it. But I will have this story, too, transcribed and sent to you as soon as possible. Perhaps later on these two pieces and the "Judgment" from *Arkadia* will make up quite a decent book whose title might be *The Sons*.

With cordial thanks for your friendly words and with best wishes for your journey,

sincerely yours, Franz Kafka

To Kurt Wolff

[Prague,] April 11, 1913

Dear Herr Wolff,

Many thanks for your friendly letter; I am fully and happily in accord with the terms you offer for the publication of "The Stoker" in *Der jüngste Tag*.[15] I have only one request, which I have already mentioned in my last letter. "The Stoker," *The Metamorphosis* (which is one and a half times as long as "The Stoker"), and "The Judgment" belong together, both inwardly and outwardly. There is an obvious connection among the three and, even more important, a secret one, for which reason I would be reluctant to forgo the chance of having them published together in a book, which might be called *The Sons*. Would it be possible, then, for "The Stoker," apart from its publication in *Der jüngste Tag*, to appear eventually along with the other two stories in a book all their own, at some reasonable time which however I would leave entirely to your discretion? And would it be possible to include a statement of this pledge in the present contract for *The Stoker?* You see, I am just as much concerned about the unity of the three stories as I am about the unity of any one of them.

Cordially yours, Dr. F. Kafka

To Kurt Wolff

[Prague,] April 20, 1913

Dear Herr Wolff,

I was already beginning to fear that I was asking too much and here you have so kindly granted[16] all I asked without even considering whether my request made sense. My warmest thanks.

Sincerely, Dr. F. Kafka

To Gertrud Thieberger

[Inscription in the first edition of *Meditation*. Probably spring 1913] For Fräulein Trude Thieberger, with cordial regards and a word of warning: this book is not yet in conformity with the proverb "A closed mouth gulps no flies" (as it says in *Carmen* by Mérimée).[17] That's why it is full of flies. You would do best to keep it tightly shut.

F. Kafka

To Kurt Wolff

[Prague,] April 24, 1913

Dear Herr Wolff,

Enclosed I am returning the proofs of *The Stoker,* and must ask you by all means to let me see the revised proofs. There are, as you can see, so many small corrections that this set of proofs cannot possibly be adequate. However, I will send the revised set back by return mail, no matter when I receive it. And might I also see the title page? If it is at all possible, I should very much like to have on the title page, under the title *The Stoker,* the subtitle *A Fragment.*

Cordially yours, Dr. F. Kafka

To Max Brod

[Picture postcard. Prague; postmark: May 14, 1913] Dearest Max, Tomorrow morning I set off for Aussig[18] and must prepare for that a bit before going to bed. The hour, in any case, would never be late enough for me to tell you what I did in Berlin.[19]

Franz

To Kurt Wolff

[Prague,] May 25, 1913

Dear Herr Wolff,

Many thanks for the package. Of course I cannot venture to give a business judgment on *Der jüngste Tag*, but in and for itself it strikes me as a splendid project.

When I saw the picture[20] in my book, I was at first alarmed. For in the first place it refuted me, since I had after all presented the most up-to-date New York; in the second place, the picture had an advantage over my story since it produced its effect before my story did, and a picture is naturally more concentrated than prose; and thirdly, it was too pretty. If it were not an old print, it might almost be something of Kubin's.[21] By now however I have completely come to terms with it and am very glad that you surprised me, for had you put the matter to me, I would not have been able to agree and would have been robbed of this beautiful picture. I feel my book has been definitely enriched by the print and that already an exchange of strengths and weaknesses has taken place between picture and book. By the way, where did the print come from? Once again, my gratitude.

Yours sincerely, F. Kafka

May I place an order for one copy, in paper, of *Beauty of Ugly Pictures*,[22] five copies in cloth of *The Stoker*, and as an advance order three copies in cloth of *Arkadia*.

To Max Brod

[Picture postcard. Prague; postmark: May 31, 1913]

Dear Max, Unless you go to the *Tagblatt*, the article[23] is doomed. At least, that was my impression. So please, please.

Franz

To Lise Weltsch[24]

[Prague,] June 5, 1913

Dear Fräulein Weltsch,

It can only have been a mistake, you owe Löwy nothing, the accounts were closed long ago and since they balance perfectly, I cannot accept any more and must send back the stamps. Please don't be angry with me over this. But if you persist in your mistaken belief concerning Löwy, with whom I am entirely at one in this affair, and continue to feel that you are under some obligation toward him, then please settle it by being so kind as to accept the little book I am sending to you. I have long been wanting to do something of this sort, but no opportunity came my way. I therefore seize on this occasion, though suspecting that it is not the right occasion nor this the right sort of book. Despite these reservations, it gives me great pleasure.

With warmest regards, yours sincerely, Franz Kafka

To Max Brod

[Postcard. Prague; postmark: August 29 (1913?)]
Dearest Max, It occurs to me that I must have struck you yesterday as an awful person, chiefly by the way I laughed when we said goodbye. At the same time I knew, as I know now, that with *you* no explanations are needed. Nevertheless, I must say, more for my own sake than for yours, that what I displayed yesterday and what only you, F.,[25] and Ottla are aware of in this form (though even with you three I ought to have suppressed it) is of course only what happens on one of the floors of my interior Tower of Babel, and what lies above and below is beyond the ken of folks in Babel. Anyhow, it is more than enough, even if I, as I might so easily do, were to try to make the most extensive retouching with an ever so practiced hand. It remains as it is, frightening and not frightening at all. Which calls for another such laugh, to be followed within five minutes by another such card as this. Beyond doubt wicked people exist, scintillating with wickedness.

Franz

To Max Brod

[Picture postcard (Rehobot Colony). Vienna;[26]
postmark: September 9, 1913]
Dear Max, Killing insomnia; I don't dare put my hand on my brow because the fever alarms me so. I am running away from everything, literature and the Congress, just when it gets most interesting.

Regards to all, Franz

To Felix Weltsch

[Picture postcard. Vienna; postmark: September 10, 1913]
Little enjoyment, more responsibilities, even more tedium and more insomnia, more terrible headaches—this is my life here, though now I have

ten minutes of peace in which to watch how the rain falls in the courtyard of the hotel.

Franz

To Max Brod

[Venice; postmark: September 16, 1913]

My dear Max, I am not sufficiently coherent to write anything coherent. I would wish to tear those days in Vienna out of my life, tear them up by the roots. It was all a useless business. It is hard to imagine anything more useless than such a congress. I sat in on the Zionist Congress[27] as if it were an event totally alien to me, felt myself cramped and distracted by much that went on (at the moment a young man and a handsome gondolier are looking through my window), and if I didn't quite throw spitballs at the delegates, as did a girl in the opposite gallery, I was bored enough to. As for the literary people there, I know almost nothing about them. I was with them only twice, and while on a certain level they impress me, basically I did not like any of them, except perhaps for Stössinger[28] who happened to be in Vienna and had a fine decisive manner of speech and then E. Weiss,[29] who is again very obliging. There was much talk about you, and while you may have Tychonian[30] notions about these people, here this chance group sits around a table, all of them good friends of yours, and constantly refer to one or another of your books in the most admiring terms. I do not mean that this sort of thing has the slightest value, I only mean to say that it goes on. I will tell you about it in detail; if any objections were voiced, it was only because of your too great visibility, which is somewhat painful to these dull eyes.

But all that is behind me; I am now in Venice. If I were not so slow-moving and sad, I would not have the strength within myself to endure Venice. How lovely the city is and how we at home undervalue it. I will be staying longer than I thought. It is good to be here alone. Literature, which has long shown me no favor, has again remembered me, by keeping P.[31] in Vienna.

My experiences in the past have shown me that you are the only one I can travel with; much worse but still bearable is to travel alone.

Regards to all, Franz

To Oskar Baum

[Postcard. Riva; postmark: September 24, 1913]

I am living now, at least as long as there is sun, in a miserable shack at the lakeside, with a long diving board over the water which I have so far used only for sunbathing. The establishment as a whole has its good side, and since I am quite alone here, I wallow in it slowly and shamelessly. Warmest regards to all.

Franz

To Max Brod

[Letterhead: Dr. von Hartungen, Sanatorium and
Hydrotherapy Institute, Riva on Lake Garda][32]
[Postmark: September 28, 1913]

My dear Max, Both your cards reached me but I lacked the strength to answer. Not answering also has the effect of creating a silence about one, and my dearest wish would be to sink into that silence and never emerge from it. How I need solitude and how soiled I feel by every conversation. At any rate, I say nothing at the sanatorium; at table I sit between an old general (who also says nothing but when he does he speaks very sensibly, at least far more so than the others) and a small Italian-looking Swiss girl[33] with a low-pitched voice who is quite unhappy about her table partners.

However I have just noticed that not only can't I talk, but I can't write. I have a lot to tell you but I cannot fit it together or it goes off in a wrong direction. In fact, I have not written anything for two weeks: I keep no diary, write no letters. The thinner the days trickle away, the better. I don't know but I think that if someone had not spoken to me, today on the boat (I was in Malcesine[34]), and I hadn't agreed to meet him tonight at the Bayerische Hof, I would not be here, writing to you, but would actually be out on the square.

Otherwise I am living quite reasonably and improving my health; since Tuesday I have been swimming every day. If only that *one* thing[35] would loosen its hold over me, if only I did not have to think of it constantly, if only there were not those times, mostly in the morning when I am getting up, when it leaps at me like a living thing. Yet it's all perfectly clear and has been over and done with for the past two weeks. I had to say I couldn't go through with it and I really cannot. But why, even as I am thinking this, without any special reason do I suddenly have this great uneasiness in my heart, the way I did in Prague during the worst times? But I can't convey to you in writing what comes upon me so starkly and always so terribly at moments when there is no letter paper before me.

By comparison with this nothing has any meaning and I merely keep traveling around inside these caverns. You might think that solitude and silence give these ideas such dominance. But that is not so; the need for solitude exists independently. I hunger for solitude. The idea of a honeymoon trip fills me with horror. Every honeymoon couple, whether or not I put myself in their place, is a repulsive sight to me, and when I want to disgust myself I have only to imagine placing my arm around a woman's waist. So you see—and still, and even though it is all over, and I write no more letters and receive none, still, still, I cannot free myself. For here in my imagination impossibilities stand as close together as they do in reality. I cannot live with her and I cannot live without her. By this one act my life, which was at least in part mercifully veiled from myself, is now completely unveiled. I ought to be whipped out into the desert.

You cannot know how much pleasure your cards brought me in the midst of all this. That you are pushing ahead with *Tycho*[36] (I can scarcely believe that it came to a standstill) and that Reinhardt is considering *Goodbye!*[37] It would be ludicrous for me to try to fight your jitters from my own resources. You will do that yourself and soon and thoroughly. Regards to your wife and to Felix (for whom this letter is also meant; I cannot write too many letters but also expect no reply, either from you or from him).

Franz

To Felix Weltsch

[Letterhead: Dr. von Hartungen, Sanatorium]
[Riva, September 1913]

No, Felix, things will not get better, things will never get better for me. Sometimes I think I am no longer in the world but am drifting around in some limbo. If you[38] imagine that I derive some help, some solution, from a sense of guilt, you are wrong. The reason why I have this sense of guilt is that it is for me the finest form of penitence. But one must not look too closely into this matter lest the sense of guilt become merely a form of nostalgia. And once that happens, there immediately rears up, far higher and more threatening than penitence, the feeling of freedom, of redemption, of relative contentment. This evening I received Max's letter. Do you know about it? What shall I do? Perhaps I won't answer; that is the only way to handle it.

Our fates lie in the cards. A few evenings ago six of us were sitting together and a young Russian woman, out of boredom and despair, for elegant people feel far more lost when thrown among inelegant people than the other way around, began to read our fortunes by the cards. In fact she read each fortune twice over, according to two different systems. The cards yielded this or that, mostly silly or half-serious stuff, which, even if one believed it, would mean nothing in the end. Only in two cases did something definite emerge, which everyone could check and which in fact coincided in both systems. There was one young lady in our group who, the cards foretold, would be an old maid, while for me the cards behaved as they did for no one else—namely, all the cards with human figures moved out to the margins, as far away from me as possible. Moreover, there was a great scarcity of such figures, at one time only two, and once, I believe, none at all. Instead of such remote figures there constantly revolved around me "Troubles," "Wealth," and "Ambition," the sole abstractions, outside of "Love," known to the cards.

To all appearances it would be folly to believe the cards literally. But there is a certain inherent rationale for using them or some other happenstance to introduce clarity into what is otherwise a confused and opaque realm. Naturally I am speaking here not of the effect of my reading upon myself but of the effect of such readings upon other people. I can test this by my reaction to the case of the young lady who by the cards was to be an old maid. She is a perfectly nice girl whose appearance, except for the way she does her hair, perhaps, in no way revealed the future spinster. Yet, though I had not had the slightest clear idea about this girl beforehand, I had pitied her right from the start and not because of her present condition but unequivocally because of her future. Ever since the cards fell out that way I have been convinced that she will be an old maid.

Your situation, Felix, may be more complicated than mine, but still it is more unreal. In its most extreme, most painful manifestations, after all, it is only theory. You strain to solve an admittedly insoluble question, whose solution as far as can be seen will be of no help to you or anyone else. But I am far beyond you as a poor wretch. If I had the slightest hope that it would be any use, I would cling to the pillars at the entrance to the sanatorium, so as not to have to leave here.

Franz

To Kurt Wolff Verlag

[Prague,] October 15, 1913

Dear Sirs,

I hear that about two weeks ago—in addition to the review of *The Stoker* in the *Neue Freie Presse*,[39] which I have seen—a review appeared in another Viennese paper, I believe in the *Wiener Allgemeine Zeitung*.[40] If you know about it, would you be so kind as to tell me the name of the paper and the issue and date.

Very truly yours, Dr. Franz Kafka

To Kurt Wolff

Prague, October 23, 1913

Dear Herr Wolff,

First of all my thanks for *Das bunte Buch*[41] which came to me today.—
About ten days ago I sent a little request to your office, sending it however, as
I now see, to the old address, and so have had no answer yet. I had heard that
some two or three weeks ago a review appeared in a Viennese paper (I do not
mean the review in the *Neue Freie Presse*, which I have seen), I believe in the
Wiener Allgemeine Zeitung, and so I was asking your office, if it had any
knowledge of this review, to inform me of the name of the paper and the
issue. Now I hear that in the last few days a review appeared in the
Börsenkurier.[42] I would be much obliged if you would let me know the issue.
Finally, may I ask you to send me a paperbound copy of *Intuition and Concept*.

Cordially yours, Dr. Franz Kafka

To Lise Weltsch

[Prague,] December 29, 1913

Dear Fräulein,

Many thanks to you and your parents for the kind invitation. Naturally I
shall be very glad to come. But naturally also—(when I enter the room, you
must put on an especially friendly face to show that you too consider it
natural and are not angry with me about it—for in that case I would
immediately flee)—but naturally also I will not come until after dinner.

Cordially yours, F. Kafka

To Max Brod

[Probably 1913]

I rejoice, my dear Max, over your happiness, over the happiness of you both,
only regret that it does not make you a bit more communicative. But that's
the way it is, and I agree with you, it is hard to write when one is traveling
and hard to write when one is happy. To try to fight that would be fighting
happiness. So swim without qualms, dear Max.

The only trouble is that since you sent me no informative picture postcard
of Lake Geneva, when I think of you I must fall back on my knowledge of
geography. But while my geography is in general excellent, it comes down
pretty much to excellent generalities and is poor in detail.

What is it really like? Do you go down to the lake at Riva, take a bit of a swim, reach one of the Borromean Islands—what is its name?—and, lying in the grass, read the letter I am enclosing? It is a nice letter, isn't it? You will recognize the sender from the handwriting.

So long.

Yours, Franz K.

1914

To Max Brod

[Prague,] February 6, 1914

My dear Max,

I sit at home with toothache and headache, and for the past half hour have been sitting at one corner of the table in the dark overheated room. Earlier I spent half an hour leaning against the stove, still earlier I sprawled half an hour in an armchair, before that paced between stove and armchair for half an hour, and only now will tear myself free and go to my own room. For your sake, Max, for if I hadn't made up my mind to write to you, I would not have had the energy to light the gas.

That you want to dedicate *Tycho* to me is the first unalloyed pleasure I have had in a long time. Do you know what such a dedication implies? That I am raised up and placed on the same level as Tycho, who is so much more vital than I. And even though this is only a semblance, some gleam of light from this semblance still warms me in reality. How small I shall be, orbiting around this story! But how glad I shall be to have a semblance of property rights in it. As always, Max, you are good to me beyond what I deserve.

You found Haas's study[1] easy to understand? To every last big word? And if he confirms your own viewpoint, then what about Fikher[2] (whose name certainly can't be spelled that way), who could be so deeply shaken by it?

You should definitely not have given Musil[3] my address. What does he want? What can he, and could anyone, want from me? And what can he get from me?

All right, now I turn back to my toothache. I have had it for three days in ever-increasing intensity. Only today (yesterday I was at the dentist's; he found nothing) was I able to tell with any exactness which tooth it is. Of course, the dentist is to blame; the pain comes from a tooth he already filled, from under the filling. God knows what is cooking beneath that lid; my glands are also beginning to swell.

It is hardly likely that I will come tomorrow to Fanta's.[4] I don't much like going there. Won't you write me when you can read something to me next week. Apparently I think I now have the right to issue orders in matters concerning *Tycho.*

Franz

To Kurt Wolff Verlag

[Prague,] April 22, 1914

Dear Sirs,

I would be greatly obliged if you would send a review copy of *Meditation* to the following address: František Langer,[5] Kgl. Weinberge No. 679, Prague. Langer is an editor of *Umělecký Měsíčník,* an influential monthly, and wants to publish a few excerpts of the book in translation. Would you also be kind enough to let me know that the copy has been sent.

Very truly yours, Dr. Franz Kafka

To Lise Weltsch

[Prague,] April 27, 1914

Dear Fräulein,

Many thanks for your good wishes. But now you must let me shake your hand and offer my felicitations for your project in Berlin. For what you are doing is what I have wanted to do for a long time. It is wonderful to get away from home and even more wonderful to get to Berlin. Do you really want to give me the pleasure of definitely and by prearrangement meeting you there? I shall be there at Whitsun;[6] will you too? Would you also care to meet Dr. Weiss someday?—he lives there permanently. From the first of June a friend of mine, a young woman,[7] will also be there (she is a Berliner who after a longish absence is returning to Berlin to stay) who I feel might become as dear to you as she is to me.

Please don't forget to drop me a few lines about this.

With warmest regards, yours sincerely, Franz Kafka

To Lise Weltsch

[Prague,] May 18, 1914

Dear Fräulein,

A mangled thumb prevented me from thanking you sooner in readable script for your kind letter. It does not surprise me that you have so quickly adapted. You would surely have done so even without the good luck of having friends there. And it is still a wonderful thing to get away from home, although you deny it. At the moment only an outsider can judge that, and the person who is in the midst of the wonderful new life must take the other's word for it, for the wonder is just beginning to penetrate.

At the outset I had not considered that you would be immediately stepping into a large circle of people with whom you would have so many and important ties, so that you would scarcely have the time and in any case no urgent need to meet new people, with all the small formalities such meetings involve. It will be enough of an effort for you, even though a healthy one, to deal with the necessary acquaintances. Had I not realized this, I would have written to you at once, even with a bleeding thumb.

Nevertheless, I would very much like to see you at Whitsun, if you can at all manage it. But if you are not visiting Prague then, you will probably be off on some outing and so will not be in Berlin. I am coming the Saturday before Whitsunday and staying until Tuesday afternoon. Can I reach you by telephone? If so, it would be best if I call you Sunday morning and ask.

With warm greetings, yours, F. Kafka

To Martin Buber[8]

[Prague,] May 25, 1914

Dear Dr. Buber, It was so kind of you to invite me to visit for Whitsun. I shall be in Berlin from Saturday evening to Tuesday afternoon, have many family affairs to attend to, but am definitely tied up only for Whitmonday morning and the early afternoon.[9] I shall take the liberty of telephoning on Whitsunday morning to inquire whether and when you can spare a little time for me and my fiancée, who has been reading your stories and thus become extremely eager to see the children.

Very sincerely yours, Franz Kafka

To Lise Weltsch

[Prague,] June 6, 1914

Dear Fräulein,

Here I am back in Prague and did not see you either here or there. Not here, because I was not free that evening and besides hoped to see you in Berlin in the midst of your new life, while in Berlin, from which moreover I was gone by Tuesday afternoon, I was so dragged hither and thither, reduced to the last remnants of my feeble strength, that I did not even telephone. What sort of apparition would you have seen if I had actually paid you a visit! Enough.

The remark in your letter, "I have already learned something, etc.," seems to indicate that I was right to congratulate you on your move. Perhaps one learns little in a foreign place, but that little is a great, great deal as long as one has not yet learned it. Nothing superhuman happens anywhere, if one looks at it in the right perspective; but what a girl from Prague in her first month of observations finds superhuman about a Berlin girl is worth investigating, experiencing, and only then can perhaps be smiled at. I don't know why I use the example of a girl from Prague; it would be more pertinent to speak of the tall oldster who is writing this letter, who greets you warmly and rejoices for your sake.

Yours, Franz Kafka

To Yitzhak Löwy

[Prague, June/July 1914]

Dear Löwy,

Your remembering me has given me far more pleasure than the tardiness of this reply suggests. I am perplexed and preoccupied, though I cannot see that being so does me or anybody else much good.

One piece of news: I have become engaged and think that in this I have done something good and essential, although of course the world is so full of doubts that even the best causes are gnawed by them.

How sad that you are still in trouble and see no way out. It is amazing that you have stayed so long in Hungary of all places, but I suppose there are unpleasant reasons for that. It seems to me that we were both more hopeful back in the days of our evening strolls through Prague. I used to think that you would somehow have your breakthrough, and by a single stroke. Still and all, I must tell you I have not given up those hopes for you. You despair easily but are also easily made happy, as you should bear in mind when you are feeling desperate. Take care of your health for good times in the future. What you have to endure seems bad enough, so do not make matters worse by injuring your health. I would very much like to hear more detailed news about you and your friends. Aren't you going to Karlsbad this season?

With warm regards, yours, Franz Kafka

To Ottla Kafka

July 10, 1914

Dear Ottla, Just a few words in haste before my attempt to go to sleep, at which I quite failed last night. Your card made an agonizing morning bearable for a few moments. That is the true massage and let us continue with it when occasion offers, if you agree. No, I have no one else in the evening. I will of course write you about Berlin.[10] At the moment there is nothing definite to say about the question or about me. I write differently from what I speak, I speak differently from what I think, I think differently from the way I ought to think, and so it all proceeds into deepest darkness.

Franz

Regards to all. You mustn't show my letter or let it lie around. You had best tear it up and throw the shreds from the *pawlatsche*[11] to the hens in the courtyard from whom I have no secrets.

To Robert Musil (?)[12]

[July 1914?]

Dear Herr Doktor,

We are faced here with an injustice to me and surely to you as well. The story was given careful consideration; it was kept long enough at the office for it to be considered in every respect, including its length, and was finally accepted unconditionally, or rather with the one proviso that I have more than adequately met, that I consent to wait a considerable time before publication. And now that months have passed after this acceptance I am being asked to shorten the story by one-third. This is undignified conduct. To tell the truth, dear Herr Doktor, for I know you will admit that I am completely right, if this request had been made to me at the beginning, before the acceptance, you and I would have been spared the present embarrassment. But I would not have shortened the story then any more than I would today. I am sure you will also approve of this stand—there is no other possible course.

As far as I can see, there remain only two possible compromises. Either the magazine publishes only the first chapter of the story, in accordance with the offer I made right at the start, which would at once represent an abridgment by two-thirds, or else the entire story is published, though at a still later date than scheduled, perhaps sometime in the course of the next year. I would be completely content with either of these two possibilities.

Cordially yours

But perhaps they no longer want the story at all and are now belatedly employing, toward you as well, this form of a disguised yet clear rejection. In that case this whole affair, which has caused you more unpleasantness than was necessary, would be finally settled and I would be left only with the consolation that I am in no way responsible for this last unpleasantness, rather that I myself bear the brunt of it.

To Alfred Kubin[13]

[Postcard. Postmark: July 22, 1914]

Dear Herr Kubin,

Many thanks for the card, which found me in a stupid state from which I am not yet wholly recovered; that is why I have not answered. Now I am traveling up and down the Baltic. You are no doubt working hard in the peace of your beautiful estate. Perhaps I will someday find words for saying again what your work has meant to me.

Yours, F. Kafka

To Max Brod and Felix Weltsch

[Letterhead: Marielyst Østersøbad]
[Before July 26, 1914]

Dear Max, dear Felix,

This letter is late, isn't it? But listen to what has happened to me. I am disengaged, have been in Berlin for three days, where everyone was my good friend and I was everyone's good friend. In addition I clearly perceived that this was all for the best and so am not so uneasy as you might think about the step, whose necessity had become so clear. But other things are not going so well. I then went to Lübeck, went bathing in Travemünde, and in Lübeck received a visit from Dr. Weiss who was on his way to this Danish resort, and so I went along instead of going to Gleschendorf.[14] A rather dreary beach with a few truly typical Danes. I have put aside my apparent stubbornness, which has cost me my engagement, and eat almost nothing but meat. As a result my stomach is upset and after terrible nights I wake early, with open mouth and feeling my abused and punished body in the bed like something alien and disgusting. I won't recuperate at all here, but will at any rate distract myself. Dr. W. is here with his lady friend.[15] Saturday night I will probably arrive back in Prague.

Regards to all your dear wives and brides.

Franz

To Felix Weltsch

[Visiting card. Prague, September 1914]

My dear Felix, I hear that you and your wife are slightly offended because I have not yet paid you a visit. If that is so, you are wrong. It is not only that in staying away I respect your honeymoon, but I am also in a wretched state due to my perpetual sleeplessness. In addition, I have much to do and furthermore live at the opposite end of the city, far beyond Rieger Park.[16] For all these reasons I am sending these books instead of bringing them. Important as the choice of these books was—since they are meant to represent me and all my good wishes for you in your new home—I begin to worry that I have not chosen well.

A pity that my inner voice never speaks before my choices are made.

Cordial regards, Franz

To Max Brod

[Prague, probably December 1914][17] Dear Max, I couldn't finish sooner. Stayed in bed until a quarter past one, without being able to sleep and without feeling especially tired.

Here is the manuscript.[18] Now that Blei is no longer with *Die weissen Blätter*,[19] I wonder if we couldn't try to have the story appear there. I wouldn't care when the story came out, next year or the year after that.

I am not bringing the Fontane; I would feel too uneasy to have that book going off on a journey. Wait till you're back. I'll bring you Sybel[20] instead. Read it and weep, both of you!

Please, Max, if you should see any French papers in Germany, buy them at my expense and bring them back for me.

And finally do not forget that you have the choice between Berlin and the Thuringian Forest, and while in Berlin there's nothing but Berlin, in the Thuringian Forest you can go ahead with *The New Christians*[21] and just at the critical moment when he is coming up from the depths.

And so goodbye.

Franz

1915

To Felix Weltsch

[Postcard. Prague; postmark: January 13, 1915] Dear Felix, Please have patience until Monday. If the book[1] has not turned up by then—though how it can, I simply can't imagine—I will have to pay for it.

Cordial regards to you and your wife, Franz

To René Schickele

Prague, April 7, 1915

Dear Sir,

[...] I do not insist at all on speedy publication of this story,[2] but do request you to inform me as soon as possible whether you can take it at all. Since you wish to avoid installments, finding room for my story must make problems; of course I realize that. If I nevertheless do not withdraw it of my own accord, my reason is solely that I am especially eager to see it published. But if it is completely out of the question, I could offer you another story,[3] that I also have ready and that comes to only some thirty typewritten pages, so that it would be less dubious a matter, at least in regard to its size.

Sincerely yours, F. Kafka

To Ernst Feigl[4]

[Postcard. Prague; postmark: September 18, 1915]

Dear Herr Feigl, I would have written sooner had it not been for the state of my head (which has shown no improvement for inconceivable ages nor can I conceive an age when it will improve). I have read your poems[5] many times over and think I have gained a certain intimacy with them. I find them highly attractive and to a certain degree even compelling. How strange the mixture of hope and despair in them and the impenetrability of this mixture, which however has a tonic effect. In almost every poem I think I hear your voice. Please do come to see me at my office, anytime you like. I am there every day until two; it would be highly unusual for me to be away. Let me stress again what I said to you earlier about my inadequacy as a judge of poetry.

With cordial greetings, Kafka

To Kurt Wolff Verlag

[Letterhead: Workers' Accident Insurance Institute]
Prague, October 15, 1915

Dear Sir,[6]

My warmest thanks for your letter of the 11th inst. Your news, especially that about Blei and Sternheim, has made me very happy and on several counts. As for your questions (which were no questions, really, since *The Metamorphosis* is already being set), I could answer them better if I knew exactly what the Fontane Prize is.[7] I gather from what you have written, and above all from what you wrote to Max Brod, that the prize is going to Sternheim, but that he would like to give the money to someone else, possibly to me. Kind as such a gesture is, it raises the question of need. But not of need regarding the prize *and* the money, but need in regard to the money alone. But to my way of thinking it would also not matter at all whether the recipient might need the money sometime in the future: rather the decisive factor should only be whether he needs it at the moment. Important as the prize or a share in the prize would be for me, I would not want to accept the money alone without a share in the prize. My feeling is that I would have no right to it, since I do not at all have that requisite immediate need for money. The only passage in your letter that contradicts my own view is the following: "The Fontane Prize will call attention ... etc." In any case the situation remains obscure and I would be grateful if you could clarify it somewhat.

As for your proposals, I completely trust your judgment. I would really have preferred to publish a sizable collection of stories (let us say, the story from *Arkadia*, *The Metamorphosis*, and still another novella,[8] under the collective title of *Punishments*). By the way, Herr Wolff agreed some time ago to this, but I suppose in the present circumstances it would be better temporarily to proceed as you have outlined. I also quite agree with the idea of reissuing *Meditation*.[9]

I enclose the corrected proofs of *Metamorphosis*. I am sorry that it is not to be in the same typeface as *Napoleon*,[10] since when you sent me the latter I assumed that *Metamorphosis* would be printed in the same way. The appearance of the page in *Napoleon* is pleasantly open and legible, while *Metamorphosis* looks dark and cramped, although the letters are, I believe, of the same size. If something can still be done about that, I would be most pleased.

I do not know what binding you have used for the later volumes of your *Der jüngste Tag* series. *The Stoker* was not handsomely bound. There was something sham about the binding which after a while produced a kind of disgust. So I would ask for another binding.

It's a pity that you could not come last week.[11] Perhaps it will be possible soon. I would be delighted.

With cordial regards, yours sincerely, F. Kafka

Might I have five more copies of the October issue of *Die weissen Blätter*?[12] I could well use them.

Herr Wolff once sent me several reviews of *The Stoker*. Should you need any for some reason, I can send them to you.

Proofs enclosed.

To Kurt Wolff Verlag

Prague, October 20, 1915

Dear Sir,

Many thanks for your letter of the 18th, for the *Napoleon*,[13] and for word that *Die weissen Blätter* will be coming.

I still do not fully understand the matter of the Fontane Prize; nevertheless I trust your general opinion on the question. However, the fact that Leonhard Frank[14] was a candidate (I suppose the prize cannot be awarded to the same person twice) suggests that what is involved is only and exclusively the distribution of the money. Nevertheless, again following your advice, I have written to Sternheim; it is not very easy to write to someone from whom one has received no direct word and to thank him without knowing exactly what for.

Of course I agree about the *Napoleon* binding. Have the earlier numbers in the series by any chance been rebound in this way?

I enclose the proofs herewith. I don't mind hurrying, but there are some days when I cannot manage to spare even the small amount of time they require.

I am also enclosing the reviews. They were sent to me as a supposedly complete collection, but are not complete. So far as I know, reviews from *Berliner Morgenpost, Wiener Allgemeine Zeitung, Österreichische Rundschau,* and *Neue Rundschau* are missing. Unfortunately I don't have any of those. At any rate, the most important one is that by Musil in the *Rundschau* issue of August 1914; the friendliest by H. E. Jacob, enclosed. On *Meditation,* the friendliest are by Max Brod in *März* and by Ehrenstein in the *Berliner Tageblatt.* But I don't have these either.[15]

You advised me to thank Sternheim, but don't I also have to thank Blei? And what is his address?

I imagine you have received the small piece for the almanac,[16] "Before the Law," and the first signature of the proofs for *Metamorphosis.*

With cordial regards, sincerely yours, F. Kafka

To Kurt Wolff Verlag

Prague, October 25, 1915

Dear Sir,

You recently mentioned that Ottomar Starke[17] is going to do a drawing for the title page of *Metamorphosis.* Insofar as I know the artist's style from *Napoleon,* this prospect has given me a minor and perhaps unnecessary fright. It struck me that Starke, as an illustrator, might want to draw the insect itself. Not that, please not that! I do not want to restrict him, but only to make this plea out of my deeper knowledge of the story. The insect itself cannot be depicted. It cannot even be shown from a distance. Perhaps there is no such intention and my plea can be dismissed with a smile—so much the better. But I would be very grateful if you would pass along my request and make it more emphatic. If I were to offer suggestions for an illustration, I would choose such scenes as the following: the parents and the head clerk in front of the locked door, or even better, the parents and the sister in the lighted room, with the door open upon the adjoining room that lies in darkness.[18]

I imagine you have already received the proofs and the reviews.

With best regards, sincerely yours, Franz Kafka

To Martin Buber

November 29, 1915

Dear Dr. Buber,

Your kind request[19] is a great honor to me, but I cannot comply with it. I am—of course an obscure hopeful impulse says "for the present"—far too burdened and insecure to think of speaking up in such company, even in the most minor way.

But please allow me, dear Dr. Buber, to take this opportunity to thank you for that afternoon I spent in your company almost two years ago.[20] Belated thanks, but not too belated from my point of view, for the hours together will always remain vivid in my mind. They signify in every respect the purest memory I have of Berlin, a memory that has often served me as a kind of refuge, all the more secure because I had not expressed my thanks and therefore no one knew of this treasure.

1916

To Max Brod

[Two postcards. Marienbad;[1] postmark: July 5, 1916]

Dear Max, Here I am in Marienbad. If I had written every day since our parting, which seems to me to be stretching on for too long a time, it would have been an inextricable confusion.

Take the last days alone: the bliss of leaving the office. Head remarkably clear for a change, almost all the work disposed of, everything left behind in exemplary order. If I had been leaving the office behind forever, I would have been ready, after six solid hours of dictation, to scrub the whole stairwell on my hands and knees, from attic to cellar, thereby showing every step how grateful I was to be leaving. But the next day, what stupefying headaches: Brother-in-law's[2] wedding, for which I had to stay on in Prague Sunday morning. The whole ceremony nothing but an imitation fairy tale; the well-nigh blasphemous marriage sermon: "How fair are thy tents, O Israel,"[3] and more of the same sort. What contributed to the mood of the day was a horrible dream, the more remarkable because nothing horrible happened in it, only an ordinary meeting with acquaintances on the street. I cannot remember any of the details, but I believe you were not there. The horrible part, however, lay in the feeling that I was face to face with one of these acquaintances. I may never have had a dream of this sort before. Then to Marienbad, where F. sweetly met me at the station; nevertheless a ghastly night in an ugly room on the courtyard. But then again it was the usual ghastly first night. Monday moved to an unusually attractive room; I am presently housed in no less a place than "Balmoral Castle." So I will try to put my vacation to good use; I am starting to work on the headaches, so far with little success. F. and I send warmest regards to both of you.

Franz

To Max Brod

[Postcard. Tepl,] July 8 [1916]
Dear Max, In Tepl[4] for a few hours. Out in the fields, away from the madness of the head and the nights. What kind of person am I! What kind of person am I! I am tormenting her and myself to death.

Franz

To Max Brod

[Postcard. Marienbad; postmark: July 9, 1916]
Dear Max, Many thanks for the letter. The review in the *Tägliche Rundschau*[5] is truly astonishing. How *Tycho* is sweeping everything before him! Moreover it was the first book they recommended to me in the local bookshop, as one they are selling briskly. I do a bit of reading in the Bible, but nothing else. However, we do a lot of walking, in the immoderate rain, with here and there a flash of sunlight. It is remarkable, today for instance in Tepl the weather was unspeakable, as it was yesterday and the day before, but this afternoon it was suddenly wonderfully mild and lovely. Yet the clouds do not disappear; how could they? Will soon write more.

Otto's[6] address, please.—Need a picture by Nowak[7] as an anniversary present for my parents. I can spend 100 to 200 crowns. Would you be kind enough to approach him on the matter? Would he sell for so little? Will write again tomorrow.

Warmly yours, Franz

To Felix Weltsch

[Postcard. Marienbad; postmark: July 11, 1916]
Dear Felix, Why no answer? For someone so punctual as you, it's hard to understand. Has something happened to your hand again? But then your wife is there, who is, I have always sensed (without being certain of my sense of it), well disposed toward me, and now she too doesn't write. The balcony room is still waiting for you, but won't much longer.

Regards from Franz

[THERE FOLLOW SOME LINES FROM FELICE BAUER]

To Max Brod

[Marienbad, July 12-14, 1916]
Dearest Max, Mustn't be constantly postponing and today is the day for answering you fully, since this is my last evening with Felice (or rather my next to last; tomorrow I am accompanying her to Franzensbad to visit my mother).[8]

The morning of the penciled card (I am writing this from the lobby, a wonderful institution for getting on peoples' nerves, disturbing them with slight irritations and making them jumpy) marked the end (but there were a number of transitions I cannot account for) of a series of frightful days, spawned in still more frightful nights. It really seemed that the rat had been driven to its very last hole. But since things could not have become worse, they took a turn for the better. The cords with which I was trussed were at least somewhat loosened; I straightened out somewhat while she who had constantly been holding out her hands to help but reaching only into an utter void, helped again and we arrived at a human relationship of a kind I had so far never known and which came very near in its meaningfulness to the relationship we had achieved at the best periods of our correspondence. Basically I have never had that kind of intimacy with a woman, except for two cases—the time in Zuckmantel (but there she was a woman and I was a boy) and the time in Riva (but there she was half a child and I was altogether confused and sick in every possible way). But now I saw the look of trustfulness in a woman's eyes, and I could not fail to respond. Much has been torn open that I wanted to shield forever (I am not speaking of anything in particular, but of the whole); and through this rent will come, I know, enough unhappiness for more than a lifetime, but this unhappiness is nothing summoned up, but rather imposed. I have no right to shirk it, especially since, if what is happening were not happening, I would of my own accord make it happen, simply to have her turn that look upon me. I did not really know her up to now. Aside from other doubts, last time I was hampered by an actual fear of the reality of this girl behind the letters. When she came toward me in the big room to receive the engagement kiss, a shudder ran through me. The engagement trip with my parents was sheer agony for me, every step of the way. I have never feared anything so much as being alone with F. before the wedding. Now all that has changed and is good. Our agreement is in brief: to get married soon after the end of the war; to rent an apartment of two or three rooms in some Berlin suburb; each to assume economic responsibilities for himself. F. will go on working as she has done all along, while I—well, for myself I cannot yet say. Should one try to visualize the situation, there is the picture of two rooms somewhere in Karlshorst,[9] say, in one of which F. wakes up early, trots off, and falls exhausted into bed at night, while in the other room there is a sofa on which I lie and feed on milk and honey. So there the husband lolls about, the wretched and immoral lout (as the cliché has it). Nevertheless, in this there is calm, certainty, and therefore the possibility of living. (In retrospect these are strong words which a feeble pen can hardly hold in check for long.)

For the present I will not write to Wolff,[10] for it is not so urgent and he too sees no urgency. The day after tomorrow I will be all alone and will then (I have time until next Monday)

do a little revising, I was going to say, and in the meantime Wednesday became Friday. I was with F. in Franzensbad visiting Mother and Valli. Now F. is gone and I'm alone. Since the morning in Tepl I have had such lovely and easy days, such as I never thought I would experience again. There were of course some darker intervals, but the loveliness and ease predominated, even in the presence of my mother, and this is quite extraordinary, is so extraordinary that at the same time it frightens me. Well—

Here at the hotel they had an unpleasant surprise for me; by deliberate or intentional confusion they assigned my room to a new arrival and so gave me F.'s room, which is far less quiet, with double rooms to either side of it, a single door, no windows, only a balcony. But I will scarcely summon up the energy to look elsewhere for lodgings. Nevertheless, as I write this the elevator door bangs shut and a heavy tread moves toward its room.

Back to Wolff: For the time being I am not writing to him, as I said. It is not such a good idea after all to come out with a collection of three novellas, two of which have already been published. I would do better to keep still until I have something new and complete to present. If I can't do this, then better for me to keep still permanently.

I am enclosing the *Tagblatt* article,[11] written, imagine, by a Privy Court councillor. Please keep it for me. It is very friendly, and all the friendlier for having contrived to be placed on the table at the café in the Egerländer[12] just at the moment we were thinking our heads were about to explode. That was truly heavenly unction. I would have liked to thank the councillor for that and perhaps will do so.

I am sending you the two pictures for your collection, which I don't approve of, but understand. What is remarkable about them, among other things, is that both are listeners, the observer on the ladder and the student bent over his book. (What an amount of trampling outside my single door! At least, the child is not disturbing the student.)

9–14 thousand! Congratulations, Max. So the world is grabbing at it. In Franzensbad especially, *Tycho* is in all the windows. I happened to read the *Tägliche Rundschau* yesterday and noticed the ad for the book by a bookseller named Gsellius. Could you send me the *Rundschau* review?

I herewith repeat my two requests: Otto's address and arranging about buying that picture. But I have a third. Could you send F. a prospectus of the Jewish People's Home[13]—(Her address: Technical Workshops, Markusstrasse 52, Berlin O–27). We talked about the project and she would very much like to know more about it.

You've always had a tender spot for "Richard and Samuel," I know. Those were wonderful times, but does that prove that it was good literature?

What are you working on? Will you be in Prague a week from Tuesday? This letter can of course be shown to Felix, but not to the ladies.

Yours, Franz

To Max Brod
[Letterhead: Schloss Balmoral & Osborne, Marienbad]
[Mid-July 1916]

[IN THE MARGIN] Once more in the busy lobby. It lures me.

Dear Max, Thanks for letting me know;[14] the news came on a headache day, such a headache as I didn't think I would ever have again, at least not here. Nevertheless I ran over there right after dinner.

I shall only describe the externals, since I cannot speak of more than I could see. But all one actually sees is the most minute details; and this is indeed significant in my opinion. It testifies to sincerity, even to the worst idiot. Where truth is, all one can see with the naked eye is such minute details.

To begin with, Langer could not be located. The place has several buildings and annexes, all clustered together on a knoll, that belong to one owner and can only be entered by partly underground stairways and passages. The names of the houses are designed to confuse: Golden Castle, Golden Bowl, Golden Ball, while some houses have two names, one in the front and another in the back. Then again, the restaurant may have a different name from the house of which it is a part, so one does not find one's way right off. Later, however, a certain degree of order becomes apparent: what we have here is a small community, arranged by social class and framed by huge, elegant buildings, the Hotel National and the Hotel Florida. The Golden Ball is the poorest of the lot. But even there no one knew Langer. After a moment, though, a girl remembered some young people who lived in the attic. If I were looking for the son of the Prague brandy dealer, I might find him there. But at the moment he was probably with Herr Klein at the Florida. When I went there, Langer was just coming out of the entrance.

I don't intend to report on what he told me, but only on what I myself saw.

Every evening at seven-thirty or eight the rabbi goes out in a carriage. He drives slowly toward the forest, some of his entourage following along on foot. Once in the woods he stops at a more or less predetermined spot and walks here and there along the forest paths with his entourage until nightfall. He returns home in time for prayers, at about ten.

I therefore came at about seven-thirty to the Hotel National, where the rabbi is staying. Langer was waiting for me. The rain was coming down unusually hard, even for this rainy season. It had not rained at this particular time of day for about the past two weeks. Langer maintained that it would surely stop, but it did not, only streamed down the harder. Langer said that it had been rainy only once during the rabbi's drive and that the rain had stopped when the rabbi came to the woods. But this time the rain did not stop.

We sit under a tree and see a Jew with an empty soda-water bottle run out of the house. He's fetching water for the rabbi, Langer says. We join the man. He is supposed to bring water from the Rudolph Spring, which has been prescribed for the rabbi. Unfortunately he does not know where the spring is. We blunder about in the rain. A man we meet shows us the way but tells us that all the medicinal springs are closed at seven. "How could the springs be closed?" the water bearer asks, and we trot along. In fact the Rudolph Spring is closed, as we can see long before we get there. Nor does the situation change as we draw nearer. "Then fetch water from the Ambrosius Spring," Langer says. "That one is always open." The water bearer agrees heartily and we hurry there. In fact women are still washing up the water glasses there. The water bearer bashfully approaches the steps, twirling the bottle which is already filling with a little rainwater. The women irritably turn him away, telling him this spring has also been closed since seven o'clock. So we hurry back. On the way we meet up with two other Jews who attracted my attention earlier. They walk along like a pair of lovers, looking affectionately at one another and smiling, one with his hand thrust into his low-slung back pocket, the other looking more citified. Firmly locked arm in arm. We tell them the story of the closed-down springs; the two simply cannot believe it, the water bearer once again cannot believe it, and so the three of them trot off without us back to the Ambrosius Spring. We go on to the Hotel National, while the water bearer catches up with us and runs ahead, calling out to us breathlessly that the spring is really closed down.

To escape the rain we are about to enter the hotel vestibule when L. suddenly jumps back and to one side. The rabbi is coming. No one must ever stand in front of him, there must always be a free passage before him, which is not easy to provide, since he often suddenly turns around and in the throng it is not easy to take evasive action speedily. (It's supposed to be still worse in his room, where the crowding is so great as to endanger the rabbi himself. Recently he is said to have cried out: "You are Hasidim? You are murderers.") This custom makes everything very solemn, the rabbi literally having the responsibility—without leading the way, since there are people to the right and to the left of him—of setting the pace for everyone. The group is continually reshaping itself so the rabbi's view will not be blocked.

He looks like the Sultan in a Doré[15] illustration of the Münchausen stories which I often looked at in my childhood. But not like someone masquerading as the Sultan, really the Sultan. And not only Sultan but also father, grammar-school teacher, gymnasium professor, etc. The sight of his back, the sight of his hand as it rests on his waist, the sight of his broad back as he turns—it all inspires confidence. I can detect this peaceful, happy confidence in the eyes of everyone in the group.

He is of medium height and rather broad of beam, though not sluggish in his movements. Long white beard, unusually long sidelocks (which he prefers in other people too; he is well disposed toward anyone who has long sidelocks; thus he praised the good looks of two children whom their father was holding by the hand, but by good looks he could only have meant their sidelocks). One eye is blind and blank. His mouth is twisted awry, which gives him a look at once ironic and friendly. He wears a silk caftan which is open in front; a broad belt about his waist; a tall fur hat, which is the most striking thing about him; white stockings; and, according to L., white trousers.

Before leaving the building he exchanges his silver cane for an umbrella. (It went on raining with undiminished force and at ten-thirty has not yet stopped.) Now begins the walk. For the first time he is not going out in the carriage; apparently he doesn't want people trailing after him as far as the woods in this downpour. About ten Jews are walking behind and to either side of him. One of them carries the silver cane and the chair on which the rabbi might want to sit, another carries the cloth with which to wipe the chair dry, another carries the glass from which the rabbi will drink, while another (Schlesinger, a rich Jew from Pressburg) carries a bottle of water from the Rudolph Spring, evidently bought in a store. There are four gabim[16] (or something like that) who play a special role among the entourage—they are his "intimates"—employees, secretaries. The highest of the four, according to Langer, is an exceptional rogue; his huge belly, his smugness, his shifty eyes seem to bear that out. However, one must not hold this against him, for all the gabim go bad; people cannot bear the continual presence of the rabbi without suffering damage. It is the contradiction between the deeper meaning and the unrelenting commonplaceness that an ordinary head cannot sustain.

The walk proceeds very slowly.

At the outset the rabbi walks with difficulty; one of his legs, the right one, gives him trouble. He also must have a good cough, while his followers stand respectfully around him. After a little, however, there seem to be no other obstacles, though now the rabbi begins to do his sightseeing, which brings the procession to a halt every other minute. He inspects everything, but especially buildings; the most obscure trivialities interest him. He asks questions, points out all sorts of things. His whole demeanor is marked by admiration and curiosity. All in all, what comes from him are the inconsequential comments and questions of itinerant royalty, perhaps somewhat more childish and more joyous. At any rate they reduce all thinking on the part of his escort to the same level. Langer tries to find or thinks he finds a deeper meaning in all this; I think that the deeper meaning is that there is none and in my opinion this is quite enough. It is absolutely a case of divine right, without the absurdity that an inadequate basis would give to it.

The next house is a Zander Institute.[17] It is set high above the street on a stone embankment with its front garden surrounded by iron railings. The rabbi makes some comments on the building, the garden catches his interest and he asks what kind of garden it is. Just as some governor in the presence of the emperor would do in such a case, Schlesinger (whose Hebrew name is Sina) tears up the steps to the garden and then, without spending a moment up there, tears down (all this in pouring rain), and reports (what, of course, he had already ascertained from below) that it is only a private garden belonging to the Zander Institute.

The rabbi turns around once he has looked his fill at the garden, and we come to what is called the New Bathhouse. Behind the building, which is where we go first, is a sort of ditch in which run the pipes for the steambath. The rabbi bends over the railing and cannot take his eyes off the pipes, concerning which various opinions and counteropinions are exchanged.

The building is of a neutral and indefinable eclectic style. The ground floor consists of a sort of blind arcade with a window set into every arch, and each vertex ornamented by an animal head. All the arches and all the animal heads are uniform. Nevertheless the rabbi comes to a halt before each of the six arches of the building's side, studies them, compares them, and passes judgment on them, from close up and from a distance.

We turn the corner and are now standing before the façade. The building makes a great impression on him. Golden letters over the door read NEW BATHHOUSE. He has the inscription read to him, asks why the building is called this, whether it is the only bathhouse, how old it is, and so forth. He repeatedly says with that characteristic East European Jewish wonderment: "A handsome building."

All along he has been taking note of the rain gutters, but now that we are passing close to the building (having already surveyed the front from across the street) he makes a detour in order to come close to a downspout that runs in a corner formed by a projection of the building. He is delighted at the water's thumping inside; he listens, looks up along the pipe, touches the pipe, and has the whole apparatus explained to him. [LETTER BREAKS OFF IN THE MIDDLE OF THE PAGE]

To Felix Weltsch

[Postcard. Marienbad; postmark: July 19, 1916]
Dear Felix, If it were really as you write, it would really be a summons for me to come and I would come. But it is not so, and in any case no longer so next day. Only the boils have gone; may they stay away. On the other hand, I don't feel at all well. Headaches, headaches! (A correspondence between two krauts, Langer would say.) Yes, Langer is here, since at the moment Marienbad is the center of the Jewish world, for the Rabbi of Belz is here. I have twice joined his retinue for evening walks. He alone would justify the

trip from Karlsbad to Marienbad. Do you know that Baum is in Franzensbad at the Sanssouci?

Cordial regards and all good wishes for you and yours,

Franz

To Kurt Wolff Verlag

Prague, July 28, 1916

Dear Herr Meyer,

Upon my return from a journey I found your letter of the tenth, as well as the books. Many thanks for both.

I share your opinion in regard to the publication of a book, although my view is necessarily more radical than yours. In fact I feel that the only right thing would be for me to present a new and complete work; if I cannot do this, perhaps I should rather keep quiet. At the moment I do not have anything at hand, and my state of health is such that I hardly feel capable of any such effort under existing circumstances. In the past three or four years I have squandered my forces (which makes the matter ever so much worse, I assure you) and am now suffering the consequences. There are other factors too.

For a wide variety of reasons I cannot at this moment accept your kind suggestion that I take a day off and come to Leipzig. Four years ago, three, and even two, my outer circumstances and my health might have allowed me to do so. Now, however, all I can do is wait until the only remedies that still may be of help are available—a little travel and a great deal of rest and freedom.

For the present I cannot offer you a longish work and so the only question remains whether there is any point in publishing *Punishments* (the stories "The Judgment," "Metamorphosis," "In the Penal Colony"); I personally would think not. If however you were to decide that such a publication would make sense, even if no longish work were to follow in the near future, I would entirely defer to your undoubtedly better judgment.

With my best regards, which I would ask you to convey to Herr Wolff also, I remain,

yours sincerely, F. Kafka

To Kurt Wolff Verlag

Prague, August 10, 1916

Dear Herr Meyer,

From your remark about me in a letter to Max Brod I see that you are inclined to retreat from the idea of publishing the book of stories. As things stand I feel you are completely right, for it is most unlikely that this book will represent the salable book you want. On the other hand I would be very pleased to have "In the Penal Colony" published in *Der jüngste Tag* series, but then not only "In the Penal Colony" but also "The Judgment" from *Arkadia*, each story in its own separate volume. This latter type of publication offers the advantage over the novella collection that each story can be seen individually and have its individual effect. Should you agree, I would ask that "The Judgment," which means more to me than any of the others, appear first; "In the Penal Colony" could follow at your discretion. "The Judgment" is in any case short, but scarcely shorter than *Aïssé* or *Schuhlin*. If you use the same print as for *Bats*,[18] the story should come to more than thirty pages, while "In the Penal Colony" would exceed seventy pages.

With best regards, yours sincerely, F. Kafka

To Kurt Wolff Verlag

[Postcard.] Prague, August 14, 1916

Dear Herr Meyer,

Our letters seem to have crossed. To come to the point: I would not like publication of "The Judgment" and "In the Penal Colony" in a single volume by themselves. In that case I would prefer the bigger book of stories. But I would gladly give up the bigger volume, which Herr Wolff himself proposed as far back as *The Stoker*, in exchange for having "The Judgment" appear in a separate format. "The Judgment," which means a great deal to me, is admittedly very short, but it is more a poem than a story; it needs open space around it and, moreover, deserves that, I think.

With best regards, yours sincerely, F. Kafka

To Kurt Wolff Verlag

Prague, August 19, 1916

Dear Sirs,

In reply to your kind letter of the 15th, let me sum up the reasons for my request that "The Judgment" and "In the Penal Colony" be published as individual volumes.

Initially there was no talk of issuing them in *Der jüngste Tag* series, but only of a volume of stories, *Punishments* (containing "The Judgment"— "Metamorphosis"—"In the Penal Colony"), which Herr Wolff projected a long while ago. These stories have a certain unity and as a group would naturally have bulked up to a more substantial volume than any of the numbers of *Der jüngste Tag*. Nevertheless I would gladly give up the book if I saw the possibility that "The Judgment" could be issued as a separate work.

The question is hardly whether to publish "The Judgment" and "In the Penal Colony" together as a *Jüngste Tag* book, for "In the Penal Colony" is quite long enough, as you yourself have estimated in your last letter, to suffice for a volume of its own. I only wish to add that to my mind "The Judgment" and "In the Penal Colony" would make a dreadful combination; "Metamorphosis" might still mediate between them, but without that story you would have two alien heads knocking violently at each other.

May I cite the following special arguments for publishing "The Judgment" by itself. The story is more poetic than narrative and therefore needs open space around it if it is to exert its force. It is also my favorite work and so I always wished for it to be appreciated if possible by itself. Since the idea of the volume of stories has been dropped, now would be the best opportunity for this. Incidentally—if "In the Penal Colony" were not to appear right off in *Der jüngste Tag*, I would be able to offer it to the *Weissen Blätter*. But that is really only incidental, for my principal concern remains that "The Judgment" be published by itself.

Are the technical problems really so insurmountable? I agree that a giant typeface would not be suitable. However if you use the same print as in *Bats*, the text will amount to thirty pages. Moreover not all *Der jüngste Tag* volumes come to thirty-two printed pages—*Aïssé*, for example, has only twenty-six, while various other volumes which I don't have to hand at the moment, like Hasenclever and Hardekopf,[19] consist of still fewer pages.

I thus believe that your firm might do me the favor—I would always regard it as such—of publishing the story by itself.

Respectfully and sincerely yours, F. Kafka

To Kurt Wolff Verlag

[Prague,] September 30, 1916

Dear Herr Meyer,

Enclosed is a selection of poems by a Prague writer, Ernst Feigl,[20] which I take the liberty to send for your kind consideration. I myself would judge them an important addition to *Der jüngste Tag*, to which they would bring a new somber tone which in many respects is truly timely. I also have the impression that Feigl has strong potentialities which have not yet come to the fore. The enclosed poems are only a sampling of a collection conceived and organically developed as a unity. It probably contains twice as many lines as there are here. The whole is intended to bear the title of the first poem,

"Getting Older." Should you want to see the rest of the poems before making a final decision, I would send them at once.

With best regards, yours sincerely, F. Kafka

To Kurt Wolff

Prague, October 11, 1916

Dear Herr Kurt Wolff,

First of all may I extend my warmest greetings now that you are once more near us.[21] Though these days there is little difference between being near and being far. I am very pleased to have your kind words about my manuscript.[22] Your criticism of the painful element accords completely with my opinion, but then I feel the same way about almost everything I have written so far. Have you noticed how few things are free of this painful element in one form or another? By way of clarifying this last story, I need only add that the painfulness is not peculiar to it alone but that our times in general and my own time as well have also been painful and continue to be, and my own even more consistently than the times. God knows how much farther I would have gone along this road had I written more or better, had my circumstances and my condition permitted me, teeth biting lips, to write as I longed to. But they did not. The way I feel now, all I can do is wait for quieter times; in saying which I am representing myself, at least superficially, as truly a man of our times. I also agree entirely that the story should not appear in *Der jüngste Tag*. I suppose it is also inappropriate for a public reading, though I am scheduled to read it in the Goltz Bookshop in November and I mean to do so.[23] Your offer to publish the book of stories is most obliging but I believe (especially since "The Judgment" is going to appear separately, thanks to your kindness) that the book of stories only makes sense if it closely precedes or follows a new and larger work and so not at the moment. Your remark in your letter to Max Brod suggests, I think, that you hold the same opinion.

About a week ago I sent Herr Meyer some poems of Ernst Feigl (he is the brother of the painter Fritz Feigl,[24] who has illustrated, among other things, a Dostoevski book for Georg Müller[25]). I welcome the possibility that you too may read the poems, now you are back in Leipzig. Perhaps the firm will see its way clear to publishing these fine poems; it would not have to be immediately, though of course "immediately" would be cause for rejoicing. At first reading one may think the poems confusing because the various associations lead into too many different directions. But on reading further one discovers that the unity of the whole makes the minor associations really minor, the major ones major in a good sense, that is, as one tongue of flame in the common fire. That is how it seems to me.[26]

Cordially yours, Franz Kafka

To Dr. Siegfried Löwy

[On the title page of a *Guide to Marienbad and Its Environs* which Kafka sent to his Uncle Siegfried]

[1916]

Of course Marienbad is the only place to go! Breakfast at the Dianahof (fresh milk, eggs, honey, butter), then quickly to the Maxtal for a snack (sour milk), quickly on to the Neptune where Headwaiter Müller presides over lunch, to the fruit vendor to stock up on fruit, a brief nap, then a bowl of milk at the Dianahof (place your order beforehand), quickly to the Maxtal for sour milk, on to the Neptune for supper, then sit awhile on a bench in the public park and count over your money, then to the pastry shop, then write me a few lines, and so to bed, sleeping as many hours in one night as I managed in twenty-one.[27]

All this is even better done in rainy than in fine weather, for then there is none of the bother of taking walks, and at all the more outlying cafés, supplies are always spotty: at Café Alm, for example, they are out of milk, at Café Nimrod they are out of butter, and at all of them they are out of rolls, which one should always make a point of bringing along.

No need to buy newspapers, for the Dianahof carries the *Berliner Tageblatt* and always has the latest edition, while other newspapers (though not magazines) are available in the Reading Room of the Town Hall. Every rooming house subscribes to at least one copy of the evening bulletins of the *Marienbader Tagblatt*.

Fruit, cheap, though not perfectly clean, may be had at the beginning of Judengasse.

If I had my choice, I would prefer the cottages you noted near the Waldquelle, not only because I did stay there and the Dianahof is nearby, but also because I think the other group of cottages faces northwest.

Recommended items at the Neptune: Vegetable omelette, Emmenthaler cheese, Kaiser stew, raw egg with green peas.

Should you want to work in the evening, take a room with balcony (with no other balconies too near) and move your lamp out on the balcony table. Then you have two rooms and special quiet out on the balcony.

There is good fruit on the way to the Maxtal, too. (So ran my thoughts, out on the balcony in the peaceful night.) Should you have any complaints, or the like, go to the Town Hall to see Fritz Schwappacher, the "indefatigable press chief," who has founded a club for journalists who happen to be visiting Marienbad.

But this is enough and now you[28] can go. The thought of you there as my representatives is very pleasing.

1917

To Felix Weltsch

[Postcard. Prague; postmark: January 2, 1917]

Dear Felix, Yesterday I wanted to wish you two a Happy New Year, but could not. I saw you so peaceful, deeply relaxed, reading, then opening your writing case, taking out paper, and writing, so that it was out of the question for me to disturb you. To be sure there was a cup at your elbow and the door to the lighted living room stood half open—so I told myself that if you should begin to apply yourself to the cup or your wife should come in, then I too might enter. But I guessed wrong.—Then finally your wife did come in, and you, chewing something with relish, began talking to her, and I, naturally ashamed of looking on further, removed myself and so could not determine whether the interruption was a fairly long one. Next time. Many regards. By the way, the news is good.

Franz

To Gottfried Kölwel[1]

Prague, January 3, 1916 [1917]

Dear Herr Kölwel,

Your poems have just come. Thank you. I had almost given up expecting them and was full of regret, for all details tend to flee my memory with senseless speed. So though I had a powerful general impression of the poems, I was eager to check it against reality. Now I can do so with three of the poems which best revive my Munich impressions, especially "We Drifters."[2] I read the poems there under unusual circumstances. I had come, borne by my story, to a city that was no concern of mine except as a meeting place[3] and a deplorable youthful memory, read my filthy story there to complete indifference, no empty stove could have been colder than that hall, then spent some time with people I don't know—which seldom happens to me here. Among them, Pulver[4] absolutely took me in for a while, but I thought you too uncomplicated to bother about. Then, next day in the coffeehouse, I wondered at the contentment with which you told me of your life, your work, and your plans, could make nothing of your retelling of a prose piece, and finally—in saying all this I have certainly not touched on all I thought and felt in Munich—was handed your poems. Some lines of these literally drummed in my head. They were so pure, so clean of any sin, were spoken with such pure breath; I wished I might have used them to clean up the mess I made in Munich. And now I again find many of these qualities. Please think of me again and send me something as occasion offers.

With best regards, sincerely yours, Kafka

To Gottfried Kölwel

Prague, January 31, 1916 [1917]

Dear Herr Kölwel,

I have been sick and am still; my stomach won't behave. Otherwise I would have written to you long ago and thanked you for your poems, which gave me pleasure, as will anything you may want to send me in the future, that I know. They are rich in consolation, songs of consolation, all of them; they are hanging on to the darkness with only one hand, perhaps so they will not be wholly broken loose from the earth, while otherwise they are steeped in good and truthful brightness. Precisely because you have the bent for it, I am troubled sometimes by a certain cold emotional turn, as skillfully performed as if it were done on a trapeze (no matter that it might be the highest trapeze of all) rather than inside the heart; the act is flawless but no doubt you are the last to be satisfied by that. For example, that phrase in the "Song of Consolation"—the poem after all is aiming at the highest truth—yet that phrase clogs it as with two huge buttresses. The same thing happens to a certain extent in the crucifixion poem, in which however there are lines that are totally absorbing. A good example of what to my mind would be the right direction is the "Autumn Song," which as a whole is weightless and can therefore carry weight.

I am not surprised that you have difficulty publishing; you neither startle nor frighten, but one thing is certain: that in the long run your poems will make their way. Hence I do not believe—though you may have evidence to the contrary—that anyone is really acting against you. Rather, without believing in such antagonisms—for believing such things has an embittering effect—one can understand the difficulties of getting started. As far as Kurt Wolff is concerned, I will of course try to find out everything you want to know. Not directly; for that my relationship is much too tenuous and without influence, but through my friend Max Brod. Just write me what is specifically involved, or rather what specifically should be asked or done, and in what way.

With best regards, yours sincerely, Franz Kafka

To Gottfried Kölwel

Prague, February 21, 1917

Dear Herr Kölwel, Thank you very much for the new poems. If I am not mistaken, they really are new poems. A great deal of new world opens out in them, by contrast with the earlier poems. How vast your realm is!

I am delighted that Wolff has yielded. It proves that in the long run his discernment cannot miss things of worth, and that for him the road from a bad no to a good yes is after all not so very long. Or perhaps it is even very short, if your suspicion in regard to intrigues was correct.

With best regards to you and Dr. Sommerfeld,[5]

sincerely yours

To Kurt Wolff Verlag

Prague, March 14, 1917

Dear Sirs,

On the twentieth of last month I sent you a registered postcard confirming the royalty statement for the year 1917[6] for the book *Meditation,* and asking that the royalties, amounting to some ninety-five marks, be transferred to Fräulein Felice Bauer, Technical Workshops, Markusstrasse 52, Berlin O-27. At the same time I asked whether and when a statement for the second printing of *The Stoker*[7] and *The Judgment* would be forthcoming.

I have so far not received an answer to this card nor has the money reached the abovementioned address. This is all the more embarrassing for me because I announced the impending arrival of the money at the same time as I sent the card to you. May I ask you to be so kind as to take care of this matter.

Very truly yours, Dr. F. Kafka

To Martin Buber

April 22, 1917

Mr dear Herr Doktor,

My reply has been delayed for a few days because the items had to be copied. I am sending twelve pieces.[8] Two of them, "The New Advocate" and "A Country Doctor," are at present with *Marsyas.*[9] If, however, precisely these two pieces should seem to you usable, I can recall them from *Marsyas;* that will probably not be too difficult. All these pieces and some others are to be published sometime in the future as a book, collectively entitled *Responsibility.*[10]

Cordially yours, F. Kafka

To Martin Buber[11]

Prague, May 12, 1917

Dear Herr Doktor,

Many thanks for your friendly letter. So I shall be published in *Der Jude* after all, and always thought that impossible. May I ask you not to call the pieces parables; they are not really parables. If they are to have any overall title at all, the best might be: "Two Animal Stories."[12]

Cordially yours, Franz Kafka

To Felix Weltsch

[Prague, summer 1917]

Dear Felix, You have carried that off very well and I absolutely would not want it to be otherwise. It is hard for me on weekdays but perhaps I'll come Sunday. Shouldn't I bring Oskar? A pity that I never know whether I'll be alive the next day or will only stagger through it, and that the latter is always more probable. I will bring along an excellent article by Heimann in the *Rundschau*[13] on politics and the franchise. Heavy going but perhaps with your help we can unravel it.

Warm regards to you and your wife, Franz

To Martin Buber

Prague, June 28, 1917

Dear Dr. Buber,

Assuming that you intend to continue publishing nonfiction, I think the enclosed poems important for the *Jude,* and if not these particular poems, at any rate the writer[14] himself and other work by him. A word from you would mean a great deal to him.

With my best wishes, cordially yours, Franz Kafka

Four enclosures.

To Kurt Wolff

Prague, July 7, 1917

Dear Herr Kurt Wolff,

I am most happy to hear from you directly once again. I had an easier time of it this winter, which in any case is now well behind us. I am sending some of the better work of this period, thirteen prose pieces.[15] It is a far cry from what I would really like to do.

With cordial regards, sincerely yours, F. Kafka

To Martin Buber

[Prague,] July 20, 1917

Dear Dr. Buber,

I received your letter just as I was leaving for a short journey; it accompanied me in Vienna and Budapest.[16] "Something that one cannot name" and "which would be useful to all these"—there are no truer words.

In Vienna I talked with Rudolf Fuchs; he will send you some other things as soon as he can, but his manuscripts are in Prague and he must have them forwarded. For the present, I am enclosing a small item by him.

In Budapest I happened to run into an old friend, a Yiddish actor.[17] Would you be interested in receiving an article for the *Jude*, written from the heart of personal experience, on the situation, that is the distress, that is the mental distress (for the real distress is almost counterbalanced by the long years of habituation to hardship) of the Yiddish actor? My friend might be competent and certainly would be most eager to write such an article.

With sincere regards, cordially yours, F. Kafka

To Irma Weltsch

[Prague,] July 20, 1917

Dear Frau Irma,

Your letter, which only arrived after our departure (we left Wednesday afternoon) has just now reached me; to be sure I have been back since early yesterday, but only went to the shop this afternoon, where my cousin[18] had kept the letter. Hence this belated reply.

I found the purse in my sister's place, shortly after I had been visiting you. Unhappy over the loss, for I am painfully miserly, I went through the apartment, which had already been searched, crawling about on my knees and systematically covering every inch of the floor, until I found the purse curled up small and lying innocently under a trunk. Naturally I was terribly proud of my accomplishment and would have liked to rush off to your house. But first I had to tell them at home, where there was every imaginable delay. We were supposed to be leaving the following afternoon, informing you was repeatedly put off, I did not want to write you a note because I wanted to go over and tell you myself, and finally I didn't even write because it was already too late even for this. Moreover I gave Max the message for you, and besides told myself that you could not have seriously believed, any more than my fiancée and I did, that the purse could have been left at your house. I also had told you repeatedly, as later proved to be the case, that my fiancée was convinced she had the purse with her when she left your place and that I had come back to ask about it only as a formality, to leave no stone unturned.

So much for my apologies. There are plenty of them, perhaps too many. Were it not for your letter, I would feel myself almost guiltless. But since you apparently went on thinking about the purse and possibly even searching for it, all apologies are of course inadequate, and I must resort to asking you not to spoil my pleasure in finding the purse by being angry with me for my negligence. For that would be—even though the purse contained 900 crowns (which may explain my haste in telling you)—a tremendously high finder's fee which I would be obliged to pay to lucky chance. You won't do that, I'm sure.

With cordial regards, yours, Kafka

To Kurt Wolff

Prague, July 27, 1917

Dear Herr Kurt Wolff,

Your kind opinion[19] of the manuscripts has given me a certain reassurance. Should you think this was the proper time to publish the short pieces (which could be supplemented by at least two other short items: "Before the Law," which appeared in your almanac, and "A Dream," which I enclose), I would be very agreeable to that and would leave the question of format entirely to your discretion; at the moment I am not concerned with royalties. After the war, however, that would change entirely. I will give up my job (giving it up is really my most intense hope), will marry and move away from Prague, possibly to Berlin. To be sure I will not depend entirely on the proceeds of my writing (or so I still have reason to believe). Nevertheless I—or the deep-seated bureaucrat inside me, which is the same thing—have an oppressive fear of this future. I do hope that you, dear Herr Wolff, will not quite desert me, provided, of course, that I halfway deserve your kindness. In the face of all the uncertainties of the present and the future, a word from you at this point[20] would mean so much to me.

With cordial regards, yours sincerely, Kafka

To Martin Buber

Prague, August 3, 1917

Dear Dr. Buber,

The scene by Fuchs actually was left out; I am herewith enclosing it. In addition a few poems by Ernst Feigl. I truly don't mean to press you; Feigl doesn't even know I am sending the poems (although we spoke about the matter once and he would of course be overjoyed if you liked them); besides, for the foreseeable future he is the last writer I can introduce to you. Your reception of Fuchs was so friendly that I thought Feigl is also worth your attention.

Since you want to see the actor's recollections I shall try to obtain them in the best possible shape from my friend—Yitzhak Löwy is his name. However he is an unpredictable person; if he musters all his powers he might produce, I think, a richly characteristic work. But it is equally possible that he will produce something hardly usable, or that—in spite of the enthusiasm with which he greeted the plan in Budapest—he will not write it at all. For that reason I would ask you not to count on this article in planning your next few issues. At any rate I shall write at once, as soon as I hear anything specific.

With cordial regards, sincerely yours, F. Kafka

To Kurt Wolff

Prague, August 20, 1917

Dear Herr Kurt Wolff,

Rather than disturb you once again during your vacation,[21] I waited until today to thank you for your last letter. What you said in it concerning my anxieties was extremely kind and for the moment totally suffices me.

May I propose *A Country Doctor* as title for the new book, with the subtitle *Short Tales.* For the table of contents I would suggest:

The New Advocate
A Country Doctor
The Bucket Rider[22]
Up in the Gallery
An Old Manuscript
Before the Law
Jackals and Arabs

A Visit to a Mine
The Next Village
An Imperial Message
The Cares of a Family Man
Eleven Sons
A Fratricide
A Dream
A Report to an Academy

With best regards, cordially yours, F. Kafka

To Kurt Wolff

Prague, September 4, 1917

Dear Herr Wolff,

I could not wish for a finer proposal for the *Country Doctor*. Of my own accord I would certainly not have dared to choose type of that size, not for my sake, not for yours, not for the book itself. But since you yourself offer this, I accept it joyfully. And may I assume that the handsome format of *Meditation* will be used?[23]

Perhaps there is some misunderstanding concerning the "Penal Colony." I have never been entirely wholehearted in asking for it to be published. Two or three of the final pages are botched, and their presence points to some deeper flaw; there is a worm somewhere which hollows out the story, dense as it is. Your offer to publish this story in the same manner as the *Country Doctor* is of course very tempting and excites me so much that I am ready to drop my defenses—nevertheless please do not publish the story, at least for the present. If you stood in my place and saw the story from my viewpoint, you would not think I was being overscrupulous in this matter. Besides, should my powers halfway hold out, you will receive better work from me than the "Penal Colony."

My address from next week on will be:

Zürau, P.O. Flöhau in Bohemia[24]

The disease[25] which for years now has been brought on by headaches and sleeplessness has suddenly broken out. It is almost a relief. I am going to the country for a longish while, or rather I must go.

With cordial regards, sincerely yours, F. Kafka

To Max Brod and Felix Weltsch

[Prague,] September 5, 1917

Dear Max, A carbon of this letter is going to Felix. The first explanation to my mother was amazingly easy. I simply and casually said that I would perhaps not be renting an apartment[26] for the present; I wasn't feeling well, was somewhat nervous, and would try and secure a longer vacation and go to visit Ottla. With her limitless willingness to grant me a vacation on the slightest pretext (were the matter up to her), she found nothing suspicious in my words, and so it will remain at least for the present. The same is true for my father. Therefore if you talk to anyone about the thing (in itself it is of course no secret, my earthly possessions have on the one hand increased by the addition of tuberculosis, on the other hand somewhat diminished), would you please warn people at the same time or, if you have already spoken of it, afterward not to mention the matter to my parents, even if the conversation should somehow prompt it. When it is so easy to keep a worry from one's parents for a while, one should surely try to do so.

Once more—without the carbon—thank you, Max. It was very good that I went to the doctor and without you I surely would not have gone. By the way, you told him I was irresponsible, but on the contrary I am too calculating, and the Bible tells us what the fate of reckoners will be. But I certainly am not complaining, less than ever today. What is more, I predicted it myself. Do you remember the open wound in "A Country Doctor"? Today some letters came from F., quiet, friendly, entirely without reproaches, exactly as I see her in my highest dreams. Now it is hard to write to her.

To Max Brod

[Zürau, mid-September 1917]

Dear Max, I did not get to writing the first day because I liked everything so much here; besides, I did not want to exaggerate as I would have had to—thus giving the devil his due. However, today everything is already looking natural, my inner weaknesses (not the disease, of which I know almost nothing as yet) are asserting themselves, from the farmyard across the way come an assortment of Noah's Ark sounds, an eternal tinsmith hammers his tin. I have no appetite and eat too much; there's no light in the evening, and so on. But the good still hugely predominates, as far as I can yet see: Ottla is literally bearing me up on her wings through the difficult world, the room (though it faces northeast) is excellent, airy, warm, and all this in an almost completely quiet building; all the things I am supposed to be eating surround me in abundance and goodness (only my lips lock themselves against them; but that always happens in the first days of any change) and freedom, freedom above all.

However there is still the wound of which the lesions in the lungs are only the symbol. You misunderstand it, Max, to judge by your final words in the hallway, but perhaps I also misunderstand it and there is no understanding these things (the same would be true of your inner affairs) because there is no seeing it whole, so turbulent and ever-moving is the gigantic mass which yet at the same time never ceases to grow. Misery, misery, but what is it but our own natures? And if the misery were ultimately to be disentangled (perhaps only women can do such work), you and I would fall apart.

In any case my attitude toward the tuberculosis today resembles that of a child clinging to the pleats of its mother's skirts. If the disease came from my mother, the image fits even better,[27] and my mother in her infinite solicitude, which far surpasses her understanding of the matter, has done me this service also. I am constantly seeking an explanation for this disease, for I did not seek it. Sometimes it seems to me that my brain and lungs came to an agreement without my knowledge. "Things can't go on this way," said the brain, and after five years the lungs said they were ready to help.

But if I choose, I might say that put in these terms the whole thing is totally wrong. The first step to insight. The first step on that stairway which culminates in a made-up marital bed as the reward and meaning of my human existence (which however would then have been well-nigh Napoleonic). The bed will never be made up and I, that is my destiny, shall never leave Corsica behind me.

These thoughts were not arrived at in Zürau, but were already with me on the train journey, in which the letter-card I showed you formed the heaviest part of my luggage. But of course I will go on mulling over them.

Regards to all, and especially to your wife, from the Tartuffe. Her insight is not bad but too concentrated: she sees only the nucleus; to follow the radiations from that nucleus asks too much of her.

Affectionately, Franz

To Oskar Baum

[Zürau, mid-September 1917]

Dear Oskar, I wasn't able to come, had to miss your reading. Anyhow one shouldn't go trotting around with this disease.

At present I am feeling quite content and starting my new life with a measure of confidence. Yesterday at lunch a counterpart of mine sat opposite me at table. A real tramp. Sixty-two years old and has been tramping the roads for ten years. His face above the well-groomed imperial is clean and rosy. From the table up he looks like a retired medium-grade civil servant. Has sustained himself for ten years, except for short spells of work, entirely by begging. For instance he was on the road all last winter, in the same clothes he is wearing now (except for a weskit, which is now too warm to wear, so he has sold it), yet has no serious rheumatism, or any other kind of sickness.

Only in the last few years he has felt a bit muddled in his head. He often feels low for no reason, takes no pleasure in anything, and then doesn't know how to go on. I asked him if belief in God wouldn't help. No, that could not help him, on the contrary, that's what leads to speculating and feeling low. People are raised religious, that's why that sort of thing goes through the head. His great misfortune was that he had never married. Troubles? Yes, then he would have some troubles, but he would have a home, pleasure in the children, and peace inside his head. Several times he had chances to marry, but his mother, who lived until he was fifty-two, had always advised him against marriage. His two sisters, too, and his father, with whom he ran a small business in the Egerland,[28] also advised him against it. And when everyone advises you against something, you lose desire for it. And when one doesn't marry, one takes to the bottle, and so had he. Nowadays he tramps the roads and often he meets good people. For instance in Böhmisch-Leipa[29] some years back an attorney (another Herr Doktor, but unlike me, the real thing)[30] gave him a meal and two crowns.

He passed through Zürau a few days ago, stopped at my sister's, and has come back a second time without meaning to. He tramps about without any particular plan (he has a map, to be sure, but it doesn't show the villages), and so he often travels in a circle. It does not matter, people hardly ever recognize him when they see him again.

He has a real profession which does not allow him to waste time. Hardly had he eaten his last bite (I did not bother him with my questions, most of the time we sat opposite each other in silence, and I swallowed my food down surreptitiously, from embarrassment) when he rose and left.

Would you send us your beer recipe, so we can offer something good to our guests? Perhaps this will lead to something good for you too.[31]

Cordial regards, Franz

I will not be taking the apartment on the hill. Apart from the fact that for the present I don't need a place and that the future is uncertain, the apartment seems to me too large, too low, too close to the street and workshops, and too melancholy.

To Max Brod

[Zürau, mid-September 1917]

Dear Max, The exquisite instinct you and I both have! A vulture, seeking quiet, I fly upward and swoop, straight as a die, into this room, opposite which a piano, wildly thumping its pedals, is playing, surely the only piano in this whole region. But I toss it, unfortunately only figuratively, into the mix, along with the many good things that have come my way here.

Our correspondence can be very simple: I do my writing, you yours, and that is answer, verdict, consolation, inconsolability, whatever one likes. For it is the same knife against whose blade our throats, our poor pigeons' throats, one here, one there, are cut. But so slowly, so insidiously, with so little blood, so heartrendingly, so hearts-rendingly.

In this context the morality is perhaps the last consideration, not even the last, the blood is the first and the second and the last. The question is how much passion is there, how much time it will take, for the walls of the heart to be pounded thin, that is if the lungs do not give out before the heart.

F. has sent a few lines saying she is coming.[32] I don't grasp her, she is extraordinary, or rather I do grasp her but cannot hold her. I run all around her, barking, as a nervous dog might tear around a statue, or to present an equally true but converse picture, I gaze at her as a stuffed animal head mounted on the wall might look down at the person living quietly in his room. Half-truths, a thousandth of a truth. All that is true is that F. is probably coming.

So many things trouble me, I can find no way out. Was it false hope, self-deception, when I told myself I wanted to stay here forever, I mean in the country, far from the railroad, near to the relentless twilight, which descends without hindrance from anyone or anything? If it is self-deception, then it comes because my blood is tempting me to a reincarnation of my uncle, the country doctor, whom I (with all due and indeed the greatest respect) sometimes call the Twitterer, because he has such an inhumanly thin old-bachelor's birdlike wit that squeaks out of a constricted throat and never deserts him. And he lives this way in the country, won't be budged from it, contented, the way a faintly burbling madness which one takes for the melody of life leads to contentment. But if the longing for the land is not self-deception, then it is something good. But have I the right to expect something good, at the age of thirty-four, with my highly fragile lungs and still more fragile human relationships? Country doctor is more probable; if you look for confirmation, the father's curse is there at once. Lovely nocturnal sight when hope wrestles with the Father.

Let's drop the wrestlers. The plans you have for your novella are exactly what I would wish. The novella is going to be splendid. But in the face of these plans, can the first two chapters stand? They are after all too lightweight. To my feeling, not at all. What are those three pages like, that you have written? Do they decide anything for the whole? Is it painful that the whole thing will refute *Tycho*? It will not refute it since all truth is irrefutable, though it may throw him down. But as all the war correspondents write, isn't the best assault technique still: stand up, run, throw yourself down? A procedure that must be incessantly repeated in the assault upon the tremendous bastion, until in the last volume of the Collected Works, blissfully weary, one drops or—with worse luck—remains on one's knees.

I do not mean this sadly. Nor am I basically sad. I live with Ottla in a good minor marriage; marriage not on the basis of the usual violent high currents but of the small windings of the low voltages. We run a fine household, which all of you, I hope, will like. I will try to put some supplies aside for you, Felix, and Oskar, which isn't easy; there is not much food around here and the many family mouths to feed have priority. But there is always something, which however everyone must procure in person.

As for my sickness—I have no fever. Weight on arrival was 61½ kilos but I have already put on a little. Beautiful weather. Been lying in the sun a good deal. At the moment do not miss Switzerland; in any case your news from there can only be badly dated.

All the best and may Heaven shower some comforts on you.

Franz

[IN THE MARGIN] Should you need help with letters, I could easily ask my typist.[33]

I imagine you have already received a letter from me. Letters take three or four days one way.

To Oskar Baum

[Zürau, mid-September 1917]

Dear Oskar, Many thanks for the beer recipe. We will be trying it out soon, hoping to charm the neighborhood. One has to do some charming if one wishes to get anything of consequence. There seem to be ample supplies for the local demand, but not enough to accumulate much, especially when parasites like me, who have put on a kilogram in the first week (or so the scales say), have plumped themselves down here. But I will manage to save up something for you, Felix, and Max. All my Prague connections have left me in the lurch, especially the major supplier. Some kind of denunciation is hanging over his head, so he must keep in the shadows for a while.

I am quite satisfied with my life here, as Max may already have told you. However the peace and quiet which you especially asked about is not to be found here either and I will give up looking for it in this life. My room, to be sure, is in a quiet builidng, but across the way is the only piano in northwest Bohemia, and a large farmyard, in which the various animals outdin each other. Almost all the neighborhood teams drive by my window early and all the geese pass me on the way to their pond. But the worst are two hammerers somewhere in the neighborhood. One hammers on wood, the other on metal. They are tireless, especially the first, who works far beyond his strength. He is wearing himself out, but I can have no pity for him when I have to listen to him from six o'clock in the morning. If he actually stops for a little while, it is only so the metal hammerer can take the lead.

In spite of this and in spite of some other things, I have no wish to return to Prague, not at all.

Warmest regards to you and your wife from Franz

I imagine you have received an earlier letter from me. The postal connections here are not only slow (a letter from Prague takes from three to four days) but also unreliable.

To Max Brod
[Zürau, mid-September 1917]
Dearest Max, How did you mean that last goodbye wish on the staircase— remember? If you meant it as a sort of test, I'm afraid I am not passing it. For me, tests are in no way bracing; I don't wait for the blows to come toward me but run toward them and disappear under their impact. Should I give thanks that I have not been able to marry? I would then have become all at once what I am now becoming gradually: mad. With shorter and shorter intermissions—during which not I but It gathers strength.

The remarkable thing, which I have finally begun to realize, is that everyone is excessively good to me, I might even say self-sacrificing, in matters great and small. From this I have drawn conclusions about human nature in general, and as a result feel more oppressed. But that is probably wrong; people behave that way only to one who is altogether beyond the reach of human help. People have a special scent for cases of this sort. Many people are good to you, too, Max, and self-sacrificing, though not all, but then you are forever repaying the world for this, so that it is a normal kind of commercial exchange (hence you can handle human affairs which I hardly dare to touch), while I pay nothing back, or at least not my debts to other people.

Enclosed a letter from Janowitz's father,[34] as always cheering. I imagine it deserves a friendly answer. The letter has just now been forwarded to me. Please give my regards to Felix and Oskar. What things are going on in Palestine![35]

Franz

To Max Brod

[Picture postcard (Zürau). September 20, 1917]
Dear Max, Many thanks for the package. The girl's letter (I am now in
Ottla's room; the mice have been carrying on outrageously) is by far the
finest of the lot. This prudence, calm, superiority, and knowledge of the
world is gloriously and horribly feminine—. I will send it all back shortly. If
you look carefully at the picture, you will see my circled window. Ottla's
house is located behind the marked tree. In reality, though, everything looks
much better, especially in the sunshine we are having now.

Franz

Just had a telegram from F.; she's coming this afternoon.

[NOTE ADDED BY OTTLA: We will meet you at the station, with a carriage, no
less. Otherwise you would have gone, according to Franz's mark, to Herr
Feigl's house, instead of to ours. I won't mark our house. You will soon be
seeing it yourself.

Ottla Kafka]

To Felix Weltsch

[Zürau, September 22, 1917]
Dear Felix, There seems to have been some misunderstanding. We have
invited you, that is to say both of you, in order to have you here, not so that
you might carry away the not much that is available here. If I hinted
anything of the sort, it was meant only as a temptation. The chief difficulty
seemed to me to lie in obtaining the vacation, but this is the difficulty you
take most lightly. We have beds for both of you. But there is actually not
much in the way of food. For the time being, there is enough for local needs
and for the patient from outside; in fact there is even a degree of abundance.
But very little of this can be tapped and that only gradually. But at any rate
something will be set aside for you.

I have taken this move in stride, where far lesser things bowl me over. The
tea cure does not appeal to me, but with my lungs I should perhaps keep quiet
where health matters are concerned. I might only say that this cure calls for a
jacket in whose side pocket one carries a half-visible thermos flask.

What club was the invitation from? The Jewish Club?[36] If you should give
a lecture and if it is announced in time, you will have one person there who

has come all the way from the provinces to hear you, provided of course that he is still transportable.

For the present I undoubtedly am, have gained a kilogram in the first week and feel the disease in its initial stages more like a guardian angel than a devil. But its further development may well be the diabolic aspect and in hindsight what seemed angelic will be the worst part of it.

Yesterday there was a letter from Dr. Mühlstein (I had sent him a note informing him that I had been to Professor P.[37] and enclosing a copy of the professor's opinion) in which he among other things stated that I could expect to improve (!) though the improvement would show up only after a considerable passage of time.

So he has gradually come to take a darker view of my prospects. At my first examination I was almost entirely well, after the second I was even better, later there was a slight left bronchial catarrh, still later, "not to minimize the matter and not to exaggerate," there was tuberculosis of both the right and left lungs, which however would clear up fairly soon and in Prague, and now at last I may someday, someday, expect to improve. It is as if he had wanted to shield me with his broad back from the Angel of Death which stood behind him, and now he gradually steps aside. But neither he nor it (alas?) frightens me.

My life here has been splendid, at least in the fine weather we've had so far. To be sure my room isn't sunny, but I have a marvelous spot for sunbathing. A hillock or rather a little plateau in the center of a broad semicircular valley, which I have taken over. There I lie like a king, surrounded by undulating hills all more or less of the same height. Because of the favorable lie of the land, hardly anyone sees me, which suits me very well, in view of the complicated positioning of my reclining chair and my seminudity. Only rarely do a pair of protesting heads appear at the edge of my plateau and shout: "Get offa that bench." More radical shouts than that I cannot understand because of the dialect. Perhaps I will become the village idiot, for the present one, whom I saw today, seems to live in the neighboring hamlet and is already old.

My room is not as good as this sunbathing spot, not sunny and not quiet. But it is well furnished and you will like it, for that is where you will be sleeping. I can perfectly well go somewhere else to sleep, as I did yesterday, for instance, when F. was here.

In connection with F. I have a library request. You know our old dispute over *bis.* It seems I have misunderstood her. She thinks *bis* means *until*—and can be certainly used as a conjunction but only in the meaning of *until,* not in the meaning of *when.* Thus one may not say, for example: *Bis* you come here, I will give you five hundred kilograms of flour. (Hush! This is only a grammatical example.) Would you please decide, on the basis of Grimm[38] (the examples have already slipped my mind) or other books, whether F. is right. The matter is not unimportant, bearing as it does on my dual relationship toward her as an earthly dog or a hellhound.

One more request, which fits right in. In the second volume of *Pathological Disturbances in the Sexual and Emotional Life (Masturbation and Homosexuality)* by Dr. Wilhelm Stekel,[39] or some such title (you must know this Viennese who reduces Freud to small change), there are five lines on *Metamorphosis*. If you have the book, please be so kind as to copy out the passage for me.

And one more request, it goes on forever but this is the last: I limit my reading here to Czech and French, and nothing but autobiography or correspondence, naturally in fairly good print. Could you lend me one book of each sort? I leave the choice to you. Almost anything in this line, if it is not too narrowly military, political, or diplomatic, is highly rewarding to me. The number of such things in Czech is apt to be rather small, and besides I may have already read the best of the lot, a collection of letters of Božena Němcová[40] which for its psychological acumen is unsurpassed.

How far along are you with your political book?[41]

Many regards, Franz

It occurs to me that *Love in the Romantic Age* would also not be bad. But the above two books are more important. Should some deposit be necessary, I'll have it paid. I imagine you have already received the four volumes *(Stony Bridge* and *Prague)*.[42] If you send word that you have the books, someone from our shop will pick them up and I will receive them in one of the packages they send me from time to time.

Ottla has been in Prague since yesterday; otherwise she too would have written.

The crossed-out words on the previous page are the beginning of a question which I then thought better of, for there was so much raw professional curiosity in it. Now that I have confessed, I feel better and can ask: What do you know about Robert Weltsch?[43]

To Max Brod

[Zürau, end of September 1917]
Dearest Max, Your letter at first reading had a distinctly Berlin intonation, but by the second reading that had already faded away and it was your voice again. I have always thought there would be time to talk about my illness when the time comes, but since you insist: I've taken my temperature every so often and have absolutely no fever. So there are no graphs, and after collecting

the first week's data, Dr. Pick has lost all interest in the matter for the time being.—Cold milk for breakfast. Dr. Pick has said (when on the defensive my memory becomes magnificent) that the milk should be drunk either ice cold or hot. Since we are still having warm weather, there is no objection to cold milk, especially since I am used to it and sometimes can take half a liter of cold milk and at most a quarter of a liter when it is warmed. Unboiled milk. Unresolved dispute. You think, the bacilli receive reinforcements. I think, the matter is not so mathematical and unboiled milk is more strengthening. But I'm not stubborn, I drink boiled milk as well, and when it gets colder will drink only warm or sour milk.—Nothing between meals. Only at the beginning, before I began putting on weight, or when I have no desire for food at all; otherwise, in the midmorning and midafternoon I am supposed to take a quarter of a liter of sour milk. To eat more often is quite beyond me; life (in general) is dreary enough.—No rest cure? I spend about eight hours daily resting. Not, to be sure, in a proper reclining chair, but on a contraption I find far more comfortable than the many reclining chairs I've encountered. This is an old broad easy chair with two hassocks set in front of it. The combination is excellent, at least for the time being, when I need no blankets. Do I wrap myself up? But I lie in the sun and regret not being able to remove my trousers which for the past few days have been my only clothing. A proper reclining chair is on the way.—Going to the doctor? When have I ever said I will not go to the doctor? I shall go reluctantly, but I will go.

Schnitzer[44] has not answered.—You think I am taking too portentous a view of the disease? No. How could I, when I find living with it far too easy, and in this matter feeling is the decisive factor. If I ever said anything of the sort, it was empty affectation, in which I am so rich in poor times, or else it was the sickness speaking, rather than myself, because I asked it to. All that is certain is that there is nothing to which I would surrender with more complete trustfulness than death.

I will say nothing about the long preliminaries to F.'s visit or the visit itself, since your own letter keeps to generalities in its laments. But laments, Max, are to be expected; this nut has still to be cracked.

You are right: to call this indecision or something else depends solely on perspective. We are also always beginners at indecision; indecision is never old, for time itself grinds it up. It is strange and dear of you that you do not really understand my case. Even if I were able to speak much more clearly about F., and I ought to, this case, absolutely contrived to last a lifetime, would still not vanish into thin air. But on the other hand I absolutely do not dare to say that if I were in your situation I would know what you could do for me. I am as helpless, in my own case as in yours, as the dog who is now barking outside. I can only aid you with the feeble warmth I have in me, nothing more.

I have done some reading, but in consideration of your state it is not worth mentioning. At most an anecdote of Stendhal's which might have come out of *Education*.[45] As a young man and a newcomer to Paris, he was at loose ends, hungering for life, depressed, disgruntled with Paris and with everything. A married woman, an acquaintance of the relative with whom he lives, is friendly to him. Once she invites him to go to the Louvre with her and her lover. (Was it the Louvre? I begin to doubt. Well, some place of that sort.) They go. Upon leaving the museum, they find it is raining hard, the streets are a sea of mud, home is a long way off, and they take a cab. In one of those moods characteristic of his present state, he declines to ride with them and makes his cheerless way alone on foot; he is close to tears when it occurs to him that, rather than go back to his room, he might pay a visit to this woman, who lives on a nearby street. He arrives totally distraught and of course finds the woman in the midst of a love scene with the man. Appalled, the woman exclaims: "Why in heaven's name didn't you get into the cab with us?" Stendhal runs out.—On the whole he well understood how to conduct himself in life.

Franz

In your next letter please write above all about yourself.

To Max Brod

[Zürau, end of September 1917]

Dear Max,

Your second package of printed matter reached me only by chance, the mailman having dropped it off at some peasant's. Mail here is very uncertain, as is the delivery of my letters (perhaps the fact that our post office is not even on the railroad line has something to do with this), and it might be advisable for you to number the items you mail, so I can complain when they go astray. I would have been particularly sorry to miss the last batch. The hasidic stories in *Jüdische Echo*[46] may not be of the best, but for some reason I don't understand, all these stories are the only Jewish literature in which I immediately and always feel at home, quite apart from my own state of mind. With all the rest I am only wafted in and another draught wafts me out again. I will keep the stories for a while, if you have no objection.

Why have you turned down the request of Jüdische Verlag,[47] let alone the request of Dr. J.? It is of course a large demand to make and your present state of mind stands in the way, but does that justify your refusal?—I suppose you don't want the essay collection, because everything is being saved for *Esther*,[48] is that it?

Löwy writes from a sanatorium in Budapest, where he has been staying for three months. He sends me the opening of his essay[49] for *Der Jude*. I consider the piece very usable but naturally it needs to be polished up grammatically ever so slightly and this would take an incredibly subtle hand. I will soon send you a typed copy of the piece (it is quite short) for your consideration. An example of the difficulties:

He comments on the Polish theater's audience, as opposed to the audience for the Jewish theater: tuxedoed men and ballgowned ladies.[50] Excellently put, but the German language balks. And there is a great deal like that; his highlights are the more effective since his language veers between Yiddish and German, inclining a bit toward the German. If only I had your skill at translating!

Franz

The partridges are meant for you and Felix, a pair for each of you. Good appetite.

To Oskar Baum

[Zürau, beginning of October 1917]

Dear Oskar, The trip here is amazingly simple. You take the train for Michelob,[51] which leaves the main railroad station before seven in the morning; the express train brings you here a bit after nine. Or you can take the local train at two and be here by five-thirty in the evening. If you let us know by telegram, we will come with our horses to pick you up and you will be in Zürau in about half an hour. The trip can be made as a day's outing (return to Prague before ten o'clock at night) or for a longer while, since my room has two excellent beds. Meanwhile I would sleep in another room which is so good that I would gladly make it my permanent lodgings if it had a stove. Milk and what goes with it can easily be provided, and even a few comestibles to take back to the city.

Nevertheless I cannot advise you wholeheartedly to come. During the first week and perhaps still in the second it was different. Then I wanted to have all of you here, and if I did not ask you individually to come on a visit, it was only because on the one hand it seemed to me a matter of course that you would all have to come, and on the other hand because the mail, which here takes the form of a moody and unreliable lout, makes far too long a circuit

(Zürau–Prague–Zürau = 8 days or not at all) to be entrusted with such urgent arrangements. But now, the third week of my stay, things are changing and I no longer know what point there would be in inviting you. Zürau remains the same for me, and I plan to sink my teeth so deeply into it that people will have to wrench apart my jaws before they drag me out of here. (But no, that is an exaggeration, and when I wrote it, I was not considering everything.) Still and all, it is good for me here. But for anyone else, there are some things that no one could possibly like, even you two, obliging as you are. Among these things may be myself, or perhaps "among" is wrong and it is just myself. And so I beg you, to whom I may speak frankly, almost as warmly as I earlier asked you to come, I must ask you: do not come now.

All this of course has nothing to do with my medically certified illness. Whether my condition is better than it was I have no idea. That is to say I feel as well now as I did in the past. Up to now I have never had an illness so easy to bear and so restrained, unless it is this very quality that is sinister— which perhaps it is. I am looking so well that my mother, who came here Sunday, did not recognize me when I met her at the station. (By the way, my parents know nothing about the tuberculosis, so you will be careful, won't you, if you should by chance run into them.) In two weeks I have gained one and a half kilograms (tomorrow I have my third weighing). My sleep is highly variable, but the average is not too bad.—Besides I will soon (I say "soon" and mean "end of month"—I have become such a master of time here) be coming to Prague and you will be able to confirm it all for yourself, the bad and the good.

The new recipe you were so kind as to send put us to shame. This matter too has undergone a Zürau evolution. At first we were delighted and the lack of corks and a corking machine seemed only a minor obstacle. Then the delight trickled away and all I had left was the certainty that the corks and corking machine could in no way be obtained. Now you write that the bottles can also be sealed. This might give the matter a new lease on life. However, there is much to do in the household at present and Ottla is perpetually and heroically at work.

One of my major concerns, though it occupies me only when I am dreaming in my reclining chair, is how I can get you something to eat. Alas, there is little to be had and we ourselves are dependent on this little, since we have neither hens nor cows nor sufficient grain. Whatever butter and eggs we can round up, the family in Prague clamors for. Would you like game? For the present I have saved up for you four kilograms of lovely flour. It is yours and you shall have it as soon as I come to Prague, at the latest; I know that in the darkness of the forthcoming winter that is only a tiny light.

To Elsa and Max Brod

[Zürau, beginning of October 1917]

Dear Frau Elsa, You are bothered because you can't seem to state the meaning of the Lucerna? But that is something you ought to be glad about. Whatever is happening there is happening on some high window ledge of humanity; if one stands too long on it, one is bound to fall, in which case it is better to fall into the room than out into space. The whole thing is an extreme and W.[52] is another manifestation of it. In the picture he is disarming. He even stoops to spitting at himself, as the position of his lips in the picture and in reality shows; you misinterpret the seeming smile. Besides, he is not entirely unique, as you seem to think. In comparing him to a pig, I mean no insult. In amazingness, decisiveness, self-obliteration, sweetness, and whatever else pertains to his profession, his place in the cosmos is perhaps after all side by side with the pig. Have you ever looked as carefully at a pig as at W.? It is amazing. A pig's face is a human face, in which the lower lip is folded down over the chin; the upper lip, without affecting the eyes and nostrils, is folded up to the brow. With this snout-face the pig actually grubs up the ground. We take that for granted and it would be an amazing pig who did not do so, but of late I have often seen the creature from close up, and you must believe me when I say that it is even more amazing that the pig does so. You would really think that just for testing purposes it would be enough to poke at the thing in question with a foot, or to smell it, or if necessary to sniff at it from close quarters—but no, all this will not do, and the pig does not even try but thrusts his snout right in, and if it has plunged into something horrid—all around me lie the droppings of my friends, the goats and the geese—then he snorts with delight. And—this above all reminds me of W.—the pig's body is not dirty, the animal could even be called fastidious (although this is not the kind of fastidiousness you would want to embrace). He has elegant, delicately stepping feet, and the movements of his body seem to flow from a single impulse. Only his noblest organ, his snout, is hopelessly piggish.

So you see, dear Frau Elsa, we in Zürau also have our "Lucerna" and I would be so happy if I could repay you for the picture of W. by sending you a ham from our piglet. But in the first place it doesn't belong to me and in the second place the animal gains weight so slowly, for all its good living, that to our (my and Ottla's) joy it will be a long time before it can be slaughtered.

I am thriving among all the animals. This afternoon I fed goats. Out in my sunning place there are several bushes whose tastiest leaves are too high for the goats and so I bent the branches down for them. These goats, by the way, look like thoroughly Jewish types, mostly doctors, though there are a few approximations of lawyers, Polish Jews, and a scattering of pretty girls in the flock. Dr. W., the doctor who treats me, is heavily represented among them. The conference of three Jewish doctors whom I fed today were so pleased with me that they would hardly let themselves be driven home in the evening for milking. Thus their days and mine come peacefully to a close.

Please don't shame me by mentioning the flour. It deeply grieves me that I can't scrape up something of consequence for you, though with some skill that should be possible.

With warmest regards, yours, Franz K.

I have just reread this letter; it is not really suitable for a lady, but W. is to blame for that, not I.

Dear Max, Many thanks for the *Foster Daughter*.[53] It will serve as tomorrow's treat in my reclining chair. Strange the news of Schreiber.[54] By the way, Flaubert's father, as I have just read, was also tubercular. Perhaps for a good many years it was a moot question whether the child's lungs would be shot, too, or whether he would turn into Flaubert.—I heartily approve of what you are doing for Grünberg.[55] How happy he will be if it succeeds!—No news about your novella?[56]— You should have received two letters from me in the past few days.—I will be coming to Prague at the end of October.

Franz

Did a *Selbstwehr*[57] come out last week, that is, on September 28?

To Max Brod

[Zürau, beginning of October 1917]

Dear Max, You ask about my illness. Confidentially I will tell you that I hardly feel it. I have no fever, don't cough very much, have no pain. True, I am short of breath but don't feel it when lying or sitting, and while I am walking or doing any work, I manage by breathing twice as quickly as previously, no great hardship. I have come to think that tuberculosis, or the kind of tuberculosis I have, is no special disease, or not a disease that deserves a special name, but only the germ of death itself, intensified, though to what degree we cannot for the time being determine. In three weeks I have put on two and a half kilos, and have thus made myself a considerably heavier weight for shipment out.

The good news about Felix[58] delights me, although it may be already outdated. At any rate it does contribute to making the cross-section or the perspective of the whole somewhat more comforting; though that may do him more harm than good.

I wrote to him more than two weeks ago but have no answer as yet. I hope he isn't angry with me? If he is, I would be so dastardly as to remind him of my illness and say that it isn't right to be angry at a poor invalid.

A new section of the novel. Is it quite new or a reworking of the part you have not yet read to me? If you think the first chapter fits in, then it will be all right.—How odd that strikes me. "Problems which I now see before me." In itself that is something one takes for granted, but for me it is something incomprehensible that has been brought home to me by my observing you. This is real struggle, the life-and-death kind, and remains so whether or not one comes through. At least one has seen the enemy or at any rate the flashes against the sky. When I try to think it out, I end by feeling literally unborn; dark myself, I chase about in the darkness.

But not quite. What would you say to this brilliant piece of self-knowledge which I have just copied from a letter to F. It would make a good epitaph:

"If I try to discover my ultimate aim, I realize I am not really striving to become a good person and to satisfy some supreme tribunal. Rather, very much to the contrary, I am trying to survey the whole community of men and animals, to recognize their fundamental preferences, desires, ethical ideals, and then to develop myself as quickly as possible toward being pleasing to everyone and, moreover—and here's the twist—so pleasing that without forfeiting universal love I would ultimately be the sole sinner who is not being roasted, who is permitted to perform before the eyes of all the acts of baseness that dwell within me. In short, only the verdict of men and beasts matters to me, and what is more, I intend to evade that, although without evasion."[59]

From this focal point of self-knowledge, one might possibly arrive at various conclusions and justifications.

I have received *Jenufa*. Reading it is music. The libretto and the music have made the essential contribution, of course. But you have translated it into German like a giant. How wonderfully you've handled those repetitions, making them breathe life!

May I, by the bye, call your attention to a few small points? Only this: Can one run away from *Schaffen*? "*Siehst Du, dann soll man Dich lieben?*" Isn't that the sort of German we have learned from the lips of our un-German mothers? "*Mannsverstand—ins Wasser gefallen*" is artificial German. "*Bange Inbrunst*"—does that belong here? [. . .][60] I would have expected better texts for the songs; I suppose they aren't very good in the Czech either. I would gladly have left "grinning death" to Reichenberger;[61] you also mention the end of the second act as botched, but I seem to recall that this passage gave you particular trouble and that you had a similar translation, perhaps only as a variant, in the manuscript. Shouldn't there have been a note on the meaning of the sacristan's widow?[62]

I'll write about Scheler[63] in my next. Am eager to read Blüher.[64] I'm not writing. What's more, my will is not directed toward writing. If I could save myself like the bat by digging holes, I would dig holes.

Franz

Haven't you heard anything about Gross,[65] Werfel, and the magazine? What about your trip to Komotau and Teplitz?

You said nothing about Ottla's drawing; she was so proud to send it to you (in her defense). That was why the letter was sent registered.

To Felix Weltsch

[Zürau, beginning of October 1917]

Dear Felix, So you aren't angry—that's good, but that "lies" may have a glow of deeper truth surrounding them is no comfort to the liar. I could make a few more remarks about the matter itself, but to you that isn't necessary. (By the way: Today, after a day that went fairly pleasantly, I feel so dull and so prejudiced against myself that I really would do better not to write.)

It's astonishing, what a range your teaching[66] covers—not astonishing as far as the pupils are concerned, for I always predicted that, and as I saw it they were all too slow in crowding around you—but astonishing on your side. What self-control, lack of moodiness, presence of mind, assurance, true workingman's qualities, or to venture the big word: what manliness it takes to enter into such things, to stick with them and in the face of the strongest countercurrents to turn them to your intellectual profit, as you are in fact doing, even though you try to disparage it. So, that needed to be said, and even I am feeling better in this regard.

Now all you have to do is take the children's noise as jubilation over these triumphs of teaching. In any case the noise is bound to subside as autumn advances, just as people here, where there is nothing to be jubilant about, will be gradually shutting in the geese, ceasing to drive out to the fields, having the blacksmiths work only in their workshops, and keeping the children at home; only the bright, singing dialect and the barking of the dogs will not stop, whereas the racket outside your house must have quieted down long ago and the schoolgirls will be able to stare at you undisturbed.

So your health is better (odd, your secret partiality for boils, exceeded only by your fondness for iodine), mine no worse. I regard my gain in weight, which already amounts to three and a half kilograms, as neutral. As to the causes of my sickness, I am not obstinate, but hold to my opinion about the "case," since I am more or less in possession of the original documents and can actually hear the lung immediately concerned literally rattling its approval.

➤Of course you're right that the essential thing needed for recovery is the will to recover. I have that, but to the extent that this can be said without affectation I also have the opposite will. This is a special and, if you will, an illness conferred on me, quite different from the others I have had to deal with previously. Just as a happy lover might say: "All those times in the past were only illusions; only now do I truly love."

Thank you for the explanation of *bis* [until]. The example, *Borge mir, bis wir wieder zusammenkommen* [lend me money until we meet again], is useful to me only on the assumption that it means: *Du sollst mir* erst dann *borgen, bis* [when] *wir zusammenkommen,* and not, say: *Du sollst mir für so lange Zeit borgen, bis* [until] *wir . . .* From the mere quotation I can't make out which it is.

You've misunderstood about the books. I most want to read books that are originally Czech or French, not translations. I'm familiar with the series, by the way; I find it (at least the Rakowitza volume)[67] too poorly printed. The light here, with my north windows, is certainly no better than in the city. Of course there are countless things in French for me; if there is nothing else in Czech I would take something from the similar but scholarly Laichter series.

On the whole I am not reading much; the life in the village suits me so well. Once you get over the feeling, with all of its unpleasant aspects, that you are living in a zoo arranged on the most modern principles, in which the animals are given complete freedom, there is no more comfortable and above all no freer life than that in a village, free in the intellectual sense. You're minimally oppressed by the milieu and by the past. This life is not to be equated with that of a small town, which is probably frightful. I want to live here always. Week after next I'll probably be going to Prague; I'll find it hard.

Cordial regards to you and your wife. It's already twelve o'clock. I've been staying up late this way for the last three or four days; it isn't good, neither for my appearance nor for the supply of kerosene, which is very meager, nor for anything else. But it's extremely tempting; that alone, nothing else.

                                                                    Franz

To Max Brod
                                          [Zürau, October 12, 1917]
Dear Max, I have long wondered how you could have applied the expression —"happy in unhappiness"[68] to me and to others, and that you mean it not as a mere statement, or with regret, or as an admonition when all else fails, but as a reproach. Don't you realize what this means? With this phrase, this secret thought, which of course carries with it the implication "unhappy in

happiness," the mark was probably printed upon Cain. When someone is "happy in unhappiness," it follows that he has fallen out of step with the world and that everything has fallen apart for him, or is falling apart, that no clear call can reach him any longer and so he cannot follow any call with a clear conscience. Things are not quite so bad with me or have so far not been so bad. I have met with both happiness and unhappiness in full measure. You are quite right as to what my average experience has been, and you are also largely right about my present state, but you must say so in a different tone.

Your attitude toward this "happiness" is paralleled by mine toward another concomitant of "inveterate sorrow": I mean smugness, which almost always goes with the latter. I have thought about that often, most recently after reading the Thomas Mann piece on *Palestrina*[69] in the *Neue Rundschau*. Mann is one of those writers whose works I hunger for. This essay, too, is a wonderful broth, but because of the quantity of (figuratively speaking) Salus-like[70] hairs floating around in the soup, one is more inclined to admire than to eat. It would seem that when one is full of sorrow, in order to heighten that sorrowful view of the world one has to stretch and bend as women do after a bath.

Of course I will come to Komotau.[71] Don't misunderstand my fear of visitors. I would not want people to make a long trip, at considerable expense, to come in this autumnal weather to this village which is bound to strike a stranger as dreary, to this household of ours which a stranger is bound to find mismanaged, rife with little inconveniences and even unpleasantness, and all this simply to see me—who am sometimes bored (a state that is not the worst for me), sometimes oversensitive, sometimes fretting over a letter that is supposed to come, or has failed to come, or is threatening to come, sometimes calmed by a letter I have written, sometimes immoderately concerned about myself and my own comforts, sometimes inclined to spit myself out as utterly repulsive, and so on, in all the circles the poodle traces around Faust.[72] But if in spite of this, you should be passing through, not on my account but on account of the Komotauers, I could wish for nothing better. Moreover the visit in Zürau will scarcely be feasible unless you can get away from Komotau early enough on Sunday (at the moment I have only a rough idea of the train schedule) to be at Zürau by noon. Then you can very handily get back to Prague by the evening train. There would be no point staying overnight since you would have to leave terribly early on Monday if you want to get back to Prague by noon, and since in any case the wagon could hardly be spared at this time, since right now there is much to do in the fields. Besides, I shall probably go back to Prague with you, since I can hardly face going back alone—just the friendly letters from the office and the necessity of putting in an appearance there terrify me.

So I have thought out this arrangement, that I get aboard your train in Michelob on Saturday, that we go together on Sunday to Zürau, and in the evening go together to Prague.

The reasons you give for the need to get well are very fine, but utopian. This assignment you give me might have been carried out by an angel hovering over my parents' marriage bed, or even better, over the marriage bed of my people, assuming I have one.

All good wishes for the novel. Your brief mention seems to signify great things. It will help me halfway keep my balance in Prague in spite of the complication of the office.

Warm regards to you and your wife. I am not in the mood for a cabaret, but then I never was. What about her? Besides, cabarets are out of bounds for me now. Where would I crawl off to, when all the big guns start booming, with my toy pistol of a lung? However this disproportion is nothing new for me.

                                                                      Franz

Please let me hear in time when you will be finished in K. on Sunday, so I will know whether we can go on to Zürau, whether the wagon should pick us up, and what I should do about my luggage.

To Felix Weltsch
                                              [Zürau, mid-October 1917]
Dear Felix, To give you some idea of the impression your courses have made upon me, here is a dream I had today. It was wonderful, that is to say, not my sleep (which was very bad, as it generally has been of late: if I were to lose weight and Dr. Pick made me leave Zürau—what would I do?) nor the dream itself, but your activity in it.

We met on the street. I had apparently just come to Prague and was very glad to see you. I thought you remarkably thin, nervous, and professorially peculiar (you held your watch chain so affectedly and clumsily). You told me you were on the way to the university where you were giving a lecture. I said I would gladly go with you, but I had to drop into this shop for a moment—we were standing right in front of it (all this took place near the end of Langengasse[73] opposite the large tavern located there). You promised to wait for me but while I was inside you changed your mind and wrote me a letter. How I received it I no longer remember, but I can still see the handwriting of the letter. It said among other things that the class began at three o'clock, that you couldn't wait any longer, that Professor Sauer[74] was going to be in the audience and you could not offend him by coming late.

Many women and girls were attending the lecture mainly on his account, so if he stayed away, thousands would stay away. So you had to hurry.

But I quickly followed and found you in a sort of lobby. There was a wild field in front of the building where girls were playing ball. One of them asked you what you were going to do. You said that you were giving a course and set forth the reading list, mentioning two authors, their works, and the chapter numbers. It was all very learned. I remember only the name of Hesiod. The second author escapes me, all I know is that his name was not Pindar, though he was very much like that, only far more obscure, and I asked myself why "at least" you weren't reading Pindar.

We entered the lecture room, where the class had already started. You had probably given your introduction and had only gone out to see me. On the podium sat a tall, strong, womanly, plain, black-clothed, knobby-nosed, dark-eyed girl; she was translating Hesiod. I understood not a word. Now I can identify the girl—in the dream I had no idea who she was—she was Oskar's sister, only a bit thinner and much larger.

Obviously remembering your Zuckerkandl[75] dream, I felt myself wholly a writer, and comparing my ignorance with the fantastic knowledge of this girl, I kept saying to myself, "Pathetic, pathetic."

I did not see Professor Sauer, but many ladies were present. Two rows in front of me (the ladies, strange to say, sat with their backs to the podium) sat Frau G. Her hair was in long curls which she kept tossing. Next to her was another lady whom you identified as Frau Holzner[76] (though she was quite young). In the row in front of us you pointed out the other school directress who runs a school on Herrengasse. They were all pupils of yours. In the other section of seats I spied Ottla, with whom I had recently quarreled about your course. (She had not wanted to come but now, to my gratification, she was here and in fact had come early.)

Even those who were only chattering were talking about Hesiod. I was somewhat soothed because the girl who was reading had smiled when we entered the room, and with the audience's approval for some time could not contain her laughter. This however did not prevent her from translating and elucidating correctly.

When she was done and you were on the point of beginning your lecture, I leaned over toward you in order to read out of your book, but then saw to my enormous amazement that all you had in front of you was a dirty Reclam[77] edition, read to tatters; for you knew the Greek text, ye gods, by heart! This expression came to my aid out of your last letter. Now, however, perhaps because I perceived that under the circumstances I would not be able to follow the lecture, the whole scene became less distinct. You took on somewhat the looks of one of my former fellow students, a boy moreover whom I liked very much—this boy shot himself and, as it now occurs to me, had a certain resemblance to the girl on the podium. So you became someone else and the course also changed midstream, becoming a music course, less detailed, and conducted by a short, dark, youngish man with red cheeks. He resembled a distant relative of mine who (this has some bearing on my attitude toward music) is in life a chemist and probably crazy.

So that was the dream, as yet far from worthy of your courses. I now lay me down for perhaps another, even more impressive dream of your course.

Franz

To Max Brod

[Zürau, mid-October 1917]

Dear Max, Let me be as little of a nuisance as possible, since I can't do anything about all your other nuisances.

I have that issue of *Aktion*[78] as well as a few other things and will bring them to you all at once. Everything you send gives me great pleasure. The "Radetzky March"[79] did not of course make quite the same impression as when you read it to me, almost like a poem. But something else is missing. Is the cutting to blame? That can't be. After rapture, hate rears up, but no one has seen it growing. Perhaps there is not room enough inside the story for the antithetical twist to develop, perhaps not enough room even in the heart.

Teweles'[80] article is probably meant for Kuh,[81] who has recently written a brilliantly nasty piece on Werfel, no doubt as an exercise in delicacy. One simply can't fathom from what state of mind such a thing is written. And I sat at table with this enigma, sat quite close to him.—

I particularly noted that Goethe was "also not of stone."[82] The whole thing is probably most embarrassing for the old lady[83] who thought she had written a poignant book about Frau von Stein and who now has it pointed out to her that all the while, evidently in the confusion of grief, she was preoccupied with Goethe's trousers.

The Komotau committee has placed some complications in the way of my trip to Prague, though of course I will go anyhow. But I will first send Ottla on ahead, so she can see "how the land lies." I will come at the end of the month.

The editorial in *Selbstwehr* might almost be yours, judging from its quick insights, the vigor of its protest, and its boldness. There were a few places, though, that made me stop and take a second look. Probably by Hellman?[84]

Cordially, Franz

To Felix Weltsch

[Zürau, after October 17, 1917]

Dear Felix, I do not specially choose the days on which I write to you, but today is one of those days (they are not all like this) when I feel low-spirited, lumpish, leaden-stomached, or rather that's how I felt at midday. Now, after our supper together (Ottla is in Prague), that mood once more comes over me, only more strongly. And now I find in addition that after today's big housecleaning, for which I was so grateful, the bottom of the lamp chimney has sprung a crack, admits air, and though I have closed up the crack with a bit of wood, the flame flickers. But perhaps all this is somehow conducive to letter-writing.

This village life is lovely and remains so. Ottla's house is located on the Ringplatz, so when I look out the window I see another cottage on the opposite side of the square, but right behind that the open fields begin. What could be better, in every sense, for breathing? As far as I am concerned, I catch my breath in every sense, least of all physically. Elsewhere I would be close to suffocation, which state, however, I know from active and passive experience, can be sustained for years.

My relationship with the people here is so loose, it is hardly like being among the living. This evening, for instance, I met two people on the dark highway; there was no telling whether they were men, women, or children. They greeted me, I responded. Perhaps they recognized me by the shape of my overcoat. Even by daylight I would probably not have known who they were, nor did I recognize them by their voices, since that seems to be an impossibility with people who speak dialect. After they had passed me, one turned around and called "Herr Hermann" (my brother-in-law's name; so it has become mine), "Might you have a cigarette?" I: "Sorry, no." And that was it, words and misunderstandings of the shades. In my present state, I do not wish for better.

I think I understand what you mean by the "intrusion of the contrary will." It belongs to that realm of damnedly psychological theory, which you have no love for but which obsesses you (as it apparently does me). The nature-cure theories are as wrong as their psychological counterparts. But that has little bearing on the question of whether the world can be cured from a single point.

I would like to have heard the Schnitzer lecture. You are right in what you say about Schnitzer,[85] but people of that sort are all too easily underestimated. He is totally artless and therefore magnificently sincere; therefore where he's out of his depth, as a speaker, writer, or even a thinker, not only uncomplicated as you say, but downright stupid. But sit down opposite him, study him, try to analyze him, especially his effectiveness, try for just a little to approach his point of view—he cannot be so easily dismissed.

"That book" of mine might actually be worth while. I too would like to read it. It is sitting somewhere in the heavenly bookshelves. But that a seventy-seven-year-old lady should ask to have the book for a birthday gift (perhaps from her great-grandson: "I am but small, my gift is small ..."), that my book should cause the family blood of the Clemenceaux to race, that the Hofrat[86] deigns to speak of it without adding a reprimand (a circumstance that undoubtedly proves how deeply contemptuous he is of the whole thing), all this—it is too much, that is the trouble.

In any case I have always felt special respect for the Hofrat, not because, as far as I can remember, I did so badly under him,[87] but because he, unlike others who brought the full weight of their self-importance to the podium, presented a clean outline that could be drawn in five strokes. In other words, there was more to him than he showed and one somehow sensed that and bowed to it.

Three courses? How can you fit that into your half-day week? It is too much, would almost be a full load for a gymnasium professor. What does Max say about it?

The offer you made to lecture to your former pupils may have been somewhat unpedagogical. By which I mean truly alarming. You loomed up in front of them like a giant, and with all the energy girls have, they reduced you to "Young Germany."[88] Which after all isn't as alien to you as you complain while under duress. By the way, they are launching a magazine next month called *Das junge Deutschland*. It is being published by the Deutsche Theater, edited by Kornfeld.[89]

And what about *Der Mensch?*[90] Granted the announcement sounds long-haired and bristly, but it may turn out a good thing. You do not mention it at all.—Many regards to you and your wife.

Franz

[IN THE MARGIN] Don't be daunted by Wolff.[91] He has to play it coy. How many writers are bombarding him! Overwhelmed as he is, he cannot sort things out.

To Max Brod
[Postcard. Zürau, October 22, 1917]
Dear Max, All right then, the 27th, at Komotau. The way those Komotauers change their mind is of course upsetting, especially for you. But for me as

well. To be frank with you: if it were not for your Komotau trip, I would not be going to Prague yet, not for two weeks at least. It is not only the life here that is beneficial, but also its continuity, and that is what the journey would destroy. Besides that, these last few days, though I feel perfectly good, I have absolutely no appetite. What if I should lose weight and Dr. Pick should take me away from Zürau, the best place for me? These are the worries which keep me from crying out my joy at seeing you and talking with you. Another thing: I will probably have to stay on in Prague at least three days to have work done on my teeth, and the office also has a claim on me. In any case an exchange of freedom for servitude and sorrow.

But are the arrangements for the Komotau trip fixed? If it is cancelled, you will telegraph me. I would not want to make the trip by myself. Aside from wanting to hear you there, I would also enjoy retracing with you the footprints of your earlier life.[92]

Franz

To Oskar Baum

[Zürau, October/November 1917]

Dear Oskar,

I simply cannot write to Director Marschner. It's been more than three months since he has heard a peep from me;[93] he enters my life only as a kind Providence,[94] endlessly forbearing and patient and paying the bill. But fortunately there is no need to write him; the head of the office of the Administration for the Care of Returning War Veterans, Poříč 7, is Secretary Dr. F.[95] (he is the first, myself the second and last and crumbling Jew of the organization)—a distinguished man, who brings love to his job and is favorably disposed to any request that is halfway fulfillable. I have just written him about the facts of the case, and that probably would be sufficient. But it might be better still if you yourself would drop in at his office between nine and one. I have already prepared him for your coming. I advise this especially because (though I know nothing about the details of the program for the care of the blind) the 8000 crowns strikes me as a fantastically large sum when compared to the usual allowance for the war-injured, so a few words of personal explanation would be useful.

Let me at any rate give you a sketch of Dr. F.: He is three-quarters Czech and four-quarters Social Democrat. His mother tongue is German (feel no hesitation about speaking German with him, as I always do), has had a hard' youth behind him, was among other things secretary to old Klaar of the *Vossische Zeitung*,[96] used not to care about literature, has only recently in his mid-forties married a Czech typist; his father-in-law is a poor carpenter—so

that all in all here is a man with whom one can speak easily and openly.
Should you manage to say a word of praise for the way he handles his job,
you will make him happy and will not moreover be lying. By the way, he
might extort such a word from you, half against his will—a little weakness he
has. But don't stay long—he has a lot to do but gets carried away in
conversation and is annoyed with himself later. He will be especially moved
by P.'s concern for his sister. He knows what that means from his own
experience.

The Assistant for the Care of Blinded Veterans, to whom he may send you
(though once he has taken up a matter he does not delegate it elsewhere), is
Dr. T. (he is not a Dr. but call him that anyway). He is a completely
different sort, was in the war, with regular features, pale, thin, of medium
height, his face marked by deep lines of duty. He speaks very slowly, in a
rasping voice, and the substance of what he says does not justify the long
pauses, stresses, violent movements of his lips, and so in general he is rather
disconcerting. But in my experience that does not mean much; he is a good
and pleasant man, though one must adjust to his tempo.

When my name is mentioned his office mate, Herr Vice Secretary K. (let
me write that name again, so it will be quite legible: K.; it is a real name, not
something you invented), may also want to put his oar into the conversation.
He is my closest colleague, and as long as I am here I love him (as Dr. F. does
not); and so you will be gradually surrounded by three friends who, let us
hope, will do everything to help Herr P.

I was sorry to hear that that summer place has proved unavailable, even
though I too may not be able to stay here for the summer.—Kierkegaard is a
star, although he shines over territory that is almost inaccessible to me. I'm
glad that you will be reading him. I know only *Fear and Trembling*.[97]
Couldn't you send Krastik[98] in manuscript to me, or rather to us? You have
three[99] faithful readers here, each in his own way. Warmest regards to you
and your wife.

To Max Brod

[Zürau, beginning of November 1917]
Dearest Max, Today we had visitors, much against my will. The girl from
the office (well, Ottla had invited her), but then she toted along a man[100]
from the office (perhaps you will remember—once we were walking along the
quay with some guests at night and I turned around to greet a couple), an
excellent fellow and I find him pleasant and interesting (Catholic, divorced),
but they came by surprise, when even a prearranged visit is surprise enough. I
am not up to such things and I ran through emotions ranging from a spasm

of jealousy to intense discomfort and helplessness vis-à-vis the girl (I advised her, without conviction, to marry the man) all the way to utter dreariness throughout that whole long day, and I am not even mentioning a variety of altogether nasty intermediate feelings. Yet there was a little sadness about saying goodbye, which was utterly nonsensical, must be due to some reaction of the stomach or the like. All in all it was a visit like all others, that is to say instructive, a monotonous lesson, which one cannot repeat often enough.

I tell you all this only because of one thing which relates to our conversation—I mean the "spasm of jealousy." That was the only good moment in the day, the moment when I had an enemy—for otherwise it was a clear field, a steep downhill drop.

I won't send anything to Frankfurt,[101] for I don't feel this as anything I have to bother with. If I send it, I would be doing so out of vanity alone. If I don't send it, it is also vanity, but not vanity alone, therefore something better. The pieces I might send mean little to me; I respect only the moments in which they were written. What's the point of having an actress, who can find far more effective vehicles for displaying her talents, spend one moment in an evening raising them out of the void into which they will fall more or less swiftly. It's a waste of effort.

Shortness of breath and coughing. You are not far wrong; since Prague I have become much more careful than I used to be. Possibly I could find other places where I could lie outside more, where the air is more bracing, and so on, but—and this is very important for the state of my nerves, which in turn is important to my lungs—I would not feel so much at ease anywhere else. Nowhere else would there be so few distractions (except for visits, but these are spaced far enough apart so that they sink into the peacefulness of this life, leaving little trace). Nowhere else would I tolerate the boarding and hotel arrangements with less resistance, vexation, and impatience than here with my sister. There is some kind of alien element in my sister to which I can most easily adjust in this particular form. (I do actually have that "fear for the presonality" that Stekel[102] once attributed to hordes of patients such as myself, but I find it perfectly natural, even when it is not equated with "fear for one's salvation." There is always the lingering hope that some day one may need one's "personality," or that it will be needed by others, and therefore must be kept in readiness.) Nowhere, then, do I accept an alien element so readily as I accept it in my sister. Here I can submit. I can also submit to my father lying outstretched on the ground. (I would gladly do so when he is standing erect, but that is not permitted.)

You read me three sections out of the novel. I joyfully absorbed the music of the first, the strong clarity of the third. (In the first the actual "Jewish passages" make one rather blink, as though in a dark room lights were

quickly turned on and off at certain points.) Actually, I balk only at the
second section, but not because of the objections you mentioned. The
bowling—is that a Jewish game as you define what is Jewish? At best it is
Jewish in the sense that Ruth[103] inside her own head was playing a different
game, but that is not the point. If the austerity of the game is self-torment,
and torment of her sweetheart, then I understand it. But if it springs from an
independent belief, which has no direct causal connection with the condition
of either Ruth's or your life, then it is a desperate belief, which can conjure
up a vision of a Palestine only in dream, as in fact happens. The whole thing
is, you know, almost a war game, built around the famous notion of
breakthrough—a Hindenburg affair. Perhaps I misunderstand you, but if there
do not exist innumerable possibilities for liberation, possibilities at every
moment of our lives, then perhaps there are none at all. But I really do
misunderstand you. After all, the game is continually replayed; the
momentary misstep means only that the moment is lost, not the whole thing.
But in that case this would have to be stated, if only for therapeutic reasons.

                                                                    Franz

Today I received the statement from Wolff on 102 copies of *Meditation* for
'16–17, amazingly high sale, but I haven't received the statement he promised
you he would send, nor the one for *A Country Doctor*.

Enclosed your ration application, which you left inside the notebook.
Please, Max, always send the *Jüdische Rundschau*.[104]—Ottla intends to go to
Prague in two weeks and arrange to have me retired on pension.

To Felix Weltsch

                                        [Zürau, beginning of November 1917]
Dear Felix, Had I gone to the theater[105] that night you would surely have
had to come along and would have come away, I think, with a good idea of
Zürau. But I still had some things to do the following morning, then went to
Max's where your real self was not present, nor were conditions favorable for
a meaningful talk, since a telegram sent the previous day prevented me from
staying, and my thoughts tended to revolve around a tooth broken off by the
dentist. Nor has my decisiveness improved any while I was in Prague. So
that's how it was, and I left by myself. On my return I found Zürau in no
way disappointing. But this is not the moment to sing its praises as truth
requires, for my stomach is slightly upset, and there is some unfamiliar noise
about the house, never before noted at this time of day, which bothers me as I
occasionally try to reassess my resources (certainly a sensible thing to do).
You see, from the start I brought a great deal of swinishness here from

Prague, something I must always reckon with. Agricultural metaphors will always be useful out here.

The life in your apartment presents so strong a contrast to the life here that my thoughts keep coming back to it. It amazed me. Your previous apartment was fancy enough, but this one is positively smothering. What kind of independence of mind you must have and how carefully balanced you have to be to bear this not only without harm to yourself—as I must confirm from all I saw—but also to be able to move about inside such a life without any barrier and take it all, not to be sure as your proper element, but as a congenial one. Max may be right, when he sets you up so high that you only see the tops but no longer the base of the towering ruin. But a friend feels he ought to speak some word of warning, and can't manage to do it convincingly, and so remains in detestable suspension.

My trip to Prague among other things cheated me of half a letter from you. In recompense I ask only for two brief explanations: How is it that you are so tentative about the evolution that your Ethics[106] is undergoing? And secondly: What is the situation in regard to your courses (Young Germany), which after all belong among the half-conquered demons of your life?

Franz

[IN THE MARGIN] I suppose you are going to many of the Urania[107] lectures? No answer from Wolff?

To Max Brod

[Postcard. Zürau; postmark: November 13, 1917]

Dearest Max, I drop this card to acknowledge the arrival of the card from you, the letter, and the printed matter (*Jüdische Rundschau, Aktion,* special issue of *Selbstwehr*[108]). For incomprehensible reasons the letter and card only arrived today, the 13th, but that does not matter; the joy your letter brings me does not depend on time.—I cannot help Langer[109] in this way. The Institute is closed to Jews. It would not amuse me to put such a fearful imposition upon the director—for that is what a prospective employee's request to be excused from work on Saturday would be. There is no explaining how two Jews, with the help of the third Jew, got in, and it won't happen again. But perhaps there is some place for Langer in our shop, if that could be justified to Father—and why couldn't it? If you want to drop by one of these days and talk the matter over with Mother, Sister, or Cousin,[110] I will let them know. But Langer is strong; why doesn't he hire himself out to some Jewish tenant farmer?—The "Greetings to Uncle Franz" is very nice, but tame. An aunt cannot spank someone whom her nephew loves.

Franz

According to Ottla, there's not the faintest hope for a job for L. with us and she knows Father and the business better than I do.

To Max Brod

[Zürau, mid–November 1917]

Dearest Max, What I am doing is simple and self-evident: in my relations to city, to family, to profession, to society, to love (you can put this first, if you like), to the existent or prospective community of our people, in all these relations I have not acquitted myself well, and moreover I have failed in such a fashion—I know from close observation—as has no one else around me. At bottom it is only that child's idea: "No one is as bad as I am," which later, when corrected, only produces a new pain. But here we are no longer dealing with badness and self-reproach, but with the patent psychological fact of not acquitting oneself. Nonetheless this idea persists and will persist. I don't want to make much of the suffering associated with the unlived life, for in retrospect this suffering seems (and has always seemed so at all the small stages along the way) all too undeservedly mild compared to the facts whose pressure it has had to withstand. Still and all it was often too great to be borne much longer, or if it was not too great, was too meaningless. (In these morasses, the question of meaning is perhaps admissible.) The most obvious escape from all this was, from childhood on, perhaps, not suicide but the thought of suicide. In my case what deterred me from suicide was no particular cowardice, but only the thought, which similarly ended in meaninglessness, "What, you, who can't do anything, imagine you can do this? How dare you think so? If you could kill yourself, you more or less don't have to." And so on. Later more understanding slowly followed. I stopped thinking of suicide. What now lay before me, when I was able to think clearly, over and beyond the confused hopes, the lonely raptures, the swollen vanities (this "over and beyond" that I was able to achieve only very rarely, as rarely as my staying alive permitted)—what lay before me was a wretched life and a wretched death. "It was as if the shame of it must outlive him" are more or less the closing words of my *Trial*.[111]

I now see a new way out, which in its completeness had so far seemed impossible and which I could not have discovered with my own resources (unless the tuberculosis is to be reckoned among my own "resources"). I have only seen this way, I imagine I have seen it, I have not yet begun to take it. It consists in this, or would consist in this—that I not only privately, by an aside, as it were, but openly, by my whole behavior, confess that I cannot acquit myself properly here. This means I need do nothing but continue to follow with the utmost resolution the lines of my previous life. As a result I would assume a coherence, not dissipate myself in meaninglessness, and keep a clear-eyed view.

This is my aim—which even if it were carried out, which it isn't—has nothing "admirable" about it, but only a certain consistency. If you call it admirable, you make me vain, send me in fact into an orgy of vanity, though I know better. That would be a pity. Even the flimsiness of a house of cards comes tumbling down when its builder becomes puffed up with pride. (Luckily a false image.)

But I see your way, insofar as I have any view of it here, as totally different. You can acquit yourself, so acquit yourself. You can hold all the disparate elements together. I cannot, or at least not yet. Our ever-closer intimacy will consist in this—that we are both walking; previously I felt too often that you were carrying me.

What you call suspicion sometimes seems to me merely the play of surplus forces which you, because you are not fully concentrating, have not thrown into your writing or into Zionism—the two are really one, of course. So in this sense it may be called, if you like, a justified suspicion.

Of course I totally approve of your wife's reading the story,[112] *but not at all at this occasion.* My objection is the same as I had about Frankfurt. You have the right to step forward, while I, and perhaps Fuchs and Feigl[113] (address: Union), have the right to keep still and we should take advantage of that.

How do you feel about *Daimon?*[114] Would you please let me know Werfel's address? If any magazine seemed tempting to me for any length of time (they all seem tempting enough at the moment) it was Dr. Gross's—perhaps because I felt the warmth of a certain personal connection glowing from it, at least for that evening.[115] Perhaps a magazine can only be a sign that people are moving toward a common point. But what about *Daimon?* All I know about that review is the picture of its editor which I saw in *Donauland.*[116]

If I go on to say that in a recent dream of mine I gave Werfel a kiss, I stumble right into the midst of Blüher's[117] book. But more of that later. The book upset me; I had to lay it aside for two days. However it shares the quality of other psychoanalytic works that in the first moment its thesis seems remarkably satisfying, but very soon after one feels the same old hunger. That is "of course" easily explained psychoanalytically: Instant Repression. The royal train gets fastest service.

I'll just add this: Health excellent. (Even Dr. Pick said nothing about the south.) Your announcement of visit welcome and good; your view of presents highly dubious, will be refuted in my next.

Franz

No, let me refute it right away, because I have the proof down pat. We are "giving" exclusively for our own pleasure. Which is harmful to the two of you in both an emotional and material sense. For if we didn't make presents but sold the stuff, we would of course be able to send you much more than we have, while because of the differential between prices here and prices in Prague you would make far more of a profit than the value of the "gifts" and in addition would have more food. But we do not do that, we harm you and we give presents recklessly, because we enjoy doing so. But tolerate it on that account. In fact we send only too little and that little is steadily becoming less.

To Elsa Brod

[Postcard. Zürau, mid-November 1917]
Dear Frau Elsa, Certainly. But avoid any mention of it in the newspapers.[118] No matter what you choose, it will be only a trifle that might do for a filler and not worth mentioning. And should the text contain something dirty, don't leave it out. If you really tried to clean up the text, there would be no end to it. And good luck! You once read the song from *Intensity of Feeling* so beautifully. Perhaps you ought to do your recitations with a musical background. You must try that sometime with a melodrama, even if it goes against the grain.—Will you be the only one reading this time?

Cordial regards, Kafka

To Felix Weltsch

[Zürau, mid-November 1917]
Dear Felix, The first fatal flaw of Zürau: a night of mice, a fearful experience. I myself came through unscathed and my hair is no whiter than yesterday, but it was still gruesome. Here and there previously (I may have to stop writing any minute, you will learn the reason), here and there in the night I had heard a delicate nibbling, once in fact I started out of bed all atremble and had a look around and the noise stopped at once—but this time it was an uproar. What a frightful mute and noisy race this is! Around two A.M. I was wakened by a rustling around my bed, and from then on the rustling did not stop until morning. Up the coal box, down the coal box, across the room they ran, describing circles, nibbling at wood, peeping softly while resting, and all along there was that sense of silence, of the secret labor of an oppressed proletarian race to whom the night belongs. To preserve my sanity, I decided that the noise was concentrated around the stove, which stands at the other end of the room. But it was everywhere, and reached its peak when a whole swarm of them leaped down together somewhere. I was completely helpless, could find nothing in my whole being to cling to. I did not dare get up, light

the lamp. All I could manage was a few shouts, with which I tried to intimidate them. So the night passed, and in the morning my disgust and misery were such that I could not get up but remained in bed until one o'clock, straining my ears to hear what one tireless mouse was doing in the wardrobe, either finishing the work of the night before or getting a start on the next night's assignment. Now I have taken the cat (which I have secretly hated all along) into my room, and must often shoo her away when she tries to jump into my lap (writing interrupted); if she dirties I must go fetch the maid from the ground floor; when she (the cat) is good, she lies by the stove while at the window one early riser of a mouse scratches unequivocally. Today everything is spoiled for me here; even the good coarse smell and taste of the farm bread is mousy.

Anyhow I was already uneasy when I went to bed last night. I wanted to write to you, had already written two pages of two letters, but it wouldn't go, I could not strike the earnest note. Perhaps it was because you began your letter in such a flippant way, made fun of yourself where there cannot possibly be anything to be made fun of. If you were as frivolous as you pretend to be, you would surely not have reached your present age: I mean, given the same circumstances. So it can't be true that alongside "rocklike faith" you simultaneously hold "frivolous theories" which basically eradicate the faith, and alongside these that "tail-end thought" which in turn eradicates the theories, so that finally nothing but this "tail-end thought" is left, or rather not even that, since it cannot wag itself of its own accord. If so, you would be content to be totally eradicated, but fortunately you are still around, you know, and that is fine and good. But you should really ponder that, see it as a remarkable intellectual achievement, or in other words agree with Max and me.

In other respects, too, you are mistaken. (Amazing, she scents something and makes a spring toward the dark place behind the wardrobe. There she sits and waits. What a relief for me!) Take the word of this rathole owner, your apartment is fancy, and it is disturbing (aside from other disturbing matters, which, to your credit, don't disturb you at all) because the "spatial surplus" produces the "temporal deficit." For example, your time lies like a rug in the vestibule. Let it lie there, it makes a handsome enough rug and is good for guarding the household. But future time ought to remain unchanged by that, for your and for everyone's sake.

My question about the Ethics, as I now see, was really a request for written lectures which I now withdraw as a monstrous imposition. However, that being the case, I do not know what to make of your remark about faith and grace and the parting of ways with Max or even with me.

My health is quite good, assuming that mouse phobia does not carry me off before tuberculosis does.

An interesting item for the military program of the Central Powers for 1918: The expiration date of my exemption has been set for January 1, 1918. For once Hindenburg has come a bit too late.

Cordial regards to you and your wife (with whom, alas, since that affair of the purse, I no longer have anything to lose).

Franz

To Max Brod

[Zürau, November 24, 1917]

Dear Max, Plenty of leisure time but oddly enough none for letter-writing. Figure it out. Since the plague of mice, which you may have heard about (long interruption: I had to paint a box and a pot), I've really not had a room (that is, with the cat, but only with her, I can just about spend the night there). But I am in no mood to sit there and hear rustling, sometimes behind the basket, sometimes at the window (one hears every claw). There is also the cat; she is a very good little creature, but I must always be on guard, while I am reading or writing, lest she jump into my lap, or be ready with the ashes when she does her multiple jobs, and that's a great bother. In short, I don't like being alone with the cat. With other people around it is less embarrassing but then it's a considerable nuisance to undress in front of her, do one's exercises, go to bed.

Therefore I fall back on my sister's room, a very pleasant one despite the alarm you feel when you first view it from the threshold (ground level, barred windows, crumbling wall). But as a shared room it is not good for writing, when one wants to do some writing in the evening. Then by day—but the days are very short, when one breakfasts in bed, gets up late, and by two o'clock it is already dark in the ground-floor room—so that the day consists of not much more than three hours, provided that the sky is not too cloudy, in which case it is even shorter and will be even more so as the winter advances—by day I either lie out in the open or at the window, reading. This time between darkness and darkness in which one wants to snatch something out of a book (and in the meanwhile Honved are cleaning up the delta of the Piave, the offensive is waged from the Tyrol,[119] Jaffa is conquered,[120] Hantke received,[121] Mann's reading was a great success, Essig's a dismal failure,[122] Lenin's real name is not Zederblum but Ulyanov, and so on)—one does not want to use this interval for writing, and no sooner has one thought this than dusk begins to fall and one can only see the geese dimly on the pond, these geese (of whom I could tell a good deal) who might be very nasty, were it not that they are treated more nastily. (Today a slaughtered goose lay outside in the basin looking like someone's dead aunt.)

So there is no time, as has been proved, and it now remains only to prove that this is as it should be. For so it is. I do not always recognize this but that is my fault, and one I do always recognize, at least a second before I commit it. If I still clung to the old principles—my time is the evening and the night—things would be bad with me, especially since the lighting is troublesome. But since that is no longer so, since I am not writing at all, I don't have to strive for quiet, mouseless, brightly lit evenings and nights, though I don't dread them either. Instead I have the free morning hours to spend in bed—(hardly is the cat put out in the morning when little scratchings begin to be heard somewhere behind the wardrobe. My sense of hearing has become a thousand times sharper and has become more uncertain by the same proportion—if I rub my finger over the sheet, I no longer know for certain whether I am hearing a mouse. But the mice are not fantasies of mine, for the cat comes to me in the evening thin and is taken out in the morning fat)—a few moments with a book (now it is Kierkegaard), toward evening a walk on the road, and this suffices me in my solitude. It is fulfillment enough and there's little need to complain. Unless I were to complain that it is humiliating to be cared for and surrounded by others who are working, while I myself, without any visible signs of illness, am to all appearances incapable of any kind of decent work. Lately I tried to work just a little in the vegetable garden, and keenly felt it afterward.

Ottla is in Prague.[123] Perhaps she will come back with a more detailed account of the Vienna evening. You could not have a better audience than young people. Like you, I trust in youth, though I did not trust in my own youth; and yet, simply as futureless, purely young youth, I might equally have deserved it. How fine it must be to be able to show such trust, as you, for example, recently did in Komotau, where sentiment (you wrote of this) was entirely my affair.

Franz

Today it strikes me that last night I viewed everything, that is to say my inner situation, all too lightly and casually.

Your packet No. 5 has come (Rundschau, Hiller,[124] Marsyas).

What is Oskar doing? I don't write to him and he has not sent the promised novel. But he is going to visit for a few days at New Year's.

A new development: I have been straining my ears all morning and now I see a new hole near the door. So there are mice here too. And today the cat is unwell, vomits continually.

To Oskar Baum

[Zürau, end of November/beginning of December 1917]

Dear Oskar, I haven't written to you at all, you haven't sent the promised novel. But these are outward matters and otherwise nothing has changed here and I hope not with you either.

Zürau is as lovely as ever, though becoming wintry. The goose pond outside my window is already freezing over now and then, the children are skating, and my hat, which the evening gale blew into the pond, had to be pried loose from the ice in the morning. As cannot have been concealed from you, there has been a frightful invasion of mice. I have driven them off a bit with the cat, whom I fetch from across the square every evening, "holding her warm in my arm." But yesterday a crude bakery rat, who perhaps had never been in a bedroom before, broke in here with an incredible thumping and I had to call in the cat from the next room, where I had confined her, due to my incompetence at teaching her sanitation and my fear of her leaping onto the bed. How readily the good animal sprang out of a box of unknown contents, which however was never meant for sleeping in, and belongs to my landlady; then all was still. Other news: One of the geese died of excessive stuffing, the sorrel has mange, the goats have been to the buck (who seems to be a particularly handsome young fellow; one of the goats, who had already been taken there, had a flash of remembrance and ran back to him again all the way from our house), and soon the pig is going to be butchered without more ado.

This is the brief picture of life and death you will be encountering at the turn of the year. What my own condition will be I really cannot say for certain. According to Dr. Pick's opinion of last month, I should already be back at the office, although I am far from healthy by ordinary standards (in spite of which I have scarcely ever felt physically better). But if I can avoid the office at least a while longer—and I wish nothing else so fervently—then this is what I will do: at the end of December I must in any case go to Prague, for my exemption expires the first of January and I must present myself. Since they probably have no interest in feeding me in Pleš,[125] when I do it for myself here, they will no doubt (and I may have some additional aid besides the common sense of the draft board) dismiss me. Then I will hurry back to Zürau and you can conveniently travel with me. That would be the best way, for me especially. As for you, you must come here in any case, whatever my fate should be. Ottla is looking forward to your visit. Bed and cat have been prepared, snow and frost will come of their own accord.

And the novel?

Warmest regards to you, your wife, and child, Franz

To Felix Weltsch

[Zürau, beginning of December 1917]

Dear Felix, Max has already told Ottla how well things are going with you and your letter confirms it in spite of yourself. What work! Three to four books a day,[126] even though they are the same ones! What is remarkable is not the quantity, of course, but the intensity of the search this represents. I too am reading, by comparison with you almost nothing, but I can bear only those books whose nature is close enough to mine to rub against me. All the others march right past me. So I am not one to search.

If you could recommend a well-printed and easily purchasable edition of Augustine's *Confessions* (that is the title, isn't it) I would gladly order it. Who was Pelagius?[127] I have read so much about Pelagianism, but retain not so much as an iota—was it some heretical Catholic stuff? When you read Maimonides,[128] you might want to supplement it with *Solomon Maimon's Autobiography* (edited by Fromer, published by Georg Müller),[129] an excellent book in itself, and a harsh self-portrait of a man haplessly torn between East and West European Judaism. But it also summarizes the teachings of Maimonides, whose spiritual child he feels himself to be. But probably you know the book better than I do.

You are surprised that you are being drawn toward religion? You began by building your ethical system—that is the one thing I think I know definitely about it—without a foundation—and perhaps you now realize that it does have foundations after all. Would that be so remarkable?

I control the mice with a cat, but how shall I control the cat? You imagine that you have nothing against mice? Naturally, nor have you anything against cannibals either, but if they should start crawling about in the night behind every chest and chattering their teeth at you, you surely could not bear them any longer. However I am now trying to harden myself by taking walks and observing the field mice. They are not bad, but the room is not a field, and going to sleep is not the same as taking a walk.

To be sure, we have no trumpets here—but I imagine yours has finished trumpeting by now—and the children, who have always been splendidly noisy and yet haven't really disturbed me, have, since the goose pond froze over, become gentle and lovely a hundred paces away.

A request: The daughter[130] of a wealthy peasant here, perhaps the wealthiest, a very pleasant girl of about eighteen, wants to spend three months in Prague. Her purpose: to learn Czech, to continue piano lessons, to go to housekeeping school, and what is perhaps her main purpose but cannot be precisely defined, to attain to something higher. For her position here has something desperate about it; because of her wealth and her convent education she has not a single girl friend who is her equal and does not know what her own place is. In this way a fine and radiantly Christian girl comes to resemble a Jewish one. I say all this on the basis of a superficial impression, for I have exchanged barely fifty words with her.

I turn to you for advice in this matter because I myself have none to give and because you know a great many Czechs who might be glad to take the girl into their home, and might be of real help to her along the lines she wishes, *since with her connections there would be no food problem.* But please give your advice soon.

I am not too worried about my army call-up, especially since the Institute has also put in a word for me there, perhaps unnecessarily. I am more inclined to brood over my relationship to the Institute, concerning which some decision must be made in the near future. If Dr. Pick had his way, I would already be back in the office.

Cordial regards, Franz

To Max Brod

[Zürau, beginning of December 1917]

Dear Max, Pure chance that I have not answered until today; other reasons are room, light, mice. But it is not a question of nervousness or adjusting from city conditions to village. My reaction toward the mice is one of sheer terror. To analyze its source would be the task of a psychoanalyst, which I am not. Certainly this fear, like an insect phobia, is connected with the unexpected, uninvited, inescapable, more or less silent, persistent, secret aim of these creatures, with the sense that they have riddled the surrounding walls through and through with their tunnels and are lurking within, that the night is theirs, that because of their nocturnal existence and their tininess they are so remote from us and thus outside our power. Their smallness, especially, adds another dimension to the fear they inspire. For instance, the idea that there should exist an animal who would look exactly like a pig—in itself amusing—but is as small as a rat and could emerge snuffling out of a hole in the floor. That is a horrible idea.

For the past few days I have found a quite satisfactory, if only provisional, solution. Overnight I leave the cat in the empty room next to mine, thereby preventing her from dirtying my room. (How hard it is to arrive at an understanding with an animal on this question. There seem to be only misunderstandings, for the cat knows, through blows and other explanations, that there is something undesirable about taking care of her needs of nature, and that the place for it has to be carefully chosen. So what does she do? Well, for example she chooses a spot that is dark, that will in addition show me her affection, and will have other qualities she finds pleasant. But from the human side this spot happens to be the inside of my bedroom slipper. So here is another misunderstanding, and there are as many of these as there are nights and needs of nature.) This also averts the possibility of her jumping into my bed. But I also have the reassurance that I can let her into my room should things get bad. These past few nights have been quiet, at least there were no unequivocal signs of mice. Moreover it does not help one get to sleep to take over a portion of the cat's assignment, and sit upright or leaning forward in bed with pricked ears and glowing eyes. But that was only on the first night. It is getting better now.

I remember the special traps you often used to tell me about, but I suppose they are unavailable now, and besides I wouldn't want to use them. Traps actually lure more and exterminate only the mice that they kill. Cats, on the other hand, drive away mice by their mere presence, perhaps even by their mere excretions, so that these should not be entirely despised. This was particularly striking on the first cat night, which followed the great mouse night. To be sure, the room did not yet become "as still as a mouse," but none of them continued running around. The cat sat in the corner by the stove, depressed by the enforced change of place, and did not stir. But that was enough; it was like the presence of the teacher, there was only some chattering here and there in the mouseholes.

You write so little about yourself, so I retaliate with the mice.

You write: "I am waiting for deliverance." Fortunately your conscious thoughts and your behavior don't completely match. Who these days does not feel "sick, guilt-stricken, powerless" in the struggle with his problem, or rather who does not feel that he is himself a problem which must solve itself? Who can offer deliverance if he is not himself given deliverance? Even Janáček (whose letter my sister would very much like to see) runs around Prague the day of his concert. What is more, you are not self-pitying and these are but momentary discouragements. And I would tell the Talmud story[131] differently: the righteous weep because they thought they had so much suffering behind them and now they see that all that was nothing in comparison to what stretches before them. However the unrighteous—but are there such?

You haven't answered a single word to my letter before last, nor sent me Werfel's address, for which reason I have to ask you to send on my letter to him. I suppose you are responsible for my receiving an invitation from Anbruch?[132]

Franz

To Max Brod
[Postcard. Zürau, beginning of December 1917]
Dearest Max, A good deed. That was the first we heard of it here. I received the news while still in bed and it turned all my morning fantasies upside down. Also two batches from you have recently come in, the second today (*Jüdische Rundschau, Panideal* (a ghastly sheet, quite apart from the cause), *Proscenium* (a rival to *Der Artist*), the Löwit catalogues (may I keep them?), *Aktion, Tablettes, Alžběta* (Janáček's mention of a Leipzig premiere must be a mistake. Doesn't he mean Dresden? What did the *Hudební Revue* say?)).[133] Such a lot. You are in a position to give gifts, we're not. The butter deal has not satisfied us here; a mouth thirsting for kisses can't be pasted shut with a mere banknote. (At this moment I hear from the kitchen, as interruption of a horrid song, the cry of fright: "A mouse!" Keep cool.) A request, Max. *Donauland* has asked me to contribute; there's a postscript by Dr. Körner.[134] I have to answer him but cannot send my answer to the office, especially in view of a printed instruction on the invitation. Frau Fanta must surely know Körner's home address. Please be so kind as to get it for me, but quickly, if you can.

Franz

Won't you be going to the rehearsals in Dresden?

To Max Brod
[Zürau, postmark: December 10, 1917]
Dear Max, A misunderstanding; the mice caused me no sleepless nights except for that first fantastic one. In general perhaps I do not sleep so very well, but on the average my sleep here is at least as good as it ever was in my best times in Prague. As for the "glowing eyes," I only meant that I tried unsuccessfully to give myself cats' eyes that could penetrate the mouse darkness. And now all that is unnecessary, at least for the time being, for a box of sand now collects almost all that the cat formerly strewed over rugs and sofa. Wonderful when one comes to terms with an animal. After having her evening milk, she goes like a well brought-up child to the sandbox, gets into it, hunches up, for the box is too small, and does what she has to. And so at the moment this matter is no longer a worry to me. A "Mouseless Sanatorium": if a place is mouseless, it is also catless, and that is to be sure an impressive phrase, but not so impressive as the word sanatorium, which fails to impress me. So I don't want to go there. My health is consistently good: my appearance satisfactory, I cough less, if possible, than in Prague. There are even days, though I do not

keep count, when I do not cough at all. The shortness of breath to be sure persists; that is to say, it doesn't show up at all in my generally unstrenuous life, doesn't bother me even on my walks, only when I have to talk to someone while walking—that is a strain. But that is a concomitant of the whole condition, and when I mentioned it to Dr. Pick, as well as to Dr. Mühlstein, neither of them took it too seriously. I don't know why the question of a sanatorium should have to be settled just now. It doesn't, but the question of the Institute will have to be, for when I next see Dr. Pick he will want to send me back to the Institute for the winter. But I will not go or else be so endlessly hesitant about going that from the management's window it will look like not going. But none of this is very enjoyable, because they are really very kind to me and certain things cannot be explained to certain people, especially by a certain person.

Second misunderstanding: I am not trying to comfort you by expressing doubts about your illness. How could I doubt it, since I see it. I am only more resolutely on your side than you are, because I feel your dignity, your human dignity, is threatened by the way you are suffering from illness. It is easy to make such a judgment in a calmer period, and you will do the same. But in any comparison between, say, my former state and your present state, distinctions have to be made. If I was desperate, I was not accountable for being so. My sickness and my suffering from being sick were one and the same: that was virtually all I had. But that is not the case with you. The thing to be said in your case is not that there ought not to be, but rather that there must not be, so strong an attack that you yield to it, as you are doing or as you seem to be doing, seem to yourself to be doing (this is what I believe; it's not intended to comfort you but is merely what I believe).

I do not think I could have given you more vital advice than the insignificant, vague things I told you. I wish I could have spent hours sitting with you in your office, listening to you. It was especially nice there. But that would only have given me pleasure and would have nothing to do with the goodness or badness of what you read; it wouldn't have prompted me to offer you any decisive advice, any specifically useful advice. I have never been able to give such advice to anyone, but nowadays I cannot for different reasons. I believe that such advice can only be given in the spirit of that get-a-grip-on-yourself pedagogy, which I see as only more and more impotent. An example out of Foerster[135] comes to mind, although very vaguely, showing how one can unfailingly convince a child not only that every person must shut the door behind him when entering a room, but that this child must shut this door.—I would be utterly at a loss if I had to do this, but then I consider being at a loss toward that sort of thing as right. Certainly it is difficult to train a child to close doors, but it is also senseless, or one might even say it is wrong.

By that I mean: Perhaps it is possible to advise, but it is better not to distract.

Max—I miss you at least no less, but the knowledge that you exist, that I have you, that letters come from you, gives me peace in this respect. Moreover, I know that you have your novel, and that gives you happiness for which there is no need to apologize.

Franz

[IN THE MARGIN] I asked about the invitation from *Anbruch* because I could not understand how otherwise they knew my Zürau address. Then you did tell them?

Please let me know in good time when you are going to Dresden. On account of my trip to Prague.

To Oskar Baum

[Zürau, mid–December 1917]

Dear Oskar, Of course in a few days I will be coming to see you but I must write about this matter, since you have broached it: the only reservation I have had about your visit (except for my first period in Zürau, when perhaps I needed complete solitude in order to solidify certain adjustments) is that you might possibly—and Ottla tries to dissuade me from this—not like Zürau or me or something or other. But should something here give you pleasure, then I will—this is certain—feel this same pleasure twofold. Now no more discussion on this matter.

What I wrote about the mice was only in fun. It would only become serious when you heard the mice. I hardly think any writer or musician can sleep so soundly as not to hear them, or that any sensitive heart could not be overcome, if not by fear, at least by disgust or sadness. But that too is only said in fun, since thanks to the cat I have not heard anything suspicious for quite a while, which means something, since in Prague I won't have the cat and will doubtless hear mice here and there. However, Max has called my attention to a trap that can catch forty mice at one time (I don't know whether it does this all at once or gradually), and it has already been ordered and will be happy here with me. As will you be under its protection.

For the present, this is the most important point. The other important points—for instance, the social conventions of Zürau—are matters we will discuss orally: for instance that the geese have to be force-fed not by a mere hired girl but by a daughter of the house. We'll also discuss your novel, which has resisted coming so that I'll probably have to go and fetch it and the three of us will read it here.

To Josef Körner

[Zürau; postmark: December 17, 1917]

Dear Herr Doktor,

You were once kind enough to come to see me in the office in order to discuss D.[136] with me. At that time I said I would send a contribution to the magazine, but sent nothing. (However you said you would send me your piece on Arnim,[137] but didn't send it either.) Then your article[138] in D. appeared and the passage concerning me heaped praise on me beyond all imaginable limits. This produced in me an orgy of vanity but also an anxious feeling of having seduced you. And now your invitation has come.

You will surely allow me to speak frankly: D. strikes me as an unmitigated lie. It can have the best people connected with it, its literary department can be run, as you will no doubt run it, with vigor and the best of intentions. But the impure cannot be made pure, especially when it inevitably must go on pouring impurities from its source. By this I do not mean to say anything against Austria, against militarism, against the war, for it is not any of these that repels me in D., but rather the special mixture, the studied and outrageous mixture, out of which the magazine is concocted.

Do not think, dear Herr Doktor, that I write this way from arrogance. You yourself would surely view it not too differently, were you to view it from the standpoint of Prague civilian life, or from this rustic quiet (I have been here three months, sick, but it is really not so bad). But as an associate of the magazine, though under coercion, you have to take it seriously as an intellectual organ that has been entrusted to you. So you see not the magazine as it is, but your own goodwill which you bring to its service.

For my part, I can imagine only three motives for associating myself with the magazine: first, the thought that you are an editor. But just this should deter me, since I would not like to link you in my memory with the fact that I, on your account, yet voluntarily, should have lent myself to something patently untruthful. There is the further consideration that you would in no way be harmed by my absence from the magazine, since the invitation to join it was prompted by your special kindness toward me and nothing else.

The second thought is that participating in the magazine might have some useful bearing on the question of my military service. But that does not matter in my case, because I am sick.

Thirdly, the thought of a possible remuneration. But at the moment I do not need it and will let the future take care of itself.

Under different circumstances all that I have said might represent quite honorable grounds for my association with the magazine, but as things stand, it is out of the question.

So, dear Herr Doktor, you must now send me your Arnim essay (you said, I think, that you had only one copy, but I will return it promptly) in order to show me that, while you may not entirely accept my arguments, you are not angry with me. That would give me great pleasure.

With cordial regards, yours sincerely, F. Kafka
Zürau, P.O. Flöhau (Bohemia)

To Max Brod

[Zürau, December 18/19, 1917]

Dear Max, I should long since have thanked you for *Esther*,[139] but it reached me on the very worst days—psychologically—for there are such days—I have so far had in Zürau. There is this unrest, this great tide of unrest, which will never cease as long as Genesis is not rescinded. But it is different from your griefs, inasmuch as no one but myself is involved in it, except for that one other person, who possibly, I hope, will gradually cease to feel.

So your affair has advanced in a direction from which I hardly expected more developments.[140] But I still think that the decision here will come neither from the left nor the right, that is, not from the women themselves. For however things may be elsewhere, I do not see you unconditionally loving either one or the other. The negative element in one drives you forth, the negative element in the other drives you back. Perhaps you could decide in favor of Ruth, but between *these* two women you do not act as though you could, or as though it were being asked of you, or as though it were your business to do the deciding. Your weeping does not seem to apply to the woman for whom you are ostensibly weeping. So with the one you weep for the other and vice versa, and although it is certainly not as clear cut as I am putting it here, you probably do not want to settle for either. Could not this be interpreted to mean that you are meant to break with both of them? Naturally this interpretation all too plainly bears my signature.

What women do is superhuman? Certainly. Perhaps only supermanly, but of course that is supernatural enough.

I read *Esther* aloud to Ottla in a single session. (A feat of breath, wouldn't you say?) All in all, the impression I had in Prague was reinforced, that is, my admiration of a large part of the prelude, almost everything that pertained to Haman— A truly long break here, as a result of which I am tearing up the page I started, chiefly because of the interruption. Our Fräulein[141] went to Flöhau today and so brought the mail this evening which would ordinarily not have come until tomorrow morning; most of it your presents, the batch of printed matter, the card, of which there is nothing to be said (Werfel always erupts that way, and if you regard it as good feelings toward me, let it be), the newspaper, and *Selbstwehr,* then a long letter from my supervisor,[142] with whom I am on an extremely friendly footing; he has come here for a visit; and finally, and this was the interruption, a letter from F., who announces her arrival at Christmas, although we had earlier agreed on the senselessness, even the harmfulness, of such a journey. For various reasons not worth listing, then, I shall probably—though I was not due there until after Christmas—be coming to Prague this Saturday, toward evening.

So now back to *Esther,* as best I can after all this.

Admiration of the second act, which moved me greatly, and the whole section on the Jews. All my objections to petty details, which you know, remain, since I can still justify them to my own satisfaction.

On the other hand I knew from the start that the play would read differently here than in the midst of the commotion of Prague. The result however is that I think I understand it less well, even while I am the more struck by the play's importance. By this I mean, I grasped it earlier—the way one might grasp something by its handle—as a work of art, but I did not grasp it in the round and so my comprehension of the play was faulty. Perhaps this may be attributed to the basic problem that the play throughout posits something notably untrue: that the three actors Haman, the king, and Esther are one and the same. A triad, as artificial as it is artful, whose meshing parts engender such premises, tensions, insights, and conclusions which only partly—though possibly the greater part—are true, or rather are unconditionally essential to the story of the soul. One example of this, surely an erroneous one because I don't entirely grasp it: Haman and Esther leap up precisely at the same time, on the same evening. In fact, there is something marionettelike concealed within that, within the whole play. (For example in the despair of the last act, which I forgot when I gave you my list of passages.) Also that Haman sits looking on for seven years at the king's table is very fine but very inhuman. But would they really have made their first appearance on this evening? The king already has a critical stretch of life behind him; he has sinned, suffered, overcome himself, yet lost. Perhaps all that lies on a plane lower than the present events. But then again perhaps, seen from the highest vantage point, it is all quite the same. At any rate, it would not have been possible without Haman and Esther. The repeated visits to the grotto almost suggest that. In a general way, of course, the king in the first act knows and understands the scene where everything unfolds, just as if it were an old play that has already taken place. And in the farewell conversation in the last act, more is discussed and lamented, though with a certain opaqueness, than merely the events of the play. But if too little is said in the exposition of these scenes, what has been stored up is discharged in the history of the millennia in the second act.

The result is, I think, that certain wrong tracks are followed. Even though they may strengthen the play as a work of art, they are hard going, and I for one cannot follow them. If I look at the matter closely, in fact, there is something in me that refuses to take these wrong tracks because they represent a sacrifice to art, and are harmful to you. I mean: harmful to you in something like the way a tripartite division of your nature takes place in your novel (as you recently wrote) and each separate part pities and consoles the other. What results here, perhaps, is a harmful antithesis between art and true humanity. In the former a certain poetic justice is required. For that reason you carry the king—concerning whom, in truth, the decision was made long ago—on to the end and beyond the end into the future. The same striving for poetic justice makes you show Esther, who after all is sustaining the world, as proceeding alongside Haman insignificantly and ignorantly. She has to be that way, of course, but within the perspective of the play her being so takes on a different meaning. She, the immutable, changes her nature when he is killed. And in the realm of true humanity, on the other hand, all you demand is resoluteness.

Too late and too much. We'll see each other soon, after all. Though I admit I am even more helpless in talking about these matters than in writing about them.

Franz

[IN THE MARGIN] Trap already ordered.—Yes, address of *Anbruch* from Fuchs; he wrote me about the "wretched *Anbruch*" which he had asked to send me an invitation to contribute. I long ago informed those people—in all sincerity, because I liked the circular letter—that I would not contribute.

To Elsa Brod

[Zürau,] December 19, 1917

Dear Frau Elsa, I write on the spur of the moment. The moment afterward I might not write, and the moment after that not send the letter. Hence this letter is fundamentally mistaken and cannot measure up to that store of human knowledge which is basically yours.

If we, dear Frau Elsa, want to discuss Max, we must first take care to be on the same plane. We must therefore speak only as Max's friends, only as friends, and must leave everything else aside, matters that I will not venture to touch, even if you should, in the error of the moment, try to draw my hand toward them. But as his friends we are not his doctors, not his teachers, nor his judges, but only fellow human beings at his side who are fond of him.

As such, I feel, we must not influence him, where his whole life is concerned, by advice, by suggestions, by insinuations, but only by that which comes most natural, that is to say by our beings, by love, kindness, restraint, friendship. You too have done this, as I have often seen and been greatly moved by it. But of course you have also done more, which is to say less, just as all of us do; for what I said above is meant only as an ideal. Recently I too have tried to give him advice, once in your presence, I think, advice that perhaps was not exactly as you would like it but was certainly not directed against you. That advice, however, was given against my own will, wrested from me by Max's appearance, from which you, who are constantly in his presence, must suffer incomparably more, to the very limits of your strength. I can well understand that, here I understand unreservedly. However the truth remains that while one can try to hold Max back when one sees him in danger of stumbling over a stone, it is not permissible to knock him over—assuming, which is quite unlikely, that one would be able to do so—in order to stop him from rushing into what one thinks will be bad for him. For me to try to advise him in this realm would be like my reproaching him for not having long ago advised me to contract tuberculosis.

In the light of this conviction, the errors of your letter become clear to me, though I do not, let me repeat, ascribe the errors to you. For this reason I also should not keep your letter, and am herewith sending it back. These errors are approximately as follows: Your grief springs from love. But you have the true opportunities of love. You are looking for an advocate. But Max, when he is clearheaded, is your strongest advocate. You see (or at least you let your eyes drift that way) a possibly remote incidental as the main thing. You grow confused and thereby neglect to be calmly what you are.

In the tone of your own letter, you might now think: "It is very easy to spout principles at someone in distress." And you would be right, and every time I think about you, this feeling shames me. But should shame make us keep silent or even lie? Especially in this, where we are both at one in our concern for Max.

Franz K

To Felix Weltsch

[Zürau, December 20, 1917][143]

Dear Felix,

If only you had come! You could have come here simply for a haven (not just to see me or Zürau—that would not have been enough) and everything I am and have in Zürau (whatever there is "of mice and men") would unreservedly have been at your disposal.

I do not really believe that such irritation is necessary for work. That craving for a haven essential for work has already been provided for by the universal ancient miracle of the rib, and the expulsion which followed from that.

I would not have thought it would be so hard to find a place for a girl. Evidently the difficulty is part of her malediction, which she by the way—I wouldn't want to give you the wrong impression—bears very cheerily. Perhaps we will find something together, for in all likelihood I am coming to Prague the day after tomorrow. If I had my own way, I would come later, but F. is coming.

Franz

I'm very pleased to hear about the contract with Wolff.[144]

To Max Brod
[Prague, end of December 1917]
Dear Max, Here are the manuscripts—my only copies—for your wife. Don't show them to anyone. Please have copies made at my expense of "The Bucket Rider" and "An Old Manuscript" and send them to me—I need them for Kornfeld.[145]

I am not enclosing the novels.[146] Why stir up the old struggles? Only because I haven't burned them yet? (A letter has just come from F.[147]—she thanks me for *Esther* and asks whether she should thank you.) Next time I see you, I hope it will have been done. What is the point of saving such "even" artistically misbegotten works? Because one hopes that these fragments will somehow combine to form my whole, some court of appeals upon whose breast I shall be able to throw myself when I am in need? I know it is not possible, that no help comes from there. So what should I do with these things? Since they cannot help me, am I to let them harm me, as they must, in view of this knowledge? The city saps me, otherwise I would not have said I would bring the manuscripts.

A brief note about last night: the way the matter presents itself to me, who do not suffer the real pain, is something like this: in her chief reproach your wife has perhaps touched on something more essential than you in yours.

It is too late, I must still go to the office. I will be writing you from Zürau very soon. Perhaps it is just as well today of all days not to be acting as an intermediary between you two.

Franz

One more request: Would you send me the military registration forms which I believe have to be filled out in January.

1918

To Max Brod

[Postcard. Zürau, beginning of January 1918]

Dear Max, Today I write only as Oskar's[1] secretary, in happy irresponsibility:

"So you can now appoint the day for reading the final section of your novel[2] to me and Felix. After the promising beauties Franz has told me about, I am even more eager than before. I'll be back on Sunday, so from Monday on, every evening is free. Perhaps you'll drop me a card when you have made arrangements with Felix. I don't want to tell you how lovely and peaceful it is here, in case you should not have the opportunity to follow my example." Recently when I read aloud the Troeltsch article[3]—this is me, Franz, who will shortly be writing to you at greater length—it occurred to me that the affirmative conclusion of your novel actually points to something simpler and more obvious than I at first thought, that is the building of a church, an asylum, something of that sort, which will almost undoubtedly come about and is already rising around us as everything crumbles and in the same tempo.

We are having a nice time with Oskar.

Franz

To Max Brod

[Zürau, probably January 13, 1918]

Sunday

Dearest Max, I didn't write while Oskar was here, partly because I am so used to being alone (not to silence but to being alone) that I could hardly write, partly because he would soon be telling you about Zürau himself. He assumed a greater distinctness for me in some respects; a pity that one is not strong enough perpetually to show a distinct face toward distinctness. No doubt your judgment of Oskar has on the whole been more accurate than mine, but you seem to have gone wrong on certain details. Many passages in the novel[4] are amazing. Up to now I have felt there was too much superficiality in Oskar's new technique. That is not so. Rather, there is truth here, but it beats against the far-flung and yet too narrow limits and the result is weariness, error, weakness, rhetoric. I would be very glad if Zürau had helped him somewhat, though I doubt it—glad both for his sake and mine. Perhaps you'll write me about it.

Thank you for the *Tablettes*, *Aktion*, and the blanks.

May I make a present of *Tablettes* to F. this time?

Our last evening together wasn't good; I would have liked to hear from you since. The evening wasn't good because I (at a loss, of course, but I'm used to that) saw you at a loss, which I find almost unbearable, even though I try to explain this haplessness by the following: that when one's old yoke is being shaken for the first time and is obviously being moved, one cannot immediately fall into the proper step. So your pacing the room was uncertain, while you were saying uncertain things. And it seemed to me that your wife had more right on her side, as perhaps wives in general have always had more right, in recompense for other things. The charge that you are not fit for marriage sounds valid, at least from her lips. If you object that that is precisely why you suffer, she can answer that you had no right to make her suffer on that account, since that is not her trouble. To which you can answer that she is a woman and suffering is her business. But in so doing you transfer the matter to so high a court that it will never deliver a verdict, but let the trial begin again from the beginning.

She sees this unfitness for marriage, and I too see it with her (no, I will not side with your wife completely, she probably sees it differently), as consisting in this: that you need marriage, but only in part, while the other part of your nature draws you away from it and also tugs at your husbandly side, and so uses it in spite of itself to shatter the foundation of marriage. Of course you married with your whole being, but your eyes continued to be fixed on the distance, in keeping with that division of your nature. At first, you forced yourself to squint, which really would not do. Thus, for example, you married your wife—and along with her and beyond her, wedded literature. Thus, for example, you would now marry someone else, and along with her and beyond her, Palestine. But these are impossibilities, although they may be necessary. A true husband—so the theory might go—would on the contrary be wedding the whole world in his wife, but not in such a way that he would see the world to be married beyond his wife, but would see his wife through the world. Anything else means torment for the wife, but would perhaps mean the salvation or the possibility of salvation for the husband, just as much as in that ideal marriage.

                                                                    Franz

To Felix Weltsch

                                                        [Zürau, January 1918]

Dear Felix, I hope the business worked out well. I felt quite sad in your office, for you had already left, and sick as I am, I was completely exhausted after walking over there, which I did in the hope that you would revive me. To make matters worse, a stern man in the next office was stern with me. But if that piece of business turned out well, I hope the benefits will make up for all that.

However, the business opportunities here are much better, though it means being on the spot. Couldn't you come down here for a few days on this pretext? There is a bed for you. My sister, who saw you recently, thinks that you are not looking well. A few days here might do something about that, too. Of course the invitation also applies to your wife, and though at the moment I don't know of any suitable accommodations, something probably can be found. How about it?

Warmly, Franz

How are things with Robert Weltsch?

To Oskar Baum

[Zürau, mid-January 1918]

Dear Oskar, First my thanks for the magnificent gift. When I consider that all you received in return for your beautiful and altruistic piano-playing was the pleasure of hearing me talk to Herr R. (I would gladly have passed on your message to him, but I didn't understand it)—while I, on the other hand, had the privilege of seeing Ottla unexpectedly take these two surprises out of her suitcase, earned only by my desire—then it seems to me, not for the first time, that something is amiss with the world. The raspberry syrup, especially, pure pleasure from the first drop to the last. Greedy as I am, I almost spoiled it, in my impatience pushing the cork back into the bottle. But Ottla saved it for me and goes on saving it every day by not having any herself. And the juice has still another virtue, for because it is something noble, it even dispels greed, and now I drink it in the spirit of freedom and because it is there and because it reminds me of your goodness toward me.

Here nothing has changed, which is as it ought to be, except that you are gone. So when you come back everything will be entirely as before, you have only to come. Only that I, perhaps to fend off any suggestion that I am a lucky fellow, have in the last few days been droopier than usual, but that is only the ups and downs of the times.

But you were a lucky fellow, for you were spared the mice. Some three days after you left—I no longer take the cat into my room—noise woke me up in the night. My first thought was that it must be the cat after all, until it became clear that it was a mouse, who, impudent as a young child, was playing with the trap—that is, it carefully plucked away at the bacon while the trap's door clattered up and down without opening wide enough for the mouse to fall through. This trap, recommended by Max in such good faith, is more alarm clock than trap. By the way, the next night the bacon was stolen out of another trap also. I hope you aren't thinking that I, half asleep, go creeping under the sideboard to take the bacon myself. Besides, all this has quieted down in the last few days.

So the Sicilian singer didn't care for the *Diary*.[5] Is that surprising or does it not rather reveal a certain deficiency of feeling and good sense? Feeling and good sense were lacking in giving her the book to review; one might as well have given it to Countess Tolstoy. What would a woman say, when she suddenly enters the diary, still all heated up from the tennis game she has been playing beneath the count's windows. "Conservatism is always harmful to art" is practically a quotation from the *Diary* itself, for we have read it.

How was Krastik when he arrived in Prague with you? And what about your book of dramatic stories?[6] Has Wolff written? What about your sleep?

With cordial regards to you and your wife, Franz

To Max Brod
[Zürau, middle or end of January 1918]

Dear Max, Your letter was especially important to me this time (once again, quite apart from its content—I have often said this before and feel it very clearly) because I have lately had two or three bad experiences—or perhaps only one—which have so increased my permanent bewilderment as though I were, for instance, in the last class of gymnasium and were suddenly, through some educational decree whose basis was beyond my ken, demoted to the first grade of elementary school. And yet—please understand me rightly—these were only relatively bad experiences, whose good aspects I appreciate and can rejoice in and have done so. But within the limits of that "relatively" they are, I must say, "absolutely" bad.

The principal such experience was Oskar's visit. While he was here I did not have the slightest grasp of the real nature of the thing, or perhaps just a little during the final day, but this was only the usual feeling of weakness, of tiredness, which always manifests itself between two people more explicitly than within an individual. All week long we had been jolly, perhaps too jolly, after we had mulled over Oskar's problem until we were wearied. In any case I seem to weary more easily than anyone in my acquaintance. But this is not the place to talk of that, and if I were to go into it here I would have to delve into the history of old sufferings.

Oskar's problem doesn't exactly fit into this context. But you asked me about it and until now I have only mentioned it in a general way, since it was only recently entrusted to me. not so much as a secret but as a confession. In addition I did not want you to have these thoughts in your mind the next time you saw Oskar. And finally because it was not really essential, since you were already pretty close to the truth. The problem has, if one wants to put it this way, three aspects (but for the present let's really keep it our secret) but becomes even more complex when regarded more closely. First, for a host of reasons which he has analyzed endlessly, Oskar cannot bear his marriage. He has been married, I believe, for seven years and has been in this state of mind for five. Secondly, though he always begins by saying how impossible his wife is, it turns out under questioning that she is a good sexual match for him and that he finds her within her limits very lovable. The impossibility of his marriage really comes down to the impossibility of marriage in general. Granted, an undissolved residue remains; it is typified by an unfinished novella of his on the subject of his marrying a series of women and girls of his acquaintance, all of which marriages also prove to be totally impossible. Thirdly—and here the great uncertainties begin—he might be able to leave his wife, for though he feels this step as a great cruelty, he believes he has sufficient tangible and intangible justification for it. But he cannot take the guilt upon himself because of his son, though not really from paternal emotions. Nevertheless he knows that separation is the only right thing to do and that in evading it he will never have a sense of peace. Taken all in all, with his wealth of "secular" projections and incubi (we slept in the same room and exchanged the germs of disease for incubi), with his sufferings which I cannot sympathize with nearly enough, he is a close cousin of Dr. Askonas,[7] as the latter is representative of our West European Judaic age. In this sense, that is in the sociological sense, the novel is a magnificently candid statement, and will, if I am right, truly reveal itself only when it affects a wide audience. Perhaps it is no more than such a statement, such a reflection of the times, but that too is a grand enterprise. During our first few nights we spoke about the novel as if it were a historical document that was being used to provide evidence of this or that. Of course it was that way with *Nornepygge*[8] also, but at the time I was not sufficiently affected by it.

As for my attitude to Oskar's problem, it was very simple, or at least I meant it to be so. In spite of my settled opinion, which may have been nothing but prejudice, I vacillated with his vacillations; I said yes and no when I thought I heard yes and no, so that all I really did was this interpreting. It was enough to influence him for good or ill, and it is just this that I would like to hear you comment on. Besides, Zürau acted as an influence partly in spite of my intentions, and along with Zürau what has happened to me here up to now. Other influences were Troeltsch and Tolstoy, whom I read to him.

But all this reacted upon me, as I only afterward realized. I had halfway passed the test of the visit, but afterward, when the bell had already rung, I found I had flunked. I have just written Oskar that it is hard to adjust to his absence after a week together and that we miss him. That is true, at least as far as I am concerned, but it is true only in conjunction with the week together and this is not the whole story. I am still feeling the effects of having been with this person, dear as he is to me, but not in the sense that I agonize over his agonies, or that any specific suffering of my own has been stirred up. Rather it is that in an almost totally abstract way, the direction of his thought, the basic desperateness of his condition, the laying bare of the insolubility of his conflict, the confusion of his fundamentally senseless, self-damaging, self-mirroring defense mechanisms—a technical term from your novel—piled one atop the other, have all been pouring into me as into the stagnant loop of a river which in a single week has been filled with living waters.

What gigantic strength is necessary, what gigantic strength and prepara-tory solitude, not to succumb to a person with whom one has walked awhile among alien-familiar demons, no less their prey than their proper owner.

I am exaggerating a little here; there are certainly other elements. But the basic truth remains. Moreover, partly as a consequence of the visit I started reading *Either/Or*,[9] with a special craving for help, the evening before Oskar's departure, and am now reading Buber's most recent books,[10] sent by Oskar. Hateful, repellent books, all three of them. To put it correctly and precisely, they are written—*Either/Or* especially—with the sharpest of pens (almost the whole of Kassner[11] comes rolling ponderously out of *Either/Or*), but they drive you to despair. And as can happen when you are reading passionately, you occasionally have the unconscious feeling that they are the only books in the world, and even the healthiest lungs feel short of breath. Of course this statement requires an elaborate explanation; it's only my present state that permits me to talk this way. They are books that can be written as well as read only if one has at least a trace of real superiority to them. As things are, their hatefulness grows under my hands.

In regard to your problem, you don't convince me. I wonder whether you are not misunderstanding me and whether we may possibly have already met at some point without knowing it? I am not saying that you married your wife for the sake of literature, but in spite of literature, and that because you *also* had to have an honest reason for marrying, you have tried to wipe out this "in spite of" by persuading yourself that you entered into a literary commonsense marriage, a "marriage of convenience." You introduced "commonsense reasons" into the marriage because you were unable to marry wholeheartedly with the usual bridegroom's emotions. And the situation seems to me rather the same right now. It seems that you are not vacillating between two women, but between marriage and outside-of-marriage. The woman is supposed to be a steadying force without hurting either one of the two elements; that is the meaning of your wish for a woman to "take the lead." But aside from the question of whether this conflict can be solved at all at one blow, perhaps it is not woman's task to solve it, but your task, and this effort to shift the burden involves a kind of guilt.

So in a sense this guilt continues into what you no longer call guilt, or more correctly what you still call guilt but to which you add the name of kindness. Certainly you are softhearted, but this is no place to prove it. You remind me of a surgeon who has been suffering pangs of conscience on behalf of principle rather than on behalf of the organism, which bears the guilt of sickness. He has bravely cut and slashed, but now he hesitates to make the final incision—hesitates out of softheartedness and also out of sadness, because then he must bid goodbye to this important case forever ("my wife, without breaking the secondary, intellectual ties with me, would have to . . ."). Yet this final cut is precisely the decisive one that may save the patient, may cause further illness, or may kill.

I haven't read *The Sunken Bell*,[12] but from what you say I assume the conflict is yours, but can see only two persons caught in it, for the one in the mountains is not a human being.

And Olga? She has not been created in her own right, but is deliberately intended as Irene's[13] counterfoil, as a salvation from Irene.

But aside from all that, the vision you have, and have with such certainty— "calm, complete peace in eros"—is something so tremendous that you can't really swallow it; which fact should prove how untenable it is. I'd have some belief in it only if you called it by a less fancy name. But—and here I revert to my opinion—because you do give it that name, it's likely to indicate a different conflict.

What Werfel said was surely only said by the bye, and he isn't so constituted that where other people react with despair, say, he reacts with anger. But still it is significant; he is tacitly referring to the moment of the poem, just as you and I and all of us do; it's as if there were something here that we are obliged to refer to, rather than something we really should try to divert our gaze from whenever we are called to account. Incidentally, there is also something brotherly and revealing in that "only empty days are unendurable"; it hardly fits in with that anger.

Franz

I enclose "Message."[14] Thanks for *Tablettes*.

To Josef Körner

[Zürau, end of January 1918]

My dear Herr Doktor,

I would never have thought that *Donauland* could have given me such pleasure. Only yesterday morning I had a reverie about what it would be like if I were to receive the Arnim piece and along with it a letter running approximately thus and thus. And then it actually came. Many thanks.

What you say about Oskar Baum is quite right; the more that can be done for him, the better. Wouldn't it be possible—I ask although this probably does not lie within your editorial province—to ask Dr. Felix Weltsch (university librarian) to be a contributor? He would be in a position to collaborate in a wide variety of ways that would be a credit to D. Wolff will shortly be publishing his *Organic Democracy;*[15] he has also had a share in the second volume of Hiller's *Ziel.*[16] Of course these pieces would not be suitable for D., but a good many other things would be.

The essay on Arnim is very subtle and truthful; not everyone could have maintained that tone to the end, certainly not without love and broad insight. You know, there is really a fantastic mixture of slackerism and bellicosity in Arnim; he has literally been standing in full armor behind the door all these years, and is still standing there. The arrangement of the quotations provides a good defense without sounding too slanted. The fundamental conflict, and the anguish thereof, comes from the fact that there are not only two kinds of truth, but three: it is necessary to offer one's life, it is even more necessary to spare one's life, and it is still more necessary to lay down one's life. Arnim, too, did not go beyond that, and his view of himself will not get any better with the passage of time. I would, however, have written the passage about marriage differently on the basis of his idea: "War is like marriage, sad, but in ways different from what the bachelor fears."

The article has one fault—and that leads to your question about Wolff—that it is written out of too great knowledge which naturally cannot be properly presented there. While certainly not hopeless, it would be difficult to publish it, particularly just now, when the paper shortage is especially bad and Wolff is taken up with many matters outside of publishing, and is deeply concerned with his latest project, "Der Neue Geist."[17] At the moment I am out of touch with him, and my last letter, in response to an urgent one of his, has gone unanswered for some four months. But it might still be possible. In this connection I recall that Wolff is himself a literary scholar. I believe he edited Merck's writings for Insel Verlag and a study of Eulenberg in the Bonn Seminar Series.[18] So he can be approached in terms of literary scholarship, especially with so relevant a figure as Arnim. He would probably turn down the idea of publishing the collected works; that would not be in his line, but an edition of the letters with an introductory essay might be. In fact he recently brought out Lenz's correspondence.[19] Perhaps your project would tie up with that. You might read this correspondence, which I myself am looking forward to eagerly, and do an article about it for *Donauland*. A better way to initiate negotiations with Wolff (and a more dignified one), I could not imagine. One has to shout if one wants to be heard by such a publisher who is besieged by authors. I would be very glad if this succeeded.

Most cordially yours, Dr. Kafka

To Felix Weltsch

[Picture postcard. Zürau, end of January 1918][20]
Dear Felix, Six to eight degrees below freezing, sleeping with open windows, washing up early, breaking the layer of ice in the pitcher, ice which will form again in the washbowl, standing quite naked, of course, and after a week still not a trace of a cold, after having become accustomed to the stove going day and night; you must have a try at this. But it is really wonderful; you'd find you can easily sacrifice a week in the library for it. I will tempt you a lot more when we talk. Warmest regards to Oskar. There is even a piano here, Frau Irma!

Everything officially corroborated by the Sanatorium Director and Chief Invalid:

Franz

To Kurt Wolff Verlag

[Zürau, January 27, 1918]
Dear Sirs,

Enclosed I am returning the proofs. May I ask you to kindly take note of the following: The book is to consist of fifteen short tales; some time ago I indicated their order in a letter to you. I do not exactly recall this order at the moment, but "A Country Doctor" did not come first, but second; the first story was "The New Advocate." In any case, may I ask that you arrange the stories in the order I indicated. May I further ask that a dedication page

inscribed "To My Father" be inserted. I have not yet received the proof of the
title page, which should read

A Country Doctor
Short Tales

Very truly yours, Dr. Kafka

Please send me a copy of the Lenz correspondence, charging it to me at
author's discount.

To Max Brod

[Zürau; postmark: January 28, 1918]

Dear Max, Since no answer has come from you, I will add only this about
your affair: I too believe that woman takes the lead, as for example she
demonstrated in the Garden of Eden—where as usually happens she was ill
rewarded for doing so. Your own wife, for example, is in this sense the leader,
by virtually leading you over her own body to the other woman. Her
holding on to you after leading you to this fits into another category and
perhaps only then has she fully taken the lead. You are right in saying that
the deeper realm of real sexual life is closed to me; I too think so. That is why
I avoid judging this aspect of your case, or confine myself to the statement
that this fire, which you consider sacred, has not the strength to burn away
those resistances whose basis I now understand. I don't know why you ascribe
the meaning you do to the case of Dante, but even if it were so, the case is
quite different from yours, at least as yours has developed so far. His girl died,
but you are making yours die, by feeling obliged to renounce her. By the
way, Dante also renounced his girl after his own fashion, and chose to marry
someone else, which does not fit in with your interpretation.

But come, just come, so you can disabuse me of all this. Only you must
telegraph beforehand in good time so we can meet you and so that your visit
should not coincide with my departure (if I should have to report to the
military about the middle of February). I should also like to avoid your visit's
overlapping a visit of my brother-in-law, who is due at the beginning of
February, though it now occurs to me that I needn't do anything about it,
since he will surely not be coming on a Sunday, as you will. So if you
telegraph beforehand, February is all clear, and if Ottla were here (she is in
Prague now and will probably look you up on Monday but won't find you,
because of your lecture trip) she would not be able to list enough (enough for
her) enticements to lure you here.

You leave, if you cannot leave by Saturday morning (but in that case you might just as well leave Friday afternoon), after two o'clock on Saturday from the Staatsbahnhof and at half past five you will be at Michelob, where we will be waiting for you with the horses. (The round trip can no longer be fitted into Sunday: since January 1 the morning express train no longer stops at Michelob.)

Thank you very much for the copies of the manuscripts (although I no longer need them, at least not for Kornfeld,[21] since I have found another solution) and the big batch of printed matter. Also my thanks for having reminded Wolff of me. It is so much pleasanter to have this done through you than to remind him myself (providing that you don't find it unpleasant), because he can then be frank when he doesn't want something or other, whereas otherwise, at least this is my impression, he does not speak frankly, at least not in letters. Face to face he is much more candid. I have already received proofs of the book.

Since Ottla is not likely to reach you to ask you this (she will be returning here Monday afternoon)—the Writers' Association[22] informs me of an unauthorized reprinting of "Report to an Academy" in an Austrian morning newspaper and requests permission to collect on my behalf a fee of thirty M. (of which they would keep 30%). Shall I consent? The twenty marks would be very welcome to me for, say, more Kierkegaard. But this association is a dirty business, so is collecting, and the newspaper might be the Jewish *Österreichische Morgenzeitung*. So should I consent? Could you order the issue for me through Wltschek[23] (it must be a Sunday edition, either in December or January)?

By way of thanks for this, may I quote you a sentence from an appeal for the Frankenstein Sanatorium,[24] since I have no one else to share my delight:

A Herr Artur von Werther, a captain of industry, delivered a major speech at the first meeting of the board of directors at Frankenstein. Apparently he wanted to see his words in print and offered it to the institution for use as a leaflet. It is a better example of this type than most, with fresher and more artless language, etc. Recently in Prague I contributed the final paragraph. This is turn seems to have stimulated revisions and additions on his part and now in print I read the following: "Laboring long years in the vineyards of practical life, my philosophy, untrammeled by visionary theories, sounds its ultimate note in the perception: Being healthy, working efficiently and successfully, honorably acquiring a modest fortune for ourselves and our families, leads humanity to contentment on earth."

[IN THE MARGIN] Please, Max, ask Pfemfert[25] in what respects the Rubiner edition of the Tolstoy *Diary* differs from the Müller edition.[26]

To Felix Weltsch

[Zürau, beginning of February 1918]

Dear Felix, Many thanks to you and also of course to Fürth.[27] This way is very good. The project will succeed, as in fact it would have succeeded without any assistance. I offered my help, but said explicitly that I put little store in this help. I shall repeat the offer afterward. And a beneficent, mendacious glitter will remain upon me, even if the project itself fails. What does this mendacity come from?

A great loss for me not to be hearing your lectures, since you apparently are going to address yourself to the most important themes. Couldn't you let me take part in some way? Don't you for instance have a readable draft or outline for the first lecture on Literature and Religion?

Your comments about Zürau on the basis of the picture postcard are quite right. There is an order here, a daily order and a seasonal one, and if one can adjust to that, all is well. The church, too, has some importance. I was recently there for a sermon. It had a businesslike simplicity. The text was Luke 2:41-52, and three lessons were drawn. 1. Parents should not permit their children to play outside in the snow but should bring them into the church (see, all the empty seats!). 2. Parents should be as tenderly concerned for their children as the Holy Family was for their son (and this even though he was the Child Jesus, about whom they did not need to worry). 3. Children should speak as piously to their parents as Jesus did to his. That was all, for it was very cold, but there was a kind of ultimate power in the whole thing. And yesterday, for instance, there was a funeral for a poor man from a nearby village which is even poorer than Zürau, but it was very solemn and could hardly have been otherwise, with the big market square covered with snow. Because of a trench cutting halfway across the square, the hearse could not go straight to the church but had to make a big circle around the goose pond. The mourners—the whole population of the neighboring village—were all standing at the church door while the hearse still continued slowly making its circle at peaceful plowhorse pace, in the van a small band of frozen musicians entwined by a tuba, and in the rear the fire company, our steward among them. And I lay in my reclining chair at the window and watched it all to my edification, simply as a neighbor of the church.

Cordial regards and good luck with the lectures, Franz

To Kurt Wolff

[Zürau, beginning of February 1918]

Dear Herr Wolff,

Many thanks for your note[28] and for the handsome gift of Lenz's letters.

That is a book I wished for long before I knew of your intention to publish it. Your giving it makes it doubly precious.

With cordial regards, yours, F. Kafka

To Felix Weltsch

[Zürau, before February 13, 1918]

Dear Felix, I do have plenty of time, you're right, but free time, in which I can do what I freely wish, that I don't have. You have too high an opinion of me if you think that. The days pass so quickly and even more quickly when, as sometimes happens, one thinks one is losing in a single day all one has sacrificed the preceding days for. But you know this as well as I, and it can be overcome. Still there is not much free time.

Naturally you are now excessively busy. That is clearer to me than to you. Every week, not under the aegis of an official job but solely on your personal responsibility, to step forth before an audience, who insist on their claim to hear fundamentals from you, and whose right to make such a demand you fully grant—there is something grand about that, almost priestly. It has made so strong an impression that I again had a dream about it. This time you were lecturing on some botanical subject (tell this to Professor Kraus).[29] You showed your audience some dandelionlike flower, or rather several of this sort. There were single large specimens, one above the other, reaching from the platform to the ceiling, which were displayed to the audience. I could not understand how you alone managed to do this, with just your own two hands. (Some people dressed for Carnival[30] have just come in—a hideous business—it happens several times almost every evening. It tries the nerves, for the masked figures say not a word in order not to give themselves away; they go around the room as though they owned it, and one has to chat with them and try to appease them.) Then from somewhere in the background or perhaps from the flowers themselves came a light, and they shone. I also noticed various things about the audience but I have forgotten.

You mention nothing about the important matter, the lectures themselves, yet it is those I asked for. But probably you cannot do anything about that now and when the lecture series is over you will send me the entire manuscript. But if you can do anything of the sort sooner, please do.

Whatever bee I am supposed to have put into Oskar's bonnet, the poor fellow had already brought with him aplenty to Zürau. I would be pleased to hear how things are with him, but I am possibly coming to Prague next week[31] (about the army, if it can't be avoided). I have recently had a surprisingly calm letter from Max.

The son of my supervisor has got off. I have been thanked for that, but no one seems to have noticed anything unusual. The boy, who is very grieved at the way it turned out, comforts himself with the thought that he was only rejected because he was one of the last.

I consider myself to be entirely healthy at the moment except for a thumb which I cut while spading a bit in the garden and which will not heal. I am weak; the smallest peasant girl has more working energy than I. Of course that was so in earlier days too, but with all these fields around it becomes more humiliating and sad as well, for it removes all desire to do anything of the sort. And by this roundabout route I come back to the past: I prefer to sit in the armchair at the window and read, or not even read.

Cordial regards, Franz

To Max Brod

[Zürau, mid–February 1918]

Dear Max, Your last letter seemed relatively so tranquil, requiring so little support, and on the other hand so restless, written in spite of the amount of work you are doing (for which I can think of no practical comparison), that I preferred not to answer right off, so as not to be a bother to you. By the way, I will be coming to Prague next week, unless in the meantime a letter to the contrary comes from the Institute. I have to present myself to the military again. Then we will be able to talk about the two matters that I especially missed in your letter: news of Oskar and some news about your visit, for you wrote as though my last letter had not reached you at all.

Dante is all very well, but by every token something else is involved and you coincide with him on a plane of extreme generality. And how easy and essential to coincide on that plane! Recently I found a letter of Vrchlický's[32] telling how in Leghorn, I believe it was, he met an old ragged artisan, who, weeping, recited cantos from Dante.

The acceptance from Königsberg[33] is certainly a great triumph since it is truly one of the foremost literary experimental theaters that is now going to produce you in your quintessential drama. I'm delighted.

We can talk about everything else. At any rate, in Zürau no one is worried about me. People (anonymous authors) have made up rhymes about almost everyone in Zürau. Mine, except for its shaky meter, is most comforting:

The doctor is a goodly man.
God will forgive him all He can.

Warmest regards, Franz

To Max Brod

[Zürau, mid-March 1918]

Dear Max, I am answering immediately, even though it is such a beautiful day. You misunderstand my silence; it was not consideration for you, which would have been better expressed by my renouncing any attempt to answer; it was inability. I began three letters in this long period and dropped them all. It was inability, but not "ennui" in the strict sense of the word. For it was "my affair" which by dint of great effort can be put into words but not communicated—but that makes me all the more incapable of putting it into words. Because I myself can do this simple thing only with great effort, in contrast to the happily-unhappily transported Kierkegaard, who so wonderfully steers the undirigible airship even though to do so is not his primary concern. And to his mind what is not a primary concern ought not to be doable. And my silence also suits the countryside, suits it when I return from Prague (after the last trip[34] I arrived as if I were intoxicated and as if I had come to Zürau to sober up and whenever I was well on the way to sobriety would promptly set out for Prague again, to go on another bender). But the silence also suits the place when I stay on for longer times, always. It happens of its own accord: the stillness keeps impoverishing my world. I have always felt it my special misfortune that I (the symbols taking a physical form) literally do not have the lung power to breathe into the world the richness and variety that it obviously has, as our eyes teach us. Nowadays I no longer take the trouble to try; there is no room for it on my day's schedule, and the day is no darker for my not trying. But making any kind of statement comes even harder, if possible, than it used to and what I do state is almost against my will.

Perhaps I have really lost my way in Kierkegaard; I realize this with astonishment when I read your lines about him. It is in fact just as you say: the problem of arriving at a true marriage is his principal concern, the concern that is forever rising into his consciousness. I see that in *Either/Or*, in *Fear and Trembling*, and in *Repetition*. (I have read the latter in the last two weeks and have ordered *Stages*.)[35] But though Kierkegaard is always in my mind these days, I have truly forgotten this point, so much am I roaming in other fields, even though I never completely lose touch with it. The "physical" similarity to him that I imagined I had after reading that little book *Kierkegaard's Relationship to "Her"* (Insel Verlag[36]—I have it right here, you know, and will send it to you, but it isn't really essential, though it might later serve as corroboration) has by now entirely evaporated. It's as if a next-door neighbor had turned into a distant star, in respect both to my admiration and to a certain cooling of my sympathy. For the rest, I do not dare to say anything definite; aside from the abovementioned books I am familiar only with the last, *The Instant*.[37] And *Either/Or* and *The Instant* are certainly two very different lenses through which one can examine this life forwards or backwards and of course also in both directions at the same time. But either way he certainly cannot be called merely negative. In *Fear and Trembling*, for example—which you ought to read now—his affirmativeness turns truly monstrous and is checked only when it comes up against a perfectly ordinary helmsman. What I mean is, affirmativeness becomes objectionable when it reaches too high. He doesn't see the ordinary man (with whom, on the whole, he knows how to talk remarkably well) and paints this monstrous Abraham in the clouds. But all the same one cannot call him negative on that account (unless at most you're applying to him the terminology of his early books); and who can say all that was involved in his melancholia.

As far as perfect love and marriage are concerned, you two are probably in agreement on the basis of *Either/Or*; only the lack of perfect love makes A. incapable of perfect marriage with B. I still cannot read the first book of *Either/Or* without repugnance.

I understand Oskar's sensitivity (aside from the fact that he shouldn't have been introduced to someone so unpleasant, or at least that's how the person struck him). The whole things seems to him so painful (being urged into something that felt wrong from the start) that he cannot restrict himself to self-torment but must also torment you a little. In this respect I can understand him and also do not regard these matters as inconsequential.

Fortunately I have not yet heard from Pick,[38] would probably politely refuse; it's a temptation that does not lead me astray but that really is a great one. But that should not apply to you. (I have received a friendly invitation from Reiss Verlag;[39] from Wolff nothing has come since the first batch of proofs.)

Liebstöckl's[40] note about you was a nasty outburst of hatred and differed from the rest of the reviews of *Jenufa* in the nastiness of its style. My feeling is that the reply propped him up a bit, since it made the reader aware that such trash as his can be a subject for discussion.

Good luck and many pleasures in Germany.

Yours, Franz

[IN THE MARGIN] Please give my regards to Felix and Oskar; I don't know whether I will get to writing to them in time.

Did you ask Pfemfert about the Rubiner edition of the Tolstoy *Diary?*

What are all these errands, troubles you speak of?

I continue to fret about my relationship to the Institute. I intend to stay on here as long as I can.

Many thanks for the two packages. You are very good to me, only you shouldn't talk about "changing, fading."

To Max Brod

[Zürau, end of March 1918]

Dear Max,

Amazing that things went off so well in Dresden.[41] How did they manage to grasp it—I mean the actors, the theater people. Amazing and splendid. And I can well understand the happiness of having your parents there. Your wife didn't come? Anyhow, those were good days and their goodness can for the time being compensate you for the loss of freedom of will. I say this so flippantly because my eye simplifies to such an extent, to the point of total vacancy, that I have never been able to fix the concept of freedom of the will at a specific point on the horizon as readily as you do. Anyhow you too can hold on to freedom of the will, or at least don't have to give it up for lost, either by temporarily refusing to accept it as a grace, or by accepting it as a grace but regarding it as of no consequence. This sort of freedom of the will remains with us; it is inalienable. And do you really know what you have achieved by the most honest kind of work, over long years? Do you know that the ripples of what you have set in motion will go on spreading endlessly? I say this for you, not for me.

Thanks for interceding with Wolff. Ever since I decided to dedicate the book to my father, I am deeply concerned to have it appear soon. Not that I could appease my father this way; the roots of our antagonism are too deep, but I would at least have done something; if I haven't emigrated to Palestine, I will at any rate have traced the way there on the map. That is why—since Wolff has cut me off, doesn't answer, sends me nothing, though this one is probably my last book—I wanted to send the manuscripts to Reiss, who made such a friendly offer. I wrote to Wolff once more, an ultimatum, which so far hasn't been answered either, but in the meantime a new batch of proofs came some ten days ago, whereupon I called if off with Reiss. But should I after all go elsewhere? Meanwhile I have also received an invitation from Paul Cassirer.[42] How, by the way, does he know my Zürau address?

Have you by any chance also talked with Adler[43] about Kierkegaard? He is no longer so much on my mind, since I have not read his old books for some time (in this lovely weather I have been working in the garden) and *Stages* has not yet arrived. You mention his "carefully thought-out quality" and evidently feel as I do that one must surrender to the power of his terminology, of his conceptual innovations. I think, for instance, of his concept of the dialectical, or his division into "knights of infinity" and "knights of faith," or even the concept of "motion." From this concept one can be carried straight into the bliss of knowing, and even a wingstroke further. Is that altogether original? Are Schelling or Hegel[44] (he studied both of them intensively, if only to oppose them) somewhere in the background?

At any rate the translator has behaved disgracefully. I thought he had made "changes in consideration of the author's youth" only in *Either/Or*;[45] has he now done the same in *Stages?* That is disgusting, especially the feeling of how helpless we are. Yet the German of the translation is not all that bad, and here and there in the Afterword one finds a useful remark. That is because so much light radiates from Kierkegaard that some of it penetrates even to the deepest abysses. But the publisher certainly did not have to summon up these "abysses" to translate Kierkegaard.

I do not see how his having published books ran counter to his basic aim (I don't know *Stages*, but in this sense all his books are compromising, after all). The books are not unequivocal, and even if he does later develop to a kind of unequivocalness, it, too, is only one component of his chaos consisting of mind, sorrow, and faith. His contemporaries may have felt that even more clearly than we do. Besides, his compromising books are pseudonymous, and what is more, their pseudonymous quality is almost of the essence. Taken as a whole, in spite of the wealth of confession in them, they might well pass for perplexing letters by the Tempter[46] himself, written behind clouds. And even if all this were not so, under the softening influence of time, they must have made his fiancée[47] breathe a sigh of relief at having escaped that torture machine whose motor was now merely idling, or which at any rate was only occupied with her shadow. At that price she may well have patiently endured the "tastelessness" of his almost annual publications. And as the best proof of the validity of Kierkegaard's method (to scream in order not to be heard and to scream falsely just in case you are heard), she remained, after all, virtually as innocent as a lamb. Perhaps in this way Kierkegaard succeeded somewhat against his will, or unintentionally, in reaching his tangential path.

Kierkegaard's religious situation doesn't come across to me with the extraordinary clarity it has for you, although your explanation of it strikes me, too, as highly seductive. Simply Kierkegaard's standpoint—before he's even said a word—seems to refute your idea. For as he sees it, the relationship to the divine is primarily not subject to any outside judgment; perhaps this is so much so that Jesus himself would not be permitted to judge how far a follower of his has come. To Kierkegaard that seems to be more or less a question of the Last Judgment, which is to say answerable—insofar as an answer will still be needed—only after the end of this world. Consequently the present external image of the religious relationship has no significance. Granted, the religious relationship wishes to reveal itself, but cannot do so in this world; therefore striving man must oppose this world in order to save the divine element within himself. Or, what comes to the same thing, the divine sets him against the world in order to save itself. Thus the world must be overpowered by you as well as by Kierkegaard, in one place more by you, in another place more by him; these distinctions count only on the overpowered world's side. And the following passage is not from the Talmud: "As soon as a man comes along who has something primitive about him, so that he does not say: One must take the world as it is (this sign that one is a stickleback and therefore not worth catching), but who says: However the world is, I shall stay with my original nature, which I am not about to change to suit what the world regards as good. The moment this word is pronounced, a metamorphosis takes place in the whole of existence. As when the word is spoken in the fairy tale and the palace that has been enchanted for a hundred years opens its gates and everything comes to life: the whole of existence becomes sheer attentiveness. The angels have work to do and look on curiously to see what will happen, for this interests them. On the other side, dark, uncanny demons, who have long sat idle, gnawing their fingers, leap up and stretch their limbs; for, so they say, here there is something for us, for which we have long waited, etc."

Apropos the god of self-torment: "I share the assumptions that Christianity makes (suffering in more than the ordinary measure and guilt of a special sort) and I find my refuge in Christianity. But to proclaim it imperiously or directly to others—this I cannot properly do, for I cannot provide them with the assumptions."

Apropos Freud (concerning the observation that Jesus was always healthy): "To lead a truly spiritual life while remaining in perfect health physically and psychically—this no man can do."

If you say he is no example, you mean, no ultimate example. Certainly, no human being is.

Franz

To Max Brod

[Zürau, beginning of April 1918]

My dear Max, Was my letter so very impersonal? Hard to understand in connection with Kierkegaard, easy to understand in regard to me. Realize also that this is a time for bidding goodbye to the village; in Prague they are taking the best line they can (assuming they want to keep me); they hold their peace, are patient, pay, and wait. It isn't easy to endure this, and next month I might be back on the job in Prague.

Thanks for the letters, which I enclose. Pick's letter is not one of the bad consequences of the war, although it is plain that your previous letter, which I haven't seen, leads him by the hand; in addition some of his major misgivings remain unclear to him, which need not be so. For the rest, I repeatedly have the same experience: the test of the writer is in his works; if they harmonize, all is well; if their disharmony is beautiful or melodic, all is also well; but if there is a clashing disharmony, it is bad. I don't know whether such principles are valid; I'd gladly disclaim them if I could; a world is conceivable to me that is governed by a living idea, a world in which art has the place it deserves, which in my experience it never has had. (In the meanwhile I went with the mare to a village called Schaab to visit the stallion; now it is already too cold in the room, but very warm here in the garden in a half-finished cucumber bed. Goat manure, which Ottla has just carted over, is prickling my nose.) I mean: An analysis such as would be a prerequisite to the application of those principles cannot possibly be undertaken upon us; we always remain integral (in this sense). When we write something, we have not coughed up the moon, whose origins might then be investigated. Rather, we have moved to the moon with everything we have. Nothing has changed; there, we are what we were here. A thousand differences are possible in the tempo of the voyage, none in the fact itself. The earth, which has shaken off the moon, has since held itself more firmly, but we have lost ourselves for the sake of a homeland on the moon. Not finally, there is nothing final here, but still we're lost. For that reason I cannot sympathize with your distinction between will and feeling in regard to the work (or perhaps only because of the nomenclature you use; and besides, by way of reservation, I am really speaking only for myself, therefore ranging too far, but cannot help it, have no other horizon). Will and feeling—everything is always, and rightly so, present as a living whole; nothing can be separated out (amazing, without realizing it I am arriving at a conclusion like yours); the only separation that can be made, the separation from the homeland, has already taken place, can be observed by any critic with his eyes closed, but he can never evaluate its differences, which anyway are insignificant in the face of infinity. Therefore any criticism that deals in concepts of authentic and inauthentic, and seeks to find in the work the will and feelings of an author who isn't present—any such criticism seems to me nonsensical and follows only from the critic's also having lost his homeland. And since everything is all of a piece, of course I mean: having lost his conscious homeland.

Königsberg will represent an even greater test of the theater and the audience. All my good wishes go with you there, Max.

Franz

Your mention of Ehrenfels[48] made a great impression upon me. Could you lend me the book? By the way, the books I ordered haven't come. Nobody is delivering anything.

To Felix Weltsch

[Zürau, end of April 1918][49]

Dear Felix,

A renewal of contact: one last greeting from Zürau, the next in Prague. To you I do not have to apologize. You have surely understood my silence or at least had an inkling of what it was about, and I understand it no better. I do not feel like writing or even talking. I have thought a great deal about you, not only in connection with *Frieden* and the *Rundschau*.[50]

Until we meet, Franz

To Johannes Urzidil

[Prague, spring 1918]

Dear Herr Urzidil,

Many thanks for your kind invitation and the copy of your magazine[51] but I must ask you not to expect any contribution from me, at least for the present, since I have nothing I could publish.

With cordial regards, F. Kafka

To Felix Weltsch

[Picture postcard (Rumburk). Probably fall 1918][52]

This summer has taught me something, Felix; I will never enter a sanatorium again. Now, when I am beginning to be really sick, I will never again enter sanatoria. Everything topsy-turvy. Your sister left today. I wanted to wait on the road for her wagon to pass and give her flowers, but delayed too long with the gardener, missed the wagon, and can now decorate my room with the flowers.

Warm regards to you and your wife, Franz

To Max Brod

[Picture postcard (Turnau,[53] Bohemia). Postmark: September 27, 1918]

Dear Max, Thank you for the letter and your caution. Your Hebrew[54] is not bad; there are a few mistakes at the beginning, but once you get into it, you make no errors. I learn nothing, seek only to hold on to what I know, nor would I have it otherwise. I spend the whole day in the garden. I copied your remarks about the novel for Dr. W.[55] to give him a little pleasure (not altogether unalloyed). He thinks highly of your judgment.

I look forward to seeing you Monday after next. Regards to Felix and Oskar.

Yours, Franz

To Felix Weltsch

[Turnau, September 1918]

Dear Felix, First of all, information derived from a talk with the sensible young manageress here and from my own experience: the chances of finding anything in the vicinity are extremely slim, for the country hotels will soon be shutting down, if they have not done so already, or have not even opened. So your sister would feel very lonely here in late fall or winter, even if a most unlikely opening should turn up (which could only happen on the basis of extremely close personal realtionships). Besides, all these hotels are said to suffer from great shortages (even of coal), whereas in Turnau itself some supplies still come through.

These considerations all point to my hotel, which I thought of right off, and the manageress has at least not been discouraging. Merits of the hotel: good management, remarkable cleanliness, and in my opinion excellent cuisine. Disadvantages, but not of this hotel only: exclusively meat diet (although as much as you want) and eggs; very rarely anything else; you don't even get vegetables.

Thus far, despite my offers of good soap and cigarettes, I have not been able to obtain milk and butter, even in the smallest amounts, and I have tried in all sorts of ways. However women are more adept at these matters. The bread distributed by the municipality is very bad and will get worse; I cannot tolerate it.

The woods are very beautiful, quite as good as the woods of Marienbad, with lovely inspiring views everywhere.

Another advantage of Turnau: excellent apples and pears. Your sister, I think, doesn't speak Czech very well. That will make staying here a lot more difficult, but not at the hotel, which has many guests from northern Bohemia, which gets the *Reichenberger Zeitung*, the *Prager Tagblatt*, and *Zeit*, and provides a German version of the menu.

Prices, at least at this moment: Room 3 crowns. Beef with sauce and potatoes 4.50. Roast pork, dumplings, cabbage 11 crowns. Roast veal 7–9 crowns. Plum dumplings (a great exception) 4 crowns. Scrambled eggs with potatoes 6 crowns, and so on.

Perhaps there are special prices for a longer stay, though the hotelkeeper refused any such arrangements the first day, with a great deal of outcry and laughter. But we were soon friends again.

That's about all, though I will look around further.

Cordial regards, Franz

[ON A SEPARATE PAGE, ENCLOSED] Dear Felix, a postscript. There is a hotel-pension at Kacanow near Turnau which to my great astonishment has put up posters here, soliciting the esteemed public, et cetera. This afternoon I went out there. It is an hour's walk from Turnau, a handsome spacious building, surrounded by slopes with woods and meadows, not plump in the valley bottom, with windows facing south. There is a new manager, a man you can talk to. He is plainly ambitious, but except for the posters has not gone to any great lengths so far. The place looks rather neglected: you can only get drinks there, not food. He explains that he does not yet have his wife with him; she is still at the inn he was formerly managing, but will be coming here in two weeks' time, at which point he will be able to be more specific about menu and prices. However he says he will be able to accommodate your sister then. This is surely a highly uncertain business and will have to be looked into more carefully.

When we see each other I will give you more detailed information about Turnau. At present I don't even know how your sister is. I will be in Prague by Saturday or Sunday. Perhaps I will drop in on you Sunday afternoon, or you drop in on me at the office Monday.

Warm regards, Franz

To Kurt Wolff Verlag

Prague, October 1, 1918

Dear Sirs,

Many thanks for the information.[56] If I understand your remark about printing, I am not to receive any proofs. That would be a pity. The order you list is correct, except for one mistake which cannot stand: the book must begin with "The New Advocate." The piece which you have down for the first item, "A Homicide," is simply to be discarded, since, except for trivial differences, it is the same as the later piece correctly entitled "A Fratricide." Please do not forget the dedication of the whole book "To My Father." I enclose the manuscript of "A Dream."

Very truly yours, Dr. Kafka

To Kurt Wolff

[Prague, November 11, 1918]

Dear Herr Kurt Wolff,

Almost my first writing after a long spell in bed[57] must be to thank you warmly for your friendly letter. Regarding the publication of the "Penal Colony," I gladly concur with all your proposals.[58] I have received the manuscript, have cut out a small section, and am sending it back to the firm[59] today.

With cordial regards, as ever, yours, Dr. Kafka

My address is: Poříč 7, Prague.

To Kurt Wolff Verlag

[Postcard. Prague,] November 11, 1918

Dear Sirs,

This is to inform you that I am sending the manuscript of the "Penal Colony" by special delivery, registered mail along with a letter. My address is: Poříč 7, Prague.

Very truly yours, Dr. Kafka

To Kurt Wolff Verlag

[Prague, November 11, 1918]

Dear Sirs,

Through an apparent error you are addressing your letters to me to Zürau. That is incorrect and such letters reach me only roundabout and virtually by accident. My present address is Poříč 7, Prague. Enclosed I am sending you a somewhat shortened manuscript of the "Penal Colony." I fully concur with Herr Kurt Wolff's plans for its publication.

Please note that after the paragraph ending with "iron spike" (page 28 of the manuscript) a largish space should be inserted, to be marked with asterisks or some other means.

Very truly yours, Dr. Kafka

To Max Brod

[Prague, November 29, 1918]

Dear Max,

I meant to leave last Sunday,[60] but on Saturday had to take to my bed with fever and so have spent the entire week half lying, half sitting. I will leave tomorrow. Please, Max, a favor. As you can see from the enclosed letter, the manuscript has not reached Wolff. As the enclosed receipt shows, I sent a postcard, as well as the manuscript with a letter, to Wolff on the same day. The card (Wolff refers to it as a letter) has arrived, the manuscript not. Both were sent special delivery, registered. Would you file a complaint? I have never known how to deal with the postal system and know nothing at all about postal arrangements under the new government.[61] Many thanks and keep well. Once I am in Schelesen I may send you a list of questions on Hebrew matters. It will not mean much work for you; the questions are such as can be answered with a word or a shake of the head and we will have a correspondence in Hebrew.

Yours, Franz

To Max Brod
[Pension Stüdl, Schelesen bei Liboch, beginning of December 1918] Dear Max, A pity that I didn't find you home last time. Anyhow I will soon be coming back, perhaps by Christmas and surely by the beginning of January. It is not as good here as at Zürau, though of course it isn't bad, and as everywhere instructive. Besides it is startlingly cheap: 6 frc. per day (according to the current exchange rate as given by the Viennese newspapers of 1 crown = 10 ctm.).

I am enclosing my list of questions. I scarcely learn a thing, the day is short, kerosene is scarce, and I spend many hours lying out in the open. I am not even reading my books, just those in the pension library (among which I found *Tycho Brahe*) and *The Story of My Life* by Meissner,[62] an extraordinarily lively and honest book filled with endless vivid portraits and anecdotes about the whole Czech, German, French, and English political and literary worlds of the mid-nineteenth century; in political terms its relevance to the present day is dazzling.

So long. My regards to your wife, and Felix and Oskar. Have you filed a complaint at the post office?

Franz

[ENCLOSURE: TWO PAGES OF QUESTIONS ON HEBREW GRAMMAR, MANY IN HEBREW SCRIPT]

To Ottla Kafka

Schelesen bei Liboch [beginning of December 1918]
[SIX SMALL DRAWINGS OF KAFKA'S ON A POSTCARD, WITH THE LEGEND] Scenes from my life.

And how are you? Bring notebooks and books at Christmas. I will be giving you tests. Or should I come to Prague? I am just as well off here as in Zürau, only it is somewhat cheaper. I mean to stay four weeks but could very well come to Prague for Christmas.[63]

Many regards, Franz

To Max Brod

[Postcard. Schelesen; postmark: December 16, 1918]
Dearest Max, It will not be taken care of but taken note of. By the way, for quite a while my wallet has contained a visiting card addressed to you with similar very simple provisions (including financial matters).—For the present however we are still alive and your essay on writers and the community[64] is splendid. While reading it I kept grimacing with pleasure. It is incontrovertible, true, translucent, deeply knowledgeable, sensitive, and dazzling besides.— As far as the organic coherence of the individual in moral terms is concerned, in my experience its causes are even worse. This coherence is in large part morally nourished solely by mental reservations. But all people are obviously social, with the exception perhaps of those who linger on the margin and soon drop off, or those who are superhumanly able to concentrate all of society in their own narrow breast. All others are social through and through, only that they have to vanquish their various difficulties with their various strengths. Perhaps some such statement should complement the essay. To be sure the essay is not a judgment, but at least it supplies the data for a judgment. Moreover, perhaps there is misunderstanding implicit in the fact that, for example (this is purely by way of example), a Workmen's Circle will be full of many splendidly social people, while a girls' club[65] will have fewer of these.—But again and forever I abide by this essay. If only your new book[66] were to be wholly shaped this way!

Franz

To Max Brod

[Postcard. Schelesen; postmark: December 17, 1918]
Dear Max, You invincible, and even you laid low. But now you are already

out of bed. I did not know, my mother did not write me about it, no one did. Write me a few words about your condition. During my fever you represented something like the warranty of life for me. I hope you will at least be spared all those little aftereffects which I had, after my flu. Still and all you seem to have been sick in bed for more than a week. Has your wife stayed well? Shouldn't you go to the country to recuperate? Unfortunately there are a few reasons here for not inviting you, but if necessary it could be managed and I would nurse you fairly well, for I do have some experience in being nursed. I wonder whether I ought to ask my mother to pay a sick call on you, whether that will be a bother to you or whether she will no longer find you at home, since you might already be in the Jewish National Council.[67] Perhaps I will ask our Fräulein[68] to call on you.

Be well, write soon, regards to Felix and Oskar.

Franz

1919

To Oskar Baum

[Schelesen, beginning of 1919]

Dear Oskar, How are you getting on this winter? Truly, things are not fairly parceled out. Here I am, having a second winter in the country, while you, who so enjoyed being in Zürau, must stay in Prague in snow and cold. And this although I am not writing any tragedy,[1] none at all, and certainly not like yours[2] concerning which, or at least the fate of which, I would really like to hear something.

I think I may soon be coming back, in about ten days, unless the doctor[3] here advises against it. I won't say it is less lovely here than in Zürau, but more difficult. This is my second time here, but I may have to come here ten times over, each time making a fresh start, before I conquer the place. In Zürau it was so easy. However my health was somewhat better.

This house still harbors a memory of you, or rather of your boy. A small Pomeranian belonging to the letter-carrier at whose house you boarded could not endure Leo's pesterings and was bought by Fräulein Stüdl,[4] that is, rescued. The dog has long been dead, but you, as father of your son, will not be forgotten. The dogs are just now barking gloriously outside the house; they take their revenge against me for the Pomeranian every night. But that is no great matter; the inner dogs are more dangerous to sleep.

Warmest regards to you and yours, Franz

To Max Brod

[Schelesen, January 1919]

Dear Max, I recently dreamed of you; the dream in itself was nothing special. I often have this dream: I take some stick or just break off a twig, jab it at an angle into the ground, seat myself astride it, as witches mount their broomstick, or merely lean against it the way one leans against a walking stick in the street, and that is enough for me to go flying off in long low leaps, up hill, down dale, as I like. When the impetus gives out, I need only push against the ground again and on it goes. I have had this dream often, but this time you were somehow involved and were looking on or were waiting for me. It sometimes seemed as if this were happening in the Rudolphinum grounds.[5] And then it turned out that I continually did you some harm or at least made demands upon you. To be sure these incidents were only trivial; once I lost a small iron rod belonging to you, and had to admit the loss to you; another time I let you wait a long time while I went flying—yes, it was all quite trivial, but it was wonderful with what goodness and patience and serenity you bore it all. Either—the dream ended with this reflection—you were convinced that though I seemed to have everything easy, things were actually hard for me, or at least you clung to this belief as the only explanation of my otherwise incomprehensible behavior. And so you did not once spoil my nocturnal pleasures with the smallest reproach.

In general even the daytime is not too bad, at least as far as the lungs are concerned. No fever, no shortness of breath, and less and less coughing. On the other hand, my stomach is upset.

When are you going to Switzerland?

Warm regards, Franz

Please give my regards to Felix and Oskar.

To Ottla Kafka

[Schelesen, February 1, 1919][6]

Dear Ottla, Last night, at midnight between January 31 and February 1, I woke at about five and heard you at the door of the room calling "Franz," softly but I heard it distinctly. I answered at once but nothing more happened. What did you want?

Yours, Franz

To Max Brod

[Schelesen; postmark: February 6, 1919]

Dear Max, How you fight with your destiny and yet your destiny speaks out in such a fine, loud, reverberating voice. What should others say whose destiny whispers or is even mute?

While you are still suffering for your ideas in your dreams,[7] I am driving around in a troika in Lapland. This happened last night, or rather I was not yet driving but the three horses were being hitched up. The wagon shaft was an enormous animal bone and the coachman gave me a technically rather clever and remarkable explanation of the troika harness. It was long and I won't go into it here. For a homely note in the Nordic scene, my mother was present, either in person or in voice. She commented on the man's national costume, declaring that the trousers were made of a kind of paper fabric manufactured by the firm of Bondy. This would seem to refer back to some memories of the previous day, for there is a Jewish element here, and there was talk of paper fabric and of some Bondy.

The Jewish element is a young woman,[8] only, it is to be hoped, slightly ill. A common and yet astounding phenomenon. Not Jewish and yet not not-Jewish, not German and yet not not-German, crazy about the movies, about operettas and comedies, wears face powder and veils, possesses an inexhaustible and nonstop store of the brashest Yiddish expressions, in general very ignorant, more cheerful than sad—that is about what she is like. If one wanted to classify her racially, one would have to say that she belonged to the race of shopgirls. And withal she is brave of heart, honest, unassuming—such great qualities in a person who though not without beauty is as wispy as the gnats that fly against my lamp. In this and other traits resembling Fräulein Bl.,[9] whom perhaps you remember with aversion. Could you lend me for her *The Third Phase of Zionism*[10] or other reading matter of that sort, whatever you think suitable? She will not understand it, she will not be interested, I will not press it upon her—but anyway.

I don't have much time, do believe me, the day is hardly long enough, it is already a quarter past eleven. Lying out in the open consumes most of the time. I lie alone on a balcony, looking over wooded hills.

My health is not bad, though stomach and intestines are out of order. The nerves too, or whatever one calls by that name, could be tougher, as I have discovered already with two people. To take in a new person, especially his sufferings and above all the struggle he wages, which one thinks one knows more about than the person himself—all this is the counterpart of giving birth.

Be well. Regards to Felix and Oskar.

Franz

I have received *Selbstwehr.* Just what do you mean by your remark "Palestine totally unclear"?

To Max Brod

[Schelesen,] March 2 [1919]

Dear Max, I haven't even thanked you for the fine book. It has done me good to live awhile in its spirit. I've also been, fortunately or unfortunately, visited by all sorts of youthful memories and emotions, which intermingle with everything.

The young lady also sends thanks. She has read the book from cover to cover and has even understood it remarkably, though with a special kind of girlish momentary understanding. Besides, she is not so without connection to Zionism as I initially thought. Her fiancé, who was killed in the war, was a Zionist, her sister goes to Jewish lectures, her best friend is a member of the Blue-White[11] and "never misses a lecture by Max Brod."

As for me, I pass my time gaily (roughly estimated, in the last five years I have not laughed so much as in the last few weeks) but it is still a difficult period. Well, for the moment I am bearing up, but it is not accidental that my health is not doing so well. Besides, this period is coming to an end in its present form[12] within a few days and I may be staying here awhile longer, if the Institute accepts the affidavit of the doctor here.[13]

The first mistakes of life, I mean the first visible ones, are so curious. One should probably not try to analyze them because they have higher and wider significance, but sometimes one has to. It reminds me of a race in which, as is only right, every participant feels sure he will be the winner, and given life's richness, this should be possible. Why does it not happen that way, even though everyone apparently does have that belief? Because the lack of faith is not expressed in the *belief* but only in the *method of running* that is used. It is as if someone were firmly convinced that he would win, but he would do so only if he broke out of the course at the first hurdle and never returned. To the referee it is clear that the man will not win, at least not on this plane, and it must be enormously instructive to watch how the man, right from the start, devotes his efforts to breaking out, and all this in dead earnest.—Luck with the book.[14] And time in plenty!

Franz

To Josef Körner

[Prague; postmark: June 3, 1919]

Dear Herr Professor,

Many thanks. Such studies are so peaceable and pacifying. I would gladly have read more, especially since the handling is delicate and sympathetic to the man.[15] However, Bettina gives the impression of having been a distraught half-Jewish young man dressed in woman's clothes and I don't understand how she could have had that happy marriage and those seven children. Should the children have led halfway normal lives, it would have been a miracle.

Incidentally, in the offprint the greater part of the essay on Schlegel and the literary parallels are missing. A pity.

With best regards, yours sincerely, Kafka

To a sister of Julie Wohryzek[16]

[Prague,] November 24, 1919

My dear Frau, I have only a brief acquaintanceship with you from Schelesen, but I felt at once that I could place my trust in you—of course I was also influenced by J.'s loving attachment to you. You seem to be basically very kind, also controlled and deliberate, though somewhat too melancholic, a trifle dissatisfied, a trifle hapless, and because of these very qualities capable of an understanding that goes beyond the immediate sphere of your life and experience. This encourages me to hope that you will at least listen patiently and attentively to me, all the more so since we are both united by our being very fond of J., each in his own fashion.

You know how J. and I met. The beginning of our acquaintanceship was extremely curious, and to the superstitious did not exactly augur happiness. For several days we laughed continually whenever we met each other, at meals, while walking, while sitting opposite each other. On the whole the laughter was not pleasant; it had no apparent reason, was painful, shameful. It contributed to our keeping away from each other, giving up eating together, seeing each other more rarely. That, I think, was in keeping with our general intentions. It is true that (aside from my illness) I had a relatively free, happy, peaceful year behind me, but still I was like a person who is sore all over and gets along tolerably well as long as he does not bump into anything, but at the first really direct contact is thrown back to the worst of his early pain, and not just as if the old experiences are being revived—for they are and remain part of the past—but rather what lingers is the formal aspect of pain; there is literally the channel of an old wound and every new pain immediately runs up and down it, terrible as on the first day and even more terrible because one is already so weakened. I don't know whether anything like this lies within your experience. But I felt that way in the first days; I had one of my first sleepless nights for a whole year; and I comprehended the threat. J. likewise was reserved toward me. She is naturally reserved; besides, my nature, my reading aloud, my anxieties which seem so incomprehensible to her with her happier disposition, must initially have struck her as exceptionally strange.

In the long run that would not remain the case between two people who were so fully and forcefully in harmony as we are, so that each of us is a compulsion to the other, quite independently of joy and sorrow, simply a necessity just as much as joy and sorrow. In addition, on the surface level, there was the literally enchanted house in which we two were almost alone and to which we were restricted because of the wintry conditions outside. Nevertheless the two of us—let this be the only time I compliment myself; later I shall find no more grounds for doing so—remained magnificently brave. Perhaps it was easier for J., both as a girl and also because she is a wonderful mixture, hard for outsiders to spoil, of warmth and coldness. But I truly suffered to the full the anguish of all animal nature; though what does that signify?—Compared to the sufferings of this latest period it was child's play.

Anyhow, we made it, although the strain certainly did our health little good; I in particular would have liked to see the doctor every day for treatment of my heart; but we made it. It was established between us that I regarded marriage and children as the most highly desirable things on earth in a certain sense, but that I could not possibly marry. (The proof of that remained, since everything else turned out to be not plain enough, my two broken engagements.) Therefore we must part. So we did. It was certainly very mournful, but alleviated by the unacknowledged feeling that this could not be the end of it. Still, even when we said goodbye we did not yet address each other as *du;* and except for a brief exchange of letters inside the pension, what must have been the most significant event of those six weeks, so far as I can recall, was my holding her little hand in mine longer than was quite necessary.

J. naturally did not have such clear views of marriage as I did. She said she was not going to marry; she did not say, like me, that she did not want to or could not marry. That is, I grant, the way girls usually talk in certain situations, but I soon really believed her. Lacking any central axis, but scarcely feeling the worse for that because of the beautiful equilibrium of her nature, she had a vague longing for glamor, the world, pleasure (I can no longer find much of that in her anymore; can you?) that perhaps could be slightly satisfied by remaining single but not at all satisfied by the ordinary possibilities of marriage that were available to her. Moreover, she scarcely had anything left of her original longing for children; as you know, women in our kind of life (seemingly) dispense with that quickly and thoroughly. So why should she have married?

So we were in agreement in regard to not marrying, but not in regard to the reasons, and this disparity barred us from remaining together. At that time there were only two possibilities for me: either approach the matter with full seriousness, and the only possible seriousness between man and woman seems to me to be marriage, or else to tear ourselves violently apart. This second possibility was extremely hard, but in Schelesen we managed it. As a result of my error, I grant. You see, for various reasons that are of no further interest right now, I thought that the whole thing was merely a Schelesen affair which both of us would be free of once we were back in Prague. I was deceiving myself, perhaps deliberately, in order to keep myself halfway on my feet there in spite of all the self-torment.

Actually, during the three weeks that I stayed on alone in Schelesen we did not write to each other once. But when I returned to Prague we flew to each other as if driven. There was no other possibility, not for either of us. But the shaping of events was admittedly in my hands.

And now there came a relatively happy and peaceful time. Since it was beyond our strength to stay away from each other, we abandoned those efforts. For you, as her sister and friend, there may not have been much that was cause for rejoicing in all this. We could be seen together in the deep woods, in the streets late in the evening, swimming in Černosič, and if at any time anyone had asked us whether we were going to be married we would both have said no, J. honestly and I even then with constraint. I could not rest content with this life, at least at the time; what was good about it was only a halfway thing, and not even that; what was bad about it was thoroughly bad. It was I who insisted on marriage, I alone; I deliberately destroyed a completely peaceful life, and I don't even regret it; or rather I am very unhappy about the trouble I caused but I would not know how I might have acted differently. I had to insist on marriage.

What gave me the right to do so, since I had already had such bad experiences (exclusively with myself)? The situation in this case was so much more favorable than in the past; in fact nothing more favorable could be conceived. I don't want to justify this statement in detail, but merely say that we were (and are) so close to each other, closer than J. herself realizes. Furthermore, it could be assumed that all the preparations could be taken care of very quickly and simply, and that my father's opposition,[17] given the unhappy relationship I have with him, could only serve me as a further strong proof of the correctness of what I wanted to do. In my view it was going to be a love-marriage, but even more a marriage of prudence in the higher sense. Admittedly, there were a number of small matters that bothered me among J.'s acquaintances, but that sort of thing occurs everywhere; and besides, the attitude of your family, as far as I was made conscious of it, was almost touchingly delicate and considerate compared with the somewhat coarser though of course very well meant actions of my father.

So what were the obstacles within me, which in spite of everything had not vanished but were lying in ambush, as it were, and carefully watching developments? I can actually speak of them as though they were something alien to me, for they by far surpass my personal strength and I am wholly at their mercy. First of all, financial problems may be excluded almost entirely; I have never had them, therefore may possibly fear them, but since I can never imagine such problems in their reality they cannot, for the present, be a decisive factor for me. It is something else; since the financial problems have too little meaning for me, the inner obstacle exerts diabolical cleverness in intermingling them with other problems, and addresses me more or less in this vein: You who have to fight incessantly for your inner stability, using all your strength and that is not even enough—you now want to found a household of your own, perhaps the most necessary but at any rate the most affirmative and boldest act there can possibly be? You who can barely manage to bear the responsibility for yourself from moment to moment now want to add on the responsibility for a family? What reserve of strength do you expect to draw on? And you also want to have as many children as are given to you, since after all you are marrying in order to become better than you are and the idea of any limitation of children in marriage horrifies you. But you are not a peasant whose land feeds his children, and descending to the last rung, you are not even a businessman, in your inward disposition, I mean, but (probably a reject of the European professional class) a civil servant, moreover excessively nervous, one who long ago fell prey to all the perils of literature, with weak lungs, exhausted by the meager scribbling in the office. Given these preconditions (though it must be granted unreservedly that marriage is essential), you want to marry? And given such intentions you also have the brazenness to want to sleep at night and afterward by day not run around half mad with headaches as if your head had been set afire? And this is the morning-gift with which you hope to make a trustful, yielding, incredibly unselfish girl happy?

These are the chief questions; many subsidiary questions remain attached to them. Of course there are innumerable answers to all these questions, and innumerable countering questions to all the answers, and so on; the nights could be illuminated bright as day with all that. But the final result is once again the magnificently calm reappearance of the initial questions, and the inability to answer them with equal calmness.

You will interject, dear Frau, that I obviously knew all that earlier and therefore had no reason to push the thing so far, to the anguish of everyone concerned. I have several responses to this. First of all, one never knows such things, even if one has had similar experiences; one has to go through them all over again in all their terrible novelty. Secondly, I had no choice, for since my nature was striving toward marriage I regarded the relatively peaceful happiness of the existing state as unjustified and thought that I might at least provide it with a subsequent justification by marriage or at least by an extreme, unsparing effort to arrive at marriage. It was a psychological predicament. Thirdly, in all other respects the situation was, as I have already said, exceedingly favorable, and I had a right to hope, if I were not deceived about the contrary forces within myself, that I might achieve what I wanted. The greatest scruples do at first creep away and hide when confronted with firm decision, but then they try to disrupt everything by all the torments of sleeplessness, although for a long while they do not dare to appear in their own form. Upon this I founded my hope. The whole thing was a race between the outward circumstances and my inner weakness. There were various phases, first a delay of the medical examination because Dr. Pick was on vacation—that was bad; then my father's rather short-lived opposition—that was good, partly because it provided distraction and diverted my thoughts from the real dangers; then came the possibility of a halfway decent apartment available immediately. Everything was already worked out—the banns had already been published, one quick little week and we would already have been married. But on Friday it turned out, since the apartment had slipped through our fingers, that we could not marry on Sunday after all. By that I don't mean to say that this was a misfortune; perhaps an even worse collapse would have followed and buried a married couple in its ruins. I am only saying that my hope of being able to arrive at marriage was not unjustified and that, measured against the facts, I myself am only a poor human being and in view of my poverty dependent on luck, but that I was not a liar.

That was the turning point. Afterward, the denouement could no longer be put off. The respite that had been given me this time was used up; the warnings that had hitherto been distant rumblings now thundered day and night in my ear. From my behavior J. could roughly guess what was happening. Finally I could not go on and had to tell her. Aside from her, I spoke to no one about it, except my sister.

At the present moment there seem to be only two possibilities.

The first is that we part. From what I hear, that seems to you the most desirable course. And even though J. is wholly bound up with any future I can conceive for myself, I would agree to our parting under two conditions. The first is: if there were a halfway reasonable prospect of J.'s marrying, and fairly soon, some good man whom she is willing to accept, having children, and living with him as purely and decently as is possible for ordinary people in our situation. Of course such a marriage would be a stroke of good fortune compared to anything that can be expected from me at present. But I also believe that if everyone would stop badgering J. she would, with her to me enchanting nature, be content with fidelity or love outside marriage, or what is called marriage nowadays. Such a relationship would not involve any great sacrifice of personal happiness for her. And so I would agree to our parting— this is my second condition—only if I were mistaken in this belief. If these two conditions were fulfilled, I am ready and willing to sign, confirm, and publicize any declaration setting forth our separation, no matter what its contents, whether it makes me out disgraceful, ridiculous, or contemptible. No matter what the statement, it will always be true to the extent that I have inflicted so much suffering upon J., the most innocent and the kindest of souls, that by comparison any purely social penance would be utterly trivial.

If these conditions cannot be fulfilled, and so I believe, then please leave us to ourselves, for we feel we belong together despite all my frailties. In February I will be going to Munich,[18] with certain hopes, for about a quarter of a year. Perhaps J., who has been wanting for a very long time to get away from Prague, might also come to Munich. We would see another part of the world; some things might undergo a slight change; many a weakness, many an anxiety, will at least change its form, its direction.

I will say no more; it seems to me that at the end I have said too much and too crudely. Be patient, not indulgent but patient and observant, so that insofar as is possible you do not overlook anything or read anything into my words.

Yours sincerely, Dr. Franz Kafka

To Minze Eisner[19]

[Prague, winter 1919–20]
Saturday

Dear Fräulein Minze, or rather since Fräulein and Minze hardly go together, dear Minze. Of course you have given me great pleasure, with the photos but above all because you are what I thought you, that is trustworthy, true to your word and good. That is the main thing. And therefore I can tell the truth about the photos: they reveal, as every image of a good thing reveals, a great deal for which one is grateful and which one might not have recognized with one's own eyes. You really are an amazingly good actress or more accurately you have the amazing potentiality of an actress or a dancer—the divine forwardness (in the best sense) of enjoying being looked at, the power of standing up to public gaze. This I would not have thought. But I am afraid the photographer, excellent person though he may be otherwise, has not handled this potentiality well and sensibly. Whatever is good in the photographs is simply you yourself. In No. 1 he makes you into a character out of Schnitzler's *Anatol.* In No. 2 he makes you the Dame aux Camélias,[20] in No. 3 someone out of Wedekind,[21] while in No. 4 you are Cleopatra (as she was the first evening) if not Fern Andra.[22] So he mixes things up and yet there is something partially right in all of them. On the whole, though, to my mind you have slipped through his fingers. This is not to say that you should avoid such photographing. I feel sure that it has done you no harm inwardly. But you should always keep your skepticism toward such things, as you should keep it toward the Dahns and Baumbachs[23] in your notebook, against insipidity, untruthfulness, affectation, since by nature you are better than any of this, and will surely dance over all these perils as over a frozen path to the sacred well, on which so many others have either stupidly fallen or insipidly stumbled. I continue to feel that it is a very good thing that you are going to Holzminden,[24] for it is a bit of the wide world without the red background of Teplitz.

But I may keep the photos, may I not, since there were no directions to the contrary in your letter. And write to me again, especially when you are in some new place. It may not be so bad to have a good friend.

Goodbye, Minze. Give everyone my best regards, and especially the Fräulein.

Yours, Kafka

1920

[Prague, January/February 1920]

Dear Minze,

I did receive your previous letter and was of course very glad to have it and often thought of it and of you and—I don't exactly know why—am only today answering it. Perhaps because the letter was so self-sufficient, seemed so little in need of help, or even in need of answer.

Today it is different. You are feeling so uncertain? That sounds bad, but your present uncertainty, like your uncertainty back there in Schelesen, has a quality of gaiety, carefreeness, and confidence about it. One worries about you, but would not have you otherwise. That is my attitude, while your relatives, who indeed may well be having a hard time of it, have only the worry. I don't remember exactly if you told me whether your father (apart from your running his business and looking after him when he was sick) was satisfied with you, whether you caused him worry, how he conceived of your future, and so on. That would interest me. But I think you did mention some sudden outburst of anger on your father's part.

That you have abandoned your plans for school is a great pity, and I don't quite see why. You had already been accepted at Holzminden, you told me. And besides, Holzminden cannot be the only possibility. In northern Bohemia alone there are several other such schools. And you do seem to be still serious about your intentions since you are also considering working on a farm as a volunteer, should circumstances warrant. At the moment I can think of no possibility, but there must surely be such openings; if I am not mistaken, you yourself spoke of the state farm in Grosspriesen[1] where you could be taken on. Has that too fallen through? Well, we will think the matter over again.

How did you spend your time in Schelesen and afterward? With Rolf and running through the fields? That would have been very good, but too little or too much. It is good to pursue one's dreams but bad, as it mostly turns out, to be pursued by them. And after all it's a big world and a wide one, as you write, but not a hairsbreadth bigger than people are able to make it. The immensity of the world, as you now see it, springs from both the truthfulness of a brave heart and the illusions of your nineteen years. You can easily verify that by noticing that an age of, say, forty years likewise seems immense to you, and yet, as all the people you know will demonstrate, does not have that immensity you imagine.

What are you doing in Karlsbad? Are you well by now? I think there is a relative of Fräulein Stüdl in Karlsbad; Fräulein Stüdl spoke highly of her to me. Do you know her? I may go to Meran in a month. Have you ever been to Meran?

With cordial regards, yours, F. Kafka

To Minze Eisner

[Prague, February 1920]

Dear Minze, No, I was not trying to rob you of your belief in life's immensity (for it has such immensity, but not in the ordinary sense), nor could I rob you of that belief, since basically you do not have it, I mean, not when you think about it. If I said something about the matter, I only wanted you to believe yourself, that is, your better self. After all, Minze as a weeping willow would also be pretty—or at least approximately ten times prettier than Minze as Cleopatra.

Odd how in your letter the "wonderful times" and the "silliness" stand so close together. They cannot be the same things, rather they must be opposites. I rather think that wonderful times are those when one is better than usual and silly times when one is worse. One doesn't buy the wonderful times by doleful moods; on the contrary, wonderful times send light out over the gray future. But one pays dearly for "silliness" and right off, even when one doesn't know it, and commits silliness with the left hand, while with the right hand one keeps paying endlessly, until one has no more left to pay. And everyone alive, dear Minze, commits "sillinesses," so many, so many. One is so busy doing that that one scarcely has time to do anything else. Which however is no reason to resign oneself to it, and you surely do not do so, or you would not be the same dear Minze.

Who is this uncle who gets along so well with you and you with him?

Why do you mention nothing about the possibility of volunteer work on the Grosspriesen state farm?

I enclose an advertisement which I often saw in a Jewish magazine up to 1918. Perhaps you should write to this address, by registered mail: "Immenhof (Henny Rosental), Dessow, Mark,[2] Germany." I think this is not so far from Berlin. I have also heard the place praised.

Do tell me the details of the Holzminden business.

What are you doing in Karlsbad? To do nothing is one of the biggest sillinesses and one that's fairly easy to conquer. What are you reading?

What were those wishes of yours that I have forgotten? You're surely not referring to my photo. I deliberately did not send one. If you remember my eyes really as clear, young, tranquil, then let them remain so in your memory, for they are better conserved there than with me. Here they are dim enough and ever more unsure, with little flickerings from being open these thirty-six years. Of course that does not come out in the photograph, but then it's all the more unnecessary. If my eyes should ever become finer, clearer, then you will get a picture, but then again it would be unnecessary, for then they would be able to see all the way to Karlsbad and straight into your heart (such power have clear human eyes), whereas now they can only painfully drift about in your sincere, and for that reason precious, letter.

With cordial regards, yours, Kafka

To Kurt Wolff

[Prague, February 1920]

Dear Herr Wolff,

I have forgotten nothing, but when I was practically sure of a vacation, back in December, I caught a slight cold.[3] The doctor looked me all over, and when he heard about Munich strongly advised against it and instead recommended Meran or similar places. I had to agree that my health was unreliable, and I could not have spent my vacation with that sense of freedom and peace of mind which would have made the holiday useful to me. But since I could not have Munich, or the kind of vacation I preferred, I chose not to have any at all. In any case the whole scale was prepared to be tipped in that direction. So I stayed. I also did not answer you, for what would have been the point of long explanations, when I had only recently tried to interest you even in my milk requirements (I really only did that in order to invest the plan with the greatest possible reality right at the beginning).

So things have not worked out for this health leave—which is the only kind I wanted. Perhaps it is being kept in reserve for me later on. But a sick leave will be necessary before spring. Since I was already headed toward Bavaria, I sent away for a prospectus of Kainzenbad[4] Sanatorium near Partenkirchen. But only today I received word from its slow and almost reluctant directorate that they won't have a room free until the end of March—which is almost a bit too late. Basically I have no need either for a sanatorium or for medical treatment—on the contrary, both do me harm—but for sunlight, air, country, vegetarian food. But outside Bohemia I know I can obtain these things at this season only in some sanatorium. If you, Herr Wolff, could give me some word of advice about the problem, I would of course gratefully accept it. Otherwise I would probably be going to Kainzenbad at the end of March.

With many thanks and cordial regards, yours sincerely, F. Kafka

To Minze Eisner

[Prague, February 1920]

Dear Minze, It makes me happy to hear that you are going to be in school. You exaggerated the difficulties of being accepted by a school, I mean: to yourself also. But if you get into this school now, things will be turning out splendidly. First of all, the suggestion has come from your uncle, that is, from the family, and that gives a good cast to things. Secondly, Dr. Ziegler's[5] recommendation probably carries some weight in the school. And finally it is a Jewish school, or so I assume, and therefore especially beneficial for an at the moment somewhat drifting child (a term that is more flattering than otherwise).

So that is how it was in Karlsbad? Who would have thought it! But as far as that "rather pretty face" is concerned, it hardly struck me that way. Of course youth is always lovely; one dreams of the future and stirs dreams in others, or rather one is oneself a dream, and how could that help being lovely. But this is the sort of loveliness common to all youth and one has no right to appropriate it to oneself. But you mean something different by that "rather pretty face," and whatever this was, it passed me by. I did notice the way you wear your hair and the snakelike movements of your arms, but this was only half cute, half comic, and half (Minze being an exception to the natural order of things and having three halves) actually unpretty, and would have been forgotten in two days. But this "for the rest" which she treated so scornfully emerged as something more significant.

All that insistence that I ought to feel young does not touch me in the least, Minze. I do not complain that I feel old, rather the opposite, or rather I don't complain about anything of the sort. You know the saying: old eyes become farsighted, and it was the lack of farsightedness I was talking about.

It is not likely that I will be going to Meran, it is a bit too expensive, but I may be going to the Bavarian Alps. My head, I think, prefers the north, my lungs the south. But since the lungs usually sacrifice themselves when it becomes too hard on the head, so the head in reciprocation has gradually conceived a longing for the south.

As for the photos, Minze, let's drop the matter, shall we, if only because in the dark (I mean, when people do not see each other) they hear each other better. And we want to hear each other well. For the same reason it would be much better if we do not see each other in Prague now, either deliberately or by accident. I do mean that.

But I will be one of the first, won't I, to have news of your acceptance at the school. I consider that a great honor.

With cordial regards, yours, Kafka

To Kurt Wolff

[Prague, February 1920]

Dear Herr Wolff,

An unexpected telegram has just arrived from Kainzenbad in which, rescinding earlier messages, they tell me that a room is reserved for me at the beginning of March. This is as welcome to me as the taming is to a shrew. But in other respects also it may be a good thing, inasmuch as my condition does not admit much delay and perhaps it is also good for me to be in a sanatorium while the weather is still cold. Perhaps a better place will turn up later. For the present, please do not go to any more trouble on my account, and be assured of my warm gratitude for all your kindness.

Sincerely yours, F. Kafka

To Minze Eisner

[Prague, February 1920]

Dear Minze, Of course one may send such letters, especially such letters. Other letters, better put together, less distracted, can often conceal some important thing without meaning to, while such a jerky letter, made up out of several pieces, conceals nothing. How much one sees depends on one's own sharpness. A letter of that sort is so intimate, as if we shared an apartment, only separated by a thousand rooms whose doors stood open all in a line, so that one could see you, though of course only a tiny dim glimpse, in the last room of all, and what one sees, Minze, is neither very lovely, nor very gay, nor very good.

For the rest, Minze, you are (or rather would be if you tried) as keen and rightly self-righteous as a little rabbi. Of course you will not have the necessary backbone crammed into you in school, but must have it in yourself. But perhaps being there will help you find it in yourself; that is quite conceivable. For though on the surface Minze seems to be uncomplicated enough, inwardly she is as infinitely unfathomable as everyone else, and in her everything can be found if it is honestly searched for.

I have in front of me an illustrated brochure from the Ahlem Gardening School.[6] It seems so marvelous there, and for my next birthday I could wish for nothing better than to be nineteen and be going to Ahlem, for this is your Simon's School. The Gardening School for Girls was set up only after the war. Before that they only had a Gardening School for Boys and a Housekeeping School for Girls. Perhaps that too gives more reason to hope you will be accepted. May that happen soon!

Yours, Kafka

To Minze Eisner

[Prague, end of February 1920][7]

Dear Minze,

Here I lie sick in bed. I have a mild fever out of old habit that I can no longer shake off. And then you come along and announce that you were not accepted at Ahlem. They could well have found a little place for you; obviously they had no idea how you could roll yourself up into such a small ball. In the meantime I have heard of still another Jewish place, Opladen near Cologne,[8] but they are all full up and there are only vague prospects for the next semester, which begins in April. Perhaps I will get more definite information on this. And Immenhof—or has it another name—has not answered at all? And what about your working as an apprentice in Grosspriesen—you persistently say nothing about Grosspriesen—and then going next year to Ahlem—that isn't practicable? Why not? To be planting vegetables on ladies' hats in the interval is a poor substitute and not very cheering, since it takes place in Teplitz. I can't endure Teplitz, though I have never been there. It is your hometown, and for any halfway restless person the hometown, even when he willingly deceives himself about it, is highly unhomelike, a place of memories, of dolefulness, of pettiness, of shame, of being misled, of misuse of energy.

The narrow mental confines of the hometown also cause you to see yourself in that opposition to other people, or rather to other girls. Certainly there are oppositions, simply because the world has some of the same chaotic qualities as your head, but you cannot make the division so simply: here are the other girls and here am I. Wicked Teplitz.

My sickness has delayed the letter. It is by the way not a real sickness, but certainly cannot be called health. It belongs to that class of illnesses which do not originate in the place where they seem to lodge and which the doctors are even more helpless than usual in dealing with. Of course it is the lungs, but then again it is not the lungs. Perhaps I will go to Meran after all, or else to the moon, where there is no air at all and where the lungs can take a rest.

The pictures gave me great pleasure, most of all because it was a great sign of your trust to lend me something as precious to you as your father's pictures must be. I suppose a good deal must have been lost in the copying; after all, this is only a portrait at second remove. But still I think I can make out a good deal, such a fine forehead, delicate temples, energy, a hardworking life. The strained position of the hands is also remarkable.

The child is splendid. The body with the animal charm of a seal on its ice floe in the arctic sea, the face with its human charm. By the way, it's rather girllike, the expression of the eyes, the fullness of the mouth. It may well be a comfort to have it, especially when it's one's own child, and after all a nephew is virtually an aunt's child. But you must not let the grip of even the prettiest little hands hold you in Teplitz.

Yours, Kafka

To Max Brod

[Prague, about March 1920]

Dear Max, I was too bemused yesterday by the story and by the rigor of the thought from which it stemmed, so that I failed to tell you what my attitude is toward Ottla's project in Cologne.[9] I am very much more concerned about it, more than about Slovakia and Paris, and I would leave far more contentedly if it succeeded. I don't know whether and what you could do to help bring about the realization of the plan for her. At any rate I wanted to tell you. Perhaps a good word to Fräulein Löwy[10] would be enough, or something of the sort. I silently pledge a thousand crowns to the National Fund.[11] After all, this may not really be a bribe to fate, since all I ask in return is an opportunity for Ottla to labor and toil. What makes me even happier than the cause is that the cause has such an attraction for Ottla. So if it were possible—

Franz

To Felix Weltsch

[Spring 1920]

Dear Felix, Thank you for your patience. But last week I was particularly distracted, I also wanted to do it justice,[12] which meant reading it twice, and so much time went by.

I corrected some unquestionable small points right on the galleys—corrections which you of course must go over. On the other hand I don't think I overlooked any of the printers' errors. There were a few more small questions and suggestions which I jotted down on the enclosed pages. You will find the relevant places marked in the margins of the galleys.

But all these are only trifles. I do not presume to bring up larger questions, not vis-à-vis you, not vis-à-vis this work. As a work of edification—and this is what it is, far more than I imagined—it means a great deal to me and will mean even more in the future.

Please don't forget me as new galleys come in.

Yours, Franz

[A LIST FOLLOWS WITH SOME FORTY PROPOSED EMENDATIONS AND QUERIES]

To Minze Eisner

[Prague, March 1920]

Poor Minze, poor dear Minze, I don't mean to blame anyone, no one has done it on purpose, but when people would obviously much prefer to keep you at home, and you apparently let these same people, who don't want you to go, take care of the travel preparations, then you probably have not done everything you might have done. And why can't the school obtain an entry permit?[13] And if it cannot obtain the permit (though it obviously hopes that once you are there, it will be able to keep you there), why at least can't it write you a letter, so that you can prove to the consulate that you mean to stay only for two or three days, for the purpose of having an interview or taking a test, and you would surely be granted a visa for those two or three days, even without the entry permit. And if you have missed a few school days, that does not matter. But I would not give in any more, or rather I myself would give in or would long since have given in, for I could not have held out against such a heavy assault of old grown-up relatives closing in from all sides. But you are no coward, Minze.

Now as to the other matter—you see, Minze, this grief is one I also know and one everyone knows, and for how few people does it take a happy turn. But then in a very particular way I probably know much less about it than other people and you know much more about it than other people, so I will not try to compare myself with you but will greatly respect your grief, as we must everyone's grief. But perhaps you overlook something. Everyone has his sharp-toothed sleep-destroying devil inside him, and this is neither good nor bad, but is life. If one did not have him, one would not live. What you curse in yourself, therefore, is your life. This devil is the material (and basically what wonderful material) that you have been endowed with and with which you are supposed to make something. When you worked on the land, that was to my knowledge no escape but rather you drove your devil out there like a cow who up to now had grazed in the streets of Teplitz and was now to graze in better pastures. In Prague we have this statue of a saint on the

Charles Bridge,[14] and on its base is a relief that tells your story. The saint is plowing a field, with a devil hitched to the plow. The devil is still furious (which marks a transitional phase; until the devil himself is pacified, the victory is not won), gnashes his teeth, looks back malignantly at his master, and tenses his tail, but he is still forced under the yoke. Now of course, Minze, you are no saint and are not meant to be, and it is not at all necessary and would be a shame and a pity if all your devils were set to drawing the plow. But for a good number of them it would be excellent, and you would have put them to excellent use. I don't say this because only I think so—in your heart you are striving for the same thing.

You write that you would get married—if the two suitors "were not so disagreeable"—so that you could have "peace and a home," and then you compare yourself to your mother. But this is a contradiction, for did your mother have "peace and a home"? Perhaps peace and a home cannot come as a gift, out of sheer weariness, but have to be earned, have to be something of which you can say: this is my doing. What kind of home will it be if your devils sit in every warm corner, not one of the lot missing and all of them growing ever stronger to the same degree that you grow ever weaker?

But I do not insist absolutely on this point. Perhaps the two candidates only seem disagreeable because you shrink from marriage out of defiance. And then I do think there is one major respect in which you differ from your mother: that having a child of your own would have a decisive, perhaps redeeming, meaning for you. Don't you think so?

But there's one thing that reassures me in spite of your letter: that you surely can—don't deny it, Minze—still laugh the way you did that time on the veranda (though on the balcony the laughter no longer rang so clearly).

Yours, Kafka

To Felix Weltsch[15]

[Prague, spring 1920]
Dear Felix, Once again I have been very slow, but this time I kept it around at home; I finished it some time ago, but Ottla is a bit ill and I have no messenger.

This section was very scholarly; in many passages I came across nothing familiar except your hand guiding me, but I managed to make my way through almost everywhere.

By the way, I think I found the essence of this chapter, or what to me is the essence, in the earlier chapters as well. Only the logical junctures were new to me here, the supplementary props, and certainly also that last genuflection (distinction between doctrine and religion), which is as selfless as the whole remarkably selfless book.

Warm regards, Franz

To Kurt Wolff

[Prague, end of March 1920]

Dear Herr Kurt Wolff,

Bavaria remains recalcitrant. I had the room, but they don't want to give me the visa for a longish sanatorium stay without the entry permit from the Bavarian municipality. I have telegraphed to Kainzenbad asking them to get it for me. Instead of my permit they telegraphed back that from the 15th on there has been a ban on foreign visitors and that I should apply to the county authorities. I suppose they want me to apply in writing and after a month my request would no doubt be denied. That was too much for me. So I have scraped together all my money and will be going to Meran. I am not really so glad about it because although it may be better for my lungs, my head was set on Bavaria, and since the head governs the lung disease, Bavaria would somehow have been right.

With cordial regards, yours, Kafka

You recommend a Sanatorium Schönberg in Württemberg, but that can hardly be the complete address.

To Minze Eisner

[Prague, beginning of April 1920]

Dear Minze,

The picture is spendid, worth 500 Cleopatras, and has given me great pleasure. The pensive eyes—which do not quite match, by the way—the pensive mouth, the pensive cheeks, everything is pensive; and there is so much to be pensive about in this curious world. When I was a child, we had a small album of pictures of women out of Shakespeare. One of the ladies, I think it was Portia, was always my special favorite. The photo reminds me of this long-forgotten picture. She too had her hair cut short.

Tomorrow I leave for Meran. That I am going alone is—contrary to your opinion (which in fact is not an opinion but the expression of a good heart)— the best part of it, though in this matter too the best is far from good.

I will write you from Meran. Except for the photo, the nicest thing in your letter was the news that you have not given up on Ahlem. Perhaps this explains the expression on your face in the photo, that your eyes are turning away from Teplitz in the direction of Bohemian-Saxon Switzerland,[16] for the snapshot seems just the right size for a passport.

All good wishes, Kafka

To Max Brod and Felix Weltsch

[Meran, April 8, 1920]

Dear Max, On this first evening in my new room,[17] it seems to be very good; the torments of looking, of making up one's mind, and above all of bidding goodbye to the old room (which seemed the only secure ground under my feet and I throw it away on account of a few lire and other such trifles which only acquire any importance under more stable conditions)—all these torments naturally cannot be balanced out by the new room, nor is that necessary; they are past already and only their source remains, waxing more tropically than all the vegetation here.

I am writing on the balcony. It is seven-thirty in the evening (summer time), still a little cool. The balcony is sunk into a garden, almost a bit too low. I would have preferred a higher one (but just find such a high balcony, when there are thousands of such balconies and not one to be had), but this one has no tangible disadvantage, for the sun shines strongly upon me until six in the evening, the surrounding green is lovely, birds and lizards come close to me.

Up to now I stayed in one of the best hotels, or rather the best, since the others of the same category are closed. The guests consisted of some distinguished Italians, then a few other interlopers, while most of the rest were Jews, some of them baptized (but what horrid Jewish energies live on close to bursting inside a baptized Jew, only to be modulated in the Christian children of a Christian mother). One of the guests, for example, was a Turkish-Jewish rug dealer, with whom I exchanged my scanty words of Hebrew—a Turk in physique, imperturbability, and peacefulness, an intimate friend of the chief rabbi of Constantinople, whom he oddly enough considers a Zionist. Then there was a Prague Jew, who until the break-up[18] (this in confidence) was a member of the Deutsche Haus as well as of Městanská Beseda,[19] and now, thanks only to his high connections, has obtained his release from the Casino [SOMETHING DELETED AND MADE ILLEGIBLE] and promptly had his son transferred to the Czech Realschule,[20] "now he won't know either German or Czech, so let him bark." Naturally he voted "according to his denomination." But all this does not characterize him at all, comes nowhere near touching his vital nerve; he is a good, lively, witty old gentleman, capable of great enthusiasms.

The company in my present pension (I found it by chance, by chance rang the doorbell after long hapless searching, overlooking, as I now perceive, a warning given me shortly before, when an overexcited churchgoer—it was Easter Monday[21]—called out to me on the street, "Luther is a devil!"), the company, then, are all German and Christian. Conspicuous are a pair of old ladies; one former or present—it is all the same—general and a similar colonel, both sensible, pleasant people. I asked to be served at a separate little table in the common dining room, for I saw that others were served that way; moreover, that way my vegetarian diet attracts less attention, and above all one could chew better and on the whole it is safer. But it also became rather comical, especially when it turned out that I was the only one who sat by myself. Later I mentioned the matter to the proprietress, but she reassured me, knew something about "Fletcherizing,"[22] and wants me to put on weight. But today when I went into the dining room the colonel (the general was not there yet) invited me so cordially to the common table that I had to give in. So now the thing took its course. After the first few words it came out that I was from Prague. Both of them—the general, who sat opposite me, and the colonel—were acquainted with Prague. Was I Czech? No. So now explain to those true German military eyes what you really are. Someone else suggested "German-Bohemian," someone else "Little Quarter."[23] Then the subject was dropped and people went on eating, but the general, with his sharp ears linguistically schooled in the Austrian army, was not satisfied. After we had eaten, he once more began to wonder about the sound of my German, perhaps more bothered by what he saw than by what he heard. At this point I tried to explain that by my being Jewish. At this his scientific curiosity, to be sure, was satisfied, but not his human feelings. At the same moment, probably by sheer chance, for all the others could not have heard our conversation, but perhaps there was some connection after all, the whole company rose to leave (though yesterday they lingered on together for a long while; I heard that, since my door is adjacent to the dining room). The general, too, was very restless, though from politeness he brought our little chat to a sort of end before he hurried out with long strides. That hardly satisfied my human feelings either; why must I be a thorn in their flesh? But otherwise it is a good solution; I shall be alone again without ridiculously sitting off by myself, provided that they do not invent some disciplinary action for me. However I will now drink my milk and go to sleep. Keep well.

Yours, Franz

Dear Felix, My little bits of news belong to you too. As for sun, I never believed, deep down never believed, that they have an unbroken succession of clear days here, and in fact it is not true so far. Today it is Thursday evening.

We have had one and a half such days and even these were cool, though the coolness was extremely pleasant, while the rest were rainy and almost cold. How could one expect anything different so close to Prague? Only the vegetation fools you, for in weather when in Prague the puddles would be freezing over, here in sight of my balcony the blossoms are slowly opening.

Best wishes. Give my regards to the ladies and to Oskar.

Yours, Franz

Could you please send me the copies of *Selbstwehr*? (I have already seen the issue with your *Miracle* essay.)[24]

To Minze Eisner

[Postcard. Meran, April 1920]

Cordial regards from the warm southland (warm, that is, when the stove is going and I am almost leaning against it). Lovely in spite of this because it is at least two steps away from Prague (the head measures differently from the feet). In case you have news about Ahlem, here is my address: Pension Ottoburg, Meran-Untermais, South Tirol.

Cordially yours, Kafka

To Max Brod

[Meran, end of April 1920]

My dear Max,

I haven't heard from you for so long a time, though it's my fault, since I could well have followed up my first letter, which seems somehow to have gone astray, with another. Or rather I could not have so easily. I live here very comfortably, putting on weight, though troubled by the usual devils of my days and nights. But I still live in such a manner that the most accurate report on my life could only be conveyed by not writing. While you probably—and this is not entirely the opposite—are so overwhelmed with work that you don't have the necessary freedom of choice that letter-writing requires. But you are looking well, my mother writes, thereby taking various uncomfortable thoughts off my mind, thoughts about overwork in connection with the election campaign,[25] disappointment in the results, and so on.

Besides I have heard a bit more about you, for my doctor, Dr. Josef Kohn (a Prague Zionist), in the course of his trip here saw you get out at the Munich station, which I found very surprising in view of the election, until he later brought me news of the commotion in the Munich theater.[26] What Orosmin had to listen to!

Yesterday I received the enclosed letter, registered, from Janowitz.[27] If you think my enclosed answer is halfway suitable, please mail it; if not, I will of course revise it in accordance with your wishes. But the whole thing is degenerating into a game of patience, which can only start working out when either he or we begin to swear. However if we don't want to be impolite, it would be better to rest content.

Please give my warm regards to Felix and Oskar and the ladies, especially Frau Elsa.

Yours, Franz

To Felix Weltsch

[Meran, April/May 1920]

Dear Felix, Thanks for the card and *Selbstwehr.* I really missed the *Selbstwehr* as though it were a message from you; that you should write me specially was more than I expected, for the amount of work you accomplish and above all the courage you bring to it and invest in it truly amaze me. And with what mastery, calm, and loyalty to yourself you carry it all out. As for your own personal troubles, which you mention in the card—I have scanned between the lines and find that not the slightest trace of them shows. Running the magazine that way is like being transfigured in one's own lifetime. Yet your political skill is something I can hardly judge.

Recently I saw some issues of *Selbstwehr* on the counter of one of the local bakers, Holzgethan's it was. A young man borrowed them from the proprietress, some words were said about magazines, I had no chance to put in my oar on the subject. At any rate I was very much surprised and wanted to write you at once what I had observed about the distribution of *Selbstwehr.* Unfortunately I let the moment pass and now it is too late, for I have discovered that these were my own issues, which I had loaned to my doctor, a Prague Zionist—and which I had earlier lent to an old lady from Prague—and which he had left at the baker's by accident and never recovered.

Recently I wanted to send you an issue of the local Catholic paper which had an editorial on Zionism but it struck me at the time as too tedious. It was a discussion of a book by Wichtl,[28] published in Vienna, concerning Zionism and Freemasonry. According to him, Zionism was created by Freemasonry—a creation already partially absorbed by Bolshevism—for the destruction of all existent institutions and the establishment of Jewish domination of the world. All this was decided at the first Basel Congress,[29] which ostensibly was negotiating about various trifling matters in order to gain outward approval for the organization, but privately was concerned only with the methods for achieving that domination of the world. Fortunately, one copy of these secret protocols was stolen and was published by that great Russian scholar Nilus[30] (the editorial, curiously enough, explicitly asserts "he really lived and was a great Russian scholar"). There were some quoted passages from these protocols of "The Elders of Zion," as the participants in the Congress called themselves. The quotations were at once stupid and frightening, just like the editorial.

Your news from Langer[31]—please thank him warmly—made me very glad. I know that this gladness is largely childish, but I am shamelessly given to it. The child has apparently not been satisfied and climbs the ladder of the years until he gets giddy.

I am feeling well when I am not having trouble sleeping—but I have this often and acutely. Perhaps the mountain air is to blame. Perhaps something else. The fact is I don't much like living in the mountains or at the seashore— all that is too heroic for me. But these are only jokes, and sleeplessness is serious. Nevertheless I will be staying on here for a few weeks more, or else moving to the vicinity of Bolzano.

Warm regards to Max, Oskar, and the ladies, also to your parents and your brother. Isn't the crucial time drawing near? All good wishes to the brave woman.[32]

Yours, Franz

To Max Brod

[Meran, beginning of May 1920]

Dearest Max, Many thanks. I had imagined Munich rather like that; the details are curious. It is understandable; perhaps the Jews are not spoiling Germany's future, but it is possible to conceive of them as having spoiled Germany's present. From early on they have forced upon Germany things that she might have arrived at slowly and in her own way, but which she was opposed to because they stemmed from strangers. What a terribly barren preoccupation anti-Semitism is, everything that goes with it, and Germany owes that to her Jews.

As for my little circle here, the antagonisms have long ago been settled. I exaggerated them at the time, but then so did the others. The general, for example, is friendlier toward me than toward others, which however does not surprise me, for I have one indubitably good social trait (unfortunately at the cost of all the rest): I am an excellent listener, and listen sincerely and happily. This trait must have gradually developed in our family. There is an old aunt of mine, for example, who devoid of any special interest nevertheless has an extraordinary listener's face: open mouth, smile, wide eyes, continual nods, and inimitable way of stretching her neck which is not only humble but seems to want to facilitate the discharge of words from the other's lips, and does so. And so I, without too much strain, gave truth and life to my act, for my aunt's face, which is quite a large one, is still superimposed on my own.

But the general misinterprets and considers me something of a child. Recently, for example, he ventured to suppose that I had a fine library, but then quickly corrected himself in view of my youth and said I must have begun to put together a library. So although they are not obliged to show much consideration for me, the anti-Semitism at the table displays itself in all its typical innocence. The colonel, talking to me in private, charges the general (who on the whole is treated unfairly by everyone) with "stupid anti-Semitism." When they talk about Jewish rascality, brazenness, coward-ice, they laugh with a certain admiration and, to boot, apologize to me. (War stories provide many opportunities for this sort of thing, also for terrible anecdotes; for instance that a sick East European Jew, the evening before his unit was marching to the front, sprayed germs of the clap into the eyes of twelve other Jews; is that possible?) It is only Jewish Socialists and Communists who are not forgiven; these are drowned in the soup and cut up small with the roast. But even here, not all of them; for instance, one of the people here is a manufacturer from Kempten[33] (they had a soviet government there too for a few days, an unbloody and un-Jewish affair) who is perfectly well aware of the difference between Landauer, Toller, and the others, and had impressive stories to tell about Lewin.[34]

I would be doing well, as far as my health goes, if I could sleep; to be sure I have put on weight, but the insomnia of the past few days has checked my gains. There may be various reasons for it, of which one perhaps is my correspondence with Vienna.[35] She is a living fire, of a kind I have never seen before, a fire moreover that in spite of everything burns only for him. Yet at the same time she is extremely tender, courageous, bright, and commits everything she has to her sacrifice, or to put it another way perhaps, has gained everything she has by her sacrifice. Yet what kind of man must he be, who could evoke that.

Because of the sleeplessness, I may be coming back earlier than I should. I will hardly be going to Munich, for much as I might be interested in the publishing house,[36] it would be a passive interest.

Warm regards to you, your wife, and everybody, especially Oskar, whom I have not yet written. Even when nothing prevents me, I find it so hard to write letters that necessarily have to be public.[37]

Yours, F.

To Minze Eisner
[Two postcards. Meran, spring 1920]
Dear Fräulein Minze, I only today received your forwarded letter. The enclosure has not come at all, will be waiting for me in Prague, so I shall have to breathe life into it again there.

In case I have not yet said this to you, I shall say it now: you are sweet and good.

Today I went up to this castle.[38] Don't the loggias remind you of the balcony at Schelesen? But they are somewhat grander, and you do not see the two small villas in the distance, but have a view of nothing less than the Ortles range.[39] For all that, it is a loggia and at the full moon the olden knights must have sat out there. All the best; by which I especially mean Ahlem.

Kafka

I am sending the picture because it apparently shows Meta's[40] last litter.

To Max Brod
[Meran, June 1920]
Thanks, Max, your letter did me good. The story, too, was written at the right moment. I have read it ten times and trembled at it ten times and also repeated it in your words.

But the difference between us remains. You see, Max, it is really something else again. You have this mighty fortress; one of the girdling walls has been taken by unhappiness, but you are in the keep, or wherever you prefer to be, and you work, work, badgered, restless, but working. While I am burning up, suddenly I have nothing but a few beams; if I didn't prop them up with my head, they would collapse and the whole hovel catch fire. Have I complained? I am not complaining. My appearance complains. And I realize what is vouchsafed to me.

The second bit of news delights me, of course. It partly dates from my time. In the interval I have done the worst possible harm to this person,[41] and perhaps in the worst way. Just as a woodsman would hack at a tree. (But he was doing it on orders.)[42] You see, Max, I still have some shame.

I wish I could have been with you in May and I am looking forward very much to seeing you.

There is only one wrong note in your letter, where you speak of my getting well. No, for the past month there is no longer any talk of that. After all, it was you who wrote the "Island of Carina."[43]

Yours, Franz

Regards to your wife.

Do you happen to know anything about Ottla? She writes little to me. The wedding[44] is set for the middle of July.

I will write to Oskar, but what should I write, when I have only one subject.

To Felix Weltsch

[Postcard. Meran; postmark: June 12, 1920]

Dear Felix, Many thanks, no I haven't read the *Weltbühne*.[45] If you can, please save it for me. But the *Selbstwehr* has stopped coming; after the first batch, for which I have already thanked you, nothing more has come. And just at this moment, when Palestine, according to a newspaper story, has been overrun by Bedouins and perhaps the little bookbinder's workbench[46] in the corner has been smashed.

Warmest regards to you and your wife.

Yours, Franz

Please give my regards to Oskar, too. I'll be coming back at the end of the month.

To Oskar Baum

[Meran, June 1920][47]

Dear Oskar, I should have written long ago if there had been some good news about my recovery. In medical terms this is simply a hopeless case, in jest and in earnest. Would you care for a lay diagnosis? The physical illness is only an overflow of the spiritual illness. Should one want to channel it once more, then the head naturally defends itself. For the head in a time of need has spawned the lung disease and now they are trying to force it back into him, just when he feels the strongest urge to spawn still other illnesses. Moreover to begin with the head and cure him would require the strength of a furniture mover, which for the aforementioned reasons I will never be able to summon up. So everything remains as before. In the past I always had the silly idea, though it was understandable enough in the early years of self-medication, that on one or another occasion, for this or that accidental reason, I had not been able to relax properly. But now I know I carry this reason around with me all the time.

Otherwise it is lovely here, especially in this rainy and sunny June, under the caress of the mild and fragrant air which pleads so guiltlessly to be forgiven that it cannot make me well.

Max has written about your reading of the story. I look forward happily to being with you again at the end of June.

Greetings to your wife, your son, and sister.

                                                          Yours, Franz

I notice that I have slipped far too much into gloom. It's really not all that bad.

To Minze Eisner

                                                    [Prague, summer 1920]

Dear Minze, How was I supposed to know all this? You are now on a farm and in the fall will be in Ahlem! If you had thought out hard what you could do to give me the greatest pleasure, a real pleasure moreover, the kind that when a person comes to the office[48] tired, without proper sleep and literally shriveled (but it isn't quite that bad), could make him fresh and confident, you could not have hit on anything as effective as your letter and the snapshot. Of course one must not exaggerate: you have the title of Assistant (what a fine title! Today one is simply an ordinary individual and tomorrow one is already an Assistant) but perhaps it is only a sort of summer vacation and a way of making yourself useful (but this is not said mistrustfully; I am merely marveling at the fact that you have accomplished something so easy and yet not at all easy). But then I read Whitmonday[49] on the snapshot and that is already far in the past and you are still there, which is highly significant. And you can already hold a small pig, choking it a little but still holding it firmly, and have brown, glistening, strong arms. No, how much more I like Minze riding on the dung cart than Cleopatra on her golden throne.

And you certainly mustn't be scared of Ahlem. Even if your life there won't be so free as your present life (how do you use your leisure?), you will be in a foreign land, among foreign people, with new things, new goals, so it will be almost good to be a bit tied down at first, or else you might become frazzled. And this ostensible freedom in Teplitz was possibly rather a being bound down hand and foot with the tightest fetters, was helplessness rather than freedom. It is a wonder that you managed to break away.

Surely you are well again and have no more of those backaches. Your letter reminded me that I recently saw Herr Stransky and another time saw Herr Kopidlansky,[50] but very briefly, as indistinctly as a dream, I don't quite know where. Both of them did not look very well. My health is just about tolerable. Meran has not helped very much. It is simply the "inner enemy" wasting me and permitting no real recovery. If only one could take it on one's lap like a living piglet, but who can drag it out of its den? But this is not a complaint. To complain about this is to complain about life, and that would be very stupid.

Cordial regards and again many thanks, yours, Kafka

Incidentally, Minze, you mustn't think that I cannot visualize Milsau a little from the picture. Something like this: flat, with gently rising slopes toward the south, black loam rich in humus, mixed with lime and sand. Clay subsoil, with basalt formations. Not very big, hardly 60 hectares of arable land, wheat, barley, sugar beets, rye. Some 42 houses with approximately 268 inhabitants (and Minze). To attend church one must go to Brunnersdorf.[51]

Pretty good from such a small picture, isn't it? And yet I haven't even had enough time to look around the place, for I've been held by your look, the critical look of a peasant lass watching the weather.

To Elsa Brod

[Prague, August 5, 1920][52]

Dear Frau Elsa, Unfortunately the doorman did not find you at home. Is being duly reported. For the rest, I only wanted to say that according to a letter of Otto Abeles the *Jüdischer Nationalkalender*[53] is not to be published this year. So you don't have to copy and send anything.

Cordial regards, yours, F.

To Max Brod

[Prague; postmark: August 7, 1920]
Friday

Dear Max, Surely, assuming good weather, a piece of rare good fortune when you are so abnormally lazy. For me it would be nothing special, for I am always lazy, in the country, in Prague, always, and most of all when I am occupied, for this occupation is no real work, is merely a dog's grateful basking in the sun.

I read "Paganism" right off Monday in one session, but have not yet read "Song of Songs,"[54] for we've had swimming-school weather ever since. I was continually astounded anew by the inclusiveness, logic, and coherence of the chapter, although I expected as much, for paganism is in part your spiritual homeland, even when you don't want it to be. The chapter is magnificent and I became your wholly uncritical Galician pupil,[55] and as I read, like her, kept covertly squeezing your hand and taking you by the arm.

Yet I cannot say that I am in sympathy with you, or to put it more correctly, perhaps I am openly displaying nothing more than your covert sympathy with paganism. In general, when you express your own feelings I am very close to you. When you become polemical, I too feel the urge to become polemical (as well as I am able, of course).

You see, I do not believe in paganism in your sense of the word. The Greeks, for instance, were well acquainted with a certain dualism; how otherwise could *moira* and many other such concepts be accounted for? Only they happened to be unusually humble people—in regard to religion—a sort of Lutheran sect. They could not put the determining divine principle at sufficient distance from themselves; the whole pantheon was only a means by which the determining forces could be kept at a distance from man's physical being, so that human lungs could have air. A great national educational institution, which captured and held men's gaze. It was less profound than the Law of the Jews, but perhaps more democratic (scarcely any leaders or founders of religion among the Greeks), perhaps freer (it kept its hold, but I don't know how), perhaps more humble (for the sight of the gods merely made men aware of this: so we are not even, not even gods, and if we were gods, what would we be?). The closest approach to your conception might be to say: There exists a theoretic possibility of perfect human happiness, that is, to believe in the determining divine principle and not to strive toward it.[56] This possibility of happiness is as blasphemous as it is unattainable, but the Greeks perhaps were closer to it than many others. But not even this is paganism in your sense. And you have also failed to prove that the Greek soul was desperate, but only that you would be desperate if you had to be a Greek. I grant you that applies to both you and me, but even then not quite.

Actually one experiences three things in reading the chapter: your positive side, which remains unshaken and which all that I have said above was not meant to shake; then your exciting, many-sided attack on Hellenism; and finally its quiet self-defense, which you too are conducting.

I met your wife the day before yesterday at the Sophieninsel[57] and had a long talk with her there and on the way home. She was cheerful, wistful too, as she said, but cheerful. A story about the engagement of your brother-in-law upset her a bit, but it also indubitably set her up a bit too, as such things always do—I too felt that way.

For a long time I heard nothing from Abeles and was already fearing the worst when his answer came yesterday afternoon, very friendly. However, Löwit Verlag is to blame, since Abeles was going on vacation the 2nd of August and has given the thing to his friend, one Dr. Ornstein, who is an editor at Löwit Verlag. It will, he assured me, "be conscientiously taken care of." His letter does not mention money, so he is probably calling for it at Löwit's. At the same time he asked me to inform you that this year's yearbook is not going to be published. He does not know your present address and he feels it important "to release this very busy man in good time from his amiable promise." Since your wife probably has something to copy for the yearbook, I went to see her toward evening, but she was not at home, so I left a message.

Things are going tolerably well with me. The answer to Vienna can wait awhile. Recently Otto Pick came to see me; he mentioned an Englishman who wants to translate your *People's King*[58] into English for American performance.—That is all and now I am going to bed. I hear that you sleep so well. Blessings upon your sleep.

Franz

To Leo Baum

[Picture postcard (Dürer's *Squirrel*). Prague, autumn 1920?][59]
Dear Leo, I was sick and so have only now received news about you from your parents. I am happy that things are going well for you, though I never doubted that they would (allowing for the inevitable incidental unpleasantnesses that have to be borne with manly courage). It has always been hard for me to overcome my envy; now I try to do it by thinking of the "terrible" styptic pencil, but don't succeed.—Do you already have Bonus[60] as your teacher? Years ago I read a good many of his pieces in *Kunstwart* with great respect.—The picture shows you that the woods had schools even back in Dürer's time. One of the squirrels has just received a food package from home; his schoolmate has nobly turned away, but is peeping back. The first squirrel, therefore, is hurrying.

Warm regards, all my best wishes, yours, Kafka

To Minze Eisner

[Prague, November/December 1920]
Dear Minze, You give me great pleasure, really you do, and the days when I received your card and now your letter are distinguished above all others. This pleasure has almost nothing to do with you personally. What pleases me is rather the fact that someone has succeeded, in the face of all the difficulties

(in themselves the difficulties were not so great, but by comparison they were tremendously great), in getting out of Teplitz, which I conceive as a dreadful place for a person like you, much more dreadful than you can grasp at this point—that this person has succeeded in breaking out and breaking into an indubitably much larger world. This really spreads courage all around the person. That the person concerned should be you, and that I should somehow have had a part in all this from infinitely far off, from the back of the beyond, naturally makes the pleasure even greater.

And now that you are finally there, you may legitimately [CROSSED OUT: curse Ahlem] (no, perhaps I should not write that) be dissatisfied with many things at Ahlem. Surely you are right; why should it be so very wonderful. It is an affair of West European Jewry, where all such things may be on the verge of breakdown. Perhaps you yourself will someday carry a beam from Ahlem to Palestine. No, that is no joke, even though it is not meant seriously.

But however it may be at Ahlem, you at any rate are starting to discover—every sentence of your letter shows this—that the world, the world of the mind most of all, is far larger than the damned Teplitz-Karlsbad-Prague triangle. And this vital discovery is an achievement worth freezing for. However if you get that stove everything will be much better. (This story about the stove truly staggers me, and perhaps there are a good many things about Ahlem that I don't quite understand as long as I sit in my dressing gown in a heated room with about ten times more food than I can handle.) (My comprehension is also a little impeded by your handwriting. People at Ahlem write so small. Of course you were writing in bed, but one doesn't realize this right off, your letter is so sprightly and healthy.)

Gogol, Hafiz, Li-Po: a somewhat random choice (the two latter evidently in translations by Bethge or Klabund,[61] which are none too good. There is one excellent small book of translations of Chinese poetry by Heilmann,[62] but I believe it is out of print and no new edition has been issued. It is part of Piper Verlag's "Fruchtschale" series. I lent my copy to someone or other and never got it back). But in any case it is much better than your Schelesen reading of Dahn and Baumbach. When you have some time for reading, borrow a copy of Lily Braun's *Memoirs of a Socialist*[63]—you can find it in any lending library. It consists of two very thick volumes but you will race right through, one cannot help it. When she was your age, I believe, she too was entirely on her own and suffered a great deal from the morality of her class (such a morality is at any rate a tissue of falsehood, but beyond it conscience obscurely begins). She struggled through like a conquering angel.

To be sure, she lived among her people. But I do not take what you say about that as conclusive and also would not believe, far from it, that you ought to feel fondness for an individual Jew because he is Jewish, or that twenty Jewish girls or even a hundred grouped around you can give you the support of a nation, but only intimations of that possibility. And further: It may well be that women have less need of a nation for themselves, but men need it and therefore women need it for them and for their sons. Something of that sort.

I don't altogether understand about your future in gardening and would like to hear more about it. What kind of settlements are these you write about? Are the girls in the Institute all Jewish? And the teachers are also Jewish? You say not a word about the boys. How far is Hanover? Are you allowed to go there? (By the way, this Judaism that looks down so haughtily on the Germans is more than I bargained for. Similarly, Germany is more than Hanover.)

I would enjoy sitting in your room (why do you mention the view in your letter?) when you have lots of people in (how old are the girls?)—if possible sitting on the stove, because I feel cold so easily, and listening and joining in the talk and laughter (as well as I could). As things stand, I will be leaving in two weeks for an Austrian sanatorium,[64] though I am in a tolerable state of health. Good luck with your battle!

Yours, Kafka

To Max Brod

[Prague; postmark: December 13, 1920]

That was very sweet of you, Max. I want to thank you at once. When I was upstairs at your wife's and twirled the little Grimmenstein residency permit in my hand, it seemed like a grand present to me. I would not like to lose that feeling, even though I am not going to Grimmenstein. I am not going because I cannot overcome myself, or rather because I find it overwhelming. It was by no means easy to change the direction of one's journey, but now it has been done. I am going to Tatranské Matliary (management: Forberger),[65] at least for the present. If it should not be good, I will transfer to Szontagh's Sanatorium,[66] in Nový Smokovec, about an hour away. I am leaving on the 18th, would have liked to see you in Prague before I left but did not want to linger any longer.

Your wife told me a good deal about the trip, saying things that were acute and bitter and sweet, as she in her special and sometimes touching way habitually divides her verdicts between the bitter and the sweet. I came away with the impression, as I did from the reviews, that it was an unalloyed success[67] and that all your intentions came through. *Esther*[68] seems to have paved the way for it remarkably well.

I will write to you from the Tatra. By the way, Ottla is coming along for a few days.[69]

All good wishes, Franz

Best regards to your sister, brother-in-law, and Thea.

To Minze Eisner

[Picture postcard. Tatranské Matliary, end of December 1920] Dear Minze, I received your letter just before my departure. Astonishing things! Scarcely are you on the ship at last when it sinks. However it is not quite clear, at least I did not understand your hints. And what are these Baltic Sea plans? These were never clear to me. But you are brave and that is fine. Be kind and let me follow your further adventures from my reclining chair. I forgot to ask lately: are you entirely well now?

Cordial regards, yours, Kafka

To Max Brod

[Matliary; postmark: December 31, 1920] Dear Max,

You imagine that your letter did *not* make me hot? And I certainly would not receive the kingdoms of the world and all its glory either, even if they were offered to me, but not because I would not yield, but because out of sheer greed I would have broken my neck casting myself down. Nothing but great weakness and poverty kept me from Berlin, and so prevented the "offer," but nothing would have prevented me from succumbing to the "offer." I would have gone at it tooth and nail; you don't know how ambitious I am.

It is different for you. The way you claim to view the vitality of Berlin is the way I actually view your vitality. You had the opportunity and resisted it with a firmness that to me is utterly convincing. Your decision in this regard is so firm and convincing to me that I would accept it just as readily if it were now to turn out differently.

Incidentally you have not yet mentioned the possibility of moving to Berlin. The interesting thing about the lure of Berlin is that the intensity there lures you, but you seem to feel that your life in Prague could not be intensified in the Berlin manner. Rather it would have to become a Berlin life through and through. But perhaps when you were in Berlin you did not hear the command to come to Berlin, but only to leave Prague.

I would need further explanations to understand the theater matter. The

Berliners have read the notices as·well as I. You yourself have spoken. Everything imaginable and unimaginable is being performed, so are people to shrink from your *Forgers?*

F. was not at your readings? Because of her condition, I suppose.[70] To have been in Berlin and not seen F. strikes me as not right, though of course it would have been the same with me. I feel for F. the love that an unsuccessful general has for the city he could not take, but which "nevertheless" became something great—a happy mother of two. Hadn't you heard about the first child?

As for myself, I have found a good place here, good, that is, insofar as one wants something that has the look of a sanatorium yet is not one. Thus it also caters to tourists, hunters, and just about anyone; there is no undue luxury and one has to pay only for what one has actually eaten. Yet it is a sanatorium since it has a doctor,[71] the facilities for the rest cure, one's choice of food, good milk and cream. It is situated two kilometers beyond Tatra-Lomnitz, so it is two kilometers closer to the great Lomnitz peaks, and is itself at an altitude of 900 meters. A good doctor? Yes, a specialist. If only I had become a specialist! How the world is simplified for him! My stomach trouble, sleeplessness, nervousness, all, that is, which I am and have can be traced to the infection of the lungs. So long as the disease was not manifest, it masked itself as stomach trouble, bad nerves. Some lung trouble—this I too believe—remains masked in this way. And since the suffering of the world is so clear to him, he goes around with a small leather case no bigger than a National Fund collection box, in which he keeps the salvation of the world; and if the world wishes, he will inject it into the world's blood for twelve crowns. And in fact he is also, for the sake of consistency, a handsome, red-cheeked, strong man with a young (obviously Jewish) wife, whom he loves, and a pretty little daughter, who is so astoundingly bright that he cannot speak of it, precisely because she is his own child and he doesn't want to boast. He pays me a daily visit; it is useless but not unpleasant.

In general this might be said: If I can endure this regimen both physically and mentally for a few months (especially staying in the same place), I will come very close to health. But probably that is a fallacy and only means: If I am well, then I will get well. In the first week I gained 1.6 kilos, but that proves nothing, for I always come on like a lion in the first week of a cure.

There are about thirty permanent guests here. I took most of them for non-Jews, such full-blooded Hungarians they were; however the majority turn out to be Jews, beginning with the headwaiter. I speak little and with few people, for the most part out of shyness, but also because I consider that proper. (If someone is shy of people, he should show it.) But there is one person here, from Kaschau,[72] twenty-five years old, with miserable teeth, one

weak eye mostly kept closed, perpetually upset stomach, nervous, also a
Hungarian who has learned German only since coming here, not a word of
Slovakian, but a young man to fall in love with, charming in the East
European Jewish sense. Full of irony, unrest, moodiness, confidence, but also
neediness. Everything is "interesting, interesting" to him, but that does not
carry the usual meaning, but rather something like, "It's burning, it's
burning." He is a Socialist, but produces a great deal of Hebrew from his
childhood memories, has studied the Talmud and the *Shulhan Arukh*.[73]
"Interesting, interesting." But has forgotten almost everything. He attends all
kinds of groups, has heard you speak, reports that Kaschau was wild about
the talk, was also present when Langer founded the Mizrachi[74] group.

May Berlin turn out well for you, and do drop me another word about it. Or
won't you be taking a trip to Slovakia one of these days? Have you begun the
novel[75] you once spoke of?

Regards from me to your wife and to everyone. I sent my thanks to you
for the Grimmenstein residence permit care of the Ewer Bookshop in Berlin.
It seemed and still seems to me to have been a very special kindness on your
part.

Yours, Franz

1921

To Max Brod

[Matliary, January 13, 1921]

Dearest Max, In the last three days I was not much inclined to defend
Matliary or to write at all. A triviality. One guest, sick but cheerful, sings a
bit under my balcony or chats on the balcony above mine with a friend (the
young man from Kaschau who is as considerate toward me as a mother
toward her child). At any rate, this little incident takes place and I writhe on
my reclining chair almost in paroxysms. My heart cannot bear it, every word
bores into my temples, and the consequence of this nervous shock is that I do
not sleep at night either. I wanted to leave today, to move to Smokovec,
much against my will, since everything here suits me. Moreover my room is
very quiet, no one alongside, under, or over me. What I hear about
Smokovec from unbiased people confirms my reluctance (no woods there,
lovely ones here, two years ago everything was leveled by a cyclone; cottages

and balconies face on a townlike, dusty, trafficked road). Nevertheless I would have had to go, except that they have just hit on an arrangement that presumably guarantees me quiet from tomorrow on: instead of the two friends, a quiet lady will take the room above mine. If not, then I will surely go. In any case I would surely leave after a while, simply from my "natural" restlessness.

I mention all this because I am so full of it, as though the world were composed of nothing but the balcony over me and its noisiness, and also in order to show you how unjustified your criticisms of Matliary are, for the balcony noises (the coughing of the severely ill, the ringing of room bells) are much worse in crowded sanatoria, and come not only from above but from all sides. I simply will not hear of any other criticism of Matliary (unless it were to be the lack of elegance of my room, but that is no objection). And thirdly, I mention it in order to show you my psychological state of the moment. It reminds me a little of the old Austria. Sometimes things went quite well; one lay on the sofa in the evening in the well-heated room, thermometer in mouth, the milk jug nearby, and enjoyed a certain measure of peace. But it was only a certain measure, not real peace. Only a triviality, I don't know what, say the question of the Trautenau District Court,[1] was needed to make the throne in Vienna begin to sway. A dental technician—that is what he is—studies half out loud on the upper balcony and the whole empire, but really the whole thing, goes up in flames.

But enough of these endless matters.

I don't believe that we differ essentially on that major question, as you would have it. I would put it this way: You want the impossible, while for me the possible is impossible. I am perhaps only one step below you, but on the same stairway. For you the possible is attainable: you have married, you have had no children, not because it was impossible for you but because you did not want them; you will have children, too, I hope; you have loved and been loved, not only in marriage. But this hasn't been enough for you, because you want the impossible. Perhaps for the same reason I could not attain the possible, only that this lightning struck me one step before it did you, even before I reached the possible. That is a great difference, to be sure, but hardly a difference in our essential natures.

For instance, your Berlin experience strikes me as distinctly impossible. That it involved a chambermaid[2] certainly doesn't demean you: on the contrary it shows how seriously you take the relationship. From the superficial point of view this girl was very far removed from the aspects of Berlin that you found fascinating. Everything else you were experiencing should really have diminished the girl in your eyes. Nevertheless, because of the seriousness with which you took the relationship she was able to hold her own. But—please don't be angry with me for what I am going to say—perhaps it is stupid and false, perhaps I have misread this part of your letter, perhaps what has happened in the meantime already confutes me—are you taking the girl as seriously as you take the relationship? And when one takes something not entirely seriously, but wants to love seriously, doesn't it mean that one desires the impossible, as if one who has taken one step forward and then taken one step back should, contrary to every evidence of reality, claim to have taken two steps forward, just because he has after all taken two steps and no less? I am not thinking of what you quote the girl as saying, for that may conform very well with seriousness, but rather how you can give no thought to what you mean for the girl. A foreigner, a guest, even a Jew, one of hundreds who take a liking to the pretty chambermaid, someone in whose serious desires she can believe, for a single night (even if he does not have this seriousness). But what more can there be? A love spanning the distance between countries? A correspondence? The hope of a mythical February? And are you asking for this much abnegation? And that *you* remain faithful to the relationship (this is something I understand very well, really deep faithfulness)—do you call this faithfulness to the girl? Isn't this heaping one impossibility on top of another? The misery in all this is certainly terrible, this much I can see from afar, but the forces that drive you to the impossible—even if they are only the forces of longing—are very intense and cannot have vanished when you returned, defeated, but bear you up to face each new day.

You say you do not understand my position. It is very simple as long as one does not try to look too deep below the surface. You don't understand it only because you assume something good or tender in my behavior, but then cannot find it. In this matter I behave toward you as a first grader who has been flunked eight times behaves toward an eighth grader who stands on the verge of the impossible: graduation. I can appreciate what you have behind you. But when you see me, a lubber of a boy, sitting stooped over a multiplication example, you can't understand it. "Eight years," you think. "This must be an amazingly thorough person. He is still working on multiplication. But no matter how thorough he is, he really ought to be able to do it by now. Therefore I don't understand him." But that I could be totally lacking in any faculty for mathematics, or that I don't cheat out of sheer funk, or most likely—that I had lost that faculty out of funk—none of this occurs to you. And yet it is nothing but the commonest sort of funk, the fear of death. Like a person who cannot resist the temptation to swim out into the sea, and is blissful to be so carried away—"Now you are a man, a great swimmer"—and suddenly for no particular reason he raises himself up and sees only the sky and the sea, and on the waves is only his own little head and he is seized by a horrible fear and nothing else matters, he must get back to the shore, even if his lungs burst. That is how it is.

But now let's compare your way and mine—or rather be considerate and let's leave my way out—with the great days of old. The only true misfortune then was women's barrenness, but even if they were barren, fertility could be gained by prayer. I—I must necessarily speak in personal terms—I no longer see any barrenness of this sort. Every womb is fruitful and smirks uselessly at the world. And when one hides one's face, it is not in order to protect oneself from this smirk, but not to let one's own smirk be seen. Compared to this, the struggle with the father doesn't mean much. After all, he is only an elder brother, also a scapegrace son, who from jealousy is merely pitifully trying to distract his younger brother from the decisive struggle and moreover does so successfully.—But now it is quite dark, as it must be for the final blasphemy.

Franz

[IN THE MARGIN] Would you have a copy of the Schreiber article[3] which you could lend to me? I will send it back promptly.

Shouldn't you also have new proofs of the poems?[4] And perhaps also of your big book?[5]

Please give my regards to Felix and Oskar; when I feel calmer I will write to them. I have read over what you say about Matliary and see that after all I must answer it point by point*: You know Slovakia, but not the Tatra country. This was vacation territory for the Budapesters, so everything is clean and the cooking is good. I admit that for us a German or an Austrian sanatorium would be a little more confortable, but those are only the feelings of the first few days. One soon gets adjusted, one of my virtues, by the way, which you want to undermine (and the family tries to do the same).

I am taking the matter as seriously as you insist, Max. In fact I even see the antithesis as far worse. It is not life or death but life or one-fourth life, breathing or gasping for breath, slowly (not much faster than a real life lasts) burning down with fever.

Since I see it this way, you can trust me not to omit anything I can do to make it turn out halfway well. But why should the doctor——? When I read your letter the first time, that sentence frightened me so that I smudged it over with my pencil to make it unreadable. At bottom what he says is not stupid and certainly no more stupid than what all the others say. It is biblical,

---

* My plans (behind the back of the Institute) are far more ambitious than you imagine. Until March here, until May Smokovec, over the summer Grimmenstein, over the fall—I don't know.

in fact: Whosoever cannot take in the creative breath of life must ail in every part.

I did prove that I can be cured without meat; I showed that in Zürau where I ate scarcely any meat and in Meran, where after the first two weeks people didn't recognize me, I looked so good. To be sure, the Enemy intervened, but eating meat doesn't fend him off or not eating meat bring him on. He comes in either case.

I have improved a great deal here and if it weren't that here too I have been troubled by a good many things—not connected with M.[6]—I would be further along.

I regret for the sake of my parents, for your sake, and finally for my sake (because in this respect we are one) that I didn't go to Smokovec right at the beginning. But since I am here, why should I risk a bad exchange and, after barely four weeks, leave here where everybody makes an honest effort to give me all that I need.

To Max Brod

[Matliary, second half of January 1921]

Dearest Max, Another postscript, so that you can see how the Enemy proceeds. No doubt there are certain inner laws, but it almost looks as if things were set up according to outer laws. Perhaps because you are physically detached from this you'll understand it better.

I had nowhere near recovered from the balcony misery. To be sure, the upper balcony is now quiet, but my fear-sharpened ears hear everything, even the dental technician, although he is separated from me by four windows and one floor.

[A DIAGRAM OF THE ROOMS FOLLOWS]

And even though he is also Jewish, greets me modestly, and certainly has no wicked intentions, he has become for me absolutely "the foreign devil." His voice gives me heart trouble; it is toneless, lethargic, actually low, but penetrates through walls. As I said, I have still to recover from the misery. At the moment everything upsets me. Sometimes it almost seems to me that life itself is what upsets me; how otherwise could everything be so upsetting?

And here is what happened yesterday: There is only one bed case here, aside from a patient whom I have not yet seen, a Czech, whose room is under my balcony. He has tuberculosis of the lungs and larynx (one of the variants of this disease, in addition to life and death), and because of his illness and because besides himself there are only two Czechs here, who however pay no attention to him, he feels isolated. I only exchanged a few words with him twice from the corridor and he sent a request through the housemaid that I drop in on him. A friendly, quiet man of about fifty, father of two grown-up sons. I went to see him shortly before supper, in order to keep the visit short, and he asked me to drop in again after eating. Then he told me about his illness, showed me a little mirror which he has to insert deep into his throat when there is sun, in order to expose the abscesses to the light, then showed me the large mirror with which he can look into his throat in order to place the small mirror properly. He then showed me a drawing of the abscesses, which by the way first appeared only three months ago, then told me briefly about his family and that he had had no news of them for a week, so he is worried. I listened, occasionally threw in a question, had to take the mirror and the picture in my hand. "Nearer the eyes," he said, when I held the mirror far away, and finally, there was no particular transition, I asked myself (this has occasionally happened to me before; it always begins with this question), "What if you should faint just now?" and I already saw this fainting fit coming toward me like a wave. I managed to keep conscious, or so I believe, to the last, but how I would get out of the room without help was beyond me. Whether he went on speaking, I don't know; I heard nothing. Finally I pulled myself together, said something about a lovely evening, which was supposed to be some sort of explanation for my staggering out on his balcony and sitting on the railing there in the cold. There I came to sufficiently to be able to say I was not feeling well, and to leave the room without saying goodnight. With the help of the corridor walls and a bench on the landing, I made it to my room.

I wanted to do the man a good turn and did him a very bad one; as I heard next morning, he did not sleep the whole night because of me. In spite of this I can't reproach myself, rather I don't understand why everybody doesn't faint. What you see in that bed is much worse than an execution, yes, even than a torturing. To be sure, we have not ourselves invented the tortures but have learned about them from diseases, no man dares to torture the way they do. Here torture goes on for years, with pauses for effect so that it will not go too quickly, and—the unique element—the victim himself is compelled, by his own will, out of his own wretched inner self, to protract the torture. This whole wretched life in bed, the fever, the shortness of breath, the taking of medicines, the painful and dangerous business with the mirrors (one little awkward motion and he can burn himself)—all this has no other purpose but to slow down the development of the abscesses, from which he must finally suffocate, to prolong this wretched life, the fever and so on, as long as possible. And his relatives and the doctors and visitors have literally built some scaffoldings over this not burning but slowly smouldering pyre, so that without danger of contagion they can visit, cool, and comfort the tormented man, cheer him up to endure further misery. And back in their room, they wash themselves with dread, like me.

Anyway, I too hardly slept, but I had two comforters. First: strong cardiac pains, which reminded me of another kind of torturer, who however is much milder in that he is much quicker. And then I had, among a swarm of dreams, this one which came last: To the left of me sat a child in a little shirt (it was not clear, at least as far as I can remember the dream, whether this was my own child, but that didn't bother me)—while Milena sat on my right. Both snuggled against me and I told them the story of my wallet. It had been lost and then I found it but I hadn't opened it yet and so didn't know whether the money was still in it. But even if it had been lost, that didn't matter, if I only had the two of them at my side.—I can no longer feel the happiness that swept me toward morning.

This was the dream. But the reality is that three weeks ago (after many similar letters, but this was the most decisive, in keeping with the extreme necessity of putting an end to the affair) I asked her for one favor: not to write any more and to prevent our ever seeing each other.

By the way, I also gained weight this week, all told 3.4 kilos in four weeks. Regards to Felix and Oskar, please. Has anything come of Oskar's Sicilian trip? And what are they both doing? Ruth?[7]

By poorish light on the balcony in the evening:

I let the letter lie for a few days, perhaps because I wanted to include what would "happen" next. It was nothing so very bad.

After your letter today, I am very ashamed of what I said about you and the girl. If I were married and had done something of the sort to my wife, I would—to express it in somewhat exaggerated terms but no more exaggerated than the premise—go into a corner and kill myself. But you forgive me to such an extent that you don't even mention it. Granted that in your letter before last you wrote in much too general terms. But I should have interpreted the generalities in a different way. Nevertheless my basic feeling on the question has not changed, only it is no longer so facilely demonstrable.

Perhaps I can get a bit nearer to it by speaking about myself. I don't have your letter right to hand (and to get it I would have to crawl out of my heavy wrappings) but I think you say that if the striving for perfection makes the attainment of women impossible for me, it would also have to make everything else impossible, eating, the office, and so forth.

That is correct. The striving for perfection is only a small part of my huge Gordian knot, but in this case every part is the whole and so your charge is correct. But this impossibility also actually exists, the impossibility of eating, etc., only that all this is not so crudely obvious as the impossibility of marriage.

Let us compare ourselves in this respect: we both have a physical problem. You have gloriously overcome it.[8] While I was having these thoughts, skiers were practicing on the slope across the road, not the usual ones I see around here, hotel guests or soldiers from the nearby barracks who are impressive enough in their grave smooth processions along the highway, gliding down from above, marching up from below. But this time there were three strangers who had come from Lomnitz. They too were probably not such experts, but how skillful they were! A tall fellow led, the shorter two followed. For them there were no slopes, no ditches, no embankments; they glided over the terrain like your pen over paper. Downhill it went much faster, they were simply tearing along, but even going up the slope it was at least like flying. And what a display they put on, coming down. I do not know whether it was really the great telemark swing (is that the right term?), but it was like a dream, like the way a healthy man glides from waking into sleep. It went on that way for about a quarter of an hour, almost in total silence (which is partly why I love it), and then they were once more on the road and—there is no other way to express it—swooped down toward Lomnitz.

I watched them and thought of you, that that was how you had overcome your physical problem.

I on the other hand—I intended to continue.

But then came several bad nights, the first two resulting from fortuitous, temporary single-night causes, the others from an abscess on the small of my back which keeps me from lying down by day and won't let me sleep at night. These are petty matters and if nothing else of this sort occurs, I will easily repair the damage. I only mention it to show that if a someone exists who wants to prevent my gaining weight and strength (up to this point my weight was consistently going up: I put on 4.2 kilos in five weeks), he is firmly in the saddle on my back.

I will not go into further comparisons today, Max; I am too tired. It is also too complicated. The material has increased so monstrously with the passage of time and is so diffuse that one necessarily becomes garrulous when one starts on it again.

Should you come? Of course you should come, if it is possible without too much trouble, but I see no possibility, unless you are making a trip to

Slovakia. From your letter I gather that you would want to combine it with a trip to Berlin, by way of Oderberg,[9] say; no, that would be too much trouble. Do not do it, for my sake as well, for it would impose too much responsibility on me. Or could you stay longer than three days, as a vacation for yourself?

I feel tempted to go on with the previous discussion, so does my talkativeness boil over. You underlined "Fear of what?" Of so much, but on the earthly plane above all fear that I will not suffice, not physically, not mentally, to bear the burden of another person. As long as we are almost united, it is merely a groping fear: "What? Are we really almost united?" And when this fear has done its work, it becomes an absolutely irrefutable, unendurable fear. No, no more of this today, it is too much.

You mention letters of Dehmel's. I only know the ones in the December issue,[10] only half-human, married-man stuff.

I have to come back to it. You write: "Why be more afraid of love than of all the other affairs of life?" and just before that: "In love I have come closest to experiencing surges of divinity." Taking both sentences together, it is as though you wished to say: "Why be more afraid of the burning bush than of any old thornbush?"

You see, it is as if my life task had consisted in taking possession of a house.—

This, too, remained unfinished. A few days' break, fatigue, slight fever (probably from the abscess), raging snowstorm outside, now it is better, although this evening a new disturbance has come up which I hope will be so minor that I can suppress it by merely noting it: a new table mate, an elderly spinster, repulsively powdered and perfumed, probably severely ill, also unhinged by nervousness, talkative in company, as a Czech partly dependent on me, also deaf in the ear on the side away from me. (Now there are a few more Czechs here, but they are leaving.) I have one weapon which I hope will be effectual: today she mentioned (not to me) that her favorite paper was *Venkov*,[11] especially because of its editorials. Delighted, I have been thinking of that all evening. (By the way, she comes from Smokovec and has been in many sanatoria and praises one excessively: Grimmenstein; but as of March it has been sold, to the government.) Perhaps the most cunning method will be to wait until she says something that she cannot possibly retract. About Grimmenstein she remarked: *má to žid, ale výtečně to vede.** But I suppose that wasn't sufficient.

* The owner is a Jew but he runs the place remarkably well.

You mustn't conclude, Max, from everything I have written that I suffer from paranoia. I have learned by experience that no place remains unoccupied and if *I* do not sit high on my horse, the persecutor will be sitting there.

But now I will close (or else you won't get the letter before you go on your trip), although I have not said what I wanted to and certainly have not found the way to you through the detour through myself; that way to you which, at least at the start, was obscurely clear to me. But this is simply the pattern of a bad writer, who finds the material lying in his arms like a heavy sea-serpent and wherever he gropes, to right, to left, it goes on forever, and he cannot endure even what he embraces. Especially when he is a person who returns from supper to his quiet room trembling almost physically from the painful aftereffects of mere contact with someone at table.

Yet all through this letter my thoughts have dwelt principally on your two options. The first strikes me as impossible, the newpaper a kind of *Gazette des Ardennes*,[12] impossible, the chief editorship impossible, the work load too great (you would surely not be the only music critic?), the political position (everyone connected with such a paper must take a position) too strong, the whole thing unworthy of you. The only advantage would probably be the high salary.

But the second option, why should that not be possible? For which the government would pay? The government is so totally improvised, so precarious, that it is bound to do some first-rate things now and then. And this would be something of that sort. It would simply be a way of thanking you for what you have done and for what you might possibly do. (Would you be under any bureaucratic restrictions in regard to it? After all, there were whole long years when you felt no impulse to get involved in anything of the sort.) Besides, things of this kind are not happening only in Czechoslovakia; they are the happy legacy of the press arrangements improvised in wartime.

Odd—I must add this, and it has some of the certainty of your decision about Berlin, although it is not so immediately persuasive—odd that you hesitate to throw all your professional energies—I mean the energies you want to commit to this—into Zionism.

I enclose the article[13] which I read all at once, rapidly, several times in succession, so dazzlingly is it written (except for a few evasive little flourishes about business papers). But is it intended as an indictment? Probably not. And is it directed specifically at Berlin? And not at every big city, at least in the West, where inevitably the conventions that supposedly make "life" easier grow stronger and more strangling.

You mention your novel[14] along with the studies of the Kabbalah—is there a connection?

The poems came yesterday. You are thinking of me.

Please give my regards to Felix and Oskar; I hope they too will not forget me, even if I don't write.

By the way, about a week ago I had another letter from M., a last letter. She is strong and unalterable, somewhat in your style. You too are unalterable; but no, that's not how the women speak of you. Yet so you are, in a certain sense, and I particularly value that; even in regard to women you are unalterable.

To Dr. Josef David

[Matliary, end of January 1921][15]

Dear Pepa,[16]

Well done, well done, and I am only putting in a few small mistakes not in order for there to be some mistakes in it but because, forgive me, even in your letter my director[17] would find mistakes, as he would find them in any letter. I only do it so that the letter will contain a suitable quota of mistakes.

Here I am trying to live quietly. A newspaper hardly ever comes my way; I don't even read the *Tribuna*[18] and have no notion of what the Communists are doing or what the Germans[19] are saying, but only of what the Magyars are saying. This I hear, but I don't understand. Unfortunately they talk a good deal and I would be happy if they said less. Why a poem, Pepa; don't put yourself to such trouble, why a new poem? Horace has already written many beautiful poems and we have read only one and a half of them. Besides, I already have a poem of yours. Near here there is a small military infirmary and all evening there is marching along the road and it's always the "Panthers" and "turning round and round."[20] The Czech soldiers are not the worst; they go skiing and laugh and shout like children, though children with soldiers' voices. But there are also a few Hungarian soldiers among them, and one of them has learned five words of the Panther song and apparently has lost his mind to it; wherever he goes, he bellows out the song. And the lovely mountains and forests round about look down on all this so gravely, as if they liked it.

But all this is not bad; it only goes on a little while every day. Much worse in this respect are the devilishly noisy voices inside the house. But that too can be endured. I won't complain. We are in the Tatra Mountains and the Sabine hills are elsewhere and perhaps nowhere.

Please give my regards to your parents and sisters. How has it worked out with the National Theater?

Yours, F

To Max Brod

[Matliary, February 1, 1921]

Dear Max, I sent an endless letter to your Koschel[21] address. But I imagine it would not have arrived until around the first of February. Perhaps you will still get it, but if not, nothing is lost, for just as it had no end, so it had no middle, only a beginning, only a beginning. I could start all over again, but what would Berlin make of it?

The letter was delayed by various interruptions which are listed therein, but the newest was not included, since I only had an inkling of it when I was sending the letter off. You see, I have caught cold, or rather I did not catch cold, for I can't imagine what would have made me catch cold. The bad weather, almost two weeks of heavy winds without letup, simply tossed me into bed without more ado. I was in bed for four days, am still in bed today, only this evening did I get up a little. It wasn't bad, it was more a precautionary going to bed, I only coughed and spat, had no abnormal fever. The doctor, who listened to my lungs today, said there is nothing new there, in fact it is better than it was a couple of days ago. Still I am tired out from it; and my weight, which at the end of the fifth week had shown a gain of 4.2 kilos, will surely tomorrow, at best, stay level. But in spite of all the fatigue and all the disturbances, I won't complain at the moment, for everything that had happened in the past six weeks, taken and firmly kneaded together, would scarcely have had the punch of three days and nights in Meran, even though back then I may have had more stamina.

Wednesday

I was disturbed last night, but in a pleasant way. There's a twenty-one-year-old medical student[22] here, a Budapest Jew, very ambitious, intelligent, also highly literary; incidentally he greatly resembles Werfel in appearance, though somewhat coarser on the whole. He has a hunger for people, the way a born doctor does. Is anti-Zionist; his guides are Jesus and Dostoevski. He came over from the main building around nine o'clock to put a compress on me (hardly necessary). His special friendliness toward me seems to spring from the effect of your name, which he knows very well. The possibility of your coming here was sensational news, of course, both to him and the young man from Kaschau.

Concerning this possibility, I wrote in the Prague letter that I would be very glad if you came but only on condition that you were going to be traveling in Slovakia anyhow, or that you can come for your own health's sake, that is, for a longer time. But if it is to be a special trip, whether from Prague or from Brünn or (you seem to imply that you could combine it with the trip to Berlin) from Oderberg or some other distant place, please don't come; it would impose too much responsibility on me.

And be happy and gay in Berlin. If I wrote something nasty about the Dehmel letters, it surely has no bearing on you. To love a woman and be unassailed by anxiety, or at least able to cope with anxiety, and moreover to have this woman to wife is for me such an impossible happiness that, in the manner of class struggle, I hate it. Besides I have only seen the letters in the December issue.

And in fact how could insubstantial fears affect the fullness of life? That fullness is in your book,[23] it is there in the way the women and the times part company, and most powerfully of all in the early poems. You have scarcely hitherto spoken as powerfully as you have done in "The Kiss." I am really just beginning to read the book with clearer vision on the first fair day after weeks of bad weather and my first day out of bed, which I am beginning now.

If you come, would you bring along a kabbalistic work? I assume it is in Hebrew.

Yours, F

To Minze Eisner

[Matliary, about February 8, 1921][24]

Dear Minze, Tired from the day's work (it's like greenhouse work), the last glass of milk has not yet been drunk, the last temperature not taken. I lie on the sofa with the thermometer in my mouth. Minze, where are you running about in the wide world? I imagine, if you were a man, you would have become Robinson Crusoe or Sinbad the Sailor and children would read books about your adventures.

How did you leave Ahlem? On good terms or bad? And the gardening school there no longer exists? And your present firm[25] took you as an apprentice without any previous training? For two years in exchange for board and room? What are your obligations for those two years?

These are a few of the unclear points but otherwise it seems that what you have done is excellent, brave and proud. Your letter consists of two letters, one long and cheerful, and one short and sad. But that in itself shows that you are walking on your own feet, for the general way of the world, as it may manifest itself on the streets of Teplitz, is neither cheerful nor sad, but even if it momentarily looks cheerful or sad, is always merely a desperate confused mixture.

Your letter came just on the last day of a relatively good spell. I read it on the balcony, which is quite like the one in Schelesen, except that it is much nearer the snowcapped mountains and therefore a bit poorer and more tumbledown. So I read the letter there, was happy over your happiness, not so cast down over your sadness, and though my feet were bundled up in the blankets, I traced your walk on the Brocken. (Once years ago I spent some weeks at the foot of the Brocken, at the Jungborn sanatorium.[26] Perhaps you passed by it. It is not far from Harzburg. I was there for several weeks, and though I was then in good health, I never made the expedition to the Brocken. I don't know why. One of the people there once made the climb quite naked one warm night; all he had with him was his coat strapped to his back. But I preferred to sleep in my open-air hut—in those days sleep was still sweet and Minze the Hiker was scarcely born; no, she was already a few years old and a more or less well-behaved Teplitz schoolgirl.)

Yes, that was the last good day, but then everything got worse, all sorts of things, finally catching cold and having to take to my bed, three weeks of almost uninterrupted windy weather. Now it is better at last, in heaven and on earth.

Dear Minze, Again an interruption of many days. I wasn't feeling quite well, but also not quite bad, only a little too tired to raise my hand to write. Perhaps the wind was to blame, always wind, and a roaring in the woods as though it were the Baltic Sea. But now it has been fair for the past few days, bright sun by day and at night such sharp cold that if you go out for a few minutes without earmuffs, your ears suddenly begin to burn so that you think you will never be able to reach the house, even if you are only two hundred yards away. May it stay like this.

And what about you, Minze, are you working so hard? Will you be able to keep it up? At the Pomological Institute[27] in Prague I once met many gardeners who spoke of their experiences. They agreed that running a nursery involved the most work. Then I happened to be in the largest nursery in Bohemia (Maschek, Turnau) and it was not half so bad there; it was mostly a tree nursery, and except for the shipping season in spring and fall the workmen there led a very good life. To be sure, this operation was already a bit on the downgrade and was a long way from German efficiency.

Books? Have you time to read any nongardening books? I'll have a little book[28] sent to you which will give you a wonderful picture of life in those small Baltic resorts a century ago. And I will write to you again soon. Courage, Minze, courage!

Yours, Kafka

[IN THE MARGIN] What do you mean by "if the doctors are right"?

To Max Brod

[Matliary, beginning of March 1921]

Dear Max,

I see this won't be a real letter. I am returning in two weeks[29] and then can perhaps answer your letter in person.

When I received your letter, which affected me deeply in many ways, I answered it in my head literally in a single outburst. But nothing was written down. A few letters lay about which had to be answered (I still have not got around to them); the young man from Budapest of whom I wrote recently took up almost all of my time for a while. But above all the fatigue increased. I lie for hours in the reclining chair in a twilight state, like that of my grandparents, which I used to marvel at when I was a child. I am not doing well, even though the doctor maintains that the trouble in the lung has remitted by half. But I would say that it is far more than twice as bad. I never had such coughing, such shortness of breath, never such weakness. I do not deny that in Prague it would have become much worse. But when I consider that the outer circumstances here, except for various interruptions, were favorable enough this time, then I do not know how it might possibly improve at all.

But it is stupid and vain to talk this way and to take it so seriously. In the middle of a little coughing fit, you cannot help regarding it as extremely important. But when it has abated, you can help it and ought to. When it gets dark, one lights another candle, and when that candle is burned down, one lies quietly in darkness. Just because there are so many mansions in my Father's house, one should make no noise.

I am glad enough to be leaving here. Perhaps I should have done so a month ago, but I am so immobile and all sorts of people here have been so incomprehensibly friendly to me that if my leave were any longer, I would stay on here for quite a while, especially since the weather is finally turning fine. In the pavilion in the woods I have several times been able to lie with my trunk bare, and on my balcony once totally naked.

From the above you might end up thinking that I have not been taking the cure seriously. On the contrary, I take it with furious seriousness. I am even eating meat, though with greater repugnance than for other foods. It was a mistake that I did not previously live with consumptives and as yet have not looked the disease straight in the eye. I have done that here for the first time. But the last chance to get a bit better was probably offered in Meran.—Now enough of this. I am writing it down in order not to have to talk about it in Prague.

You write about Solomon Molkho[30] as though I had ever heard about him. I have really missed a lot in these three months.

See you soon!

Franz

The Wickersdorf[31] circular letter fits in with this subject. I happened to have seen the Essig letter by chance in a newspaper and wanted to send it to you as an example of particular horridness. "Those dear little eyes which so tickled his heart." Of course there is basically nothing so horrid about it except that the letter has now been published and further that the letter-writer is by now food for the worms.[32]

To Max Brod

[Matliary, beginning of March 1921]

Dearest Max,

This letter, I hope, will arrive at the same time as my letter of yesterday. Yesterday's doesn't count; I did not mention under what circumstances it was written. I was lying on my sofa, knocked out by the exertion of eating. An agonizing lack of appetite brings sweat out on my face when I see the horror of a full plate in front of me. However, I have been eating much meat for the past two weeks, because a less capable cook has replaced the previous cook who liked me. The meat caused my hemorrhoids to flare up and I had intense pain night and day. I was in that state when I wrote the letter. But it was not accurate. For if the coughing seems harder to me, the shortness of breath worse, there are positive factors to offset that: the doctor's findings, the weight gain, though that is at a standstill, and the favorable temperature. Well, we'll soon see each other. To write such exaggerations! Who directs my hand?

Yours, F

To Max Brod

[Matliary, March 11, 1921]

Dearest Max, May I ask you to do me a very great favor which moreover has to be done immediately. I want to stay on here, not right here but in the Tatra, probably in Dr. Guhr's Sanatorium in Polianka, which has been highly recommended, though it is also much more expensive than Matliary.

I want to stay for the following reasons:

1. To begin with, the doctor warns me of the possibility of a total collapse if I should return to Prague and promises approximate recovery if I stay until

autumn, so that every year a six-week spell at the ocean or the mountains will suffice to keep me going. Both predictions, the second more than the first, are exaggerated, yet he torments me every morning with them, in a fatherly spirit, in a friendly spirit, in every sort of spirit. And even though I know that his predictions would be greatly toned down if he knew that I want to transfer to Polianka, it still makes an impression on me.

2. Everyone at home asks me to stay, though with more reason than they know. I am firmly convinced, now that I have been living here among consumptives, that healthy people run no danger of infection. Here, however, the healthy are only the woodcutters in the forest and the girls in the kitchen (who will simply pick uneaten food from the plates of patients and eat it—patients whom I shrink from sitting opposite) but not a single person from our own town circles. But how loathsome it is to sit opposite a larynx patient, for instance (blood brother of a consumptive but far sadder), who sits across from you so friendly and harmless, looking at you with the transfigured eyes of the consumptive and at the same time coughing into your face through his spread fingers drops of prurulent phlegm from his tubercular ulcer. At home I would be sitting that way, though not quite in so dire a state, as "good uncle" among the children.

3. Perhaps I would be able to bear the spring and summer in Prague quite well; at least Dr. Kral wrote advising me to come, but in talking to my parents he seems to have retracted this advice. (These vacillations can be explained by the vacillations of my own letters.) But perhaps it would be wiser suddenly to do something halfway decisive if, as the doctor maintains, it would really lead to improvement. And where could I better spend the warm season than in the high mountains? (Polianka's altitude is more than 1100 meters.) I can imagine where I would be better off: in a village, doing some light work. But what village I don't know.

4. The decisive factor, though, is my subjective state, which is not good—though of course there are still endless possibilities of its worsening. Coughing and shortness of breath are worse than they have ever been. In the middle of winter—it was a hard winter, not in respect to cold but with incessant savage blizzards—the shortness of breath was occasionally desperate; now, in good weather, it is of course better. I now tell myself this: that either my subjective condition is right, in which case it doesn't matter what happens to my job. But no, there I'm mistaken: in that case it particularly matters what happens to the job, for then I especially need it. But if I were to approximately regain my health, then I would need it less.

My leave is over on the 20th of March. I have been too long considering what to do. From pure anxiety and scruples I have waited until now, until practically the last days, when the request for an extension of leave becomes all but indecent extortion. For the proper procedure would be as follows: that I first ask the director what his opinion would be; then, depending on his answer, a petition would be submitted; then this petition would be presented to the administrative committee, and so on. Naturally it is now too late for all this. Nothing can be done by letter any longer, and the extortionary aspect can only be softened by a personal appeal. Thus I should go to Prague, but should I waste time on traveling? I could ask Ottla to go, but should I ask her to do this in her condition?[33] Also, I don't want to explain the whole matter to her as thoroughly as I have to you. So there is only you, Max, upon whom I can lay this burden. The favor I ask is this: that as soon as possible you go to my director, Dr. Odstrčil, with the medical certificate[34] that I enclose (I will not be getting it until the afternoon, or so I hope, as the doctor and I agreed). The best time to go would be about eleven A.M. You will naturally know better than I what should be said. I just want to sketch my idea of it, something of this sort:

I am undoubtedly capable of going to the office (as an aside, also capable of handling the work(!) I have there)—but this was also true before I left. However, there is also no doubt that I would have to go away again in the fall and once again in somewhat worse shape than last fall. The doctor now promises that a stay of four to six months will put me in a dependable state for work. I am therefore asking for an extension of my leave, for two months, say, after which time I will again submit a detailed medical affidavit. I am asking for this leave in whatever way they want to grant it, at whole, three-quarters, or half salary. I only don't want to be left entirely without salary— and I also want them to wait awhile before retiring me on pension. Incidentally, this half year can also be subtracted from my vacation privileges and my retirement benefits. In fact such a restricted leave would actually be a relief to me, since I am all too aware of how much time off I have already received from the Institute. The manner in which I am asking for this leave is of course improper, and can only be excused by the fact that up to this point I have been struggling with scruples, and therefore have only now fully discussed the matter with the doctor. I also know that a petition must first be submitted and so on, but perhaps it would be possible for me to submit the petition subsequently, with the understanding that I can count on being granted permission to stay on here without having to start work on the 20th. But if that is not possible, then I could still come to Prague for a while.

I would suggest saying something like this. And would you then, Max, telegraph me: "Stay there" or "Come here."

Now a few words about the director. He is a very good, kindly man, has been remarkably good to me in particular, though political motives have played a part, for then he could say to the Germans that he had treated one of theirs with exceptional kindness, even though the man was only a Jew.

Please don't speak carelessly about the salary question and don't mention my father's wealth, first because probably it doesn't exist and secondly certainly not for me.

Emphasize that my procedure is incorrect; he places great weight on correctness, on proper due being paid to his authority.

The talk will surely move on to generalities, with him leading it in that direction, in view of who you are. In that case you might be able to mention in passing—not to bribe him, for I don't want anything of that sort, but to give him a pleasure, for I feel greatly obligated to him—that I have often spoken of his creative use of language and first learned to admire the vitality of spoken Czech through him. Perhaps you won't see much of this in the course of your talk, for since he became director he has almost lost this vigor. Bureaucracy does not let it emerge; he has to talk too much. Incidentally, he is a professor of sociology and a writer on the subject, but you needn't know anything about that. Of course you can speak to him in either German or Czech.

So that is the assignment. When I consider that I am adding something of this sort to your other work, I don't much like myself, I assure you. But one is encircled by scruples and must break out somewhere and you, Max, must bear the brunt. Forgive me.

Yours

One thing more: It would not be impossible that Ottla, of her own accord, has initiated something similar.[35] It might be wise to ask the family beforehand.

Perhaps it seems to you that I am too worried about my relationship to the office. I'm not. Consider that the office is not in the least responsible for my illness, that it has had to put up not only with my illness but with the five years in which it was developing, in fact that the office kept me on my feet when in my unawareness I was only staggering through the days.

If I were to stay here, then perhaps I would see you here. That would be good.

Many regards to your wife and to Felix and his wife and Oskar and his wife.

To Minze Eisner

[Matliary, second half of March 1921]

Dear Minze,

First and foremost, what is this mild fever with which you wake up every day? Is it really fever, measured by the thermometer? And there must have been a school doctor at Ahlem; did you speak to him about it? And to the doctor in Barth? I don't know, without asking again, since that snapshot of you with the manure cart I have had great confidence in your health; you seemed so sturdy in the picture, so much healthier than in Schelesen—and even in Schelesen you were in general healthy—how I panted to keep up with your long strides. And now mild fever? But there is no such thing as a mild fever, only an abominable fever. "The faster and more beautifully to squander life, the better," you write. All right, if that's how you want it. But believe me, fever is not a beautiful way to squander life, nor a fast one. This is not a real sanatorium, in a real sanatorium the impression would be much stronger, but even here, when I look about me, I don't see any beautiful and fast squanderings. No one is squandering his life; he is being squandered. But with your fresh youth it is possible to put up a stout fight against it and you must do so. Assuming that an attack has taken place, which I don't know and would rather not believe. But if it is really fever you have, consistently 98.6°F or more, measured with the thermometer in the mouth, then you must go to a doctor at once, that goes without saying. Then goodbye to Robinson Crusoe, at least for the present. For Crusoe himself, when he had fever one time, was rescued by a ship, and only after he had recovered his health at home was he allowed to depart again and become Robinson Crusoe. He cut out this chapter in his book, because he was ashamed of this episode, but at any rate he was always very anxious about his health and what was right for the great Robinson Crusoe must also be right for little Minze.

Otherwise you are right, Minze, and I am exaggerating when I find your present life so splendid. But I can't help it. Somewhere the philosopher Schopenhauer made a comment on this question which I can quote only very loosely, to this effect: "Those who find life beautiful would seem to have an easy time proving it so: all they have to do is to point out the world from a balcony. However it might be, on bright or overcast days, the world and life will always look beautiful, the region, whether varied or monotonous, will always be beautiful, the life of nations, of families, of individuals, whether easy or difficult, will always be interesting and beautiful. But what does this prove? No more than that the world, if it were nothing but a peepshow, would really be infinitely beautiful. But unfortunately it is not that; rather this beautiful life in a beautiful world has really to be lived through in every detail of every moment and that is no longer so beautiful, but simply toilsome." That's more or less what Schopenhauer said.[36] Applied to your case it would mean: It certainly is fine and amazing and heroic that Minze is off in the cold north earning her bread and in the evening after a hard day lies on a straw pallet wrapped in horse blankets and Lisl is already asleep nearby and outside it is snowing and it is wet and cold and tomorrow comes another hard day—all that looks beautiful from the balcony of a villa in the Tatra—

But in the evening, looking into the kerosene lamp at my elbow, it is no longer so beautiful at all and almost to be wept over a little.

I intended to write something of that sort, but was interrupted, this time not by blizzards and having to take to my bed; on the contrary there have been seven perfect days of continual sunshine and lying nude in the woods on the very edge of deep snow, and going coatless and being able to breathe a little more freely. But people interrupted with their troubles. As though I could be of any help. In connection with this there is this little classic story which is always pertinent: Grillparzer was once invited to a party at which he would be meeting Hebbel.[37] However, Grillparzer declined to go, saying, "Hebbel always asks me about God and I can't tell him anything and then he is cross."

In the meantime your second letter has arrived, a little more cheerful if I am not mistaken. In spite of the injured hand. Yes, it is not easy to handle the pruning knife. I always preferred injuring the trees rather than myself. But when I did cut myself, they would say for comfort, "Clumsy fingers must be cut off." And you are going to the doctor's. I suppose he won't only look at your hand. 51 kilos: not enough, not enough.

As for the Baltic resorts, they are lovely; I know only one in the extreme west: Travemünde, where I wandered about one whole hot day disconsolate and undecided in the crowds of bathers.[38] It was about a month before the outbreak of the war.—But to go there now, Minze, would be—apart from everything else—a breach of our agreement, for we decided we would never see each other again. In which, however, the "never" is somewhat exaggerated, as is your Robinson Crusoe dream. Yet I wish you, too, a great big garden and blue skies and the south.

Dear Minze, how many days have passed since the foregoing was written; I can hardly count them and what has happened in the interval I cannot say. Probably nothing; I cannot, for instance, remember reading a real book in this whole period. Rather, I must often have lain in a complete daze, like that of my grandparents which I used to marvel at when I was a child. The days passed unnoticed, very quickly; there was no time for writing. I had to force myself to scribble a card to my parents, and to write to you, Minze, was like having to strain to stretch out my hand across all of Germany, which after all is impossible.

The outcome of this period is this: that while I intended to be in Prague on March 20, I will be staying here longer. The doctor here threatened me with all possible evils if I left and promises me all possible good if I stay, so I will stay for a while longer. But rather than lying here on the balcony or in the outdoor pavilion (the woods are still inaccessible because of snow), I would rather be working somewhere in a garden "in the sweat of my brow," for that is what we were made for. Everyone feels this basically, even if he doesn't do it. But you do it, bless you! It is probably in many respects not pleasant—how could it be, since it is the fulfillment of a curse; but to evade the curse is even worse.

I hope the sun is shining upon your work as wonderfully as it does on my rest cure (for the past few days I have been able to lie naked on my balcony in the afternoon, as naked as a child under the eyes of an invisible great mother), and the Baltic resorts are lovely, certainly, but I don't want to see you except in your own garden (may it be in the south by a lake; I will not shirk the journey to Lake Garda or to Lago Maggiore) with your husband and your children, a whole long string of them, how much more beautiful than the handsomest wolfhounds. Besides, why does it have to be a European lake, for Lake Kinneret, the Sea of Galilee, is also lovely. The enclosed clippings, read to tatters in keeping with their importance, deal somewhat with this matter.

Perhaps the little book of Fontane's disappointed you in regard to life on the Baltic, but perhaps one must know Fontane, especially his letters, in order to understand these reminiscences. I cannot exactly say where I found this Baltic life so well described, whether in these sketches or in some novel of his. Moreover I don't exactly know the title of this novel, *Cecile* or *Beyond Recall*[39] or something else. I don't know; when I am in Prague I could check.

Your birthday is in April? But you are not at all fickle, so how did you come in April? What day?

I enclose the contract; it seems sensible and not as cruel as I feared.

And now I want to hear something about that fever soon.

Yours, Kafka

To Max Brod

[Postcard. Matliary; postmark: March 31, 1921]
Dear Max, I wasn't quite well and still am not well; the digestion. Either it comes from eating meat or from other things; we will know in a few days. Then I will write more fully to you. Anyway you have written to me, but always only about me, not about you, not about your job, your trips, about Leipzig,[40] about Felix and Oskar. In a few days, then, I will write. Be well.

Yours, Franz

Please give my regards to your wife; as I say that I realize how long I've been away from Prague.

To Max Brod

[Matliary, mid-April 1921]

Dearest Max, How could you fail with the novella[41] now, since you have the
calmness with which to sustain the tension and the novella must be born like
a good child of life itself. And how sensibly everything arranges itself for you,
in the office too. In your earlier job you were a lazy official, for your work
outside the office counted for nothing, could at best be tolerated and forgiven,
but this time it is the principal thing and gives what you do in the job its
unique value, beyond the scope of any other official, so you are always
diligent, even in the eyes of the office, even when you do nothing there. And
finally and above all, how masterfully you manage your marriage and Leipzig
besides and give yourself fully to both, and through the strength of reality are
convincing in both, even though I do not comprehend how you can be. May
all go well for you on your hard, high, proud course!

Myself? When the news about you, Felix, and Oskar is all set down, and I
compare myself with you others, it seems to me that I am wandering like a
child in the forests of maturity.

More days have passed in fatigue, in doing nothing, in watching the clouds,
and in worse. It is really so, all of you have been moved up into man's estate.
Imperceptibly, for marriage alone is not the decisive factor. Perhaps there are
destinies that evolve historically and others that do not. Sometimes for fun I
imagine an anonymous Greek who comes to Troy without ever having
intended to. He has not got his bearings yet when he finds himself in the
thick of the battle. The gods themselves don't yet know what the issue is, but
he is hanging from a Trojan chariot and being dragged around the city. It is
long before Homer has yet begun to sing, but he is already lying there with
glassy eyes, if not in the dust of Troy, then in the cushions of the reclining
chair. And why? Hecuba is nothing to him, of course. But Helen too is not a
decisive factor. Just as the other Greeks, summoned by the gods, set out and
under the protection of the gods gave battle, so he set out, impelled by a
father's kick, and gave battle under his father's curse. Lucky that there were
other Greeks there, or else world history would have remained restricted to
two rooms in his parental house and the threshold between them.

The illness I wrote about was an intestinal catarrh, so much worse than
any I have had yet that I was convinced it was intestinal tuberculosis (I know
what intestinal tuberculosis is like—I watched while Felix's cousin died of it).
There was one day when I had 104° fever, but it passed, I think, without ill
effects, though the loss of weight will have to be made up. By the way, the
tortured man of whom I once wrote has made an end to himself. Apparently
half deliberately, half by accident he fell down between two cars of a moving

express train, through the buffers. He had left the sanatorium almost out of his mind, leaving early in the morning, as though for a little walk, without his watch, wallet, or luggage, pushed on until he reached the tramline, went on to Poprad,[42] took the express train, heading toward Prague as if to make an Easter visit to his family, but then he changed direction and jumped down. All of us here share the blame, not for a suicide but for his despair of late. Everyone shrank from him, a very sociable man, in the most unfeeling way, as people will elbow their way to the lifeboats at a shipwreck. I except the doctor, the nurse, and the housemaid, for I have a great respect for them in this regard. Later we had a similar patient arrive, but he soon left again.

In a *Prager Tagblatt* which accidentally came my way—a tourist from Mährisch-Ostrau was here for a few days and, though we hardly spoke to each other, he always pressed heaps of newspapers on me in the kindest fashion; he was reading, they tell me, *In the Struggle for Judaism*—I read that Haas has married Jarmila, which doesn't surprise me, for I always expected great things from Haas. But the world will be surprised. Do you know anything more about it?[43]

You write of a little post you might find for me. That is sweet of you and very comforting to read about, but it is not for me. If I had three wishes (putting aside the dark lusts), I would wish first for approximate recovery. The doctors promise this, but I see no signs of it. How often in the past years I've gone off on a cure and I always felt much better than now, after more than three months' cure. What has improved in the course of these three months is surely more the weather than the lungs, although, this must not be forgotten, my previous hypochondria which was diffused throughout my body has not become concentrated in the lungs. My second wish would be for a foreign land in the south. (It would not have to be Palestine. In my first months here I read the Bible a great deal; that too has stopped.) And third: a modest handicraft. That surely isn't wishing so very much. Not even wife and children are among the wishes.

To Max Brod

[Matliary, mid-April 1921]

Dearest Max, The moment I received the book[44] I read it twice, almost three times, then promptly lent it out so that it would quickly be read by someone else. After it was returned I read it for the fourth time and now have lent it out again—I was in such a hurry. But it is understandable, because the book is so vital, and when one has stood in deep shade for some time and sees such life, one is drawn toward it. It is not really a memorial; rather, it is a wedding

between you two, vital and sad and desperate as a wedding is for those who
are marrying, and happy and eye-opening and heart-pounding for those who
are looking on; and who would be able to look on without at the same time
also marrying, though he were couched in the most solitary room in the
world. And this vitality is actually intensified by the fact that you alone are
reporting it, you, the strong survivor, and doing so with such delicacy that
you do not drown out the deceased, but allow him to speak out too and be
heard in his toneless voice, and to put his finger to your lips in order to mute
your voice where that suits his purposes. That is wonderful. And nevertheless,
so much does the book yield to the reader's will, so much does it give him
freedom of the will despite all its inner power, that only the survivor is, if you
will, there, only the speaker in all the immensity which life, as against death,
has for the living. It stands there like a funeral monument, but at the same
time like a pillar of life; and what grip me most immediately are precisely
those passages that are probably unimportant to you, such as this: "Now was I
mad or was he?" Here stands the man, the faithful and unalterable soul, the
eternally open eye, the never-failing spring, the man who—I put it
paradoxically, but mean it plainly—cannot comprehend the comprehensible.

That was yesterday. I wanted to say a few more things, but today a letter
from M. came. I am supposed not to tell you anything about it, because she
says she promised you not to write me. I tell you this right off, and now as far
as M. is concerned it is as if I had not told you anything; I know that. How
lucky, Max, to have you.

But I must write you about the letter for the following reasons: M. writes
that she is sick, consumptive; she already was in the past, shortly before we
met, but at that time it was a light case, totally inconsequential—that
tentative approach the disease sometimes takes. Now it is said to be more
severe. Well, she is strong, her vitality is strong; my imagination is incapable
of conceiving of M. as sick. And in fact you had different news about her.
Still, she has written to her father; he was kind and she is coming to Prague,
will stay with him and later go to Italy. (She has dismissed her father's
suggestion that she go to the Tatra Mountains, but is Italy wise now, in the
middle of spring?) It's odd that she will be living in her father's home; if they
are so reconciled, where does that leave her husband?

But all this is not my reason for writing you about it; naturally the
question is where this leaves me. What I am asking you is to let me know
when M. comes to Prague (you will no doubt hear of that) and how long she
is staying, so that I don't happen to come to Prague at this time. And I would
like you to inform me if M. does go to the Tatra Mountains, so that I can
leave here in plenty of time. For a meeting would no longer mean that

desperation tears its hair, but that it scratches bloody welts on head and brain.

But in doing this for me, you mustn't again tell me that you don't understand me. I wanted to write you about that quite a while ago, but was too tired. Still, I suppose I've hinted at it a good many times before. It won't be anything new to you, but I haven't yet said it right out, crudely. Moreover, in itself it's nothing special. One of your earliest stories deals with it, moreover in sympathetic terms. It's an illness of instinct, a product of the age; depending on vitality there are ways to deal with it one way or the other. But in accord with my lack of vitality I cannot find any such ways, or at most the way of fleeing, though I am in a condition that makes it impossible for the outsider (and incidentally even more so for me) to see what there is left to save. But people don't always run away to save themselves; the ashes the wind blows away from a fire don't fly away in order to save themselves.

I am not talking about the happy—in this respect happy—times of childhood, when the door was still closed, the door behind which the tribunal conferred (the father-juryman who filled all the doors has since then, a long time since, emerged). But later the fact was that the body of every other girl tempted me, but the body of the girl in whom I placed my hopes (for that reason?) not at all. As long as she withheld herself from me (F) or as long as we were one (M), it was only a menace from far away, and not even so very far; but as soon as the slightest little thing happened, everything collapsed. Evidently on account of my dignity, on account of my pride (no matter how humble he looks, the devious West European Jew!), I can love only what I can place so high above me that I cannot reach it.

I suppose that is the kernel of the whole thing, of the monstrously swollen whole that even includes "fear of death." And not everything is merely superstructure of this kernel; some of it is certainly substructure as well.

But in this collapse it really was terrible; I cannot talk about that. Only this one thing: About the Hotel Imperial you were mistaken; what you thought was enthusiasm was funk. Only fragments of four days torn out of the night were happiness; fragments which were already locked up in the closet literally unassailable; the moaning for this achievement was happiness.

And now I again have her letter here. It asks nothing but that I let her have some news of me; she will not answer. My temples were throbbing in the afternoon that is now behind me; the night is still before me, but that will be all. She is unattainable for me; I must resign myself to that, and my energies are in such a state that they do so jubilantly. Which adds shame to the suffering; it is as if Napoleon had said to the demon that summoned him to Russia: "I cannot go now: I haven't drunk my evening glass of milk yet"; and as if he then, when the demon asked, "Will that take so long?" replied: "Yes, I have to Fletcherize it."

So now do you understand it?

To Max Brod

[Matliary, April 1921]

Dear Max, Can it be that you haven't received my last letter (about Schreiber and about M.)? I might have addressed it wrongly. I should be sorry if a stranger happened to receive it.

Many thanks for the feuilleton, the page from your Paris diary. You don't know how much joy that gives me, for if you did you would send me everything of yours that is published. I don't even hear about everything that appears in *Selbstwehr*; for instance, I know only the second part of the essay on Kuh (a little wild, a little high-pitched, a little hasty, but such a joy to read). And do you often write such reviews as the one on Racine?[45] (Well done, incidentally, the way you fall asleep in the first column and, in the last, awakening, are annoyed that the audience is so small. Wonderful, too, how, desperate but also glad that you're alive, you seek Racine's purpose at his old grave. And of course it's hopeless because in such a quest one flies off in all directions unless one steps aside and lets one's imagination do the work, as you do there.)

Thanks, too, for what you say about the medical student. He deserves it, although perhaps he will have to stay out of the city well beyond the autumn. Yet he shows no outward signs of his illness. He's a tall, strong, broad, red-cheeked, blond fellow; when dressed he is almost too heavy, has no complaints, doesn't cough, at most runs a temperature now and then. Since I've introduced him somewhat by his appearance (in bed, in nightshirt, with tousled hair, he has a boyish face like an engraving from Hoffmann's[46] children's stories, earnest and tense, yet also dreamy—he's actually good-looking that way)—now that I've introduced him, I want to ask two things in his behalf. With your experience you'll probably be able to answer the first without much trouble. What can he hope for in Prague in the way of support or help with practical things? He has two recommendations, one sealed one from a Budapest rabbi to Rabbi Schwarz, and a very good one from the Budapest religious community to the Prague religious community, with an especially cordial note appended by a Rabbi Edelstein, whose pupil he was. What I fear, though, is that every foreigner who comes to Prague has such recommendations. Secondly: Would it significantly help his admission to the university and his life otherwise if he were to acquire Czechoslovak citizenship? (He might be able to do that; he has a noncommital name, Klopstock, and his father—long deceased—came from Slovakia.) ...

You ask about my health. My temperatures are favorable. Fever is extremely rare; even 98.4 isn't anything like a daily occurrence, and that measured in the mouth where it is two- to three-tenths warmer than in the armpit. If there weren't so many fluctuations it could almost be called normal; but then I spend most of my time lying down. Coughing, phlegm, shortness of breath have decreased, but decreased precisely to the degree that the weather has improved, so that I should speak of improvement in the weather rather than in my lungs. I have gained about 6½ kilos. What is annoying is that I am not completely healthy two days in succession, even aside from the lungs and my hypochondria. I am not disregarding your advice at all. But the Lokopan salve is unknown here; the pretty, slim, tall, blonde, blue-eyed girl in charge of the pharmacy in Lomnitz looked sharply at me to see whether I was trying to make a fool of her. After all, anybody could invent a comical name for a joke and ask whether this salve is available. The injections—well, Dr. Kral is for them, my uncle against them, the doctor here for them, Dr. Szontagh in Smokovec against them, and of course in this conclave I vote against them. You really can't object to that, Max, especially since you warn against them in your book. I had already read the article on injections; the *Ostrauer Morgenzeitung* is the only paper I get almost every day. I have also read the medical supplement, part of which is obviously written by a humorist. (This seems to be the only professional reading of the doctor here, whom, however, I'm very fond of.) The article presents the usual artificial statistics which the proponents of nature therapy will say are meaningless. ("Inoculations are fine until they kill you.") The foreshortened time span in which conventional medicine deals is ludicrous, and nature therapy has nothing but contempt for it. I am willing to believe that tuberculosis will be controlled; every disease will ultimately be controlled. It is the same with wars—each one will come to its end but none ever stops. Tuberculosis no more has its origins in the lungs than, for example, the World War had its cause in the ultimatum.[47] There is only a single disease, no more, and medicine blindly chases down this one disease as though hunting a beast in endless forests.—But I have not disregarded your advice. How could you think so.

Franz

To Oskar Baum

[Matliary, April 1921]

Dear Oskar, So you haven't forgotten me. I am almost tempted to reproach *you* for my not having written. But in this great inactivity writing is almost an action for me, almost like being born again, and again working one's way through the world, after which one must irrevocably take to one's reclining chair. So one shies away from it. By which I don't want to give the impression that I think I am right; no, not at all.

I have heard hardly anything about you, though I read about your Weininger[48] lecture. (Don't you have a spare manuscript, perhaps a proof of the essay?) Rumors about jobs as a critic, that's all. I am always chattering to Max about myself, and give him hardly a chance to write about other matters. And what all could have happened, in these intervening years; you might have made a few trips to Sicily, and how much work you might have done, and Leo might almost be ready for the university. It is hard to keep track of time in the reclining chair. It seems as if four months have gone by, but the mind is well aware that many years have passed.

It is a comfort that aging keeps pace. For example a young thing from Budapest has just left us. (Her name is Aranka; every third girl is called that and every other, Ilonka. These are pretty names. Some are also called Clarika. And all are addressed only by their given names: "How are you, Aranka?") So this young thing has left. She was not especially pretty; the curve of her cheeks was somewhat wrong, her eyes were not perfectly set, her nose was thick. But she was young, so youthful, and everything she wore suited her pretty body, and she was gay and affectionate and everyone was in love with her. I deliberately kept at a distance from her, did not introduce myself. She was here for three months and I never exchanged a single direct word with her, which in such a little circle is not easy. And now on the last day at breakfast (I have my lunch and supper alone in my room) she came over to me and began a longish speech in her laborious Hungarian German: "May I take the liberty, Herr Doktor, to say goodbye to you," and so on—the way one speaks, all blushing and unsure of oneself, to an aging dignitary. And while this was going on, my knees were really shaking.

I am happy to be reading the book[49] again. For reasons that in a certain sense will not bear inspection, it is one of my favorites among your books. It is so good to live in it, warm; it's as though the reader were crouching forgotten in a corner of a room where he can participate all the more intensely in what is happening there. Unfortunately I had to lend it away, but I will get it back tomorrow. My table partner, this time Ilonka, saw it and asked for it in such a way that I had to lend it to her—the more willingly because she has evidently never read a good book in her whole life. Her prettiest feature is a delicate, almost translucent skin, and I wanted to see how she will look when her face is lit up with pleasure over your book.

Warmest regards to you, your wife, child, and sister.

Yours, Franz

To Ottla Davidová

[Matliary, April 1921][50]

Dearest Ottla and Věruška[51] (? Mother spelled the name that way—what sort of name is it? Věra, or is it Vjera, like the name of Frau Kopal's daughter? What sort of considerations led you to that name?), an errand, please. For her brother[52] the stamp collector, Frau Forberger needs:

100	2-heller special-delivery stamps	
100	80-heller stamps	} with pictures of Huss
100	90-heller stamps	

Please take the money from my account; I will be repaid here. These stamps are going to be withdrawn from circulation toward the end of May, so have to be bought immediately and are supposed to be had only in Prague. If the errand is too much for the two of you (I wonder how you would get the baby carriage up into the lobby of the main post office. Do you have a nice baby carriage? Is Frau Weltsch[53] a bit envious?), then perhaps Pepa will be so kind. (By the way, isn't he going to Paris?) You can then offer the enclosed article from the Brünn *Lidové Noviny* to him for his opinion; if he thinks well of it, we must of course speak of it to Dr. Kral, so that he might inquire where passage may be booked on such sanatorium ships and how much it would all cost. But you must not tell him right off that the article unfortunately appeared in the April 1st issue, where it seemed totally on the up-and-up. A poor patient here, his hopes aroused, went with it to the doctor for his opinion; the doctor brought it to me to read, since he doesn't know Czech, and I was so weakened at the time by the intestinal catarrh that for an hour or two I took it seriously.[54]

These are my pretexts for writing to you. In fact I have been wanting to write for a long time, but I was too tired or too lazy or only too depressed, it is hard to differentiate. Besides, I've always had some little trouble or other, for instance right now a savage abscess with which I'm battling. I am happy the two of you are so spry, but you shouldn't be too spry. We have a young farm woman[55] here, moderately sick, though she is merry and sweet and pretty in her dark peasant costume with its wide swaying ballerina skirt. Her mother-in-law was always heaping too much work on her, even though the doctor there kept warning against it and would say:

> A young woman you must spare,
> As if she were a golden pear

which to be sure is not very logical but still instructive. For which reason I refrain from thinking up more errands for you.

Nevertheless one errand will be necessary, to the director; it is very disagreeable. My leave runs out on May 20. (Did he really tell you that the leave had been officially approved?) What then? Where I go then or whether I stay here until the end of June is a secondary consideration. (Since the intestinal catarrh, which in my view was caused by eating meat, it has been arranged that one of the kitchen girls spend, I think, a good part of her time thinking up menus for me. At breakfast they make suggestions about lunch, at teatime about supper. Recently the girl was standing dreamily at the window, dreaming, I thought, of her hometown Budapest, when she suddenly said, "I really wonder how you will like the salad vegetables tonight.")

But how can I ask for my leave to be extended? And where will it end? It is very difficult. Should I ask for a leave at half pay? Is it easier to ask for such a leave? It would be easy to ask for a leave if I could tell myself and others that the office was somehow responsible for the illness or its aggravation. But in fact the opposite is true; the office kept the illness in check. It is difficult and yet I shall have to ask for the leave. I will of course be able to include a medical report; that part is very simple. Well, what do you think?[56]

But you must't imagine that I am entirely occupied with such thoughts here. Yesterday, for instance, I spent half the afternoon laughing, and not laughing at anyone's expense, but laughing out of tenderness and deep emotion. Unfortunately the story can only be sketched in, impossible to tell it in all its glory.

We have a General Staff captain[57] here; he is attached to the barracks hospital, but lives down here, as do many other officers, because it is too dirty up there in the barracks. He has his food brought down. As long as there was plenty of snow, he went on tremendous ski trips, almost to the peaks, and often by himself, which is very rash. Now he has only two occupations, one is sketching and doing watercolors, the other is playing the flute. Every day at fixed hours he paints and sketches out of doors, while at other hours he blows away at his flute in his little room. Apparently he prefers to be alone (except when he is sketching, at which times he does not seem to mind being watched). Naturally I respect this preference. So far I have hardly spoken to him five times, only when he calls something out to me from a distance, or when I unexpectedly come upon him somewhere. If I meet him when he is sketching, I offer a few compliments. His drawings are not bad; they are good or even very good amateur work. That's about all, I see; nothing very special here. As I say, I know quite well there's no conveying the essence of the thing. Perhaps if I tried to describe how he looks: When he goes for a walk on the road, always holding himself very straight, walking in slow, easy strides, his eyes always raised to the Lomnitz peaks, his coat flying in the wind, he looks like Schiller. When you are close up and see his thin, lined face (partly lined from flute-playing) the pale color of wood, his neck and his whole body also dry and wooden, then he reminds you of the dead rising from their graves in the fresco of Signorelli[58] (I think it is in the collection *Masterpieces of Art*). And then there is a third resemblance he has. He hit on the fantastic idea of having his pictures—

No, it is too big a subject. I mean inwardly. In brief, he arranged to have a show. The medical student wrote a review in a Hungarian newspaper, I in a German paper,[59] all in secret. The captain went to the headwaiter with the Hungarian newspaper and asked him to translate. But it was too complicated for the headwaiter, so in all innocence he brought the captain to the medical student, saying he could do a better job of translating the review.

The medical student happened to be in bed with a slight fever. I was there visiting him; that's how it began. But enough. Why am I telling the story when I am not telling it right.

But to come back to the original point, you must by no means think that we are laughing all the time, really not.

I am enclosing the bill from Taussig,[60] also a clipping for Elli concerning Felix.[61] It might also be of interest for your little one in about ten years. That isn't very far away; one turns over once from the left side to the right side on the reclining chair, looks at the clock, and ten years have passed. Time seems to go by more slowly only when one is moving about.

Of course I send special regards to Elli and Valli. What are you thinking? That I send regards because that is easy and don't write because writing is hard? Not at all. I send regards because they are my dear sisters and I don't write especially to them because I am writing to you. By and by you will say that I only send regards to your daughter because writing is hard. And yet writing is not harder than anything else, rather a bit easier.

All the best to all of you, F

Please give my regards to the Fräulein.

To Max Brod

[Matliary, beginning of May 1921]
Dear Max, Have I still not made myself plain? This is odd, but so much the better, for what I wrote was incorrect, incorrect as a single instance, and only true when it is extended to my entire life. (Extended? Therefore blurred? I don't know.) You are going to speak to M. I shall never again have this joy. When you speak to her about me, speak as you would of someone dead. I mean as far as my "externality" is concerned, my "extraterritoriality." When Ehrenstein saw me recently,[62] he said in effect that in M. life was reaching out

its hand to me and I had the choice between life and death. That was somewhat too magniloquent (not in regard to M. but in regard to me), but in essence it was true. It was only stupid in that he seemed to believe I had such a choice. If there were still a Delphic oracle, I would have asked it and it would have answered: "The choice between death and life? How can you hesitate?"

You go on writing about getting well. That is out of the question for me (not only in regard to my lungs but also everything else. Lately, for instance, a wave of restlessness has come over me, sleeplessness, suffering from the slightest noise. And sounds materialize in the empty air. I could tell you long stories about this, and when all the possibilities of the day and evening are exhausted, then a small group of devils gets together in the night, as now, and has a merry chat at midnight outside my house. In the morning it turns out that these are clerical workers coming home from a Christian Socialist meeting—good, innocent people. No one can assume as many masks as the devil). So that is out of the question. Just look at this reluctantly living body, which the brain, alarmed at what it has done, now wants to force back toward life. Reluctantly living: it cannot eat and an ulcerous wound has to be kept under bandages for a whole month before it indecisively heals. The bandage was removed only yesterday. (Of course the cheerful doctor has remedies at hand: arsenic injections. No, thanks.) So it is out of the question, but it is also not that which is most to be desired.

You write about girls. No girl is holding me here (especially not the ones in the picture; besides, these left months ago), and no girl will ever hold me anywhere. Amazing how little discernment women have; they only notice whether they attract you, or whether you have pity for them, or finally whether you look for compassion from them. That is all, though in general that is enough.

Actually I associate only with the medical student; everything else is incidental. If someone wants something from me, he tells it to the student. If I want something of anyone, I do the same. Nevertheless it is not loneliness, not loneliness at all; a semicomfortable life, outwardly semicomfortable in an ever-changing group of extremely amiable people. Granted, I am not drowning in plain sight of everybody and no one has to rescue me. What is more, they too are so amiable as not to drown. Then much of the amiability is due to quite obvious reasons. For instance, I tip lavishly (relatively lavishly; it is all cheap enough), which is essential. For the headwaiter recently wrote to his wife in Budapest (the letter somehow became public knowledge) classifying the guests by their tips. "Twelve of the guests can stay, but the devil take the rest." Then he begins to list the guests by name in a sort of litany: "Dear Frau G. (who is actually a sweet young, rather childish peasant woman from the Zips[63] region): may the devil take her," etc. I was not in the list; if the devil does take me, it would certainly not be because my tips are too small.

So Oskar is with the *Presse*, not with the *Abendblatt*?[64] Is the quality of the newspaper such that you could recommend it? Has he given up the lessons? Could you send me an issue with an article of Oskar's one of these days? I have not yet seen the paper. Is Paul Adler also on it? And Felix? Such things have happened before. The demands are getting worse? It's really reaching him? Up to now it did not really do so. Basically he was still living in Rome and the wars with the barbarians went on at the borders of Asia. Have things deteriorated? The child? Is he at a summer place now? Be well.

Franz

To Max Brod

[Matliary, end of May/beginning of June 1921]

Dearest Max, My debt is already so large, I have received so much from you, you have done so much for me. And here I lie stiff and still, in anguish over the man who is installing stoves in the adjacent rooms. He begins at five in the morning every day, even on holidays, hammering, singing, and whistling, and goes on without pause until seven in the evening, then steps out for a bit and goes to sleep before nine o'clock. I do the same, but without being able to sleep because the other people have a different schedule, and I am like the father of Matliary and can only fall asleep when the last squeaking chambermaid is in bed. And of course what disturbs me is not precisely this man (the chambermaid told him at noon that he wasn't to whistle—though I tried to stop her by force—how should I, lazing away on my reclining chair, forbid an excellent workman anything?—So now he hammers away without whistling except for certain intervals when he forgets and is probably cursing at me, though to tell the truth, it really is pleasanter for me). When he stops, then every living being here is ready and willing to take his place and will do so and does so. But it isn't the noise here that is at issue, but rather the noise of the world, and not even this noise but my own noiselessness.

But apart from my protracted sleeplessness, I did not want to write you anything before your meeting with M. I can't help entangling myself in lies when I write about her and I did not want to influence you any more—not so much for your sake as for mine. So now you have seen her. How she can have become reconciled to her father I cannot fathom, and I suppose you don't know anything about that either. I had an idea that she would be looking good. Strba is situated at the opposite end of the Tatra. (It has the highest altitude, but is not an actual sanatorium.) Forgive me for having imposed this on you; it happened in the first senseless agitation over her letter. However, even after due consideration I would have asked you. I didn't at all doubt that she would immediately tell you about her letter. Even so, she has the right to hold me to silence about it. What you write about the "superfluous letter" and "it can't go on this way" seems to hint that she doesn't want to hear anything more about me. (I entangle myself in lies, as I said.) "Flinging opinions about"—yes, that is the crucial thing which you, as a detached observer, of course, must keep well in mind when dealing with a girl of this sort. You sense the false notes, I never could, though I was on the alert. I do not want to exaggerate the amount of truth in such opinions. They are not fixed, a word can mollify them. I would not want to be a ship under such a pilot. But they are brave, grand, and lead the way to the gods, at least to the Olympic ones.

I also don't think I said anything explicit to you about M.'s relationship to your wife. M.'s judgment in this matter is also narrow and she has almost changed her mind. I cannot remember any connection with Lisl Beer. But I do recall a remark of M.'s to the effect that she once spent some time with Haas and your wife, and your wife had spoken about you and M. found this tone of humble admiration hateful. But don't be so hard on M., Max, because of this. This is a somewhat difficult situation to which I have often given thought. Try drawing up a list of your wife's women friends, those you consider unquestionably her friends, and you may discover that all these friends are women whom your wife at bottom despises. I can speak more frankly on that subject than anyone else. In a certain societal, social sense (particularly in that sense which is the decisive factor in your wife's isolation) I remarkably resemble your wife (which however doesn't mean that we are close), so much so that a casual glance might decide that we were alike. And this resemblance, so it seems to me, is not even restricted to our present state. It even includes our original endowment, the endowment of good, ambitious, but somehow tainted children. Nevertheless there does exist an actual difference between us, though one not perceptible to my merely scientific eye; it is a trifle, a worthless nothing, but yet it suffices, in the absence of any other social data, to make me fond of someone who, like M., asserts that she hates your wife. Granted, as a consequence of marriage, your wife has ventured farther into life than I have. It will occur to no one to measure my value by my situation in life, and anyone to whom it does occur will not believe his results.

M. may have made up with Staša[65] again. In the course of six months that relationship has also reversed itself once or twice. As to me, Staša showed a keen eye. At the very first meeting she recognized that I was not reliable. Yet such feminine stuff has never made a great impression on me, or rather all too much of an impression. If I hear such stuff as: She is splendid, he is not splendid, he loves her, she loves him, she is unfaithful, he ought to take poison, all this presented in an undifferentiated, deeply convinced, passionate spirit, then a dangerous feeling comes irresistibly over me, a feeling that only seems to be boyish, but is actually deeply life-shattering.

I wanted to say: All that seems to me [BREAKS OFF]

The first quieter day after an ordeal of some two weeks. This by and large out-of-the-world life which I lead here is not in itself worse than any other. I have no reason to complain about it. But if the world shouts a ghoulish cry into my gravelike peace, then I fly off the handle and beat my forehead against the door of madness which is always unlatched. A trifle is enough to bring me to this state. It is enough if under my balcony, his face turned toward me, a young half-pious Hungarian Jew lies in his reclining chair, comfortably outstretched with one hand over his head, the other thrust deep into his fly, and all day long cheerfully keeps on humming temple melodies. (What a people!) Something of that sort is enough and other things rush in to follow. I lie on my balcony as in a drum while people bang away at it top and bottom and on all sides. I have lost all faith that quiet is to be had anywhere on the earth's surface. I cannot wake, I cannot sleep. Even if it's quiet for once, I cannot sleep anymore because I am too distraught. I also cannot write and you reprove me, but I cannot even read. Three days ago, with the help of the medical student, I found a lovely little clearing in the midst of the woods, not too far—it is actually an island between two brooks. There it is quiet and there in three afternoons (mornings there are soldiers there) I recovered sufficiently so that I was able to take a brief nap. I am celebrating this today by a letter to you.

You are going to the Baltic—where? Recently I read about many lovely and cheap Baltic resorts: On the recommended list were Thiessow, Scharbeutz, Nest, Haffkrug, Timmendorf Beach, and Niendorf. None of them were more than 30–40 marks a day. With whom are you going—with your wife, by yourself, or with the other one? I also sometimes think of the Baltic, but it is more dreaming than thinking.

Your sister[66] wrote a friendly letter and sent me the salve. I am very glad to have it. In winter the outbreak was bad (now sunbaths take care of me) but the salve, if it works so effectively and prevents boils, can easily become what is called a scourge of mankind, since salves are not going to keep down the numbers of souls consigned to the Hounds of Hell, only add to them.

I would like to add to the foregoing that all that feminine stuff strikes me as comical, presumptuous, self-important, pitilessly ridiculous, compared with the wretched physicality implicit in it. They play their game, but what do I care.

And yet even here I have taken one or two morning walks with a girl in the woods and the walks were like what used to be said of the king's tables: They were bowed down under the weight of their abundance. And nothing happened, hardly a glance. Perhaps the girl noticed nothing and it is really nothing, and is already far in the past, and will also have no consequences, apart from the fact the the constellation is very favorable. For the rest, it is nothing to be surprised about, if

[IN THE MARGIN] I am sending this for the time being. To be continued tomorrow.

I write you so scrappily—the insomnia—without any present cause, only the legacy of earlier times—permits nothing else. Thanks for the telegram.

To Felix Weltsch

[Matliary; postmark: June 5, 1921]

Dear Felix, Please, there are no "walls of not-writing." Nothing of the sort. I am writing to Max and therefore also to you, and Max is writing to me and you are sending me *Selbstwehr,* so you are writing to me too. I am so very sorry that you are ... —I cannot possibly write the word down—there is not the faintest trace of it in your articles and therefore in your thinking.

Selbstwehr has gained a new subscriber here. He is the resident physician, Dr. Leopold Strelinger, Tatranské Matliary, P.O. Tatranská Lomnica. Would you please have the magazine sent to him, starting with the next issue. My only contribution to the cause was to lend him a few issues. He was delighted, to my surprise, since he seemed to me to be occupied with quite other matters.

Cordial regards to you, your wife, and child.

Yours, F

To Robert Klopstock

[Matliary, June 1921]

My dear Klopstock,

In the pavilion, with my old sleeplessness, with the old burning in the eyes, the tension in the temples:

[...] in this respect I was never disbelieving, but surprised, fearful, my head as full of questions as this meadow is full of gnats. I was in somewhat of the situation of this flower beside me, which is not wholly healthy, and though it lifts its head to the sun—who wouldn't do that?—is full of secret griefs because of the painful processes in its roots and in its sap; something has happened there, is happening still, but it has only very vague, painfully vague information on that and cannot at this point bend over, scratch up the soil, and have a look, but must act like its brothers and hold itself high. Which it does, but wearily.

I can imagine another Abraham,[67] who, to be sure, would not make it all the way to patriarch, not even to old-clothes dealer—who would be as ready to carry out the order for the sacrifice as a waiter would be ready to carry out his orders, but who would still never manage to perform the sacrifice because he cannot get away from home, he is indispensable, the farm needs him, there is always something that must be attended to, the house isn't finished. But until the house is finished, until he has this security behind him, he cannot get away. The Bible perceives this too, for it says: "He put his house in order." And Abraham actually had everything in abundance long before: had he not had his house, where would he have reared his son, into what beam would he have stuck the sacrificial knife?

Next day: Have been meditating a good deal about this Abraham, but these are old stories, no longer worth discussing; especially not the real Abraham; he had everything long before, was brought up for it from childhood, I cannot see the break. If he already had everything and yet was to be led even higher, then something must have been taken away from him, at least seemingly— that is logical and no break. It was different with the above-mentioned Abrahams: they stand on their building sites and suddenly are supposed to go to Mount Moriah. Possibly they do not even have a son and are called upon to sacrifice him. These are impossibilities and Sarah is right to laugh. All we can do is suspect that these men are deliberately not finishing their houses, and—to name a very great example—are hiding their faces in magical trilogies[68] so as not to have to lift their eyes and see the mountain that stands in the distance.

But another Abraham. One who certainly wants to carry out the sacrifice properly and in general correctly senses what the whole thing is about but cannot imagine that he is the one meant, the repulsive old man and his dirty boy. He does not lack the true faith, for he has this faith; he wants to sacrifice in the proper manner, if he could only believe he was the one meant. He is afraid that he will, to be sure, ride out as Abraham and his son, but on the way will turn into Don Quixote. The whole world would have been horrified, back then, had it been looking on, but this Abraham is afraid that the world will laugh itself sick over him. But it is not the ridiculousness in itself that he fears—though he also fears that, above all his joining in the laughter—but chiefly he fears that this ridiculousness will make him still older and more repulsive, his son dirtier, more unworthy to be really summoned. An Abraham who comes unsummoned! It is as if the best student were solemnly to receive a prize at the end of the year and in the expectant silence, the worst student, because he has misheard, comes forward from his dirty back bench and the whole class falls apart. And it is perhaps not that he has heard wrong, for his name was actually spoken, because it is the teacher's intention that the reward for the best is to be accompanied by the punishment of the worst.

Terrible things—enough.

You complain about solitary happiness—and what about solitary unhappiness? Truly they are almost a pair.

Nothing has come from Hellerau, which depresses me. If Hegner were considering, then he should have sent a card at once informing us that he was considering. We are indissolubly united in our interest in Hellerau.[69]

To Max Brod

[Matliary, June 1921]

Dearest Max, I put away the to-be-continued memo a few days ago because suddenly it occurred to me that you might be angry with me. When I wrote the letter, I did not remotely consider that. And in theory I was performing a far deeper bow to your wife than I would ever venture in real life. But then the possibility of your being angry occurred to me. Now, fortunately, it isn't so. In any case, my example was wrong. M. hates almost all Jewish women and literature may also have played a part. But your example of the contrary is weak—these "Christian" friendships[70] hardly exhaust the ethnic attraction; how could they possibly go deeper? But above all I did not want to emphasize the negative aspect so much, the absence of friendships. Therefore the theory stands; it is fixed like the thorn in my flesh.

Already made such progress on the book?[71] And so happy? And I know nothing about it, so far from you, so far. Nor shall I hear anything about it, at the Baltic either. Now I may speak frankly: I cannot imagine anything better than to have gone along with you. I could not entirely suppress it, or say it outright, but in fact it would have been a sort of ambulance trip. When for example I try to put myself in your place in regard to this, I see that if I were well, I would find consumption in someone near me very upsetting, not only because of the constant danger of infection but above all because this continual illness is filthy, filthy, this contradiction between the appearance of the face and the lungs, all of it filthy. I can only watch with disgust when the others bring up sputum, and I myself don't have a sputum jar, as I should have. However, all these scruples no longer count. The doctor has categorically forbidden me to go to a northern sea. Nor has he any interest in keeping me here through the summer; on the contrary, he authorizes me to go away to forested areas, to wherever I please, but not to the seashore. However, I am allowed to go to the sea and am even supposed to, but in winter and to Nervi.[72] That is how it is. And I had already anticipated it with such pleasure: you, the journey, the world, the song of the sea. The brooks that bound my clearing also sing, and the trees, and it is also soothing, but it is not reliable there—the soldiers come and now they are there all the time and make a tavern of the forest clearing—then the brook and forest are filled with their noise. One spirit, one devil is in them all. I try to get away from here, as you advise, but are there any possibilities of peace anywhere but in the human heart? Yesterday, for example, I was at Taraika, an inn in the mountains, at an altitude of more than 1300 meters, wild and beautiful. I had important sponsors, they were ready to do everything possible for me, in spite of an excess of expected guests; they were ready to provide me with vegetarian cooking, much better than here, would bring me my food from the lofty

Old stories by now. It was noisier there than here, what with tourists and gypsy music. So I have continued on here, unable to move, as though I had put down roots, which has surely not happened. To be honest, what I fear most of all—without in general giving too much thought to it—is the Institute. I have never been away from it this long, except for Zürau, but it was different there. I was different there. Also my old supervisor was backing me up somewhat. My debt to the Institute is so enormous, so unpayable, that it can only go on increasing—there can be no other development. Well, I usually solve problems by letting them devour me. Perhaps that is what I am doing here also.

I haven't yet thanked you for the clippings. They all display happiness and confidence and the effect of these on your writing. How much sadder Oskar's articles appear—contorted, often laborious, defective especially in a certain social sense—on the whole, however, he knows how to do that too, intransigent though he is. Felix neglects me. He has not sent me the last several issues of *Selbstwehr*, and though I put through a new subscription for the physician here, Dr. Leopold Strelinger, he too has not received the magazine.

Some time ago I read Kraus's *Literature*.[73] I suppose you know it. My impression at the time, which of course has greatly faded by now, was that it was exceedingly acute, piercing straight to the heart. In this small world of German-Jewish writing he is really dominant, or rather the principle represented by him. · He has so admirably subordinated himself to that principle that he has actually confounded himself with it and involved others in his confusion. I think I am distinguishing fairly well what in the book is only wit, although magnificent wit, what is whimpering, and finally what is truth, at least as much truth as there is in this hand with which I write, just as distinct and frighteningly physical. The wit principally consists of Yiddish-German—*mauscheln*[74]—no one can *mauscheln* like Kraus, although in this German-Jewish world hardly anyone can do anything else. This *mauscheln*—taken in a wider sense, and that is the only way it should be taken—consists in a bumptious, tacit, or self-pitying appropriation of someone else's property, something not earned, but stolen by means of a relatively casual gesture. Yet it remains someone else's property, even though there is no evidence of a single solecism. That does not matter, for in this realm, the whispering voice of conscience confesses the whole crime in a penitent hour. This is not to say anything against *mauscheln*—in itself it is fine. It is an organic compound of bookish German and pantomine. (How expressive this is: "So he's got talent? Who says?" Or this, jerking the arm out of its socket and tossing up the chin: "*You* think so?" Or this, scraping the knees together: "He writes? Who about?") What we have here is the product of a sensitive feeling for language which has recognized that in German only the dialects are really alive, and except for them, only the most individual High German, while all the rest, the linguistic middle ground, is nothing but embers which can only be brought to a semblance of life when excessively lively Jewish hands rummage through them. That is a fact, funny or terrible as you like.

But why should the Jews be so irresistibly drawn to this language? German literature existed before the emancipation of the Jews and attained great glory. After all, that literature was, as far as I can see, in no way less varied than today—in fact, today there may be less variety. And there is a relationship between all this and Jewishness, or more precisely between young Jews and their Jewishness, with the frightful inner predicament of these generations. This is something Kraus especially recognized, or more precisely, this was something that came to light by being contrasted with him. He is in some way like the grandfather in the operetta, differing only to the extent that instead of simply saying *Oy*, he composes long tedious poems. (With a certain justification, by the way, the same justification with which Schopenhauer lived a tolerably cheerful life even though he recognized that man was continually plunging straight to hell.)

Psychoanalysis lays stress on the father-complex and many find the concept intellectually fruitful. In this case I prefer another version, where the issue revolves not around the innocent father but around the father's Jewishness. Most young Jews who began to write German wanted to leave Jewishness behind them, and their fathers approved of this, but vaguely (this vagueness was what was outrageous to them). But with their posterior legs they were still glued to their father's Jewishness and with their waving anterior legs they found no new ground. The ensuing despair became their inspiration.

An inspiration as honorable as any other, but on closer examination showing certain sad peculiarities. First of all, the product of their despair could not be German literature, though outwardly it seemed to be so. They existed among three impossibilities, which I just happen to call linguistic impossibilities. It is simplest to call them that. But they might also be called something entirely different. These are: The impossibility of not writing, the impossibility of writing German, the impossibility of writing differently. One might also add a fourth impossibility, the impossibility of writing (since the despair could not be assuaged by writing, was hostile to both life and writing; writing is only an expedient, as for someone who is writing his will shortly before he hangs himself—an expedient that may well last a whole life). Thus what resulted was a literature impossible in all respects, a gypsy literature which had stolen the German child out of its cradle and in great haste put it through some kind of training, for someone has to dance on the tightrope. (But it wasn't even a German child, it was nothing; people merely said that somebody was dancing) [BREAKS OFF]

[A QUESTIONNAIRE ENCLOSED IN MAX BROD'S PREVIOUS LETTER AND FILLED OUT BY KAFKA]

Questionnaire
Weight Gain: 8 kilos
Total Weight: more than 65 kilos
Objective Condition of the lungs: the doctor's secret. Allegedly favorable
Temperatures: in general free of fever
Breathing: not good; on chilly evenings almost as bad as in winter
Signature: the only question I am at a loss to answer

To Ottla Davidová
                    [Postcard. Matliary; postmark: August 8, 1921]
My first outing.
I identified Věra right off, had a little trouble identifying you, though your pride was instantly recognizable. My pride would be even greater, would

hardly fit on this card. She seems to have an open, honest face and I think that there is nothing better in the world then openness, honesty, and reliability.

Yours

To Max Brod

[Postcard. Matliary; postmark: August 23, 1921]

Dear Max, I have been in bed for almost a week.[75] Fever, not a cold. One of those incidents with the lungs which there is no preventing. It is practically over now except for the cough and has procured me a few last sunny days. Besides, I don't tear myself free from Matliary all at once (which has less to do with Matliary than with my lack of mobility), only bit by bit, in keeping with my nature. I will probably be in Prague at the end of the week, will come to see you right off. I hope you will not yet have left for Karlsbad.

Yours

To Elli Hermann[76]

[Prague, autumn 1921]

Dear Elli, I really would have expected a less negative letter, or at least a more cheerfully decisive one. Don't you see how fortunate this is? Or do you know any better educational opportunities? There are more radical schools or schools that show the personal stamp of their director—or more distinguished schools—for example, Wickersdorf;[77] there are blander schools or odder schools abroad, which can't be assessed from here. There are schools in Palestine which are more akin to us and perhaps more important. But for proximity and minimal risk there is probably nothing except Hellerau.[78] Too young, because he is a few months short of ten? But seven-year-olds are taken there; there are three elementary grades, you know. One can be too young to be put to work, too young to marry, too young to die. But too young for a gentle, unconstrained education that brings out the best in a child? Ten years are not many, but in some circumstances ten can be an advanced age: ten years without physical training, without hygiene, of a pampered life, above all of a pampered life without exercising the eyes and ears and hands (except for counting over his spending money), caged with the grown-ups, who basically—it can hardly be otherwise in ordinary life—take their frustrations out on the children. Ten years of this sort are many. Granted that they have not had such a bad effect on Felix; he is vigorous, calm, bright, cheerful. Nevertheless these ten years have been spent in Prague where prosperous Jews are affected by a particular spirit from which children cannot be shielded. I am not referring to individuals, of course, but to this almost tangible general spirit, which expresses itself somewhat differently in everyone, in each according to his character, which is in you as well as in me—this small, dirty, lukewarm, squinting spirit. To be able to save one's own child from that, what good fortune!

Franz

To Elli Hermann

[Prague, autumn 1921]

Dear Elli, No, it is not energy, don't let yourself be either alarmed by it (as though I could force you to do anything against your will by means of this energy of mine) or falsely encouraged (as though this energy of mine could supply you with the will you lack to send Felix away—the will you want to have but lack). It is not energy, or at most an energy in words, and even this too will run out, in fact has already run out. It is not energy, rather it is the same thing you feel with amazing acuteness but interpret incorrectly, when you write that you, too, "want to get out of our milieu" and therefore (therefore!) you cannot send Felix away. You want to get out of our milieu and to do this with the aid of Felix. Both aims are fine and feasible; children are there to save their parents. Theoretically I do not understand how there can be childless people. But how do you mean to accomplish this "getting out"? Simply through an act typical of this milieu—by stinginess (I won't give him away), by despair (what would I be without him), by hopelessness (he won't be my son any longer), by telling yourself lies, by false pretexts, by glossing over your weakness, by dolling up the "milieu" ("making life bearable," "meeting one's responsibilities," "even from a distance the examples of such mothers can —" and so on). Of course I would do all this too if I were in your place, and on an even grander scale.

As for your story about "the facts of life"; in addition to all that is charming and touching about it, I see the following elements: First: you came too late. 2. Felix did not go to you with the stuff he had been hearing from the Prague boy. 3. He did not just question you about Věra, either, but rather crossexamined you, since he already had the other boy's explanation. 4. Of course the only explanation you could use was an abstraction, Love. But that is bad enough. (The story of the stork has a certain merit, in its unexaminable and rather remote reality.) Even worse is the fact that this abstraction is juxtaposed to the reality of pregnancy, which for the boy is terrifying and surprising. Good, you are not lying and he is not concealing things from you. 5. It was very good, your remarking that one could, if one wanted to, make anything ridiculous and bad. Unfortunately this can be done not only

through words but also by actions, and the distorted good then becomes
indistinguishable from the very worst. So what remains of your remark? And
isn't the Brüx[79] boy right, in terms of his milieu? 6. You have established a
connection between your explanation and that offered by the boys. I would
be interested to know how you did that. But in itself that cannot be difficult,
for everyone necessarily does that somehow in the course of his life. I am not
speaking of women, but in every man there is something of the Brüx boy.
The difference is that with the boy this common trait, irrespective of the form
in which it manifests itself, is nevertheless sanctified by his awe of the things
that are beyond him and by his craving for knowledge. That is why I am on
the side of the boy as against men, and in a certain sense against your kind of
explanation. For only the boy is the incorruptible seeker after truth, and he
must then relentlessly pass that truth on. As for what he still lacks in
knowledge and experience, we can feel confident that by virtue of his
ordinariness—for after all, he is blood of the blood of the others—he will fill in
the blanks by guess and feeling, and will do so more or less correctly.

Consider, for instance, the two boys who instructed me. Today they surely
know no more than they did then. However, they were, as it turned out,
unusually consistent characters whose lives turned out all of a piece. They
instructed me simultaneously, one from the right, the other from the left, the
one on the right merry, fatherly, worldly wise, with a laugh whose particular
tone I was later to hear from men of all ages, myself included (to be sure,
there is another kind of laughter that is above things, a free sort of laughter,
but I have yet to hear it from a living soul). The one on the left was matter
of fact, theoretic, and this was far more repugnant. Both of them married
years ago and stayed on in Prague. For many years now the one on the right
has been ravaged by syphilis to the point where he is scarcely recognizable. I
do not know if he is still alive. The one on the left is a professor of venereal
disease and the founder and president of a society for fighting venereal disease.
I do not want to weigh them against each other. Besides, they were not
friends and had only accidentally converged, that time, to see to my
instruction.

But relatively speaking, it is fairly unimportant whether his instruction
comes from your explanation or from the boy's. All that matters is what he
will himself decide, when his body begins to stir. By this I am not thinking of
specific acts or abstentions, but of the spirit that will guide him. And in
general he will make his decision (unless he is gripped by overwhelmingly
strong urges) on the basis of his life pattern. If he has been overindulged,
softly bedded spiritually and physically, overstimulated by the big city,
without religion, and bored, then he will decide accordingly, even if you were
to stand behind him every moment with loving admonitions, which would
of course be temporally and pyschologically impossible.

You cannot, for instance, do what would seem to be easiest—that is, fend off boredom, that breach through which all evil spirits enter. You yourself have admitted this, and I too have seen him in states that were dismal in this regard. Moreover such states are bound to grow worse and more dangerous from year to year, since they assume forms that both you and he will find harder to recognize. In childhood these states of boredom were still vague and one could more or less do something about them. But gradually the states of the worst tedium come to resemble the very best kind of diversion. The boy reads, he learns music, he plays soccer, and all this does not have to but very possibly may contain terrible boredom and aimlessness which neither he nor others can recognize but which reveals itself by its consequences.

To Elli Hermann

[Prague, autumn 1921]

[...]⁸⁰ For myself I have (among many others) one great witness, whom I quote here, simply because he is great and because I read this passage only yesterday, not because I presume to have the same opinion. In describing Gulliver's travels in Lilliput (whose institutions he praises highly), Swift says: "Their notions relating to the duties of parents and children differ extremely from ours. For, since the conjunction of male and female is founded upon the great law of nature, in order to propagate and continue the species, the Lilliputians will needs have it that men and women are joined together like other animals by the motives of concupiscence, and that their tenderness toward their young procedeth from the like natural principle. For which reason they will never allow that a child is under any obligation to his father for begetting him or to his mother for bringing him into the world, which, considering the miseries of human life, was neither a benefit in itself or intended so by his parents, whose thoughts in their love-encounters were otherwise employed. Upon these and the like reasonings, their opinion is that their parents are the last of all others to be trusted with the education of their own children."⁸¹ He obviously means by that, altogether in keeping with your distinction between "person" and "son," that if a child is to become a person, he must be removed as soon as possible from the brutishness, for so he expresses it, the mere animal conjunction from which he has his being.

You yourself admit that selfishness plays a part in your hesitation. But isn't this selfishness in a certain sense self-damaging? It is as if you, for instance, did not want to send the winter coats to the furrier's over the summer, because when the things come back to you in the fall, they will inwardly strike you as alien, whereas if you yourself keep the coats by you, come fall they will completely belong to you, both inwardly and outwardly, but will be eaten by moths. (I am not being spiteful, really not; it is only a handy example.) [...]

This, then, is my view of your resistance. There is only one counterargument that I could completely accept, but you do not mention it. Perhaps it is on your mind. It is this: How can my advice about the education of children have any value when I have never been able to give myself advice on how to have children of my own?—This argument is irrefutable and hits me hard. But good as it is, I think it hits me harder than it does this advice of mine. Don't blame my advice because it comes from me.

To Elli Hermann

[Prague, autumn 1921]

[...] Swift's main point is not what you stress (children do not have to be grateful to their parents for their existence). Basically, this is something no one would assert, in this simplified form. The weight lies on the final sentence: "Parents are the last of all others to be entrusted with the education of their own children." To be sure, it is said far too succinctly, as is the whole of the argument leading up to this sentence, and so I will try to explain it to you more fully. Let me repeat, though, that all this is only the opinion of Swift (who, by the way, was the father of a family[82]), and though my opinion tends in the same direction, I do not presume to be so decided about it.

This, then, is what Swift thinks:

Every typical family at first represents merely an animal connection, as it were, a single organism, a single bloodstream. Cast back on itself, it cannot get beyond itself. From itself it cannot create a new individual and to try to do so through the education within the family is a kind of intellectual incest.

The family, then, is an organism, but an extremely complex and unbalanced one, and like every organism it continually strives for equilibrium. As long as this striving for equilibrium between parents and children goes on (the equilibrium between the parents is a separate matter), it is called education. Why it is called that is incomprehensible, since it shows no trace of real education, that is, the quiet, unselfish, loving development of potentialities of a growing human being or merely the calm toleration of the child's independent development. Rather it is usually a violently convulsive attempt at equilibrium of an animal organism condemned, at least for many years, to the most acute imbalance. This organism, to distinguish it from the individual human animal, might be called the family animal.

The reason for the absolute impossibility of an immediate, just equilibrium (and only a just equilibrium is a real one, only this has any stability) within this family animal is the inequality of its parts, that is to say the monstrous superiority in power of the parents vis-à-vis the children for so many years. In consequence of this, the parents arrogate to themselves the sole right, during the childhood of the children, to represent the family, not only to the outside world but also within the intimate intellectual organization. They therefore step by step deprive the children of their right to personality and from then on can make them incapable of ever securing this right in a healthy way, a misfortune that later will weigh no less heavily on the parents than on the children.

The essential difference between true education and family education is that the first is a human affair, the second a family affair. In humanity every individual has his place or at least the possibility of being destroyed in his own fashion. In the family, clutched in the tight embrace of the parents, there is room only for certain kinds of people who conform to certain kinds of requirements and moreover have to meet the deadlines dictated by the parents. If they do not conform, they are not expelled—that would be very fine, but is impossible, for we are dealing with an organism here—but accursed or consumed or both. The consuming does not take place on the physical plane, as in the archetype of Greek mythology (Kronos, the most honest of fathers, who devoured his sons; but perhaps Kronos preferred this to the usual methods out of pity for his children).

The selfishness of parents—the authentic parental emotion—knows no bounds. Even the greatest parental love is, as far as education is concerned, more selfish than the smallest love of the paid educator. It cannot be otherwise. For parents do not stand in a free relationship to their children, as an adult stands toward a child—after all, they are his own blood, with this added grave complication: the blood of both the parents. When the father "educates" the child (it is the same for the mother) he will, for example, find things in the child that he already hates in himself and could not overcome and which he now hopes to overcome, since the weak child seems to be more in his power than he himself. And so in a blind fury, without waiting for the child's own development, he reaches into the depths of the growing human being to pluck out the offending element. Or he realizes with horror that something which he regards as his own distinction and which therefore (therefore!) should not be lacking from the family (the family!) is lacking in the child and so he begins to pound it into the child. Which effort is successful, but at the same time disastrous, for in the process he pounds the child to pieces. Or else, for example, he finds in the child things that he loved in his wife but hates in the child (whom he continually confuses with himself, as all parents do), as for example he can love the sky-blue eyes of his wife but would be extremely disgusted if he were suddenly to have such eyes himself. Or, for example, he finds things in the child that he loves in himself or longs to have and considers necessary for the family. Then he is indifferent to the child's other qualities. He sees in the child only the thing he loves, he clings to that, he makes himself its slave, he consumes it out of love.

Thus tyranny or slavery, born of selfishness, are the two educational methods of parents; all gradations of tyranny or slavery. Tyranny can express itself as great tenderness ("You must believe me, since I am your mother") and slavery can express itself as pride ("You are my son, so I will make you into my savior"). But these are two frightful educational methods, two antieducational methods, and likely to trample the child back into the ground from which he came.

The love that parents have for their children is animal, mindless, and always prone to confuse the child with their own selves. But the educator has respect for the child; and for the purposes of education that is incomparably more, even if there is no love involved. I repeat: For the purposes of education. For when I call parental love mindless and animal, that is not to denigrate it. It is as much an inscrutable mystery as the intelligent creative love of the educator. Only for the purposes of education we cannot denigrate it enough.

When N. calls herself a mother hen, she is right. Every mother is basically that and the one who isn't is either a goddess or, probably, a sick animal. But if Mother Hen N. wants to have not chicks but people for her children, she must not educate her children entirely by herself.

I repeat: Swift does not wish to disparage parental love; in fact he considers it so strong a force that under certain circumstances children should be shielded from this parental love. Should a mother, who in some poem or other rescues her child from a lion's paws, not be able to protect the child from her own hands? And does she do this without any reward, or better, without the possibility of reward? Another schoolbook poem, which you must surely know, tells of the wanderer who, after many years, returns to his native village and whom no one recognizes but his mother. "The mother's eye her son did know."[83] That is the true miracle of mother love and a great truth is expressed here. But only half a truth, for the corollary is missing, that if the son had stayed at home, she would never have known him, for her daily association with the son would have made him completely unrecognizable to her and so the very opposite of the poem would have happened and anyone else would have known him better than she. (Granted that she would not have had to recognize him, since he would never have come back to her.) Perhaps you will say that the wanderer went forth in the world only after he was eleven years old. But I know for a fact that he was only a few months shy of ten. Or in other words that his mother was not the kind who greedily wanted to bear the responsibilities and greedily wanted to share the joys and, what is perhaps even worse, the sorrows (he was not to have the whole of anything!), not the kind of mother who made arrangements to be saved by her son, and who therefore trusted him. (Mistrust is a Prague failing. Moreover the consequences of both trust and mistrust are equally risky, but mistrust is risky in itself.) And so for this very reason she was saved by the homecoming of her son. (Perhaps her danger was from the beginning never so enormous. For she was no Jewish woman of Prague, but some pious Catholic from Styria.)

What then must be done? According to Swift, children should be taken from their parents. That is to say, the equilibrium the family animal needs should be postponed to a time when the children, independent of their parents, should become equal to them in physical and mental powers, and then the time is come for the true and loving equilibrium to take place, the very thing that you call "being saved" and that others call "the gratitude of children" and which they find so rarely.

Besides, Swift knows how to qualify his dictums and holds that it is not absolutely necessary to remove the children of poor people. For the world presses in upon the poor, their working life cannot be kept at a distance from their hut (as for example at the birth of Christ in the half-open hut, the whole world was immediately present, the shepherds and the Wise Men from the East), and so there is no place there for the oppressive, poison-laden, child-consuming air of the nicely furnished family room.

Of course Swift does not deny that parents under certain circumstances can be an excellent unit for educating children, but only strangers' children. That, then, is how I read the Swiftian passage.

To Robert Klopstock

[Prague, September 2, 1921]

Dear Robert, the trip[84] was very easy; I mention it only because of the multitude of dreamlike and interlocking accidents that assured me a good seat. The train was jammed; at first one could sit here and there on a suitcase, later one could hardly find room to stand. Two empty cars were supposed to be coupled on in Vrutky, so there would be seats there. At Vrutky I got off, ran to the cars, but these two were filled up and were old dirty cars in addition. So I ran back to my own car, did not find it at first shot, climbed into another one; that too was the same, everything was filled up. In this car three women, among others, were pressed against the walls. They were going from Lomnitz to Prague. One of the three was an old schoolteacher whom I knew casually from Matlar, where she once brought the engineer G. to my table, there being no other place in the dining room. Now on the train I do a few small services for them. The schoolteacher, with the combined forcefulness of an indignant old lady and a schoolteacher, decides to go from compartment to compartment and insist on a seat. In fact she does find an empty place in a distant first-class compartment and by chance a second seat is vacated at that moment. So two of the women are provided for, while the third goes along with them. Immediately the following scene takes place in the compartment: Of the remaining four passengers, two are low-level railroad officials or something of the sort, and with great effort they persuade the conductor (since they themselves only have passes for second class) to declare the compartment a second-class one—the conductor has the right to effect this metamorphosis in exceptional cases. Finally he agrees, but the other two passengers in the compartment, who have first-class tickets, are incensed and demand an empty first-class compartment. The conductor provides them with one, which means that there are now two more empty seats, one for the third woman and one—since the women want to show their gratitude for my services—for me. They call me down the crowded corridors. I hardly know how, since they not only do not know my name, but, as later becomes evident, the schoolteacher cannot remember when it was she first spoke to me. Nevertheless I hear them calling me and I migrate to where they are just as the conductor is pasting a big 2 on the glass door.

The best food on the trip was the plums, excellent plums.

Several changes in Prague. For example, the death of a strange old uncle.[85] He had died a few months ago; a few days ago I sent him my first card from Matlar: "Cordial regards; looking forward to seeing you again shortly."

It quickly turned out that I have very good connections, through relatives, with Professor Münzer. If there is any chance of a position[86] for you there, it is imperative that you begin to prepare the ground well ahead of time: for example, you must begin now if you want anything in February. Do send me some documents, the professor's letter, and so forth.

Perhaps I will be going to a German sanatorium for another three months. The best of everything and thanks for everything.

Yours, K

To Minze Eisner

[Prague, beginning of September 1921]

Dear Minze, Right off in haste. Your two letters have reached me only now, for I have been in Matliary all this time and letters were not sent on to me. When are you coming? In the meantime I will try to get what information I can. But please, Minze, when you come, do not surprise me: I take surprises so very badly. Being sick a long time has frayed my nerves. The little spider that is climbing the wall at the moment frightens me, as will the great big Minze, the working girl, should she suddenly come into the room. So please, Minze, write beforehand, where and when we can see each other.

Hoping to see you soon, yours, Kafka

To Minze Eisner

[Prague, beginning of September 1921]
Dear Minze, So you are coming in the middle of September. That is very good. (Late in September or beginning of October I will again be leaving Prague.) Perhaps you can avoid coming on the 13th or the 14th, since that is my father's birthday. But if you can't avoid it, you may come on those days also. You are welcome any day. If you come on a weekday morning, I could hardly meet you at the station (in return for many alms I must at least sit at my desk in the Institute for a few weeks). In that case you can simply come from the station to my office (Pořič 7) "to present yourself." I am there until 2 o'clock; the doorman will call me down. A pity that you did not come this past week, since you would have been able to sleep at my youngest sister's (whose husband is away on a trip this week, and who lives in the same house as I do) and would thus not tire yourself with continual traveling. In addition you could have taken in the Congress in Karlsbad.[87]

Let me know when you are coming, to what station and at what time. (You used to be friendly with a family in Prague; are you no longer?)

Best wishes, yours, K

To Robert Klopstock

[Prague, beginning of September 1921]
Dear Robert, I haven't yet acknowledged even your registered letter. [...]

I have talked with Pick; he knows about my letter to Hegner. Hegner has the good habit—which could not have been foreseen, and which however tends to be unnerving to people—to keep quiet when he cannot say "Yes." Casually, he once said to Pick: "Kafka writes me that I should employ a friend of his for a year in the printing shop. What should I answer to such a request?" This rhetorical question settled our affair. But Holzmann—Pick tells me—has nothing to fear and will be received cordially. Perhaps you have already had news of that.

My health is not very good; if I didn't go straight to bed after leaving the office, and stay there, I couldn't bear up. The first days I did not do this and it took its revenge on me. And the weather is still very good. I am also so tired that I cannot even lift my hand to send some picture postcards to Matlar. Please give my regards to all.

I read this fine anecdote in Flaubert's diaries. One day Chateaubriand and some friends visited Lake Gaube (a lonely mountain lake in the Pyrenees). They all sat and picnicked on the same bench where Flaubert had breakfasted. The beauty of the lake enchanted everyone. "I would like to live here forever," Chateaubriand said. "Oh, you would die of boredom here," answered a society lady. "What would that matter," answered the poet with a laugh, "I am always bored."[88] Actually it is not the wit of the story which delights me, for that is nothing special, but the cheerfulness, the almost majestic happiness of the man.

                                                      Best wishes, yours, Kafka

To Robert Klopstock

                          [Postcard. Prague; postmark: September 7, 1921]
Dear Robert, What's all this about, you say I haven't written? Two letters and a card—they could not all have gone astray. [...] I am tired and weak and everyone here is strong and lively. Ernst Weiss was just here, not at all angry, friendly and on the whole gentler than usual. He obviously keeps himself healthy, and very healthy, by sheer will. If he wanted to, he could be as sick as anybody else.

                                                      Best regards, K

To Robert Klopstock

                                        [Prague, mid-September 1921]
Dear Robert, This is only a stopgap answer. I will write more fully on Monday. At the moment I am somewhat reeling from the letter, but will give it more consideration and will discuss it with Ottla and Max (who has been back in Prague for some time—the Congress ended a few days ago and he did not even stay until the end) [...]. Today, but as I say this is not yet final, I would advise, out of fear of the city, your at least seizing upon the Barlangliget opportunity, and if it isn't available, to make it so. But I mean this for the winter; the few days until the middle of October of course don't amount to anything. If B. or Smokovec are not possible (what about the English manufacturer?), then possibly there is only Prague, as far as I know. For Norddach, even if it were possible, could surely not be arranged in a few days, and if it can be no doubt that will be easiest done from Prague [...]

So much for the time being. I am feeling quite well. I have just taken my temperature: 98.2 at six o'clock in the evening.

Yours, K

To Robert Klopstock

[Prague, mid-September 1921]

Dear Robert, Things are not so bad, they are simply not good and I am surely going away, probably to Görbersdorf.[89] It seems to be no more expensive than Matlar. Admittedly I would rather go farther, to the Rhine or Hamburg, but I have not received any proper answers from there. My temperature does not go up over 99, but it does go up above 98.6 daily.

Why don't you write about yourself? Your health, Smokovec, letter of recommendation, Aussee, and the like.

Ilonka has sent chocolate; that is very dear of her. Like a little vassal she sends tribute and does not dare add a word of her own. How quiet she was, and in memory has grown even quieter.

. . . .

Janouch[90] was here the other day, only in from the country for a day; he announced himself by letter. He is not at all angry and your letter especially gave him great pleasure. He called on me at the office, crying, laughing, shouting, brought me a pile of books which I am supposed to read, then apples, and finally his sweetheart, a little friendly daughter of a forester; he lives out there with her parents. He considers himself lucky, but now and then makes a disquieting impression of being badly confused, and also doesn't look well. He wants to get his diploma and then study medicine ("because it is quiet, modest work") or law ("because it leads to politics"). What devil stokes this fire?

So Holzmann is going to study in Heidelberg? Then he didn't go to Hegner's? A pity. Then he already belongs partly to Stefan George[91]—not a bad but a stern master.

What is everyone in Matlar up to, Glauber especially, with his plans for Poprad? What answer did he get from the Munich academy? Is Szinay there yet?

Best regards, yours, K.

To Robert Klopstock

[Picture postcard (Matlar). Prague; postmark: September 16, 1921]

Since in my thoughts I am in Matlar (and have no other card), I am sending this one of Matlar. I did not telegraph because I don't have anyone to send downstairs and the elevator is out of order. Also because my letter must have already reached you, then because I am ashamed to telegraph concerning my health, then because it is expensive, then because it is surely permissible to slightly exaggerate one's troubles to one's personal doctor with impunity; if not, to whom else? And finally because a letter is already lying ready, which cannot be mailed until the passages dealing with health have been made illegible.

K.

To Robert Klopstock

[Postcard. Prague; postmark: September 23, 1921]

Dear Robert, [. . .] the sniffles developed into strong cough. I was not at the office today, though tomorrow I hope to be there again. But just this moment a telegram has come from the little gardener[92] in Pomerania (who is also not at all angry) in which she announces herself for tomorrow. She is staying only a day, but still and all I shall have to collect all my strength and yet she is friendly and sweet and patient. She wants advice, but good advice dangles among the stars—that is why it is so dark up there—how can it be hauled down?

I am glad that Barl. may work out. I can hardly ask anything of Max in this connection—he is so busy and harassed [. . .]

I cannot go to the seashore; where would I get the money? Even if I wanted to "take" it, I wouldn't be able to. Also it is too far for me: for reasons of health I am willing to go to the ends of the earth, for reasons of sickness at most ten hours.

K

How is Szinay? Regards to Glauber.

To Robert Klopstock

[Prague, end of September 1921]

Dear Robert, Good to hear that I still have a few days' grace in which to see the professor. The Pomeranian visit went very well, was also quite short. But now something bigger has developed. The letter-writer[93] whose sharp and even penmanship you know from her envelopes is in Prague and so the sleepless nights begin.

If Fräulein Irene takes the view you did in your last letter, then all is well and all that remains is to regret the husband from Zips. But she would probably have been too delicate for him. I am very glad that she is getting away. It was like a dice game: At first it seemed that your pupil was going to win Hellerau, then my nephew had prospects, then you (with me backing you up), then Holzmann, and finally the winner was Fräulein Irene, whom we did not even know was playing. Has there been a telegram from Dresden yet?

So your cousin is staying longer in Berlin? Is she painting?

I won't be coming to Barl., Robert. I could have stayed in the Tatra much longer, but to return there would be as though I wanted to reinfect myself with my own disease which stayed there (not that I have any the less of it). I want to take the sickness somewhere else. Besides, the doctors want a proper sanatorium, with rubdowns, compresses, quartz lamps, and better food. In addition Görbersdorf is no more expensive than Matlar, though I admit that I am not looking forward to going to Görbersdorf. Our Lake Geneva plan was after all the best.

Amazing how the will plays with the disease, though also how frightfully the will can be played with. For two days I have hardly coughed, which would not be so strange, but I hardly have any phlegm either, when I had been bringing up quantities of phlegm. But I would much prefer to be honestly coughing than to be carrying around this "pneumothorax."

Just like you, I have not been receiving *Selbstwehr* and the Congress newspaper.[94] Won't you be getting to Matlar?

Is Szinay consumptive too? Where is he bound for, to Unterschmecks?[95] (Oh, but Unterschmecks—that isn't a lung sanatorium, is it?) And Frau G.?[96] Is Fräulein Ilonka going anywhere?

Keep well, yours, K

To Robert Klopstock

[Prague, September/October 1921]

Dear Robert, Only Fräulein Irene's problems for today. I went to see Pick; he knew nothing [...] but Paul Adler was there, very helpful, and at a gathering to which I would have had to go anyway dashed off the two letters which you will find enclosed. He is a splendid person; that he would be so in this regard was beyond my expectations. One letter is addressed to Prof. Dreher, a professor at the Academy of Art. He is about forty-five, very friendly, as is his wife. He is a friend of Gross, who is mentioned in both letters and who is the director of the Academy for Arts and Crafts. If the address Waisenhausgasse 7, Dresden A, is not exactly right, she can inquire at the Art Academy. In fact Fräulein Irene can look him up at the Art Academy, but her chances are better if she looks him up at home, since she can make the acquaintance of his wife there and come under feminine protection. I know Georg von Mendelssohn casually; no doubt he will not remember me, but he is someone you cannot forget, a huge, tall Scandinavian-looking man with a small, horribly energetic, birdlike face. One is put off by his manner, his staccato speech, his forbidding appearance which seems ready to reject every possible request. But one should not be frightened, he does not mean ill, at least not usually, and is absolutely trustworthy. He is a central figure in the German craft movement, has a metalcrafts studio in Hellerau, and belongs in every respect to the "cognoscenti" in the crafts.

Inasmuch as I have secured these two letters (which of course apart from their obligingness are full of all sorts of nonsense which Fräulein Irene will no doubt ignore, as I do, for the sake of their good intentions), I would consider it wise for her to confine herself to Dresden. There Fräulein Irene will have the opportunity of studying (depending on how things turn out) either at a small, personally conducted school or in the School of Arts and Crafts itself. In addition, Dresden is a beautiful, pleasant, and above all relatively healthful city (much more healthful, more of a garden city, than Munich) and also closest to her native region.

For these reasons I have sent the application only to Dresden. Should there be no reply or a rejection, it does not matter, for the letters of recommendation will put everything right. Should the answer be favorable, she will be able to present her testimonials to her new friends in Dresden. So I am temporarily returning (enclosed) the money and the stamps for the other applications. I sent along 20 crowns with the application to Dresden; 10 crowns seemed to me too little. I am writing to you because Hunsdorf strikes me as somehow unreliable as a postal destination; besides, the young lady may already be in Matlar.

Cordial regards to her and to you, K

So that Fräulein Irene may become a bit acquainted with the letter-writer, I enclose a review of his. Is there a post office in Hunsdorf? For the telegram is supposed to go there.

On a separate sheet, enclosed:
And now a few words *in confidence* to you; as long as it concerned only the hopeless experiment of sending in an application, the matter interested me, but only from a distance, as for example in Jules Verne,[97] when one sees the children playing in the boat. The boat is not going to come unmoored by accident, one tells oneself, and drift off into the vast ocean. But the remote possibility of that does exist and precisely that is interesting. But now that it is turning serious and I myself am involved, it is no longer interesting. I am more inclined to accept the opinion of the Munich principal[98] than yours, as expressed in your letter. But that too is not the decisive factor. Even if no vigorous talent were present—and that appears, not to my ignorant eyes but to my knowledge of character, to be the case here—that would not be so bad in itself, for the discipline of the school, the influence of the teacher, the despair of her own heart, might well generate something useful. But that could only happen in early youth; at Fräulein Irene's age, it is no longer possible. To be sure, she has lived all her life in the wilderness of the Zips region (for so it will seem to the sophisticated minds of the Dresden gentlemen), and this gentle awkwardness, modesty, her human, artistic, all-encompassing inexperience has a certain tangible value. The radical change in her mode of life will have a strong effect. If she has some degree of robustness, she will be able to bear this effect without harm, but unfortunately, because of her age, also without benefit. And what a responsibility we would bear, sending her out into the world this way. Precisely in those years in which she might still save herself by a marriage she will be abroad, will discover that this hope too is in vain, will shamefacedly return, and only then will see that everything is truly lost. My heart sinks at the thought that she will pass through here on her way to Dresden, that I will see her (though I am too weak to show her around the city) and so will have to act as though I had confidence in the project. And when I imagine the art school professor, the good Saxon, saying: "Well then, my dear young lady, show us your work," and the professor's wife standing by, I immediately want—even though I would physically be as far from the scene then as I am now—to creep into a hole in the ground to hide from the horrors of the world. The letters of recommendation are good, but it would be better to tear them up.

Yesterday I went to a party gathered to hear a young actress doing a recitation. (Her artistic future—she is studying with Reinhardt—strikes me as no less desperate than Fräulein Irene's.) Then I went to the coffeehouse for a while, out of weakness, came home in a state of nervous trembling, for nowadays I cannot endure the eyes of people (not out of misanthropy, but merely the eyes of people, their presence, their sitting there and looking across at me, all that is too much for me), then coughed for hours,* finally dropping off to sleep in the morning, and would just as soon have floated out of life, which seemed easy because of the apparent shortness of the distance.

I won't be going to see Münzer for another day or two.

Why doesn't Fräulein Irene rather go to a gardening school? Maybe there is something of the sort even in Dresden.

I have just noticed that Fräulein Irene is not twenty-eight, as I thought, but twenty-six. This small detail perhaps makes her chances a bit more hopeful.

* Don't telegraph! I was not coughing for hours but not sleeping for hours and along with that did a bit of coughing.

To Robert Klopstock

[Two postcards. Prague, postmark: October 3, 1921]
Sunday
Dear Robert,
I don't understand your not having had word. A card and a letter must have reached you. I am all tied up until Thursday,[99] though in reality less so than in my mind, but then quiet returns. I am not as bad off as I feared, in my first great panic, but dangers remain and are increasing.[100]

Cordial regards, K

[IN THE MARGIN] When is Fräulein Irene coming?

To Ludwig Hardt[101]

[Prague, beginning of October 1921]
Dear Herr Hardt, I will be in the lobby of the Blaue Stern[102] this evening at six. I come so late and will leave so soon because I have to conserve my feeble strength to be able to come for sure on Wednesday evening. Of course I cannot assume that you will be free just at this particular time: should you not be free, then a note from you will send me away; I will inquire of the doorman. If for this reason I cannot see you on Tuesday, may I make this one request of you: If it is at all possible and if you would be so kind, would you include the Kleist anecdote in Wednesday's program?

Cordially yours, Kafka

[PENCILED POSTSCRIPT] Dear Herr Hardt, Your letter has just come. Certainly this evening would be best but I do not trust myself to go out two evenings in a row in this rainy weather. I will therefore try to meet you at six. If that doesn't work, I will try to come at half past eight and will leave a note with the doorman to that effect. What complications! Please do not be annoyed with me.

To Robert Klopstock
                    [Postcard. Prague; postmark: October 4, 1921]
Dear Robert, Please don't be angry or, what is much the same, don't be so disturbed. I too am disturbed, but in another fashion. The situation is clear, the gods are playing with us both, but different gods for you and for me and we must exert all our human energies to equalize it. I cannot say much about the main thing, for this is, even for myself, locked within the darkness of the breast. I imagine it lies there beside the disease, on the same bed. Thursday or Friday I will be alone again and then I may perhaps write to you about it, though even then not thoroughly, for there is no human being, myself included, who could deal with it thoroughly. I have had to devote a little of my time (with me, unfortunately, little is much) to an actor (though, but here there are no thoughs, an admirable one) who is here for a few days.
                                                        Yours, K

To Robert Klopstock
                    [Postcard. Prague; postmark: October 8, 1921][103]
Dear Robert, It was held over a day, now it is past. Hardt is still around, admirable in many respects, very lovable in some. He will be leaving Tuesday, then it will quiet down. All through these days I hardly had a chance to lie down during the daytime, but am not very tired, very energetic in my coughing, as a matter of fact. Tomorrow I am going to have to look at the Czech sanatorium, for Göbersdorf won't have a room free until the end of November and besides they are antivegetarian. I suppose by now the decision concerning Barl. has been made at last. And what about Fräulein Irene?

You may have troubles, Robert, naturally. But you can put the blame on others, or if you like blame no one, which is even better. What a fine, free life.
                                                        Yours, K

To Robert Klopstock

[Prague, second week of October 1921]

Dear Robert, Can't be done, my sister was there. A new passport would cost 191 crowns, but aside from the fact that this would be a tremendous price to pay for nothing, they do not want to issue a new passport; the old one is still in good shape, they say, they have handled far worse passports, and so forth and so on. They say it was against the rules to sew the loose pages together, but even that does not matter. Anyhow, to be on the safe side they have now rubber-stamped all the pages. That was all she could get out of them. At most one could have told them the truth, but that would have meant paying that high price.

Yesterday Fräulein Irene was here. My mistrust of the project is not allayed. It is an insane undertaking, so insane it is not even pleasant to look on. I will be overjoyed if it turns out even halfway well; not only will I have been wrong in this case, but my whole view of the world will be influenced. She left this noon. Perhaps she went to see Hardt this morning and obtained a recommendation from him.—The whole thing makes me think about myself. It's as though I were to give way to a dream of mine and want to join a scout troop of ten-year-old boys.

As far as you are concerned, Fräulein Irene had nothing to report. She had nothing to say about Barl., nothing about Matlar, nothing about Frau G.— But of course she is sweet and gentle and my crude judgment does not affect that.

At last I have a little rest, but am very tired from the exertions of the last few days, general condition not too bad.

All the best, yours, K

To Minze Eisner

[Picture postcard. Prague; postmark: October 11, 1921]
The Lazybones and the Working Girl[104]

Dear Minze, I've been submerged for a long time, have simply pocketed your pretty snapshots with pleasure, have read your two cards and letter, as if you were sitting by the sofa and telling me all that had happened, and for the rest have been taken up with various agitating and exhausting visits, have also now and then been confined to bed, had not a moment's time, what with things to attend to, what with tiredness, and knew moreover that it did not matter between us whether I wrote today or tomorrow, for we do not become nervous when one or the other of us does not write; each of us knows that the other has an iron constitution.—Did nothing come of the trip to Holland? Pity, pity.—I will be staying awhile longer in Prague. Warmest regards, to your girl friends also.

Yours, K.

My sister sends cordial greetings. Her address:
    Ottilie David, Altstädter Ring 6, Prague.

To Robert Klopstock

[Prague, mid-October 1921]
Dear Robert, You are always dissatisfied with me. That's hardly good for my health. I am exactly the same person I was in Matlar, yet there you were not always dissatisfied with me, though, granted, the living together mercifully blurs lines. From the whole pattern one might conclude that once you had caught on to all my tricks, you did not want to know anything more about me.

The comparison with your cousin is like a switch you are always threatening me with. And yet surely I have nothing significant in common with her except yourself. In earlier years, whenever I committed some apparent stupidity which was in reality a consequence of a fundamental flaw of my nature, my father used to say, "Rudolph all over!" comparing me to a stepbrother of my mother's whom he found extremely ridiculous, an indecipherable, too friendly, too modest, solitary, and yet almost loquacious man.105 Basically I had hardly anything in common with him except the critic. But the painful repetition of the comparison, the almost physical difficulty of avoiding at all costs a route I had not the slightest intention of taking, and finally my father's persuasiveness, or rather, if you like, his curse, resulted in my at least starting to resemble this uncle of mine.

The whole pneumothorax story was only a joke; I was preoccupied with other things than my lungs. The lungs realized the justification for this and were quieter for a while but have since made up for it.

That you are alone is not good, though this too cannot be said with certainty. Are you studying? How are your temperatures?

Don't you hear anything from Ilonka, from Frau Galgon? So Szinay is consumptive—is that possible?

Best wishes, yours, K

[IN THE MARGIN] What was this book you were talking about, that I am supposed to have promised you?

To Robert Klopstock

[Prague, October 1921]

Dear Robert, Here is the passport; I was sick again, which is why this was delayed. I hope you can use it soon. In your case the worst thing is not the sickness, depressing and incomprehensible though the fever is, but that it coincides with your occasional spells of despair, which in turn arise out of nothing, out of youth, out of Judaism, and out of the general sorrows of the world. In ordinary daily life the only real comfort is the experience that, incredible as it is, one emerges time and again from the bottomless pits of so many a moment.

Yours, K

To Robert Klopstock

[Prague, November 1921]

Dear Robert, Perhaps I do not fully understand your letter: Does it mean that the Britishers don't want to give any money for a cure in the Tatra either, although the doctor, as I recall, virtually assured you that you could stay in the Tatra? And do you now want to go straight to Prague, to the city? To walk in the inner city on a warm afternoon, no matter how slowly, affects me as though I were in a long unventilated room and did not even have the strength to open the window to get some air. And to stay here permanently? In the dissection room? In winter, in heated and unaired rooms? And without transition, straight from your pure mountain air? Do you really mean that you want to come right away? [...]

The girl's letter is lovely, as lovely as it is abominable. These are the seductive voices of night, this is how the sirens sang. We do them an injustice when we think they intended to seduce. They were well aware that they had talons and barren wombs; that is why they lamented. They could not help it that their lament sounded so lovely.

You are well provided, then, with letters from girls. Who Heddy is, I have no idea. Poor Glauber. But perhaps it will hasten matters and give them a favorable turn, for the girl really has to sympathize with him and therefore oppose her father, while at the same time overcoming her scruples concerning the chief thing and so on.

There have been no new issues of *Selbstwehr* since then. The Congress newspaper sometimes comes to me here, sometimes goes to Matlar. Except for the last issue (but this too would hardly interest you; it deals with proposals for intensive agriculture)[106] it was not worth reading—dry extracts from speeches.

The children delight me. Yesterday, for instance, my next-to-newest niece[107] (I once showed you her picture) sat on the floor while I stood in front of her. Suddenly for no discernible reason she took great fright of me, and ran to my father, who had to take her on his knee. Her eyes were full of tears and she was trembling. But since she is very gentle and delicate and friendly and also was somewhat reassured by Grandfather's arm, she answered all our questions, for instance, that I am Uncle Franz, that I am nice, that she likes me very much, and so on, but all the while she was trembling with fear.

Cordial regards, yours, K

To Robert Klopstock

[Prague, November 1921]

Dear Robert,

The fear is gradually subsiding but it was alarming.

The temperatures are still worrisome. And without any particular cause? Are you at any rate lying down as much as in the summer? And what is your situation in Matlar? [...]

I have had a letter from Fräulein Irene, written before she began on her probation period. Apparently people there are very friendly toward her, as are both the girls Hardt put her in touch with, who seem to have made friends with her. Even though Hardt, as he told me privately, did not hope for much from these Russian-Jewish girls, so very different in nature, with their fiery intellectuality. I hope all this is not going according to the old law: Those who can't be helped are offered help by all. (Do you know *The Robbers?* Only the great hero helps the man who can be helped. The majority flock to help those who are beyond rescue.)[108] May things go well for Fräulein Irene! Her letter was exciting.

Are you reading *Goat Song*[109] in the *Prager Presse?* It is most interesting. This struggle with the waves—and time and again [Werfel] comes through, great swimmer that he is. I am supposed to see him tomorrow but I will not be going.

I will send you *Selbstwehr* Monday. It won't hurt you to hunger for it a little, after you so often despised it in the past. I am also sending the textbook.

As yet I have nothing much to say about the new cure.[110] The doctor sublimely, childishly ridiculous, like most of them. Afterward I end up being very fond of them. After all, what matters is that they do the best they can, and the less that is, the more touching it is. And sometimes they spring a surprise.

All the best, yours, K

Regards to Glauber and Szinay.

To Robert Klopstock

[Prague, December 1921][111]

Dear Robert, When will you finally stop retouching the picture and see me as I really am, lying so powerless here on the sofa? High on the topmost onion dome of the Russian church opposite, roofers are banging, working, and singing in wind and rain. I marvel at them through the open window as though they were giants of the antediluvian world. If I represent contemporary man, what could they be but such giants? No other reason for my not writing but this, or rather yet another: that no matter what I write, I am powerless to convince you.

Many thanks. Gradually, with a little outside help, this great man[112] is being unearthed here and there from Hungarian obscurity. However, a flock of false conceptions and false analogies also intrude upon the process. Such a translation reminds one somewhat of the complaints of ghosts over the painful incompetence of mediums. Here we have the mediumistic incompetence of reader and translator. But the prose is more direct and gives us a somewhat closer view of him. There's much I don't understand, but I take in the whole. As always in such a case, one feels happy that he is there and that one is in some way or another related to him. "Without antecedents," his work is said to be, and therefore we are also related in this respect. The translation of the poetry is clearly deplorable, only here and there a word, perhaps a tone. By way of measuring the relationship of the translation to the original, I take as my standard the relationship between myself and the roofers.

You are somewhat unfair to the editor. What does it matter that he reaps profits? And what objection can be made against parasitism when it acts openly, honestly, with inborn flair, and for the good of all concerned? Aren't we also parasites and he our leader? Moreover, the sight of the two of them together is highly dramatic and instructive, the one who says so much and the other who holds back so much. The epilogue also contains some new things, at least new for me.

My life, fortunately, has been very regular lately. Only Max sometimes comes to see me, and once Werfel was here, to invite me to Semmering,[113] which was very good of him, but the doctor did not allow me to travel. Finally I had a visitor for four days. That is all.

Now the anniversary of my arrival at Matliary is approaching and my acquaintance with the wealthy, plump young man who sat so snugly between two pretty women, reading the Christmas number of the *Neue Freie Presse*.

Be well, yours, K

Your special-delivery letter has just arrived. Apparently there is no other way for you to know me except through the hatred my behavior must ultimately generate in you.

Please give my regards to Glauber.
   What is Frau Galgon doing?
   Fräulein Ilonka wrote to me recently.

To Robert Klopstock

                            [Prague, beginning of December 1921]
Dear Robert, What a fellow you are! Fräulein Irene has been accepted. A girl who in 26 years (obviously in keeping with her talents) never did any artwork except for a bad copy of a bad postcard, has never seen an art show aside from Captain Holub's, has heard no lectures aside from one by Saphir,[114] has read no newspaper other than the *Karpathenpost*—this girl has been accepted, writes half-happy letters not lacking in subtlety, is the friend of an apparently interesting girl. Wonder upon wonders and all conjured up by you. I warm myself on it in this dreary winter.[115]

                                       Yours, K

To Robert Klopstock

                            [Prague, beginning of December 1921]
Dear Robert, The story of your uncle is amusing, like a part acted by Pallenberg.[116] I feel the air of the room in your letter. But you did not write me about what followed, only about the citizenship matter.

   Your vocational choice—well, ever since I've known you it never entered my mind that you were meant to be anything but a doctor. That medicine is a profession for the well-to-do only may be true of Central Europe, but it is not true of the rest of the world and especially not of Palestine, which is now happily beginning to enter your frame of reference. And it also involves physical activity. Then again, the half-and-half professions, that is to say professions that are not serious, are abominable, no matter whether they are physical or intellectual. Whether physical or intellectual, they become glorious when they are concerned with people. It is terribly easy to perceive this and terribly difficult to find the living pathway to it. However in your case the matter is not even so difficult, for you are a doctor. In general it can be said of the average set of lawyers that they must first be ground to dust before they may reach Palestine. Palestine needs earth but it does not need lawyers. I happen to know one Praguer who after a few years of studying law gave that up and became an apprentice mechanic. (Along with the change of profession, he married and already has a little boy.) His training period is about over and in the spring he will leave for Palestine. I grant you that when people go into such new professions, nonacademics normally need three years of study while the academics need six years and more. However I was recently at an exhibition of apprentice work and saw how astonishingly far people can go in all the crafts after only one or two years (though these were all people without higher education).

Odd that your cousin is not going to stay on in Berlin; after all, there's something to giving Berlin a try as a halfway free person. That she so lightly turns away from Berlin speaks either greatly for her artistic abilities or against them. But the rest, that she is not going home by way of the Tatra and that she doesn't want to speak to me—that is not odd and does not surprise me.

If you don't have *Javne and Jerusalem*[117] by Bergmann, I will send it to you.

How are you living at the moment? What are you working at? I haven't yet gone to see my cousin again.[118] I am beginning to belong to that group of people who haven't any time. The day is carefully divided between lying down, taking a walk, and the like, and I haven't time or strength even for reading. Fever again, after a few fever-free days. The doctor has only prescribed a special tea which, if I understand the doctor rightly, contains silicic acid, and he has read somewhere (I hope not in some humor magazine) that silicic acid is supposed to promote scarification. Perhaps you should try it too. I will copy out the recipe for you when I get back to my place. I am writing this at my sister's, for my room, that icy hell, is unheated.

Cordial regards, also to Glauber and Steinberg.

Yours, K

Write me about Ilonka and Frau Galgon.

You should have received a letter from me and the textbook.

To Robert Klopstock

[Prague, December 1921]

Dear Robert, Aren't you exaggerating somewhat in your opinion of Ilonka? She is fearful, is weighed down by the world, doesn't trust her own judgment, but has sound enough nerves to conduct herself according to standards not her own—or we hope she has such nerves. And I grant is sensitive enough not to make a heroic thing of that, but rather to confess the misery of it to herself and others. Unfortunately she has such sensitivity. Besides I do not consider it entirely a misfortune that she has obeyed her father. Someone who trusts his own judgment need not necessarily be in the right, whereas someone who doesn't trust his own judgment is probably bound to be in the right. And besides, marriage is a relative happiness, at least most of the time, only you have to survive the engagement period. In my letter to Ilonka, I have tried to buck her up in this matter. Have you heard anything new from her? And why don't you write a word about Frau Galgon?

You exaggerate in regard to Ilonka, I in regard to Irene. I exaggerate out of happiness, that such a children's dream should be acted out somewhere in close proximity to me, at least so it seems, that there should be so much naïveté and thus so much courage and thus so many possibilities upon this earth. One should not dwell so much on the details, though it is just these that delight me. Compared to this, what are Kraus, Kokoschka,[119] and so on? These names are daily mentioned in certain Dresden circles just as the Lomnitz peaks are mentioned in Matlar, and at best for the same reason: The eternal monotony of the mountains would induce despair if one could not sometimes force oneself to find them beautiful. What you call those "miracle-working" letters were three penciled scraps in which I congratulated her and myself.

My condition is no worse than in Matlar in the winter. Temperature and weight are not quite as good as in Matlar, but otherwise there has been no deterioration, certainly not. When Werfel was here, I was probably in worse shape than now, but that was not the basis of the prohibition. The doctor is in general down on Semmering because of its raw climate and in general against any prolonged and extreme change, and in addition against anything that would interrupt his treatment. Nevertheless it is somewhat paradoxical that toward the end of January he means to take a trip to Spindelmühle (in the Riesengebirge)[120] with his family and wants to take me along, although only for two weeks.

Did you happen to read an article by Upton Sinclair on Dr. Abram[121] in the *Prager Presse?* I took it for a joke but that has been disclaimed.
. . . .

Nothing yet has been done about your affair, partly because of my negligence and partly not my fault. First my cousin took the matter over, since he is related to Münzer through his wife. But this cousin was always sickly and now he is sick in earnest.[122] Therefore I took the papers away from him and gave them to Felix Weltsch. Perhaps I will hear something about it on Sunday.

Yours, K

Regards to Glauber, Szinay, Steinberg. And what about Holzmann? Did he send you George?

Among the newspapers I am sending you will find a *Reformblatt* with an article on X-ray treatment. Should there be anything significant there, please write me a few words on the subject at your convenience. The newspapers are already packed up and I don't want to undo the package.

To Robert Klopstock

[Prague, December 1921/January 1922]

Dear Robert, What confirmation I have of the Abram stuff is not as clear as all that. My sister has only spoken to Rudolf Fuchs who told her that was well-known stuff, the so-called Abram theory, and books had already been written on the subject. I don't think he was making a joke. But where he heard about the Abram theory, whether through his editorial connections, I don't know. I myself talk to nobody except Max (sometimes to Oskar and Felix) and my doctor, and both know nothing about it, besides which neither of them has read the article. (Could you tell me which issue?) My doctor (whose fault it is that I had to throw away the first beginning to this letter, in which I chattered on about the doctor) is younger than I am, is passionate about medicine, is interested especially in cancer, and showed me, upon my raising the question, a book about radioactivity he has just been studying, but knows nothing about Abram.

Your self-reproaches about Abram! Such things, such confessions, are what have forever and a day kept the world far from me. Should such a sin be something out of the ordinary, unique, or especially terrible, then not only don't I understand the world anymore, for that goes without saying, but the world is also made up of other substance than myself. For me such a sin would only be a drop in life's river, on which I am sailing, happy if I do not drown. To single out such a sin seems to me like someone's examining the sewer water of London and finding a single dead rat in it and on the basis of this concluding: "London must be an extremely repulsive city."

Anxiety over the amount of one's work is always, probably, a blockage in life itself. In general one doesn't suffocate because of lack of air but because of lack of lung power.

Your explanation of the Abram theory is very good. Only the electrons are incomprehensible to me; I do not even know the word.

To be sure the *Reformblatt* is an absurd sheet, but its absurdity does not devaluate it, is merely an additional feature. The aspirations of this paper and others like it are perhaps more vital than those of the people who promote them and are only crouching in this semidarkness, biding their time. [. . .]

Best wishes, yours, K

How is your health and your work? And why still nothing about Frau Galgon?

To Minze Eisner
[Picture postcard (Spitzweg's *The Bridegroom*). Prague, winter 1921–22]
It is very sweet of you, Minze, not to forget me. This does not mean that I take your card for a sign of forgiveness of my long silence—forgiveness is easy—but rather for a sign that you understand my special case, or more precisely, not that you clearly understand but that you are forbearing. And that is really very sweet. Are you a little more cheerful than the last time you wrote me and I was truly at a loss how to answer? I often am apt to beat my forehead against such a barrier.

Cordial regards, yours K

1922

To Robert Klopstock
[Prague, end of January 1922]
Dear Robert, Another letter of reproof, insofar as I understand it. (The German—but this is not what makes it hard to understand—is a bit odder than it had been, not exactly wrong, not at all, but odder, as if you had been spending little time with German-speaking people.) Must you always be reproving me? Don't I do that enough myself? Do I need help with that? But of course I need help with that. And you are basically right, but I am so busy chasing after an imaginary spar in the perpetual and actual shipwreck that probably I can only be nasty about everything else. Especially where letters are concerned, letters from men or women. Letters can cheer me, can move me, can seem worthy of admiration, but they mattered much more to me in the past, too much for them to serve me now as a significant form of life. I have not been deceived by letters but deceived myself with letters, literally warmed myself for years in advance in the warmth that finally was engendered when the whole pile of letters went into the fire. [. . .]

Max's novel[1] meant a great deal to me. A pity that I am not able to snatch some of it out of your sight (for example the spy story, the youthful journal part) so that you can see into the book's depths. At least in my opinion, those stories get in the way, but for the novel as a whole—and this is its weakness—they are nevertheless necessary. Take the trouble to look behind them—it's worth it.

You say nothing about *Goat Song.*

I suppose you have received the messages from Münzer.

I will be sending various newspapers tomorrow. I have received only the first issue of *Feuerreiter.*[2]

I'll be leaving Friday for Spindelmühle[3] for two weeks. I hope these weeks will be an improvement on the last sleepless three weeks, which brought me to extremities I had not yet reached in Matlar.

What arrangements are you making toward your future? I do not yet have a place, but at the YMCA, so Max tells me (he gave a lecture there a few days ago), there are fine, quiet, comfortable sitting rooms and study rooms for students, lounges, bathrooms, and so on, but no accommodations for the night.

Be well and give my best regards to Glauber.

Yours, K

To Robert Klopstock

[Postcard. Spindlermühle, end of January 1922]

Dear Robert, I'm in Spindelmühle, under outwardly excellent conditions; in the first few days everything was good, now sleepless, sleepless to the point of despair. But still I can go sledding and mountain climbing, high and steep enough, without any special ill effects. The thermometer is ignored. Ottla has surely written to you when the semester begins. Keep well, and looking forward to seeing you. After a year and a half of living in the mountains and the wilds, how you will throw yourself into the city!

Yours, K

To Max Brod

[Picture postcard. Spindlermühle; postmark: January 31, 1922]

Dear Max, The first impression was very good, much better than in Matlar;

in the second impression the phantoms of the place awoke, but I am very satisfied, it could not be better. If it stays this way, I will mend. I have already gone sledding and perhaps may try skiing. Be well. You have helped me a lot in the last few days. I await news from Schandau.

Yours

To Max Brod

[Postcard. Spindlermühle; postmarked on arrival: February 8, 1922] Dearest Max, Pity, pity that you can't come *for a few days.* If luck were with us, we would spend all day mountain climbing, sledding (skiing, too? So far I have taken five steps), and writing, and with the last especially would be speeded closer to the end, the imminent end, a peaceful end, or don't you want that? For me it's like it was in gymnasium, the teacher is pacing back and forth, the whole class have finished their assignments and gone home, and only I am still toiling away at extending the fundamental mistake in the mathematical assignment and keeping the good teacher waiting. Of course this will be paid for, like all sins committed against teachers.

Up to now I have had five good nights, but the sixth and the seventh were bad, my incognito having been penetrated.[4]

Yours

To Johannes Urzidil

[Spindlermühle; postmark: February 17, 1922] Dear Herr Urzidil,

Many thanks for the book.[5] In essence but also in structure it reminded me so of "Ivan Ilyich."[6] First Werfel's plain and fearful truthfulness (true also that uncanny "joyous will to deception"), then the death of this young man, the three days and nights of screaming, though in actuality one heard not a sound, and if it had been audible, one would have moved a few rooms farther off, for there is no "way out" except for this, and finally your manly and comforting epilogue, in which one would naturally like to concur if only it did not come too late, after the execution, as is the nature of comforts. It was much the same with "Ivan Ilyich," only here in *Legacy* it is even clearer, because every stage is specially personified.

With cordial regards, yours, Kafka

To Minze Eisner
[Picture postcard ("Winter in the Riesengebirge").
Vienna;[7] postmark: February 22, 1922]
Cordial regards from a sun spa.

Kafka

Dear Minze, I'll write you from Prague. I have had some bad times, not because of the lungs but because of the nerves. Your letters reached me only the other day because they were addressed to the office and it has been a long time since I have gone there. Best wishes.

Yours, Kafka

To Robert Klopstock
[Prague; postmark: February 23, 1922]
Dear Robert, I stayed in Spindelmühle a few days longer.[8] I didn't want to write from there anymore, weary days. I had barely arrived when the telegram came; my mother answered it, which explains the odd wording, then came the telegram from Pick (I am angry with him or he is angry with me; he knows nothing about me except that the day before yesterday we passed each other on the street). Then came the letters, the whole thing a painful embarrassment for me, forgive me. This morning the passport arrived, I went there right away, it is not so simple. Nothing is so simple. They told me: This passport has been extended to its limit. A new passport has to be issued, for which a new photograph is mandatory. Still and all, I do not claim that an imperious or diplomatic person would not have achieved a renewal of the passport. My sad story about your Budapest trip, the direct trains, your poverty was listened to in a friendly spirit but otherwise produced no result. Therefore, Robert, you must send the photo. Have you no certificate of poverty? What does the note from the sanatorium say? Why have you enclosed it?

Cordial regards, yours, K

To Robert Klopstock
[Postcard. Prague; postmark: March 1, 1922]
Dear Robert, It's nothing at all. Everything is fine, as soon as your letters show a little insight into the true state of affairs. You must simply keep in mind that you are writing to a wretched little person possessed by all sorts of evil spirits. (It is indubitably to the credit of medicine that in place of the

concept of possession it has introduced the comforting concept of neur-
asthenia, which, however, makes cure more difficult and in addition has left
it an open question whether weakness and illness induce the possession or
whether weakness and illness are not rather a stage of possession, preparing a
bed for rest and fornication for the unclean spirits.) And you torment the
person if you don't recognize that, whereas otherwise you might get on quite
well with him.

Everything went wrong for me today at the passport office, even though I
came earlier than last time. It was so crowded that they sent me away.
Tomorrow I will go still earlier. There is little hope for exemption from fees.
My sister tells me that she has already tried for it in vain. And you sent me,
instead of a certificate of poverty, a photo in which you look like a young
nobleman, some son of Ludendorff.[9]

Cordially, K

To Robert Klopstock

[Prague, end of March 1922][10]
Dear Robert, It's long since I wrote, I know, but I must first allow time to
dispose of the shame you sometimes heap upon me in your fond and angry
letters.

I always find it extremely odd when here and there—in your last letter it
takes up disproportionate space—you deplore your relationship to people:
"Dear, good people," you write. I too feel this way about "dear, good," but
when I see the phrase written down and written not by myself, it strikes me
as more ludicrous than true, a sort of birthday wish offered to humanity,
with all those attendant mental reservations that cancel out the words.

A third letter from you, so much unanswered and I don't know what to say
and am only tired. I can only tell you to come, pull yourself loose from
Matlar where you are drying up and come among people whom, despite all
you say, you well know how to deal with, how to invigorate, how to lead.
And you will easily recognize that this phantom, which first appeared in your
letters, was built up in your letters by your own hand, which was not present
in Matlar, and which I am supposed to be, and frightens me to the point of
running away, to the point of keeping silent (not because the phantom is
frightening in itself, but in relation to me)—you will quite painlessly see that
this phantom does not exist, but only a man who is hard to put up with, who
is buried in himself and locked away from himself with a strange key, but
who has eyes to see and would rejoice at every step forward that you take and
at your great encounter with the world that rushes to meet you. Otherwise?

Lately I have begun to write a little[11] in order to preserve myself from what is called nerves. From seven in the evening I sit awhile at my desk, but it is nothing, like trying to scratch a dugout with one's fingernails in the midst of the World War, and next month that too will end and the office will begin.[12]

Have a good time in Budapest!

And regards to Ilonka. Say what you will, it is sad. This negative form of heroism: breaking an engagement, renouncing, defying parents—it is so little and cuts off so much.

Yours, K

I have a few books I would like to give you to read, but it is so complicated and risky to send them, since they don't belong to me.

To Robert Klopstock

[Prague, beginning of April 1922]

It is perhaps better to answer the letter in writing.[13]

On the whole it contains what I already knew and which you may twist as you like without being able to make it any different from what it is: You are disappointed with the substance and maintain to yourself and to me that you are disappointed with the relationship. Of course that is painful not only for you but is also a pain that you are inflicting on me. You are surely beginning to discover this error but as yet have a good way to go. Nor will the discovery bring any salvation. All in all, only disappointment is to be found in this; the deeper one digs, the deeper the disappointment.

You are wrong when you make so sharp a distinction between Matlar and Prague. You were just as consistently disappointed in Matlar. Its "great mountains" are certainly not those among which Eden lay.

As for the remark concerning [ONE WORD MADE ILLEGIBLE]—that is more or less a meaningless triviality. But was I so wrong to protest—that time when you started to tell something which I had foolishly confided to you as a great secret, to a third person, even though this person was only Fräulein Irene, who was totally uninterested, and you went on with a kind of complacency and I tried to stop you and you repeated it, all smiles and satisfaction—why I was wrong there passes my understanding.

But you are right in what you say about the question of sorrow. That was a dishonest, embarrassed question, but why should I not be permitted to ask such embarrassed questions, I for whom such questions were invented?

Our alleged "inferiority" consists in this, that we are desperate rats who hear the footsteps of the master of the house and flee in various directions—for instance, toward women, you toward this one or that one, I toward literature. But it is all vain. We ourselves see to the vanity of it by our choice of refuges, by the choice of this or that woman, and so on. That is the inferiority.

Yet I will admit that there is a difference between how I was in Matlar and how I am in Prague. In the interval, after being lashed through periods of insanity, I began to write, and this writing is the most important thing in the world to me (in a way that is horrible to everyone around me, so unspeakably horrible that I don't talk about it)—the way his delusion is important to the madman (should he lose it, he would become "mad") or the way her pregnancy is important to a woman. This has nothing to do with the value of the writing—I know that value only too precisely, just as I know the value it has for me. [...] And so with trembling fear I protect the writing from every disturbance, and not the writing alone, but the solitude that is part of it. And yesterday when I said that you should not come on Sunday evening but rather on Monday and you twice asked, "So you don't want me to come in the evening?" and I had to give you an answer, at least when you asked the second time, and said, "Get yourself some rest for a change," then that was a total lie, for all I was thinking of was my own solitude.

This is the difference, then, between here and Matlar, but there is no other, and certainly not that I am less "powerless" here (as you so accurately put it) than I was in Matlar.

The foregoing was written in the evening, while I was feeling in fairly good condition. During the partly sleepless, partly sleep-wrecked night I thought out a different letter. But now in broad daylight it seems to me inappropriate after all. Only this: In view of the truth and beauty of your letter and the truth and beauty of the look in your eyes, you deserve to have me reply with my truth and my ugliness. But that is what I have always done, in speaking and in writing, ever since that first afternoon in the reclining chair, since that first letter to Iglo.[14] And the most painful part of it is that you don't believe me (whereas I believe you), or even worse, that you both believe and do not believe me, but strike out at me with both your belief and your disbelief. At any rate you are constantly piercing me, searing me with that question which touches me to the quick: "Why aren't you different from the way you are?"

Incidentally your letter does contain a new element, which only became clear to me in connection with your stammering in the doctor's presence, but which I don't after all believe. In discussions and in letters we have always been agreed on the following: You cannot study in Budapest for three main reasons: because you must get out into the world; because you cannot live near your cousin, since her presence disturbs you too much; and above all because of the political conditions.[15] You have confirmed that in almost all your letters. Thus in your recent letter asking for the passport you stated that the residence permit from the Pressburg[16] ministry absolutely must be transferred to the new passport because under present conditions not being able to escape from Hungary was tantamount to death. (This did seem to me exaggerated, but even if you only remotely believed that, it would suffice to make Budapest impossible as a place for you to pursue your studies.) And in your very last letter from Budapest you said again that you cannot live near your cousin. So Budapest was impossible; I recognized that, but there was no talk about me; the talk about me came up only in connection with choosing among the universities outside Budapest. It seemed to me right that you should choose Prague in consideration of me and other factors, but right only on the assumption that Budapest was impossible, impossible quite apart from me. Now your letter of yesterday is trying to recast the story. You are wrong there.

To Robert Klopstock

[Prague, mid-April 1922]

Dear Robert, I can only answer as before that a letter like your last one, for instance, is simply another cause for anxiety, or that your impatience is to blame, or a remark like "... not being able to pin you down, though more than any of us"—a remark totally without a shred of truth. Above all, however, and apart from all that, it is fear of any indissoluble bond at present—I will say nothing about the future—a bond emphatically, outrightly (I leave aside tacit agreements), magniloquently laid before heaven and sealed with all the sacraments of inseparability. I can no more have that kind of bond with men than with women. What's the use of such grandiose things on this pilgrimage, in this beggarly scrimmage? Every moment we are presented with inescapable, rapturously seized opportunities for the most shameless kind of swagger. Why look for still more opportunities? Moreover the loss is perhaps not so great as it sometimes seems: If one feels some sort of shared direction, there is bond enough in that. Leave the rest to the stars.

And all this anxiety about which you keep asking, as though it concerned you, after all concerns me alone. If there were anything to be gained by penance or something of the sort, I would have to impose it on myself. But then, is there anything so strange about this anxiety? A Jew, and a German besides, and sick besides, and in difficult personal circumstances besides—those are the chemical forces with which I propose to straightway transmute gold into gravel or your letter into mine, and while doing so remain in the right.

To Robert Klopstock

[Prague, June 1922]

Dear Robert, I have given the translation to Felix, though he does not know whether he will publish it. It seems there is something of the same sort, although without so many interesting details, in the *Prager Tagblatt*. Nevertheless he wants to thank you.

I have at last written a letter to a young lady, the first in a long time, though it deals only with a humble plea about her piano-playing, which drives me to despair. The amount of quiet I need is not to be found on the face of this earth. For at least a year I would like to hide myself away with my notebook and talk to no one. The merest nothing shatters me.

I am supposed to start working at the office at the end of the month.[17] But the doctor has been raising objections. I don't know what will happen. To be honest, my feeling is that the spring was harder on my lungs than the fall and winter.

Fräulein Irene was here, visibly rejuvenated and prettified. (Except for an ugly Tatra cap with which she covered her lovely hair; back in Matlar she also always wore such an ugly cap, a white one I believe. This time it was gray. But I did not venture to say anything about it.) The visit could not have been much pleasure for her because of my sometimes incredible tiredness. But it was a pleasure for me to see Fräulein Irene and I silently congratulated you on your good deed.

What is to be done about housing for you here? I haven't yet found a solution; I hope something will turn up.

Yours, K

Perhaps the enclosed review will interest you. To be sure, if the purpose of such a review is to make one want to read the book, it misses its aim, at least with me.

To Max Brod

[Two postcards. Planá nad Lužnici;[18] postmarked on arrival: June 26, 1922]

Dear Max, I am well lodged, though Ottla made incredible sacrifices of her comfort for my sake. But even without these sacrifices it would be good here "as far as I can see at present" (since one musn't forswear oneself), more peaceful than it's been at any previous summer resort "as far as etc." At first, during the trip, I was afraid of the country. So Blüher says there is nothing to see in the city? But only in the city are there things to see, for everything that streamed past the train window was cemetery or could have been, nothing but things that grow above corpses, whereas the city after all stands out in strong and vigorous contrast to that. But on my second day here everything is all right; it is strange to associate with the land. There is noise here; there wasn't any the first day but by the second it was here, I having come on the express train and it having followed on a freight. I divert myself during an unsuccessful afternoon nap thinking how you wrote *Franzi* close to the construction job. Good luck with the work, let the stream stream.—At the office I found a month-and-a-half-old letter from Wolff,[19] so very friendly that it put me to shame. My self-denigration has two aspects. On the one hand there is truth to it and as such it would make me happy if I could take the repulsive little story[20] out of Wolff's desk drawer and wipe it out of his memory. His letter makes me wince. But then the self-denigration is also inevitably a strategy, which, for example, makes it impossible for Wolff to agree with it, not out of hypocrisy which he surely does not have to practice toward me, but because he is forced to by the strategy. And I am always astonished when, for example, Schreiber, whose self-denigration also had this dual character, as truth and also inevitably as strategy, had no success—not with the truth (for truth produces no successes; truth only shatters what is shattered) but with the strategy. Perhaps because real necessity hampered him. Necessity does not permit such gossamer successes to occur.

What speculations! There are things that only the Inspector General[21] may meditate on, only to say in conclusion, "What story is this I have told?"

Yours

To Robert Klopstock

[Postcard. Planá; postmark: June 26, 1922]
Dear Robert, The trip was very good, thanks to your help, only that the young lady in the compartment did not forgive me for the disappointment of your not coming along, as it seemed at the outset you would. I have been very well received here. Ottla, who sends you regards, looks after me no less tenderly than after Věra, and that is saying a great deal. But since Planá has its living inhabitants and its animals, there is also noise here which blasts sleep and shatters the head. (Otherwise it is remarkably beautiful, with woods and river and gardens.) This in spite of Ohropax;[22] just having it is a sort of comfort; this morning, to be sure, having the plugs in my ears did not make the Sunday horn-playing of a peasant youth inaudible but eventually prevailed on him to stop. Why must someone's pleasure always spoil the pleasure of someone else? Even my habit of sitting at the table has driven Ottla from her previous big, two-windowed, and warm room into a small

chilly one along with her baby and maidservant, while I lord it over the big room and suffer at the good cheer of a numerous family which in innocent noisiness is turning the hay almost under my window.

How are you getting along?

Yours, K.

To Felix Weltsch

[Postcard. Planá, end of June 1922]

Dear Felix, Am I mistaken or are you already at Schelesen? I believe you once called July your working month. May it be glorious! I had no chance to say goodbye to you; moreover I had committed that idiocy that time at the theater of lending the textbook to you, with twofold consequences: that you no longer bothered about me and that I never recovered the textbook. But it was a fine evening, wasn't it? Isn't the play, when all is said and done, even finer than the production? This scene, for example: The sleigh bells are ringing outside. Khlestakov, who has just acquired two new lady friends in short order and in his excitement has almost forgotten that he must leave, remembers and hurries out the door with the two women. The scene is like a bait thrown out to the Jews. In fact it is impossible for Jews to imagine this scene without sentimentality, even impossible for them to recount it without sentimentality. When I say: The sleigh bells are ringing outside, that is sentimental. Max's review[23] is also sentimental. Yet the play itself has not a trace of it.—I am feeling tolerably well here. If only—I hope you are not aware of this in Schelesen—there were not so much noise in the world.—Good wishes to you, your wife, and child.

Yours, F.

To Oskar Baum

[Planá, end of June 1922]

Dear Oskar, I herewith announce my readiness to leave around the 20th of July if you so write. I have the passport. The new and reformed procedures for issuing passports are wonderful. Our fumbling interpretations are powerless to deal with the complexities of which the bureaucracy is capable, and what is more, the necessary, inevitable complexities springing straight out of the origins of human nature, to which, measured by my case, the bureaucracy is closer than any social institution. Otherwise, describing the details is too wearisome, for you, that is, who did not stand for two hours in a crowd on the stairway to an office, happy to have a new insight into the machinery, and who, in answering a trivial question while the passport was handed to him, trembled in truly profound respect. (Also in ordinary fear, though even in that, too, feeling the same profound respect.)

Don't forget me in Georgental,[24] but also don't wear yourselves out looking for lodgings for me. If nothing turns up, it will be sad for me but not a misfortune. For after all the whole world is open to a pensioned-off official, so long as it isn't asking more than a thousand crowns per month.

To Max Brod

[Planá; postmarked on arrival: June 30, 1922]

Dear Max, It is not easy to extract the cause of your melancholy mood from your letter, for the points you mention are hardly sufficient. First and foremost, the novella[25] is alive; isn't it enough to justify your life? (No, it is not enough.) But isn't it enough to sustain your life? Yes, it is enough for that, would be enough to allow one to live joyously with coach and six. The other matter? E. writes, but irregularly; but why worry about that, if the letters are irreproachable? Rosenheim's letter—a diplomatic blunder on the part of Dreimaskenverlag,[26] isn't it? But a little diplomacy can repair this. The ghastly news? Are you referring to something else besides the assassination of Rathenau?[27] It's incomprehensible that they let him live as long as they did. Two months ago a rumor of his assassination was going around in Prague. Prof. Münzer spread it—so credible was it, so consistent with the linked destinies of Jews and Germans. And it was accurately described in your book.[28] But I am already going on too much about this. The subject extends far beyond my horizon. The horizon outside my window is already too big for me.

Political news reaches me nowadays—unless, to my vexation, someone sends me a different newspaper, which I devour—only in the truly excellent form of the *Prager Abendblatt*. Reading this newspaper alone, you feel as well informed about the world situation as you used to be about the progress of the war from reading the *Neue Freie Presse*.[29] According to the *Abendblatt*, the whole world now is as peaceful as the war was then; the paper caresses all your cares away even before you have any. Only now do I appreciate the real position of your articles in this newspaper. Assuming that they are read, you cannot wish for a better setting. Nothing disturbing could creep in from the wings to interfere with your words; it is completely silent around you. And reading your articles here is such a fine way to commune with you. I also read them to keep track of your moods. Smetana and Strindberg seem to me subdued, but "Philosophy"[30] comes out as clear and good. The dubious aspect of "Philosophy," by the way, seems to me to be a distinctly Jewish complex of problems, springing from the confusion that the natives are too alien to one, thus distorting reality, and the Jews too close, distorting reality, and therefore one cannot treat the latter or the former with the proper balance. And how this problem is aggravated in the country, where even total strangers greet you, but only some, and where, when a dignified old man trudges past you with an axe over his shoulder, you no longer have the chance to catch up with him again and respond to his greeting.

It would be lovely here if it were quiet; there are a few hours of quiet but not nearly enough. No composing hut.[31] But Ottla is wonderfully solicitous. (She sends regards. Your regards were a great consolation to her in her grief over a somewhat unsuccessful cake.) Today, for example, is an unlucky day: a woodcutter has spent the whole day splitting wood for the landlady. What he inconceivably bears all day long, both with his arms and with his brain, I cannot bear with my ears, not even with the aid of Ohropax (which is not altogether bad; when you insert it in your ears you hear exactly as much as you did before, but after a while a mild stupefaction of the brain ensues and a faint sense of being protected; well, it is not much). Also the noise of children and the like. Today I also had to change rooms for a few days; this room, which I have had up to now, was very fine—big, light, with two windows and a wide view, and its furnishings, though utterly poor and utterly unhotellike, had a quality that might be called "holy sobriety."[32]

On such a noisy day, and a few more such are in store for me, certainly a few and probably many, I feel like someone expelled from the world, not by a single step as in the past, but by a hundred thousand steps.—Kayser's[33] letter (I haven't answered it; the question of non-German publication is both too hopeless and too petty to discuss) of course pleased me (how need and vanity lap such things up). But he is not unmoved by my method and the story,[34] moreover, is bearable. I mentioned the story[35] sent to Wolff, which an unprejudiced person cannot be in doubt about. Regards to you and your two ladies. Also to Felix, to whom unfortunately I was unable to say goodbye.

Yours

[IN THE MARGIN] I hear Frau Preissová[36] lives here. I would very much like to have a talk with her but my fear and discomfort in the face of such a venture are equally great. Perhaps she is very high and mighty, or perhaps she is as shattered by every interruption as I am. No, I do not want to have that talk.

How will you answer Kayser? Hauptmann is so close to you, you can hardly refuse to write about him.

To Robert Klopstock

[Planá; postmark: June 30, 1922]

Dear Robert, Many thanks for the newspapers, but there is no need to send them; I get the *Abendblatt* every day, an adequate paper and with Max's articles a rich feast. I also receive clippings of the novel, at least occasionally. Instead may I ask you for something else: If a new issue of *Die Fackel*[37] has come out—I have not seen one for a long time—and it isn't too expensive, would you send it to me, after reading it yourself. I do not want to deny myself this tasty dessert made up of all the good and bad instincts.—*Secessio Judaica?*[38] Won't you write something about it? I would be very glad if you would, if not in German then in Hungarian. I cannot do it; when I try, my hand immediately goes dead, even though I, like everyone else, would have a great deal to say about it. Somewhere in my ancestry I too must have a Talmudist, I should hope, but he does not embolden me enough to go ahead, so I set you to it. It does not have to be a refutation, only an answer to the appeal. That ought to be very tempting. And there is indeed a temptation to let one's flock graze on this German and yet not entirely alien pasture, after the fashion of the Jews.

Yours, K.

To Robert Klopstock

[Planá, beginning of July 1922]

Dear Robert, You are completely right, of course. If you are devoting yourself to other things in this single-minded way, then there is no room for anything else and everything else has to take second place. I did not mean my suggestion to summon you to a decisive battle, like the battle between Goliath and David, say, but only to a sidelong glance at Goliath, to a casual assessment of the power relationship, to a revision of our own stock in trade, that is to say to a work of repose, to a job that can always be done and for which there is no time in the blissful-desperate matutinal state you are in and in which everything inevitably is directed at achieving representativeness. Even the position of critic would not have been suitable. And what is more, critic on a Christian Socialist paper. Have you received any answer yet about the translation of Max's books?

Strange, this long letter from the usually reserved girl. I cannot imagine its contents.

Thank you for the *Prager Presse*. I have no need for the *Abendblatt* novel; do you follow it?

My sister[39] will be staying in Hellerau in any case. Perhaps she is there today. She has had an answer from Frau Neustädter.

Not a word from Oskar; in his Thuringian happiness he has forgotten me.

Yours, K.

To Oskar Baum

[Planá, July 4, 1922]

Dear Oskar, What good, conscientious, and sensitive people you two are! All your arrangements and all your advice are necessary and splendid. So I will come, perhaps not exactly on the fifteenth but probably before the twentieth. I even welcome the opportunity to come early, since my uncle from Madrid is due in August, though the date has not yet been set, and so I might have to be back in Prague somewhere around the 20th of August in order to see him (he generally stays about two weeks). I will telegraph the exact date of my arrival between the 15th and the 20th of July, if you would be so good as to attend to the arrangements with the landlady, on top of everything else you have done for me. There are still other reasons why the date is convenient for me, because while it is very nice here at Ottla's, some guests are due just around this time and things may be somewhat crowded. However I will be able to come back here at the end of August. Ottla will probably be staying until the end of September.

You may notice that I scramble the essentials and inessentials and there is a reason for this, which may be good or bad. Apart from everything else, what impels me to Georgental (the pleasure of spending some time with you, with both of you; to be near your work; to relive the time in Zürau, which has quite fled from me, with all that I was back in those days; to see a bit of the world and convince myself that there is breathable air elsewhere—even for my lungs—a discovery which to be sure does not make the world any wider but does quiet certain gnawing yearnings)—apart from all this, I have one specially important reason for going: my fear. You can surely imagine this fear to a certain extent, but you cannot really know it in its depths—you are too brave for that. I have, to be frank, a horrible fear of this journey, of course not exactly of the journey itself, and not at all fear of the journey alone, but of every change. The bigger the change, the bigger the fear, but it is only relative. If I were to confine myself only to the very smallest changes—though life does not permit this—it would end with the moving of a table in my room being no less terrifying than the journey to Georgental. Moreover, not only is the journey there terrible but the departure from there will also be. In the last or in the next-to-the-last analysis, it is of course nothing but a fear of death. Partly also the fear of calling the gods' attention to me. If I just go on living here in my room, one day passes as regularly as the last. Of course someone has to look after me, but that is already being done, the hand of the gods is only mechanically holding the reins. So lovely, it is so lovely to be unnoticed. If any fairy stood beside my cradle, it was the fairy named "Retired on Pension." But now to leave this happy situation, to set off freely with one's luggage under the vast sky to the railway station, to stir up the world, though to be sure nothing shows but the stirring up within one's own self—that is horrible. And yet it must be done. Otherwise—and it would not take too long—I would completely unlearn how to live. Between the fifteenth and the twentieth, then. Regards to everybody. Thanks also to your Madame Secretary. Wonderful that I can be at Georgental that same evening. Is the station really Georgental-Ort?

Yours, Franz

To Max Brod
[Planá; postmark: July 5, 1922]
Dear Max, After a sleepless night, the first of the sort in Planá, though unfit for anything else, I can perhaps understand your letter better than I usually can, better than you. But perhaps I am oversubtle and understand it too well, for your case is different from mine to the extent that although it is not real either, it is nearer to reality than mine is. This is what has happened to me: As you know, I was supposed to go to Georgental. I never had any objections to that. If I once said that there would be too many writers there, that was perhaps a premonition of what was to come, but it was not meant as a serious objection, rather a bit of coquetry. On the contrary, I admire every writer I get close to (that was why I also wanted to meet Preissová, though your wife advised me against it). To be sure, every human being commands my admiration, but the writer especially and above all the writer I don't know personally. It is inconceivable to me how he has so comfortably established himself in this airy and terrifying realm and how he conducts such an orderly economy in it. Most writers I know impress me, at least personally, as very agreeable, for example even Winder.[40] The way I am, a threesome would have suited me very well, for I would not have mattered, I would have been able to keep out of the way and yet not be alone there, which is what I fear. And Oskar, whom I am fond of and who is good to me, would be a support. And I would see a new bit of the world again, see Germany again for the first time in eight years. And it is cheap there and healthy. And though it is fine here at Ottla's, and especially now that I have my old room back again, still toward the end of the month and the beginning of next month there will be guests from my brother-in-law's family and things will get rather crowded,

so it would be very good if I were to take a trip, and then I could come back since Ottla is staying until the end of September. Therefore there is no rational or emotional gap here—the trip is unreservedly to be recommended. And yesterday I had a very dear, elaborate letter from Oskar: He has found a fine quiet room with balcony, reclining chair, good food, and a garden view for 150 marks per day. I have only to accept it, or rather I have already accepted it in advance, for I told him that if anything of the sort could be found I would surely come.

And what has happened? To put it first of all in general terms, I fear the traveling. I had an inkling of this in the last few days when I was glad that a letter from Oskar failed to come. But it is not only fear of traveling itself; after all, I came here by train and although it was only two hours and the trip there would be twelve hours, I found the journey tedious but was otherwise indifferent to it. So it isn't fear of travel, as was recently described in connection with Myslbeck,[41] for example, who wanted to go to Italy and had to turn back when he got no farther than Beneschau.[42] It isn't fear of Georgental, for once I get there I will surely adjust to it the very same evening. Nor is it weakness of will, for in that state every decision is postponed until the mind has precisely calculated the contingencies, which most of the time is impossible. Here is a borderline case where the mind can really calculate the contingencies and repeatedly comes to the same result, that I ought to go. Rather it is a fear of change, a fear of attracting the attention of the gods by what is a major act for a person of my sort.

Last night as I lay sleepless and let everything continually veer back and forth between my aching temples, what I had almost forgotten during the last relatively quiet time became clear to me: namely, on what frail ground or rather altogether nonexistent ground I live, over a darkness from which the dark power emerges when it wills and, heedless of my stammering, destroys my life. Writing sustains me, but is it not more accurate to say that it sustains this kind of life? By this I don't mean, of course, that my life is better when I don't write. Rather it is much worse then and wholly unbearable and has to end in madness. But that, granted, only follows from the postulate that I am a writer, which is actually true even when I am not writing, and a nonwriting writer is a monster inviting madness. But what about being a writer itself? Writing is a sweet and wonderful reward, but for what? In the night it became clear to me, as clear as a child's lesson book, that it is the reward for serving the devil. This descent to the dark powers, this unshackling of spirits bound by nature, these dubious embraces and whatever else may take place in the nether parts which the higher parts no longer know, when one writes one's stories in the sunshine. Perhaps there are other forms of writing, but I know only this kind; at night, when fear keeps me from sleeping, I know only this kind. And the diabolic element in it seems very clear to me. It is vanity and sensuality which continually buzz about one's own or even another's form—and feast on him. The movement multiplies itself—it is a regular solar system of vanity. Sometimes a naïve person will wish, "I would like to be dead and see how everyone mourns me." Such a writer is continually staging such a scene: He dies (or rather he does not live) and continually mourns himself. From this springs a terrible fear of death, which need not reveal itself as fear of death but may also appear as fear of change, as fear of Georgental. The reasons for this fear of death may be divided into two main categories. First he has a terrible fear of dying because he has not yet lived. By this I do not mean that wife and child, fields and cattle are essential to living. What is essential to life is only to forgo complacency, to move into the house instead of admiring it and hanging garlands around it. In reply to this, one might say that this is a matter of fate and is not given into anyone's hand. But then why this sense of repining, this repining that never ceases? To make oneself finer and more savory? That is a part of it. But why do such nights leave one always with the refrain: I could live and I do not live. The second reason—perhaps it is all really one, the two do not want to stay apart for me now—is the belief: "What I have playacted is really going to happen. I have not bought myself off by my writing. I died my whole life long and now I will really die. My life was sweeter than other peoples' and my death will be more terrible by the same degree. Of course the writer in me will die right away, since such a figure has no base, no substance, is less than dust. He is only barely possible in the broil of earthly life, is only a construct of sensuality. That is your writer for you. But I myself cannot go on living because I have not lived, I have remained clay, I have not blown the spark into fire, but only used it to light up my corpse." It will be a strange burial: the writer, insubstantial as he is, consigning the old corpse, the longtime corpse, to the grave. I am enough of a writer to appreciate the scene with all my senses, or—and it is the same thing—to want to describe it with total self-forgetfulness—not alertness, but self-forgetfulness is the writer's first prerequisite. But there will be no more of such describing. But why am I talking of actual dying? It is just the same in life. I sit here in the comfortable posture of the writer, ready for all sorts of fine things, and must idly look on—for what can I do but write?—as my true ego, this wretched, defenseless ego, is nipped by the devil's pincers, cudgeled, and almost ground to pieces on a random pretext—a little trip to Georgental. [...] The existence of a writer is an argument against the existence of the soul, for the soul has obviously taken flight from the real ego, but not improved itself, only become a writer. Is it possible that separation from the ego can so weaken the soul? (I don't dare let this stand. Put this way it is also wrong.) Since I was not at home, what right have I to be alarmed when the house suddenly collapses. After all, I know what preceded the collapse. Did I not emigrate and leave the house to all the evil powers?

I wrote to Oskar yesterday, did mention my fear but promised to come. The letter has not yet been mailed. In the interval there was the night. Perhaps I will wait one more night; if I don't get through, I will have to cancel after all. This will mean that from now on I may not go out of Bohemia, next I will be confined to Prague, then to my room, then to my bed, then to a certain position in bed, then to nothing more. Perhaps at that point I will be able to renounce the joy of writing voluntarily—voluntariness and joyousness are what count.

To underscore the whole story in terms of my writing—but I do not do the underscoring, the thing underscores itself—I must add that my fear of the journey is partly compounded by the thought that I will be kept away from the desk for at least several days. And this ridiculous thought is really the only legitimate one, since the existence of the writer is truly dependent upon his desk and if he wants to keep madness at bay he must never go far from his desk, he must hold on to it with his teeth.

The definition of a writer, of such a writer, and the explanation of his effectiveness, to the extent that he has any: He is the scapegoat of mankind. He makes it possible for men to enjoy sin without guilt, almost without guilt.

The day before yesterday I chanced to be at the railroad station (my brother-in-law meant to leave, but then didn't go); by chance a Vienna express train had stopped here, because it had to wait to connect with the express train to Prague. By chance your wife was on it. What a pleasant surprise. We talked for a few minutes. She told me you have finished the novella.

If I do go to Georgental, I will be in Prague in ten days, will happily lie on your sofa and you will read aloud. But if I don't go—

I have sent Oskar a telegram, canceling. There was no help for it. It was the only way I could deal with the agitation. Yesterday's first letter to him struck a familiar note for me. That is how I used to write to F.

To Oskar Baum

[Planá, July 5, 1922]
Dear Oskar, The enclosed letter was written yesterday, on July 4, immediately upon receipt of your letter.

It skirted the truth in two respects: It did not give a fair picture on the one hand of my joy at going to Georgental, on the other hand of my fear. The two things are too greatly at odds. If one wanted to put them both in a letter, one had to skirt the truth. As I was going to the post office with the letter, I met Ottla. She advised that it would be best to set the exact date for my arrival, and I saw her point. Since I had no pencil with me, I took the letter back home. Anyway I continued to feel upset and then, as I had feared, I could not sleep all night—my first sleepless night in Planá. There are some ten nights before the fifteenth and even if I wanted to leave right away, there would still be three or four. I wouldn't be able to endure them, and so I cannot go. I admit that, put in this way, it is quite incomprehensible. Today I wrote Max a whole treatise about it—even before I knew I was going to telegraph you. I will spare you that—not add this, too, to all that I have done to cause you pain. There is no point elaborating on it. I have experienced something like this qualitatively before, but not yet quantitatively. Even for me it is a fearful intensification. It implies, for instance, that I won't be able to go outside Bohemia from now on. Tomorrow my limits can narrow and the day after tomorrow can narrow still further and in a week come to their final narrowing. Think of that and perhaps the two of you may be able to forgive me. It would ease my mind if Frau Horn would fix some fine for me which I would send promptly.

Be well.

Yours, F

I am telegraphing you today: Unfortunately cannot come. Letter follows.

Ottla tries to explain the fear partly (more than this she dares not venture) as springing from physical weakness. A very mild explanation, if one remembers that last year I was possibly even weaker and yet managed to go to the ugly Tatra Mountains (from which, I grant, I was also unable to tear myself away) and moreover that the physical weakness, which certainly does exist, springs from psychic weakness.

To Felix Weltsch

[Planá, beginning of July 1922]

Dear Felix, What you say about my noise is almost right. At any rate I have taken the idea over from you and it has become one of my few psychological props, one of those more or less monstrous scaffoldings with which I work on my wretched shed, the idea that because of the density of the world, each overcome noise is replaced in endless succession by a new one that has still to be overcome. But yet that is only almost right, and to attempt to use it to answer what you adduce would be folly or baseness. Rather this noise (and this is not just a descriptive phrase but the literal truth) is likewise a howling reproach to those who are caring for you—who are revealed as weak and helpless and with open eyes dodging their responsibility, thus assuming a still heavier responsibility. Noise also has something fascinating and narcotic about it. If I sit in one room—I am fortunate in sometimes having two rooms to choose from—and, just as for you, there is a sawmill across the road, which is bearable for short intervals, but when the circular saw takes over, as has been happening continually of late, it makes one curse life—if I sit in this ill-fated room, I cannot leave it, even though I am free to go into the adjoining room and must do so, for the sound of the saw is unbearable. But I cannot change rooms, only go back and forth and perhaps observe that the second room isn't quiet either, and children are playing in front of its window. That is the situation. I keep hoping that, as once happened, the circular saw will suddenly stop. I have a casual acquaintance with the bookkeeper there and this gives me what little hope I have. Of course he does not know that his circular saw disturbs me and he is otherwise in no way concerned about me. On the whole he is a reserved man, and even if he were the most openhearted he could not halt the circular saw when there was work for it. But I look desperately out of the window and think about him. Or else I think of Mahler, whose summertime life is described somewhere, how every day at five-thirty—he was very healthy in those days and slept so soundly—he would bathe out in the open and then run into the woods, where he had a "composing hut"[43] and where he would find his breakfast prepared, and he would work there until one in the afternoon, and the trees, which later would make so much noise in the sawmill, stood still in their host about him, protecting him from noise. (In the afternoon he would take a nap and only from four o'clock on would live with his family and only rarely would he, to his wife's delight, say anything in the evening about his morning's labors.) But I wanted to tell about the saw. Left to myself, I cannot get away from it: my sister has to come and with unbelievable sacrifices of her comfort vacate the other room for me (which however is no composing hut but I will not speak of that at present), and now I am rid of the saw for a while. Thus, now and then, others ought to lead you, too, into a quiet room.

The first impression of your letter was splendid. I initially turned it about in my hand, glad to have it, and in rapidly glancing over it, I noted only two passages, one where there was something about ethics, and the other saying that "Ruthie is wonderful," and so naturally I was very pleased. Granted, I have other letters of yours, about the Parents' Evening (particularly fine) or the one about Rathenau. (Have you read H.'s article about Rathenau? What amazing tastelessness on the part of him who is ordinarily so infallible—this irony with which a petitioner treats his murdered benefactor. One involuntarily feels that this reporter, who speaks with such egalitarian irony about a dead man, must at least be partly dead himself. And to crown the whole, it turns out to be self-irony, for if H. expected Rathenau to say, "We Rathenaus are workhorses," I, likewise, felt the utmost confidence that sooner or later H. would write, "I, a poor dog of a subeditor." By this I do not mean any offense to H.; I would surely have written in the same tone and much worse, only I would not have published it, perhaps because it would have been still worse written.)

There are a few things I might say and ask in connection with the fact that I am not going to Germany, out of "fear"—imagine—even though I asked Oskar to arrange for a room there for me and he so kindly and splendidly took care of it. It is not fear of the journey—worse—it is fear in general.

Cordial regards, powerless good wishes, regards to your wife and child.

Yours, F

[REGARDS FROM OTTLA]

To Max Brod
[Planá; postmark: July 12, 1922]

Dearest Max, I have been dashing about or sitting as petrified as a desperate animal in his burrow. Enemies everywhere. Children outside this room and also outside the other. I was just about to go away when quiet descended—probably only for the moment—and I can write to you. You must not think that things in Planá are completely or almost completely fine and that that accounts for my remaining here. To be sure, the lodgings themselves are very cleverly arranged, insofar as domestic peace is concerned. The arrangements have only to be used, and Ottla, who looks after everything, does so, with the result that though we live wall to wall, I am not in the least disturbed by her, the child, or the maid, either by day or by night. But yesterday afternoon, for example, children were playing outside my window. Right under me there was a nasty group, while a bit off to the left there was a nice one, lovely-looking children, but the noise made by both was the same. It drives me from my bed, out of the house in despair, with throbbing temples through field and forest, devoid of all hope like a night owl. And when I lie down at night in peace and hope, I am awakened at half past three and don't fall asleep again. At the nearby railroad station, which however is not in itself disturbing, timber is perpetually being loaded. This involves constant hammering, though it is usually gentle and intermittent. This morning, however, and I don't know whether from now on it will be this way always, they began hammering very early and the noise rings through the quiet morning and the sleep-famished brain in quite another way than it does by day. It was very bad. And then I get up in the morning; there is no reason to get up at all, given the state of my temples. And yet I have been really very lucky. For the past few days some two hundred Prague schoolchildren have been quartered here. A hellish noise, a scourge of humanity. I cannot imagine how it happens that the people in the affected part of town—and it is the biggest and choicest quarter—have not gone mad and rushed out of their houses into the woods, and in fact they would have to rush far, for the whole margin of these lovely woods is infested. On the whole I have been spared all this, but every moment can bring surprises; already there have been smaller surprises and sometimes I look searchingly and expectantly out of the window, poor sinner that I am. I am also losing any taste for good noise, and how people flock together in theaters merely for the sake of the noise will soon become incomprehensible to me. Only I hope I shall always be able to understand the reviews you are now writing, which are particularly fine or which make particularly fine reading here. If one went only by the printed account, one would imagine that here was someone who, in the deepest quiet of night and the working day, emerges in the evening, and all by himself, inwardly joyful, and blessed with the very best eyes and ears, wanders through the theaters in steady pursuit of a life-giving mystery. The fine study of Jirásek, or else a felicitous sketch like the one about *Potash and Perlmutter* (did everything go all right that evening?). Or about the Arena,[44] although here the little paragraph about the benches bothers me somewhat, not incidentally but fundamentally. I do not know in what respects we differ from each other on this point. Is my vision at fault here, or my judgment?

What you say about my case is right. Seen from the outside, that is how it is. That is a consolation and at certain hours also a cause for despair, for it indicates that nothing of the terror comes out and so it is all reserved for me alone. This darkness, which only I am forced to see, but even I far from all the time—in fact I no longer saw it the day after that day. But I know it is there and waiting for me, if—well, if I don't show some forbearance toward myself. How well and correctly you explain it all, and if you invite me to Berlin that way, I will surely go and possibly I could have gone with Baum, if we had both left Prague together. And my physical weakness must also be thrown into the reckoning, as Ottla does, and the nastiness of being a hard-currency traveler who is going to Germany for no other reason than that it is cheap, and the not unjustified fear of political unrest—many reasons and yet only one, one that once as a child I thought I saw somewhere, the size of a pin, and that I now know is the only fear there is.

And the writing? (This is going ahead here, less than average in quality, no more, and constantly endangered by noise.) Possibly my explanation will not make sense to you and only comes down to the fact that I want to have your writing as close as possible to mine. And certainly there is this difference, that I, should I ever have been happy, outside of writing and whatever is connected with it (I don't rightly know if I ever was)—at such times I was incapable of writing, with the result that everything had barely begun when the whole applecart tipped over, for the longing to write was always uppermost. This does not mean that I am fundamentally, innately, and honorably a writer by nature. I am away from home and must always write home, even if any home of mine has long since floated away into eternity. All this writing is nothing but Robinson Crusoe's flag hoisted at the highest point of the island.

To make myself feel a little better by grousing: Today from half past three on, again the loading ramp, hammering, rumbling of logs, cries of the loaders. Yesterday at eight in the morning it was finally over, but today the freight train brought a new load, so that probably this morning—and mornings up to now have been mostly fine—is going to be like this. To fill in the interval, some hundred paces away they have just started a winch going. For the most part it stands still or is operated by sensible horses who work without directions. But today oxen were hitched to it and these have to have every step explained to them with *gee* and *ho* and *sakramenská pakáž* [you goddamned beasts]. Why go on living?

The villa at Wannsee, Max! And for me, please, a quiet attic room (far from the music room) from which I will not stir; no one will ever notice I am there.

But for the present there are only your recurrent ailments. What was the cause this time? They are inconceivable, but when one hears of them, they seem real enough, over and above any comfort one can offer. But how can it be that you are ill and yet at the same time dream of Swan Lake.[45] (It is enchanting, I have just read your piece again—this gliding over the surface of all that melancholy, the melancholy mood spreading out on the sofas, the old Russian palace—the ballerina—the drowning in the lake—everything.)—Your health must have significantly improved in the last few days. (*Whoa!* cries a boy under my window. The chains at the railroad station clank; only the oxen pause; it is going to be a tough morning. You see, it is cool, otherwise the sun protects me from the children. Today I might have had the strength to go to Georgental.) Surely you have never suffered physically as much as this time, even if you deny it. I cannot forgive E. for these physical sufferings even if she is not to blame for them; I cannot forgive her if only because of the connection you make.

I too received a complaining letter from Felix. I think that of us all he would be the easiest to help, yet no one helps him.

Have you received my card? Can you leave the novella behind in Prague? Have you written something on Hauptmann?

Best wishes, more than ever.

F

Do you know anything about Klopstock? For some time he hasn't written to me—very understandably in view of my unsatisfactory replies.

How did the Parents' Evening go (on the personal plane)? How did my sister speak? Have they pupils for next year?[46]—Ottla has just brought me news that she (unprompted, for I did not call her attention to the matter and down in the kitchen which faces on the courtyard she can barely hear the children) has sent the children away and that they—this is the nice group—dispersed obligingly. There remains the loading ramp and the unslept head and the relatively late hour, a lost day made more bearable by Ottla's solicitude.—No, the naughty group, uncontrollable because the landlady of this house is their aunt, is now outside my window. You ask about the woods. The woods are lovely, quiet is to be found there, but no "composing hut." A walk through the woods (which are highly diversified) in the evening, when the noise of the birds becomes muted (had I been Mahler, the birds would perhaps have disturbed me) and only here and there anxious twitterings sound (one might think it was fear of me, but it is fear of the evening), and sitting on a certain bench at the edge of the woods where there is a great view (but here the horrible voices of the Prague children already dominate)—that is very lovely, but only when a peaceful night and a peaceful day have preceded it.

To Robert Klopstock

[Postcard. Planá, mid-July 1922]

Dear Robert, So it goes, I am still in Planá and will remain here, even though Oskar was so wonderfully considerate as to find what was evidently a very fine room in Georgental for me. But I cannot make the journey out of fear—not fear of travel but a general fear—so I called it off by telegram and am staying on here. Even though it is otherwise beautiful, it is dizzyingly turbulent here, for someone like me. Well, there is no escaping, not to the plains.

How have you been? The colloquium? The parting with Hermann? (Semiannual bill 2700 crowns, of which 1900 is for my father. Whatever may be said against my lungs, they are not unprofitable.)[47]

Cordial regards from myself and Ottla.

Yours, K.

To Oskar Baum

[Prague, July 16, 1922]

Dear Oskar, Only a few words today. Outwardly I am justified for not coming, as it now turns out I could not have joined you in any case. According to the original plan I was to leave on the fifteenth, but on the afternoon of the fourteenth I received a telegram in Planá that my father who became very sick in Franzensbad was being brought back to Prague. I left for Prague immediately, where my father was operated on that very evening. It is probably nothing malignant, nothing organic—an obstruction of the intestine resulting from navel hernia or something of the sort (I don't dare ask questions of doctors, and when they tell me something nonetheless I don't understand them), but all the same a very serious operation, a man of seventy, weakened by preceding illness which might have been connected with this condition, and with heart disease besides. However, so far, two days after the operation, things have been going miraculously well.

But I want to say something more about my not coming. I had resolved to examine your card very closely, weighing each word of it and reading between the lines. At first reading and still at second, the card seemed extremely kind and reassuring. But later—my study of it having been suspended when I had to leave for Prague—I was taken up short here and there, especially by the "attack of exaggerated solicitude." How dare you, Oskar, write such a phrase. "Exaggerated solicitude," when I bother you day after day, disturb your work, and try to wheedle out of you the most favorable railroad connections in the secret hope that if I only ask often enough it will turn out that Georgental can be reached by streetcar! So let's hear no more of fits of solicitude, please! And don't misconstrue my anguish and think that it was only the beauty of Planá that kept me from coming. True, Planá is beautiful, but I am seeking a respite from its beauty, and before and after the imaginary trip to Georgental I have experienced there such days of noise, that I have cursed my life and needed many days to recover from the fear of noise, from my invariably successful lying in wait for the noise, from the confusion in my head, the pain in my temples, and afterward all of Ottla's measures—she who takes the greatest care of me—had lost all efficacy and new and terrible noise was lying in wait.—Enough for today and all the best to you and yours.

Yours, F

Why no word from Frau Horn?

To Max Brod

[Planá; postmark: July 20, 1922]

Dearest Max, I had no time to come to see you yesterday morning and it was already urgent for me to get away. I had had more than enough of the irregular life (although Planá is even worse suited to the regular life than Prague, but only because of the noise; otherwise it's fine. I have to repeat that constantly for fear of contradiction from "on high"). Still and all I might have stayed had I seen that my father needed me in any way. But yesterday that was not at all the case. His affection for me diminished day by day (no, on the second day it was at its peak, but then went down steadily). And yesterday he could not get me out of the room quickly enough, while he forced my mother to stay. For my mother there now begins a special, new, wearing period of suffering, even if everything goes on progressing as well as it has done so far. For while my father, in the grip of terrible memories, has so far felt staying in bed as a blessing, he must now adjust to the ordeal of lying still. Moreover he has a scar on his back which in the past made prolonged lying almost impossible for him; in addition there is the difficulty of every change of position for his heavy body, his irregular heart, the bulky bandage, coughing, with its painful effect on the incision, but above all his restless, unresourceful, and benighted mind. From now on he faces a torment that, as I see it, exceeds all that has gone before. This torment is coming to the fore precisely because of the improvement in his condition. Yesterday he gestured with his hand as the nurse, whom I find wonderful, was leaving, a gesture that in his language can only mean "Bitch!" And this state of his (which perhaps only I can grasp in all its dreadfulness) will, with the very best prognosis, go on for ten days, and whatever of this can be visited upon my mother will be fully and richly visited. Ten such day-and-night vigils as now stretch before my mother!

Therefore I had no time to come to see you, but probably I would not have come even if I had had the time, the more so because I would have been embarrassed if you had already read my notebook,[48] this notebook which I ventured to give you after your novella, even though I know that it exists only to be written in, not yet to be read. After your novella, which is so perfect, so pure, so shapely, so young, a sacrifice whose smoke must be so pleasing on high. May I ask you, and only because it is so dear to me, if you wouldn't look it over, not just the very beginning but up to the part about the professor's family and then the very last lines. The beginning wanders somewhat, at least for someone who does not know the whole. It's as if it were looking for those side effects that provide pleasant diversion to the reader but are harmful to the whole; in fact they are completely discarded within the whole. But in the course of this beginning they provide a little heat lightning. On the other hand, the story's last breath takes too long, while the reader, who is still gasping for air, is confused and loses the point of view. But this is not to say anything against the epistolary form, which I find convincing. I have not the faintest idea how this novella fits into my concept of the "writer." That doesn't bother me a bit and I am simply happy that the novella exists. But yesterday I found good material for my concept when I spent the train trip reading a little Reclam paperback: Storm's *Memoirs.* A visit to Mörike. These two good Germans sit peaceably together in Stuttgart chatting about German literature. Mörike reads aloud *Mozart on the Journey to Prague.*[49] (Hartlaub, Mörike's friend, who knows the novella very well, "followed the reading with worshipful enthusiasm, which he could barely restrain. At a pause in the reading he exclaimed to me, 'But, I ask you, isn't it almost unendurable?'" It is 1855, they are both elderly men, Hartlaub is a minister.) And then they also talk about Heine. Storm has already said in the *Memoirs* that for him the gates of German literature were flung open by Goethe's *Faust* and Heine's *Buch der Lieder,* those two magical works. And Heine meant a great deal to Mörike as well, for among the few original and highly prized holographs which Mörike owns and which he shows to Storm is "the heavily corrected manuscript of a poem" of Heine's. Nevertheless Mörike says of Heine and this is, although it is probably only a repetition of a common view, at least in one of its aspects a brilliant and still mysterious summary of what I myself think about writers (though what I think is also in another sense a common view): "He is a poet through and through," Mörike said, "but I could not have spent fifteen minutes with him, because of the mendacity of his whole being." Call in a Talmudist to give us a commentary on that.

Yours

You said you were short of material for the *Abendblatt.* I can think of something that might do very well. Do a piece on the sculptor Bilek.[50] More on that presently. You surely know his monument to Huss in Kolin, don't you? Has it made such a matchless impression on you too?

To Robert Klopstock

[Planá; postmark: July 24, 1922]

Dear Robert, You must not be so despairing over this apparent defeat, which while I do not thoroughly understand it, I can sympathize with in my way. If we were on the right road, such a defeat would be boundlessly depressing, but we are only on some road or other, which must first lead to a second and this to a third and so on, and even after a long while we may not reach the right one, perhaps may never reach it, so we are exposed entirely to uncertainty but also to inconceivably beautiful diversity. So the fulfillment of hopes and especially of such hopes remains the ever-unexpected but ever-possible miracle.

As for me, I could use quiet, quiet, but unfortunately cannot believe in what you have there[51] and would at least have to turn off the fountain. And the fear, which does not let me travel, is something I have known for a long time; it is more alive than I am and is out to prove it.—Anyway I would not have been able to leave; my father had an operation (navel hernia with intestinal obstruction) nine days ago; it is taking a remarkably favorable course. Max talked about your visit in even warmer and more unreserved terms than before.

Yours, K

I could not get along without Ohropax either by day or by night.

To Max Brod

[Planá, end of July 1922]

Dearest Max, Already a quarter past nine in the evening, almost too late for writing, but the day is often too short, partly because of the children, since only the interludes in their activities count as usable day, and partly because of my weakness and sluggishness. Ottla aptly says that I shall have to have myself pensioned twice over.

But these are trivialities. What troubles you have! What is this vast chimera which is working against you—which cannot be deflected or even mollified by the novella?[52] Though I don't entirely understand your allusion, which you promptly withdraw, to the "family council." E's relationship to you is after all nothing new to the family; her three sisters and her brother-in-law have become reconciled to it, willy-nilly, and therefore all that remains is her father and of course her brother. From a distance it seems, at least from what I gather from your accounts, as only a very small and hardly successful intrigue on the part of the Leipzig sister, whom I imagine as very enterprising in this respect.

I would have liked to read the letter from the Berliner. So you see, she has answered after all. Still as chatty and confiding as before, tempting one to further correspondence? The "truly proper person" is on the one hand an anticipatory quotation from your novella, on the other an inducement to really take a closer look at her. What holds you back is a dash of self-punishment, not to speak of understandable trepidation—you have built her up so high, higher than the mountain dweller of the novella.

I do not exactly know whether you received my last letter. You do not mention the novella at all—many thanks for the newspaper installment as well as for the synopses. It would intrigue me to write a commentary on the novella sometime, although I don't yet have a precise notion of how I would go about it—nor Mörike.—Recently at André's I leafed through a survey of contemporary literature just published by Diederichs (the author is one Otto von der Leyen[53] or something of the sort), moderate German position, though its arrogant tone would seem to be the author's personal accent, not a part of his position.

Seven forty-five in the morning, the children,* after the astoundingly good day that yesterday was, are here so early, at first only two with a toy haywagon, but that is enough. They are my "family council." Once I notice they are here—and I can see them even from the middle of the room—it is as though I had pried up a stone and saw underneath the obvious, the expected, and yet the dreaded, the wood lice and all the creatures of the night. But this is obviously a transference. It is not the children who are the night's creatures, rather it is they who in the course of play pry up the stone from my head and "favor" me with a glance into it. And indeed in general neither they nor the family council are the worst, for both are harnessed to existence. Rather the worst thing, of which they are innocent and which ought to render them loved rather than feared, is that they represent the last stage of existence. Whether they appear terrible by their noise or delightful by their silence, beyond them begins that chaos invoked by Othello. Here we arrive from another angle at the problem of the "writer." It may be possible, I would not know, for a man who has conquered chaos to begin to write; those will be holy books. Or begin to love; that will be love, not fear of chaos. Lieschen is wrong, though only as far as terminology goes. Not until the world has been ordered does the writer begin. Does your reading of Anna,[54] which I have long been looking forward to reading myself, mean that you are after all writing something about Hauptmann? But now you should also read Osterfeier; perhaps you can do it on your trip.

To return to the survey: I had only a minute to look into it. It would be interesting to read it more carefully. It seems accompanying music to the Secessio Judaica and it is astonishing how within a minute a reader, to be sure a well-disposed one, can organize things with the help of the book, how the crowd of half-familiar, surely honest creative writers who turn up in a

---

* [INSERTED] who were then driven away by Ottla

chapter entitled "Our Land" are classified by landscapes: German property not to be annexed by any Jews.

And even if Wassermann[55] should rise at four in the morning day after day and his whole life long plow up the Nuremberg region from end to end, the land would still not respond to him and he would have to take pretty whisperings in the air for its response. There is no index in the book, so that I found only one mention of you in the text, a not unfriendly one; I think it was a comparison between a novel of Löns[56] and your *Tycho*. *Tycho* was found, in all due respect, suspiciously dialectic. I am actually praised, though only by half, as Franz Kaffka (evidently Friedrich Koffka)[57] who is credited with having written a fine play.

You also do not mention Bilek, though I wish you would take him in your arms. I have long been thinking of him with great admiration. Lately a remark in a *Tribuna* article dealing with other matters (I think it was by Chalupný) reminded me of him again. It is a wanton and senseless impoverishment of Prague and Bohemia that mediocre stuff like Šaloun's *Huss* or wretched stuff like Sucharda's *Palacký* are erected with all honors, while on the other hand sketches of Bilek's for a Žižka or Komenský monument, sketches of incomparable quality, remain unexecuted.[58] If it were possible to rectify this disgrace, that would be doing a great deal, and a government organ would be the right place to begin. Granted, I do not know whether this wrong should be rectified by Jewish hands, but I know no other hands that could do it, and I trust everything to yours. Your comments on the novel[59] shame and gladden me, much as I gladden and shame Věra, when she, as happens often now that she toddles around, abruptly plumps down on her little backside and I say, *"Je ta Věra ale šikovná"* ["Isn't Věra a clever girl!"]. She perfectly well knows, because she feels it in her backside, that she has sat down clumsily, but my exclamation has such power over her that she begins to laugh happily and is convinced that she has just carried out the difficult trick of properly sitting down.

What Herr Weltsch reports[60] is hardly convincing. He simply takes it for granted that a father can only love and praise his son. But in this case what is there to cause a father's eyes to light up? A son incapable of marriage, who could not pass on the family name; pensioned off at thirty-nine; occupied only with his weird kind of writing, the only goal of which is his own salvation or damnation; unloving; alienated from the Faith, so that a father cannot even expect him to say the prayers for the rest of his soul; consumptive, and as the father quite properly sees it, having got sick through his own fault, for he was no sooner released from the nursery for the first time when with his total incapacity for independence he sought out that unhealthy room at the Schönborn Palace.[61] This is the son to rave about.

F

What is Felix doing? He no longer answers me.

To Robert Klopstock

[Planá, end of July 1922]

Dear Robert, So you are all right. I would not have become worried (not writing in itself is nothing bad, though I cannot say it is something good, for my desire not to write was hardly ever prompted by a better desire, as it seems to have been for you) had it not been for the newspaper story, which preyed on my mind, about the students who took their meals at the YMCA and came down with typhus at the end of the school year. Since the disease apparently takes about four weeks to incubate, many of the students carried the germs along with them on their vacation. We have been spared that, spared for struggles, as you hint. Good luck with them, and peace, and woods and solitude. I am, with interruptions, tolerably well.

Did you receive my card about my father's operation?

Yours, K

To Max Brod

[Planá; postmarked on arrival: July 31, 1922]

Dearest Max, A quick last greeting before leaving (to the extent that the people downstairs permit: the landlady, nephews and niece—the landlady's, that is).

Keeping to your sequence:

Bilek: It's a great delight to me that you really mean to try something that I dared to mention only as a purely fantastic wish; I don't have the strength for more. In my opinion it would be a fight on a par with the fight for Janáček, if I understand the matter rightly (I almost wrote: with the fight for Dreyfus). I'm not suggesting that Bilek would be the Janáček or Dreyfus of the struggle, for one hears, and it seems plausible, that he is fairly well off; the article said that he has commissions and that already the seventh copy of a statuette called *The Blind Man* had been ordered. Moreover, he isn't unknown; the article—which in general dealt with government expenditures on art—actually called him *velikán* [great man]. So while campaigning for him would not be especially original, the fight is worth while nonetheless. What we would be campaigning for is sculpture itself, and the human pleasure in the visual. In saying this I keep thinking of the *Huss* at Kolin (not so much the statue in the Modern Gallery[62] and the monument in Vyšehrad Cemetery[63] and still less the mass of relatively inaccessible small pieces in wood and graphic which used to be shown and are growing dim in my memory). At Kolin you come out of the side street and see before you the big square with the small houses bordering it, and in the center the *Huss*. At all times, in snow and in summer, it has a breathtaking, incomprehensible, and thus seemingly arbitrary unity, which is nevertheless imposed anew at every moment by that powerful hand and even takes in the spectator himself. The Weimar Goethe House achieves something of the sort, perhaps largely through the blessing of time. But it would be rather difficult to campaign for the creator of that, and the door of his house is always closed.

It would be very interesting to find out how the *Huss* monument came to be erected. As far as I can recall from the stories of my deceased cousin,[64] all the municipal authorities were opposed to the monument beforehand, and even more afterward, and probably to this day.

The novella: A pity I won't have a chance to see the final version.

Lieschen is certainly much easier to understand than M. We learned in school that girls are like that; but we didn't learn that they are to be loved and thereby made incomprehensible.

Felix: The magic psychiatrist sounds improbable, but F. would certainly deserve the finest of improbabilities. Why should he not be able to take over *Der Jude?* That would certainly be extremely fine, and if it didn't work out, extremely sad. Granted, at the moment it brings in less than *Selbstwehr,* but surely enough for him to get by (I am assuming that if *Der Jude* could be edited from Heppenheim,[65] it can be edited from Prague). It would be a prestigious job for him and would involve far less work than *Selbstwehr.* Granted, good old *Selbstwehr* would be in danger; that was noticeable during the Epstein period, when things of this sort were perpetrated and perpetuated: "The Russian *halutz*[66] appears on the scene." *Selbstwehr* cannot be put out with the left hand but needs the devotion that Felix gives to it.—As far as I am concerned, it is unfortunately only in joke or in a semicomatose moment that my name should come up in connection with the vacant editorship at *Der Jude.* How could I think of such a thing, with my boundless ignorance of affairs, my complete lack of connection with people, the absence of any firm Jewish ground under my feet? No, no.

Hauptmann: The piece in the *Abendblatt* was exceptionally fine and I am very much looking forward to the *Rundschau* article.[67] However I do not know how you can, except with the inscrutable rights of love, establish a relationship between Jorinde and Anna (as you did in your exegesis). Jorinde is quite different, at once more comprehensible and more mysterious than

Anna. Anna has unquestionably fallen. Her motives are baffling but her fall is beyond doubt. *Her* greatest mystery is her judgment upon herself and her self-punishment, a mystery that in a way makes her more comprehensible to me than Jorinde, not rationally but because of my own inner requirements. Jorinde, on the other hand, hasn't done anything bad at all. If she had, given her nature, she would confess it, just like Anna. But since she hasn't anything to confess, she cannot confess anything. Given her character—and perhaps this could have been said of Anna before her fall—it seems impossible for her to say of herself with conviction: "I have done wrong." Therein perhaps lies her enigma, but it is an enigma that cannot, as it were, develop, because she has done nothing bad. In this way one almost ends by finding her lover baffling, who exaggerates his weakness to the point of darkening the entire world. This weakness is undeniably there and consists in his inability to terminate his association with the mechanic. Which is not only a momentary weakness but the prelude to further weaknesses, so that if he could end this association, that would only make room for another equally disturbing to him.

Jorinde's innocence disturbs him almost as much as the mechanic does—and innocence here means inaccessibility. He is, as you certainly have also said, literally in pursuit of something Jorinde does not possess, to which she rather represents only the barred door. And when he rattles it, he inflicts great pain on her, for she cannot give him what she does not possess. But he cannot refrain because he wants what she is barring, which she herself knows nothing about and could not possibly learn anything about from anyone. Not from him, either, even though she tried her best to learn.

I will surely write to you at Misdroy,[68] but not to E., for that would be a farce and would be so viewed by her. On the other hand, when I write to you, I will do it in such terms that you can show her the letter and that will not be a farce at all. Incidentally, postal connections with Germany are very slow at the moment.

Keep well.

F

Please drop me a card from Berlin and also from Misdroy.

The case of Bilek is more remarkable than the case of Janáček, first because Austria still existed at the time, so Bohemia was under a cloud, and secondly because Janáček was truly totally unknown, at least in Bohemia. Bilek, on the other hand, is very well known, highly esteemed, and is seen by hundreds and thousands as he takes his evening strolls among the ten trees of his dusty villa garden.

To Max Brod
[Planá, beginning of August 1922]
Dearest Max, I have spent almost four days in Prague and have returned to the relative peace here. This pattern, a few days in the city, a few months in the country, might be the right one for me. Four days in the city in summertime are to be sure a great deal: for instance, one could scarcely put up a longer resistance against the half-naked women. Not until summer does one really see their curious kind of flesh in quantities. It is soft flesh, retentive of a great deal of water, slightly puffy, and keeps its freshness only a few days. Actually, of course, it stands up pretty well, but that is only proof of the brevity of human life. How short human life must be if flesh one hardly dares to touch because of its perishability, because its shapely contours last only a moment (which contours, as Gulliver discovered—but most of the time I cannot believe it—are disfigured by sweat, fat, pores, and hairs)—how short human life must be, if such flesh will last out a good portion of that life.

Here in the village women are altogether different, though there are also many summer visitors here, for example an unusually beautiful, unusually fat blonde woman, who, just as a man tugs at his vest, must stretch herself every few steps in order to straighten out her belly and breasts; she is dressed like a fine poisonous toadstool and smells—some people know no limits—like the best edible mushroom (of course I do not know her, I know hardly anyone here). But one ignores the summer visitors, who tend to be either comical or nondescript. I admire most of the native women. They are never half-naked, and even though they own little more than one dress, they are always completely clothed. They do not get fat until deepest old age, and only an occasional young girl is buxom. (There is a hired girl in a half-tumbledown farm which I often pass on my evening walk; she will sometimes stand in the doorway of the stable and literally send her breasts into battle.) But the women are dry, a dryness one can probably fall in love with only at a distance, women who seem not at all dangerous and yet are magnificent. It is a special kind of dryness, produced by wind, weather, work, cares, and childbearing, but there is nothing of urban misery about it, rather a tranquil, upright cheerfulness. Next door lives a family—they would not have to be named Veselý ["cheerful"]—the wife is thirty-two and has seven children, five of whom are boys. The father works in the mill, usually on the night shift. I revere this couple. He looks, as Ottla says, like a Palestinian farmer; well, that may be so. He is of medium height, somewhat pale-skinned, but the pallor is partly the effect of his black mustache (one of those mustaches you once described as sucking up energy). He is quiet, moves hesitantly; were it not for his calmness one might say he was shy. His wife, one of those dry types, forever young, forever old, blue-eyed, cheerful, with laughter wrinkles about her mouth, in some incomprehensible way carries this pile of children through life (one boy goes to the technical school in Tábor) and of course is endlessly harassed. Once when I spoke to her, I felt I was almost married to her, for though the children harass me, too, outside my window, now she protects me. Granted, it is hard, for her husband must often sleep by day and so the children have to be out of the house and there is hardly anywhere for them to go but the area outside my window, a bit of grass-grown road and a bit of fenced-in meadow with a few trees which her husband bought to pasture the goats in. One morning he tried to sleep there and lay there, first on his back, his arms under his head. I sat at my table and continually kept him in sight, could scarcely look away from him, I could not do anything else. We both needed quiet, that was something we had in common, but the only thing. If I could have sacrificed my share of silence for him, I would gladly have done so. However it was not quiet enough, other children, not his own, were making noise; he turned over and tried to fall asleep with his face in his hands, but it wasn't possible and he stood up and went into his house.

But as I am gradually beginning to notice, Max, I am telling you stories that cannot interest you and only tell them in order to have something to tell and to remain in some sort of connection with you, for I came back from Prague feeling gloomy and dull. Initially I did not want to write to you at all, for while letters might do in the noise and unhappiness of the city, the way you were living there, I did not want to disturb you in the silence of the seashore. The card you sent me from Prague before leaving confirmed me in this feeling. But it is different now that I am back from Prague. I am somewhat saddened by my father's persistent suffering. Perhaps it will take a turn for the better; for a whole week now he has been able to take a daily walk, but he constantly has pain, discomfort, restlessness, and fear. I am sad about my mother, too, for though she is marvelously brave and strong in spirit, she is destroying herself looking after him. I am sad about several other, far less important but almost more oppressive things. The question of self-destruction brings you to my mind. Last night I dreamed of you, all sorts of things of which only one bit remains, that you looked out of a window, shockingly thin, your face an exact triangle. I have been shaken out of my relative equanimity by the "unnatural" life of the past few days and suddenly see the road, if there ever was one, breaking right off at my feet. Because of all this I am writing to you after all, in spite of the scruples and inner difficulties. For considering the way you were spending your time those last days in Prague, always on tenterhooks for the letters from Leipzig (and often after a letter had come, suffering more than before), it might well be that you look the way you did in my dream. Unless the vacation has already helped you, as I wish with all my heart. It may well have done so, since now, instead of the continual torment of the letters, you have the happiness of continuous living communication. I would like to send regards to Fräulein S.[69] but cannot, for I know her less and less. I know her from what you have told me of her, as the wonderful friend; I further know her as the goddess of the novella, who, to be sure, is inscrutable but never blameworthy. But finally I also know her as the letter-writer who is working to destroy you, and *at the same time denies that she has any such intention.* There are too many contradictions here; they do not add up to a person and so I do not know who walks at your side and cannot send regards to her. But for you, so long and come back sound and well.

F

To Max Brod

[Planá; postmark: August 16, 1922]

Dear Max, I will set down what I think I understand better than you and then what I do not understand. Perhaps it will then become clear that I understand none of it, which might well be the case, for the subject is vast, the distance likewise, and in addition there is the worry about you, worry that things may be going worse for you than you admit, and so only a foggy picture emerges from all this.

First and foremost, I do not understand why you so strongly emphasize W.'s[70] advantages in order that (but now this quiet letter-writing is over. There is a thunderstorm. My brother-in-law, somewhat at loose ends, has come in and is sitting at my table. My table? It is his table and it is incomprehensible magnanimity on his part that I am given the use of the fine room while the family of three sleeps in a tiny cubicle—though the big kitchen should not be left out of the reckoning. This is especially so when I recall how in the first days, when the division was different, my brother-in-law would so happily stretch himself in his bed and would remark that the best thing about their summer place was that one awoke to such a magnificent view from the bed, with the woods in the distance and so forth, and only a few days later he was sleeping in the tiny room with the neighbor's courtyard for view and the chimney of the sawmill. I mention all this in order—no, let the reason remain unspoken). But back to what concerns you. From all you have said, W. by no means occupies a dominant position, but the scale seems carefully adjusted, at least at the moment, in such a way as to cause everyone the utmost torment. W. has no dominance, he cannot marry, he cannot help, he cannot make E. a mother, for if he could he would already have done so and the situation would have defined itself

toward you far more drastically. Therefore let's not talk about his motives
being decent and yours bad. He loves E. and you love her. Who will decide
the matter, since not even E. can fully decide? On his side he has the looks
and the attractiveness of youth, which is a great deal, especially for an older
woman, the more so since your Jewishness did not so much handicap you as
enhance him. But you have obviously much more to offer and of a more
lasting nature—you have manly love and manly support, and give continually
now the dream, now the reality of the artist's being. So what is there in the
situation that causes you to despair? Clearly not the way the struggle is likely
to end, but the struggle itself and its developments. Here, I grant, you are
right. I couldn't stand it, couldn't stand the slightest hint of that sort of thing.
But how much you endure from which I flee or which flees from me. For
that reason I am probably overestimating you. I haven't even a halfway
intelligent notion of your strength.

Now the second point: E. lies and lies endlessly, which is evidence rather of
her distress than of her mendacity. And also it seems to be a kind of after-
the-fact mendacity; for example, she asserts that she does not use *"Du"*
toward W., which is true, but right after that she does begin to use it, partly
seduced by the very assertion and now incapable of taking that assertion back.
Nevertheless, I would not have expected this and still don't understand it,
and also cannot understand how you can speak of self-abasement, for it is
actually the collapse of her structure and an appeal to you, as a man and a
source of strength, to somehow make up for it. She takes refuge entirely in
you, at least when you are with her. The letter, which she wrote to me in
spite of your pleas, was after all written all too much as you would have
wished, if I understand it rightly, much like her tormented yet true postcard
to me.

Leaving aside all the complicating side issues, of which there are more than
enough in this affair, I see the basic pattern this way: You want the
impossible, out of a persistent hunger. That would not be anything
extraordinary; many want that, but you push further than anyone I know
and almost reach your goal, but not quite, for the goal is the impossible. And
this almost-but-not-quite causes you suffering and must do so. There are all
degrees of the impossible; you will remember that the Count of Gleichen[71]
also attempted the impossible—and whether anyone ever succeeds is a question
probably not even the grave can answer. But what he wanted was not as
impossible as what you want. He did not leave one woman in the Orient and
try to keep a marriage going over the Mediterranean Sea. But even this last
would have been possible had he been bound to his first wife against his will.
For then the new woman's yearning, or feeling of emptiness, or need for
protection or the devil knows what else, would be matched on his part by

despair over his first marriage, along with a sense of consolation and gratitude. But this is not the case here; you are not in despair and your wife in fact makes your difficult life easier. But then, as I see it, if you want to avoid destroying yourself (I shudder when I consider that you also have to write letters home) there is nothing for it but to attempt the frightful step (though in comparison with what you have suffered in the past years, the step merely appears to be frightful) and actually bring E. to Prague, or if for various reasons this should be too painful, take your wife to Berlin, that is, move to Berlin, and openly, or at least openly among the three of you, live as a threesome. Then almost all the previous evils would vanish (though new and unknown evils may appear): your fear of W., your fear of the future (which would otherwise remain even after you had worsted W.), your concern for your wife, the anxiety over children, and your life would be easier even economically (for the expense of maintaining E. in Berlin would otherwise be ten times greater than your present burden). Only I would lose you in Prague. But where there is room for two women around you, why should there not be some sort of room for me?

For the present I would be glad to see you come back safe and sound from this hellish holiday.

F.

Your wife: Perhaps it would not be so desperately hard to win her over to the plan. While in Prague I talked with Felix and he thinks it is impossible that she does not know. Which means that she suffers fairly cheerfully. I also recall the letter of Storm's which she used to like to show around.

To Emmy Salveter

[Draft of a letter. Planá, August 1922]

Many thanks for the card and the letter. They did not surprise me at all; nor did I feel that this was the first letter I received from you, for I have heard so much about you and your name is so familiar to me. The only lack is that I have so far not seen or heard you, but that too is not always felt, for you come so alive in Max's stories. And I will have to be content with that, for the doctor does not permit me to travel to the Baltic.

But I would very much like to meet you, for separated as we are by distance and silence, yet with so very many common references between us, misunderstandings can easily arise and even letters may do more harm than good. Thus such an inevitable misunderstanding already threatens to arise out of your good letter. Distant faces, especially those one knows only from photographs, too easily take on a wicked and hostile aspect in the imagination. Thus, my name is Franz, which readily evokes a scoundrel;[72] at the moment it almost strikes even me that way. But in reality—how can anyone who is concerned with Max's life and work think ill of you; how could anyone arrive at any other relationship with you than that of deepest gratitude? Max's life and work is based upon the joy he takes in your being and well-being, and to want to drive you apart is tantamount to driving him from his life and work. Must not the unity of you and Max and me that results from this be a perfect unity? I admit there are days, like those days before his last trip, when the picture is reversed, when the very thing that gives him life appears to want to take it from him. I would not venture to get mixed up in the immediate causes; I also see, of course, that much senseless self-torment is involved, explicable only by the distress of a person who is threatened in what is dearest to him.

Be that as it may be, if you, my dear young lady, had seen him then or on similar occasions—a view of him you can never have; it is reserved for me, for with you Max is immediately consoled—shattered, frightfully emaciated in two or three days, with sleepless eyes, indifferent to everything but the one thing that inflicts pain on him, yet going on working with that energy which even then does not desert him, and so continuing to destroy himself—if you were to see him, my dear young lady, then you would surely, I think I know this much about you, not be satisfied with acting like me, that is sitting quietly and helplessly by him, at best as if crushed by the same pain, but you would rush to Max's side and be far more helpful and comforting than I. A pity, such a pity that at such moments you are not there, for surely you would not be writing to me if you were.

So much for your good letter. Apart from this I understand that I am supposed to give you my report on the meeting in the café with Fräulein F.— or rather I understand that I am not to give you my report but craftily let Max dictate what I am supposed to say. Since these two duties cannot be reconciled, you must content yourself, dear young lady, with my saying that this meeting was one of the most meaningless incidents of my life.

To Robert Klopstock

[Planá; postmark: September 5, 1922]

Dear Robert, I was in Prague for several days and only now find your card here. I will probably be staying in Planá for at least another month; from time to time one has to go to Prague to recognize the value of Planá, or rather, one is always conscious of it, but one does not always have the strength to appreciate it. You are wavering about coming to Prague? In any case, you should unquestionably go to a city. I only flee it because I cannot cope with it, because the few scanty meetings, conversations, sights I have there bring me to the verge of fainting. Nevertheless I will probably spend October and November in Prague, but afterward would like to go and stay with my uncle[73] in the country, if that should prove feasible. To say anything about your future, I would have to know the nature of these offers you have received. Prague would be the best place for you, not under all circumstances but under many.—Max is already in Prague. His address is Břehová ul. 8.— Write me about the offers.

Yours, K

To Max Brod
[Planá; postmarked on arrival: September 11, 1922]
Dear Max, Say nothing about the "right instinct" guiding me not to come to Germany. It was something else. I have been back here for about a week, and have not spent the week very happily (for I will evidently have to drop the Castle story forever, cannot pick it up again since the "breakdown" which began a week before my trip to Prague, even though the part written in Planá is not quite as bad as the part you know). But if the week has not been a happy one, it has been serene and I am almost becoming fat, since I feel especially serene when I am alone here with Ottla, without my brother-in-law and guests. Yesterday afternoon, again very quiet, I passed by the landlady in the kitchen and we started chatting. (Up to now she has been outwardly friendly, but cold, hostile, hypocritical. However in the last few days, for no visible reason at all, she has become frank, cordial, and friendly to us. It is a complicated business.) At any rate we started chatting, about the dog, about the weather, about my appearance *(jak jste přišel, měl jste smrtelnou barvu)* [when you first came, you were as white as a corpse], and some devil or other inspired me to brag that I like it very much here and that I would much prefer to stay on, that only the prospect of eating at the inn deters me. She remarked that I would perhaps be afraid to stay on alone, but I treated this as ridiculous, and then something happened that was completely unpredictable within the framework of the entire relationship (moreover she is a woman of means): She offered to have me as a boarder, for as long as I liked, and was already specifying details, for instance, what I would have for supper and suchlike. I thanked her delightedly for her offer and the matter was settled: I would surely stay the whole winter. I thanked her once again and left. There and then, as I went up the steps to my room, I had this "breakdown," the fourth I have had in Planá. (The first was on one of the days the children were making noise, the second when Oskar's letter came, the third when the question arose of Ottla's going back to Prague on

September 1 and I staying on a month and taking my meals at the inn.) I don't have to describe the outward symptoms of such a state; you too know what they are like, though you must think of the most intense form you have ever experienced, where the emotion is already on the point of reversing itself. Above all I knew I would not be able to sleep, that the faculty of sleep had had its heart bitten out. In fact I was already sleepless, I literally experienced insomnia beforehand as though I had had a sleepless night behind me. I then went out, could think of nothing else, was totally preoccupied by unspeakable fear, and in clearer moments by fear of this fear. At a crossroads I ran into Ottla; it was by chance the same place where I met her with my letter of reply to Oskar. This time things went a bit better than last time. What Ottla would say was now of the utmost importance. Should she assent to my plan by the least word, then I would be pitilessly lost for at least several days. For I myself on my own could not have the slightest objection to the plan; it was rather the realization of a great wish: to be alone, quiet, well looked after at reasonable cost, spending autumn and winter in these parts which I found especially pleasant. Then what was there to object to? Nothing but the fear, and after all that was no objection. Consequently, if Ottla raised no objections, I was doomed to a battle with myself, a battle of annihilation which would have no outcome other than that I stay. But fortunately Ottla immediately said that I could not stay, the climate was too raw, the fog, and so on. With this, the tension was relaxed and I could make my confession. Of course there was still the difficulty of the offer I had accepted, but this was a small matter, in Ottla's view, although to me it still loomed as monstrous, since the whole thing still loomed monstrous to me. At the moment I was somewhat calmer about it, or rather my mind was calmer, insofar as it played a part in all this. I myself was not calmed; too much had been raked up which now lives of its own accord and could no longer be calmed with a word, but which would need a certain time span to subside. I then walked into the woods by myself, as I do every evening. Being in the dark woods is my favorite time. But this time I could feel nothing but that fear. It lasted for the whole evening and in the night I could not sleep. Only in the morning, in the sunny garden, it lifted a little, as Ottla took occasion to speak with the landlady about the matter in my presence and I took a small part in the discussion and to my vast astonishment (which is totally detached from my mind) heard this world-shaking matter cleared up with a few casual sentences. I stood there like Gulliver listening to the giant women conversing. It even came out that the landlady had not taken her proposal all that seriously. But I was hollow-eyed for the rest of the day.

What, then, is it all about? Insofar as I can think it through, it is only one thing. You say I should test myself on larger matters. That is correct in a certain sense, though on the other hand the proportions do not decide the issue. I could still test myself in my mousehole. And this one thing is: fear of complete loneliness. If I stayed here alone, I would be completely lonely. I cannot talk to the people here, and if I did so, it would only be a heightening of loneliness. And I have a nodding acquaintance with the terrors of loneliness, not so much of lonely loneliness as of loneliness among people, as it was during my first days in Matliary or for a few days in Spindelmühle, though I do not want to speak of that. But what is it about loneliness? Fundamentally, loneliness is my sole aim, my greatest temptation, my opportunity, and assuming it can be said that I have "arranged" my life, it was always with the view that loneliness can comfortably fit into it. And in spite of this, this fear of what I love so much. Far more understandable is the fear of being robbed of loneliness, which is equally strong and rushed to the fore at the first challenge ("breakdown" when the children made noise, when Oskar's letter came); and even more understandable the fear of the tortuous middle way, and yet this fear is the weakest of the three, and I am ground between these two fears—the third only comes to their aid when it becomes clear that I want to escape—and finally some great miller in the background will growl out that for all his toil, he has not netted much nourishment from me. In any case, a life such as my baptized uncle[74] has led would be a horror for me, even though it lies along my course, to be sure not as a goal, but it was not my uncle's goal either but only happened in the last period of decline. It is significant that I feel so good in empty apartments, but not in those that are entirely empty. I like them when they are full of memories of people and stand in readiness for further living—apartments with furnished marital bedrooms, children's rooms, kitchens, apartments where the morning mail comes through the letter slot, addressed to others, where someone else's newspaper is thrust into the door. Only the real tenant must never show his face, as recently happened to me, for then I am deeply disturbed. Well, that is the story of the "breakdowns."

Your good news cheers me; three days ago, when the letter arrived, I could still feel cheered, and today I am slowly becoming capable of feeling cheered again. I am not yet prepared to go with you to Berlin. Ottla has stayed on another month here, almost entirely for my sake, so how can I leave now? (Why are you going on the 30th of October?) Besides I want to attend the premiere and to go twice strikes me as too grandiose. As far as E. is concerned, she hates me anyhow and I am almost afraid to meet her, and as far as you are concerned, my influence, if I have any, is stronger when I am buried away somewhere than when I step forth.

You yourself have put your finger on what I didn't like in Speyer.[75] The boarding school, the early pages on Christine and Blanche are uncommonly fine and would win over the sternest critic. But then his hand falters; one can scarcely read further. To be sure, there are enough honorable passages, but no more than that. On the other hand, in the first half there are already signs of the book's later deterioration: in the too facile characterizations of the other pupils, or in the introductory chapter. If anyone throws open a window on a November night in order to compare the silence of Germany with the silence of Tibet, all one wants to do is slam the window shut again. These are exaggerations of the Storm mood.

Anna also somewhat depressed me and at any rate gave me little pleasure. Moreover I read it through almost twice, once for myself, and then again, some sixteen cantos, for Ottla. I recognize the master's touch in the structure, in the witty and animated dialogue, in many passages, but the whole thing is such a bag of wind! None of the characters, except for Just, has any life for me. In saying this I am not thinking of the completely absurd, undignified comedy, of Erwin, for instance, who has never lived and never died and is constantly being torn out of his dummy grave (reading about him can only make us laugh), of Thea or the grandmother. But also almost all the others; one's sense of one's own poor life is certainly enhanced when confronted with such wretched waxworks.

You are not in love with Anna but with E., and don't love Anna for E's sake but love E only for her own sake, and even Anna cannot keep you from this. My favorites are the Moravian Brethren, and the author is by no means as unsympathetic to them as you represent. "And undeniably they had in their eyes a strange radiance, deep and good."[76]

Good luck in Berlin!

F

To Robert Klopstock

[Planá, September 1922]

Dear Robert, The pen feels almost strange in my hand, it's so long since I have written. But this time the occasion is important enough to make me attempt it. I advise you without question to spend the winter semester in Berlin, and for the following reasons:

An opportunity of this sort to live in Berlin without financial cares and do independent work comes but once in a lifetime and so in no event should be thrown away. (What is Dr. Steinfest paying you for? Is it a gift?)

To meet the challenge of changing your place of study is something you have a knack for; make good use of your inner resources.

Prague is of questionable worth. Quite apart from the clearly personal aspect, Prague also has some special charm. I can understand that and I think it is the tinge of childlikeness in its people's minds. However, the childlikeness is so mixed with childishness, pettiness, and inexperience that it constitutes a danger to nonnatives, not a major danger but a danger nonetheless. Prague is more useful if one comes from Berlin, though to my knowledge no one yet has done this on any grand scale. In any case Prague is a medicine against Berlin and Berlin is a medicine against Prague, and since the West European Jew is a sick man and lives on medicines, it is essential for him, if he is to move in these circles, not to pass up Berlin. I have always told myself this but have not had the strength to stretch out my hand from my bed and reach for the medicine. I have also tried, quite wrongly, to disparage it with the thought that it is only a medicine. However Berlin today is a good deal more; one also has, I think, a stronger view of Palestine from there than from Prague.

As far as Max is concerned, it will be almost easier to maintain contact with him this winter in Berlin than in Prague, since for a special reason Berlin will now become his second home. You might also be able to do him invaluable services there. (Besides he is to have a premiere there, to which I will probably come.)

As for myself, except for a few weeks which I will be spending at my uncle's (in Moravia, which is almost farther from Prague than Berlin), I will be staying in Prague, since I am not intellectually transportable. But I will very much enjoy having you somewhere as my billeting officer.—All this applies only to the winter. Perhaps one winter in Berlin is sufficient. (Doesn't your cousin[77] also wish to spend the winter in Berlin?) Then you can come back to Prague as a much-traveled man, who can draw comparisons (if you still feel like it and do not prefer a south German university). The fact that from May on your patron will be in Prague will fit in with that.—In sketching all this, I also assume that you are in good health; otherwise you would not be toying with such plans.—You can count on Max and Felix to provide you with introductions to Berlin, as well as on me for one to Ernst Weiss, should you wish it. In spite of Dr. Steinfest's money, you probably will also have to call upon the rich man's help, for as Dr. Weiss reports, one can hardly get by with 10,000 marks.

So we will see each other in Prague (for I will probably be there by the first of October) when you pass through on your way to Berlin and we can discuss whatever is necessary. Is Fräulein Irene going back to Dresden? Where is Glauber? In Lomnitz? Please send him my regards. And Szinay?—My little niece[78] will not be sent to Hellerau, of course. I did succeed in having my sister, brother-in-law, and the children pay a visit to Hellerau, but through this partial victory I lost all hope of the eventual victory. Frau Neustädter frightened them off, for she malignantly contrived to have both sniffles and boils on her face the day they were due. Herr Neustädter, the Englishman, a teachers' aide, and a Dalcroze[79] student made a very good impression, but could not prevail against the sniffles. The children were off on an outing; it was Sunday. It is simply that my sister does not have the strength to make the decision. I cannot blame her for this. For months I have wanted to make a ten-minute train trip and have not managed to.

All good wishes, yours, F

To Oskar Baum

[Prague,] September 21, 1922

Dear Oskar, Thank you for your letter which has reached me by way of Planá (I have been in Prague since Monday).[80] I was very much afraid that you were angry, and am still afraid, for how could you remain well disposed toward me after such conduct. Unless one strenuously considers how this terrible conduct rankles in my own flesh.

I will be coming to see you in the next few days. Except for a number of interruptions, I got along very well in Planá, and it was only at the end that I was almost glad to be leaving. There would be nothing nicer than to stay there the winter, for a heroic sleeper, that is, and that I am not. I would not have been able to bear it among the unleashed nature spirits. And you, tied up by the musical season, would have been able to come for only a few days at best. Fortunate Leo! All praise to his parents! So grown-up and healthy and strong and skillful and physically seasoned, and what is more, admired by the excess of girls, who further and guide the development by their admiration.

Ask Max to lend you *Melancholy of the Seasons* by Speyer, which describes a boarding school. In contrast to this, those of us whose education basically took place in a lonely, too cold or too hot boy's bed would have to say, "I am accursed." It is not quite accurate, but one feels strongly impelled to say it.

Cordial regards to you, your wife, and sister.

Yours, F

To Robert Klopstock

[Prague, autumn 1922]

Dear Robert, A few words, the Fräulein is waiting. From what Fräulein Irene told me, I had the impression that the worst is over and that going to the hospital is no longer in question. However if you should feel that the hospital would make things even the least bit easier for you, we can try to arrange it (you are surely being very badly tended at home). It would not be a matter of begging; I would go to my colleague and the matter could be arranged through him in a perfectly dignified fashion [...] So speak up. I have had news just today from Dr. Hermann, but it was very brief and hazy; he spoke of a mild grippe. I will be going to see him tomorrow.

How high is your fever? Exactly.

I had already answered your letter when Fräulein Irene came here yesterday. In view of the fever, what I had to say is even less important than it had been. I am holding the answer.

All good wishes, yours, K

Tell me frankly what you need.

To Minze Eisner

[Prague, autumn 1922]

Dear Minze, Your letter gave me great pleasure, for it shows me you have not given up before obstacles which I think I know and others which I am unacquainted with. Instead you are going forward with your brave and self-reliant life. Of course I accept the invitation;[81] how could I not accept it. To see you as a housewife, and in addition quiet and woods and garden. Though admittedly my transportability has become limited, not so much physically as mentally. For example, in the summer I was supposed to go to see some friends in Thuringia, but even though my physical state was quite good I could not manage to. It is difficult to explain. But perhaps I will make it to Kassel. What kind of villa is it and what kind of grounds? A nursery garden? Or only a countryseat? Though that is hardly likely. And you surely cannot live there all by yourself. With what kind of people are you living? There is a story called "Two Sisters" among Stifter's *Studies*,[82] about a magnificent garden created by a girl; do you know the story? Curiously enough, it takes place near Lake Garda, the same locality, I think, we once talked about in a similar connection. Apparently it is a dream many people have.

The confession. To be chosen to hear it is already an inescapable and grave obligation. Please, though, do not hope for anything from this. What sort of man would it have to be from whom one could hope for anything when one made a confession to him. To confess to a person or to cry into the wind is largely one and the same, whatever good intentions the poor weak will might bring to the task. To flounder about in the confusion of one's own life, and having to hear someone else's confession, what can one say except, "True, that's the way it is, that's how it goes," which of course may be a comfort, but not a great one. But please write to me, dear Minze, if you feel the urge. You can count on my respect and sympathy, to the limit of my strength.

You ask about my illness: It is not as bad as it looks from outside the closed door of the sickroom, but the building is a bit fragile. However I am better by now and two months ago was in fine shape. It is merely a somewhat confused war situation. The disease itself, viewed as combat troops, is the most obedient creature in the world; it keeps its eyes fixed entirely on headquarters and carries out whatever orders are issued there. Up there, though, they are often indecisive and there are other causes of misunderstanding. Something should be done to end the split between headquarters and troops.

Be well, Minze, and my best wishes for your journey and your undertaking.

Yours, Kafka

To Kurt Wolff Verlag

[Prague; received: October 21, 1922]

Dear Sirs,

Many thanks for the two books and especially for the regards transmitted to me,[83] which I cordially reciprocate.

I take this occasion to notify you, as I have already done several times, that my address is no longer Pořič 7, but solely:

Altstädter Ring 6, Prague.

Not only is it unpleasant, for various other reasons, to be receiving mail at Pořič 7, but also these items reach me only after lengthy, sometimes months-long delays. The books, too, were late in reaching me. Therefore please be so kind as to take note of this change of address.

By chance I heard from a third party that *Metamorphosis* and "The Judgment" appeared in Hungarian translation in the Kaschau newspaper *Szebadság* and that "A Fratricide" appeared in the Easter issue of *Kassai Naplo,* again in Kaschau. The translator is the Hungarian writer Sandor Márai,[84] who lives in Berlin. Did you know of this? In any case may I request that any future rights to translate my works into the Hungarian be reserved for Robert Klopstock,[85] a Hungarian man of letters with whom I am well acquainted and who will surely do an outstanding job.

Very sincerely yours, F Kafka

To Max Brod

[Prague, December 1922]

Dear Max, Chiefly for your information, because Werfel will be coming to see you, and incidentally to comfort myself with thoughts of you:

Yesterday Werfel came to see me, with Pick; the visit, which otherwise would have given me pleasure, left me in despair. Werfel was well aware that I had read *Schweiger*[86] and I foresaw that I would have to talk to him about it. Had I felt only an ordinary dislike for the play, I could somehow get around it. But the play means a great deal to me; it hits me hard, affects me horribly on the most horrible level. It had not remotely occurred to me that I would someday have to talk to Werfel about that. The reasons for my repugnance were not entirely clear to me because I had not had the slightest inner debate over the play, but merely the desire to shake it off. Though I may have been deaf to Hauptmann's *Anna*, I hear every nuance of this Anna and the tangle involving her with agonizing, uncanny acuteness. Ah well, these auditory phenomena are closely linked. If I now try to sum up the reasons for my repugnance, then it comes to something like this: Schweiger and Anna (and of course the immediate group around them: the terrible Strohschneider, the Professor, the Lecturer) are not people. (Only the peripheral group, the Curate, the Social Democrats, possess some semblance of life.) In order to make this bearable, they must invent a legend to transfigure their hellishness, the psychiatric history. But in view of their nature they can only invent something as inhuman as they are themselves, and so the horror is redoubled. But it is multiplied tenfold by the pretence of innocence and straightforwardness of the whole.

What was I to say to Werfel, whom I admire, whom I even admire in this play, although in this case only for his having the strength to wade through these three acts of mud? Moreover my feeling about the play is so personal that perhaps all this applies only to me. And he comes to see me in charming friendliness, and I must greet him, when he comes once in years, with such undigested, indigestible criticisms. But I could not do otherwise and babbled away, getting a little of my disgust off my chest. But I suffered from the consequences the whole evening and all night. In addition I may have insulted Pick, since I was so agitated that I hardly paid attention to him (though it was only after Pick left that I talked about the play).

My health is better.

All good wishes in life and on the stage.

F.

To Franz Werfel (probably not sent)

[Prague, December 1922]

Dear Werfel, After the way I behaved at your last visit, you could not come again. I realized that. And I would surely have written to you before this were it not that letter-writing has gradually become as hard for me as talking, and that even mailing letters is troublesome, for I already had a letter all written for you.[87] But it is useless to go over old things. Where would it end, if one were never to stop defending all one's old wretched mistakes and apologizing for them. So let me only say this, Werfel, which you yourself must know: If what was involved here was only an ordinary dislike, then it might possibly have been easier to formulate and moreover might have been so unimportant that I might well have been able to keep it to myself. But it was a horror, and justifying that is difficult: One seems stubborn and tough and cross-grained, where one is only unhappy. You are surely one of the leaders of this generation, which is not meant as flattery and cannot serve as flattery of anyone, for many a man can lead this society, so lost in its bogs. Hence you are not only a leader but something more (you yourself have said something similar in the fine introduction to Brand's posthumous works,[88] fine right down to the phrase "joyous will to deception") and one follows your course with burning suspense. And now this play. It may have every possible merit, from the theatrical to the highest, but it is a retreat from leadership; there is not even leadership there, rather a betrayal of the generation, a glossing over, a trivializing, and therefore a cheapening of their sufferings.

But now I am prattling on, as I did before, am incapable of thinking out and expressing the crux of the matter. Let it be so. Were it not that my sympathy with you, my deeply selfish sympathy with you, is so great, I would not even be prattling.

And now the invitation; in written form, it assumes an even realer and more magnificent appearance. Obstacles are my illness, the doctor (he definitely rules out Semmering once again, though he is not so definite about Venice in the early spring), and I suppose money too (I would have to manage on a thousand crowns a month). But these are not the chief obstacles. Between lying stretched out on my Prague bed and strolling erect in the Piazza San Marco, the distance is so great that only imagination can barely span it. But these are only generalizations. Beyond that, to imagine that for example I might go to dinner with other people in Venice (I can only eat alone)—even the imagination is staggered. But nonetheless I cling to the invitation, and thank you for it many times.

Perhaps I will see you in January. Be well.

Yours, Kafka

To Max Brod

[Probably December 1922]

Dear Max, I can't come. The last two evenings I had some slight fever (100). By day it was much lower or even normal, but even so I do not dare go out.

Much luck with the battles of Berlin and otherwise, too. Cordial regards to the traveler, whose recitations I have not yet been able to hear.

Yours, F.

Please don't buy the Goethe for me. 1. I have no money, need all I have and more for the doctor. 2. Have no room for books. 3. Still have five odd volumes of Goethe.

To Max Brod

[Probably 1922]

Dear Max, I'm not coming. I have to eat at seven o'clock, otherwise I don't sleep at all. The threat of injections is highly effective. Besides this, just today, as every day, I have to get something done, which is not easy. Sometimes it's as though I were a gladiator in training. He doesn't know what they have in store for him, but to judge by the training he is being put through, it may be a great battle with all of Rome looking on.

To Max Brod

[Probably 1922]

Dear Max, Don't come. I have some fever and am in bed. I have not informed Dr. Thieberger.[89] Couldn't you do it, should you think it necessary? I am herewith sending you two issues of *Česká Stráž* and one of *Česká Svoboda*. The *Svoboda* has a different view of the question of the name, in fact two different views (see the note and the poem).

Warm regards, yours, Franz

To Max Brod

[Probably 1922]

Dear Max, Please, lest there by any mistake: It occurs to me that I might have said that our Fräulein wanted only to go to a matinee performance. That is not so. Evening tickets would also be welcome, in fact, if possible even more welcome.

F

To Minze Eisner

[Prague, winter 1922–23]

Dear Minze, Only today, I can hardly believe it, I am sending you thanks for the flowers which gave me so much pleasure, brightening the house, bringing me a bit of Kassel. But these have been deeply perturbed days. My mother suddenly learned that she had to have a very urgent and grave operation. Now the operation, though it remains just as urgent, has had to be canceled due to other complications connected with the main trouble, and is being postponed from day to day, with various extremely painful expedients. How dreadful is medicine, dreadful invention of dreadful people.

I will write again when it is over; do send me your address, or is Wilhelmshöhe near Kassel enough?

Good wishes, yours, Kafka

Even these few lines have lain about unmailed and will probably reach Teplitz too late. The operation, an unusually critical one, took place yesterday.

1923

To Oskar Baum

[Prague, mid-January 1923]

Dear Ones, My congratulations. Wicked ones, why didn't you inform me in time. I see Max and Felix only infrequently so that I learned of the ceremony[1] only a few days ago and by accident. But I thought it was set for the 16th. Only yesterday I learned—and should have known all my life (in this matter too I was not informed in time, but you are not to blame for that)—that the ceremony can only take place on a Saturday. But yesterday I was shivering so that I could not go out and get better information, and so the affair took place without me and even the books are chosen indiscriminately and by chance. Only my inner participation in a ceremony whose true importance goes far beyond all my conceptions remains, apart from date and preparations.

Be well. Perhaps I may finally pay you a visit.

F

If Leo doesn't care for any of the books or already knows them, he can exchange them at Calve's. There are other very good volumes in the same series, for example deep-sea explorations, Darwin, Sven Hedin, Nansen. Or perhaps he would like something from a similar line published by Brockhaus,[2] and also available at Calve's Bookshop.

To Minze Eisner

[Prague, January/February 1923]

Dear Minze,

My last letter most probably did not reach you in Teplitz. It concerned my mother's serious operation. The operation is now over and my mother seems to be recovering, slowly, very slowly.

This and other matters kept me from writing to you sooner, and in the interval you find youself in your wintry garden. How could I not know, Minze, that things are difficult. It is a totally hopeless Jewish undertaking, but it has, as I see it, something magnificent in its hopelessness. (Perhaps it is really not so hopeless as it appears to me at this moment, after a sleepless night that was unusually harrowing, even for me.) One cannot help imagining a child left to play by itself who undertakes some incredible adventure of climbing up on a chair or something of the sort. But the father whom it has wholly forgotten is looking on after all, and prospects are much brighter than they seem. This father might, for example, be the Jewish people.* By the way, do you know Hebrew or have you at least ever begun learning it? Is your fiancé Jewish? Zionist?

What worries me about the whole undertaking is only the physical fatigue you sometimes mention in your letters. Is it a trace of some kind of illness? Or rather largely a natural tiredness, which finds its end in that wonderful sleep which is denied to me?

When I am in a better mental state, I will write again.

All good wishes, yours, Kafka

* This would also help to explain the persistence, in the face of indifference, which strikes you as so incomprehensible, and which seems to derive from some strength greater than their own.

To Minze Eisner

[Prague, March 1923]

Dear Minze,

A beautiful great surpassingly great surprise and yet the most natural, most sensible, most logical thing in the world. The many questions that spring to mind in the face of this surprise cannot be written down. I will be very glad to see you in Prague. Give your fiancé my regards and remain joyous and strong in the great mutation.

Yours, K

To Robert Klopstock

[Postcard. Prague, mid-April 1923]
Dear Robert, I must have misunderstood you. I have been expecting you
back for several days and did not write mostly for that reason. Didn't you say
you would surely be here for the Pallenberg performance on the 12th? And
now the performances have been postponed, will be given Wednesday,
Thursday, and Friday, you will still not be in Prague and I will not, as I had
hoped, be able to go to the standing-room section with you to protect me.
Still, of course, it is a very good thing that you have stayed longer; the
difference between the two letters makes that plain. You did not notify
people and then were in despair because their doors were not immediately
thrown open to you. The big event is the arrival of Bergmann;[3] he is staying
a month; you will see him; it is exciting and tempting to be with him. The
expected Hebrew letter has not come; that was another reason for my not
writing.—Everyone to whom you sent greetings sends greetings to you; when
I mentioned the greetings Věra wanted to come to my room because she
doesn't yet understand that people can greet each other by mail and thought
you were with me.—The package has come. Thanks.

To Oskar Baum

June 12, 1923
Dear Oskar, In case I should not be able to come in the next few days—which
is likely, given the state of my head—here is the translation of the letter:
"Address: The Workers Bank Ltd., P.O.B. 27, Jaffa–Tel Aviv. Reference
number: 2485. Dr. Bergmann wrote us that E.W. has promised to take steps
concerning the shares of the Workers Bank and to sell shares among your
acquaintances. We wish herewith to remind you of your promise and to
inquire whether you need information or promotional material which we can
supply. We shall make a point of immediately sending everything you wish,
and will endeavor to do all we can here to support your work, if you will
only inform us whether you need our support. We await your reply. Yours
very truly—"

I shall hold on to the letter for a few days, for propaganda purposes. The
type of paper will make a strong impression on one of my brothers-in-law
(who is against Palestine).[4] I shall see what this letter can do.

Cordial regards, yours, F

To Oskar Baum

[Summer 1923]

Dear Oskar, I read it through the same evening, with terror, terror-stricken by that steely animal looks and by the way it creeps closer on the sofa.[5] I suppose such things occur to all of us, but who can do it as you do? I ineffectually tried it too,[6] years ago, but instead of groping my way to the desk I preferred to crawl under the sofa, where I can still be found. What is comforting in your story is the second gentle puzzle, which attempts reconciliation. To be sure, it is too weak for that; it holds out no hope, but only the prospect of the loss of hope. In human terms it is slight, also too unreal, but otherwise it seems to me very lovely, this gentle framing of the consuming fire.

I felt the beginning was a little too busy with externalities, too much hotel and detective stuff. But it's hard to say whether it should be different; perhaps that is just what is needed. At any rate it is excellent that they pass by his room so that the wildness in there can rage itself out in peace and quiet. I would probably have neither felt nor noticed this criticism did I not suspect you of a fondness for such beginnings, and have questioned whether it was necessary only because of this suspicion, not for any other reason.

Many thanks.

Yours, F

To Max Brod

[Postcard. Müritz on the Baltic;[7] postmark: July 10, 1923]

She[8] is charming. And so entirely centered on you. Whatever came up, she made it a pretext to refer to you. A train bound for the Baltic—perhaps you're on it. She was in such-and-such a place with you. It took a little while before I understood why she was having me describe the Hradčany. She often came up with remarks like: "It's strange how we take over the views of a beloved person, even when they are opposed to the ones we used to have." A truly vital originality, straightness, seriousness, a dear and childlike seriousness. I went along with her to Pua's[9] Jewish children's camp in Eberswalde, but Emmy's household god won out and we came no farther than Bernau.[10] There a stork's nest gave her the greatest joy; she spotted it with unbelievable swiftness. She was very nice to me.—Here I am tolerably well, as is always the

case during the first few days. A camp run by the Jewish People's Home[11]:
The healthy, cheerful, blue-eyed children give me great pleasure.
  Warm regards to you and your wife.

Franz

To Robert Klopstock

[Postcard. Müritz; postmark: July 13, 1923]

Dear Robert, Survived the trip and Berlin with some effort, but any effort
that lets us escape the ghosts for a moment is sweet; we literally see ourselves
vanishing around the corner and them standing there in perplexity. Not for
long, though; the hounds seem to have picked up the scent already.—During
the first few days the sea made me very happy. I am learning far less Hebrew
than in Prague. However, there's a camp affiliated with the Berlin Jewish
People's Home here, with many Hebrew-speaking, healthy, and cheerful
children. It is a substitute for Pua's camp, which I wasn't able to reach. I did
not know that Eberswalde is almost two hours from Berlin, so it was not
until afternoon that I set out (not alone) and bogged down in Bernau,
halfway there, from where I wrote to Pua. I was in Berlin only one day, tired
and a little feverish.

Cordial regards, F.

Regards to our friends and acquaintances.

To Kurt Wolff Verlag

[Postcard. Müritz; postmark: July 13, 1923]

To Kurt Wolff Verlag,
  I did not receive the inquiry of the 12th of last month to which you refer,
apparently because, like your last card, it was still addressed to Poříč 7,
although I have asked you many times not to write to that address but only
to *Altstädter Ring 6/III, Prague.* "A Hunger Artist" was published last year in
the October or November issue of the *Neue Rundschau.*[12]

Very truly yours, Dr. Kafka

To Hugo Bergmann

[Müritz, July 1923]

Dear Hugo,
  Many thanks for your greetings and good wishes. This was the first letter
in Hebrew I have received from Palestine. Perhaps the wishes expressed in it

have great force. To test my transportability, after many years of lying abed and of headaches, I pulled myself together for a short trip to the Baltic Sea. At any rate I had one piece of good fortune in connection with it: fifty steps from my balcony is a vacation camp run by the Jewish People's Home of Berlin. Through the trees I can see the children playing. Cheerful, healthy, spirited children. East European Jews whom West European Jews are rescuing from the dangers of Berlin. Half the days and nights the house, the woods, and the beach are filled with singing. I am not happy when I'm among them, but on the threshold of happiness.

All the best to you, yours, Franz

Give my regards to your brave mother and the children.

To Else Bergmann[13]

[Müritz, July 13, 1923]

Dear Frau Else, Well, I have managed to survive the short test run for the greater journey,[14] neither very badly nor very gloriously, though like a test run less for the greater than for the great journey.—Couldn't you leave your garden for a while and come to the sea somewhere? The sea has truly become more beautiful in the ten years since I last saw it, more varied, livelier, younger. But I find more pleasure in a vacation camp of the Berlin Jewish People's Home, healthy, cheerful children from whom I draw warmth. Today I shall celebrate Friday evening with them, for the first time in my life, I think.

Keep well and greet your little one for me.

Yours, K.

To Else Bergmann

[Müritz, July 1923]

Dear, dear Frau Else,

My letter has been delayed, and not only because of the difficulty of finding out the postal rate, which changes every few days.[15] I know that now I shall certainly not sail—how could I sail—but that along with your letter the ship virtually docks at the threshold of my room and that you are standing there asking me, and asking me as you do, which is no small thing. Anyhow you yourself—so incomprehensibly concerned with so odd a matter—partly provide the answer to your own question. Even assuming that I could carry out anything of the sort, it would not have turned out to be a real voyage to Palestine at this time, not at all. At the moment I cannot tell you what it would have become, for your registered letter about that silly, silly matter has just arrived. First: Had I known that the book had any value for you at all, it would not have occurred to me to write about it and I would have been simply proud and happy that it was sailing to Palestine with you. Secondly: The book would not have occurred to me at all had I not heard it mentioned here, where there is something of a gardening atmosphere, with special praise. Thirdly: However my mother handled the matter—unfortunately not at all as I would have liked her to—whatever was bad about it was certainly not directed against you personally, please believe that, but against the "Palestine danger." And with that let us leave this subject, though not before I ask you, when you are using the book, to please notice how joyfully it is serving you in the name of its former owner, in spite of your having truly and veritably purchased it from him.

Now back to where I was: It would not have been a voyage to Palestine, but in the spiritual sense something like a voyage to America by a cashier who has embezzled a large sum of money. And that the voyage would have been undertaken with you would have greatly increased the spiritual criminality of the case. No, I could not go that way, even if I had been able—I repeat. "And all the berths are already taken," you add. And once again the temptation beckons, and again the absolute impossibility answers. That is how it is, and what a pity, but in the final analysis nevertheless quite right. The hope persists for later, and you are kind and do not dash it.

Keep well, and think kindly of me.

Yours, K.

To Robert Klopstock

[Postcard. Müritz; postmark: July 24, 1923]
Robert, what is the matter now? Yesterday the package arrived (how did that old batch from Pua fall into your hands?) and the notebook (I was just considering whether to buy myself one), but no news. Is the heavy atmosphere of the Tatra as oppressive as it used to be? Is it impossible to study Hebrew there? I believe in the power of places, or rather in the powerlessness of people. I don't really have anything to tell, but a great deal to show, much experience to share. With this in view I recently brought you here in a dream. The camp, the camp, these young people. How you exaggerate the value of Prague for you, Robert, and the value of individuals you know there. One must live differently from the way we do there. You must arrange your life differently in the coming year, perhaps leave Prague, go to the dirty Jewish streets of Berlin, for instance.—As for me, none of this means that I can

sleep. Last night was horrible. Only occasionally a little somnolence blows my way from the dormitory of the children's camp.

Yours, F

Regards to Glauber and the others.

To Robert Klopstock

[Picture postcard. Müritz; postmark: August 2, 1923]
Dear Robert, I will be writing you tomorrow, today I am only sending Pua's temporary address, which may be changing as early as tomorrow: Jewish People's Home, Müritz.

All the best, F

[ADDED IN HEBREW: GREETINGS AND SIGNATURE: PUA]

To Tile Rössler[16]

[Müritz; postmark: August 3, 1923]
My dear Tile, The mail has mixed up your letters; the second came at noon, the first after it, in the evening; I received the evening letter at the beach. Dora[17] was with me; we had just read a little Hebrew. It was the first sunny afternoon for a long time, and probably for a long time to come. The children were making a racket. I couldn't retreat to my beach chair because my brother-in-law was there treating a toe he'd injured playing soccer, so I stood and read your letter while Felix threw stones over me, around me, and through me, trying to hit a stake that stood behind me. And yet I had quiet enough to read your letter, to be glad that you long for us, but also glad that by leaving you have not, at least as I feel at the moment, lost nearly so much as you think. I don't like it here as well as I did at first; I don't know exactly whether my fatigue, sleeplessness, and headaches are to blame, but why did all these things bother me so much less at the beginning? Perhaps I'm not allowed to remain too long in one place; there are people who can acquire a sense of home only when they are traveling. Outwardly everything is just as it was; all the people in the Home are very dear to me, much dearer than I am able to indicate. Dora, especially, with whom I spend most of my time, is a wonderful person. But the Home as such no longer seems so clear to me; one visible little thing has somewhat spoiled it in my eyes, other invisible little things are at work to spoil it still more. As a guest, a stranger, and moreover a tired guest, I am in no position to speak out, to clarify the situation, and so I

am defecting. Up to now I have been there every evening, but today, though it is Friday evening, I'm afraid I will not go.

The upshot is that I am not so regretful that my sister will not be staying until the 10th (her husband has come to fetch her) but will leave a few days earlier, and because it is easier and cheaper, but above all because I don't want to stay on here alone, I shall go with them. If I am not too tired I'll stay a day or two in Berlin and then I'll certainly see you, but even if I don't stay but continue straight on to my parents in Marienbad (then on to Karlsbad[18] for another day where—what a pity—instead of seeing Tile I would only see her boss), we'll see each other soon, for I hope to return to Berlin before long.

I recently had a visitor[19] here, a good friend who lives in Palestine, the one I told you about. She came along at the same time as Frieda Behr, an old friend of hers, and stayed at the Home. The visit was very brief; she stayed barely a day; but her self-confidence, her calm cheerfulness, remained behind with me as a lasting encouragement. You must meet her in Berlin some time.

It is charming the way you write Schaale with double a, the way Frage is written in Yiddish, I think. Yes, the Schale [bowl] is also intended to be a Frage [question] addressed to you, to wit: "Say, Tile, when will you get around to smashing me?"

And the vase you gave me is often the cause of a struggle I have with Christl, the three-year-old daughter of our landlord, one of those blonde little white-skinned, red-cheeked flowers that grow in all the houses around here. Whenever she comes to see me she always wants to have the vase. Pretending that she wants to look at a bird's nest on my balcony, she pushes her way into the room, but as soon as she reaches the table she stretches out her hand for the vase. She makes no bones about it, offers no explanations, but merely repeats firmly: The vase! The vase! and insists on her rights, for since the world belongs to her, why shouldn't the vase? And the vase must be afraid of her cruel child's hand, but it need have no fear because I shall always defend it and never give it up.

Please give my regards to all my friends at the Home, especially Bine, to whom I would have written long ago if I did not cherish the ambition to thank her for her fine Hebrew with Hebrew on my part, although not so fine. In my present state of restlessness, I have not found the composure to make such an effort in Hebrew.

All my relatives also send you many regards, expecially the children. When your noon letter came, there was a great quarrel between Felix and Gerti as to who should be allowed to read your letter first. It was hard to decide; in favor of Felix was his age and the fact that he had brought the letter from the letter-carrier. But Gerti could claim that she was a closer friend of yours than Felix. Unfortunately violence decided the matter, and Gerti let her lower lip droop in that splendid way she has.—Have you heard Grieg yet? That is the last clear memory I have of you—the piano being played and you standing there, bowed a little, a little damp from rain, humbling yourself before the music. I hope you'll always be able to stand that way! Keep very well!

Yours, K.

And the voice? The doctor?—My address in Prague, though it will be another two weeks or so before I'll be back there, is Altstädter Ring No. 6, 3rd floor.

To Robert Klopstock

[Müritz, beginning of August 1923]

My dear Robert, On the basis of my own experience, I shall never be able to understand, never manage to understand, that an otherwise cheerful and essentially untroubled person can be destroyed by consumption alone. Couldn't you be mistaken about Glauber? Is he really so far gone as he always maintained, though no one would believe him? And now this rainy summer on top of all else, the tumbledown "Tatra,"[20] the inexorable mountains—it is bad. For him and you.

As far as your illness goes, I am not worried. You are careless about what you eat, careless about catching cold; easy for something to go wrong without its signifying anything.

My head and sleep are bad, especially in recent days; a long time since my head has felt clear. The camp, which at the start gave me nothing but sleep, now takes sleep away from me in equal measure. But it may give it back to me again; it's a living relationship.

We are leaving here Monday[21] morning. Of course I could stay on, were I able to stay alone. In this sense I could not subsist on the camp alone, for I am only a guest there. And not even clearly a guest, which pains me; not clearly because a personal relationship cuts across the general relationship.

But whatever disturbing details it may have provided and even though it could not keep me going, the most important thing in Müritz and beyond Müritz has been the camp.

I shall stay one or two days in Berlin. If I am not too tired I'll risk going to Karlsbad en route from Berlin to Prague, which probably is not very expensive. In my mind the risk is not so great as I make it sound, because I am already used to the idea of going to see my parents in Marienbad, but now it seems that my parents will be returning to Prague sooner because of the bad weather, so that I will no longer find them there. In a certain sense, therefore, it's a smaller risk for me to go by way of Karlsbad than directly to Prague, just as the Czar of Russia, say, was not allowed to change his travel plans at will because only on the prepared route could he be protected from assassination attempts. My style of life is on no less imperial a scale.

And later on, after Prague? I don't know. Would you feel like moving to Berlin? Closer, very close to the Jews?

K

Is there something called an acute apical pulmonary catarrh?

My regards to everyone to whom they are due.

To Max Brod
[Berlin; postmark: August 8, 1923]

Dear Max, It's so long since I have heard anything important from you. I am writing to you from the garden of a Berlin tavern, and now going on with the letter in the hotel, only a few days before seeing you again, because of my need to have some physical connection with you even before I shake your hand. You were very tight-lipped during your Baltic period. I wonder how you are? As for myself: I don't know how I am. At any rate, almost with each passing hour I feel more intensely the evil effect of being alone, although the state of solitude has lasted only a day so far. Yet I am not alone at all. Last night, for example, I went to *The Robbers* with three East European Jewish girls—though I did not notice much more about the performance than my own great fatigue. I'm hardly likely to visit Emmy; I'm too weak. In addition, I don't know exactly what Emmy thinks of me, and in such cases I fear the worst. Then, too, there is the continually menacing Berlin. Day after tomorrow I'll probably come to see you. Regards to your wife and Felix and Oskar, from whom I have heard nothing at all. It now occurs to me that you may be at the Congress[22] and I won't meet you at all. That would be fine for you and sad for me.

F

To Robert Klopstock
[Postcard. Schelesen;[23] postmark: August 27, 1923]

So it is over and done with.[24] What you must have gone through, Robert, and he too. Odd that (of course there is no other comparison) the two most cheerful persons who were in Matlar when we were there should have died first. Anyhow one cannot really deal with such things as long as one is still sitting erect at table and the heart continues to beat at a barely tolerable pace. There is an inhuman but magnificent story about that in the *Maggid*,[25] the story of the vein that only shows when there is fear of death.—I did not go to

Karlsbad, am now with Ottla in Schelesen. Pua's address: Viktoria Heim II, Steinmetzstrasse 16, Berlin W 57.[26] Max is in Prague. I'll write you about Berlin. If only conditions did not keep getting worse there. Keep well, rest up, regards to all.

F

To Max Brod

[Postcard. Schelesen; postmark: August 29, 1923]
Dear Max, I would be very glad to hear a few words about how you are living and working. I read the gloomy note about your return; I hope it does not signify anything general. There isn't much to say about me; I'm trying hard to gain a little weight—when I came here I weighed 54½ kilos, have never weighed so little—but I can scarcely manage it. Too many counterforces. Well, it is a struggle. I like the region very much, and the weather has so far been pleasant, but I must be a very precious possession of those counterforces; they fight like the devil, or are it. Be well, regards to Felix and Oskar.

F

To Max Brod

[Postcard. Schelesen; postmark: September 6, 1923]
Dear Max, I don't believe in ruin. Unfortunately you sometimes have my way of looking at things, but fortunately never lose your decidedness. Why ruin? Are the strongest human relations so dependent on outward matters? If E. were now temporarily, in these worst of times, to take a job as nursemaid, say, that would be regrettable, of course, but would it be ruin? When you speak of rage, that's the kind of talk that suits neither you nor your cause. It is foolish of me to speak of things you are more positive about than I am, but I am really stupid and uncertain inside my head and therefore take pleasure in being able to offer such positive statements as these: Rage is something a child has when his house of cards collapses because a grown-up has shaken the table. But the house of cards didn't collapse because the table was shaken, but because it was a house of cards. A real house doesn't collapse even if the table is chopped into firewood; it doesn't need a foundation from somewhere outside. These are clear, remote, and glorious matters.—I sent two cards to E. and I will be with you next Friday[27] morning. When are you leaving for Berlin? How much does the trip cost now? Regards to Felix and Oskar, please.

To Carl Seelig[28]

Dear Sir,

I am in the country for a few days; your letter was forwarded to me. Many thanks for your kind invitation. Unfortunately, I cannot at this time take part in the series of books you are publishing. The writings I have on hand from an earlier period are altogether useless; I cannot show them to anybody. Recently, moreover, I have been propelled far away from writing. But will you please allow me to get in touch with you sometime in the future.

I well remember your letter of two years ago; please forgive this old debt. I was so ill at the time that I could not even reply.

I can no more fulfill your second request than your first; both are in fact linked, and not just superficially. To respond to either would call for a certain ability to assume responsibility, and at the moment that is beyond me. Moreover, I am sure I would only mention the names of writers well known to you.

That is a meager harvest as the reward for your charming letter, isn't it? The blame is mine and not the letter's.

With cordial regards, sincerely yours, Franz Kafka

To Robert Klopstock

[Postcard. Schelesen; postmark: September 13, 1923]

Dear Robert, Can it really be that they won't give you students' dining privileges? That would surely be bad; we shall have to arrange something. At any rate I'll talk to Max about it. Did the Karinthy[29] story appear in the *Tagblatt* at the time it happened?—It was only in the first intoxication of being at the Home that I thought you should go to Berlin this very semester; under present circumstances it would be too difficult. But you must keep that in mind for later; you should not go on leading this isolated life in Prague. A little literature in the coffeehouse, a little arguing with roommates, a bitter mixture of sorrow and hope between the two of us, the relationship to Max— all that is too little, or if not too little, not good nourishment. Of course it may be that to me as a native of Prague everything may seem much drearier than it is in reality. But even with this amendment it remains dreary, compared with the prospect I had a view of in the Home. In any case Palestine would have been beyond me; in view of the possibilities in Berlin it would not even be urgent. Though Berlin, too, is almost beyond me. (My temperature has gone up, and there are other problems.) And the danger remains that the voyage to Palestine will shrink to a trip to Schelesen. May it at least remain that, rather than end up as the elevator trip from the Altstädter Ring to my room. But my mother is in Paris.[30]

F

To Max Brod
                    [Postcard. Schelesen; postmark: September 13, 1923]
Dear Max, I shall probably not be coming Friday; I wanted to come for Father's birthday, but it is too lovely, the weather I mean, not my rising temperatures, and so I am staying. A pity that I did not have the *Abendblatt* sent directly here; as things stand I receive it very belatedly and incompletely. It was especially fine to see Borchardt[31] under your protection, and how powerful this protection was. Keep well.

F.

Klopstock writes: Now I am receiving the *Abendblatt* again and have been waiting as eagerly for the newspaper, for Max's articles, as for a meeting with a very dear and good friend whom I have not seen for a long time.

To Max Brod
                    [Postcard. Schelesen; postmark: September 14, 1923]
Dearest Max, "That outward matters do not influence human relationships"—I really did not mean anything so sweeping, although ordinarily I take pleasure in exploring my inner contradiction. But this time I was not speaking merely of human relations, but of the strongest, and not of the strongest outward matters, such as pain and torture, but only of the fall of the mark, and not of just anybody, but of you. Nor was it a question of "influence," but a question of "ruin." Please, Max, let that all stand and don't be angry with me. As for myself: My weight is up a little, scarcely noticeable outwardly; but that is offset by some greater defect every day. There's a trickling in the walls, as Kraus says. Only yesterday an old man paused in front of me and said: "You're not feeling so bouncy, huh?" Naturally we then came around to talking about Jews; he's a gardener in a Jewish villa, good people as far as that goes, but timid like all Jews. Timidity is their nature. Then he went back into the woods to fill a second basket strapped to his back with a vast amount of dry wood, and I began counting my pulse, far above 110.
   Luck with your work.

F.

To Robert Klopstock
[Postcard. Prague; postmark: September 23, 1923]
Dear Robert, I couldn't keep it up any longer; I'm leaving tomorrow—unless in the next twelve hours some great obstacle is thrown at me from a dark ambush—for Berlin, but only for a few days; probably I'll be back here when you come. I was able to have only a brief talk with Max; he left for Berlin today, Saturday; possibly I'll see him there. I just recall that I have been asked by two magazines—*Vers und Prosa*, Rowohlt Verlag, edited by Hessel, and *Ha-Ohel: Das Zelt*, Christinengasse 4, Vienna I, edited by Höflich[32]—to recommend promising young writers to them. Would you feel inclined? Keep well. Naturally I'm a bit keyed up.

F

To Robert Klopstock
[Postcard. Miquelstrasse 8, Berlin-Steglitz;[33]
postmark: September 26, 1923]
Dear Robert, So here I am. Of course there's nothing definite to be said as yet. I've spoken with Max here. There's nothing at the *Abendblatt;* four Hungarian editors are sitting around doing nothing in the press department. On the other hand—and basically that would be much more to the point—Max is prepared to and certainly able to get you free dining privileges at the students' dining hall; he will do so very gladly. Go to him promptly after your arrival. Do you know, by the way, that Münzer is gravely ill? Intestinal cancer. At least so my mother told me.

When conditions here, my personal ones, I mean, have clarified, I'll write in more detail or, more probably, tell you face to face. You have my card from Prague, don't you?

To Oskar Baum
[Postcard. Berlin-Steglitz; postmark: September 26, 1923]
Dear Oskar, I was in Prague for a day and a half and did not come to you, in spite of my great longing to see all of you at last. But how could I have come, faced with the foolhardy prospect of going to Berlin for a few days.[34] Within the limits of my condition that is a foolhardiness whose parallel you can only find by leafing back through the pages of history, say to Napoleon's march to Russia. Outwardly, and for the present, it is going tolerably well, as it did back then, by the way. Is there any chance of your coming to Berlin in the near future? (The play about the sculptor!) Or will your courses hold you—of

which I know nothing as yet, whether one should be sad about them or take them as routine.

Cordial regards to you and yours, F

If there is anything I can do for you in Berlin—

To Max Brod

[Postcard. Berlin-Steglitz; postmark: September 28, 1923]
Dear Max, Yesterday, Thursday, she[35] came to see me; it was my first social occasion, the "housewarming," and so several serious slips were made, which moreover I will not know how to make amends for next time either. It is true that she sweetly and delicately overlooked them, but you might casually smooth that over, if you have the opportunity. First I simply invited her by telephone to come at five, an act of uncouthness that unfortunately became even more uncouth because I could understand almost nothing over the telephone but her laughter. In addition I might possibly have done better in spite of my general state of weakness had I known that it is permissible to go to her boardinghouse. I thought that was forbidden; in July it certainly seemed that way. Furthermore she brought some flowers; I had none. Furthermore, but perhaps that was no mistake, Dora was there; she was indispensable for the occasion. But the worst of it, I must say, was that when she arrived I was asleep, for once uniquely asleep. But otherwise it went off fairly well, I think; she seems a little restless, nervous, almost overworked, but brave and terribly full of yearning. We discussed the possibility of attending the Jewish Harvest Festival[36] on Sunday, as risky a venture for her as for me. I probably won't do it.

All the best, F

To Max Brod

[Postcard. Berlin-Steglitz; postmark: October 2, 1923]
Dear Max, At the moment I am waiting for Emmy; we want to take a little morning walk in this lovely neighborhood. I went to see her Sunday afternoon, again made several serious mistakes, and am already ashamed of constantly repeating the same thing. The principal reason is that when I get out down there, at the Zoo,[37] say, I have trouble with my breathing, start to cough, become more anxious than I ordinarily am, see all the dangers of this city uniting against me. Out here I am also trying to guard myself from the real agony of the prices; in that regard I receive a great deal here, but in the city that help fails. Yesterday, for example, I had a severe fit of numerical

obsessions, and I now understand your anxieties much better, you with your poor dear indefatigable, unshakable head. My room, whose rent used to be 28 crowns a month, cost over 70 crowns in September; in October it will cost at least 180 crowns. I understand quite well that E. needs bucking up, but in her room she seemed to me more courageous, more vigorous and, stooped over your "last rose," happy.—By the way she is not coming today, telephoned to cancel our appointment, will come tomorrow, is very sweet.—Meanwhile, I have looked through the *Steglitzer Anzeiger*,[38] which up to now I have been avoiding for days. Bad, bad. But there is a certain justice in being associated with the fate of Germany, like you and me.

F

By the way, you unfortunately did not have a reassuring effect upon my mother.

To Max Brod

[Postcard. Berlin-Steglitz; postmark: October 8, 1923]
Dear Max, I have not seen Emmy for several days. One day we spent a very friendly time together in the botanical gardens; again my impression of her fortitude outweighed my sense of her nervousness. Since then the weather has been worse; Steglitz is no longer inviting for walks, and I am again afraid of the city. Yesterday, Sunday, E. was slightly unwell, as I was informed by telephone. Incidentally, I myself was not quite well at the same time; a cough, harmless in quality, irritating in quantity, cost me a whole night. I stayed in bed Sunday and it is over now. Perhaps I'll hear something about E. today.—I don't have anything to tell you yet about my schedule; imperceptibly, inactively, my days fly by. Not like Dr. Weiss, with whom I talked for the first time yesterday; he came to see me. Active, nervous, the strong person's nervousness, with a kind of bitter gaiety, even successful (opening of the Actors' Theater season with Elisabeth Bergner as Tanya).[39] I also encouraged him, by the bye, in the idea that his *Nahar*[40] might have its turn in your cycle of Prague reviews; he doesn't believe it will happen.—Klopstock is in a very bad way, I think, imagines he "has gone to the dogs" and therefore doesn't dare call on you, "but his articles continue to inspire me with delight, and the ever-increasing respect with which I read his things even restores to me a part of my vanishing dignity."

Warmest wishes, F

Regards to Felix and Oskar.

To Carl Seelig

[Berlin-Steglitz, autumn 1923]

Dear Sir,

After all I can now present something that might give you pleasure. I am sure you know the name of Ernst Weiss and probably something about his recent, to my mind often incredibly powerful though also none too accessible books (*Animals in Chains, Nahar, Star of Demons, Atua*).[41] In addition to this fictional work he has a collection of essays which he would like to publish under the title *Credo Quia Absurdum*. To my mind these essays display all the virtues of his fictional works, without being as hermetic as they are.

I am enclosing as a sample the essays "Goethe as Perfection" and the title essay "Credo Quia Absurdum"; in addition, to give you an idea of his present work, the first chapter of a novel, *Daniel*.

The titles of some of the pieces for the book of essays might be:

> Mozart, an Oriental Master
> Calmness in Art: Contemporaneity
> The Life of Rubens
> Daumier
> A Word on Macbeth
> The Genius of Grammar
> Rousseau
> The Modern Novel
> Cervantes
> On Language
> Peace, Education, Politics

Please let me know what you think about the publication of such a book,[42] or even better let him know directly (Dr. Ernst Weiss, Nollendorfstrasse 22a, Berlin W 30). In any case may I ask that the three enclosures, which he urgently needs, be returned.

With my best regards, sincerely yours, Franz Kafka

To Felix Weltsch

[Postcard. Berlin-Steglitz; postmark: October 9, 1923]

Dear Felix, Many thanks for the *Selbstwehr*. I have after all stayed longer than I thought and would not like to have missed it. I've not been to see Lise[43] yet; the days are so short, pass for me even faster than in Prague, and happily much less noticeably. Of course it is a pity that they pass so swiftly, but that is the way time is; once you've taken your hand off its wheel it starts to spin and you no longer see a place for your hand to check it. I scarcely go beyond the immediate vicinity of the apartment, but this neighborhood is wonderful; my street is about the last half-urban one. Beyond it the countryside breaks up into gardens and villas, old, lush gardens. On warm evenings there is a strong fragrance, stronger almost than anything I have encountered elsewhere. Then in addition there are the great botanical gardens, a fifteen-minute walk from where I am, and the woods, where I have not yet been, are less than half an hour. So the setting for this little emigrant is beautiful.—Another request, Felix: If you can, do something for poor Klopstock (like finding a job for him).

> Cordial regards to you and yours, F

To Max Brod

[Postcard. Berlin-Steglitz; postmarked on arrival: October 16, 1923] Dear Max, Emmy has probably already told you that I don't want to return to Prague, not now, perhaps in two months. Your fears are unfounded; I am not reading the newspapers, have so far not personally suffered from the evil consequences of the times; as far as meals go I am living exactly, but exactly, the way I did in Prague; in bad weather I stay in my room; the cough that I casually mentioned has not come back. What is worse is that in the last few days the phantoms of the night have tracked me down, but that too is no reason for returning. If I'm to fall prey to them, I'd rather it were here than there; but we haven't reached that point. Besides I shall be seeing you soon. Would you be so kind as to bring me a suitcase with winter clothes. It would go along with your own baggage; here you would simply turn the claim check over to the baggage-delivery service. You would have some bother with it in Bodenbach,[44] though. Would you do that? I have seen E. several times. She seemed to me more cheerful again, and stronger, especially after she had telephoned to Prague.

> Yours, F

Three essays, which E. turned over to me, have given me great pleasure.

To Robert Klopstock

[Postcard. Berlin-Steglitz; postmark: October 16, 1923] Dear Robert, Frýdek,[45] a good solution; I'm very glad that you have found it. When is the examination to be?—As for my needless anxieties: If it proves at all possible, I shall be very glad to spend the winter here. If my case were altogether new in history, the anxiety would be justified, but there are precedents. Columbus, too, for instance, did not turn his ships around after a few days.—As far as my eating is concerned, I do not eat in company, so am exposed only to inner embarrassment. Incidentally, life here in Steglitz is peaceful, the children look well, the begging is not frightening, the basis from earlier, prosperous times is still splendid and shaming in the contrary sense. I do keep out of the inner city, though, have been there only three times; my Potsdamer Platz is the square outside the Steglitz Town Hall. Even that is too noisy for me; happily I then duck into the wonderfully quiet tree-lined avenues.

All the best, F

I have written to Max and Felix; go to see them.

To Max Brod

[Berlin-Steglitz; postmarked on arrival: October 25, 1923]
Dear Max, It is true that I am not writing to you, but not because I have anything to conceal (except to the extent that concealment has been my life's vocation), nor because I would not long for an intimate hour with you, the kind of hour we have not had, it sometimes seems to me, since we were together at the north Italian lakes. (There is a certain point in my saying this, because at the time we had truly innocent innocence—perhaps that's not worth regretting—and the evil powers, whether on good or bad assignments, were only lightly fingering the entrances through which they were going to penetrate someday, an event to which they were already looking forward with unbearable rejoicing.) So if I do not write, that is due chiefly to "strategic" reasons such as have become dominant for me in recent years. I do not trust words and letters, my words and letters; I want to share my heart with people but not with phantoms that play with the words and read the letters with slavering tongue. Especially I do not trust letters, and it is a strange belief that all one has to do is seal the envelope in order to have the letter reach the addressee safely. In this respect, by the way, the censorship of mail during the war years, years of particular boldness and ironic frankness on the part of the phantoms, has proved instructive.

I forgot to add to my remark above: It sometimes seems to me that the nature of art in general, the existence of art, is explicable solely in terms of such "strategic considerations," of making possible the exchange of truthful words from person to person.—But I am writing so little because, as is only natural, I am continuing my Prague life, my Prague "work,"[46] of which there was also very little to say. You must also consider that I am living a half-rural life here, under neither the cruel nor the pedagogical pressure of real Berlin. That is also pampering. I was with you once at Josty's, once with Emmy, once with Pua, once at Wertheim's[47] to have my photograph taken, once to fetch money, once to look at an apartment—those are definitely all my expeditions to Berlin in these four weeks, and I returned from almost all of them feeling miserable and profoundly grateful to be living in Steglitz. My "Potsdamer Platz" is the Steglitz Town Hall square; two or three streetcars pass through it, there is also a small amount of traffic, Ullstein, Mosse, and Scherl[48] have branches there, and from the front pages of the newspapers on display there I absorb the poison that I can just manage to bear, sometimes momentarily cannot bear (just now there is talk in the anteroom about street battles). But then I leave this public place and lose myself, if I still have the strength, in the quiet autumnal avenues. My street is the last relatively urban one; then everything dissolves in the peace of gardens and villas; every street is a peaceful garden walk or can be one.

My day is also very short, you know. I get up around nine, but lie down a great deal, especially afternoons; I badly need that. I read a little Hebrew, chiefly a novel by Brenner,[49] but it is getting very hard for me, although in spite of all the difficulty the thirty pages read so far is no achievement I can offer in justification if I am asked to give an accounting for four weeks.

Tuesday. Incidentally, I am not enjoying the book very much as a novel. I have always had a certain awe of Brenner; I don't know exactly why. Imagination and things I have heard were mingled in my feeling about him. There has always been talk of his sadness. And "sadness in Palestine"?——

Let us rather talk about the sadness of Berlin, because it is closer.

The telephone has just interrupted me. Emmy. She had meant to come Sunday; a pity that she did not, for there were other visitors here who would have entertained her, a girl[50] I know from Müritz and a young Berlin painter, two fine young people of captivating charm. I had hoped meeting them would do a great deal for Emmy, who is now so deep in the excitements of the times and in those of love. (Don't imagine, by the way, that I am giving parties; it happened by chance and only once; I'm just as afraid of people as I was in Prague.) But she did not come, had caught cold. Then yesterday we talked on the telephone; she was excited. Berlin excitements. (Fear of a general strike, difficulties in changing money, which however seemed to exist only near the Zoo and perhaps only yesterday. Today, for example, money could be changed at the Friedrichstrasse station and there was not the slightest crowding.) Berlin excitements mingled with

Prague sufferings (I could only say: Max writes something about coming on the ninth), and the Berlin excitements are truly contagious; after the telephone conversation I struggled with them all night. At any rate, she promised to come this evening and I hoped that meanwhile I would have accumulated enough strength to be comforting to her, but now she has telephoned that she cannot come, gives reasons for her agitation. But evidently there is only one reason; the others are assembled around it as mere ornament. That one reason is the date of your trip. She will not accept the wedding as a reason for your postponing it—"let him break others' hearts for a change." I think I have already heard similar remarks in Prague on similar occasions. Poor, dear Max! How fortunate-unfortunate you are! If you think you can give me any advice on what I can usefully say to E., I'll certainly take it; at the moment I myself have no idea. I asked whether I could come to see her tomorrow; she said she didn't know when she would be home (all this in a very friendly and sincere manner), she had a class in the morning, in the afternoon would be seeing a girl friend "who's also crazy" (she'd already told me about her). Finally we agreed to talk on the telephone again tomorrow. That is all, little and much.

Wednesday. Just now, at nine o'clock, I talked with E. again. Things seem much better; the prospect of talking to you on the telephone this evening casts its consolation ahead. Probably she will come this evening. Another telephone talk, another change in plans. E. says she will come by afternoon. I keep thinking how love and music must have exalted but also undermined E., that she who formerly endured a hard life with such exemplary bravery now suffers intensely from superficial matters in a life that is basically much easier, in spite of all the terrors of Berlin. For my part, I understand this very well, much better than she does; but I would not have been able to endure her earlier life.

To come back to your questions: I've already spoken of my limited Hebrew studies. In addition I wanted to attend a famous gardening school in Dahlem,[51] which is barely a quarter-hour from here. But a student there, a Palestinian and acquaintance of D. (Diamant is her name), frightened me off by the information he gave me with intent to encourage me. I am too weak for the practical classes, too distracted for the theoretical instruction; moreover, the days are so short and I cannot go out in bad weather. So I dropped the idea.

I would certainly have gone to Prague, in spite of the expense and the effort, if only to be with you and at last to see Felix and Oskar (in a letter of yours to E. there is a frightful sentence about Oskar; is that remark only the product of a mood or a fact?). But Ottla advised me against it, and finally my mother did too. It's really better that way; I would not yet be a guest there. I hope I can stay away long enough to become one.

Yours, F

Give me some advice about your brother's wedding. Regards to your sister and brother-in-law.

I can very well wait until November for the winter clothes.

What things are you working on? Is the novel[52] at rest?

To Kurt Wolff Verlag
[Postcard. Berlin-Steglitz; received: October 26, 1923]
Dear Sirs,

I have received your royalty statement. Your sending a batch of books would be very welcome indeed. May I have some say in the choice of the books?[53] I am now living temporarily in Berlin (c/o Moritz Hermann, Miquelstrasse 8, Berlin-Steglitz), which would make the matter easier, wouldn't it?

Very truly yours, F. Kafka

To Robert Klopstock
[Postcard. Berlin-Steglitz; postmark: October 25, 1923]
Dear Robert, I hope you are relaxing peacefully among your friends after the feverish pace of Prague. (Max, who saw you once in passing, wrote me that you're not looking bad; I cling to that whenever I think of you.) And perhaps chemistry also leaves some room for Hebrew. I am making very slow progress in the language; the holidays and Schelesen made me forget a great deal, especially how to study regularly and intensely. Now I've been here for a month and have read thirty-two pages of a novel by Brenner, a page every day. The book is entitled *Shekhol ve-Kishalon*—solve that chemical formula. It is difficult for me in every respect, and not very good. Twice Pua helped me with the reading, but now I have not seen her for almost two weeks.—One of the possible undertakings here has failed, though it had hardly reached the point where it could fail. Near me in Dahlem is a famous gardening school that I wanted to enter; information from a Palestinian studying there, who meant to encourage me, frightened me off. I am too weak for practical

gardening work, too distracted for the theoretical side; I shall have to send my distraction in other directions.

The big package of butter arrived in excellent condition. Many thanks. How are your mother and brother?

Regards to Steinberg!

To Max Brod

[Postcard, Berlin-Steglitz; postmark: October 25, 1923]

Dear Max, Only a few words to comment on your card, since meanwhile you will have received my letter. E. came to see me Wednesday afternoon; I actually lured her here with a loaf of bread, which is obtainable in Steglitz but not in Berlin on Tuesdays, not because of any real shortage but for other, mysterious reasons that under present conditions keep changing daily. (Only Tuesdays, by the way. As it turned out, E. didn't keep the bread for herself but made a present of it to her sister.) Well, E. was agitated, which however did not prevent her from being gay and laughing at times. But it would be wrong to attribute this agitation solely to conditions in Berlin. The agitation and the Berlin conditions are connected only to the extent that a one-day shortage of bread or a one-time difficulty in changing money suffices to open the floodgates to all other woes. And these other woes, not the conditions, are hard to deal with. I had feeble excuses for everything, but could find no reply when she said that basically she was willing to forgo everything and would be completely content if only you would come for two days every month. What is there to say about that? Especially when she adds that during the Winkler period, when it was necessary or merely useful or even merely pleasant, you would have come at once at her request, or even in response to a word, a hint, ignoring all such things as weddings. And that after all she asks no more than that you come. Well, there is a good answer to that also, but in this case it isn't suitable.

For the moment, however, all that is no longer acute. After the telephone conversation with you, E. called me up, cheerful, radiating happiness, said all was well and something about being "newborn," but she used a better, stronger expression. I attributed the change chiefly to her having been engaged by the Actors' Theater, and certainly that is a really splendid, liberating thing for her—but after your card I see that shifting her suffering to you also contributed a good deal to her "rebirth." The Prague or Aussig plan[54] seems to me wrong and very dangerous; salvation lies only in work and music, and outward circumstances are so far not nearly as bad as you think; in a general way perhaps yes, but in particulars certainly not. I, for example, have so far been able to live just as I do in Prague, as far as food is concerned. It's true that butter is sent to me, but even that can be had. Just to give you an idea of the prices: on the very day of the telephone conversation I had lunch in town, in a vegetarian restaurant on Friedrichstrasse (ordinarily I always eat at home; this was only my second restaurant meal since I've been here). D. and I. We had spinach with fried egg and potatoes (excellent, made with good butter, in quantity enough to be filling by itself), then vegetable cutlets, then noodles garnished with applesauce and plum compote (the same could be said of this dish as of the spinach), then an extra plum compote, then tomato salad and a roll. The whole thing, with excessive tip, cost about eight crowns. That isn't bad. Perhaps it was an exception, influenced by chance fluctuations in the exchange rate; the rise in prices is really enormous and it's impossible to buy anything aside from food. But as I said, there is plenty of food in Berlin, and it is good. Don't worry about that.

Regards to Felix and Oskar; say a good word to them from me.

Perhaps I'll go to the theater with E. tonight. *An Enemy of the People,* with Klöpfer.[55] So far I have not been away from home a single evening.

To Robert Klopstock
                [Postcard. Berlin-Steglitz; postmark: October 31, 1923]
Dear Robert, Please, do not exaggerate in regard to Berlin. It was monstrous that I came here, but for the time being further monstrosities have not occurred, so there is no point in jinxing it by congratulations. It is not even out of the question that the fantastic inflation will drive me out—not yet, but if prices go on climbing with the same indefatigability. So far things are going well for me; I could not be better cared for than I am.—That you have made a new translation of *Klarissa*[56] has given me a painful turn. It was excellently translated; why do this work over, especially now when I—perhaps it's an illusion, but it is certainly a strong one—have felt in your last letters such a craving to do your own work, and beyond that such strength for it as you never had in the past. It might not be a bad idea if after your doctoral exams you could return to Frýdek, fleeing into silence. Even though, as I have been reading in *Selbstwehr,* just this year an overwhelming abundance of Hebrew affairs is being planned in Prague. Here I have to ride for hours for such things;[57] there I would have them a hundred paces from home, and yet unattainably far.

                                                Yours, F.

To Max Brod
[Postcard. Berlin-Steglitz; postmark: October 31, 1923]
Dearest Max, I won't write you until tomorrow, when I'll know what E. is going to do. Granted, it is a difficult problem, dismayingly difficult, though since both sides are willing to do their utmost, it would seem as if compromise were easily possible. There are a good many sides to this, which I don't entirely understand—such as the argument that coming here once a month would be too expensive. But the two weeks in Bodenbach would surely be much more expensive. At the moment I also do not understand how Bodenbach of all places would be soothing to the nerves. A small, unfamiliar country town in late fall, and to live there alone, without work and acquaintances, dependent on brief visits from Prague, and finally to have to return to Berlin again—assuming that Berlin were the cause of all the suffering. Well, the decision isn't final yet, and I'll write tomorrow.

Yours, F

I hear from Klopstock that he has done a new (!) translation of *Klarissa* and will send it to four agencies.

To Max Brod
[Berlin-Steglitz; postmarked on arrival: November 2, 1923]
Dearest Max, So you are coming, as I heard from E. As I have said in my second letter and in the card, I too regard that as the only proper step. Now there is no need to write about any of that, since we will shortly be seeing each other. Besides, today I am not in full possession of my mental powers; I've poured out too much on a tremendous event: on November 15th I am going to move. A highly advantageous move, so it seems to me. (I am almost afraid to commit this news to paper, my landlady is not to know until November 15th, and here I go writing it down among her furniture which reads it over my shoulders; but then the furniture, at least some pieces of it, is partially on my side.)

As far as the inheritance is concerned, that is really just talk, but apparently wide spread, for Else Bergmann also wrote me about it. The truth is that the gross estate amounts to about 600,000 crowns, to which three uncles[58] have a claim in addition to my mother. Even so, that would still be pretty good, but unfortunately the chief participants are the French and Spanish governments and the notaries and lawyers of Paris and Madrid.

You may be right about her girl friend; once or twice in such spots the girl friend scurried through the conversation. But along with her affection for this girl friend, E. has a very strong dislike for her which has only to be backed up.

In your fears about the future you forget that you will also be paid in stable currency by Wolff, who must truly have made a fantastic amount of money.

Nothing has yet come of my planned visit to the theater with E.; the inflation is really monstrous. I was considering two theaters, the Lessing Theater (*Crime and Crime*, with Kortner, Gerda Müller)[59] and the Schiller Theater (*Enemy of the People*, with Klöpfer); but the former is astronomically priced, the latter sold out for days in advance, and I cannot go in all kinds of weather.

Keep well, and may the Lugano sun shine upon us—innocent or guilty— once again.

F.

To Robert Klopstock

[Berlin-Steglitz, early November 1923][60]

Dear Robert, I received your letter Wednesday morning. If you are to have the story Friday, we shall have to hurry, the post office and I. In any case, it is definitely a pleasure to me to look through your translations; send along whatever you have. The story itself seems to me very good, except that in reading these stories of Karinthy's[61] I usually have an unpleasant aftertaste, as though this particular idea, in itself tolerably good, were always to be the last, as though the poor man were always spending his last penny and showing you, in addition to the coin, his empty pocket. I don't know what causes that impression, since his richness is indubitable.—The translation is very good. Just a few remarks. The title is correct, but wouldn't a simple "Without a Head" or "Headless" be stronger?

6) I would choose *schleppen*; *ziehen* also expresses anguish and is odder; *bewegen* would be without this anguish. The whole passage with *ziehen* and *Spur hinterlassen* reminds me too much of creeping caterpillars.

feinen Zeuges Stoff sounds rather good, but *Zeug* and *Stoff* are the same.

What is this: *Glaubender?*

I've noted my other comments in the text.

I've received the Kraus book;[62] it was kind, dear, and spendthrift of you to have sent it. It's jolly, though only an afterbirth of the *Last Days*.[63] Otherwise I have been reading little, and only Hebrew; no books, no newspapers, no magazines, or rather, yes, *Selbstwehr*. Why don't you send something to

Selbstwehr; the magazine is wide open to you. I should have thought you wanted to be in Prague by November 1. Yes, Vienna is beautiful; after our time in Berlin we'll move to Vienna, won't we?

I associate with very few people, have talked to Dr. Weiss once, haven't seen Pua for five weeks; she has vanished completely, doesn't answer postcards.

The state of my health is bearable.

On November 15 I am moving to a new apartment in the vicinity. I'll send you the address shortly.

Keep well, all the best for your dreams and tasks.

Yours, F

Shekhol ve-Kishalon are two nouns that I too do not fully understand. At any rate they are an attempt to set down the quintessence of misfortune. *Shekhol* means literally childlessness,[64] so perhaps unfruitfulness, fruitlessness, pointless effort; and *kishalon* means literally: stumble, fall.

To Valli Pollak

[Berlin-Steglitz, November 1923]

Dear Valli,

The table stands by the stove; I have just moved away from the fireside because it is too warm there, even for my perpetually cold back. My kerosene lamp burns marvelously, a masterpiece both of lamp-making and of purchasing. It has been assembled by borrowing and buying the separate pieces, though not by me, of course; how would I manage anything of the sort! It's a lamp with a burner as large as a teacup and a construction that makes it possible to light it without removing the chimney and shade. It has, in fact, only one flaw, that it won't burn without kerosene, but then we others are the same. And so I sit and now take up your so very old and dear letter. The clock ticks; I have even grown accustomed to the ticking of the clock, rarely hear it, usually only when I am doing things that merit special approval. This clock has certain personal relations with me, like a good many of the other things in the room. Only now, since I have given notice (or more exactly: since I have been given notice, which is in every respect good and in any case a complicated business that would require pages to describe), the objects have partly begun turning away from me, especially the calendar—I once wrote our parents about its pronouncements. Of late it seems changed, either utterly taciturn—I urgently need its advice, for instance, go to it, but all it says is "Feast of the Reformation,"[65] which probably has its deeper meaning, but who can fathom it? Or else it is sarcastic; recently, for example, something I read gave me an idea that seemed to me very good, or rather significant, so much so that I wanted to ask the calendar about it (it answers only on such odd moments in the course of the day, not when you pedantically tear off the calendar leaf at a particular hour): "Sometimes even a blind chicken finds a grain," it said. Another time I was horrified by the coal bill, whereupon it said: "Happiness and contentment are life's blessings," which along with the irony shows an offensive stolidity; the calendar is impatient, can scarcely wait for me to leave. But perhaps it only does not want to make the parting hard for me. Perhaps, after the calendar leaf for the day I move, there will be a leaf I'll no longer see that will say something like: "It is determined by divine decree, etc."[66] No, it isn't right for me to set down everything I think about my calendar—"after all, it's only human."

If I were to go on writing you in this fashion about everything I come in contact with, I'd never make an end of it, of course, and it would seem as though I were leading a very animated social life, whereas in reality all is muted around me, though never too muted. I hear little about the excitements of Berlin, the bad and the good, though more of the former, of course. By the way, does Peppa know what people in Berlin say when asked, "How are you?" I'm sure he knows; you all know more about Berlin than I do. But at the risk of telling you something altogether outmoded—after all, it still applies—people say: "Rotten, times the index number."[67] And this one: Someone is enthusiastically describing the Leipzig gymnastics meet: ". . . the tremendous sight of 750,000 gymnasts marching in!" The other, reckoning slowly, says: "So, what does that amount to—three and a half peacetime gymnasts."

How are things (this is no longer a joke, but also nothing sad, I hope) in the Jewish school? Did you read the young teacher's article in Selbstwehr? Very well meant, and zealous. I have again heard that Arnstein is doing very well and Fräulein Mauthner is said to have reformed the whole practice of gymnastics in Palestine. You mustn't take old Aschermann's commercial acumen amiss; after all, there is something tremendous in a man's taking his family on his back and carrying them across the sea to Palestine. That so many of his kind do it is no less of a maritime miracle than the one in the Red Sea.

Many thanks to Marianne and Lotte[68] for their letters. Astonishing how their handwriting, placed side by side, depicts not so much the differences in their natures as, almost, their physical differences, at least so it seems to me in these last letters. Marianne asks what aspects of her life particularly interest me. Well: What she is reading, whether she is still dancing (here in the

Jewish People's Home all the girls learn rhythmic dancing; it's free of charge),
and whether she is still wearing glasses. I have been asked to send Lotte
regards from Anni G. A dear, pretty, clever child (Lotte, I mean, but Anni
too); she is learning Hebrew diligently, can almost read already and sing a
new song. Is Lotte making progress?

But now it is high time to go to sleep. I have spent almost a whole evening
with you and your family, and it is so far from Stockhausgasse to
Miquelstrasse. Keep well. [. . .]

To Max Brod
                    [Berlin-Steglitz; postmarked on arrival: November 5, 1923]
Dearest Max, A brief account of how the matter looks to my mind—which
admittedly is somewhat battered today for various reasons. My report is
largely based on yesterday's, Thursday's,[69] talk with E., who was with me
from about seven to ten, just at the time your letter arrived, by the way, but I
did not want to open it in front of her.

You're certainly right about this: If Berlin conditions were anything like
last year's, life easy, possibilities vast, pleasant distractions, etc., there very
probably would not have been any such eruption. But not because there was
no fire in the volcano; it merely would have sought other channels. That
might well have resulted in peaceful times, but these would surely not have
been lasting. For there is a central point of suffering here where a good many
elements meet and mingle. It's always there, although at different times—
especially under the evidently overpowering influence of your presence—it
takes on very different aspects. One way to treat it is to be content with
superficial peace. That truly would be a great deal, moreover, since ultimately
such temporary peace can develop, because of expected or unexpected things,
into real peace. But Berlin as it is today cannot produce such a temporary
peace even though you were to make superhuman efforts, and unfortunately
you seem to be doing just that. But since Berlin can't, some extra help must
be given, and that extra help would be your coming once a month. That
would provide better nourishment than the best of little boxes. You do not
have to seek any other immediate causes for the latest eruption. Just two
weeks ago the demand was limited to your coming; only now has it increased
so tremendously. Therefore I too think that she would again restrict herself
under your personal influence. It was solely within the context of this hope
that yesterday I made the proposal, possibly a dreadful one to you but within
my view of the matter a solution, that the two of you during these last days
stop tormenting each other with letters and telephone calls back and forth,

and instead leave everything to eye-to-eye presence, which might once more yield that "temporary peace."

E's current principal demand is monstrous; I deeply feel that, Max, with you. But it is not only jealousy, although that too would not be "pointless" as you suggest. It is not only jealousy—I am not saying this because you don't know it, I am saying it in order to be close to you in this strange, hidden, mysterious suffering—it is also the impossibility of understanding on her part, just as it is the impossibility of explanation on your part. You surely cannot think that you have countered E. when you say "that only duty holds me fast here in marriage." How many totally incontrovertible things she can say to that! And totally obvious as well. It is not only "duty," of course; but at the moment there is no other way to express it. Don't, however, hope that in saying that you are countering anything.

Perhaps still under the impact of what she called the "happiness" given her by your telephone call (which later, I gather, was entirely canceled out by your letter), E. was looking very good. She had done well at the rehearsal, also had a prospect of singing in a church concert, so that she made a general impression by no means desperate. Only now and then she would burst out, either about that "duty" or to express fear of being swayed and lulled by you when you come.

I wrote my mother some time ago that you would be coming to Berlin; now I'll tell her that it isn't so. But it really does not matter much; I can easily have been mistaken. If you can bring the things with you—it remains a bother, no matter how it is arranged—then please do; but it's not at all absolutely necessary. No doubt some other opportunity will come along for getting them here. If you do bring them, simply give the baggage ticket to the railroad delivery office with my present address. But perhaps I'll be able to send you my new address (from November 15 on) in time, so that the suitcase can be taken right there for simplicity's sake. But more important than all this is that we will soon see each other.

F

To Kurt Wolff Verlag

[Postcard. Berlin; received: November 19, 1923]

Dear Sirs,

Many thanks for your postcard of October 29 and for the firm's catalogue. But it cannot be done this way. The catalogue contains so many tempting books, and most of them are expensive. I don't know what you mean by a "suitable selection." May I therefore ask you to tell me the value in gold marks of the books you originally had in mind to send me. Then I shall choose accordingly.

Very truly yours, F. Kafka

My present address: c/o Seifert, Grunewaldstrasse 13, Berlin-Steglitz.[70]

To Felix Weltsch

[Postcard. Berlin-Steglitz; postmark: November 18, 1923]
Dear Felix, Many thanks for sending the magazine so regularly, and for taking care of us here, difficult as it may be for you. I have moved, by the way; please see that the address is changed to: *c/o Seifert, Grunewaldstrasse 13, Berlin-Steglitz.* And one thing more: Please let me know how much I owe; I'll promptly instruct my sister to pay it. And please stop sending my Prague copy, if you haven't already done so; I'll probably stay here awhile longer, in spite of the mad inflation. I have not yet called on your relatives,[71] much as I wanted to; it is becoming too hard for me to tramp around at this season and with the days so short. Twice a week, and only in good weather, I briefly attend the Academy for Jewish Studies.[72] That's the most I can manage. Warmest regards to you, your family, and the Baums.

Yours, F

To Max Brod

[Postcard. Berlin-Steglitz; postmark: November 25, 1923]
Dear Max, These last few days I have been much occupied with you. Mother sent me the reviews from the *Abendblatt;* what fine, fresh, vital things—you're still in the saddle.—Today Ottla is here, approving of everything she sees, I think. As far as you are concerned, I have no worries.—I have money now and in the course of the week will give E. the 400 crowns. How is your new method of transferring money working out?—I have not been sick; it's just that the lamp flickers a little; otherwise it's not been bad so far. It did prevent me from going to E's performance, though; D., too, was unfortunately not altogether well that day. But perhaps the play will be repeated at Christmastime.—What you say about the defects of our meeting in Berlin is true. But it is also a defect on my part more than a defect of Berlin. May we hang on to the hope of improvement. Incidentally I have the feeling that you are living freely and firmly—which in the past you hardly ever could do—in spite of some inevitable disturbances in your complicated life, which your heroic

efforts nevertheless keep simple. The two articles prove that.—Give Felix and
Oskar a caress or two for me.—All the best.

                                                                                        F

Dora sends regards.

To Kurt Wolff Verlag
            [Berlin-Steglitz, end of November/beginning of December 1923]
Dear Herr Meyer,

From the length of time that has again passed since your kind card, you
can gather how hard I find this matter. But it is a stupendous event in these
times, to be permitted to choose books by the armful.

The books I would like, then, are the following (but let me make this
proviso, that where the binding is expensive, that is especially for the Books of
Hours, I shall be glad to have copies in boards):

Hölderlin	*Poems*
Hölty	*Poems*
Eichendorff	*Poems*
Bachhofer	*Japanese Woodcut*
Fischer	*Chinese Landscape*
Perzynski	*Chinese Gods*
Simmel	*Rembrandt*
Gauguin	*Before and After*
Chamisso	*Schlemihl*
Bürger	*Munchausen*
One volume	by Hamsun
Kafka	1 *Stoker*
	⎧ *Meditation*
	⎨ *Metamorphosis*
1 or 2	⎨ *Country Doctor*
	⎩ *Penal Colony*

So that is the list.[73] It has become, in spite of all my efforts, much too
much; but since ten more attempts would turn out no better, I may as well
send it off as it stands.

                        With many thanks and regards, sincerely, Kafka
                        c/o Seifert, Grunewaldstrasse 13, Berlin-Steglitz

To Max Brod
[Postcard. Berlin-Steglitz; postmark: December 17, 1923]
Dearest Max, It's a long time since I wrote. I have had disturbances of the most varied kinds, and every possible variety of fatigue, the sort of thing a person (living in retirement) has to fight his way through in this wild and woolly foreign land—and what is even more difficult—in this wild and woolly world. The agitation I caused by trying my unlucky hand on your article is probably over by now; surely it didn't last long, since the very next day you received, as E. has told me, a good card asking forgiveness; for that reason, too, I stopped feeling bad about it. I now very well understand the money worries. What I don't understand, after sharing in and misunderstanding the November crisis which at the time you interpreted so much better than I did, is why you allowed yourself to be so shaken by the December crisis as such (jealousy, telephone problems, etc.), since in essence it was no different from the crisis in November, which was so beautifully solved by your spending some time together that it augured well for the entire future. But in any case, if you have anything you wish done and don't too greatly fear the danger of some folly on my part, remember me.

What is the meaning of your remark about your play?[74] Has it already been performed? I no longer read any newspaper (because of the inflation); I've given up even the Sunday paper (in any case the landlady is more than prompt about informing one of the new taxes), and so I know less about the world than I did in Prague. For example, I would like to find out something about Musil's *Vincenz*[75] of which I know nothing but the title which I read on the theater placard long after the premiere, on my way to the Academy (my venture into the world). But that is truly not a major sorrow. Incidentally, couldn't you get in touch with Viertel[76] or Blei about your play? They are almost friends.

I should have written to Oskar long ago about his story at the *Rundschau,*[77] but the matter is still in progress, so to speak.

Regards from Dora, who is absolutely delighted by the essay on Křička.[78]

To Oskar Baum
[Postcard. Berlin-Steglitz, December 1923]
My dear Oskar, What a miserable spokesman you have! What use is his goodwill? When he's miserable to such a degree, he can only do harm. I was delighted, truly delighted, to have an assignment from you, and so promising a one. Now of course I did not myself run straight to the telephone (what an

idea! to the telephone! As a matter of fact it stands on my table), but with all my strength I pushed someone else over to it. Two calls were unsuccessful. I took that as a sign that a more cunning procedure was called for, wrote a letter, and had a friend carry it over. It was so planned that K.[79] would be forced to make verbal concessions. But K., even more cunning, vanished into the adjoining room and returned with a dictated letter. He was very sorry—but special issues and editorial difficulties—so far not possible—but now a new idea has turned up (to this moment I don't know whether it refers to your story) which he would very much like to discuss with me—would I come to see him or telephone him. That was unconsciously crafty, for both actions are impossible for me. I, even more crafty, send a second letter, once again by way of my friend, explaining the two impossibilities but urgently requesting him to discuss your story in detail with my friend. But how these cunning evasions pile up. In response to this second letter he says he will come out to see me sometime this week. Now he's neatly out of the whole affair, for he doesn't come. The following week I inquire again (that is, once more not I personally) about the story, whereupon he says that he will not be able to come until after Christmas; as far as the story is concerned, it has definitely been accepted, but he cannot tell when it will be published.—Odd, the way so vast an operation can slip into the machinery of the world, so delicately, without in the slightest degree changing anything. Dear, dear Oskar, please don't be angry with me!

Warmest regards to you and yours, F.

To Robert Klopstock
[Postcard. Berlin-Steglitz; postmark: December 19, 1923]
Dear Robert, First questions in the style of Robert, but more important than the kind he asks: Student dining hall? Teeth? Translations? Additional earnings? Room? Examinations? That will do for the present. As for me, you must not imagine, Robert, that my life is such that I have the freedom and energy to report, or even to write, at any given moment. There are abysses into which I sink without even noticing, only at best to creep up again after a long time. Such are not the proper occasions for writing.—It's very good that you want to go to the Ivriah.[80] Perhaps not only for the Hebrew courses; you might try the Talmud class also. (Once a week! You won't completely understand it, but what does that matter. You will hear it from far away; what else is it but news from afar.) To me the Academy for Jewish Studies is a refuge of peace in wild and woolly Berlin and in the wild and woolly regions of the mind. (I am just being asked about my condition and can say of my head only that it is "coiffured like a lion.") A whole building of

handsome lecture rooms, large library, peace, well heated, few students, and everything free of charge. Of course I am not a proper student, am only in the preparatory school, and have only one teacher there, moreover go seldom, so that in the long run almost all the glory evaporates again; but even though I am not a student, the school exists and is a fine place, and basically not at all fine but rather odd to the point of grotesquerie and beyond that to the point of intangible delicacy (namely, the liberal-reformist tone and scholarly aspects of the whole thing). But enough of this.—It's very good that you will be seeing Pua; perhaps then I'll have some news of her. I have not been able to reach her for months. How have I offended her?—All the best.

F

Another student wishes to enclose a greeting. [GREETING AND SIGNATURE OF DORA]

To Kurt Wolff Verlag
                    [Postcard. Berlin-Steglitz; postmark: December 31, 1923]
Dear Sirs,
    On the 4th you wrote me that a package of books was on the way for me. Almost four weeks have passed and I have not yet received them. Would you be so kind as to ask what has happened to the package.
                                          Very truly yours, F. Kafka
                        c/o Seifert, Grunewaldstrasse 13, Berlin-Steglitz

1924

To Max Brod
                                    [Berlin-Steglitz, mid-January 1924]
Dear Max, First I did not write because I was sick (high temperature, chills, and fever, and as a postlude to illness a single visit from the doctor for 160 crowns; later D. negotiated it down to half that; at any rate, since then I have a tenfold fear of getting sick; a second-class bed in the Jewish Hospital costs 64 crowns a day, but that only pays for bed and board, apparently not for service or the doctor), then I did not write because I thought that you would be passing through Berlin on the way to Königsberg. By the way, E. too said at the time that you would be coming in three weeks to be present at her audition, and after this idea proved wrong (how did Königsberg turn out? It

need not necessarily be so bad if people take a negative attitude toward *Bunterbart,* which by now I would really like to read; it was the same with *Klarissa* at the beginning, too, although I grant that *Klarissa* should have prepared the way for the second play)—as I say, when this idea proved wrong and your coming here was postponed to such an extent that I might well have sighed with E.—though this time I don't know how she behaved—I did not write because of a slight clouding of the mind, caused by digestive disturbances and the like. But now your card has roused me. Of course I'll try to do all I can with E., to the limits of my strength and cleverness, although the opposition of the old lady is a considerable factor; she is evidently as moody as she is hardheaded and also seems to have a knack for intrigue. What comes to my aid, though it also detracts from me somewhat, is that I take real pleasure in furthering E. and her cause in the realm of acting, which isn't so entirely closed to me as the mysteries of larynx-chest-tongue-nose-and-frontal-sinus. For this reason, though, my advice lacks authority, assuming it would have any otherwise. Still, the chief obstacle is my health. Today, for instance, a telephone call with E. was arranged; but I cannot very well go across to the cold room because I have a temperature of 100 and am staying in bed. It's nothing special, I frequently have such a temperature without any further repercussions; the change in the weather may be a partial cause, and presumably it will be over tomorrow. Still, it is a serious obstacle to freedom of movement, and moreover the figures of the doctor's fee float in fiery letters over my bed. Nevertheless, perhaps I'll be able to take the tram to the Academy in town tomorrow morning and stay a bit with E.; dragging her out constantly in this kind of weather—she too seems to have a slight cold—isn't a good idea. Furthermore, I have in mind to introduce E. to the actress Midia Pines,[1] whom I once told you about. She is coming to Berlin for a few days, will be giving a recitation in Neumann's Graphisches Kabinett[2] (she does the life story of the hermit from *The Brothers Karamazov,* reciting the whole thing by heart), and will probably visit me. Perhaps E. will take this as a good example, since Midia Pines, though still a young girl, is also a language teacher. And of course I would be very glad to have E. recite to me; I long ago asked her with the utmost sincerity to do so (if only for the sake of hearing some Goethe poems after so long a time). Only circumstances have so far stood in the way, among them the fact that we poor foreigners who cannot pay such high rents will be expelled from our wonderful apartment on February 1. You are right to add that reminder of "warm, well-fed Bohemia," but it just won't very well do; to some extent I am stuck here. Schelesen is out of the question; Schelesen is Prague. Besides, I had warmth and good feeding for forty years, and the result does not tempt me to go on trying them. Schelesen would also be too small for me, and probably for us; it isn't that I've taken up studying—aside from the fact that I am not really pursuing these studies but only doing them for pleasure without the necessary groundwork—but having a man in the vicinity who knows something about these things would be a certain encouragement to me; I'd probably be more interested in the man than in the things. At any rate, that would not be possible in Schelesen, but perhaps it really might be possible—this occurred to me on reading your suggestion—in some Bohemian or Moravian country town. I'll think about that. If the creature were not so decrepit, you could almost make a drawing of his appearance: On the left D., say, supporting him; on the right that man, say; some sort of "scribbling" might stiffen his neck; now if only the ground beneath him were consolidated, the abyss in front of him filled in, the vultures around his head driven away, the storm in the skies above him quieted down—if all that were to happen, then it might be just barely possible to go on for a while. I have also thought of Vienna, but spending a thousand crowns on the trip (as it is I am a parasite on my parents—who are behaving wonderfully—and recently on my sisters, too) is too risky, likewise passing through Prague and venturing into the unknown. So perhaps it is quite sensible to stay here a little while longer, all the more so since the grave drawbacks of Berlin nevertheless have a delightful and educational effect. Perhaps one of these days we'll leave here together with E.—All the best, especially for your work on the novel,[3] to which, so I hear, you are at last planning to return.

Yours, F.

Thank you for the food parcel. We were a little ashamed to keep it; the contents were not very tempting either, though deserving the highest praise. D. had a big cake baked and took it to the Jewish orphanage where she had been a seamstress last year. I hear that it was a great event for the children, who lead a depressed, joyless life there. In order not to burden you any longer with this, I've sent several addresses to my sister Elli; all of these are to receive packages.

Recently Kaznelson and his wife came to see me. Frau Lise said her mother had seen you in Bodenbach at Christmas; had you been here? I said no. At once, quickwittedly as if you had prompted him, Kaznelson said: "Probably he went to Zwickau." At that moment it actually struck me as fishy.

Dora knows Manfred Georg[4] of Breslau quite well (he's in Berlin now) and would be curious to hear your opinion of him. You do know him, if I'm not mistaken, and if I'm furthermore not mistaken the essay on you in the anthology[5] is by him.

What you write about Werfel[6] is very fine, very encouraging, strength-giving, and worth reading several times. But why heroic? Rather epicurean; but no, heroic after all, heroic epicureanism. If only the worm in all apples were not the real epicure.

Fine, fine, the "Theater Poiret."[7] If we confine ourselves only to these articles—what a writer you are! How often I've read the article on Musorgski (and still don't know how to spell the name), rather like a child who clings to the doorjamb at the entrance to a ballroom and looks in on a grand revel of strangers.

Have you read *Ordeal by Fire* by Weiss?[8] I've had it around for weeks, have read it one and a half times; it is splendid and even more difficult than anything else of his, although it wants to be very personal and then again by its twists and turns tries to avoid the personal. I haven't thanked him yet; I have several such burdens on my conscience. To shift a few of them from myself: Have you written about *Nahar* yet?

Please give my warm regards to Felix and Oskar (I haven't heard anything further from Kayser and probably will not be hearing from him again).

Have you heard anything about Klopstock? Has anything of his been published in the *Abendblatt?*

To Robert Klopstock
                    [Postcard. Berlin-Steglitz; postmark: January 26, 1924]
Dear Robert, I imagined that you were still in B. It was only in a letter from Max that I learned you are already in Prague. He also mentioned four translations of yours that have been published and that I knew nothing about. You are no longer sending any to me for revision; who has taken away my assignment? Meanwhile Irene has been here and told me a little about you; what was that examination that you mentioned around Christmas as having passed well? I did not see Midia; evenings I almost always have a rise in temperature. On such occasions the "other student" always goes; she was delighted by Midia. There is little to tell about myself; a somewhat shadowy life; anyone who isn't looking squarely at it cannot notice it. At the moment we have apartment troubles, an overabundance of apartments, but the fine ones march right past us, beyond our means, and the rest are questionable. If only I could earn something! But nobody here is paying wages for lying in bed until twelve. An acquaintance, a young painter, has a fine job now; I've

envied him for it more than once. He is a street book-peddler; around ten o'clock in the morning he goes to his stand and stays there until dusk; and we have already had temperatures of fourteen degrees and lower. Around Christmas he made ten marks a day, now three or four.

To Felix Weltsch

[Postcard. Berlin-Steglitz; postmark: January 28, 1924]

Dear Felix, It's true that I write to you only when I move (out of fear that an issue of *Selbstwehr* might fail to arrive; it now always comes so punctually, most faithful of the faithful in regard to punctuality and contents, coming to the most unpunctual of its subscribers), but in other respects our correspondence promises to become livelier. On February 1 (that is, for the next issue) my address will be: c/o Frau Dr. Busse, Heidestrasse 25–26, Berlin-Zehlendorf. I am possibly making a mistake (and am being punished in advance by the exorbitant rent, which as rents go is really not at all excessive for this apartment but is in reality beyond my means) by moving into the home of a deceased writer, Dr. Carl Busse (he died in 1918), who at least during his lifetime would certainly have detested me.[9] Perhaps you remember his monthly group reviews in *Velhagen & Klasing's Monatshefte*?[10] But I'm moving in nonetheless; the world is everywhere full of perils, so let this special one emerge if it will from the darkness of all the unknown dangers. Oddly enough, by the way, even in such a case a certain hometown quality comes to the fore which makes the house alluring. The allure comes about, I grant you, only because I have been given notice in my previous fine apartment because I am a poor foreigner incapable of paying the rent.

Cordial regards to you and yours.

To Lise Kaznelson

[Postcard. Berlin-Steglitz, end of January 1924]

Dear Frau Lise, Please don't be annoyed with me for straightway merging my thanks for your package with the memory of my little lady bookseller. It is so pleasant to be a benefactor and so easy (just asking someone to telephone and letting Dr. Kaznelson make inquiries among the booksellers), and since it is so easy we do not like to stop and so we bother those among our fellow men who allow themselves to be bothered. But now I promise that if Dr. Kaznelson will be so kind and let me know what success he had with his last try, I'll stop my benefactions. In any case, my warmest thanks to both of you.

Regards to your family, K.

From February 1 on my address is c/o Frau Dr. Busse, Heidestrasse 25–26, Berlin-Zehlendorf.

To Ludwig Hardt

[Berlin-Zehlendorf, February 1, 1924]

My dear Ludwig Hardt, Many thanks for the telegram; it says you are giving your reading "in the Ghosts Hall"[11]—which is not inapposite. Well, far as I am from Berlin I'm not so far that I wouldn't have known of the readings without a telegram. But sad to say, sad to say, I cannot come. Not only because I moved just this afternoon, with all the paraphernalia of the massive household I am running (the moving itself was simple enough, thanks to the help of the friendly bearer of this message, Fräulein R.F.), but chiefly because I am sick, feverish, and haven't been out of the house in the evening throughout these four months in Berlin. But couldn't I see you here in Zehlendorf—it's been such a long time. Tomorrow evening a Fräulein Dora Diamant will be coming to your reading to discuss this matter with you. Warm regards and blessings on your evening.

K.

To Ludwig Hardt

[Berlin-Zehlendorf, beginning of February 1924]

Dear Ludwig Hardt, I have just received the report of an unhappy young lady: The doorman misunderstood her when she asked whether Hardt had arrived yet and called him personally to the telephone; I have made her even more unhappy by recollecting that H. usually takes a nap before a reading (which is surely still true), but then offered the consolation that nothing can disturb H. (which is surely even truer). Not even a loquacious letter at the end of an evening of reading. But now in brief: I cannot come, am sick, sent a letter only yesterday by someone who was to attend the canceled reading. Couldn't you come out here sometime, so that I could see you again after so long a time? Not that you would be seeing anything very cheering here, but still—

Fräulein Dora Diamant, the bearer of this message, has plenipotentiary authority and more to discuss the possibility of a journey to Zehlendorf. Will it be possible?

Yours, K.

To Robert Klopstock

[Berlin-Zehlendorf; postmark: February 29, 1924]

My dear Robert, It's not possible, I cannot write, can scarcely thank you for all the good things you shower upon me (the wonderful chocolates that I received only a few days ago, or rather, not to hide the truth, that we received, and then *Die Fackel*, with which I indulged in those ennervating evening orgies of which you know, once while my uncle[12] and Dora were enjoyably—though their enjoyment was probably of a different sort from mine—away at a Kraus reading) and among which the gifts are the least part. Two letters I began and a postcard have long been drifting around the apartment somewhere. You will never receive them. Recently I looked for your letter before last, could not find it; then it turned up in a Hebrew book in which I had kept it because I was reading a little in the book every day but hadn't opened it for a whole month. It's longer than that since I last went to the Academy. Everything is very lovely out here, but I shall probably have to leave. It's a great pity that you are not well off either; that means there's nothing to counterbalance my state. I cannot begin to understand what you are living on. Is S. at least paying? And have you received tickets for the student dining hall? Very unfair that you've managed to scotch that assignment for D. Assignments make us happy. Despite various problems, your health seems—let us touch tender spots tenderly—at least not too bad. Having that much at least, one can push on.

Keep well, keep very well.

Yours, F

To Robert Klopstock

[Berlin-Zehlendorf, beginning of March 1924]
Dear Robert, No, no traveling, no such wild adventure; we'll meet anyhow, without all that, in a quieter manner, more in keeping with weak bones. Perhaps—we really are thinking seriously of it—we'll soon be coming to Prague; if a sanatorium in the Vienna woods proves feasible, then certainly. I am resisting a sanatorium, also resisting a boardinghouse, but what's the use since I cannot resist the fever. And 100.4° has become my daily bread, all evening long and half the night. Otherwise, nevertheless, it is very lovely here to lie on the veranda and watch the sun working on two tasks, each difficult in its own way: to awaken me and the birch alongside me to natural life (the birch seems to be somewhat ahead). I am very reluctant to leave here, but I cannot entirely reject the idea of going to the sanatorium since on account of the fever I have not been out of the house for weeks, feel strong enough while lying down, but if I attempt any walks, after the first step they assume the quality of a grandiose enterprise, so that sometimes the thought of peacefully burying myself alive in the sanatorium is not at all so unpleasant. And then again it horrifies me when I consider that I shall be losing freedom even for those few warm months that are predestined for freedom. But then there

comes that morning and evening coughing lasting for hours, and the flask almost full every day—that again argues for the sanatorium. But then again there is fear, for example, of the horrible compulsory eating there.

Now your later letter has arrived. So you agree, or are only forced to agree? I am glad that you take back what you said and no longer regard my uncle simply as a "cold gentleman." How, in fact, could coldness be simple? It has to be complicated if only because it probably always is a phenomenon explicable solely in historical terms. And then again: What makes him seem cold is probably that he fulfills his duty and protects the "bachelor secret."

I well remember your stories about the sick girl. Wasn't it she whose dreams were also haunted by Abraham? I thought about you a great deal while reading Holitscher's memoirs;[13] they are appearing in the *Rundschau* and I have read the second and third installments. To be sure, there is no direct connection to be drawn between you and him, except for being Hungarian and the Jewishness common to all of us; but I tend to cling to localities and think I see more in them than they openly show. Incidentally, Holitscher himself thinks he has no trace of the Hungarian spirit in him, is simply a German. You've hardly told me anything about such Budapesters. There are very good touches in the memoirs where Verlaine comes into the story, and Hamsun. The way he complains about Jewishness is embarrassing both for him and for the reader. As if someone at a party were to go on for hours expounding on the features of a certain ailment and furthermore showing it to be incurable, amid general agreement, and after all this is over someone in the corner begins to wail about this particular ailment. And yet there is something fine about it; it is sincere to the point of grotesque wretchedness. Nervertheless, one feels: it might go even further.

My personal pleasure in the book is intensified by "literary" recollections of youth, the way I would pore over every word of the Albert Langen Verlag catalogues,[14] reading them again and again, because they were inexhaustible and because I could not obtain most of the books they listed, and also did not understand most of them. For so many years what an aura of Paris and of literature surrounded Holitscher and the titles of his novels[15]—and now here is this aging man crying over the hardships of that whole period. He was unhappy then, but one cannot help thinking: If only I had been unhappy that way just once; I really should have tried to be unhappy that way. Incidentally, he has Hamsun saying—it's a crude and clumsy fiction, obviously put in solely to comfort me—that the winter in Paris took a great deal out of him, that his old lung disease has flared up again, that he has to leave for a small summer sanatorium way up in Norway, and that Paris is too expensive anyhow.[16]

Now comes the Davos surprise. How hard all this is, and what frightful sums I shall have to squeeze out of others for myself. And you, Robert, are complaining about the 1000 crowns. What a spoiled, independent, free nobleman you are.

Well, we shall probably see each other. Uncle proposed that I go direct from here to Innsbruck, but I explained to him today why I would prefer to go by way of Prague. Perhaps he will consent.

To Robert Klopstock
[Postcard. Sanatorium Wiener Wald, Ortmann, Austria; postmark: April 7, 1924][17]
Dear Robert, Only medical matters—everything else is too involved, but my treatment—its only merit—delightfully simple. Against fever, liquid Pyramidon three times a day. Against coughing, Demopon (unfortunately doesn't help) and Anästesin lozenges. Along with the Demopon, atropine, if I am not mistaken. Probably the larynx is the chief problem. Verbally I don't learn anything definite, since in discussing tuberculosis of the larynx everybody drops into a shy, evasive, glassy-eyed manner of speech. But "swelling at the rear," "infiltration," "not malignant," but "we cannot yet say anything definite"—all that in connection with very malignant pain probably suffices. Otherwise: A good room, lovely country; I haven't noticed any sign of patronizing. I had no chance to mention pneumothorax; given my poor general condition (49 kilos in my winter clothes), it is out of the question. I have no contact with the rest of the place, lie in bed, also can only whisper (how quickly that went; just a touch of it started for the first time on about the third day in Prague). The place seems to be a great gossipers' nest from balcony to balcony; for the time being it doesn't bother me.

To Max Brod
[Postcard. Sanatorium Wiener Wald; postmark: April 9, 1924]
Dear Max, It is expensive, might very well be frightfully expensive; "Josephine"[18] must help out a little, there's no other way. Please offer it to Otto Pick (of course he can print whatever he likes from *Meditation*); if he takes it, please send it to Die Schmiede[19] *later*; if he doesn't take it, then send

it *right away.* As for me, it's evidently the larynx. Dora is with me. Regards to your wife and Felix and Oskar.

F

[A POSTCRIPT BY DORA DIAMANT INDICATES THAT THE PATIENT'S CONDITION IS VERY GRAVE]

To Robert Klopstock
                [Postcard. Sanatorium Wiener Wald; postmark: April 13, 1924]
Dear Robert, I am being transferred to the University Clinic of Prof. Dr. M. Hajek, Lazarettgasse 14, Vienna IX. It seems my larynx is so swollen that I cannot eat; they must (they say) undertake alcohol injections into the nerve, probably also surgery. So I shall be staying in Vienna several weeks.

Cordial regards, F.

I am afraid of your codeine. Today I have not only already used up the flask, but am taking only codeine 0.03. "I wonder what it looks like inside?" I just asked the nurse. "Like the witch's kitchen," she said honestly.

To Robert Klopstock
                            [Postcard. Vienna; postmark: April 18, 1924]
Robert, dear Robert, No acts of violence, no sudden trip to Vienna. You know my fear of acts of violence and yet you always start that again. Since I left that luxurious, depressing, and yet ineffectual (though wonderfully situated) sanatorium I have been feeling better; the procedures in the hospital (except for details) have done me good; the pain in swallowing and the burning have decreased; so far no injections have been undertaken, only spraying of the larynx with menthol oil. On Saturday,[20] if no special misfortune intervenes, I intend to go to Dr. Hoffmann's sanatorium, Kierling bei Klosterneuburg, Lower Austria.

To Max Brod
                            [Vienna, probably April 20, 1924][21]
Dearest Max, I have just received your letter, which makes me inordinately happy; it seemed so long since I had seen a word from you. Above all forgive the epistolary and telegraphic noise that surrounded you on my account. It was largely needless, prompted by weak nerves (how boastfully I speak and yet I've cried without reason several times today; my neighbor died during

the night), and then, I admit, also by that awful, depressing sanatorium in the Vienna woods. Once the fact of tuberculosis of the larynx is accepted, my condition is bearable; for the present I can swallow again. And the stay in the hospital was not so bad as you might imagine; on the contrary, in many respects it was a gift. Thanks to your letter I have received a number of very friendly attentions from Werfel: the visit of a woman doctor who is a friend of his and who also spoke with my doctor; then he also gave me the address of Prof. Tandler, who is a friend of his; then he sent me the novel[22] (I was frightfully hungry for a suitable book) and roses. And although I had to ask him not to come (for it's marvelous here for the patients; for visitors, and in this regard therefore also for the patients, horrible), a card from him indicates that he means to come today anyhow; in the evening he is leaving for Venice. I am now leaving with Dora for Kierling.

Many thanks for all the laborious literary affairs you've so splendidly taken care of for me.

All the best for you and for everything relating to your life.

F

My address, which Dora may not have written clearly enough to my parents:
Sanatorium Dr. Hoffmann
Kierling bei Klosterneuburg, Lower Austria.

To Max Brod

[Postcard. Kierling; postmark: April 28, 1924]

Dearest Max, How good you are to me and how much I owe you these last weeks. Ottla will tell you about the medical matters. I am very weak, but very well taken care of here. We have not applied to Tandler; perhaps through him a free bed or a cheap bed might be obtainable in Grimmenstein, which is very beautifully situated, but I cannot travel now, and perhaps it would also have other disadvantages. I will shortly thank Dr. Blau[23] for his letter of recommendation, or should I not? The free subscription[24] is very welcome to me, only I haven't been receiving the paper; so far I've received only the Thursday and Friday issues, otherwise none; even the Easter issue hasn't come yet. They've mixed up the address—once it read Kieburg—do be so kind and intervene—perhaps the Easter issue* could still be sent to me. Your two packages, especially the second, have given me the greatest pleasure, and the Reclam books seem virtually predestined for me. It isn't that I am

* I have just received it from home; the mailing seems to be straightening out.

really reading (or rather, yes, I am reading Werfel's novel with infinite slowness, but regularly); I'm too tired for that. Being closed is my eyes' natural state, but playing with books and magazines makes me happy.

Keep well, my good, dear Max.

F.

To Julie and Hermann Kafka

[Kierling, about May 19, 1924][25]

Dearest Parents, Now about the visits you refer to every so often. I have been considering the matter every day, for it is very important to me. It would be so nice; we have not been together for such a long time. I don't count my stay with you in Prague; that just introduced confusion into the household. Rather, I mean spending a few days together peacefully in a beautiful locality, alone. I don't remember when the last time was—once for a few hours in Franzensbad. And then "having a good glass of beer together," as you write, from which I see that Father doesn't think much of this year's wine, and I'll agree with him there, as far as the beer is concerned. In the past, as I often remember during the heat spells, we used to have beer together quite often, in that far-off time when Father would take me along to the Civilian Swimming Pool.[26]

That and many other things argue in favor of the visit, but there is too much that argues against it. First of all, Father probably will not be able to come because of passport difficulties. Naturally that robs the visit of a large part of its meaning. But above all Mother, no matter who else accompanies her, will be concentrating too much on me, will be too dependent on me, and I am still not very pretty, not at all a sight worth seeing. You know about the problems of the early period around here and in Vienna; they got me down somewhat; they interfered with a rapid lowering of the fever, and this had the effect of further weakening me. But during the early period the shock of the larynx business was more weakening than it should rightly have been.

Only now am I beginning to work my way out of all these weakening factors, with the aid of Dora and Robert[27]—from a distance you cannot possibly imagine what a great help they are (what would I be without them). There are interruptions in my progress even now, such as, for example, an intestinal grippe these last few days that I haven't yet entirely thrown off. The upshot is that in spite of my wonderful helpers, in spite of good air and food, almost daily sunbathing, I still have not properly recovered, in fact on the whole am not even so well as I was recently in Prague. If you also count in the fact that I am allowed to speak only in whispers and even that not too often, you will gladly postpone the visit. Everything is at the best of beginnings—recently a specialist[28] announced that the larynx was significantly improved, and although I [cannot fully believe] this extremely amiable and unselfish man—he comes out here once a week in his own automobile and charges almost nothing—his words were still a great comfort to me. Everything is, as I said, at the best of beginnings, but the best beginnings don't amount to much. Since I cannot show the visitors—and what is more, such visitors as you two would be—major, undeniable progress, measurable even by lay eyes, I think we should rather let it be. So shall we not let it ride for the present, dear parents?

You must not think that you could do anything to improve or amplify my treatment here. The owner of the sanatorium is, I admit, a sick old man who cannot devote much time to my affairs, and my dealings with the highly disagreeable resident physician are more on a social than a medical basis; but aside from occasional visits of specialists, Robert is here; he doesn't stir from my side, and instead of thinking of his examinations devotes all his energy to thinking of me. Then there is also a young doctor in whom I have great confidence (I owe him, as well as the abovementioned specialist, to Ehrmann, the architect); he comes out here three times a week, though not by car but modestly by train and bus.

To Max Brod

[Postcard. Kierling; postmark: May 20, 1924]
Dearest Max, So now the book[29] is here too, just the look of it magnificent, glaring yellow and red with a touch of black, and very tempting, and moreover gratis, evidently a gift from the firm of Taubeles—it must have been in some remnant of alcohol intoxication (and since I now receive one or two injections every day, the intoxications overlap so there is always a remnant) that I bluntly and brazenly, impelled by Dora's innocence, asked you to "obtain" the book. If only I had instead used a vigorous alcohol injection to make myself somewhat more human during your visit,[30] which I had looked forward to so eagerly and which turned out so dismal. However, it was not an exceptionally bad day; you mustn't think that; it was just worse than the preceding day; this is the way the time and the fever goes on. (Now Robert is trying Pyramidon.) Along with these and other things to complain about, there are of course a few tiny items of good cheer, but it's impossible for me to communicate them or they shall have to be reserved for a visit like the one I so wretchedly spoiled. Keep well. Thanks for everything.

F

Regards to Felix and Oskar.[31]

Conversation Slips[1]

This gives one an idea of consumption: in the middle a faceted stone, at the side the saws, otherwise everything empty, dry sputum. [DRAWING]

Does my larynx hurt so much because for many hours I have done nothing with it?

I always have a nagging irritation.

You say you haven't heard anything about Schweninger,[2] Bismarck's doctor? He stood midway between conventional medicine and nature therapy which he had discovered quite on his own. A great man who had a hard time treating Bismarck because Bismarck was a magnificent glutton and a heavy drinker.

The small quantities and the continual feeling that there is an obstruction to complete cleansing, an obstruction that should be removed before any attempt is made to treat it with medicines.

Somewhere in today's newspapers there is an excellent little item on the treatment of cut flowers; they're so terribly thirsty, one more such newspaper.

Aslant, that is more or less what I thought, so they can drink more; strip their leaves.

A little water; these bits of pills stick in the mucus like splinters of glass.

If the noodles had not been so soft I couldn't have eaten them at all. Everything, even the beer, burned me.

Library of Travel and Adventure[3]
Brockhaus Verlag, Leipzig

No. 27 Arthur Berger, *In the Islands of Eternal Spring.*

I've already had several books from this series, mostly excerpts from large works for boys. Very good. One of the large retailers will probably have it in stock, Lechner, say, on the Graben, but not Heller,[4] for instance; one has to have a nose for that sort of thing, but that's something I can't expect of you in this heat. Wait with that until the clothes come.

But of course it's only a silly observation. When I started to eat, something in the larynx dropped, whereupon I felt wonderfully free and was already thinking of all sorts of possible miracles, but the feeling was soon gone.

To think that I once could simply venture a large swallow of water.

Maybe it's easier to choke over less.

I'd especially like to take care of the peonies because they are so fragile.

And move the lilacs into the sun.

Ask whether there is good mineral water, just out of curiosity.

Do you have a moment? Then please lightly spray the peonies.

Are you a connoisseur of wines, Doctor? Have you already drunk the Heurigen?

And in this condition I'm in—recuperating from it, if it's possible at all, will take me weeks.
    Please see that the peonies don't touch the bottom of the vase. That's why they have to be kept in bowls.

A bird was in the room.

Good advice: Put a slice of lemon into the wine.

Can't one bathe in the brook, or sunbathe

Mineral water—once for fun I could

I'll hold out another week, maybe, I hope; such are the nuances.

I want to obey him, especially when it's pleasant; after the lemonade tell me again how your mother drank, only water, long-lasting pain, thirst. But earlier, when she received the good water, she rejoiced.

Did she never have a complication that involved being temporarily forbidden to drink?

Have you seen the books from Die Schmiede[5] yet?

Study trip for R.[6] Government stipend 6 weeks

A third deleted from the middle.[7]

Can the pain temporarily stop? I mean, for a fairly long time.

Please be careful that I don't cough in your face.

Letter to Schmiede

How trying I am to all of you; it's crazy.

Bismarck also had his own doctor, was also trying.

The doctor was also a great man.

I've always feared them[8] more than anything else. *I'd rather have the medicine and omit everything else.* After this morning—but of course everything is deceptive—the lozenges work better than the injection, aside from the endless burning. I can't immediately after they dissolve, because then the burning is worst. The improvement shows in the fact that the pain, which also comes after the injection, is duller, as though the wounds over which the food flows were sealed a little. I am only trying to describe the effect. Besides I felt it only this morning. This might well all be wrong.

Fear again and again.

Of course it causes me more pain because you all are so good to me; in this respect the hospital is very good.

They killed the man beside me;[9] every assistant doctor dropped in and without asking
    They let him walk around with pneumonia, 106 temperature. Wonderful the way all the assistants were sound asleep in their beds at night and only the priest with his acolytes was there. He didn't have to confess. After the extreme unction the priest again

I find talking a strain today.

I'm only so sad because this insane trouble over eating is useless.

Here, now, with what strength I have am I to write it?
   They have waited so long to send me the material.[10]

It's obvious the way one devilish medicine[11] smoothes the way for the next.

Let the bad remain bad, otherwise it will grow worse.

Do you know Giesshübl?[12] It's near Karlsbad   Mineral spring
woods

If there were no main topic, there would be subjects for conversation.

How many years will you be able to stand it? How long will I be able to
stand your standing it?
   Now I want to read it.
   It will excite me too much, perhaps, and yet I must experience it all over
again.[13]

Why were we not in a beer garden?
   Long way
   Wine—Meran   Beer   Gnat

When it's quiet for a while I'm glad.
          [DRAWING (ITALY AND SICILY)]

A lake doesn't flow into anything, you know.

Milk is very good, but it is frightful the way it's getting so late again, yet I
can't help it. That is a general lament.

The trouble is that I cannot drink a single glass of water, though the craving
itself is some satisfaction.

And the wonderful memories of Giesshübl, for instance, a lovely little forest
village near Karlsbad.

If it is true—and it seems probable—that the quantity of food I consume at
present is insufficient for the body to mend of its own accord, then there's no
hope, apart from miracles.

I cannot keep up the present level of eating if this pain and coughing continue.

My father is glad to receive the special-delivery letters, but also annoyed by them.

See the lilacs, fresher than morning.

You'll have to warn the girl about the glass; she sometimes comes in barefoot.[14]

Ergo bibamus.[15] So let us drink.

I don't like that, too much work; takes too much knowledge. Cut flowers should be treated quite differently.

I am already so poisoned that the body can hardly understand the pure fruit.

It[16] can be eaten from the jar, and that is good, but not clean, but since I shall eat only a little it is best to stir it all up and put a little into the glass for me.
    I cannot swallow that without water. Yogurt would have been absolutely enough for me, enough for everybody, especially with this fever. It changes with the weather; in hot weather it is even better, thicker, besides in hot weather it is still better, not so delicate and firm.

That the ants don't eat it up.

By now we have come a long way from the day in the tavern garden when we

It was a kind of bargain in half-sleep. I was promised that I would manage to sleep through the noise, but that in return I must promise something else. I promised but have forgotten what

It[17] cannot eat, so no pain. Does it want to come back?

Always this "temporarily"; I can also apply it to myself. We always talk about the larynx as though it could take a turn for the better, but that isn't true.
    Of course mood plays its part, the exciting subject of conversation, for instance.

How could we be without R. so long?

Now I have dreamed that R. is at the door and I am to give him a sign that I am somehow ready, but at the same time I knew that you [Dora] were on the terrace and did not want to disturb you by making the sign. Difficult problem.

Even if I really were to recover a little from it all, I certainly wouldn't recover from the narcotics.

Who telephoned? Was it by any chance Max?

Tremendous amount of sputum, easily, and still pain in the morning. In my daze it went through my head that for such quantities and the ease somehow the Nobel Prize

That is why one loves dragonflies.

We'll buy a little book about these matters; one has to know such things precisely

But now enough flowers for the time being.
    Show me the columbine; too bright to stand with the others.
    Scarlet hawthorn is too hidden, too much in the dark.
    More of the water. Fruit

You praise so arbitrarily when I've eaten enough; today I ate a great deal and you reproach me; another time you praise me just as unfairly.

Where is the eternal spring?[18]

Doesn't the newspaper say: Greenish translucent bowls?

Yesterday evening a late bee drank the white lilac dry.
    Cut at a steep slant; then they can touch the floor.

I like to eat it in the comb; I suppose it can be had only in the fall, and besides fine light-colored combs are very rare.

Can't laburnum be found?

He hasn't drunk any water yet today. And the way we live here; at the Wiener Wald that would have been impossible.

Might I try a little ice cream today?

Faithful Eckart—a good, wise, fatherly guardian spirit.[19]

That time you came when I was kept in bed, how easy it was, and yet I didn't even have beer, just preserves, fruit, fruit juice, water, fruit juice, fruit, preserves, water, fruit juice, fruit, preserves, water, lemonade, cider, fruit, water.[20]

How wonderful that is, isn't it? The lilac—dying, it drinks, goes on swilling.

That cannot be, that a dying man drinks.

Even if there should be scarification—forgive all this disgusting questioning, but you are my doctor, aren't you?—it will take years; I'll have to wait just as long for painless eating.

rhetorical question

Given this limited ability to drink, I cannot yet go with my father to the beer garden at the Civilian Swimming Pool.[21]

In earlier years Venice   Riva   Desenzano   also alone Norderney,   Heligoland[22]   Uncle Siegfried

I was to have gone to the Baltic with her once (along with her girl friend), but was ashamed because of my thinness and other anxieties.
    Insofar as it was worth understanding me.[23] She was that way in everything.
    She was not beautiful, but slender, fine body, which she has kept according to reports (Max's sister, her girl friend).

Put your hand on my forehead for a moment to give me courage.

This newspaper comes in three copies, twice a week.

Every limb as tired as a person.

Why didn't I once try beer in the hospital
   Lemonade   it was all so boundless.

So the help goes away again without helping.[24]

Notes

Max Brod's notes to the original edition of *Briefe* (1958) have been revised and amplified. Grateful acknowledgment is made to the following works which furnished most of the new information presented here:

Chris Bezzel, *Kafka-Chronik*. Munich and Vienna, 1975.

Hartmut Binder, *Kafka in neuer Sicht*. Stuttgart, 1976.

——, *Kafka-Kommentar zu sämtlichen Erzählungen*. Munich, 1975.

——, *Kafka-Kommentar zu den Romanen, Rezensionen, Aphorismen und zum Brief an den Vater*. Munich, 1976.

Jürgen Born, Ludwig Dietz, Malcolm Pasley, Paul Raabe, and Klaus Wagenbach, eds., *Kafka-Symposion*. Berlin, 1965.

Max Brod, *Franz Kafka: A Biography*. Trans. by G. Humphreys Roberts and Richard Winston. New York, 1963. (Cited as Brod, *Biography*.)

——, *Streitbares Leben*. Munich, 1960.

Franz Kafka, *Briefe an Ottla und die Familie*. Ed. by Hartmut Binder and Klaus Wagenbach. Frankfurt a.M., 1974. (Cited as *Ottla*.)

Margarita Pazi, *Max Brod: Werk und Persönlichkeit*. Bonn, 1970.

Klaus Wagenbach, *Franz Kafka: Eine Biographie seiner Jugend 1883–1912*. Bern, 1958.

——, *Franz Kafka in Selbstzeugnissen und Bilddokumenten*. Reinbek, 1964.

Kurt Wolff, *Briefwechsel eines Verlegers 1911–1963*. Ed. by Bernhard Zeller and Ellen Otten. Frankfurt a.M., 1966.

References to Kafka's works in English are to the editions published by Schocken Books, New York:

> *Amerika, A Novel.* 1962.
> *The Castle.* 1974.
> *The Complete Stories.* 1975.
> *Dearest Father: Stories and Other Writings.* 1954.
> *Diaries.* Vol. I: 1910–1913; Vol. II: 1914–1923. 1948.
> *Letters to Felice.* 1973.

Letters to Milena. 1965.
The Penal Colony: Stories and Short Pieces. 1948.
The Trial. 1968.

Max Brod explained his editorial policy as follows: "Kafka did not date most of his letters. The presumptive dates were established on the basis of the postmark, if it was legible and if the envelope of the letter happened to be preserved, or on the basis of the contents. These presumptive dates, and all other additions by the editor, are enclosed in brackets. Wherever only the year in which a letter was written could be determined, the letter has been placed at the end of that year. I cannot claim that this procedure has established the absolutely correct order, but a plausible approximation has been reached. For vital assistance in the arrangement of these letters I am deeply obliged to Frau Ester Hoffe. [...]

"My gratitude goes to Klaus Wagenbach for his ever-ready help with the chronological order and corrections."

1900

1 Selma Kohn Robitschek, daughter of the chief postmaster of Roztok (Roztoky), on the left bank of the Moldau, 7½ miles north of Prague. For one summer the Kafkas lived in their house, and Franz and Selma spent much time in the forest, where he would read Nietzsche aloud.

1902

1 Max Brod explains: "Oskar Pollak was a schoolmate of Franz Kafka in the gymnasium, and their friendship continued for a while during their years at the university. Pollak, born in Prague in 1883, first studied chemistry, then philosophy, archaeology, and finally art history. As an art historian he went to Rome where he worked chiefly on the Roman Baroque; a major work of his, *Artistic Activity under Urban VIII*, was published posthumously (Vienna, 1928–31). At the outbreak of the war he volunteered and was killed on the Isonzo on June 11, 1915. The letters of Kafka published here were found among Oskar Pollak's papers, where I was able to examine them with the kind consent of Pollak's widow. At the time of the first publication of Kafka's letters in 1937, I omitted some inessential passages, quantitatively very little, and unfortunately can no longer fill these gaps since the original letters were probably lost during the German occupation of Prague."

2 *Der Kunstwart,* a cultural monthly, founded (1887) and edited by Ferdinand Avenarius (1856–1923), a nephew of Richard Wagner. Under the influence of Nietzsche's ideas it propagated the "higher values" in art, literature, and life. For a time Kafka was much influenced by its style.

3 Liběchov, village on the Elbe, 25 miles north of Prague, on the former Czech–German linguistic frontier.

4 Small town near Weimar, with mines in which Goethe was interested. Oskar Pollak was visiting the sites of classical German literature.

5 Goethe's house in Weimar, maintained as a national shrine.

6 Kafka started out to study chemistry (as did his friends Oskar Pollak and Ewald Přibram), but soon switched to jurisprudence, to which he devoted his first semester (winter 1901-2). Disgusted by the dryness of the material, he spent the second semester exclusively on the humanities (art, German literature, psychology, etc.), with German literature as his main subject. (Actually, one semester of humanities was obligatory for law students.) The chair of German Literature was then held by Professor August Sauer (1855-1926), a narrow and aggressive German nationalist for whom Kafka soon developed an intense dislike. It may have been for this reason that he went to Munich in October 1902 to investigate academic possibilities there. Nothing is known about this trip, from which he soon returned to Prague (perhaps forced by his father) to concentrate on the study of law without further digressions. After six semesters (through summer 1905) and a period of extra-academic preparation, he received his degree of doctor of law on June 18, 1906. Max Brod recollects that the deleted portion of this letter contained a violent denunciation of Professor Sauer.

7 Chotkovy Sady, small park near the Belvedere on the left bank of the Moldau, a favorite refuge of Kafka and his sisters.

8 Alfred Löwy, oldest brother of Kafka's mother, director general of the Spanish railroads.

9 Třešt', small village in western Moravia, about 80 miles southeast of Prague, where Kafka's uncle Dr. Siegfried Löwy (the "country doctor") lived.

10 Dubá, village 19 miles northeast of Liboch.

11 Now Celetná ulice, where Kafka lived with his parents and three sisters from 1896 to 1907.

12 According to Brod (Streitbares Leben, pp. 245 f.), Shamefaced Lanky is Kafka himself, while Impure in Heart is a portrait of his former classmate at the gymnasium, Emil Utitz (1883-1956), then a student of philosophy and follower of Franz Brentano. Later Utitz became a professor of philosophy in Germany and Prague and author of important books.

1903

1 Oskar Pollak had gone to Castle Ober-Studenec near Ždirek (south of Pilsen), where he had taken a position as tutor. Max Brod accounts for the deletions in this letter as follows: "Only portions of this letter are being published here; in the original it runs to twelve

pages and contains, among other things, a detailed criticism of a lecture in Prague by Professor Paul Schultze-Naumburg [(1869–1949), defender of traditional Germanic artistic values and contributor to the *Kunstwart*]. As in the fourth letter [p. 5] to the same addressee, the contrast between city and country is one of Kafka's principal themes. In another letter to Oskar Pollak, Kafka writes: '. . . whereas in truth we are half-buried ones, but you have good air for breathing in this green spring. Therefore it is presumptuous and a little sinful to write to you from the city, except to advise you, wise as city folks are where others are concerned, to throw yourself into agriculture. On the other hand, it is sensible and cautionary to have letters from the country written to oneself. I shall do that.'"

2 Now Václavské náměstí and Na Příkopě, respectively, intersecting thoroughfares in central Prague.

3 Gustav Theodor Fechner (1801–87), German natural philosopher and experimental psychologist. Johannes Eckhart (1260?–1327?), called Meister Eckhart, Dominican mystic and master of German prose.

4 Kafka was briefly in Munich in October 1902 (see note 6, 1902), but not, as far as we know, in 1903. The unlikelihood that he should refer to the 1902 visit fully fourteen months later puts the date of this letter in doubt.

1904

1 Max Brod (1884–1968), Kafka's closest friend, and preserver, editor, and commentator of his works. Kafka had met Brod for the first time on October 23, 1902, at a lecture Brod gave on "Schopenhauer and Nietzsche." Their friendship became intimate after the death of Brod's friend Max Bäuml in 1908.

2 Ewald Felix Příbram, Kafka's friend during school and university years, was the son of Dr. Otto Příbram, chairman of the board of the Workers' Accident Insurance Institute, of which Kafka was to become an employee in 1908. Max Brod observes that "aspects of Ewald Příbram's personality are clearly recognizable in the character of the 'new acquaintance' in 'Description of a Struggle.'"

3 Friedrich Hebbel (1813–63), German dramatist. A critical edition of his *Tagebücher 1825–1863*, edited by Richard Maria Werner, was published in four volumes in 1903. The set was in Kafka's library.

4 Julie Kafka, née Löwy (1856–1934), descendant of a well-to-do German-Jewish family in Poděbrady on the Elbe. She married Hermann Kafka on September 3, 1882. Franz was their first child.

5 *Byrons Tagebücher und Briefe,* ed. by Eduard Engel, 4th ed. (Berlin, 1904), in Kafka's library. The entry reads: "I have not stirred out of these rooms for these four days past; but

I have sparred for exercise (windows open) with Jackson an hour daily to attenuate and keep up the ethereal part of me." *Byron's Letters and Journals,* vol. 3: *Alas! the Love of Women,* ed. by Leslie A. Marchand (Cambridge, Mass., 1974), under date of April 10, 1814.

6 Thomas Mann's novella "Tonio Kröger" was first published in *Neue deutsche Rundschau* (February 1903) and included in *Tristan,* a collection of stories (also 1903). In Thomas Mann, *Stories of Three Decades,* New York, 1936.

7 Brod's *Ausflüge ins Dunkelrote* (a novel) was not published until 1909.

1905

1 German poet (1868–1933). Kafka was briefly interested in George and had given Max Brod two volumes of his poetry.

2 Small town in Moravian Silesia, north of Olomouc, near the former German (now Polish) border.

3 After his last semester at the university (summer 1905) and a vacation in Zuckmantel (6 miles northwest of Aussig) and Strakonitz (on the Wotawa, 33 miles northwest of Budweis), Kafka began to prepare himself for the three examinations he had to undergo. The first (Rigorosum II: Austrian civil and criminal law) took place on November 7, 1905.

4 Wilhelm von Kügelgen (1802–67), German artist and author, whose *Jugenderinnerungen eines alten Mannes* [*An Old Man's Reminiscences of Childhood and Youth*], 1870, was very popular at the time.

1906

1 For his second examination (Rigorosum III: constitutional and international law) on March 16, 1906.

2 Literary magazine (1905–6) edited by Franz Blei (writer and editor, 1871–1942), which Brod and Kafka jointly subscribed to.

3 Written immediately after the second examination, which was conducted by five professors, none of whose names began with the letter M: Frankl, Rauchberg, Ulbrich, Weber, and Zuckerkandl. The last-named was Kafka's professor for political economy (see note 86, 1917). Weber was Alfred Weber (1868–1959), brother of the sociologist Max Weber.

4 Apparently the move of Hermann Kafka's notions business from Zeltnergasse 12 to the Palais Kinsky on Altstädter Ring.

5 *Tod den Toten!* [*Death to the Dead*], Stuttgart, 1906.

6 Thomas Babington Macaulay, *Lord Clive*, published, as Max Brod recalls, in a popular series of English and French authors intended for use in schools.

7 May 27.

8 Max Brod: "A novel I worked on for years without ever being able to complete it. 'The Thousand Amusements' might have been another possible title."

9 The dean, Professor Frankl, set June 13, 1906, as the date for the third examination (Rigorosum I: Roman, German, and canonical law). Having passed it, Kafka received his doctor of law degree on June 18 from Professor Alfred Weber.

10 At this period pneumatic tubes were used to send special-delivery letters around cities within hours. There was even "tube mail" between Paris and Berlin. From door to door it was faster than airmail today.—Trans.

1907

1 In a book review in the Berlin monthly *Die Gegenwart* (February 9, 1907), Brod had praised Kafka for his style, along with three established writers (Heinrich Mann, Frank Wedekind, and Gustav Meyrink), although Kafka had not yet published a single line.

2 Gustav Meyrink (1868-1932), author of fantastic novels and tales, best known for his novel *Der Golem*, 1915 [*The Golem*, London, 1928].

3 Wladislaw Gasse was Oskar Pollak's address. Max Brod was living at his parents' house on Schalengasse.

4 Presumably the first two chapters of the first version of "Wedding Preparations in the Country."

5 Now Chomutov, city northwest of Prague, at the foot of the Erzgebirge, where Brod had "temporarily found a job with the internal revenue office of the district. The 'green baize of the office table' in the postcard of August 28 below refers to this."

6 Max Brod, *Experimente* (1907), four stories, including "Die Insel Carina" ["The Island of Carina"], "in which," as Brod explains, "one of the characters (Carus) represented Franz Kafka as I then saw him," that is, as merely an aesthete.

7 Possibly *Journal de Stendhal 1801-1814* (Paris, 1899), a copy of which was in Kafka's library.

8 Short-lived literary magazine (1907) edited by Franz Blei.

9 Brod's publisher at this time was Axel Juncker in Stuttgart (see note 13, 1912). Kafka had done a drawing for the title page of Brod's first book of verse, *Der Weg des Verliebten* [*The Path of the Lover*], 1907.

10 "Some poems," Brod recalls, "that Kafka must have found in another magazine and that he sent to me more or less as 'compensation.' "

11 Kafka had changed his handwriting from German to Latin script.

12 The discovery of the letters to Hedwig W. is due to the special ardor of Max Brod's secretary, Frau Ester Hoffe. Hedwig W., aged 19, a student of languages in Vienna, was visiting her grandmother in Triesch.

13 At this time Hermann Kafka's white goods and notions business was a retail shop; Kafka's aversion to his father's business developed later, when it became a large wholesale enterprise. The office was at the criminal court in Prague where Kafka worked during the second part of his training year (October 1, 1906, to September 30, 1907). During the first part he was at the civil court.

14 Newspaper founded in Vienna in 1889, as the official organ of the Austrian Social Democratic Party, by Victor Adler (1852–1918), the leader of the party.

15 Novel (1880) by Jens Peter Jacobsen (1847–85), Danish writer and poet, and translator of Darwin. The sentence here alluded to is in Chapter 11 and reads: "But every castle of happiness that is erected rests upon a foundation that is partly sand, and the sand collects and runs out under the walls, slowly perhaps—it may be, imperceptibly—but it runs and runs, grain by grain ... And love? — Neither is love a rock, however ready we are to believe it" (New York, n.d.).

16 Kafka's plan to study a year at the Export Academy in Vienna was not carried out.

17 On June 20, 1907, Kafka's parents (and he with them) had moved from Zeltnergasse 3 (where they had lived for eleven years) to Niklasstrasse 36 (now Pařižska), close to the Moldau. To the northwest Kafka's room commanded a view of the river and its left bank with the Belvedere Park (now Letenské Sady).

18 With the support of his Madrid uncle, Kafka was expecting to obtain a job at the Prague office (on Wenzelsplatz) of the Italian insurance company Assicurazioni Generali, Trieste; see note 20, 1907.

19 The *Prager Tagblatt* and the *Deutsche Zeitung Bohemia* were the two leading German-language dailies of Bohemia.

20 Kafka had started his job with the Assicurazioni Generali on October 1. Office hours were from 8 A.M. to 6 P.M. The salary was very low, and all employees were obliged to work overtime without pay.

21 Erected in 1650 to commemorate the liberation of Prague from the Swedes in 1648.

22 In connection with his new job, Kafka had undergone a detailed medical examination on October 1, 1907. He was found "healthy" but "fragile," almost 6 feet tall and weighing 134 lbs. Apparently a second examination was required.

23 See note 9, 1907.

24 Enclosed was a short prose piece, "Begegnung" ["The Encounter"], which Kafka later included in his first book, *Meditation,* under the title "Die Abweisung" ["Rejection"].

25 "Weissgerber" is probably an error for Weissberger. A Herr Weissberger, American Vice-Consul in Prague, "warmly recommended" Kafka for the job with the Assicurazioni Generali. His son, possibly José A. Weissberger (1880–1954), was the company's general representative in Madrid. Max Bäuml: see note 1, 1904.

26 Felix Weltsch (1884–1964), philosopher and Zionist, classmate and friend of Max Brod who had introduced Kafka to him in the fall of 1904. Kafka's friendship with Weltsch remained rather formal until 1912.

1908

1 Niklasstrasse 36.

2 The Čech Bridge (most Svatopluka Čecha), which was completed later that year.

3 The Trocadero and Eldorado were wine taverns. Kuchelbad, 6 miles west of Prague, was the site of horse races.

4 Schalengasse (Skořepka) 1 was the address where Max Brod lived at the time with his parents Adolf and Fanny Brod, his brother Otto, and sister Sophie.

5 *Jakob von Gunten* (1909), by Robert Walser (1878–1956), Swiss author highly regarded by Kafka. See below, p. 60.

6 Jakob Löwy (1824–1910), cloth dealer from Poděbrady, now living in Prague in retirement.

7 *Schloss Nornepygge* [*Nornepygge Castle*], Stuttgart, 1908.

8 Kafka had given up his job at the Assicurazioni Generali on July 15 and became on July 30 an employee of the Workers' Accident Insurance Institute of the Kingdom of Bohemia, where his office hours were from 8 A.M. to 2 P.M.

9 Tetschen, German-speaking city on the Elbe opposite Bodenbach, near the German border (now Děčín). In his new job Kafka had to make frequent official trips to the industrial region of northern Bohemia to inspect factories and check their classification as to insurance categories.

10 Černošice, village about 10 miles southwest of Prague.

11 Now Spičák (alt. 2740 ft.), near the Bavarian border, on the watershed between the Elbe and the Danube. Kafka vacationed there for a week.

12 *Schloss Nornepygge.*

13 Hermann Kafka (1852–1931), son of a butcher in the small (100 inhabitants) Czech-speaking village of Wossek, about 60 miles south of Prague.

14 Play (1903) by Victorien Sardou (1831–1908), written as a vehicle for Sarah Bernhardt.

15 Blind author, music teacher, and organist (1883–1941) to whom Max Brod had introduced Kafka in the fall of 1904. From then on the four friends—Kafka, Brod, Weltsch, and Baum—met regularly to read their works to each other.

16 *Uferdasein [Shore Life]*, Stuttgart, 1908; Oskar Baum's first book.

17 Ando Hiroshige (1797–1858), Japanese painter.

18 Max Brod's novella *Ein tschechisches Dienstmädchen [A Czech Maidservant]*, Berlin, 1909.

19 Denis Diderot (1713–84), *Le neveu de Rameau* (first published in Goethe's translation, 1805; original French, 1891).

20 Rudolf Kassner (1873–1959), Austrian philosopher, aesthetician, and critic; friend of Rainer Maria Rilke, Oscar Wilde, and Paul Valéry.

21 Friend of Max Brod, whom he married four years later.

22 Movie house favored by Brod and his friends.

23 Gustave Flaubert (1821–80), *The Temptation of Saint Anthony* (1874), which Brod and Kafka were reading together in French.

24 See note 8, 1906.

25 A cabaret.

26 *Der Vice-Admiral*, operetta (1886) by Karl Millöcker (1842–99).

1909

1 Kafka here reverts to the formal pronoun of address; previously he had used the familiar *Du* in his letters to Hedwig W.—Trans.

2 This referred to a job for Max Brod.

3 Brod had obtained a job with the postal administration in Prague, which he held until 1924.

4 Jakob Löwy; see note 6, 1908.

5 "Steine, nicht Menschen," a poem by Max Brod, published in *Bohemia*, April 11, 1909; later included in *Tagebuch in Versen* [*Diary in Verse*], Berlin, 1910.

6 Knut Hamsun (pseudonym of Knut Pedersen, 1859-1952), Norwegian novelist. The story is *Under Høststjeren* [*Under the Autumn Star*], 1906; first German edition, 1908. In *Wanderers*, New York, 1922.

7 Prague's oldest synagogue, so called (old-new) because it was rebuilt after the disastrous fire that destroyed the Jewish quarter in 1338.

8 Until 1918 a toll was collected on all bridges except the Charles Bridge.

9 Max Brod explains: "A letter to console me for some extra work my boss at the time, Postal Director Kalandra, had assigned to me."

10 Now Dobřichovice, village 12 miles southwest of Prague. Kafka is referring to Brod's description of a joint outing, "Zirkus auf dem Lande" ["Circus in the Country"], *Die Schaubühne*, July 1, 1909.

11 The second version of "Wedding Preparations in the Country." See note 4, 1907.

12 Refers to Baum's unfinished novel *Das Leben im Dunkeln* [*Life in Darkness*], which is set in an asylum for the blind. It was finished soon and published later that year.

13 Štěchovice, village on the Moldau, 19 miles south of Prague, with steamboat service from the city.

14 The mother of Felix Weltsch. He did not marry until 1914.

15 Mnichovice and Strancice, villages, 19 and 15 miles, respectively, southeast of Prague.

16 Willi Nowak (1886–), painter and graphic artist.

17 Kafka and Max and Otto Brod vacationed in Riva on Lake Garda September 4–14. During their stay they went to Brescia to watch (on September 11) a flying competition in which Louis Blériot (1872–1936) and Glenn Curtiss (1878–1930) took part. See Kafka's "The Aeroplanes at Brescia" in *The Penal Colony*.

18 Max Brod, "Ein Besuch in Prag," *Bohemia*, No. 278 (1909), an article about the visit to Prague of Flaubert's niece, Caroline Commanville.

19 Louis Bouilhet (1822–69), French poet and dramatist, friend of Flaubert.

20 A major fraud trial then in progress in Prague.

21 Max Brod explains: "Dr. Fleischmann was one of Kafka's superiors who often (unfortunately, but without meaning ill) tried to persuade him to write specialized papers of a scholarly nature."

22 Heinrich Rauchberg, one of Kafka's professors at Prague University, a specialist in administrative law and statistics.

23 *Life in Darkness.*

24 Renowned café on the Graben (Na Příkopě).

25 Baum's *Life in Darkness.*

26 One of Kafka's inspection tours, this time to western Bohemia.

27 Director Eisner, a department head at the Assicurazioni Generali, had taken an unusual interest in Kafka and tried, though in vain, to make his work easier. Max Brod comments: "This highly cultivated, skeptical, and kindly man (a cousin of the composer Adolf Schreiber) was intensely interested in literature. Apparently he had compared Kafka to one of the characters in a novel of Robert Walser [see note 5, 1908]; many of Walser's figures are addicted to sweetly contemplative idleness." Director Eisner kept in touch with Kafka until at least 1915.

28 See note 5, 1908.

29 *Geschwister Tanner* (1907), Robert Walser's first novel. Simon is the main character.

30 Max Brod recollects that Kafka at this time avidly attended the horse races in Kuchelbad (see note 3, 1908). Kafka's short prose piece "Reflections for Gentlemen-Jockeys" (included in *Meditation*) was written around this time, and he learned to ride himself (see below, postcard to Max Brod, March 10, 1910).

31 Jeschken (Ještěd), mountain rising to 3313 ft. southwest of Reichenberg (Liberec) on the

Neisse in northern Bohemia. Maffersdorf, small spa, 3½ miles southeast of Reichenberg. The other places mentioned are all in the immediate vicinity.

32 Café frequented by writers and artists, on Hybernergasse (Hybernská ulice).

1910

1 Still *The Happy Ones* (see note 8, 1906). Milada is the heroine of this novel.

2 Sophie Brod, later married to Max Friedmann.

3 A night club.

4 Possibly the second version of "Description of a Struggle."

5 Jörgen Petersen Müller (1866–1938), Danish gymnastics teacher, developed daily fifteen-minute exercises for home use, and published instruction books for men (1903) and women and children (1913). Müller exercises were a fad at the time.

6 Wran (Vran), Davle: small villages some 17 miles south of Prague. Above Štěchovice (see note 13, 1909), the St. John's Rapids of the Moldau. The steamboat trip back to Prague took 2½ hours. For Dobřichovice, see note 10, 1909.

7 Friedrich Soennecken (1848–1919), developed superior steel nibs, established a large office-supply firm in Bonn in 1875. Soennecken products were standard up to World War II.

8 According to Max Brod, the manuscript of "Description of a Struggle." He explains: "Kafka's remark is in response to my enthusiastic approval and my thanks for the manuscript, which I had asked him for and which he gave me." Kafka had read the novella to Brod on March 14 and expressed his intention to destroy it.

9 *Bohemia* was about to publish five short pieces by Kafka (later included in *Meditation*) on March 27 in its Easter supplement.

10 A mass meeting of the Realists, a Czech political party founded by Thomas Masaryk (1850–1937), then a parliamentary deputy, later first President of Czechoslovakia (1918–35).

11 Jan Herben (1857–1936), Czech writer and journalist, closely associated with Masaryk, editor in chief of *Čas*.

12 The young actress Sybil Smolová, who had impressed both Kafka and Brod.

13 Small-circulation Prague daily, the organ of Thomas Masaryk.

14 I.e., Kafka's review of a technical treatise (on the insurance of motherhood) by Robert Marschner, the director of the Workers' Accident Insurance Institute. Ferdinand Matras was the editor of *Deutsche Arbeit*, an official monthly designed to impress the Czechs with the superiority of German culture and workmanship. Kafka's review was published in the issue of June 1910.

15 Max Brod dated this letter "Spring 1919?" Kurt Krolop's suggestion (in *Weltfreunde*, Prague, 1967, p. 83, n. 106) to assign the letter to the spring of 1910 is amply borne out by the factual and internal evidence. The trial of Countess Maria Nikolaievna Tarnovska for complicity (with two co-defendants) in the murder of her fiancé, Count Pavel Evgrafovich Kamarovsky, took place in Venice from March 4 to May 20, 1910; she was sentenced to 8½ years in prison. The sensational trial, in which psychological and sexual perversions played a role, created a stir at the time. Paul Wiegler (1878–1949), author, critic, and translator, then literary editor of *Bohemia;* Willy Handl (1872–1920), theater critic, author of a novel, *Die Flamme* [*The Flame*].

16 Presumably again *The Happy Ones.*

17 By Kafka, which Max Brod had praised.

18 Saaz (Žatec), town on the Eger (Ohře), 65 miles northwest of Prague. Since August 21 was a Sunday, Kafka may have been on a weekend excursion. This year, Kafka took his regular vacation in October.

19 Kafka and Max Brod took French lessons in preparation for their trip to Paris (see note 21, 1910).

20 Kafka had to give a public lecture on accident insurance in Gablonz later in September.

21 Max Brod placed this and the following letter at the end of 1910, qualifying the year. On Saturday, October 8, 1910, Kafka and Max and Otto Brod left for Paris, with a stopover in Nuremberg. The second letter clearly antedates the trip to Paris ("as early as Saturday," i.e., October 8, when the party left). The "dislocated big toe" places the first letter immediately before the second: "lying on the sofa," "foot swollen."

22 "Kafka wrote these three cards consecutively without interruption and mailed them on the same day. He did the same with the consecutive postcards on pp. 115–16, 238, 306, and 325–26."—Max Brod.

23 In Paris Kafka developed nasty boils which forced him to return to Prague on October 17. Max and Otto Brod stayed on in Paris.

24 Arthur Schnitzler's (1862–1931) first play (1893).

25 A special whole-grain bread baked for twelve hours at low heat, introduced by Simons of Soest, Westphalia. It is still on the market.

26 The son of Oskar and Grete Baum.

27 Albert Bassermann (1867–1952), German stage and film actor.

28 After his return from Berlin, about December 9, Kafka still had ten days before going back to work on December 19.

29 Of Kafka's sister Elli (Gabriele, born 1889) to Karl Hermann (1883–1939), a native of Zürau. The new relatives were Karl's two brothers, Paul and Rudl, and their father, Leopold.

30 Possibly a fragment of "Description of a Struggle."

1911

1 Inspection tour to Friedland (Frýdlant) and Reichenberg (Liberec) in northern Bohemia, from January 30 to about February 12.

2 Friedland, 15 miles north of Reichenberg, is dominated by the Renaissance castle that Albrecht von Wallenstein, the Imperial general in the Thirty Years' War, bought in 1622.

3 Another inspection tour; in the meantime Kafka had been back in Prague. Neustadt (Nové-Město), village in the Iser (Jisera) Mountains at the foot of the Tafelfichte (Smrkem), a mountain of 3680 ft. about 5 miles east of Friedland.

4 Grottau (Hrádek), 12 miles northwest of Liberec, on the Czech-German border. The Austrian counts Clam-Gallas had a castle there.

5 The German film *Die weisse Sklavin* was produced in 1910, with Ellen Dietrich in the leading role.

6 *Der Tag der Vergeltung,* a detective novel by Anna Katharina Green, published in Lutz's Series of Crime and Detective Fiction, with several editions between 1900 and 1905.

7 *Hyperion,* literary bimonthly, edited by Franz Blei and Carl Sternheim (1878–1942), Munich, 1908–10. Both Max Brod and Kafka had published in it. When it ceased publication Kafka wrote an "obituary" ("Eine entschlafene Zeitschrift") which was published in *Bohemia,* March 20, 1911. See "Hyperion," *The Penal Colony,* pp. 313 ff. See also note 35, 1912. *Die Neue Rundschau,* founded by S. Fischer in Berlin in 1890, at the time Germany's foremost literary monthly. Kafka read the magazine with some regularity from about 1904, when he had outgrown his infatuation with the *Kunstwart* (see note 2, 1902).

8 According to Hartmut Binder *(Kafka-Kommentar* I, p. 87), the story "Unhappiness," which Kafka had read to Max Brod on March 3, 1911. Apparently Kafka gave Brod a carbon which he later reclaimed (see below, p. 76) to correct some typographical errors.

9 Zittau, industrial city in the then Kingdom of Saxony. Mount Oybin (alt. 1594 ft.), a

bell-shaped hill, 5 miles southwest of Zittau, with picturesque ruins, was a popular excursion spot. Apparently Kafka, on another inspection tour of northern Bohemia, availed himself of the opportunity (April 23 was a Sunday) to visit the site.

10 Not identified.

11 From August 26 to September 13, Kafka and Max Brod had spent their vacation traveling to Zurich, Lucerne, Lugano, Stresa, Milan, and Paris. On the 13th Brod returned to Prague, while Kafka went to Erlenbach (on Lake Zurich) for another week of rest.

12 Peter Rosegger (1843–1918), regional Styrian writer, very popular at the time. Arthur Achleitner (1858–1927), regional Bavarian writer.

13 Conrad Ferdinand Meyer (1825–98) and Gottfried Keller (1819–90), best-known Swiss fiction writers of the century. Meyer wrote mainly historical fiction and aimed at a supranational classical quality, whereas Keller and Walser (see note 5, 1908) showed more local color.

14 Abraham Goldfaden (1840–1908), Yiddish dramatist. The performance took place on October 13 (see *Diaries* I, pp. 95 ff.). Yitzhak Löwy (see note 1, 1912) was one of the actors.

15 Building on the right bank of the Moldau, accommodating the conservatory of music, concert halls, exhibition rooms, and a permanent picture gallery.

1912

1 In the intervening months Kafka had seen more performances of the Yiddish troupe and befriended the actor Yitzhak Löwy. He met him frequently and arranged an evening of Yiddish recitations for his benefit, which took place on February 18, 1912, at the Jewish Town Hall in Prague. Kafka gave an introductory speech. Apparently Löwy perished in the Warsaw Ghetto during the Nazi occupation, 1942–43.

2 Subsequently included in *Meditation*. See note 8, 1911.

3 Max Brod had a disagreement with a reviewer of *Bohemia* in connection with a concert on March 17, 1912, at which music composed by Brod was performed. The reviewer broadcast "all over Prague" that Brod had written him an anonymous letter. Brod took Kafka's advice. Subsequently it turned out that the letter was written by Brod's father (see Brod, *Streitbares Leben*, pp. 59 ff.).

4 *Arnold Beer, das Schicksal eines Juden* [*Arnold Beer, the Fate of a Jew*], a novel (Berlin, 1912).

5 See note 5, 1906.

6 Kafka and Brod started their summer vacation with a trip to Leipzig, where Kafka met his future publishers, Ernst Rowohlt (see note 12, 1912) and Kurt Wolff (see note 6, 1913), on June 29. The same afternoon both went on to Weimar.

7 Kafka had three sisters. For the oldest, Elli, see note 29, 1910. The second was Valli (Valerie), born 1890, married to Josef Pollak in 1913. The youngest, Ottla (Ottilie, born 1892), was Kafka's favorite. She married the Czech lawyer Josef David (a Christian) in 1920. All three sisters died in Nazi concentration camps.

8 On July 7 Kafka traveled alone to the ancient city of Halberstadt (now in East Germany), while Brod returned to Prague. Johann Wilhelm Ludwig Gleim (1719-1803), German poet, secretary to the cathedral of Halberstadt; he was unmarried but liked to keep open house for the poets and writers of the day.

9 From Halberstadt Kafka proceeded to this sanatorium where he stayed from July 8 to 29. The sanatorium practiced natural therapy.

10 The diary Kafka kept in Weimar; see *Diaries* II, pp. 287 ff.

11 Max Brod's sonnet "Lugano-See" ["Lake Lugano"], subsequently published in *März* (August 1913), p. 247, with a dedication to Kafka. Now in Brod, *Biography*, pp. 80 f.

12 Ernst Rowohlt (1887-1960), German publisher, established his firm in 1908 and was soon joined by Kurt Wolff (1887-1963) as partner (see note 6, 1913).

13 Axel Juncker (1870-1952), a Dane, founded his publishing house in Stuttgart in 1902 and soon moved it to Berlin. He was Max Brod's publisher up to this time.

14 Heinrich von Kleist (1777-1811), *Anekdoten*, bibliophile edition, printed at the press of W. Drugulin, published by Rowohlt, 1911. Kafka wrote a brief review of this edition. See *The Penal Colony*, pp. 312 f.

15 *Die Höhe des Gefühls* [*Intensity of Feeling*] (scenes, verses, consolations), Brod's first book to be published by Rowohlt (Leipzig, 1912).

16 *Arkadia: A Yearbook for Literature*, edited by Max Brod, was published by Kurt Wolff in 1913. Publication of further volumes was forestalled by the outbreak of war in 1914.

17 On their trip to Italy in 1911, Kafka and Brod had fantasized about issuing guidebooks to show travelers the cheapest ways to get around. See Brod, *Biography*, pp. 120 f.

18 Felix Weltsch and Max Brod, *Anschauung und Begriff* [*Intuition and Concept*], was published by Kurt Wolff in 1913.

19 During the Leipzig visit (see note 6, 1912), Max Brod had shown Rowohlt and Wolff specimens of Kafka's work, and both were interested in publishing a book by Kafka. Brod kept urging his friend to select a number of pieces to form what was to become *Meditation*.

20 The first version of *Amerika* (now lost) which Kafka had been working on intermittently for some time. See also *Letters to Felice*, p. 218.

21 Margarethe Kirchner, daughter of the curator of Goethe's house in Weimar. Kafka flirted with her during his visit. See *Diaries* II, pp. 290 ff.

22 Small village, 2 miles northeast of Weimar, with the Grand Duke's summer palace and park, where Goethe used to stage theatrical entertainments.

23 "Die Arche Noahs," a dramatic scene, included in Brod's *Intensity of Feeling*.

24 Ernst Lissauer (1882–1937), German poet, dramatist, and editor.

25 Café Louvre, meeting place of the followers of the philosopher Franz Brentano (1838–1917). In the past Kafka had occasionally attended these gatherings.

26 Village 2 miles northeast of Liboch (see note 3, 1902).

27 Of *Amerika*.

28 Elsa Taussig, Max Brod's future wife.

29 While in Lugano (September 1911) Kafka and Brod planned to write a novel jointly. It was to consist of the travel diaries of two friends and to be called *Richard and Samuel*. Only one chapter was written, published in *Herder-Blätter*, I, No. 3 (1912). See *The Penal Colony*, pp. 279 ff., and Brod, *Biography*, pp. 119, 125 f.

30 Not identified.

31 Highest peak (3747 ft.) of the Harz Mountains, in legend the gathering place of witches.

32 The song was "In der Ferne" ["Far Away"], by Albert Count von Schlippenbach (1800–1868), beginning with the lines *"Nun leb wohl, du kleine Gasse,/Nun ade, du stilles Dach"* ["Now fare thee well, you little alley,/Now goodbye, you quiet roof"]. In November Kafka sent the copy he had made to Felice Bauer (see *Letters to Felice*, p. 48).

33 Max Brod's dating ("Jungborn im Harz, July 1912") is contradicted by Kafka's diary entry for August 7, 1912 *(Diaries* I, p. 265).

34 For *Meditation*. Encouraged by Rowohlt and Wolff and constantly prodded by Brod, Kafka began to assemble the pieces to be included in the book after his return from Jungborn. Nine that had been published presented no problem. The task now was to get the "remaining pieces" into shape for the printer.

35 "Conversation with the Supplicant" and "Conversation with the Drunk," two sections from the first version of "Description of a Struggle," were published in *Hyperion*, No. 8 (March/April 1909). Now in *The Complete Stories*, pp. 29 ff. and 40 ff.

36 Paul Ernst (1866–1933), German author, began as a naturalist, then turned to neoclassical formalism. For a time he was obsessed with writing stories on the Boccaccio model. While in Weimar Kafka and Brod spent the evening of July 5 with Paul Ernst and accompanied him on a walk the next day. See *Diaries* II, pp. 298 ff.

37 Felice Bauer (1887–1960), whom Kafka had met for the first time on the preceding evening at Max Brod's. (See *Letters to Felice*, pp. 14 ff., and *Diaries* I, pp. 268 f.) Kafka was establishing the final order of the pieces to be included in *Meditation*. The book was published late in 1912 (though dated 1913).

38 Refers to "Children on a Country Road." See *The Complete Stories*, p. 380, lines 18–20. The deletion and correction were not made.

39 In his letter of September 4, 1912, Kurt Wolff had expressed his and Rowohlt's eagerness to publish Kafka's book and asked him to state his conditions and any wishes he had regarding the book's format.

40 The type size chosen was 16-point.

41 Max Brod and Felix Weltsch were in Italy (see *Letters to Felice*, p. 7). Brod was sending diary pages to his fiancée.

42 To Josef Pollak, on September 14, 1912.

43 The repellent passage is preserved in *Diaries* I, p. 214 ("that the most distant journey . . . call it Russian."). The correction Kafka sent his publisher on October 8 (see below, p. 88) may be found in *The Complete Stories*, p. 398, lines 3–5 ("which fades . . . true stature.").

44 Felice Bauer.

45 Of *Amerika*. Kafka was working on the second version.

46 Karl Hermann, the husband of Kafka's sister Elli, owned an asbestos factory in Prague, of which, under his father's pressure, Kafka had become a silent partner when it was established in October 1911. During Karl Hermann's absences Kafka was supposed to look after the factory.

47 Paul Hermann.

48 Max Brod states: "Without my friend's knowledge I sent Kafka's mother a copy of this letter (without the postscript) because I was seriously worried about Franz's life. His mother's response and additional details (which also illuminate Kafka's 'Letter to His Father') may be found in the biography" (see Brod, *Biography*, pp. 93 ff.).

49 Magazine edited by Willy Haas and Norbert Eisler in Prague from April 1911 to October 1912. "The First Long Train Journey" (Chapter I of *Richard and Samuel*, see note 29, 1912) by Brod and Kafka (May 1912) and Kafka's "Great Noise" (October 1912) had

appeared there. Willy Haas (1891–1973), critic and essayist, edited Kafka's *Letters to Milena* (1952).

50 Of the second version of *Amerika*.

51 The "venomous letter" is Kafka's to Felice of November 11. See *Letters to Felice*, pp. 37 f. and 554, n. 47, where the circumstances of Kafka's sending roses and Max Brod's telephone call are explained.

52 "The Judgment." The evening took place on December 4. Max Brod and Oskar Baum also read from their works.

1913

1 Austrian writer (1875–1936) in whom Max Brod was interested (he included a story by Stoessl in *Arkadia*). Alerted by Brod, Kafka read some of Stoessl's books and was impressed (see *Letters to Felice*, pp. 86, 101). This letter was first published in the *Neue Zürcher Zeitung*, May 31, 1974.

2 Stoessl did not review *Meditation*, but gave Kafka his opinion in a letter. Kafka, taken aback by his lack of understanding, quoted the letter to Felice *(Letters to Felice*, pp. 175–76) and lost interest in its author.

3 On October 14, 1912.

4 Max Brod and Elsa Taussig had recently married and were on their honeymoon.

5 Sister of Kafka's future Hebrew teacher, Friedrich Thieberger. She later became the wife of Johannes Urzidil (1896–1970), who also knew Kafka and wrote about him.

6 The strong personalities of Ernst Rowohlt and Kurt Wolff proved incompatible. They separated on November 1, 1912, and Wolff took over the firm. He changed its name to Kurt Wolff Verlag on February 15, 1913. Wolff (1887–1963) was a successful publisher in Germany until 1930. Among his authors were Franz Werfel, Heinrich Mann, Max Brod, and Sinclair Lewis. During the 1930's Wolff lived in France and Italy; he emigrated to the United States in 1941. The following year he founded Pantheon Books in New York. Kafka's erroneous "1912" in the date of this letter was corrected by Max Brod.

7 On Saturday, March 22, Kafka had gone to Berlin to spend Easter with Felice.

8 Otto Pick (1887–1940), Bohemian poet and writer, translator from the Czech. He had written two favorable reviews of *Meditation* (*Pester Lloyd*, Budapest, February 9, 1913; *Aktion*, Berlin, February 19, 1913). Albert Ehrenstein (1886–1950), Austrian expressionist poet and writer, was to review *Meditation* favorably (*Berliner Tageblatt*, April 16, 1913).

Carl Ehrenstein (1892–1940), Albert's brother, author of a volume of prose sketches, *Klagen eines Knaben* [*Lamentations of a Youth*] (*Der jüngste Tag*, vol. 6), Leipzig, 1913.

9 Franz Werfel (1890–1945), poet and novelist, friend of Kafka and Max Brod, was then an editor at Kurt Wolff Verlag.

10 *The Metamorphosis*, which Kafka had written in November and December 1912.

11 Paul Zech (1881–1946), poet, translator from the French. Else Lasker-Schüler (1869–1945), poet and dramatist.

12 To Felice Bauer. See *Letters to Felice*, p. 233.

13 Suburb just south of Prague.

14 Of "The Stoker" and *The Metamorphosis*. On April 2, Kurt Wolff had asked Kafka to send "the first chapter of the novel" and "the bedbug story" immediately, as he was leaving for a long trip on Sunday, the 6th, and wanted to read both before his departure. Kafka sent "The Stoker" right off. Wolff, who had postponed his departure by two days, proposed terms to Kafka on the 8th. Wolff's letter of April 2 pleased Kafka so much that he sent it to Felice (*Letters to Felice*, p. 237).

15 *Der jüngste Tag*, a series of inexpensive small books devoted to the youngest writers. The first six volumes appeared in the spring of 1913, among them *The Stoker* as vol. 3.

16 Kurt Wolff had readily agreed (on April 16, 1913) to combine the three stories in one volume at a later date, but no such book was published.

17 Prosper Mérimée (1803–70) in *Carmen* (1845): "*En close bouche n'entre point mouche.*"

18 Aussig (Ustí), industrial town on the Elbe, north of Prague. Kafka had been there on April 22 to negotiate a complicated insurance case (see *Letters to Felice*, pp. 245 f.).

19 Kafka had again visited Felice in Berlin over the Whitsun holidays (May 11–12) and met her family.

20 At the suggestion of Franz Werfel, a frontispiece was added to *The Stoker*. It was an illustration from a book by Nathaniel Parker Willis (1806–67), *American Scenery* (London, 1838), entitled "View of the Ferry at Brooklyn, New York." It was engraved by G. K. Richardson after a design by W. H. Bartlett.

21 Alfred Kubin (1877–1959), graphic artist and illustrator, author of *Die andere Seite*, 1909 [*The Other Side: A Fantastic Novel*, New York, 1967].

22 Max Brod, *Über die Schönheit hässlicher Bilder* (a collection of essays), Leipzig, 1913.

23 According to Brod's recollection, "an article written by Kafka on assignment of his office,"

though Kafka may be referring to the "notice, suggested by me and written by Pick" (announcing a recital by Yitzhak Löwy) which appeared in the *Prager Tagblatt* on June 1, 1913. The recital took place on June 2 at the Hotel Bristol. See *Letters to Felice*, pp. 264; 563, n. 96; and 579.

24 Sister of Robert Weltsch (see note 43, 1917) and cousin of Felix Weltsch, later the wife of Siegmund Kaznelson (see note 84, 1917).

25 Felice Bauer.

26 On September 6, Kafka (and Otto Pick) had accompanied the director of the Institute, Robert Marschner, and his immediate superior, Chief Inspector Eugen Pfohl, to Vienna to attend the Second International Congress for First Aid and Accident Prevention (September 2–9). Then, with stops in Venice, Verona, and Desenzano, he went to Riva on Lake Garda, where he spent his vacation.

27 The Eleventh Zionist Congress, which was held in Vienna while Kafka was there.

28 Felix Stössinger (1889–1954), writer and editor.

29 Ernst Weiss (1884–1940), novelist, born in Brno.

30 A reference to *Tycho Brahes Weg zu Gott* (Leipzig, 1916) [*The Redemption of Tycho Brahe*, New York, 1928], the novel Max Brod was then working on to clarify his religious and philosophical ideas. In its protagonists, the astronomers Tycho Brahe and Johannes Kepler, Brod treated his own ambiguous relationship to Franz Werfel.

31 Otto Pick.

32 Dr. Christoph von Hartungen and his sanatorium in Riva (then Austria) were popular among writers and artists, many of whom became the doctor's personal friends.

33 This was G.W., about whom Kafka vowed never to reveal anything. See below, p. 117; *Diaries* I, pp. 301, 303; II, pp. 112, 220; *Letters to Felice*, p. 335.

34 Resort on the eastern shore of Lake Garda.

35 Kafka's relationship to Felice. From Venice he had written to her on September 16: "We shall have to part." After a brief postcard from Verona (September 20) he stopped writing to her. See *Letters to Felice*, p. 320.

36 See note 30, 1913.

37 *Abschied von der Jugend* [*Goodbye to Youth*], a romantic comedy (Berlin, 1912). Max Reinhardt (1873–1943), stage director and theatrical manager, revolutionized the German theater; he produced Salzburg festivals from 1920.

38 Kafka was now using the familiar *Du* with Felix Weltsch.

39 By Camill Hoffmann (1878–1944), in the issue of October 12, 1913.

40 Not traced, if indeed there was one.

41 Kurt Wolff's first almanac (1914), released in October 1913. It contained Kafka's "Reflections for Gentlemen-Jockeys."

42 Review of *The Stoker*, by Leo Greiner (1876–1928), in the *Berliner Börsen-Courier*, October 12, 1913.

1914

1 Willy Haas (see note 49, 1912), "Die Verkündigung und Paul Claudel" ["The Annunciation and Paul Claudel"], *Der Brenner* (Innsbruck), July 1, 1913.

2 Ludwig von Ficker (1880–1967), founded (1910) and edited *Der Brenner* (until 1954).

3 Robert Musil (1880–1942), author of *Young Törless* (1906; New York, 1955) and *The Man Without Qualities* (1931–43; New York, 1953), had devoted an admiring review to *Meditation* in *Selbstwehr* (Prague), December 20, 1912. Before the outbreak of war, Musil was an editor at the *Neue Rundschau* for a few months; in that capacity he asked Kafka for a contribution (see *Diaries* II, p. 22). See also below, p. 109.

4 Frau Berta Fanta, wife of a Prague pharmacist, gave regular evenings where the best minds of the Prague cultural and intellectual scene lectured (among them Albert Einstein in 1911). In the past, Kafka had frequently attended.

5 František Langer (1888–1965), Czech playwright whose plays were very successful in Germany during the 1920's.

6 May 30–31. Kafka had been in Berlin at Easter (April 12–13) when he and Felice Bauer became unofficially engaged; he was to return for the official celebration.

7 Grete Bloch, born in Berlin (1892), at the time in Vienna; see *Letters to Felice*, pp. 323–24, 397.

8 Martin Buber (1878–1965), Jewish philosopher and religious writer, renewer of Hasidism.

9 Kafka and his father went to Berlin on Saturday, May 30; his mother and Ottla four days earlier. The engagement was celebrated at the apartment of Felice's parents on Whitmonday.

10 Next morning Kafka was leaving on his vacation, with a first stop in Berlin to have a discussion with Felice. It took place on July 12, with Grete Bloch and Felice's sister Erna present. The engagement was broken off. Next day Kafka went on to Lübeck. This letter was probably addressed to Radešovice, where the Kafka family had a summer place. Kafka wrote his parents a long letter from Marielyst about the broken engagement and his future plans (see *Ottla*, pp. 21 ff.).

11 *Pavlač*, a long balcony running along the inner courtyard of older houses in Bohemia and eastern Austria.

12 The German text of this letter was published by Hartmut Binder in "Kafka und *Die Neue Rundschau*," *Jahrbuch der deutschen Schiller Gesellschaft*, Marbach, 1968. In the article Binder details his reasons for identifying the addressee with Robert Musil and the story with *The Metamorphosis*, and for the dating. *The Metamorphosis* was not published in the *Neue Rundschau*, but in the *Weissen Blätter* (see note 19, 1914).

13 See note 21, 1913. Kubin lived at Zwickledt, a country estate near Wernstein on the Inn.

14 Kafka had intended to spend his vacation in Gleschendorf on the Pönitzer See (a tiny inland lake), 18 miles north of Lübeck. Marielyst: on the Baltic coast of Denmark.

15 Rahel Sansara (Sanzara), stage and pen name of Johanna Bleschke (?-1936). In the early 1920's she had a brief acting career in Darmstadt, then wrote a successful novel, *Das verlorene Kind* [The Lost Child].

16 Rigerovy Sady, east of Franz Joseph Station. Kafka lived at the apartment of his eldest sister, Elli, on Nerudagasse, which runs south of Rieger Park, extending two blocks beyond it. While her husband was at the front, Elli and her children lived with her parents on Niklasstrasse.

17 Dated by Max Brod "probably August 1915"; the present date was suggested by Hartmut Binder, "Kafka und *Die Neue Rundschau*," p. 105.

18 Of *The Metamorphosis*.

19 *Die weissen Blätter*, founded in 1913 by Erik Ernst Schwabach in Leipzig, edited by Otto Flake (1913), Franz Blei (1914), and during the war years by René Schickele (1883-1940; Alsatian writer and pacifist) in Switzerland. It was distributed by Kurt Wolff Verlag in Leipzig. Schickele was appointed editor in December 1914, and Max Brod, who knew this, seems to have informed Kafka immediately.

20 Possibly Heinrich von Sybel (1817-95), German historian, or a contemporary publicist (unidentified).

21 A novel Max Brod was working on but never finished.

1915

1 "Apparently," as Max Brod recalls, "a book borrowed from the university library, where Felix Weltsch worked."

2 Since *The Metamorphosis* was no longer to be published in the *Neue Rundschau* (see note 12, 1914), Kafka had submitted it to the *Weissen Blätter*, where it was published in its entirety in October 1915. Kurt Wolff published it in book form in November 1915. This letter was first published in the catalogue for the exhibition *Expressionismus: Literatur und Kunst 1910-1923* at the Schiller National Museum, Marbach, May–October 1960.

3 Almost certainly "In the Penal Colony," the only unpublished longer story Kafka had ready at this time.

4 Poet and writer, later popular courtroom reporter for the *Prager Tagblatt*, always in sympathy with the underdog.

5 See below, letter to Kurt Wolff Verlag of September 30, 1916.

6 The addressee of this letter (and others to Kurt Wolff Verlag until September 1916) is Georg Heinrich Meyer (1868-1931), who directed the firm from August 1914 to September 1916, while Kurt Wolff was in the army on the Western front.

7 The Fontane Prize (DM 800) for 1915 was awarded by Franz Blei. He decided to give it to Carl Sternheim (for his three stories "Busekow," "Napoleon," and "Schuhlin," published by Kurt Wolff Verlag), but with the suggestion that Sternheim, who was a millionaire, give the money to Kafka.

8 "In the Penal Colony," which Kafka had written in October 1914.

9 Meyer had proposed printing a new title page for the remaining copies of *Meditation*, in order to replace Rowohlt's imprint by Wolff's, and distributing them as a second edition.

10 By Sternheim; see note 7, 1915.

11 Apparently a slip. In his letter of Monday, October 11, Meyer had announced a quick visit to Prague on Wednesday afternoon (October 13). Kafka's letter was written on Friday, October 15. "Day before yesterday" would have been called for.

12 Where *The Metamorphosis* had appeared.

13 Presumably to show a different kind of binding. The volumes in the *Jüngste Tag* series came in different bindings (as was customary with most German publishers): paperbound, bound in boards, and bound in half-leather, with graduated prices.

14 Leonhard Frank (1882–1961), German novelist, had received the Fontane Prize in 1914 for his first novel *Die Räuberbande* [*The Robber Band*, New York, 1929].

15 Concerning the reviews here mentioned, those in *Berliner Morgenpost* and *Wiener Allgemeine Zeitung* have not been traced. The others are: *Österreichische Rundschau*, first April issue, 1914 (Felix Braun, on *The Stoker*); *Die Neue Rundschau*, August 1914 (Robert Musil, on *Meditation* and *The Stoker*); *Deutsche Montagszeitung* (Berlin), June 16, 1913 (Heinrich Eduard Jacob, on *The Stoker*); *März* (Munich), February 15, 1913 (Max Brod, "A Literary Event," on *Meditation*); *Berliner Tageblatt*, April 16, 1913 (Albert Ehrenstein, on *Meditation*).

16 *Vom jüngsten Tag: Ein Almanach neuer Dichtung* (Leipzig: Kurt Wolff Verlag, 1916), in which "Before the Law" appeared.

17 Ottomar Starke (1886–1962), stage designer and illustrator, created many covers and illustrations for the *Jüngste Tag* series.

18 Starke's design on the cover of the published book shows, in the background, a folding door with one wing ajar, and in the left foreground a man in a morning coat, hands clasped to his face.

19 Martin Buber, then living in Heppenheim on the Bergstrasse, was making preparations for a new magazine, *Der Jude*, whose first issue appeared in April 1916 (R. Löwit Verlag, Berlin and Vienna). Max Brod had written to Buber on November 17, 1915, suggesting Kafka as a contributor, whereupon Buber seems to have invited him. This letter and the letter to Buber dated April 22, 1917, were first published in Martin Buber, *Briefwechsel aus sieben Jahrzehnten*, ed. by Grete Schaeder (vol. 1, Heidelberg, 1972).

20 Kafka had first met Buber on January 18, 1913, in Prague. The visit referred to probably took place on Saturday, February 28, 1914, when Kafka was in Berlin to see Felice, who was at work in the afternoon.

1916

1 From July 2 to 12 Kafka and Felice Bauer were at Marienbad.

2 Probably Paul Hermann.

3 Phrase from the Hebrew liturgy, based on Numbers 24:5.

4 Teplá, 12 miles east of Marienbad, ancient town with a famous Premonstratensian convent.

5 Not traced.

6 Otto Brod, Max's brother.

7 Willi Nowak; see note 16, 1909.

8 Kafka and Felice went to Franzensbad on July 13. This pinpoints the letter's date, which Brod had given as "mid-July."

9 Suburb 5 miles southeast of Berlin.

10 About the proposed collection of three stories *Punishments*. See also above, letter to Kurt Wolff Verlag, October 15, 1915.

11 Not identified.

12 Hotel on Franz Joseph Platz in the northern part of Marienbad.

13 The Jewish People's Home in Berlin, a center for Jewish relief work founded by Siegfried Lehmann (1892–1958), a leading figure in Jewish education in Berlin, later in Palestine/ Israel, where the Ben-Shemen children's village was developed from the Berlin Home.

14 Max Brod comments: "I had informed Kafka that according to newspaper reports the Rabbi of Belz, one of the heads of Hasidism, had arrived in Marienbad. Kafka (as his diaries indicate) felt drawn toward everything connected with the hasidic movement with a curious mixture of enthusiasm, curiosity, skepticism, approval, and irony. He promptly went to our mutual friend, Georg Mordechai Langer [1894–1943], the brother of František Langer [see note 5, 1914]. G. M. Langer, though a particularly solitary person, born and raised in the West European Jewish culture of Prague, became an authentic Hasid and lived for years at the 'court' of the Rabbi of Belz. He wrote in German and Czech on Kabbalah subjects, and published two volumes of Hebrew poems. One of these poems is an elegy on Kafka's death. In 1939 he eluded the Nazis in Prague and escaped to Palestine on one of the illegal ships, under conditions of unspeakable misery; he died there in 1943 from the hardships he had suffered during the voyage." Kafka and Brod took Hebrew lessons from Georg Langer, probably in the fall of 1921.

15 Gustave Doré (1833–83), French illustrator and painter.

16 The word should read *gabbaim*, plural of *gabbai*, a lay communal official.

17 Dr. Gustaf Zander (1835–1920), Swedish physician, founded (1865, in Stockholm) an institute where gymnastics and massages were carried out by means of a mechanical contraption. Subsequently similar institutes were established in many cities.

18 *Aïssé*, by René Schickele; *Schuhlin*, by Carl Sternheim (*Der jüngste Tag*, vols. 24 and 21, respectively); *Fledermäuse* [*Bats*], by Gustav Meyrink (seven short stories), 1916.

19 Walter Hasenclever (1890–1940), German author and dramatist: *Das unendliche Gespräch* [*The Unending Conversation*] (*Der jüngste Tag*, vol. 2); Ferdinand Hardekopf (1876–

1954), expressionist poet, later journalist and translator: *Der Abend* [*The Evening*] *(Der jüngste Tag,* vol. 4).

20 See note 4, 1915.

21 Grand Duke Ernst Ludwig of Hesse had obtained Kurt Wolff's release from the army. Wolff was given unlimited leave in September 1916 and returned to Leipzig.

22 Of "In the Penal Colony."

23 Kafka read "In the Penal Colony," preceded by a few poems by Max Brod, at the Galerie Goltz in Munich on November 10.

24 Friedrich Feigl (1884–1966), painter and graphic artist.

25 Georg Müller (1877–1917) founded his publishing house in Munich in 1903; specialized in classics and modern authors.

26 Ernst Feigl's poems were not published by Kurt Wolff.

27 Max Brod explains that "this rather eccentric uncle above all prized close scheduling and making the best use of one's time."

28 German: *ihr* (plural). It is not known whom Uncle Siegfried planned to travel with. He was a bachelor.

1917

1 Gottfried Kölwel (1889–1958), German poet. Martin Buber had recommended Kölwel's first book of poems to Kurt Wolff, who published it in 1914 *(Gesänge gegen den Tod* [*Chants Against Death*], *Der jüngste Tag,* vol. 17). When Kafka was in Munich (November 10–12) for his reading he met Kölwel, who showed him some of his recent work.

2 "Wir Wehenden durch diese Welt" was published in Kölwel's second book, *Erhebung* [*Elation*] (Munich, 1918), as were the other poems mentioned here.

3 Felice Bauer had come to Munich to attend Kafka's reading.

4 Max Pulver (1889–1952), Swiss neoromantic poet and dramatist, subsequently a well-known graphologist.

5 Dr. Martin Sommerfeld (1894–1939), literary historian.

6 The royalty statement covered the period from July 1, 1915, to June 30, 1916, during which 258 copies of *Meditation* were sold.

7 The second printing of *The Stoker* was apparently issued early in 1916.

8 For *Der Jude;* see note 19, 1915. The stories are presumably among the fifteen listed in Kafka's letter to Kurt Wolff of August 20, 1917, to form the volume *A Country Doctor.*

9 Bimonthly edited by Theodor Tagger (1891–1958), in the 1920's a very successful playwright under the pseudonym Ferdinand Bruckner. The first issue (July–August 1917) contained Kafka's "An Old Manuscript" and "A Fratricide."

10 The final title was *A Country Doctor.*

11 This letter was first published in a paper by Robert Kauf, "*Verantwortung:* The Theme of Kafka's *Landarzt* Cycle," *Modern Language Quarterly,* December 1972.

12 "Zwei Tiergeschichten." The two stories were "Jackals and Arabs" and "A Report to an Academy," published in *Der Jude* in October and November 1917, respectively.

13 Moritz Heimann (1868–1925), writer and an editor at S. Fischer Verlag in Berlin. The article was "Politische Voraussetzungen etcetera" ["Political Premises, et cetera"], *Die Neue Rundschau,* June 1917.

14 Rudolf Fuchs (1890–1942), poet and translator; see also note 113, 1917.

15 To make up *A Country Doctor.*

16 Felice Bauer had come to Prague early in July, and she and Kafka became engaged for the second time. On Wednesday, July 11, they entrained for Budapest to visit Felice's sister, Else Braun, who was married in Arad. On July 18 Kafka returned alone, spending the day in Vienna and taking the night train back to Prague.

17 Yitzhak Löwy; see note 1, 1912.

18 Irma Kafka, orphaned daughter of Kafka's uncle Heinrich Kafka of Leitmeritz. During the war years she worked full time at Hermann Kafka's business and became a close friend of Ottla, who also worked there (until the spring of 1917). In 1918 Irma married a Herr Stein.

19 In a brief note of July 20, 1917, Kurt Wolff had told Kafka he found the pieces "extraordinarily beautiful and accomplished."

20 In answer Kurt Wolff wrote Kafka on August 1, 1917: "Most sincerely and most gladly I declare my readiness to give you, also in the time after the war, continuous material support."

21 Kurt Wolff was vacationing on the island of Herrenchiemsee in the Chiemsee, Bavaria.

22 Kafka subsequently excluded this title from *A Country Doctor*.

23 *A Country Doctor* was set in the same typeface and produced in the same format as *Meditation*, but owing to war conditions only published in 1919.

24 Ottla, who had worked in her father's business, had finally managed to break away from Prague and the family. In April 1917 she went to Zürau to run a 50-acre farm belonging to her brother-in-law Karl Hermann, who was a soldier at the front. Flöhau: about 3 miles south of Saaz (Žatek).

25 On August 10, between 4 and 5 A.M., Kafka had a hemorrhage from his mouth which lasted for some ten minutes. In the morning he went to the office as usual, before consulting Dr. Mühlstein in the afternoon. The doctor diagnosed "bronchial catarrh." After two more visits to Dr. Mühlstein, Max Brod took Kafka to Professor Gottfried (Friedl) Pick on September 4, who confirmed Dr. Mühlstein's revised diagnosis of "pulmonary apicitis" and ordered a three-month vacation to avert the danger of tuberculosis. For the time being, Kafka kept his disease a secret from his parents. On September 7 he was granted three months' leave, and on September 12 he joined Ottla in Zürau, where he was to remain until April 30, 1918, with several extensions of his leave. "To some extent," Max Brod observes, "the rural milieu of Zürau was evoked in *The Castle*" (which Kafka began to write in January 1922).

26 Until August 1914 Kafka had lived with his parents. During the war years he lived at various addresses, last at the Schönborn Palace (where he slept and where the hemorrhage occurred) and at Alchemistengasse (where he did his writing). After the hemorrhage Kafka gave notice at the Schönborn Palace and moved back to his parents' apartment, where he occupied Ottla's bedroom. At the same time he lost the use of the house on Alchemistengasse. Before the move to Zürau was definite, he briefly considered taking a place on the Belvedere (on Ovenetzergasse). See *Ottla*, pp. 41 f., 176.

27 Kafka's mother, though she lived to be 78, was of delicate constitution.

28 Region in northwestern Bohemia, bordering on Germany.

29 Now Česka Lípa, town 53 miles north of Prague.

30 Kafka had received his doctor's degree in law in 1906, but because of his boyish appearance he never felt he looked like a real "Herr Doktor."

31 During the last war years, supplies in the cities had become scarce and Kafka tried to save and send food (eggs, butter) to his family and friends in Prague.

32 Felice Bauer visited Kafka in Zürau, September 20–21.

33 Fräulein Kaiser, Kafka's secretary at the Workers' Accident Insurance Institute.

34 Gustav Janowitz had three sons who belonged to Kafka's wider circle of friends: the poets Hans (1890–1954) and Franz (1892–1917), both represented in Max Brod's anthology *Arkadia*, and Otto, the piano accompanist of Karl Kraus.

35 Field Marshall Edmund H. H. Allenby (1861–1936), commander-in-chief of the Egyptian Expeditionary Force, was then preparing his campaign against the Turks in Palestine which was to end Turkish rule in that region in November 1918. See also note 120, 1917.

36 The invitation was not from the Jewish Women's and Girls' Club, as Kafka thought, but from the Club of German Woman Artists, which had invited Felix Weltsch to give a series of lectures on his philosophical ideas. The course began in February 1918.

37 Professor Friedl Pick (see note 25, 1917).

38 The German conjunction *bis* means "until"; in the sense of "when" it is used in the vernacular in eastern Austria and Bohemia. Kafka was not aware that he had been using *bis* in the wrong sense, as these letters demonstrate. When editing the literary works, Max Brod eliminated this mistake. Grimm: the great dictionary of the German language begun by Jacob and Wilhelm Grimm (*Deutsches Wörterbuch*, 16 vols. in 32, 1852–1961).

39 Wilhelm Stekel (1868–1940), *Krankhafte Störungen des Trieb- und Affektlebens*, vol. 2, *Onanie und Homosexualität*, Berlin and Vienna, 1917. In the 3d ed. (1923), the passage occurs on p. 477, n. 1. In connection with a patient's dream about having been changed into a bedbug, Stekel cites *The Metamorphosis*.

40 Božena Němcová (1820–64), great Czech writer, collector of fairy tales and legends; her major work is the novel *Babička*, 1855 [*The Grandmother*, Chicago, 1891], which Kafka regarded highly.

41 Felix Weltsch, *Organic Democracy;* see note 15, 1918.

42 *Das Liebesleben der Romantik* and *Steinerne Brücke:* unidentified. *Prague:* probably *Das Jüdische Prag* [*Jewish Prague*], a compilation by the editors of *Selbstwehr*, Prague, 1917.

43 Robert Weltsch (1891–), cousin of Felix Weltsch, writer on politics; from 1919 to 1938 in Berlin as editor of *Die jüdische Rundschau* (see note 104, 1917).

44 Moriz Schnitzer, a manufacturer and natural therapist in Warnsdorf, northern Bohemia. Kafka met him about May 1, 1911, during one of his inspection tours. Schnitzer examined Kafka, diagnosed "poison in the spinal cord," and recommended a vegetarian diet, fresh air, sunbathing, and staying away from doctors, thereby confirming Kafka in his own preferences. Now Kafka had written Schnitzer to consult him about his disease. See also below, pp. 159–60, and Brod, *Biography*, p. 109.

45 *L'Education sentimentale*, novel (1870) by Gustave Flaubert.

46 Magazine edited by Meta Moch.

47 Publishing house in Berlin founded in 1902 by Martin Buber, Berthold Feiwel, and Ephraim Lilien; closed by the Nazis in 1938, it was reopened by Siegmund Kaznelson in 1958.

48 Max Brod, *Eine Königin Esther* [*A Queen Esther*], a play (Leipzig, 1918).

49 See above, letter to Martin Buber of July 20, 1917, and *Dearest Father*, pp. 129 ff.

50 The oddity of Löwy's German *("frackierte Herren und neglegierte Damen")* cannot be retained in translation. See *Dearest Father*, p. 133.

51 Měcholupy, on the railroad line Prague–Žatek.

52 A popular singer.

53 *Her Foster Daughter*, opera (first performed in Brno, January 21, 1904) by Leoš Janáček (1854–1928). Max Brod translated the libretto by Gabriela Preissová (1862–1946) under the title *Jenufa*, and it was largely due to his efforts that the opera eventually conquered the opera houses of the world.

54 Adolf Schreiber (1883–1920), composer, friend of Max Brod.

55 Abraham Grünberg, a young Hebrew writer, a refugee from Warsaw. See *Diaries* II, pp. 142 f.

56 *Das grosse Wagnis* [*The Great Risk*], the novel Max Brod was working on and which Kafka means when he speaks of "the novel" in subsequent letters. It was published in 1918.

57 Jewish weekly published in Prague from 1907; from 1912 the organ of the Zionist Organization of Czechoslovakia, and from 1918 the mouthpiece of the newly established Jewish Party (a national-Jewish political party). Felix Weltsch was the editor from the fall of 1919 until 1939. No issue was published on September 28, a national holiday (feast day of St. Wenceslas, patron saint of Bohemia).

58 See note 36, 1917.

59 *Letters to Felice*, p. 545; see also *Diaries* II, pp. 187 f.

60 Two additional examples that have no point in English have been omitted in translation.

61 Hugo Reichenberger (1873–1938), German conductor, from 1905 to 1935 at the Vienna Court (later State) Opera. Max Brod remarks: "He had 'improved' my translation beyond recognition. Despite my protests it was printed with his revisions. After stormy struggles I was able to eliminate some of his worst gaffes."

62 A role in *Jenufa*.

63 Max Scheler (1874–1928), German philosopher, applied the phenomenological method to

ethics with the aim of establishing an ethic of values. Kafka presumably is referring to Scheler's *Die Ursachen des Deutschenhasses* [*The Causes of the Hatred for Germany*], Leipzig, 1917.

64 Hans Blüher (1888–1955), German philosophical and anti-Semitic writer, interested in the German Youth Movement.

65 Otto Gross (1877–1919), one of the earliest followers of Freud (though not his pupil) and author of books on psychoanalysis (as early as 1901). At a party at Max Brod's on July 23, 1917 (with Kafka, Werfel, and Adolf Schreiber present), Gross had propounded an idea for a new magazine to be called *Blätter zur Bekämpfung des Machtwillens* [*Journal for the Suppression of the Will to Power*].

66 In the fall of 1917 Felix Weltsch lectured on literature at a Prague girls' gymnasium.

67 *Láska a smrt Ferdinanda Lassallea* [*Love and Death of Ferdinand Lassalle*] (Prague, 1912), apparently a translation of *Meine Beziehungen zu Ferdinand Lassalle* [*My Relationship to Ferdinand Lassalle*] (Breslau, 1879), by Helena Racowitzova (Helene von Dönniges, 1846–1911). She was the girl with whom Lassalle fell in love and whose fiancé, Janko von Racowitz, fatally wounded him in a famous duel. After Lassalle's death she married Racowitz, and committed suicide in 1911. Lassalle (1825–64) founded (in 1863) the Universal German Workingmen's Association and thereby the German Social Democratic Party.

68 Kafka copied the beginning (through the phrase "You are happy in your unhappiness") of Brod's letter for Felice; see *Letters to Felice*, p. 546.

69 Thomas Mann (1875–1955), *"Palestrina,"* first published in the *Neue Rundschau*, October 1917, later incorporated into the chapter "Von der Tugend" ["On Virtue"] in *Betrachtungen eines Unpolitischen* [*Reflections of a Non-Political Man*], Berlin, 1918. The essay deals with the opera *Palestrina* by Hans Pfitzner (1868–1949), first performed in Munich, June 12, 1917.

70 Hugo Salus (1866–1929), neoromantic poet living in Prague; popular around the turn of the century.

71 Where Max Brod was to deliver a speech; see below, pp. 160–61.

72 A reference to the black poodle in Goethe's *Faust*.

73 In March 1915 Kafka had rented a room on Langengasse (today 16 Dlouhá třida).

74 August Sauer, professor of German literature; see note 6, 1902.

75 Professor of political economy at Prague University; see note 3, 1906.

76 Lydia Holzner, head of a secondary school for girls in Prague.

77 Philipp Reclam jun., large publishing house founded by Anton Philipp Reclam (1807–96) in 1828 in Leipzig. The firm issued inexpensive paperbound editions of most authors of German and (in translation) world literature.

78 *Die Aktion,* Berlin weekly for politics, literature, and art, founded (1911) and edited until 1932 by Franz Pfemfert (1879–1954).

79 "Radetzkymarsch," a story by Max Brod, appeared in *Die Aktion* in September 1917.

80 Heinrich Teweles (1856–1927), theater critic of *Bohemia,* also wrote for the *Prager Tagblatt* under the pseudonym Bob.

81 Anton Kuh (1891–1941), Austrian critic and editor whom Kafka had met in Vienna in July. Kuh's article was "Werfel-Matinée," a review of a matinée performance of Werfel's *Besuch aus dem Elysium* [*A Visit from Elysium*], *Prager Abendblatt,* October 10, 1917.

82 An untranslatable pun: an allusion to Goethe's prolonged friendship with Charlotte von Stein.—Trans.

83 Ida Boy-Ed (1852–1928), German novelist, wrote a defense of Charlotte von Stein (1742–1827): *Das Martyrium der Charlotte von Stein: Versuch ihrer Rechtfertigung* [*The Martyrdom of Charlotte von Stein: An Exercise in Justification*], Stuttgart, 1916.

84 Albrecht Hellmann was the pen name of Siegmund Kaznelson (1893–1959), publisher and editor; after World War I on the editorial staff of *Der Jude;* author of a scientific-literary project on the role of Jews in German culture (1922–62).

85 See note 44, 1917.

86 Professor Zuckerkandl; see note 75, 1917. He was a distant relation of Georges Clemenceau. Max Brod quotes from Felix Weltsch's letter to Kafka of October 17, 1917: "A conversation with Hofrat Zuckerkandl about—you. He praised you to the skies as a writer. His mother-in-law at a spa heard from another lady about a writer named Franz Kafka whose works one absolutely had to know. She asked for the book and received it. As a consequence the Hofrat read four pages and was enthusiastic. 'I certainly must know him if he has his doctorate from us.'"

87 Zuckerkandl was one of Kafka's professors in 1903–4.

88 Apparently an allusion to the topic of one of Felix Weltsch's lectures at the girls' gymnasium (see note 66, 1917). "Young Germany" was the name of a group of revolutionary German writers in the 1830's and '40's. Its best known members were Ludwig Börne (1786–1837) and Heinrich Heine (1797–1856). See also below, p. 165.

89 Paul Kornfeld (1889–1942), expressionist dramatist, born in Prague, at the time working with Max Reinhardt in Berlin. *Das junge Deutschland,* a monthly devoted to literature and the theater, was edited for the Deutsche Theater in Berlin, published 1918–20.

90 Expressionist magazine modeled on *Die Aktion,* edited by Leo Reiss in Brno, in 1918. Oskar Baum, Max Brod, and Ernst Weiss were contributors. Johannes Urzidil was managing editor.

91 To whom Weltsch presumably had submitted the manuscript of his book *Organic Democracy.*

92 See note 5, 1907. On October 27, 1917, Max Brod gave a talk at the Komotau Zionist Club. Kafka came over from Zürau; next morning both returned to Zürau and went on to Prague in the evening.

93 Refers to the three months' sick leave Kafka was granted on September 7, 1917 (see note 25, 1917).

94 In German "Schmerzensreich," the name of the son of Geneviève of Brabant in the German chapbook, also of the son of the repudiated queen in the fairy tale "The Girl Without Hands" by the brothers Grimm.

95 Dr. Fleischmann; see note 21, 1909. Oskar Baum had approached Kafka on behalf of a blinded war veteran, a Herr P.

96 Alfred Klaar (1848–1927), writer, for many years theater critic of the *Vossische Zeitung* in Berlin.

97 Kafka was using the German edition of Kierkegaard's *Werke* [*Works*], edited by Hermann Gottsched and Christoph Schrempf, published by Eugen Diederichs in Jena. *Furcht und Zittern (und Wiederholung)* was vol. 3 of that edition. Kafka is forgetting that he had read *Buch des Richters* [*Book of the Judge*] (Jena, 1905), a selection from Kierkegaard's diaries translated into German by Gottsched, in 1913 (see *Diaries* I, p. 298).

98 Principal character in Oskar Baum's novel *Die Tür ins Unmögliche* [*The Door to the Impossible*], Munich, 1919.

99 The second was Ottla; the third may have been Fräulein Greschl (see note 130, 1917), who sometimes spent an evening with them.

100 Kafka's secretary, Fräulein Kaiser; the man probably was a Herr Klein.

101 Where an evening of readings was to take place. Max Brod had urged Kafka to participate.

102 Wilhelm Stekel; see note 39, 1917. The reference has not been traced.

103 Character in Brod's novel *The Great Risk.* She was the embodiment of a Zionist girl Brod had an affair with.

104 *Die jüdische Rundschau* (Berlin), founded in 1896 as the organ of the Zionist Union of

Germany. During the war years it was edited by Leo Herrmann and Max Mayer, then briefly by Fritz Löwenstein. From December 1919 to 1938, Robert Weltsch was the editor and chief contributor.

105 Kafka had been in Prague the last days of October, with visits to the dentist and to Dr. Pick.

106 Felix Weltsch was writing a book on ethics (freedom of will) and discovering that there was a religious foundation to his ideas (see below, p. 173). The book was published in 1920, under the title *Gnade und Freiheit* [*Grace and Freedom*].

107 A society to promote adult education.

108 *Selbstwehr* issued a special edition on the occasion of the Balfour Declaration of November 2, 1917.

109 Georg Mordechai Langer; see note 14, 1916.

110 Irma Kafka; see note 18, 1917.

111 Kafka had written the major part of *The Trial* in the second half of 1914 and consecutively read the finished chapters to Brod.

112 Elsa Brod was to read "A Report to an Academy" at the Jewish Women's and Girls' Club in Prague on December 19, 1917. See also note 118, 1917.

113 Rudolf Fuchs (see note 14, 1917) had published a book of translations (poems by Peter Bezruč [1867–1958]). Kafka had seen Fuchs while stopping in Vienna in July. For Ernst Feigl, see note 4, 1915. Neither had published poetry of his own in book form.

114 Bimonthly founded in February 1918 by a group of Viennese authors (Franz Werfel among them) who had established a cooperative publishing house. It existed, under changing names, until 1921.

115 On July 23, 1917; see note 65, 1917.

116 Illustrated monthly, founded in 1917.

117 Hans Blüher (see note 64, 1917), *Die Rolle der Erotik in der männlichen Gesellschaft* [*The Role of Eroticism in Male Societies*], vol. 1, *Der Typus inversus*, Jena, 1917.

118 See note 112, 1917. Max Brod comments: "The single time my wife ventured to give a reading, with great success. She read Kafka's 'Report to an Academy.' This was the first public reading of a work by Kafka" other than by himself.

119 Military actions in the so-called Caporetto Campaign, when German forces routed the Italian army, driving it back to the River Piave. Honved: Hungarian reserves.

120 Field Marshal Allenby took Jaffa in Palestine from the Turks on November 16, 1917.

121 Arthur Hantke (1874–1955), German Zionist leader; on November 17, 1917, on behalf of the Zionist Organization, he managed to get a pro-Zionist statement from Count Czernin, the Austro-Hungarian foreign minister.

122 A public reading by Thomas or Heinrich Mann has not been traced for the time preceding this letter. Hermann Essig (1878–1918), German dramatist and novelist.

123 Ottla was in Prague from November 22 to 25. She told her father about the true nature of his son's illness and conveyed to the Institute Kafka's wish to be retired on pension. The request was denied.

124 Kurt Hiller (1885–1972), German critic and essayist. Editor of an annual for intellectual politics, *Das Ziel*, from 1916.

125 Presumably a military barracks in Bohemia.

126 Presumably works Weltsch was consulting in connection with his manuscript on ethics.

127 Pelagius (fl. ca. A.D. 400), British monk who rejected Augustine's doctrine of predestination and asserted free will.

128 Also known as Moses ben Maimon (1135–1204), Jewish philosopher who strove to reconcile rabbinical Judaism with the system of Aristotle as transmitted by the Arab philosophers.

129 Solomon Maimon (1735–1800), German philosopher of Jewish descent, follower of Immanuel Kant. His *Autobiography*, first published in 1792, was republished in 1911 by Georg Müller Verlag in Munich, edited by Ludwig Fromer. English edition: *Solomon Maimon: An Autobiography*, New York, 1967.

130 Binder and Wagenbach *(Ottla*, p. 181) suggest that this was Fräulein Greschl.

131 Tractate Sukkah 52a.

132 *Der Anbruch: Flugblätter aus der Zeit*, ephemeral magazine, founded in 1917.

133 *Jüdische Rundschau:* see above, note 104, 1917. *Panideal:* Rudolf Maria Holzapfel (1874–1930), Austrian philosopher and poet, postulated a supreme ideal value transcending family, class, and nation; his main work was *Panideal*, a psychology of social emotions (Bern, 1901; expanded to two volumes, 1923); in 1917 he started a periodical, *Panideal*, in Bern, Switzerland, to promote these ideas. *Proscenium:* not identified. *Der Artist:* the central organ for the circus, cabaret, wandering bands, and ensembles business, edited by H. Otto, Düsseldorf, from 1883. R. Löwit: publisher in Berlin and Vienna. *Aktion:* see note 78, 1917. *Tablettes:* not identified. *Alžběta:* not identified. (The German premiere of Brod's *Intensity of Feeling* took place in Dresden in March 1918.) *Hudební Revue:* Czech music magazine (1907–20), edited by Karel Stecker and Karel Hoffmeister.

134 Josef Körner (1888-1950), literary historian and critic. See also note 138, 1917.

135 Friedrich Wilhelm Foerster (1869-1966), German pedagogue and pacifist. His *Jugendlehre: Ein Buch für Eltern, Lehrer und Geistliche* [*Youth Guidance: A Book for Parents, Teachers, and Clergy*] (Berlin, 1904) was used at the Jewish People's Home in Berlin (where Felice Bauer did volunteer work), whereupon Kafka became interested in the author. See *Letters to Felice*, passim.

136 *Donauland;* see note 116, 1917.

137 Achim von Arnim (1781-1831), German romantic poet and novelist.

138 In his article "Dichter und Dichtung aus dem deutschen Prag" ["Writers and Writing in German Prague"] *(Donauland,* September 1917), Körner had praised Kafka's "noble and clear style" and called *The Metamorphosis* his "so far most accomplished work."

139 Brod's play *Eine Königin Esther.*

140 Brod had an affair with a Zionist girl, whom he portrayed as Ruth in his novel *The Great Risk.*

141 Mařenka, a hired girl, who helped Ottla with the farm work. See *Diaries* II, p. 183.

142 Chief Inspector Pfohl (see note 26, 1913) had visited Kafka in Zürau on December 10, 1917.

143 Max Brod dated this letter "mid-December 1917" and placed it before the letter to himself of December 18-19, 1917. But Kafka wrote Brod in the first part of that letter (written on the 18th) that he had received Felice's letter (announcing her visit) on that same evening. Therefore the letter to Weltsch which mentions Felice's visit must have been written after the 18th. By announcing to Brod that he will "probably" come to Prague "this Saturday" (i.e., December 22) and telling Weltsch that he will "in all likelihood" go "to Prague the day after tomorrow," Kafka establishes the date of the letter to Weltsch as December 20. (On December 22 Kafka had sciatica, and may have postponed his trip by a day.)

144 Presumably for Felix Weltsch's book *Grace and Freedom.*

145 As editor of *Das junge Deutschland;* see note 89, 1917.

146 *Amerika* and *The Trial.*

147 Felice had been in Prague December 25-27. The second engagement was broken off.

1918

1 When Kafka returned from Prague to Zürau about January 6, he took Oskar Baum along. Ottla accompanied Baum back to the city on January 13.

2 Still *The Great Risk.*

3 Ernst Troeltsch (1865–1923), German philosopher of religion; his essay was "Luther und der Protestantismus," *Die Neue Rundschau,* October 1917.

4 Baum, *The Door to the Impossible.*

5 Leo Tolstoy, *Tagebuch,* vol. 1 (Munich, 1917), was in Kafka's library.

6 Oskar Baum, *Zwei Erzählungen* [*Two Stories*] *(Der jüngste Tag,* vol. 52), Leipzig, n.d. (1918).

7 A character in Max Brod's novel *The Great Risk.* The book was first published in a six-volume set of Brod's selected fiction, Munich, 1918.

8 See note 7, 1908.

9 Kierkegaard's main work, translated into German *(Entweder-Oder)* by W. Pfleiderer and Christoph Schrempf; 2 vols., Jena, 1911–13. See note 45, 1918.

10 Martin Buber's most recent books were *Die Rede, die Lehre und das Lied* [*Speech, Doctrine, and Song*] (1917) and *Ereignisse und Begegnungen* [*Events and Encounters*] (1917).

11 See note 20, 1908.

12 Gerhart Hauptmann (1862–1946), *Die versunkene Glocke,* 1896 [*The Sunken Bell,* New York, 1899].

13 Olga and Irene are two characters in Max Brod's novel *Jüdinnen* [*Jewesses*], 1911.

14 The manuscript of Kafka's "An Imperial Message."

15 Felix Weltsch, *Organische Demokratie: Eine rechtsphilosophische Studie über das Repräsentativ-system und das parlamentarische Wahlrecht* [*Organic Democracy: A Philosophical Study of the Representative System and Parliamentary Suffrage*], Leipzig, n.d. (1918).

16 See note 124, 1917. The second volume of *Das Ziel,* dated 1917/18, was issued in spring 1918. Like the first it was prohibited by the German government, but obtainable "under

the counter." Felix Weltsch's essay was "Erlebnis und Intention: Die aktivistische und die romantische Gefahr" ["Experience and Intention: The Dangers of Activism and Romanticism"].

17 So far Kurt Wolff had largely published books in the fields of literature and art. In the winter of 1917–18 he founded a separate branch under the name Der Neue Geist, devoted to the publication of political and intellectual works.

18 Johann Heinrich Merck (1741–91, a seminal critic during the "Storm and Stress" period and a friend of Goethe's), *Schriften und Briefwechsel* [*Writings and Correspondence*], ed. by Kurt Wolff, 2 vols., Leipzig, 1909. Kurt Wolff, "Der Dramatiker Eulenberg" ["Eulenberg the Dramatist"], *Mitteilungen der Literarhistorischen Gesellschaft Bonn*, VII (1912). Herbert Eulenberg (1876–1949) was a neoromantic dramatist (much performed before 1914) and prose writer.

19 Karl Freye and Wolfgang Stammler, eds., *Briefe von und an J. M. R. Lenz,* 2 vols., Leipzig, 1918. Jakob Michael Reinhold Lenz (1751–92), dramatist of the "Storm and Stress" period and a friend of Goethe's.

20 Max Brod dated this postcard "beginning of January." However, at the very beginning of January (to about the 6th), Kafka was still in Prague; then, during his first week back in Zürau, Oskar Baum was with him. The "warmest regards to Oskar" toward the end of the card makes a date sometime after the visit most likely. The card must precede Kafka's letter to Weltsch dated "beginning of February," since in the meantime Weltsch had commented on this picture postcard (see p. 196).

21 For *Das junge Deutschland;* see note 89, 1917.

22 The Deutsche Schriftsteller-Verband, Berlin, founded in 1887.

23 Czech: Vlček, presumably a wholesale newsdealer in Prague. The suspected reprint has not been traced. The *Wiener Morgenzeitung* was the only Jewish paper in Austria at this period.

24 Frankenstein (a suburb of Rumburk in northern Bohemia) was the site of a Veterans' Sanatorium for Nervous Diseases which Kafka, in his official capacity, was to visit several times during the following summer when he was again working at the Institute. See below, p. 205.

25 Editor of *Die Aktion;* see note 78, 1917.

26 Ludwig Rubiner (1881–1920), ed., *Auswahl aus dem Tagebuch von Leo Tolstoi 1895–1899* (Zurich, 1918); Leo Tolstoy, *Tagebuch,* complete edition in 6 vols. (Munich, 1917 ff.).

27 Walther Fürth, a member of the circle that met at the Café Arco.

28 Kurt Wolff had advised Kafka on January 29 that all his wishes regarding *A Country Doctor* would be carried out and that he was sending Kafka the Lenz *Letters* as a gift.

29 Oskar Kraus (1872–1942), professor of philosophy at Prague University, chief exponent of the ideas of Franz Brentano (see note 25, 1912). Max Brod explains: Professor Kraus "had ironically rebuked Felix Weltsch, his former student, for his lectures on political and literary subjects (frequently mentioned in the correspondence). Here Kafka proposes that Weltsch let the professor know that he is 'even' lecturing on botany."

30 In 1918, Ash Wednesday (the first day of fasting after Carnival) fell on February 13, dating the letter before that day.

31 See note 34, 1918.

32 Jaroslav Vrchlický (1853–1912), Czech man of letters, influenced by Victor Hugo.

33 Of Max Brod's drama *Eine Königin Esther* for its first performance.

34 Kafka had briefly been in Prague after the middle of February to inquire at the Institute about his military service. He returned to Zürau on Tuesday, February 19.

35 *Stadien auf dem Lebensweg* [*Stages on Life's Way*], vol. 4 of the *Werke;* see note 97, 1917.

36 There were two similar books, one with the title, the other issued by the publisher mentioned by Kafka: *Sören Kierkegaard und sein Verhältnis zu ihr*, ed. and trans. by Raphael Meyer, Stuttgart, 1905; and *Sören Kierkegaards Verhältnis zu seiner Braut* [*Søren Kierkegaard's Relationship to His Fiancée*], ed. by Henriette Lund, Leipzig, 1904.

37 *Der Augenblick*, vol. 12 of the *Werke*.

38 Otto Pick (see note 8, 1913) was an editor of the *Prager Presse* at this time.

39 Erich Reiss (1887–1951), publisher in Berlin.

40 Hans Liebstöckl; the review has not been traced.

41 The premiere of Brod's *Intensity of Feeling*.

42 Paul Cassirer (1871–1926), founded, with his cousin Bruno, an art gallery (1898) where he promoted the Impressionist painters, and in 1908 a publishing house specializing in expressionist literature, both in Berlin.

43 Paul Adler (1878–1946), Prague poet, then living in Hellerau near Dresden.

44 Friedrich Wilhelm Schelling (1775–1854) and Georg Wilhelm Friedrich Hegel (1770–1831), German idealist philosophers. In Berlin Kierkegaard attended Schelling's lectures on "The Philosophy of Revelation."

45 Christoph Schrempf (1860–1944), the editor of Kierkegaard's *Werke*, dealt rather freely (if conscientiously) with Kierkegaard's text in order to present a readable German book.

46 Reference to the "Diary of the Seducer" in vol. I of *Either/Or*.

47 Regine Olsen.

48 Christian von Ehrenfels (1859–1932), Austrian psychologist, discoverer of *gestalt*, from 1896 professor in Prague. Kafka attended his lectures during his first two semesters at the university and participated in a seminar in 1913. See *Diaries* I, index. The book was *Kosmogenie [Cosmogeny]* (Jena, 1916).

49 Max Brod dated this letter "Zürau, May–June 1918," but Kafka left Zürau on April 30, after Ottla had brought (on April 18) the news from a visit to Prague that Kafka's leave would not be extended. From May to November Kafka again lived, with interruptions, at the apartment of his parents, Altstädter Ring 6.

50 *Frieden*, a weekly dealing with politics, economics, and literature, was to serialize Chapter 2 of Weltsch's *Grace and Freedom* in 1919. Weltsch's essay "Organic Democracy" appeared in the *Neue Rundschau*, April 1918.

51 According to Max Brod, the magazine *Der Mensch* (see note 90, 1917), of which Urzidil was managing editor.

52 Apparently written from one of Kafka's inspection trips to the sanatorium in Frankenstein; see note 24, 1918.

53 Turnov, town 65 miles northeast of Prague. Kafka stayed there for a rest in the second part of September.

54 Kafka had begun to learn Hebrew around May 1917, using a textbook of modern Hebrew by Moses Rath.

55 Presumably the novel *Tiere in Ketten [Animals in Chains]* (Berlin, 1918), by Ernst Weiss.

56 On September 13, 1918, G. H. Meyer had informed Kafka in a long letter tht the printer could not complete composition of *A Country Doctor* (because of an insufficient supply of type), listed the order of the pieces to be included, and mentioned the loss of the manuscript of "A Dream."

57 On October 14 Kafka became ill with Spanish influenza, then raging in epidemic proportions. He got up for the first time on November 7 and went back to work on the 19th.

58 Kurt Wolff had suggested (on October 11, 1918) issuing "In the Penal Colony" as a deluxe edition in the newly created series Drugulin-Drucke and returned (at Kafka's request conveyed by Max Brod) the manuscript of the work.

59 Kurt Wolff was in Darmstadt at the time, hence the separate communication to the firm in Leipzig.

60 Kafka's mother had suggested to the family doctor, Dr. Heinrich Kral, sending her son to a pension in Schelesen (near Liboch) to recuperate. The trip was scheduled, as Kafka states here, for Sunday, November 24. He finally left, accompanied by his mother, on Saturday, November 30.

61 While Kafka was ill the Habsburg Empire came to its end. On October 28 a provisional government was formed in Prague; on November 11 the Austrian Emperor abdicated; and on November 14 the Republic of Czechoslovakia was proclaimed and Thomas Masaryk chosen President.

62 *Geschichte meines Lebens* (2 vols., Teschen, 1884), by Alfred Meissner (1822–85), much-traveled Bohemian writer and poet.

63 Kafka did go to Prague for Christmas, returning to Schelesen on January 22, 1919.

64 Max Brod, "Unsere Literaten und die Gemeinschaft," *Der Jude,* October 1916.

65 Volksverein: not identified (unless Kafka means the newly created Jewish National Council; see note 67, 1918). Mädchenklub: the Zionist Jewish Women's and Girls' Club, of which Ottla was a member.

66 Max Brod, *Heidentum, Christentum, Judentum* (2 vols., Munich, 1921) [*Paganism, Christianity, Judaism,* University, Ala., 1970], the book Max Brod was working on at this time.

67 Zionist organization, founded in Prague in October 1918. Max Brod was a member.

68 Marie Werner, who came to the Kafka family as governess to the children and then stayed on; she spoke only Czech.

1919

1 Refers to Kafka's dramatic fragment "The Warden of the Tomb" which, according to Max Brod, Kafka had discussed with Oskar Baum during Baum's stay in Zürau in January 1918.

2 Oskar Baum, *Das Wunder* [*The Miracle*], a play (Berlin, 1920).

3 Dr. Ernst Fröhlich.

4 Olga Stüdl, the owner of the pension where Kafka was staying.

5 Next to the Rudolphinum (see note 15, 1911) was a small park.

6 Max Brod placed this card in 1921 with a question mark. Correct date taken from *Ottla*, p. 63.

7 Max Brod explains: "Refers to a dream in which I am tormented by Jewish and Zionist disasters. The situation in Palestine was critical at the time."

8 Julie Wohryzek, daughter of a Prague shoemaker and synagogue custodian. In the summer of 1919 Kafka became engaged to her, but the engagement was broken off a year later.

9 Possibly Grete Bloch, the friend of Felice Bauer (see *Letters to Felice*, pp. 323 f.).

10 Max Brod, *Die dritte Phase des Zionismus.*

11 Blau-Weiss: Zionist youth organization on the model of the German Youth Movement.

12 Julie Wohryzek was going back to Prague.

13 On January 12 (while still in Prague), Kafka had asked the Institute for a sick leave of three months, but was granted (on January 14) only three weeks. Then he was allowed two extensions (on February 7 and March 6), the last to expire the end of March.

14 According to Max Brod, his play *Die Fälscher* [*The Forgers*], though Kafka could well have meant *Paganism, Christianity, Judaism* (see note 66, 1918).

15 See above, p. 192. Bettina von Arnim, née Brentano (1785–1859), married to Achim von Arnim in 1811.

16 This letter was first published in its entirety by Klaus Wagenbach in *Kafka-Symposion*, pp. 45 ff. (taken from a carbon copy that came to light after World War II). Max Brod could publish only the last two and a half paragraphs, corresponding to the last page of the holograph which was available to him.

17 Hermann Kafka's opposition was violent and expressed in the most humiliating terms. See *Dearest Father*, p. 187.

18 Apparently Kafka contemplated going to Munich to be near his publisher, Kurt Wolff, who was moving his business there from Leipzig at this time. See also below, p. 224.

19 After spending the summer in Prague, working at the Institute, Kafka went back to the Pension Stüdl in Schelesen for a week or so in November 1919, this time with Max Brod. It was then that Kafka wrote the greater part of the "Letter to His Father" and met Minze Eisner (1901–72), a girl from Teplitz, who was convalescing from a long illness. At the end of her brief memoir (published under the pseudonym Dora Gerrit in *Bohemia*, February 27, 1931), Olga Stüdl describes Minze as a "young girl, burdened with psychological afflictions and an empty life," and states that Kafka "warned her, adjured her, taught her to surrender herself to work and place all hope of improvement in effort and achievement."

20 Heroine of the play *La Dame aux Camélias* (1852) by Alexandre Dumas *fils* (1824–95).

21 Frank Wedekind (1864–1918), German dramatist.

22 Fern Andra (1893–1974), American-born star and producer of silent films in Germany.

23 Felix Dahn (1834–1912), German historian and historical novelist. Rudolf Baumbach (1840–1905), German poet and author of verse epics. Both were middle-class favorites before 1914.

24 Town on the Weser, in Brunswick, with an agricultural school.

1920

1 Now Velké Březno, on the Elbe, 6 miles east of Aussig (Ústí).

2 Mark Brandenburg.

3 Kafka was on sick leave from December 22 to 29. The correspondence between Kafka and Kurt Wolff for 1919 seems to have disappeared. It might have thrown light on Kafka's plan to go to Munich.

4 Small spa (alt. 2414 ft.) in the Bavarian Alps, with medicinal springs.

5 Ignaz Ziegler (1861–1948), liberal rabbi of Karlsbad; well-known preacher and religious writer.

6 Ahlem: town near Hanover. The Horticultural Training and Experimental Institute still exists.

7 Max Brod dated this letter March 1920, but the illness Kafka refers to occurred from February 21 to 24, thus dating the letter.

8 See next note.

9 Ottla wanted to attend the *hakhshara* (training for agricultural work in Palestine) in Opladen, near Cologne.

10 Not identified.

11 The Jewish National Fund, established in 1902, collected voluntary contributions. Half the money was earmarked for the purchase of land in Palestine, the other half was invested to accumulate interest to be expended on special purposes.

12 Kafka was proofreading the galleys of Felix Weltsch's *Grace and Freedom*.

13 In postwar Europe many countries required entry permits and special visas for foreigners.

14 The sculpture of the local St. Procopius (ca. 1004–53), by Ferdinand Maximilian Brokoff (1688–1731), on the sixth monument on the right, coming from Malá Strana.

15 First published in Hartmut Binder's paper "Ein ungedrucktes Schreiben Franz Kafkas an Felix Weltsch," *Jahrbuch der deutschen Schiller-Gesellschaft*, Marbach, 1976. The letter is preceded by 95 proposed emendations and queries.

16 Meaning: in the direction of Germany. Bohemian-Saxon Switzerland is a mountainous region in northwestern Bohemia and southern Saxony which Minze would have to traverse on the way to Dresden and Hanover.

17 At the Pension Ottoburg in Untermais, just south of Meran. Kafka had stayed the first few days at the Hotel Emma in Meran itself, which proved too expensive. Max Brod's date (April 10) has been changed, since Kafka mentions Thursday, which was the 8th, as the day of writing.

18 *Umsturz*, the splintering of the Austro-Hungarian Empire after World War I.—Trans.

19 The Deutsche Haus, or Casino (26 Graben), was a membership association of German-Bohemian society, with club rooms, a restaurant, and a park. Měštanská Beseda was the Czech equivalent of the Deutsche Haus.

20 High school with emphasis on science and modern languages, as distinct from the gymnasium which cultivated Latin and Greek and the humanities.

21 April 5.

22 German *fletschern* is derived (as is its English original "to Fletcherize") from the name of the American nutritionist Horace Fletcher (1849–1919), who developed a technique of chewing one's food thoroughly (up to thirty times per bite); at the time it was quite a fad in the U.S. and Europe.

23 Or Small Side: Malá Strana (German: Kleinseite), the part of Prague on the left bank of the Moldau.

24 In the fall of 1919 Felix Weltsch had become the editor of *Selbstwehr*. The essay was his review of Oskar Baum's play *The Miracle*, then being performed in Prague, in the issue of April 2, 1920.

25 The elections for the National Assembly of the newborn state of Czechoslovakia took place on April 18, 1920. Max Brod was a candidate of the Jewish Party, but lost. The Socialists emerged as the strongest party, but the government formed was a bourgeois coalition with the Socialists participating.

26 Max and Elsa Brod had gone to Munich to attend the opening night of *Intensity of Feeling* on April 20, 1920, at the Kammerspiele. It was preceded by Friedrich Koffka's *Kain* (see

note 57, 1922). Brod's gentle lyrical play (in which Orosmin is the leading character) had no chance to hold its own against Koffka's stark dramatics and was a resounding failure.

27 Probably Hans Janowitz, writer and, in 1920, coauthor of the scenario for the expressionist film *The Cabinet of Dr. Caligari*. See also note 34, 1917.

28 Friedrich Wichtl, *Freimaurerei – Zionismus – Kommunismus – Spartakismus – Bolschewismus* [*Freemasonry, Zionism, Communism, Spartacism, Bolshevism*], Hamburg and Vienna, 1920.

29 The First Zionist Congress, held in Basel, Switzerland, August 29-31, 1897.

30 The *Protocols of the Elders of Zion* were launched by the Czarist secret police around the turn of the century to justify anti-Jewish pogroms. Their fabrication was based on a French pamphlet by Maurice Joly (1821-78), *Conversations in the Underworld Between Machiavelli and Montesquieu* (1864), a polemic against the empire of Napoleon III. The *Protocols* were first published by Serge Nilus in his book *Das Grosse im Kleinen, oder Nahe ist der herandrängende Antichrist und das Reich des Teufels auf Erden* (Moscow, 1905). Otto Friedrich (*Die Weisen von Zion* [*The Elders of Zion*], Lübeck, 1920) and Hermann L. Strack (various publications), among others, exposed them as forgeries.

31 Georg Mordechai Langer; see note 14, 1916.

32 Felix Weltsch's wife, Irma, was expecting a child.

33 City in the Swabian part of Bavaria, west of Munich.

34 Gustav Landauer (1870-1919), writer and literary historian, anarchist, member of the Council Government in Munich in April 1919; assassinated. Ernst Toller (1893-1939), participated in Munich revolution 1918-19; after the victory of the right-wing forces, condemned to five years' confinement; poet and dramatist—part of his work was published by Kurt Wolff Verlag. There was no "Lewin" involved in the Munich revolution; Kafka probably refers to Max Levien, a Communist organizer, who escaped to Austria and disappeared in Russia during the purges of the 1930's. He might also mean Eugen Leviné, another Communist organizer, who was executed in 1919.

35 With Milena Jesenská-Polak (1896-1944). Kafka had first met her among her friends at a Prague café late in 1919. She was married to the Prague writer Ernst Polak, but since her father disapproved of the marriage the couple lived in Vienna. Milena, a Czech journalist, was interested in translating some of Kafka's works and wrote him several letters from Vienna, to which Kafka replied at least once while still in Prague (the second letter in *Letters to Milena* is from Prague and should be the first). In Meran he began a regular correspondence, and the acquaintance developed into love.

36 Kurt Wolff Verlag, now in Munich.

37 Since Oskar Baum was blind, letters had to be read aloud to him.

38 Tirol Castle, north of Meran, built about 1200 from the remains of a monastery,

somewhat changed since, was the seat of the counts of Tirol, who died out in 1253. Shown on the first postcard.

39 Rising west of Meran to 12,793 ft.

40 The second postcard shows a family of dogs. Meta was the name of the dog at the Pension Stüdl in Schelesen.

41 Julie Wohryzek. She had opened a ladies' hat shop in Prague.

42 Here Kafka crossed out three lines, making them completely illegible. The next sentence refers to this.

43 Early story by Brod in which he portrayed Kafka (see note 6, 1907).

44 The wedding of Ottla and Josef David took place on July 15.

45 Oppositional political and cultural weekly, founded in 1915 (as *Schaubühne;* name changed 1918) by Siegfried Jacobsohn. A review of "In the Penal Colony" appeared in the issue of June 3, 1920, by Peter Panter (pseudonym of Kurt Tucholsky, 1890–1935).

46 Max Brod remembered that "one of Kafka's plans for his future was to become a bookbinder in Palestine."

47 Max Brod dated this letter June 1918, from Zürau. The month is correct (it is mentioned twice in the letter), but in June 1918 Kafka was back in Prague. The "mild and fragrant air" suggests Meran and thereby the summer of 1920. The prospect of seeing Baum again "at the end of June" (when Kafka left Meran) is in accord with this. Kafka left on June 29, going first to Vienna where he spent a few days with Milena. He returned to Prague on July 4, met Julie Wohryzek that same day, and broke off the engagement.

48 Kafka was back at work at the Institute from July 5 to December 18.

49 May 24.

50 Two men whom Kafka met at the Pension Stüdl in Schelesen, when he was there on his second visit (with Max Brod).

51 Prunéřov, 7 miles southwest of Komotau. Milsau, about 2 miles southeast of Prunéřov.

52 Brod dated this August 7. The following letter to Max Brod was written on Friday, August 6 (postmarked the next day). On the previous day Kafka received the answer from Abeles; the same evening he went to see Elsa Brod and, since she was not home, left this note.

53 Almanac published in 1915–16 and 1921–22; Otto Abeles (1879–1945) was a writer and Zionist worker in Austria and Holland.

54 Two chapters in Brod's *Paganism, Christianity, Judaism.*

55 During the war years Brod had been giving courses for Jewish refugee children from Galicia, with Kafka frequently sitting in.

56 Compare Aphorism 69 in Kafka's "Reflections on Sin, Suffering, Hope, and the True Way," in *Dearest Father*, p. 41.

57 Slovanský Ostrov, an island in the Moldau, with the "Civilian Swimming School" Kafka liked to go to.

58 *Der Volkskönig*, a historical play by the Czech dramatist Arnošt Dvořák (1881-1933), which Max Brod had translated into German (Leipzig, 1916).

59 Max Brod had placed the postcard at the end of 1920, but if the year is correct it was almost certainly written before Kafka left for Matliary. Oskar Baum's son Leo was educated at the Odenwaldschule (in Oberhambach near Heppenheim, Hesse), founded (in 1910) and directed until it was closed by the Nazis in 1934 by Paul Geheeb (1870-1961), a pioneer in modern educational methods. Kafka's remark "the woods had schools" is an allusion to the school's name: the Odenwald is a densely wooded, hilly region. According to Max Brod, Kafka had made a strong case for sending the boy far away from his parental home. (On this topic see also Kafka's letters to his sister Elli, below, pp. 290 ff.)

60 Arthur Bonus (1864-1941), Protestant theologian and writer, frequent contributor to the *Kunstwart.*

61 Nikolai Gogol (1809-52), Russian novelist and dramatist. Hafiz, Persian poet of the 14th century; a free German rendering by Hans Bethge (1876-1946) was published in 1910. Li-Po (died A.D. 762), Chinese poet; the free adaptations by Klabund (1890-1928) were very popular *(Li tai-pe,* Leipzig, 1916).

62 Hans Heilmann, ed., *Chinesische Lyrik vom 12. Jahrhundert v. Chr. bis zur Gegenwart,* Munich, 1905. The book was a favorite of Kafka's; he liked to read aloud from it and quoted one of the poems in a letter to Felice *(Letters to Felice,* pp. 59 f.).

63 Lily Braun, *Memoiren einer Sozialistin,* 2 vols., Munich, 1909-11. Kafka was very fond of this fictionalized autobiography and gave copies to Felice, Ottla, and Max Brod. Lily Braun (1865-1916), née von Kretschmann, came from an aristocratic Prussian background, but successfully broke away from her family, joined the Socialist Party, and was very active in the feminist movement.

64 Sometime in November Kafka had asked the government of Lower Austria for a permit to stay at Grimmenstein Sanatorium. Although he obtained the permit and was granted a leave from the Institute, he could not make up his mind to go to Grimmenstein; his vacillation is reflected in the letters to Milena.

65 A sanatorium for the treatment of tuberculosis, run by Mrs. Jolan Forberger, in the High Tatra Mountains in Slovakia, some 35 miles north of Budapest.

66 Headed by Dr. Miklós von Szontagh; Kafka later went there for an examination.

67 Max Brod's play *The Forgers* had its premiere at the Königsberg Opera House. It was published by Kurt Wolff Verlag in 1920.

68 See above, p. 198, and note 33, 1918.

69 As it turned out, Ottla did not come.

70 Felice Bauer had married in March 1919.

71 Dr. Leopold Strelinger.

72 Town, then in Hungary (Kassa), now in Czechoslovakia (Košice), southeast of the Tatra Mountains. The young man probably was a Herr Szinay, frequently mentioned in the letters to Robert Klopstock.

73 The "Arranged Tables," a compendium of Jewish religious and civil law (based on the Talmud), by Joseph Karo (1488-1575), published in 1565.

74 Religious Zionist movement, founded in 1902 as a religious faction of the World Zionist Organization.

75 *Reubeni;* see note 30, 1921.

1921

1 Trutnov: capital of a district in northeastern Bohemia with a mixed German and Czech population. When a superior court with German as the official language was established there in 1891, the Czechs in Prague reacted with violent demonstrations and anti-Habsburg riots. The Imperial Government in Vienna resorted to severely repressive measures, resulting in many arrests and the suppression of Czech organizations and periodicals.

2 This was Emmy Salveter, who was to loom large in Max Brod's life and in Kafka's letters to him. When Brod first met her, she earned her living as a chambermaid (apparently in a hotel) in Berlin. With his financial support she was subsequently able to embark on a career as an actress. Brod portrayed her in three of his novels, and she lent some characteristics to Pepi in Kafka's *Castle*.

3 Adolf Schreiber (see note 54, 1917) had committed suicide in the Wannsee, near Berlin, on September 1, 1920.

4 Max Brod, *Das Buch der Liebe* [*The Book of Love*], Munich, 1921.

5 *Paganism, Christianity, Judaism.*

6 Milena.

7 The new daughter of Felix and Irma Weltsch.

8 Max Brod suffered from a deformation of the spine.

9 Starý Bohumín, border station between Czechoslovakia and Germany.

10 Richard Dehmel (1863–1920), German poet. The letters appeared in the *Neue Rundschau* (December 1920) under the title "Dehmels Fahrten in den Alpen" ["Dehmel's Wanderings in the Alps"].

11 *The Land*, organ of the Czech agrarians, with anti-Semitic tendencies.

12 A German propaganda sheet in the form of a regular French newspaper, founded on November 1, 1914, in Rethel, northern France; it was designed to demoralize the population of occupied France by slanted news.

13 Possibly the article on Schreiber; see note 3, 1921.

14 *Reubeni.*

15 Brod dated this letter "probably May 1921"; the correct date is taken from *Ottla*, p. 102, where Kafka's original Czech text is printed. In the third week of January (when he had been in Matliary for more than four weeks), Kafka sent Ottla the German draft of a letter to his director in which he reported on his health and expressed thanks for the leave. Ottla was to ask her husband to translate the letter into Czech. Kafka received this translation, and here thanks his brother-in-law, also in Czech. The English translation was made from Brod's German version.

16 Pet name for Josef David, Ottla's husband.

17 Dr. Bedřich Odstrčil, the successor of Robert Marschner as director of the Workers' Accident Insurance Institute.

18 Czech-Jewish weekly of liberal tendencies, founded in 1919, close to Masaryk. Milena contributed articles on fashion.

19 The Communist Party of Czechoslovakia was founded toward the end of 1920. Germans: the Germans in Czechoslovakia who had lost their dominant position in the new Czech state.

20 Refers to a Czech popular song of the time which is also quoted in Max Brod's novel *Franzi.* "Panthers" was then a name for teenage rowdies.

21 Small hotel in Berlin, at the time a favorite with writers and artists.

22 Robert Klopstock (1899–1972) was soon to become a close friend. He stayed with Kafka during his final illness.

23 *The Book of Love.*

24 Since the preceding letter to Max Brod mentions "almost two weeks of heavy winds" and the present letter "three weeks," the sequence Brod gave the letters has been reversed.

25 In the city of Barth in Pomerania, on the Baltic.

26 See above, p. 78, and *Diaries* II, pp. 287 ff.

27 In the summer of 1918 Kafka did light gardening work at the Pomological Institute in Troja outside Prague after office hours.

28 Theodor Fontane (1819–98), *Meine Kinderjahre* (1894), an autobiographical account of his childhood years, spent partly in Swinemünde on Usedom Island in the Baltic.

29 Kafka's sick leave was to end on March 20.

30 The antagonist of the "false Messiah" David Reubeni, in the second quarter of the 16th century (Molkho was burned at the stake in 1532). Max Brod treated their story in his historical novel *Rëubeni, Fürst der Juden,* Munich, 1925 [*Reubeni, Prince of the Jews,* New York, 1928].

31 Progressive school, founded by Paul Geheeb (see note 59, 1920) and Gustav Wyneken (1875–1964), in Wickersdorf, near Saalfeld, Thuringia. It existed from 1906 to 1933.

32 Hermann Essig (see note 122, 1917) had died in 1918.

33 Ottla David was expecting her first child, Věra, born March 27.

34 The certificate, which has been preserved, bears the date of March 11, 1921; since Kafka was going to get it in "the afternoon," the letter must have been written on the same day.

35 As indeed she had. Kafka had written to Ottla on March 9, describing his condition, though rather vaguely, whereupon Ottla went to the Institute and procured an extension of his sick leave. On March 16 Kafka submitted the medical certificate by Dr. Strelinger and asked for an extension of two months, which was granted on March 25 (until May 20).

36 See Arthur Schopenhauer, *The World as Will and Representation,* vol. II (1844), chapter 30.

37 Franz Grillparzer (1791–1872), Austrian dramatist, and Friedrich Hebbel (see note 3, 1904).

38 Kafka visited Travemünde on July 14, 1914, from Lübeck; see above, p. 110.

39 Fontane's *Cécile* (1887) and *Unwiederbringlich* (1891) [London and New York, 1964] take place in the Harz Mountains and in Denmark on the Baltic coast, respectively.

40 Reference to Emmy Salveter (see note 2, 1921), who apparently was then in Leipzig.

41 *Franzi, oder eine Liebe zweiten Ranges* [*Franzi, or A Second-rate Love Affair*] (Munich, 1921), a novel in which Max Brod treats his affair with Emmy.

42 Town and railway junction in Czechoslovakia, south of the Tatra.

43 Max Brod, *Im Kampf um das Judentum*, Vienna, 1920. Jarmila Rainer, née Ambrozova, was the wife of a Prague journalist who committed suicide because she had an affair with Willy Haas (see note 49, 1912). Jarmila was pathologically devoted to Milena; in the summer of 1920 she had written a number of letters in Milena's handwriting, whereupon Kafka intervened at Milena's request (see *Letters to Milena*, pp. 166, 179 ff.). After their marriage Haas and Jarmila moved to Berlin.

44 Max Brod, *Adolf Schreiber: Ein Musikerschicksal* [*Adolf Schreiber: The Fate of a Musician*], Berlin, 1921. See note 3, 1921.

45 Kuh (see note 81, 1917) had just published a pamphlet critical of Zionism: *Juden und Deutsche* [*Jews and Germans*], Berlin, 1921. Brod's two-part review, "Der Nietzsche-Liberale" ["The Nietzschean Liberal"], appeared in the April 1 and 8, 1921, issues of *Selbstwehr*. "Racines Bajazet," *Prager Abendblatt*, April 15, 1921.

46 Heinrich Hoffmann (1809-94), German physician, author of once widely popular children's books, illustrated by himself, among them *Der Struwelpeter* (1847).

47 The 48-hour ultimatum issued to Serbia by Austria-Hungary after the assassination of Archduke Franz Ferdinand on June 28, 1914.

48 Otto Weininger (1880-1903), Austrian philosopher, known through his book *Geschlecht und Charakter* (1903) [*Sex and Character*, New York and London, 1906], in which he sought to demonstrate the intellectual and emotional inferiority of women. Baum delivered his lecture on Weininger in mid-February. Johannes Urzidil reviewed it in *Selbstwehr*, February 18, 1921; the lecture apparently was not published.

49 Probably *The Door to the Impossible* (see note 98, 1917).

50 Max Brod's date "beginning of May" changed to April by Binder and Wagenbach (*Ottla*, p. 117).

51 Pet name of Ottla's daughter Věra.

52 His name was Julius Putsch.

53 Irma Weltsch's daughter Ruth was then about ten months old.

54 A mock-scientific article' suggesting that tuberculosis patients may gain weight (i.e., volume) simply by taking a cruise going east (in the direction of the earth's rotation), that the enlargement of measurements proposed by Einstein would then take effect and close the caverns in the lungs, and that a concern in Prague was actually fitting out hospital ships for that purpose. See *Ottla*, p. 204.

55 Susi Galgon, whose name will appear in Kafka's letters to Robert Klopstock.

56 Kafka obtained the medical certificate on May 5 and forwarded it to Ottla on May 6 with a covering note addressed to the Institute. Ottla obtained a further extension of Kafka's sick leave until August 20.

57 His name was Anton Holub.

58 Luca Signorelli (1441–1523), *The Last Judgment*, a mural in the cathedral of Orvieto.

59 Kafka's review, "Aus Matlárháza" ["From Matlárháza," the Hungarian name of Matliary], appeared in the regional German-language weekly *Karpathenpost*, April 23, 1921.

60 Taussig & Taussig, the leading second-hand book dealer in Prague.

61 The son of Karl and Elli Hermann, born December 8, 1911.

62 Albert Ehrenstein (see note 8, 1913) had visited Kafka in Matliary probably sometime in April.

63 A German-language enclave, southeast of the Tatra, formerly in northern Hungary (Szepes), now largely in Czechoslovakia (Spiš).

64 The *Prager Presse* and the *Prager Abendblatt* (Max Brod was a critic for the latter).

65 Staša Jílowská, a married friend of Milena's, whom Kafka had seen several times while in Prague during the summer of 1920.

66 Sophie Friedmann, wife of Max Friedmann, a businessman.

67 Refers to Kierkegaard's *Fear and Trembling*.

68 Allusion to Franz Werfel's "magical trilogy" *Spiegelmensch* (Munich, 1920) [*Mirror Man*, New York, n.d.], which was a polemic against Karl Kraus (see note 73, 1921).

69 Kafka was trying to obtain a job for Klopstock at the Hegner press in Hellerau (see below, p. 299). Jakob Hegner (1882–1962), German publisher and translator from the French; to ensure high quality in typography and presswork, he founded his own press, the Hellerauer Druckerei, in 1918. For Hellerau, see note 78, 1921.

70 Milena Jesenská, Emmy Salveter, and Jarmila Haas were Christians.

71 *Reubeni.*

72 Resort east of Genoa, on the Ligurian Sea.

73 Karl Kraus (1874–1936), *Literatur, oder Man wird doch da sehn* [*Literature, or We'll See About That*], Vienna, 1921. Kraus called this polemic against Werfel in the form of a farce a "magical operetta," in answer to Werfel's "magical trilogy" (see note 68, 1921).

74 *Mauschel* = Moshe = Moses = Jew = Jewish peddler; *mauscheln:* his language, a mixture of good and bad German and Yiddish accompanied by "typically Jewish" gestures.

75 Kafka was bedridden from August 13 to 19 and unable to return to Prague in time to be at his job on August 20. He made the trip about August 26 (see below, pp. 297–98.) and reported for work on August 29.

76 Brod placed Kafka's letters to his eldest sister into the autumn of 1921 because her son Felix (born December 8, 1911) was "a few months short of ten" in the first letter. Since the letters offer no other chronological evidence, Brod's consecutive presentation has been retained, although they almost certainly intermesh with some of the following letters to Minze Eisner and Robert Klopstock.

77 See note 31, 1921.

78 Hellerau was founded in 1909 as a garden city just outside Dresden. It had some light industry, such as Jakob Hegner's press (see note 69, 1921) and the German Workshops (see *Letters to Felice,* pp. 417 ff.), and Emile Jaques-Dalcroze's School for Eurythmics which Kafka had visited in 1914. In 1921 a progressive school, the Neue Schule, was established; A. S. Neill (1883–1973), later the creator of Summerhill, was a cofounder.

79 Most, town in northwestern Bohemia, near the German border.

80 When Max Brod copied these letters he omitted passages he considered unimportant. Wanting to restore the deletions after World War II, he discovered that the originals had disappeared during the Nazi occupation.

81 The quoted passage occurs in Chapter 6 of *Gulliver's Travels.*

82 Kafka was mistaken about this. Swift never married.—Trans.

83 "Das Erkennen" ["Recognition"] (1864), by Johann Nepomuk Vogl (1802–66), Viennese poet. The poem ends with the quoted line.

84 From Matliary to Prague; see note 75, 1921.

85 Dr. Richard Löwy, lawyer on Altstädter Ring, for whom Kafka clerked from April 1 to September 30, 1906.

86 Kafka was trying to find a job for Robert Klopstock through Professor Münzer, or at least arrange for his matriculation at Prague University.

87 The Twelfth Zionist Congress took place in Karlsbad September 1-11, 1921.

88 Gustave Flaubert, in the chapter "Pyrénées," *Voyages*, vol. 1 (Paris, 1948). René de Chateaubriand (1768-1848), French writer, inaugurated the Romantic movement in France.

89 On September 13, Dr. J. Kodym, the Institute's physician, had recommended that Kafka return to a sanatorium. Görbersdorf: in German Silesia, just north of the Bohemian-German border, southwest of Breslau, site of several specialized sanatoria for tuberculosis.

90 Gustav Janouch, the son of a colleague, had begun to visit Kafka at his office in March 1920, when he was 17. He made notes of his conversations and later published them (Gustav Janouch, *Conversations with Kafka*, New York, 1953; revised and enlarged ed., New York, 1971).

91 Stefan George's friend and exponent Friedrich Gundolf (1880-1931) was professor of German literature at Heidelberg University from 1916 to 1931.

92 Minze Eisner.

93 Milena Jesenská.

94 During the Zionist Congress (September 1-11) *Selbstwehr* published a daily four-page supplement with news and extracts from the speeches.

95 Spa in the Zips, south of the Tatra, developed in 1881.

96 Susi Galgon.

97 Jules Verne (1828-1905), *Une Année des Vacances*.

98 Of the Academy of Fine Arts.

99 Milena was in Prague. It was on this occasion that Kafka handed her all his diaries; see *Diaries* II, p. 193.

100 Klopstock had sent along a questionnaire with such headings as Temperature, Coughing, etc., which Kafka put aside unanswered.

101 Ludwig Hardt (1886-1947), eminent reciting artist who liked to include pieces by Kafka in his programs. The Kleist piece is presumably "Anekdote aus dem letzten preussischen Kriege" ["An Anecdote from the Last Prussian War"], which Kafka loved to read aloud himself.

102 One of Prague's best hotels, on the Graben.

103 Max Brod's sequence of this postcard and the next letter have been reversed, since in the postcard Kafka is still asking about Irene, and in the letter she "was here."

104 Kafka's legend for the picture on this postcard, which reproduces a drawing by Mikoláš Aleš (1852–1913) entitled *Autumn*. It shows a rainy field with a peasant woman driving home a flock of geese and a boy flying a kite, while a statue of St. Wenceslas is looking on from the wayside.

105 Rudolf Löwy, bookkeeper at the Košíř brewery, a bachelor and convert to Catholicism. See *Diaries* II, pp. 207 ff.

106 Presented in a speech by Arthur Ruppin (1876–1943), head of the colonization department of the Zionist Organization.

107 Hanne, born 1920, the youngest daughter of Elli and Karl Hermann.

108 The last line of Schiller's play *Die Räuber* (1782) is: *"Dem Manne kann geholfen werden"* ["The man can be helped"].

109 Franz Werfel, *Bocksgesang,* a play (Munich, 1922) [New York, 1926].

110 On October 17 Kafka was examined by Dr. O. Herrmann, who prescribed a special cure which was approved by the Institute on October 29. Kafka was granted a three months' leave (to February 4, 1922) to undergo this treatment.

111 Max Brod (or Robert Klopstock) dated this letter November 22, 1922, but internal evidence suggests a date early in December 1921. Werfel (who was then living in Vienna) was in Prague at that time (as he was again a year later, when he and Pick visited Kafka; see below, p. 364) and Kafka was supposed to go and see him, but since he didn't Werfel called on him and invited him to the Semmering. In his answer Klopstock seems to have commented on this, whereupon Kafka returned to the subject in a subsequent letter (below, p. 315). The "visitor for four days" must have been Milena (see *Diaries* II, p. 200). And it is more likely that Kafka mentioned the anniversary of his arrival in Matliary (on December 18, 1920) and his first sight of Klopstock after one year rather than after two. (When Werfel invited Kafka again in 1922, the doctor "once again" ruled out the Semmering; see below, p. 366.)

112 Endre Ady (1877–1919), Hungarian poet. Klopstock had introduced Kafka to Ady's work. A volume of German translations, *Auf neuen Gewässern* [*On New Seas*], appeared in 1921.

113 Mountain pass rising to 3215 ft., south of Vienna, connecting Lower Austria and Styria; resort with expensive hotels and a colony of millionaires' villas.

114 For Holub, see above, pp. 278–79. About Saphir, Klopstock recalled only that he was some Zips notable.

115 Kafka comments on this metaphor in *Diaries* II, pp. 200 f.

116 Max Pallenberg (1877–1934), German actor, mainly of comic roles. Kafka had seen him on October 30, 1921, in Molière's *Miser* (see *Diaries* II, pp. 108 f.).

117 Hugo Bergmann, *Jawne und Jerusalem,* a collection of essays (Berlin, 1919); for Bergmann, see note 3, 1923.

118 Dr. Robert Kafka, the son of Philip Kafka in Kolin. He was a lawyer in Prague. See Brod, *Biography,* pp. 206 f.

119 For Karl Kraus, see note 73, 1921. Oskar Kokoschka (1886–), Austrian artist and writer.

120 Kafka did go there in January 1922.

121 Dr. Albert Abrams (1863–1924), American physician, considered electrons (rather than cells) as the basic units making up the human body; defined disease as a disturbance in the harmony of the electrons' oscillations *(New Concepts in Diagnosis and Treatment,* San Francisco, 1916); and devised and marketed apparatus to determine and treat the disharmony. His ideas, though highly controversial, caught on quickly, and by 1923 there were some 3500 specialists in the "Electron Relation of Abrams" (E.R.A.) all over the world. See Upton Sinclair, "In Defense of Albert Abrams," *Survey,* March 15, 1923; no earlier publication has been traced.

122 He suffered from a disease of the spleen, of which he died the following year.

1922

1 In the course of Brod's novel *Franzi.* (see note 41, 1921), a Baron Deograt acts as a Hungarian spy in Czechoslovakia and is hoodwinked by the hero–narrator. In an early chapter the hero is visited by a cousin from Brazil who as a youngster in Prague had kept a diary recording the transgressions of the two boys, which he leaves with Franzi when he departs. What seems to have interested Kafka was the hero's speculations about platonic and sexual love and the moral reflections on the consequences of good and evil deeds, sometimes contary to the doer's intentions.

2 Late-expressionist magazine for literature and art, edited (1921–24) by Heinrich Eduard Jacob (1889–1967).

3 Name changed to Spindlermühle in 1923; in Czech Špindlerův Mlýn, resort in the Riesengebirge, at the foot of the Schneekoppe, near the Polish (formerly German) border. On January 24, 1922, Kafka had asked for an extension of his sick leave; it was granted on January 27. The same day, a Friday, he left for Spindlermühle.

4 In the hotel's directory Kafka's name was listed as "Joseph K." (see *Diaries* II, p. 213).

5 Johannes Urzidil, ed., *Karl Brand: Das Vermächtnis eines Jünglings* [*Karl Brand: The Legacy of a Young Man*], with a preface by Franz Werfel (Vienna, 1920). The book contains the unpublished work of a young Prague poet who died of consumption in 1918. Brand came from a Christian proletarian background.

6 Leo Tolstoy's story "The Death of Ivan Ilyich."

7 Kafka had left Spindlermühle on February 17. "Vienna" in the dateline is puzzling.

8 The two weeks planned for would have ended on February 10.

9 Erich Ludendorff (1865–1937), German general in World War I. He was not a nobleman, but of very arrogant appearance.

10 This and the following two letters have been redated in accordance with Hartmut Binder's *Kafka in neuer Sicht*, pp. 346 ff.

11 After returning from Spindlermühle Kafka wrote the story "A Hunger Artist" and began work on *The Castle*.

12 Kafka's leave expired on May 4. On April 17 he asked the Institute for permission to add his regular five-week vacation to his leave, which was granted.

13 Robert Klopstock was in Prague.

14 Igló, town in the Zips, southeast of the Tatra Mountains, then in Hungary, now in Czechoslovakia (Spišská Nová Ves).

15 From 1920 to 1944 Hungary was under the repressive right-wing rule of Admiral Horthy (1868–1957).

16 Bratislava, after 1918 the capital of the province of Slovakia.

17 Kafka's vacation (see note 12, 1922) ended on June 8. But his health was so bad that on June 7 he applied for his retirement. Apparently he was told he would hear by the end of the month. Then, on June 30, the Institute retired him on pension (1000 crowns a month), effective as of July 1, 1922.

18 Village, 60 miles south of Prague, on the Lužnice River, just south of Tábor. Ottla had rented a summer place there.

19 In a letter of May 10, 1922, Kurt Wolff had assured Kafka that his lack of response to two extremely friendly letters from the publisher was not being held against him.

20 "First Sorrow," which Kafka had submitted for publication in the magazine *Genius* (published by Kurt Wolff), where it appeared in III, No. 2 (1922).

21 Title character of Nikolai Gogol's comedy, a performance of which Kafka had recently seen (see below, p. 327).

22 Brand name (Oropax = ear peace) of earplugs made of wax and cotton wool, still on the market.

23 Max Brod, "Gogol's 'Revisor'" ["Gogol's *Inspector General*"], *Prager Abendblatt*, June 14, 1922.

24 Village in the Thuringian Forest, with medicinal springs, popular as a summer resort.

25 Max Brod, *Leben mit einer Göttin* [*Life with a Goddess*], Munich, 1923.

26 Publishing house in Munich.

27 Walther Rathenau (1867–1922), influential German industrialist and politician, at the time foreign minister, was assassinated on June 24, 1922.

28 *Life with a Goddess.*

29 With its notorious war correspondence Alice Schalek (1874–1956), for whom the war was a lark and who was bitterly fought by Karl Kraus.

30 Max Brod, "Das Geheimnis," a review of Smetana's opera *The Secret* (*Prager Abendblatt*, June 23, 1922); "Die böse Frau (Königin Christine)" ["The Wicked Woman (Queen Christina)"], a review of Strindberg's historical drama *Queen Christina* (*Prager Abendblatt*, June 27, 1922); and "Philosophie des Grüssens" ["Philosophy of Salutation"] (*Prager Abendblatt*, June 26, 1922).

31 A reference to Gustav Mahler's Komponierhäusl; see note 43, 1922.

32 Allusion to line 7 of Hölderlin's poem "The Middle of Life."

33 Rudolf Kayser (1889–1964), writer and critic, editor of the *Neue Rundschau* (1921–32).

34 "A Hunger Artist" appeared in the *Neue Rundschau*, October 1922.

35 "First Sorrow."

36 Gabriela Preissová, author of the play that served Janáček for his opera *Her Foster Daughter;* see note 53, 1917.

37 Critical magazine, founded by Karl Kraus in 1899 and edited (and from 1913 wholly written) by him until 1936. It was published irregularly.

38 Hans Blüher (see note 64, 1917), *Secessio Judaica* (Berlin, 1922). See also *Diaries* II, pp. 230 f.

39 Elli Hermann.

40 Ludwig Winder (1889–1946), novelist; literary editor and theater critic of *Bohemia*, 1915–38.

41 Josef Václav Myslbek (1848–1922), Czech sculptor. He had died on June 2; Kafka may have attended his funeral on June 5.

42 Benešov, 32 miles south of Prague, on the railroad line to Vienna.

43 A small one-room stone house in the woods near the villa in Maiernigg on the south shore of Wörther See in Carinthia, where Gustav Mahler (1860–1911) spent his summers from 1900 to 1907.

44 Alois Jirásek (1851–1930), Czech author of historical novels; Brod did not identify the article. The other two articles are *"Pottasch und Perlmutter"* [*"Potash & Perlmutter"*] and "Smichover Arena," both in *Prager Abendblatt*, June 28 and July 6, 1922, respectively. The former is apparently a review of a performance of the play by Montague Marsden Glass (1877–1934) and Charles Klein (1867–1915), derived from Glass's novel of the same title.

45 Max Brod, "Der Schwanensee," *Prager Abendblatt*, July 11, 1922, a review of a performance of Tchaikovsky's ballet at the Czech National Theater.

46 This first Jewish elementary school was founded by Prague Zionists in 1920; Max Brod spoke at the opening. Here Kafka means his sister Valli, who spoke at one of the parents' evenings.

47 A reference to the physician Dr. Otto Herrmann.

48 Containing parts of the manuscript of *The Castle*. On March 15, 1922, Kafka had read the beginning of the novel to Max Brod (see Brod, *Biography*, p. 185 n.).

49 Theodor Storm (1817–88), north German poet and author of short stories; the episode is told in "Meine Erinnerungen an Eduard Mörike," *Erinnerungen und Familiengeschichten* [*Reminiscences and Stories of My Family*], 1876. Eduard Mörike (1804–75), Swabian poet and novelist, *Mozart auf der Reise nach Prag* (1856). Wilhelm Hartlaub (1804–85).

50 František Bílek (1872–1941). When Kafka and Max and Elsa Brod were in Kuttenberg (Kutná Hora) in December 1914, they visited Kolín at Kafka's urging to look at the monument.

51 The letter is addressed to Tatranská Kotlina.

52 *Life with a Goddess*, which deals with Brod's relationship with Emmy Salveter.

53 Friedrich von der Leyen (1873–1966), professor of German literature, collector and editor of fairy tales. His book *Deutsche Dichtung in neuer Zeit* (Jena, 1922) was in Kafka's library.

54 Gerhart Hauptmann, *Anna,* a rustic love epic (in hexameters), Berlin, 1921.

55 Jakob Wassermann (1873–1934), born in Fürth near Nuremberg, treated his native region in such novels as *Die Juden von Zirndorf,* 1897 [*The Jews of Zirndorf,* London, 1933], and *Das Gänsemännchen,* 1915 [*The Goose Man,* New York, 1922].

56 Hermann Löns (1866–1914), editor and author popular with the German Youth Movement.

57 Friedrich Koffka (1888–1951), expressionist German dramatist. His play *Kain* [*Cain*], published 1917, was briefly successful after the war.

58 Emanuel Chalupný, Czech journalist. Ladislav Šaloun (1870–1946) created the monument to John Huss erected on the Altstädter Ring July 6, 1915. Stanislav Sucharda (1886–1916), Czech sculptor. František Palacký (1798–1876), Czech historian and politician. Jan Žižka (1360?–1424), Hussite leader. Jan Amos Komenský (1592–1670), known as Comenius, Czech theologian and educator.

59 *The Castle.*

60 Max Brod had written Kafka that Heinrich Weltsch, the father of Felix, had told him that "Franz's father spoke with pride and flashing eyes about Franz."

61 The apartment where Kafka spent his nights from March to August 1917 and where he had his hemorrhage on August 10, 1917. For a description, see *Letters to Felice,* p. 541.

62 Presumably *Golgotha* (1891–93).

63 The tomb of the Czech writer V. B. Trebizsky. Brod never wrote an article on Bílek.

64 Robert Kafka; see note 118, 1921.

65 Where Martin Buber, editor of *Der Jude,* lived.

66 Pioneer.

67 Max Brod, "Gerhart Hauptmanns Frauengestalten" ["Gerhart Hauptmann's Female Characters"], *Die Neue Rundschau,* November 1922. Jorinde, a character in Brod's novel *Life with a Goddess.* Anna, the heroine of Hauptmann's epic poem *Anna;* see note 54, 1922, and below, p. 360.

68 Small seaside resort on the island of Wollin in the Baltic.

69 Emmy Salveter.

70 His name was Winkler; see below, p. 391.

71 Legendary figure of the Middle Ages who was captured while participating in a crusade

and rescued by a Turkish girl. With the Pope's special dispensation he married the girl, although he had a legitimate wife in Thuringia, and brought her back to his castle. The subject itself or the underlying situation *(ménage à trois)* was frequently treated in novels and plays, last by Wilhelm Schmidtbonn (1876–1952) in his play *Der Graf von Gleichen* (1908). Kafka had seen the play on January 22, 1912 (see *Diaries* I, p. 223).

72 Allusion to the first name of Franz Moor, the villain in Schiller's *Robbers.*

73 Dr. Siegfried Löwy in Triesch.

74 Rudolf Löwy; see note 105, 1921.

75 Wilhelm Speyer (1887–1952), *Schwermut der Jahreszeiten* [*Melancholy of the Seasons*], a novel (1922).

76 *"Und sie hatten im Auge unleugbar ein seltsames Glänzen,/ tief und gut,"* from canto 19 of *Anna.*

77 *Kusine* (female).

78 Gerti (born November 1912), the daughter of Karl and Elli Hermann.

79 The Englishman: A. S. Neill (see note 78, 1921). Emile Jaques-Dalcroze (1865–1950), Swiss composer and musical pedagogue, devised a system of rhythmic gymnastics synchronized with music; see note 78, 1921.

80 September 18.

81 Minze Einser had invited Kafka to visit her at a villa in Kassel-Wilhelmshöhe.

82 Adalbert Stifter (1805–68), "Zwei Schwestern," 1846, in *Studien,* 6 vols., 1844–50.

83 Presumably in a letter from Wolff to Brod.

84 Sándor Márai (1900–), Hungarian writer.

85 Since Kurt Wolff did not react, Klopstock himself wrote to him on March 9, 1923 (with a postscript by Kafka), whereupon Wolff gave him the Hungarian translation rights on March 12.

86 Franz Werfel, *Schweiger,* a tragedy (Munich, 1922).

87 This draft is in *Dearest Father,* pp. 245 ff.

88 See note 5, 1922.

89 Friedrich Thieberger (1888–), the brother of Gertrud Thieberger (see note 5, 1913), Kafka's Hebrew teacher in the autumn of 1919 before Kafka left for Schelesen.

1923

1 The thirteenth birthday (bar mitzvah) of Oskar Baum's son Leo.

2 Two series of books for young people, the first, *Wissenschaftliche Volksbücher für Schule und Haus* (Braunschweig: Georg Westermann Verlag), specializing in science and exploration; the second, *Biblothek der Reisen und Abenteuer* (Leipzig: F. A. Brockhaus), dealing with travel and adventure. Sven Hedin (1865–1952), Swedish explorer in Asia, widely read at the time; Fridtjof Nansen (1861–1930), Norwegian Arctic explorer.

3 Hugo Bergmann (later Shmuel Hugo Bergman, 1883–1975), Kafka's classmate at the gymnasium, philosopher, and Zionist. He went to Palestine after World War I, where he became librarian at the Hebrew National Library and professor at Hebrew University.

4 Ottla's husband, Josef David.

5 A story by Oskar Baum, "Das Ungetüm" ["The Monster"].

6 In *The Metamorphosis*. Baum's story had a similar subject.

7 Small resort northeast of Rostock. Kafka had gone there with his sister Elli and her children at the beginning of July.

8 Emmy Salveter. Kafka had stopped in Berlin to meet her.

9 Pua (Puah) Bentovim (Frau Dr. Puah Menczel), a young girl from a Russian-Jewish family in Palestine, had come to Prague (later to Berlin) to study. She gave Kafka lessons in Hebrew in the spring of 1923, and in July 1923 was active in the education of Jewish children in Eberswalde. A friendship with Kafka developed; see Hartmut Binder, "Kafka's Hebräischstudien," *Jahrbuch der deutschen Schiller-Gesellschaft*, Marbach, 1967.

10 Eberswalde, city 29 miles northeast of Berlin. Bernau, town on the railroad line to Eberswalde, 14 miles from Berlin.

11 See note 13, 1916.

12 The story was published in the October issue.

13 The wife of Hugo Bergmann (see note 3, 1923) and daughter of Berta Fanta (see note 4, 1914).

14 While in Prague, Hugo Bergmann had tried to persuade Kafka to move to Palestine, where he could stay at his apartment. After his return, however, he wrote to his wife in Prague that "Franz could only live with them if he shared a room with the children."

15 Because of the inflation then raging in Germany.

16 Kafka had met Tile Rössler, then 16, at the camp in Müritz. Max Brod reports: "Tile Rössler, now [1958] one of the leading choreographers in Tel Aviv, has preserved two other written mementos from Kafka's hand, in addition to the letter published here. On the wrapper of chocolates he sent her he wrote: 'Not so sweet, not so seductive as M., but more undemanding, more solid and nourishing.' (M. stands for Moissi [Alexander Moissi (1880–1935), much-admired actor, famous for his Romeo and Hamlet, and his Everyman at the Salzburg festivals]). And on a box of candy: 'I am sending you the candies not because they are so good—they probably aren't very—but they are magic candies. You must not touch them at all. Stay quiet on the sofa, place the open box beside you, and far as I am from Steglitz [near Berlin, Tile's home], I will nevertheless put piece after piece into your mouth, as though I were sitting beside you. Try it!' This curious relationship has been described with poetic license by Martha Hofmann in the story *Dina und der Dichter Kafka: Franz Kafkas Briefwechsel mit einer Sechzehnjährigen* [*Dina and the Writer Kafka: Franz Kafka's Correspondence with a Sixteen-Year-Old Girl*], Tel Aviv, 1943."

17 Dora Dymant, or Diamant (1902–52), an East European girl with a hasidic upbringing, was in charge of the kitchen at the Müritz camp.

18 Where the Thirteenth Zionist Congress was to be held August 6–15, 1923.

19 Puah Bentovim.

20 The house in Matliary where Kafka stayed was called "Villa Tatra."

21 August 6.

22 The Zionist Congress at Karlsbad.

23 On the way back from Müritz, Kafka had stayed two days in Berlin, then gone straight to Prague without stopping at Karlsbad. Around the middle of August he went with Ottla and her two girls to Schelesen (until September 21). Ottla's second daughter, Helene, was born on May 10, 1923.

24 Engineer Glauber, Kafka's fellow patient in Matliary, had died.

25 Martin Buber, *Der grosse Maggid und seine Nachfolge*, Frankfurt a.M., 1921. The tale is "The Artery," in *Tales of the Hasidim: The Early Masters* (New York, 1947), pp. 263 f.

26 A boarding school for illegitimate girls where Puah had found cheap lodgings.

27 Meaning the Friday in the week following, September 14, but Kafka postponed his return; see note 33, 1923.

28 Carl Seelig (1894–1962), Swiss writer and critic, then an editor for the publishing house E. P. Tal in Vienna, was in charge of a series of deluxe editions (1000 numbered copies), "Die Zwölf Bücher," in which distinguished writers such as Maeterlinck, Hermann Hesse,

and Romain Rolland had so far appeared. Seelig had asked Kafka for an unpublished work for the series, offering him the sum of 1000 Swiss francs, a fortune in those days of inflation, and to suggest talented young writers for the series.

29 Frigyes Karinthy (1887–1938), Hungarian writer, best known for his humorous sketches and parodies. Klopstock was translating some of his stories into German.

30 Presumably her brother Josef Löwy, formerly a fruit and vegetable wholesaler in the Congo, now living in Paris, had died. See also below, p. 393, where Kafka speculates about the inheritance.

31 An article by Max Brod on Rudolf Borchardt (1877–1945), German writer, poet, and translator.

32 *Vers und Prosa*, short-lived monthly, edited by Franz Hessel (1880–1941), German writer, editor, and translator; Ernst Rowohlt, who had been in the war, reestablished his publishing house in Berlin on February 1, 1919, with Hessel among the editors. *Ha-Ohel: The Tent*, Jewish monthly edited by M. Y. ben Gavriel (pseudonym of Eugen Höflich, 1891–1965), published in Vienna, 1924.

33 Kafka left Schelesen for Prague on September 22 and went on to Berlin on the 24th. He moved in with Dora Dymant, c/o Moritz Hermann, in Steglitz, southwest of Berlin, then a suburb. The title character of "A Little Woman" is a portrait of their landlady.

34 Actually, Kafka was to remain in Berlin until March 17, 1924.

35 Emmy Salveter.

36 Sukkot; also called Festival of Booths.

37 Station on the Berlin Elevated, in Charlottenburg.

38 Local suburban newspaper.

39 Ernst Weiss's play *Tanya* (1920). Elisabeth Bergner (1897–), Austrian stage and screen actress, then a fast-rising star.

40 Novel by Ernst Weiss; see next note.

41 *Tiere in Ketten*, novel (Berlin, 1918); *Nahar*, part II of *Tiere in Ketten* (Berlin, 1922); *Stern der Dämonen*, novel (Berlin, 1922); *Atua*, three stories (Berlin, 1923).

42 Most of these essays were later published in *Das Unverlierbare* [*The Unlosable*], Berlin, 1928.

43 Lise Kaznelson; see note 24, 1913.

44 Tetschen-Bodenbach (Děčín), border station on the railway line Prague–Berlin, with customs control.

45 Small town, southeast of Ostrava (now Frýdek-Mistek), near the Polish border.

46 In the time from October to December 1923, Kafka had written the stories "A Little Woman" and "The Burrow."

47 Josty's was a well-known café in Berlin; Wertheim's, a department store.

48 The three largest publishers of newspapers and magazines in the 1920's.

49 Josef Chaim Brenner (1881–1921), Hebrew writer, born in Russia, settled in Palestine in 1909, a leader of the Palestinian workers' movement and advocate of peaceful collaboration with the Arabs. He was killed in an Arab riot. His novel: *Shekhol ve-Kishalon* [*Loss and Stumble*], Tel Aviv, 1920.

50 Tile Rössler.

51 The State Gardening Institute and Nursery in Dahlem (established in 1824) was the foremost such institution in Germany, with two-year practical and theoretical courses.

52 *Reubeni.*

53 In sending the royalty statement for the fiscal year 1922–23, Kurt Wolff Verlag had advised Kafka on October 18 that in view of the insignificant sales and the inflation they were closing his account as of July 1, but would like to send him free copies of his own books plus works by Březina, Heym, Trakl, and Franz Janowitz. They added that they were not discouraged by the lack of sales, but would continue to promote Kafka's books, because they were "convinced that at a later time the extraordinary quality of these prose pieces would be recognized." (See Kurt Wolff, *Briefwechsel*, pp. 57 f.)

54 Max Brod was contemplating the possibility of bringing Emmy Salveter to Czechoslovakia because of the catastrophic economic situation in Germany.

55 Eugen Klöpfer (1886–1950), German character actor, outstanding as Falstaff or Dr. Stockmann in Ibsen's *An Enemy of the People.*

56 Max Brod, *Klarissas halbes Herz* [*Clarissa's Half Heart*], a comedy (Munich, 1923).

57 At the Academy for Jewish Studies, see note 72, 1923.

58 Alfred Löwy in Madrid; Dr. Siegfried Löwy in Triesch; Rudolf Löwy, the convert. The fourth uncle, Dr. Richard Löwy, the lawyer, had died in 1921.

59 The play was *Brott och brott* (1899; in German: *Rausch* [*Intoxication*], 1899), by August Strindberg (1849–1912). The actors: Fritz Kortner (1892–1970); Gerda Müller (18??–1951).

60 Max Brod inserted this letter before Kafka's postcard to Klopstock postmarked October 31, 1923. Internal evidence, however, suggests the present placement.

61 See note 29, 1923.

62 Karl Kraus, *Untergang der Menschheit durch schwarze Magie* [*The End of Mankind Through Black Magic*], Vienna, 1922.

63 Karl Kraus, *Die letzten Tage der Menschheit* [*The Last Days of Mankind*], Vienna, 1922.

64 Actually, "bereavement."

65 Protestant holiday, observed in north Germany on October 31, which in 1923 was a Wednesday.

66 "*Es ist bestimmt in Gottes Rat,*" first line of a well-known poem by Ernst von Feuchtersleben (1806–49), set to music by both Mendelssohn and Schumann, concerning the transitoriness of all things and the hope of meeting again in a better world.—Trans.

67 A changing divisor, posted daily, to convert the inflated mark to its pre-inflation value. The inflation was rapidly reaching the point of one trillion marks equalling one U.S. dollar; it ended on November 15, 1923.

68 Marianne (Mrs. George Steiner, born 1913) and Lotte (born 1914, died 1929 or 1930), the daughters of Valli and Josef Pollak.

69 November 1.

70 Kafka and Dora Dymant had moved to this address on November 15, 1923. They stayed there until January 31, 1924.

71 Siegmund and Lise Kaznelson.

72 The Lehranstalt (Hochschule) für die Wissenschaft des Judentums (Berlin, 1872–1942), where Kafka attended lectures by Professors Harry Torczyner (1886–1973) and Julius Guttmann (1880–1950). An institute for the training of rabbis and scholars; its last director was Leo Baeck.

73 The Stundenbücher were deluxe editions of lyric poetry, printed on hand-made paper and bound in blue kid. The first three titles on the list belong to this series. Friedrich Hölderlin (1770–1843), Ludwig Hölty (1748–76), Joseph von Eichendorff (1788–1857), German poets. The next five titles were art books: Ludwig Bachhofer, *Die Kunst der japanischen Holzschnittmeister;* Otto Fischer, *Chinesische Landschaftsmalerei;* Friedrich Perzynski, *Von Chinas Göttern: Reisen in China;* Georg Simmel (1858–1918), *Rembrandt: Ein kunstphilosophischer Versuch;* Paul Gauguin (1848–1903), *Vorher und Nachher* (translated from the French manuscript). Next, two German classics in illustrated editions: Adelbert von Chamisso (1781–1838), *Peter Schlemihls wundersame Geschichte,* and Gottfried August Bürger (1747–94), *Wunderbare Reisen und Abenteuer des Freiherrn von Münchhausen.* The

volume of Knut Hamsun was apparently *Under the Autumn Star* (1922) (see above, p. 53), which was found in Kafka's library (along with the Gauguin volume) when inventory was taken ten years after his death.

74 Max Brod, *Prozess Bunterbart* [*The Bunterbart Trial*], Munich, 1924.

75 Robert Musil, *Vincenz und die Freundin bedeutender Männer* [*Vincenz and the Lady Friend of Important Men*], a farce in three acts, had its premiere in Berlin on December 4, 1923.

76 Berthold Viertel (1885–1953), stage and movie director, also active in the U.S.

77 Oskar Baum's story "The Monster" (see note 5, 1923), which he had submitted to the *Neue Rundschau.*

78 Jaroslav Křička (1882–1969), Czech composer, choral conductor, and professor of music. Max Brod translated the libretto of his opera Bílý pán [*White Ghosts,* after Oscar Wilde; 1929] into German as *Spuk im Schloss* [*Ghost in the Castle*]; performed in Breslau, 1931.

79 Rudolf Kayser (see note 33, 1922), editor of the *Neue Rundschau.*

80 Adult school for Hebrew studies.

1924

1 Not identified.

2 J. B. Neumanns Graphisches Kabinett, art gallery in Berlin, later in New York.

3 *Reubeni.*

4 Manfred Georg (later George, 1893–1965), German journalist. Went to New York in 1938 and made the Jewish German-language weekly *Aufbau* into a leading organ of the Emigration.

5 Gustav Krojanker, ed., *Juden in der deutschen Literatur* [*Jews in German Literature*], essays on contemporary writers (Berlin, 1922), which contained an admiring essay by Max Brod on Kafka ("Here is the truth, nothing but the truth").

6 Max Brod, "Gastspiel Ernst Deutsch" ["Guest Appearance by Ernst Deutsch"], *Prager Abendblatt,* January 10, 1924; a review of the performance of Werfel's *Schweiger,* with Ernst Deutsch (1890–1969), stage and film actor.

7 Max Brod, "Theater Poiret," *Prager Abendblatt,* December 7, 1923.

8 Ernst Weiss, *Die Feuerprobe,* a novel (Berlin, 1923).

9 Carl Busse (1872–1918), neoromantic poet and novelist; as a critic opposed to modern trends. The new address was two stops on the local beyond Steglitz, near the Grunewald Forest.

10 Illustrated family monthly, founded in 1886, published by Velhagen & Klasing.

11 Instead of "Meister-Saal" [Master Hall], the telegram read "Geister-Saal."

12 Max Brod reports that Dr. Siegfried Löwy "had come to Berlin because of Kafka's grave condition and persuaded him to enter a sanatorium near Vienna."

13 Arthur Holitscher (1869–1941), author of novels, plays, and travel books. His *Lebensgeschichte eines Rebellen* [*The Life of a Rebel*] was serialized in the *Neue Rundschau;* book publication in 2 vols., 1924–28. Max Brod also recalls that Kafka was very fond of Holitscher's *Amerika heute und morgen* [*America Today and Tomorrow*] (1913; in Kafka's library), which he first read when it was serialized in the *Neue Rundschau* in 1912. Kafka "was fond of reading aloud passages from it, and the book may have contributed to the conception of *Amerika.*"

14 Albert Langen (1869–1909), German publisher, founded his firm in 1893 in Paris, later moved it to Munich, specializing in Scandinavian literature.

15 In 1895–96 Holitscher lived in Paris as a journalist. Titles of some of his early books were *Suffering People, White Love, The Poisoned Well.*

16 Hamsun contracted tuberculosis during his first trip to the United States (1882–84) and was still consumptive when he lived in Paris from 1893 to 1896. (Later he recovered and lived to be 93.)

17 Alarmed by Kafka's condition, Robert Klopstock had come to Berlin. Max Brod arrived March 14 to attend the dress rehearsal of *Jenufa* at the State Opera. On March 17 Dora Dymant and Klopstock took Kafka to the station, and Brod accompanied him to Prague. Klopstock interrupted his studies to nurse Kafka. Dora came to Prague toward the end of March and took Kafka to this sanatorium in the first days of April. Ortmann: small location in the valley of the Piesting, near Pernitz, about 45 miles southwest of Vienna.

18 "Josephine the Singer, or the Mouse Folk," Kafka's last story, was written during his brief stay in Prague in March 1924.

19 While in Berlin, Brod had introduced Kafka to this newly established publishing house (Die Schmiede = The Forge), and Kafka had given them three of his latest stories ("First Sorrow," "A Little Woman," and "A Hunger Artist"). Now he is adding "Josephine" (see also note 7, Conversation Slips). Apparently Brod did give the story to Otto Pick, who was close to Arne Laurin (1889–1945), editor-in-chief of the *Prager Presse.* The story was published in the literary supplement of that paper's Easter issue, April 20, 1924.

20 April 19.

21 Brod's "Kierling" in the dateline has been changed to "Vienna," as Kafka makes clear he had not yet left.

22 Franz Werfel, *Verdi: Roman der Oper*, Berlin, 1924 [*Verdi: A Novel of the Opera*, New York, 1925].

23 Dr. Siegmund Blau, editor-in-chief of the *Prager Tagblatt*. He was a native of Vienna, where he had great influence which he used in Kafka's behalf.

24 Of the *Prager Presse*. "Josephine" appeared in its Easter issue.

25 First published in Brod, *Biography*, where it is dated June 2. The dating followed here is that established in *Ottla*.

26 See Brod, *Biography*, p. 206, and "Letter to His Father," *Dearest Father*, p. 144.

27 Robert Klopstock had joined Dora in Vienna and stayed with Kafka in Kierling to the end.

28 Professor Tschiassny.

29 Max Brod could not recall the title of the book which he had sent Kafka through the Taubeles bookshop in Prague.

30 Brod had visited Kafka on May 11 and 12 from Vienna, where he pretended he had a lecture.

31 Kafka died fifteen days after this letter, on June 3, 1924, shortly before noon. His body was taken to Prague. The funeral took place on June 11, at 4 P.M., at the Jewish cemetery in Prague-Strašnice.

Conversation Slips

1 Max Brod explains: "During his final illness (tuberculosis of the larynx) at the sanatorium in Kierling, Kafka was not supposed to speak, an injunction he obeyed most of the time. He communicated with Dora Dymant, Robert Klopstock, and others by scribbling notes on slips of paper. Usually these notes were mere hints; his friends guessed the rest. A small selection has been published here from the originals in the possession of Dr. Klopstock. A great many slips that refer to the patient's medical condition have not been reproduced. In the notes to this section I have leaned heavily on Dr. Klopstock's explanations. In the *Biography* [pp. 205 ff.] I have quoted examples from other such slips. All the slips show that Kafka's intellectual powers, profound kindness, and imagination remained unclouded to the end."

2 Ernst Schweninger (1850–1924) was Bismarck's physician and an advocate of nature therapy.

3 See note 2, 1923.

4 Lechner, bookshop on the Graben; Hugo Heller, book dealer and publisher, on Bauernmarkt; both in Vienna.

5 Die Schmiede had sent Kafka some books.

6 Robert Klopstock.

7 Refers to the galley proofs of the volume *A Hunger Artist*, which had reached Kafka in May. He was able to proofread only the first sixteen pages, covering "First Sorrow" and the beginning of "A Little Woman." The book was published by Die Schmiede in 1924 after Kafka's death.

8 Apparently meaning injections.

9 At Professor Hajek's clinic in Vienna; see above, p. 412.

10 The galley proofs of *A Hunger Artist*.

11 After one drug ceased to be effective, the doctors had to resort to another. Kafka hated every sort of medicine, which he considered would slowly poison him.

12 Giesshübel-Sauerbrunn (now Kyselka), a favorite excursion spot 10 miles northeast of Karlsbad, with mineral springs.

13 Robert Klopstock comments: "At this time Kafka's physical condition and the whole situation of his literally starving to death were truly ghastly. When he finished the proofs—working on them must have been a tremendous psychological effort and a shattering intellectual reencounter with himself—tears rolled down his cheeks for a long time. This was the first time I ever saw any expression of emotion of this kind in Kafka. He had always shown a superhuman self-control."

14 A glass had fallen to the floor and broken.

15 A medieval refrain, also title of a poem by Goethe which Kafka asked Dora to read to him.

16 Yogurt.

17 A fly in the room.

18 See above, p. 416.

19 Legendary medieval figure, the paragon of a devoted friend, treated by Goethe and Ludwig Tieck.

20 Refers, as Klopstock reports, to the days in Prague after Kafka's return from Berlin and before going to the Sanatorium Wiener Wald. At that time Kafka noticed the first symptoms of the disease of the larynx. Klopstock notes: "During those days he wrote the story 'Josephine [the Singer,] or the Mouse Folk,' and one evening when he had finished the last page of the story he said to me: 'I think I began to investigate that animal squeaking at the right time. I have just finished a story about it.' I didn't have the courage to ask him to let me read it. That same evening he told me that he felt an odd burning in his throat whenever he drank certain beverages, especially fruit juices, and said he was worried that his larynx might also be affected."

21 See above, p. 414.

22 Kafka is referring to his trips of earlier years which find their reflection in letters from those days, except the last mentioned: after graduating from the gymnasium, he made his first trip abroad in August 1901, going by himself to the North Sea islands of Norderney and Heligoland.

23 Apparently the question was asked whether Kafka's first fiancée, Felice Bauer, understood him.

24 After the doctor's visit.

Chronology

1883	July 3: Born in Prague.
1889–93	Elementary school (German Boys' School).
1893–1901	Altstädter Gymnasium.
1896	June 13: Bar mitzvah.
1898	Friendship with Oskar Pollak, Ewald Felix Přibram, and Hugo Bergmann.
1899–1903	Early writings (destroyed).
1900	Summer: Vacation in Roztok (Selma Kohn).
1901	August: Vacation on North Sea islands of Norderney and Heligoland.
1901–6	German University, Prague. Studies chemistry for two weeks, then law. In spring 1902, studies German literature and the humanities.
1902	Summer: Vacation in Liboch and Triesch with Dr. Siegfried Löwy (the "country doctor"). October: Trip to Munich. October 23: First meeting with Max Brod.
1903	Working on a novel *The Child and the City* (lost).
1904–5	Autumn–winter: Writes "Description of a Struggle" (first version).
1905	July–August: Vacation in Zuckmantel. First love affair. Autumn: Beginning of regular meetings with Max Brod, Oskar Baum, and Felix Weltsch.
1906	April–September: Clerk in the law office of Dr. Richard Löwy. June 18: Doctor of law degree. August: Vacation in Zuckmantel. October: Beginning of one-year legal training.
1907	Spring: Writes "Wedding Preparations in the Country." June: Family moves from Zeltnergasse 3 to Niklasstrasse 36. August: Vacation in Triesch. Friendship with Hedwig W.

October: Starts job at insurance company Assicurazioni Generali in Prague.

1908 February–May: Takes course in workers' accident insurance at Prague Academy of Commerce.

March: First publication (eight short pieces in *Hyperion*).

July: Leaves Assicurazioni Generali and begins new job at Workers' Accident Insurance Institute for the Kingdom of Bohemia in Prague.

September: Official trips to Tetschen and Černošic; then a vacation in Spitzberg.

1909 March: Publication of two sections from "Description of a Struggle" in *Hyperion*.

September: Vacation at Riva and Brescia with Max and Otto Brod. Writes and publishes (in *Bohemia*) "The Aeroplanes at Brescia."

December: Official trip to northern Bohemia.

1910 Begins to keep a diary.

March: Publication of five pieces in *Bohemia*.

August: Vacation in Saaz.

October: Trip to Paris with Max and Otto Brod.

December: Trip to Berlin.

1911 January–February: Official trip to Friedland and Reichenberg. Beginning of travel diaries. Inspection tour of northern Bohemia.

March: Publication of "Hyperion" in *Bohemia*.

April–May: Official trip to Warnsdorf.

Summer: Vacation (with Max Brod) to Lugano, Stresa, Milan, Paris. Then alone to Sanatorium Erlenbach near Zurich.

Autumn: Works on *Richard and Samuel* (with Max Brod).

October 4: First visit to a performance of an East European Yiddish troupe, followed by many more through the winter. Friendship with the actor Yitzhak Löwy.

Winter: Working on first version of *Amerika*.

1912 February 18: Evening of recitations by Yitzhak Löwy (organized and introduced by Kafka).

May: Publication of "The First Long Train Journey" (Kafka and Brod) in *Herder-Blätter*.

June–July: With Max Brod to Leipzig and Weimar. Meets Ernst Rowohlt and Kurt Wolff. Flirts with Margarethe Kirchner. Meetings with Paul Ernst. Then alone at Sanatorium Just in the Harz Mountains.

August 13: Meets Felice Bauer.

September 22–23: Writes "The Judgment" overnight.

September–October: Writes "The Stoker" and begins second version of *Amerika*.

October: Publication of "A Great Noise" in *Herder-Blätter*.
November–December: Writes *The Metamorphosis*.
November: Official trip to Kratzau.
December 4: Gives public reading of "The Judgment."
December: *Meditation* published by Ernst Rowohlt.

1913   January 18: Meets Martin Buber.
              January 24: Interrupts writing of *Amerika*.
              Easter: With Felice in Berlin.
              March: Meets Kurt Wolff, Franz Werfel, and others in Leipzig.
              April: Begins gardening work in Troja.
              May 11–12: With Felice in Berlin.
              May: *The Stoker* published by Kurt Wolff.
              June: "The Judgment" published in *Arkadia*.
              June 28: First meeting with Ernst Weiss.
              September–October: In Vienna to attend Second International Congress
                 for First Aid and Accident Prevention; Eleventh Zionist Congress.
                 Vacation to Desenzano by way of Trieste, Venice, and Verona. Then
                 in Riva; relationship with G.W., "the Swiss girl."
              November 8–9: With Felice in Berlin.
              November: Family moves to Altstädter Ring 6.

1914   February 28–March 1: In Berlin with Felice. Visits Martin Buber.
              Easter: In Berlin. Unofficial engagement to Felice.
              May 1: Felice in Prague. Search for apartment.
              May 30–June 2: In Berlin. Official engagement to Felice.
              June: With Otto Pick in Hellerau and Leipzig.
              July 12: In Berlin. Engagement broken.
              July: Vacation to Lübeck and Travemünde; then with Ernst Weiss and
                 Rahel Sansara in Marielyst (Denmark).
              August: Moves to Valli's empty apartment, Bilekgasse 10. Begins work on
                 The Trial.
              September: Moves to Elli's empty apartment on Nerudagasse.
              October: Takes leave of absence to work on *The Trial;* writes last chapter
                 of *Amerika* and "In the Penal Colony." Resumes correspondence with
                 Felice.
              December: Writes "The Village Schoolmaster" ["The Giant Mole"]
                 (unfinished). Christmas trip with Max and Elsa Brod to Kuttenberg
                 and Kolín.

1915   January 17: Stops work on *The Trial*.
              January 23–24: With Felice in Bodenbach.
              January–February: Writes "Blumfeld, an Elderly Bachelor" (unfinished).
              February 10: Rents own room at Bilekgasse 10.
              March 1: Moves to Langengasse 18.
              April: To Hungary with his sister Elli.
              May 23–24: With Felice Bauer and Grete Bloch in Bohemian
                 Switzerland.
              June: With Felice in Karlsbad.

July: At Sanatorium Frankenstein near Rumburk.
October: Carl Sternheim awarded Fontane Prize, gives money to Kafka.
October: *The Metamorphosis* published in *Die weissen Blätter*.
November: Book publication of *The Metamorphosis*.

1916   April: Official trip to Karlsbad (with Ottla). Robert Musil visits Kafka in
              Prague.
              May: Official trip to Karlsbad and Marienbad.
              July 3–12: Meeting with Felice in Marienbad; with Felice to Franzensbad;
              then alone at Marienbad.
              October: "The Judgment" published in book form.
              November 10–12: In Munich, meets Felice and reads "In the Penal
              Colony" at Gallery Goltz. Meets Gottfried Kölwel and Max Pulver.
              November 26: Begins to write (the stories in *A Country Doctor*) in Ottla's
              rented house on Alchimistengasse.

1916–17   Winter: Writes "The Warden of the Tomb."

1917   March: Moves to apartment in Schönborn Palace; continues to write at
              Ottla's home on Alchimistengasse.
              Spring: Writes "An Imperial Message" (as part of the story "The Great
              Wall of China") and "The Hunter Gracchus."
              Summer: Begins to learn Hebrew. Writes "A Report to an Academy."
              July: Felice in Prague; second engagement. With Felice to Hungary, then
              returns alone, stopping in Vienna where he meets Otto Gross, Anton
              Kuh, and Rudolf Fuchs. "An Old Manuscript" and "A Fratricide"
              published in *Marsyas*.
              August 9–10: Hemorrhage at Schönborn Palace.
              September: Moves into his parents' apartment. Dr. Friedl Pick diagnoses
              tuberculosis of the lungs. Three months' sick leave granted; joins Ottla
              in Zürau (until April 1918).
              September 20–21: Felice in Zürau.
              October: "Jackals and Arabs" published in *Der Jude*. To Komotau and
              Prague for a few days with Max Brod and Ottla.
              November: "A Report to an Academy" published in *Der Jude*.
              December (last week): To Prague. Felice in Prague; second engagement
              broken off.

1918   January: With Oskar Baum to Zürau.
              February: In Prague for a few days to clarify his military status.
              April: Leaves Zürau, returns to Prague.
              May: Resumes work at the Institute.
              Summer: Gardening work at the Pomological Institute in Troja.
              Summer and autumn: Frequent official trips to Rumburk and
              Frankenstein.
              September: Vacation in Turnau.
              Mid-October–late November: Ill with Spanish influenza; sick again after
              a few days back at work.

November 30: To Schelesen.
Christmas: In Prague.

1919

January 22: Returns to Schelesen; meets Julie Wohryzek.
March (end): Returns to Prague.
May: "In the Penal Colony" published in book form.
Summer: Engagement to Julie Wohryzek.
Autumn: Publication of *A Country Doctor*. Takes Hebrew lessons from Friedrich Thieberger.
October (end): Receives first letter from Milena Jesenská-Polak.
November: Banns issued. Wedding with Julie Wohryzek scheduled for November 2 or 9, but postponed because of apartment problems. With Max Brod to Schelesen. Meets Minze Eisner. Writes "Letter to His Father."
November 21: Returns to Prague and the office.

1919–20

Winter: Recurrent illness.

1920

January: Begins writing *He* aphorisms.
April: To Meran; then to Untermais. Correspondence with Milena.
June 27–July 4: In Vienna; four days with Milena.
July: Breaks engagement to Julie Wohryzek, but continues seeing her. Returns to work. Lives at Elli's apartment on Nerudagasse.
August 8: Moves back to his parents' apartment.
August 14–15: Meets Milena in Gmünd.
August (end): Resumes his literary work after more than three years of inactivity.
December: To Matliary in the High Tatra Mountains (until August 1921).

1921

January: Attempts to break off with Milena.
February 3: Meets Robert Klopstock.
March (end): Gravely ill (until early April).
April: "From Matlárháza" published in *Karpathenpost*.
August (end): Returns to Prague; resumes job at Institute.
September–October: Milena in Prague; Kafka gives her his diaries.
October 15: Resumes diary entries.
October 31: Sick leave granted to undergo special treatment.
November: Several visits by Milena
December: Franz Werfel in Prague.

1922

January 27: To Spindlermühle for three weeks.
February: Writes "A Hunger Artist." Begins work on *The Castle*.
April–May: Visits by Milena.
June: To Planá.
July: Pensioned off by the Workers' Accident Insurance Institute (he had not worked since October 1921). Writes "Investigations of a Dog." Two trips to Prague.

August 20: Stops work on *The Castle.*

September: Brief trip to Prague; then leaves Planá and returns to Prague.

October: Publication of "A Hunger Artist" in *Die Neue Rundschau.*

November–December: In bed most of the time.

December 2: Ludwig Hardt reads works by Kafka at an evening of recitations in Prague.

December: Visit by Franz Werfel and Otto Pick. Takes Hebrew lessons from Puah Bentovim.

1923   Winter–spring: Mostly bedridden. Continues Hebrew lessons with Puah Bentovim.

April–May: Sees Hugo Bergmann, who invites Kafka to Palestine.

May: To Dobřichovice.

June: Last meeting with Milena.

July–August: In Müritz on the Baltic with Elli and her children. Meets Dora Dymant. Returns to Prague via Berlin.

Mid-August–September: With Ottla in Schelesen.

September 24: To Berlin (via Prague) to live with Dora Dymant in Steglitz (Miquelstrasse 8). Studies Hebrew.

October–December: Writes "A Little Woman" and "The Burrow."

November 15: Moves with Dora to Grunewaldstrasse 13.

November–December: Takes courses at Academy for Jewish Studies.

Christmas: Bedridden with fever.

1924   February: Moves with Dora to Heidestrasse 25–26 in Zehlendorf. His health declines rapidly. Siegfried Löwy comes to Berlin, persuades Kafka to enter a sanatorium.

Mid-March: Max Brod comes to Berlin, takes Kafka back to Prague. Writes "Josephine the Singer, or the Mouse Folk." Larynx becomes affected.

March (end): Dora Dymant comes to Prague, takes Kafka to Sanatorium Wiener Wald, Lower Austria, on April 7.

April: With Dora in Sanatorium Wiener Wald. Tuberculosis of the larynx diagnosed.

Mid-April: For a few days at Professor M. Hajek's clinic in Vienna. Dora is with him, then accompanies him to Dr. Hoffmann's Sanatorium in Kierling. "Josephine the Singer, or the Mouse Folk" published in the *Prager Presse.*

May: Robert Klopstock joins Dora in nursing Kafka. Kafka corrects part of the galleys of *A Hunger Artist,* published in 1924 after his death.

June 3: Death in Kierling; burial June 11 in the Jewish cemetery in Prague-Strašnice.

June 19: Memorial service at the Little Theater in Prague.

Index